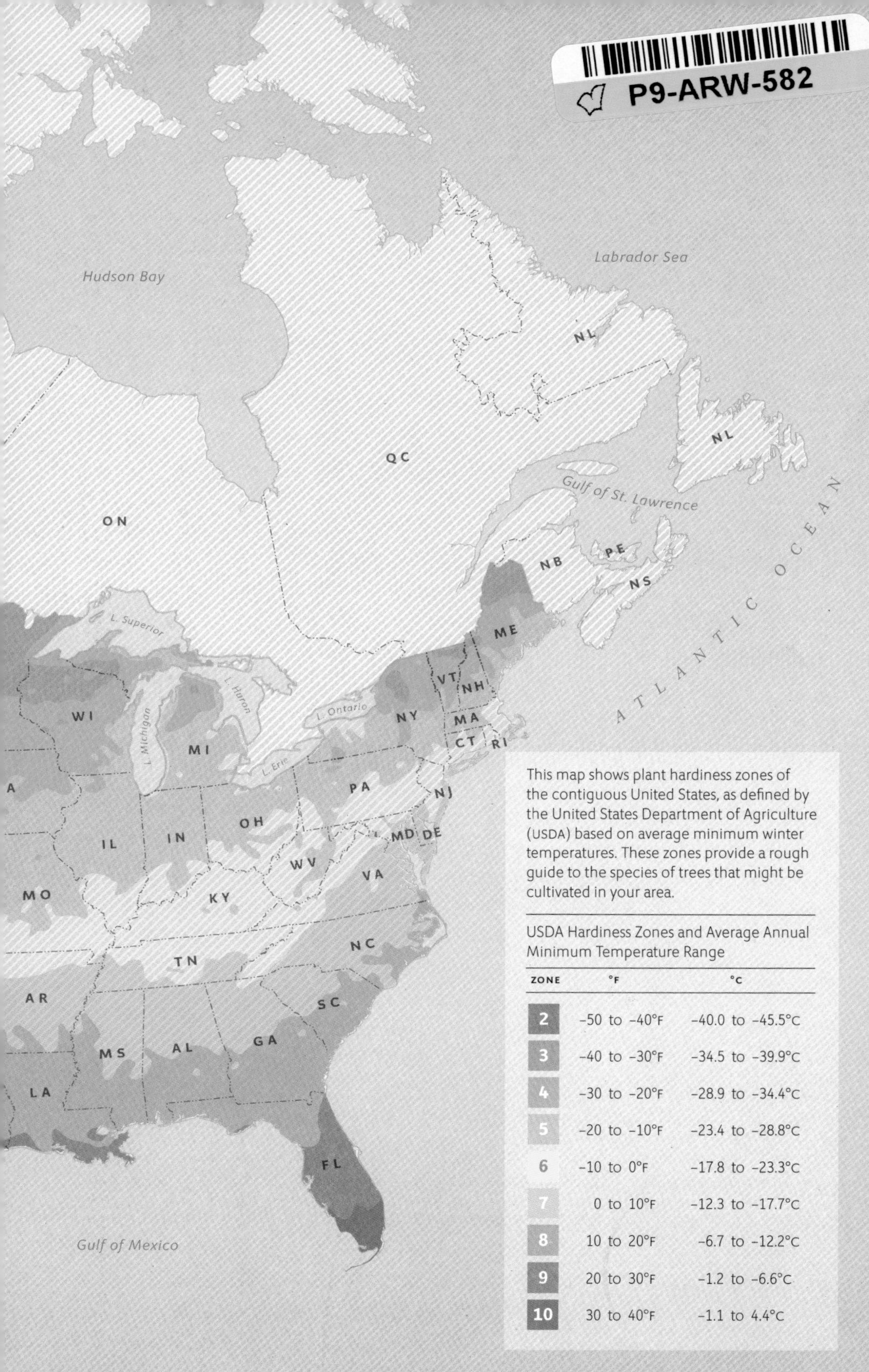

Hudson Bay
Labrador Sea
NL
QC
NL
Gulf of St. Lawrence
ON
NB
PE
NS
ATLANTIC OCEAN
L. Superior
ME
VT
NH
L. Huron
WI
L. Michigan
MI
L. Ontario
NY
MA
CT
RI
L. Erie
PA
NJ
A
IL
IN
OH
MD
DE
WV
VA
MO
KY
NC
TN
AR
SC
MS
AL
GA
LA
FL
Gulf of Mexico

This map shows plant hardiness zones of the contiguous United States, as defined by the United States Department of Agriculture (USDA) based on average minimum winter temperatures. These zones provide a rough guide to the species of trees that might be cultivated in your area.

USDA Hardiness Zones and Average Annual Minimum Temperature Range

ZONE	°F	°C
2	−50 to −40°F	−40.0 to −45.5°C
3	−40 to −30°F	−34.5 to −39.9°C
4	−30 to −20°F	−28.9 to −34.4°C
5	−20 to −10°F	−23.4 to −28.8°C
6	−10 to 0°F	−17.8 to −23.3°C
7	0 to 10°F	−12.3 to −17.7°C
8	10 to 20°F	−6.7 to −12.2°C
9	20 to 30°F	−1.2 to −6.6°C
10	30 to 40°F	−1.1 to 4.4°C

1 inch = 25.4 millimeters *1 inch = 2.5 centimenters* *1 foot (12 inches) = 0.3 meters*

0 1 cm 2 3 4 5 6 7 8 9 10

0 ½ 1 inch 2 3 4 5 6 7 8 9

The Sibley Guide to Trees

The Sibley Guide to Trees

Written and illustrated by David Allen Sibley

Alfred A. Knopf, New York

To my parents, Fred and Peggy Sibley,
for always supporting my interest in drawing birds

This is a Borzoi Book.

Published by Alfred A. Knopf.

Published in the United States by Alfred A. Knopf, Inc., New York and
simultaneously in Canada by Random House of Canada Limited, Toronto.

Distributed by Random House, Inc., New York.
www.randomhouse.com

Prepared and produced by
Scott & Nix, Inc.
150 West 28th Street, Suite 1103
New York, NY 10001
www.scottandnix.com

Range maps prepared by Steve Holzman using data provided by USDA and BONAP.

Printed and bound by C & C Offset Printing Co., Ltd., China

Digital Photography and separations of author's original art
by North Market Street Graphics, Lancaster, Pennsylvania

First Edition

Published August 2009

First Printing, May 2009

ISBN 978-0-375-41519-7

Library of Congress Control Number: 2009927625

The paper of this book is FSC certified, which assures it was made from well managed forests and other controlled sources.

This book celebrates trees and all efforts toward their protection and recognition of their environmental importance.

Contents

Preface

Trees surround us every day in many different forms. They are part of our lives not only as living plants in our yards and parks but also in furniture, pencils, oranges, the framework of our homes, and the paper in the book that you are holding in your hands. Trees are some of the most common things in our everyday lives and at the same time some of the most superlative. The tallest, heaviest, and oldest living things on earth are trees.

I have studied birds for most of my life and over the years I have written and illustrated several guides to birds and birding. When I first thought of creating a new field guide, I leaned toward the colorful, dynamic (and bird-like) butterflies or reptiles and amphibians, my childhood favorites. But these creatures are visible for only part of the year, and most can only be seen with special effort and require very close study to be identified. Both groups have relatively few species in the Northeast, where I live, with much higher diversity in the warmest parts of North America. In some very important ways, I found that tree study was more like birding. Trees, like birds, are around us all the time; not just in summer or in nature sanctuaries, but all year in our yards and along our streets. We can see and identify them at a distance along the roadside, across a pond, even from a moving car. As we go about our daily routines, most of us won't encounter many butterflies, amphibians, or native mammals, but we will see birds and trees.

Another advantage is that trees don't really move. But they still change with the seasons, so that they are never quite the same from week to week. Even after years of studying trees in your area, some small change in appearance one day might draw your attention to a tree you've never noticed before. There are many opportunities for discovery.

Trees project a different sense of time, and hold a record of environmental history that can be revealed through patient study. If you planted an acorn today, no matter how young and healthy you are, you would not live long enough to see it as a fully mature oak tree. It is possible to see trees that were alive when Columbus landed in the New World, and even some that were already old in the time of Julius Caesar.

Like birds, learning about trees can be an entry point to understanding the natural world. But if birding is a window through which we admire our feathered neighbors passing by at a distance, studying trees is a door that opens wide and invites us in. We can relax under their shade, climb their branches, or feel the texture of their bark. We can pick their fruit, plant them in our gardens, or make use of their wood. Our lives are intertwined with trees in countless ways, and they remind us that we are *not* simply neighbors, but part of an integrated community.

This book is primarily an identification guide and you can think of it as a kind of directory. It will help you find the trees and know their names, but that is just the beginning. It is up to you to get to know them, learn their stories, and appreciate how much they do for us.

—David Sibley
April, 2009
Concord, Massachusetts

Introduction

This book covers the identification of 668 native and commonly cultivated trees found in the temperate areas of North America north of Mexico. This includes most of the continental United States and Canada, an area corresponding to the United States Department of Agriculture (USDA) plant hardiness zones 1–8. A color-coded map with a key on the inside front cover illustrates the hardiness zones covered in this guide.

All native trees are included in the species accounts of this book, except those trees found only in southern Florida, which is home to over one hundred native species found nowhere else on the continent. All commonly cultivated species are covered, but the warmest climates in North America have a progressively higher diversity of cultivated trees and fewer of these species will be found in this guide.

Getting Started

If you are reading this book, you presumably have an interest in the identification of trees, and several tips and suggestions are offered below to help you get started. Just as in learning anything new and complex—a new language, playing a musical instrument, identifying birds—the key to success is study and practice. The more you look at trees, the more easily you will identify them. Simply noticing trees as you travel through your daily routine, or spending time at home browsing this or other books about trees, is an excellent way to become familiar with the basic patterns of variation and the common species of trees.

PRACTICE OBSERVING

One of the keys to identifying trees at a distance is knowing how to sort the important bits of information from the unimportant ones. The overall size and shape of a tree is usually useful only for the broadest indication of what group it might be in, while the pattern formed by twigs is a very useful identification clue. Getting out in the field and looking at lots of trees is the only way to develop this knowledge, as you will gradually, and subconsciously, begin to understand which elements really distinguish each tree. Looking at the same trees daily throughout the year and noting changes will also provide valuable experience. Taking notes or making sketches of what you see is an excellent learning tool—it forces you to focus on all the aspects of the tree and the act of recording your observations will reinforce what you have observed.

RECOGNIZE PATTERNS

Our brains are very good at pattern-recognition, so this is something that doesn't take much conscious effort, but it can be helpful to watch for and try to make generalizations. For example, all birches have slender graceful twigs and all poplars have stout stiff twigs. Learning the broader patterns of variation at the group level of trees, rather than species-by-species, can greatly enhance your understanding and enjoyment.

USE MULTIPLE FIELD MARKS

Trees are extremely variable, and no single field mark will ever be sufficient to identify a tree. You will have to look for multiple features. By using multiple clues, including range and habitat, you can begin to identify trees at a distance without seeing any smaller details, in the same way that experienced birdwatchers identify hawks from a great distance. A medium-sized tree at the edge of a marsh in the mid-Atlantic states, looking relatively flat-topped and showing some red leaves in late summer, is almost certainly a Black Tupelo. This type of observation is won by practice and understanding of the whole tree in all its parts.

PAY ATTENTION TO HABITAT

Just as in other nature study, each species has certain affinities for where it grows. In trees these preferences involve conditions such as moisture, sunlight, and type of soil. Pay attention to the surroundings where you identify each species—the soil conditions, understory, other species of trees nearby—and you will begin to develop a sense of where to expect each species.

GET TO KNOW YOUR LOCAL TREES

Many parks and refuges have "interpretive trails" where trees are labeled and described. If you are lucky enough to live near an arboretum, that can be a great resource for tree study. One way to familiarize yourself with this book and with your local trees is to make a list or mark all of the species that might be seen in your area. A species checklist is provided on page 400 of this guide where you can record tree sightings. Start small and get to know your local trees very well, and you will build a solid foundation for expanding your knowledge to places farther from home.

MEET OTHER TREE FANS

Check with a local nature center, botanical garden, or park to see if they offer nature walks or other classes or field trips that discuss tree identification. Even a garden store, nursery, or a university extension service might offer classes on many different aspects of trees.

What is a Tree?

Trees are not a well-defined biological group like birds or insects. Trees are simply very large plants, and plants from many unrelated families can grow into a "tree-like" form. Every Eastern White Pine seed has the potential to be a tree, but one that sprouts in a rocky crevice on a windswept mountaintop may only grow to a maximum of two or three feet high. In a more hospitable location, the same seed could grow into a tree over one-hundred feet tall. The tradition of bonsai is an extreme expression of this adaptability. Environmental conditions strongly influence trees and tree-like plants.

DEFINITION OF A TREE

In order to determine the species to be covered in a guide to trees, it is necessary to establish a definition of a tree. This has to be arbitrary, since there is a continuum of variation from shrubs to trees. However, most authorities use a version like this: *A tree is a perennial plant with a single woody stem at least a few inches thick (at about four feet above the ground), branching into a well-formed crown of foliage, and reaching a height of at least 12 or 15 or 20 feet.*

Every young tree can be shrub-like, although even very young plants of species like Eastern White Oak or Bald-cypress show the single trunk and upright habit indicating that they are destined to be trees. A species that is usually a shrub might grow to tree-like size only occasionally in scattered locations, or only in one region, and some cultivated shrubs can be pruned into a tree-like form. Many such species that are "shrubs or occasionally small trees" are included in this guide, but many others are not.

One could quibble endlessly over the definition of a tree. Even large species that are included in this guide could have been excluded for various reasons. Black Willow, Box-elder, and others are usually multi-trunked (like a shrub) even though they are often over fifty feet tall. Saguaro lacks a well-formed crown of foliage. Palms do not branch. Quaking Aspen often has multiple trunks arising from the same root system.

Nitpicking aside, there is a distinctive growth form that we all know as a tree, and one of the simplest and most practical definitions states simply: if you can walk under it, it's a tree; if you have to walk around it, it's a shrub. As a general rule, any plant species that is commonly over 30 feet tall with a trunk at least one foot thick is included in this guide.

CULTIVATED SPECIES

In cities and towns, most trees are cultivated—deliberately planted and maintained by people. Many cultivated trees are species native to North America (although they may be planted far outside their natural range) but many others are exotic species native to other continents, most often Europe or Asia. All of the cold-hardy cultivated trees commonly seen in North America are included in this guide.

Many cultivated species have escaped into the wild, and all have the potential to do so. Even though many exotic trees are in unnatural settings like manicured gardens or city streets, they are constantly interacting with native insects, birds, and other animals as a functional part of the urban and suburban ecosystem.

Not only does the addition of many cultivated exotic species add to the diversity of trees in North America, but domesticated varieties, or cultivars, add another level of diversity. It is estimated that there are about 7,000 cultivars of the Common Apple alone. Plant breeders have been able to manipulate the appearance of leaf shape, flower size, branching angles, fruit size and flavor, and variations of color of virtually every part of the tree.

In the same way that domesticated dogs or goldfish have diversified through selective breeding, it is now possible to see a European Beech tree with purple leaves or whitish leaves, or deeply cut lacy leaves, or one that forms a sprawling mound barely twenty feet tall, or another that forms a narrow upright spire.

Many of these cultivars are propagated by horticultural techniques such as cuttings or grafting so that all plants sold are clones of a single individual. This allows the sale of plants with consistent and reliable characteristics, but it can lead to very low genetic diversity in the trees of our yards and streets. Many plants are cultivated, especially fruit trees, by using an established growing plant as rootstock. This technique involves grafting a living branch or branches cut from one type of tree to another related type of tree. The combination of the two types of plants offer growers a variety of desired characteristics from the rootstock species and the grafted portion of the tree (called a "scion.")

Planting species native to your region is recommended, but the mass-produced cultivars of native species like Red Maple are often quite different from the local "wild" trees of the same species. Most have been cloned from individuals with desirable growth forms or bright colors, and may even be hybrids with other native or exotic species. To find truly native trees, look for a nursery that specializes in locally-grown native plants.

Taxonomy

VALUE OF TAXONOMY

The study of living things involves classifying individuals into species, and species into groups based on shared characteristics. Taxonomy seeks to find the underlying patterns and order in the tremendous diversity we observe in the natural world. Essentially, taxonomy, and the resulting levels of hierarchy creates a structure into which we can place all of our observations. In this guide, species of trees are arranged with their nearest relatives according to their taxonomic relationships.

While it is possible to classify trees by superficial features, such as their leaf shape, or by flower color, none of those methods will help us understand the relationships between species. It is easy to be overwhelmed by the incredible diversity of the over six hundred species of trees in North America. But when the relationships of different types of trees are ordered in the arrangement of genera and families, the hundreds of species become a linked network of related species—birches here, near the alders and hornbeams, plums over there right next to the cherries. This networked structure of relationships becomes clearer and more well-defined the more we learn, and in that process of discovery and understanding lies the real pleasure of the study of nature.

TAXONOMIC HIERARCHY

The system used to classify all living things involves a hierarchy of groups. All plants are in the kingdom Plantae, which is subdivided into divisions and then into successively smaller groups of related plants, down to the level of species.

KINGDOM:	Plantae
DIVISION:	Magnoliophyta
CLASS:	Magnoliopsida
ORDER:	Fagales
FAMILY:	Fagaceae
GENUS:	*Quercus*
SPECIES:	*alba*

The taxonomic classification of the Eastern White Oak (*Quercus alba*) from kingdom to species.

In this guide, the family and genus are emphasized as the taxonomic ranks most helpful for understanding and identifying species of trees. By definition, all of the species in a genus are closely related and share many features in common, while species from different genera are less closely related and can be expected to show larger differences. Trees from different families are even more fundamentally different, different orders even more so, and so on.

HIGHER GROUPS OF TREES

North American trees include members of three divisions:

PINOPHYTA includes all of the needle-leaved and scale-leaved conifers including yews, pines, spruces, cypresses, junipers, and others, as well as the podocarps. The conifers and ginkgo together belong to the group known as gymnosperms (meaning "naked seed").

GINKGOPHYTA includes only the Ginkgo.

MAGNOLIOPHYTA includes all of the broadleaf trees from palms through the end of this guide. This division is commonly known as "flowering plants" or angiosperms (meaning "contained seed").

The Magnoliophyta have traditionally been divided into two main groups: the monocots and dicots. Monocots are named for having a single cotyledon (seed leaf), and also usually have flower parts in multiples of three and usually parallel leaf veins. The monocots include tens of thousands of species (including orchids, lilies, and grasses) but few trees, and are represented in this guide only by palms and Joshua-tree. The dicots have two seed leaves, flower parts in fours or fives, and net-veined leaves. They are represented in this guide by everything from Saguaro to the end of the book (Saguaro is placed with the Joshua-tree for convenience but is actually more closely related to Tamarisk).

SUBGENERA

Within taxonomic hierarchies, further subdivisions are sometimes used to represent significant variations. For field identification, one of the most informative subdivisions is the subgenus or section, a grouping of related species within a genus. For example, the oaks are trees in the beech family and form the genus *Quercus,* which has about 400 species of trees and shrubs worldwide. Oaks can be usefully separated into three distinct subgenera. In this guide subgenera are usually given the less formal label of "group." The oaks are presented in the red oak group, white oak group, and Golden-cup Oak group. Other well-defined subgenera are found among the pines (genus *Pinus*), alders (genus *Alnus*), and plums and cherries (genus *Prunus*).

SPECIES

The species is the basic unit of study for the naturalist, and the concept is applied similarly in birds, trees, and other organisms. A species is a distinguishable population of individuals that share a high level of genetic similarity. This leaves a lot of room for interpretation, and the trees present many ambiguous or borderline cases. For example, Southern Bayberry occurs in two forms: a solitary, larger-leaved, often tree-like plant in wetter soils, and a smaller, smaller-leaved, thicket-forming shrub in drier soils. There is evidence that the differences are not simply an effect of the different soil conditions, but botanists still debate whether these should be recognized as species, subspecies, or merely forms. Plants such as serviceberries and hawthorns that can reproduce asexually, forming whole populations of clones, present another challenge to plant taxonomists. There is no consensus on the criteria for recognizing species in plants, and in fact, multiple criteria are probably needed to cover the wide range of situations encountered.

Just as in other living things, there are many closely-related populations of trees whose status is debated—some authorities consider them species, others subspecies, and others merely local variations. In these cases there is no easy solution. Lumping a varied group of populations under a single species name would be misleading, but naming poorly-defined local variations as species would be equally misleading. What is most important is simply to maintain an awareness of the variation, no matter what labels are applied to it.

When considering species in trees, it is worth remembering that natural selection does not act directly on the appearance of trees in the same way that birds evolve ornamental colors and patterns. Trees do not communicate with other trees through visual cues, so they do not care what other trees look like. We tend to focus on visible features, but the features that distinguish many plant species—pollen grain structure, flower anatomy, chromosome numbers, or sap chemistry—are not apparent to the unaided eye. Striking variations in color or leaf shape may have no taxonomic significance, while some trees that look virtually identical to us are legitimately classified as separate species.

HYBRIDIZATION

Hybrids, the offspring of parents of two different species, are common among related trees, and even some plants from different genera are capable of interbreeding. Hybrids generally show intermediate characteristics, but in many cases it is simply not possible to identify a hybrid without chemical or DNA testing. Recent studies on several different families of trees have shown that some individual trees that appear to be hybrids do not have mixed DNA, and therefore must be merely extreme variations of one species.

SUBDIVISIONS OF SPECIES

Botanists use several different categories to subdivide variation below the level of species. Individual variation (e.g. a Flowering Dogwood tree with pink flowers, or a European Beech with deeply dissected leaves) is described as a form, if it occurs in the wild, or a cultivar, only if it is produced in cultivation. This is analogous to the term "morph" in birds, such as the dark morph of the Rough-legged Hawk, which is simply an individual variation occurring as some percentage of the population.

The labels subspecies and variety are used for population-level variation, which usually involves more than just a single feature and has some geographic basis. For example, Cucumbertrees in the eastern part of their range often have brighter yellow flowers and also tend to have smaller leaves and hairy twigs and are named as a variety. Lodgepole Pines in the Pacific Northwest are always shorter, crooked trees with different needles, cones, and bark from trees in the mountains, and is named as a different subspecies.

In theory, the term subspecies should be used for well-defined variation that nearly rises to the level of species, while variety is used for somewhat less well-defined variation with differences that are relatively small or inconsistent. In practice, however, the distinction between subspecies and variety is often unclear and arbitrary, and many authorities now advocate making variety a synonym of subspecies.

NAMES OF TREES

The names and taxonomy of families of plants in this book reflect the most recent classification of the Angiosperm Phylogeny Group. The taxonomy and names at the species level is a combination of the Flora of North America, the Biota of North America Program, and the United States Department of Agriculture plants database, modified in a few cases as suggested by new research.

Many minor variations and hybrids of trees have been given formal scientific names by botanists, and this can be very confusing. Following botanical conventions, I have used single quotation marks around a name to indicate that it is not an accepted taxonomic entity (species or subspecies). These names may apply to hybrids, varieties, or cultivars, and over time some may evolve into species, but in general they should not be included in a list of "official" trees of North America.

COMMON NAMES

Over the centuries, trees have been given many different names. Common or "English" names used in this guide have been chosen from among those in common use. Sources of names include the Flora of North America project, the Biota of North America Program, the United States Department of Agriculture plants database, and various popular books on trees. In a few cases common names have been modified to distinguish them more clearly from other species. A few of the most commonly used alternate names are listed in each species account beneath the scientific name.

Size

SIZE AND MEASUREMENTS

The maximum size listed in the species accounts in this guide are for the maximum height recorded in North America and has been compiled from several sources. Seeking and documenting big trees is a popular hobby, and the official "National Register of Big Trees" is maintained by the organization American Forests.

Except as a broad indicator, size is generally not very useful for identifying trees. For example, Northern Red Oak has the potential to grow 150 feet tall, Bear Oak does not. All species begin as a seed, and their size at the time of observation depends on their age and rate of growth. Trees continue to grow larger (although not necessarily taller) as long as they live, and size is extremely variable—depending on the health of the tree, available water, local wind conditions, length of growing season, and other factors.

The sizes of leaves, flowers, and fruit are given as single values in this book. It should be understood that all species are variable, and that adding or subtracting about twenty-five percent from the given measurements should cover most of the normal variation within a species. In general, leaf size is more variable than fruit size, which is more variable than flower size. Measurements of leaves are of the whole leaf from base of the stalk to tip of the blade.

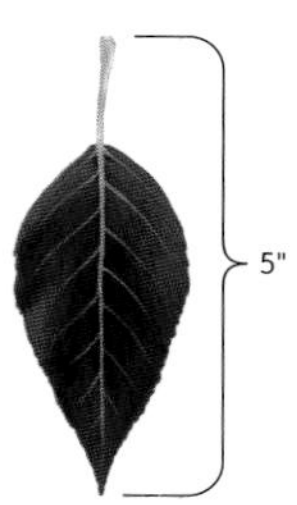
5"

Leaf measurements in this guide are an average value of the whole leaf, including the blade and the stalk. Mature leaves of Black Cottonwood average 5 inches from the base of stalk to the tip of the blade.

TREE RECORDS

Trees are some of the most extraordinary living things on earth and represent many extremes in size, age, and simple majesty:

- The tallest tree currently living (and the tallest ever recorded) is a Coast Redwood 379.1 feet tall in northern California. More than ten other living Coast Redwoods are over 360 feet tall. The second-tallest tree species in the world is the Australian Mountain-ash (*Eucalyptus regnans*) currently 331 feet tall. There are a few reports from the late 1800s of both of these species reaching over 400 feet tall, but there is no verifiable evidence of those measurements.
- The largest living single tree by volume and by weight is a Giant Sequoia (the "General Sherman" tree) with an estimated volume of over 50,000 cubic feet and estimated weight of 3.6 million pounds (more than ten times the weight of the biggest Blue Whale). That tree is dwarfed by a Coast Redwood that fell in 1905, which had an estimated volume of 88,000 cubic feet and weighed 6.6 million pounds. Even larger is a grove of genetically identical Quaking Aspens in Utah with many stems from a single root system—it covers 106 acres of land and is estimated to weigh 12 million pounds.
- The oldest living single tree is an Intermountain Bristlecone Pine in California at over 4,800 years old. Another tree in Nevada, cut down in 1964 by a researcher, was over 5,000 years old. A Norway Spruce in Sweden has sprouted a succession of relatively short-lived single trunks from a root system now over 9,500 years old. The aforementioned grove of Quaking Aspen (actually a root system) in Utah has been estimated to be at least 80,000 years old.

Maps

The range maps in this book show where each species, native or exotic, is known to be growing and reproducing in the wild with no assistance from humans. Native species range is shown in green and escaped exotic species range is shown in yellow. Within the area shown on the map, each species will be found only in suitable habitat. Some species are widespread, found in many settings and soil types throughout a region, while other species are very local and are found only in scattered locations within the mapped range.

These maps have been created by combining data on natural range from the United States Forest Service database with data on escaped and naturalized trees compiled by John Kartesz and the Biota of North America Program. No comprehensive and detailed information exists on the distribution of escaped trees in Canada or Mexico. For some species, other information was used to sketch in the approximate range in Canada, and for some introduced species, there are simply gaps in the mapped range.

Green indicates where a native species is found growing in the wild; yellow indicates where a non-native species has escaped and is growing in the wild (Eastern White Oak, left and Sawtooth Oak, right).

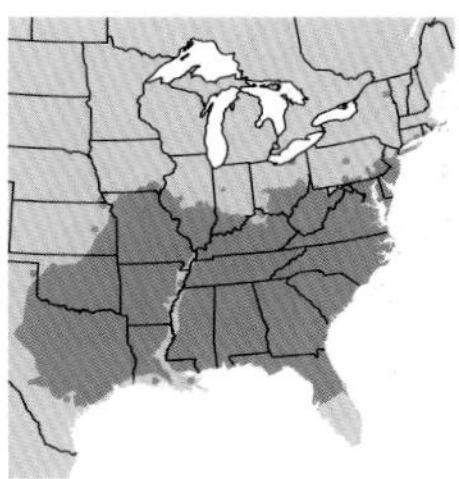

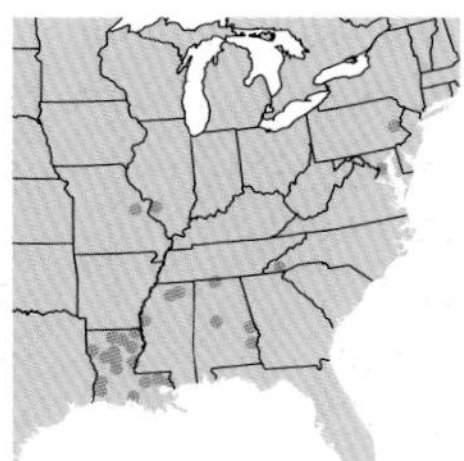

The maps show only areas where species have been documented growing in the wild, so you are likely to see many species being cultivated in areas that are not shown on the maps. For example, Pecan is one of the most frequently planted yard trees in the rural Southeast, and is grown in commercial pecan orchards there and in the Southwest, but the map only shows the relatively limited areas where escaped trees have been found in the wild. Similarly, Ginkgo is commonly planted in cities and towns nearly continent-wide, but very rarely escapes.

Many native species now grow in parts of North America where they did not occur naturally two centuries ago. After escaping from cultivation, eastern species like Northern Red Oak and Black Locust are now found at many locations in the West, and both species of native catalpas have spread far beyond their original natural range in the Southeast. The range of these species is all indicated in green (native) on the maps, regardless of whether local populations are natural or introduced.

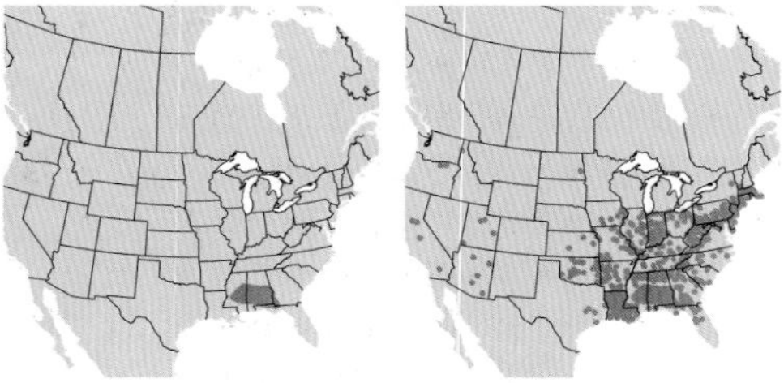

The range of Southern Catalpa was originally restricted to a small area of the South (left), but after escaping from countless plantings, the species is now fully naturalized and commonly seen growing in the wild across much of the East and as far west as central California (right). This species is also currently cultivated in many other places not shown on this map.

ZONES

The USDA plant hardiness zone system uses the average minimum winter temperature to define regions, which tend to correspond to average length of growing season (milder winter equals a longer growing season). These zones provide a simplified guide to the difference in climates and give a first indication of whether a species of plant might grow in a particular region.

The range of zones where each species will grow is included in this guide for every species that is regularly cultivated. If you know the zone of your location, then the listed range of zones will give some indication of whether that tree could grow in the area. In practice, as any gardener knows, many other factors such as amount and timing of precipitation, summer heat, soil type, and other factors, all have as big an influence on the range of a species as minimum winter temperature. So while the zones suggest where a species *could* grow, that does not mean that it *will* grow there.

NATIVE OR INTRODUCED?

Native plants are defined as those that occurred naturally in North America before European exploration and settlement. Introduced plants were brought to this continent later, by humans. But humans have been moving plants for thousands of years, and it is suspected that a few of the species we consider native may have been introduced here by humans even before Europeans arrived in the New World.

Naturalized (introduced) plants are nonnative species that are reproducing and well-established in the wild. Introduced trees may be called invasive if they spread aggressively and at the expense of native species.

Escaped plants, also called simply "escapes," are plants that have spread from cultivation into an area where they did not occur naturally. This term is sometimes used in a narrow sense to refer to plants that have escaped from cultivation but are not naturalized. These species may persist for only a short time or only in a small area.

Cultivated trees are simply growing where they have been planted by humans. Exotic trees can often be seen growing around old homesteads or farm fields, even long after the buildings and fields have disappeared, but if they do not reproduce or spread they are not considered escaped.

The line between cultivated and escaped is fine and easily crossed, and new species of trees are escaping each year. For example, the Kalkora Mimosa is an uncommonly cultivated small tree from Asia, closely related to Silktree. A few trees have been found growing outside cultivation in Duke, North Carolina, where they are hybridizing with the more common Silktrees. Whether this species will spread beyond that site only time will tell.

The cultivated species included in this guide, and many other less commonly cultivated species that are not included here, all have the potential to escape into the wild, and should be monitored.

Habitat

The preferred habitat of each species is summarized very briefly and broadly. Just like birds and other animals, some trees have very specific habitat requirements, while others are generalists. The habitats of trees involve mainly soil type, soil moisture, and microclimate, which are not very easy for the non-scientist to discern.

One of the most easily observed and easily defined aspects of a tree's habitat is the availability of water, and that is a feature that is emphasized in the habitat descriptions. Many pairs of similar species can be distinguished by the preference of one for wet soils and another for dry soils. Soils that are intermediate, neither wet nor dry, are called mesic.

Tree Conservation

Perhaps no other group of organisms has been as profoundly affected by humans as trees. Only a few thousand acres of virgin old-growth forest remain in the eastern United States, the rest has been cut, and most of the eastern forest has been cut down many times. What the average person thinks of as "mature forest" is usually fifty- to seventy-year-old new growth, covering land that was open pasture or farmland less than a hundred years ago. At the same time, a large percentage of the land is now covered by roads and structures, supporting just a few cultivated trees or no trees at all. A recent study estimated that fifty-eight percent of the land area of the contiguous United States no longer supports native vegetation.

Native trees face several distinct threats. First, and most directly, the threat of being cut down. While birds and other animals may be able to move to a new home when their habitat is destroyed (few are successful in that, but at least they have the option), trees cannot. Simply cutting trees down is not necessarily bad. Logging opens the forest canopy and allows new growth. In just a few decades, even a clear-cut portion of land, left undisturbed, may become a new forest. But if the ground is paved over, those trees are gone forever.

Second, trees face an increasing threat from introduced diseases and insect pests. The list of such pests affecting trees grows longer each year. In early 2009, tens of thousands of trees were removed from suburban neighborhoods in Worcester, Massachusetts in an effort to prevent the spread of the Asian Longhorn Beetle. Insects such as Emerald Ash Borer and Hemlock Woolly Adelgid are decimating ash and hemlock populations, since the native North American species have evolved no defense against these Asian insects. Molds and fungal diseases like sudden oak death and laurel wilt threaten to do to those species what other fungal infections did to elms and chestnuts early in the 1900s.

Third, trees face the threat of atmospheric pollution in many forms, including climate change and acid rain. One of the many poorly-known consequences of acid rain is that acidic water leaches calcium out of the soil and carries it downstream. Trees require trace amounts of calcium to thrive, and the reduced calcium in the soil of some northeastern forests is thought to be the cause of very slow growth among Sugar Maples and other trees there in recent decades. Climate change threatens trees in unknown and unforeseeable ways. Recent dry years across the western United States have made many species of conifers, from New Mexico to Alaska, more susceptible to the attacks of native Pine-bark Beetles. Weakened by drought, and without sufficient moisture to produce the sap that is their best defense against insect attacks, the trees are simply overwhelmed and killed by countless tunneling beetle larvae.

You can help by supporting land preservation, supporting conservation advocacy groups, planting native species of trees and other plants, and working towards a more sustainable lifestyle.

Tree Identification

TERMINOLOGY

Technical terms have been avoided in this guide whenever possible and replaced with simple, everyday language. For example, botanists use terms such as canescent, hispid, lanate, strigose, among other words, to describe variations of minute hairs on leaves and stems. In this guide, the terms used are simply hairy or woolly. Although botanical terms are more precise, they require a high level of understanding to be used effectively. Simple terminology is generally sufficient for most field identification of trees.

VARIATION

Like any living thing, and even more so than most animals, trees are variable in appearance. The illustrations and descriptions included here can only represent a small segment of the wide range of variation that is considered typical of each species. With experience you will gain a sense of which features are less variable, and therefore more reliable for identification. Given such variability, it is even more important to look for multiple diagnostic features to support your understanding and identification of trees.

GROWTH FORM

The eventual shape of a mature tree depends partly on genetics and partly on its environment. Each species has a certain potential which it will reach under optimal conditions. The overall growth form of a tree, known as its habit, can be a useful cue for identification, as each genus and some species tend to have characteristic shapes and branching patterns. The tips of the twigs form the crown of the tree—which can be flat, rounded, or pointed, narrow or broad—and subtle average differences between species may be helpful for identification.

Images of whole trees are shown for a few species in this guide, but growth is so variable, and differences so small, that these images have limited value as a diagnostic tool. In general young trees of all species are narrower, more conical, and more symmetrical than old trees. With age most trees become broad, flat-topped, and irregular. Leafless winter trees were used for many full tree illustrations in this book because leaves tend to obscure the structural differences in branching, so identifying summer trees by overall shape is more difficult than in winter.

Trees grown in sunlight take on a very different form than those grown in shade. Shading forces a tree to grow towards whatever light is available, while an open-grown tree is fully exposed to sunlight, and grows relatively low and broad. A tree of the same species grown in forest is competing with other trees for sunlight, and grows a tall straight trunk and relatively small crown of leaves to capture sunlight at the canopy of the forest. Such trees can sometimes be seen when individuals are left behind after the forest around them is cut down. Conversely, an open-grown tree can still survive after a forest grows up around it, and retains the massive low side branches and spreading form it developed when it had no competition.

Whether a tree is upright (relatively tall and narrow) or spreading (relatively short and broad) can be a useful general clue to identification, and depends largely on the angle of branching, which is fairly consistent within a species. Because a birch tree has relatively small angles between trunk and branches, the branches stay close to the trunk and the shape of the tree is upright and narrow. Apple trees have branches that are nearly horizontal, at right angles to the trunk, and the tree is low and spreading.

The tall narrow shape characteristic of Subalpine Fir in the Rocky Mountains is a result of slow growth and heavy snowfall. Its foliage is dense and clumped, and the branches are short to easily shed snow. A Balsam Fir growing in the temperate forest of New England, on the other hand, develops a broader conical shape with faster growth producing longer shoots and more graceful branching. Less snowfall loads allow the tree to grow longer side branches.

Compare the narrow shape of forest-grown Eastern White Oak (left) with the broad spreading shape of an open-grown tree (top right).

Common Apple (left) has branches diverging at nearly right angles to the trunk, forming a broader, more spreading shape, while Gray Birch (right) has branches angled up and a narrower overall shape.

Compare the broader shape of Balsam Fir (left) grown in the open in a region without heavy winter snow, to the narrow shape of Subalpine Fir (right) grown in an area with a very heavy winter snow load.

Monterey Pine is a relatively small gnarled and stunted tree in the few locations where it grows wild along the California coast. Planted elsewhere, however, it grows to its full potential size as a tall and stately tree, much larger and faster-growing than in the wild.

Some differences between trees are genetic, while others are a response to environmental pressures. In most cases the differences we observe in the wild probably result from a combination of genetic potential meeting environmental reality.

RATE OF GROWTH

Trees grow much more slowly under adverse conditions than they do under favorable conditions. Rate of growth can have profound effects on the appearance of a tree. Slow-growing twigs tend to be stout and gnarled with leaves tightly clustered along a short section of the twig. Fast-growing twigs are more slender, long and straight, with leaves more widely-spaced.

Photosynthesis requires sunlight, so branches that are shaded (often low) simply cannot produce the wood necessary for rapid growth. Even on the same tree, the highest branches may be long, whip-like, and fast-growing, while the lowest branches (which tend to be the ones we see and study) may be short, crooked, and slow-growing.

Both of these Pecan twigs are from the same tree: the twig above from higher on the tree is slender and fast-growing compared to the stouter, more crooked slow-growing twig found lower on the tree.

LONGEVITY

Different species of trees have very different lifespans. Some small trees such as Pin Cherry and Gray Birch rarely live more than fifty years, while larger species like Eastern White Oak can live well over 500 years. Size is not always a sign of age, as Eastern Cottonwood can become a very large tree with massive branches within one hundred years and the species usually does not live much longer than that.

Leaves

Leaves are extremely variable, both individually and among species of trees. They include everything from the large heart-shaped leaves of catalpas and the intricately divided pinnate leaves of the Silktree, to the slender needles of pines and the tiny scale-like leaves of junipers.

Leaves are the surfaces where most trees gather energy from the sun and, through photosynthesis, convert carbon dioxide and water into sugar. Water is needed to hold the leaf blade in the required position, to react with carbon dioxide during photosynthesis, and as a medium to transport the resulting sugars back to the rest of the plant. But water is usually a limited or unpredictable resource, so the leaves are adapted to gather sunlight efficiently while at the same time conserving water.

Leaves serve no reproductive or signaling function and therefore their appearance is constrained only by the need to gather sunlight while conserving moisture, which results in a wide variety of leaf shapes but also a tendency for trees in similar environments to converge on similar strategies. For example, most desert plants have few, narrow leaves to conserve moisture, while forest understory trees (or understory twigs of individual trees) tend to have broader leaves.

EVERGREEN OR DECIDUOUS

In the simplest sense, an evergreen tree is simply a tree that retains its leaves year-round, staying green all year. A deciduous tree loses all its leaves less than twelve months after they grow, and becomes bare and leafless for part of the year. Within each of these simple definitions, however, there is extensive variation. Some deciduous trees in the far north may have leaves for only four months of the year, while deciduous trees in the south may have leaves for eleven months. Evergreen trees may hold leaves for just over twelve months or up to thirty years (usually two to four years).

Deciduous trees drop their leaves as a strategy to avoid damage from freezing or drying, and most deciduous trees are found in cold or dry climates. Trees that lose their leaves during a dry season are called drought-deciduous. These species are often very flexible in their strategy, and may grow leaves only after sufficient rainfall and lose leaves as soon as the water supply dwindles. Many species in wetter climates also respond to dry periods by dropping leaves. Box-elder in particular is noted for its leaves that curl and turn brown during prolonged dry spells.

All species evolve so that the timing of leaf emergence and leaf fall match the local climate. Red Maples are fully deciduous throughout their range, but trees in the south have a much shorter leafless period in winter than trees in the north. Sweetbay is fully deciduous at the northern edge of its range, and loses its leaves for several months each winter. In the southern parts of its range, it holds its leaves for a full twelve months and appears to be evergreen. Such a tree is called tardily deciduous or semi-evergreen and these terms are both used (more or less interchangeably) to describe a tree that is nearly or apparently evergreen but does not retain leaves longer than twelve months.

Southern Live Oak is another species that appears to be evergreen, but usually holds its leaves for just one year. Most trees lose their old leaves gradually just after new growth emerges in spring, so they always appear green. But some individual trees drop their old leaves a week or two *before* new leaves emerge, and for a very brief period they are fully leafless, even while neighboring trees of the same species appear to be evergreen.

On close examination it is possible to

Leaves of the gymnosperms are quite different from the broad flat leaves of angiosperms. All trees in the pine family have slender, needle-like leaves.

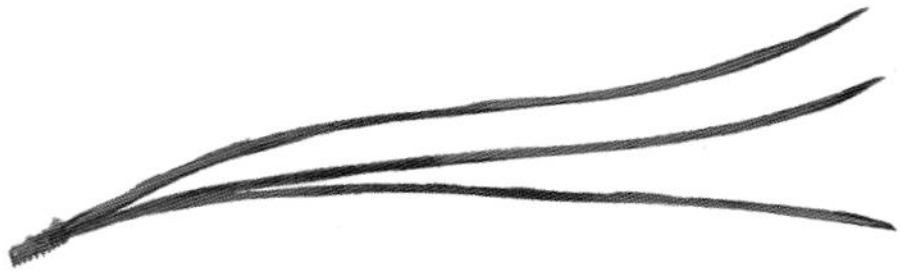

Pine needles emerge in clusters of 2 to 5, joined at the base (all other gymnosperms have solitary needles). Each cluster of needles is protected at its base by a sheath of small scales. The sheath soon falls away on white pines, but is persistent on yellow pines.

Each gymnosperm genus has distinctive variations in needles. Most trees in the cypress family have small scale-like leaves that line the twig.

Small depressions on the scale leaves of many species in the cypress family are glands that exude tiny drops of resin. The presence or absence of glands or resin can be helpful for identifying these very similar species.

determine how long leaves are retained on any tree by looking for bud scale scars to distinguish each season's growth on the twigs. A deciduous or semi-evergreen species will have leaves from only a single growing season, only on the twigs, while truly evergreen species will have leaves from at least two growing seasons, on the twigs and also on the branchlets.

BROADLEAF VS. NEEDLE-LEAF

One of the most fundamental distinctions among trees is the difference between the broad flat leaf blades of most angiosperms, with net-like veins, and the needle-like or scale-like leaves of the gymnosperms, with parallel veins. Among angiosperms, the monocots (only palms and Joshua-tree are tree-like) have parallel veins in their leaves like gymnosperms. A third pattern is shown by the Ginkgo, which has veins that simply fork into a fan shape.

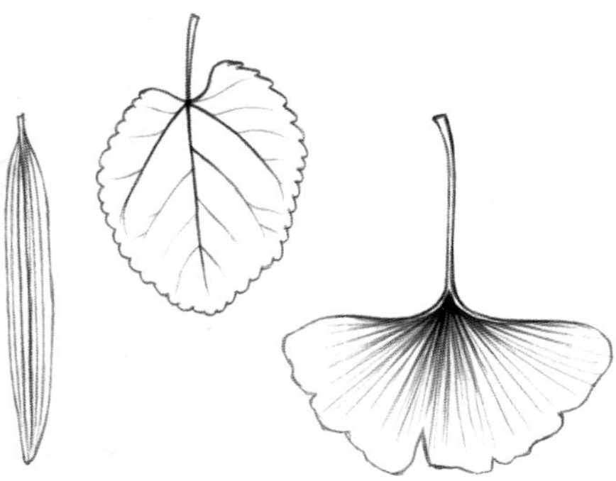

Most gymnosperms have narrow needle-like leaves with parallel veins, such as the Bigleaf Podocarp (left). Angiosperms have netted veins, such as the White Mulberry (middle). Ginkgo (right) is unique in having straight veins that fork to form a fan shape.

LEAF SIZE

The size of leaves is extremely variable and the size of an individual leaf is never very helpful for identification. Observing many leaves is the best way to get a sense of the range of variation and the average leaf size on a tree. Among other things, leaves on sprouts and other vigorous twigs are often much larger than normal, while leaves on slow-growing or unhealthy twigs can be very small.

In the oaks and many other groups, leaves in full sun in the canopy tend to be smaller and narrower or more deeply lobed than those on the more shaded lower branches. But in spite of all of this variation, the larger leaves of Eastern Black Oak and smaller leaves of Scarlet Oak, for example, can be obvious when viewing the whole tree and looking at the average leaf size.

LEAF SHAPE

Leaf shape is undoubtedly the most studied feature in tree identification. It may not be the most useful, but it is conspicuous and easy to interpret, so we tend to focus on the outline of the leaf and study it in great detail. For the novice, leaf shape provides a simple and straightforward starting point for tree identification, but it is important to recognize the limitations of leaf shape as a field mark and to put equal emphasis on other features.

Important leaf shape features include the overall shape, focusing on the shape of the base and the tip, the length of the leafstalk, whether the leaf is lobed or unlobed and the margins are toothed or smooth, and the pattern of veins.

VARIATION IN LEAF SHAPE

The overall shape of the leaf is quite variable in most species. On a single tree the leaf shape often differs between shaded twigs in the interior and exposed twigs in the crown. Leaf size and shape also differ dramatically between slow-growing twigs and vigorous twigs on the same tree. The first one or two leaves of the season (i.e., the lowermost leaves on the twig) are sometimes atypical in shape.

Leaves that are drying up tend to curl and twist and leaves that have been attacked by insects or disease often grow into odd shapes or develop scars or galls in response to the attack.

LEAFSTALK

The leafstalk can provide some very useful clues for identification. The length of the stalk is fairly consistent in most species and the difference between a poplar and an elm, or between white birch and yellow birch, is readily apparent. Maples, which have extremely variable leafstalk lengths, are an exception. Other clues to watch for include the flattened leafstalks of some poplars, and small glands along the leafstalk shown by some cherries and plums and some poplars.

LEAF TEETH

Many species have toothed leaf margins. The pattern of teeth on the leaf margins is generally less variable than the overall shape. Leaves with marginal teeth all the same size are said to be single-toothed; leaves with teeth of different sizes, such as small teeth along the contours of larger teeth, are said to be double-toothed. This feature is usually consistent within a species and can be helpful for distinguishing some very similar species such as plums. Also take note of the prominence of the teeth, which varies from fine to coarse on different species.

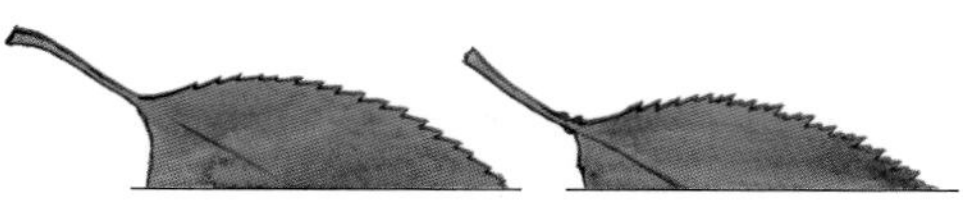

The leaf margin can have simple teeth as in Mexican Plum (left), or double teeth as in American Plum (right).

LEAF VENATION

Leaves have a network of veins (like our circulatory system) to carry water and nutrients to each cell, and to carry the products of photosynthesis back to the rest of the tree. The pattern of veins within a leaf is very consistent and useful to distinguish species and genera of broadleaf trees. Veins may be conspicuous in texture or in color, or very inconspicuous.

Most broadleaf trees have pinnate veins (feather-like), with one primary vein along the center of the leaf and many more or less parallel secondary veins branching off. These

The pinnately compound leaf of Shagbark Hickory (left) shows the central stalk with several pairs of leaflets and one terminal leaflet. A bipinnately compound leaf of Littleleaf Leucaena (right) has each leaflet divided into many subleaflets.

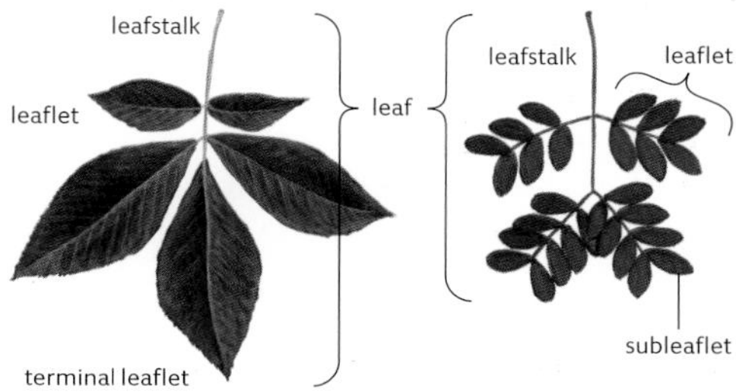
leafstalk
leaflet
leaf
terminal leaflet
leafstalk
leaflet
subleaflet

Shown below are simple, lobed, and compound leaves with pinnate venation (left) and palmate venation (right).

simple leaves

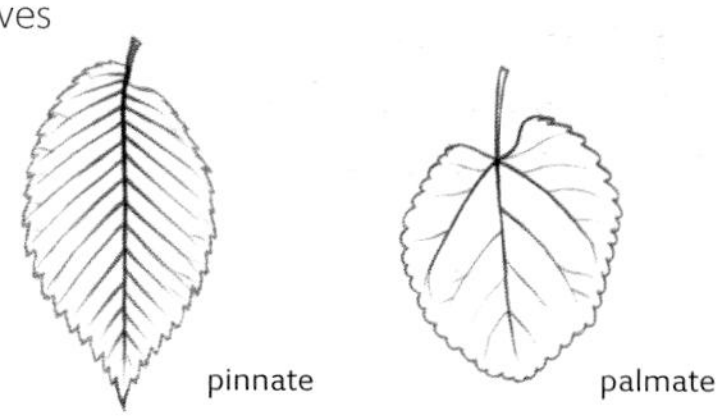
pinnate
palmate

lobed leaves

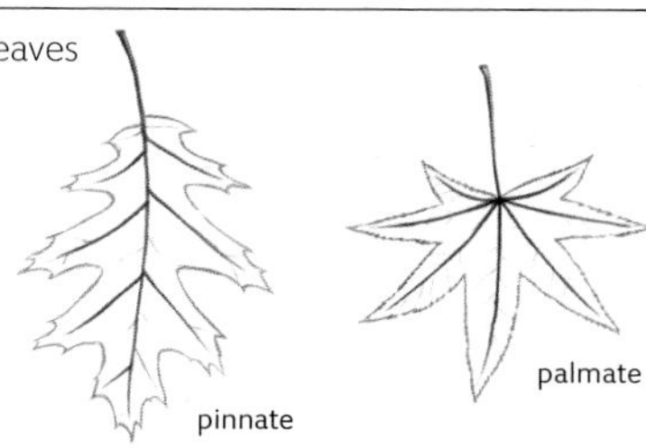
pinnate
palmate

compound leaves

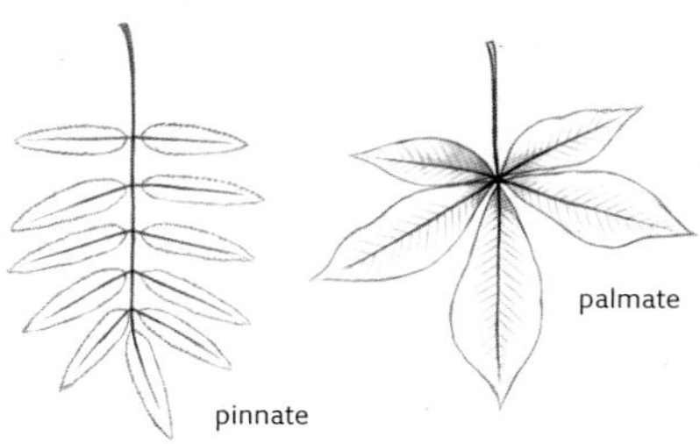
pinnate
palmate

secondary veins can continue straight to the teeth at the leaf margin, or curve towards the leaf tip and disappear before reaching the margin, or curve strongly to follow the leaf edge back towards the primary vein; this is known as arcuate veins.

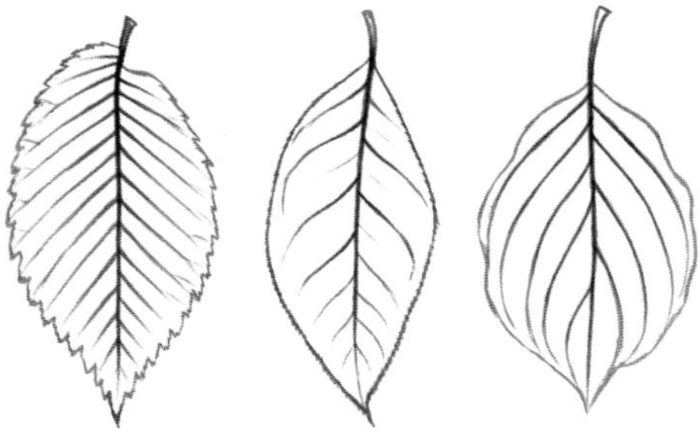

Elms (American Elm, left) have straight pinnate veins that extend to the teeth at the leaf edge. Cherries (Black Cherry, middle) have veins that curve and do not reach the leaf edge. Dogwoods (Flowering Dogwood, right) have veins that curve to follow the leaf edge.

Species with palmate veins have three to seven primary veins all radiating from the base of the leaf. The clearest examples of this involve species with lobed leaves (for example, Sweetgum), but mulberries, lindens, and some other genera have unlobed leaves with three main veins radiating from the base.

COMPOUND VS. SIMPLE LEAVES

Most trees have simple leaves, with a single flattened leaf blade on each stalk. Some trees have compound leaves, with multiple separate leaflets on a single stalk. These can be pinnately compound like a feather, with leaflets along two sides of a long central stalk, or palmately compound with all leaflets emerging from the same point at the tip of the stalk. There is a relatively small difference between a deeply-lobed leaf and a palmately compound leaf, and in fact the Rocky Mountain Maple often has lobed simple leaves and compound leaves on the same tree.

A few species have compound leaves on which the leaflets are themselves compound. These species are called bipinnately compound.

Most species with compound leaves can lose leaflets individually in the fall, and the central leafstalk may persist into winter, or the entire compound leaf can fall intact. Simple leaves can be distinguished from these compound leaflets by having a bud formed just above the point of attachment on the twig. Leaflets of a compound leaf do not have buds at their base.

LEAF ARRANGEMENT

Whether a tree's leaves grow in pairs opposite each other along the twigs, or singly on alternate sides of the twig, has generally been strongly emphasized in guides to tree identification. It is easily discerned and immediately separates the species into two groups. It is also helpful in the winter when leaf arrangement can be seen in the leaf scars on bare twigs. In this book I have chosen to de-emphasize this feature because it is rarely helpful at the species level, and serves only to place a tree in a group of genera with opposite leaves.

Leaves that grow singly from the twig, without another leaf directly across the twig, are called alternate, as they usually grow from alternate sides of the twig. Leaves that grow in pairs from opposite sides of the twig at the same level are called opposite. If three of more leaves all grow from the same level on the twig they are called whorled. On very slow-growing twigs such as spur twigs, the leaves can be clustered so closely that they appear to be opposite or whorled, when in fact they are alternate.

Three main groups of native trees have opposite leaves—maples, ashes, and dogwoods. Generations of students have memorized these trees with the acronym MAD. Opposite leaves are also shown by buckeyes and by several other smaller and less prominent species and groups of trees. Whorled leaves are shown only by the catalpas and the Buttonbush.

Parts of a lobed palmate leaf

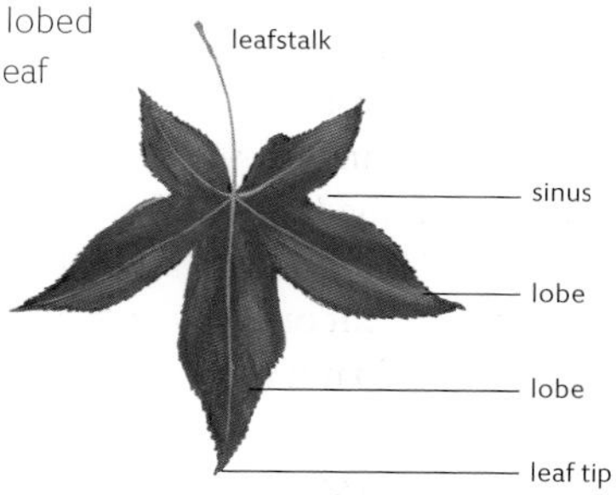
leafstalk
sinus
lobe
lobe
leaf tip

Parts of lobed pinnate leaf

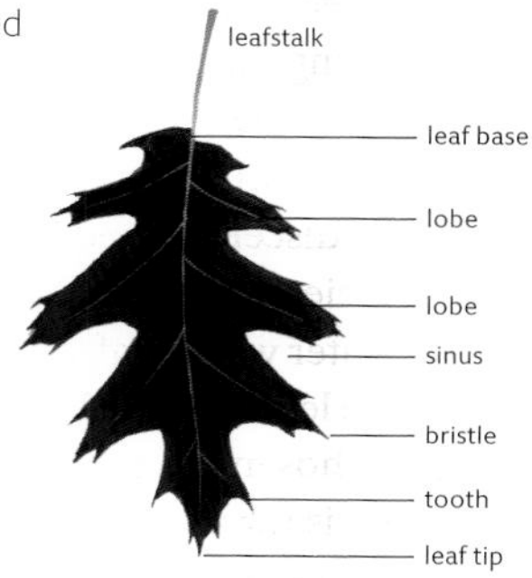
leafstalk
leaf base
lobe
lobe
sinus
bristle
tooth
leaf tip

COMPOUND PALMATE LEAVES

Only the buckeyes have truly palmately compound leaves. Several maples, such as Rocky Mountain Maple and Boxelder (and many species with pinnately compound leaves) can have just three leaflets and therefore appear palmately compound.

Common Horsechestnut, page 326
Rocky Mountain Maple, page 343

LOBED PINNATE LEAVES

Oaks commonly have lobed pinnate leaves. Several species of hawthorns can also show pinnately lobed leaves.

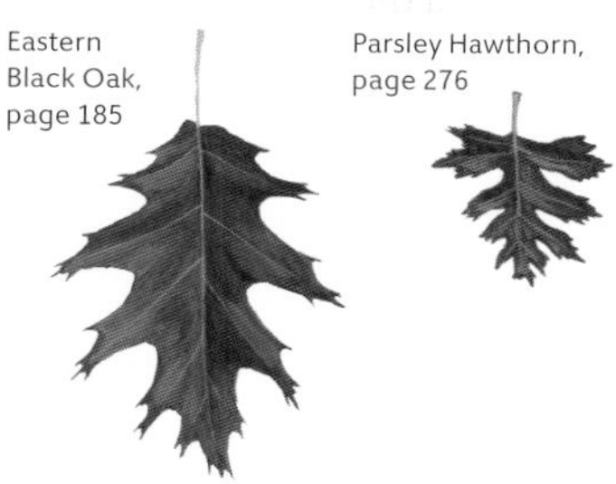
Eastern Black Oak, page 185
Parsley Hawthorn, page 276

LOBED PALMATE LEAVES

Many types of trees have leaves with veins radiating from the base of the leaf blade and ending in obvious lobes. Representative species from each genus with palmately lobed leaves are shown here.

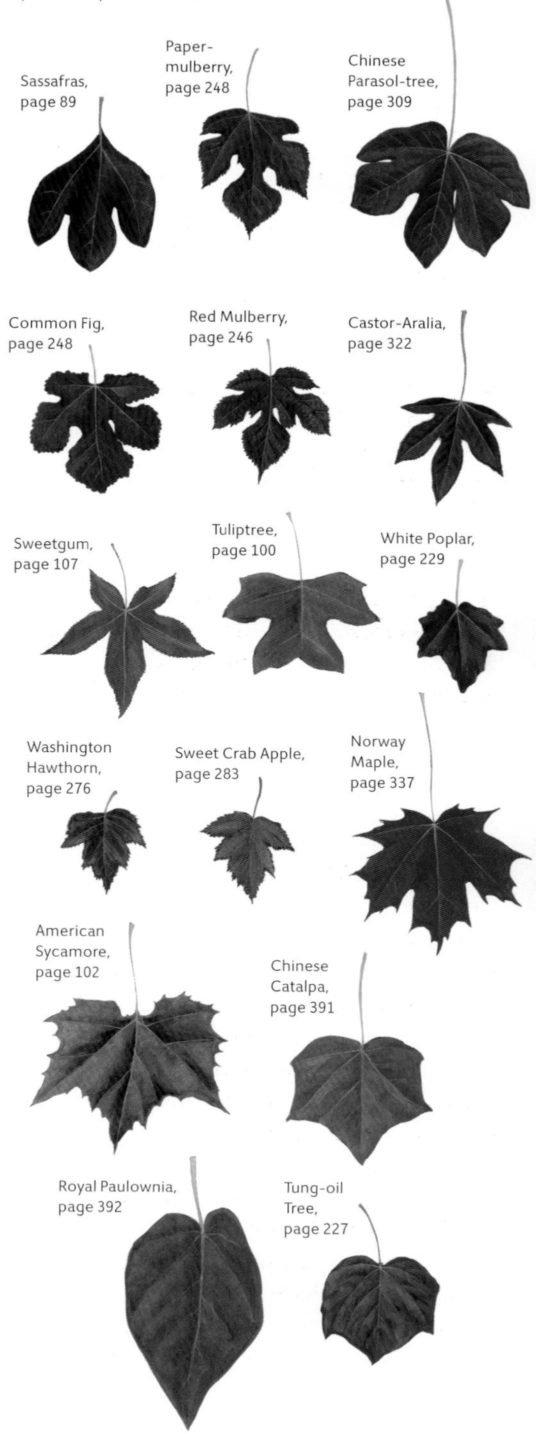
Sassafras, page 89
Paper-mulberry, page 248
Chinese Parasol-tree, page 309
Common Fig, page 248
Red Mulberry, page 246
Castor-Aralia, page 322
Sweetgum, page 107
Tuliptree, page 100
White Poplar, page 229
Washington Hawthorn, page 276
Sweet Crab Apple, page 283
Norway Maple, page 337
American Sycamore, page 102
Chinese Catalpa, page 391
Royal Paulownia, page 392
Tung-oil Tree, page 227

COMPOUND PINNATE LEAVES

Shown here are representative species from each genus of tree with pinnately compound leaves. Most genera are in the legume family, and of the remainder, only walnuts, hickories (walnut family), and ashes (olive family) are represented by more than a few species with pinnately compound leaves.

American Mountain-ash, page 290

Shining Sumac, page 316

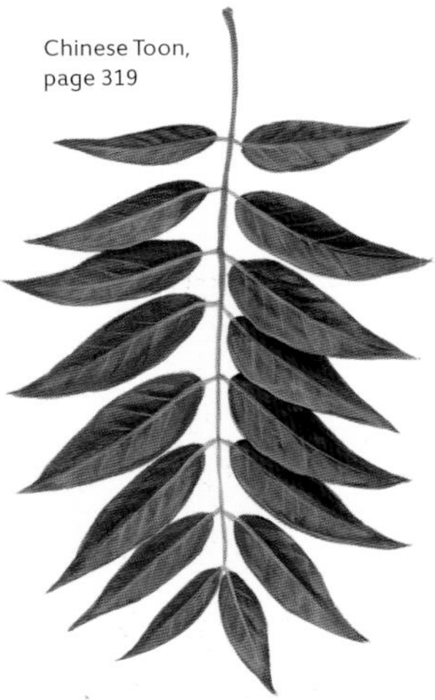
Chinese Toon, page 319

Poison-sumac, page 317

Western Soapberry, page 324

Butternut, page 140

Ailanthus, page 352

Beebee Tree, page 321

Amur Corktree, page 323

Southern Prickly-Ash, page 322

Mexican-buckeye, page 325

Chinese Pistachio, page 313

Black Hickory, page 146

Golden Rain-tree, page 325

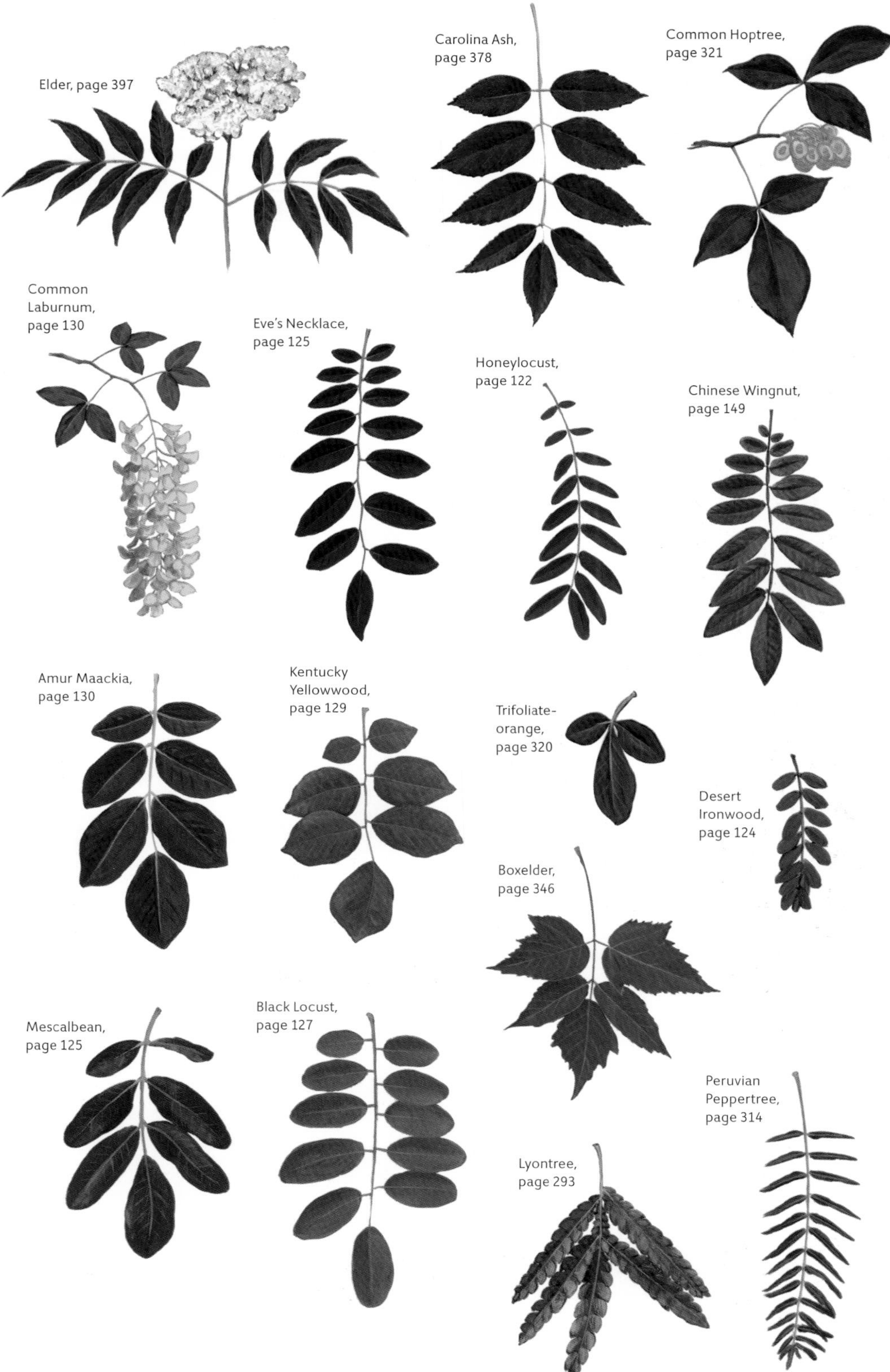
Elder, page 397
Carolina Ash, page 378
Common Hoptree, page 321
Common Laburnum, page 130
Eve's Necklace, page 125
Honeylocust, page 122
Chinese Wingnut, page 149
Amur Maackia, page 130
Kentucky Yellowwood, page 129
Trifoliate-orange, page 320
Desert Ironwood, page 124
Boxelder, page 346
Mescalbean, page 125
Black Locust, page 127
Peruvian Peppertree, page 314
Lyontree, page 293

COMPOUND BIPINNATE LEAVES

Some species leaves are bipinnately compound, meaning the leaflets are again divided into subleaflets. Representative species with bipinnately compound leaves are shown here.

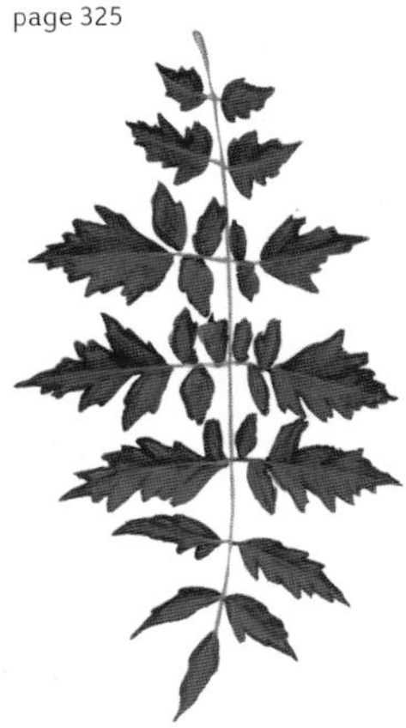

Golden Rain-tree, page 325

Chinaberry, page 318

Devil's Walkingstick, page 393

Kentucky Coffeetree, page 121

Littleleaf Leucaena, page 115

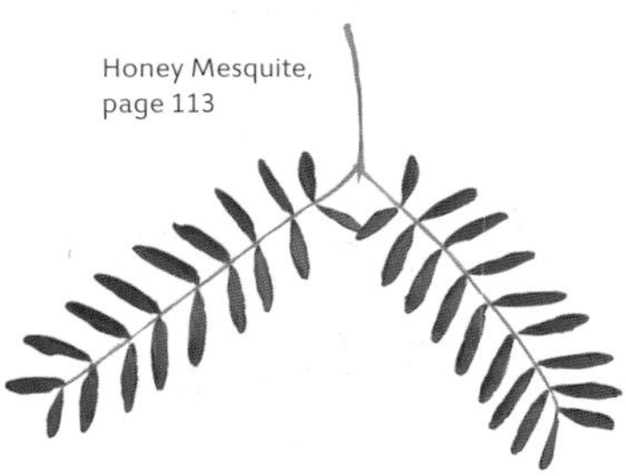

Honey Mesquite, page 113

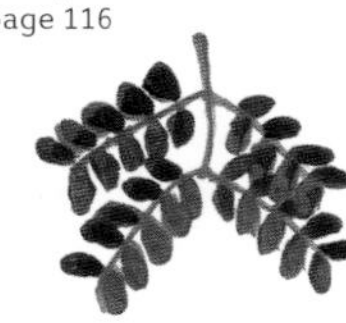

Ebony Blackbead, page 116

Yellow Paloverde, page 120

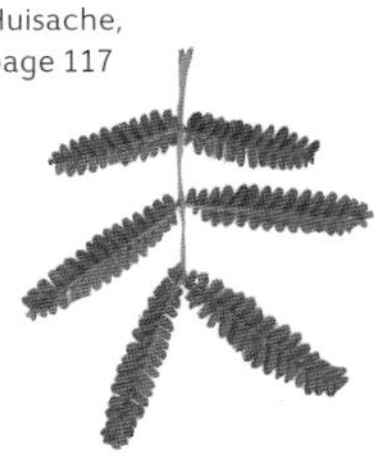

Huisache, page 117

Silktree, page 133

Honeylocust, page 122

Tenaza, page 115

Depending on the genus, leaves grow on tree branches in different arrangements. Shown from left to right are alternate, opposite, and whorled arangements.

OTHER LEAF ARANGEMENT

When we talk about leaf shape, most people think first of the two-dimensional outline of the leaf, but leaf shape also has a three-dimensional aspect. Leaves may be flat or curved, folded up along the midvein, or curled up or down at the edges. The leaf blade may be flat, or puckered, or rippled, and the surface may be very smooth or irregular with sunken veins. All of these three-dimensional variations in shape can give a leaf a dramatically different appearance, and may be especially obvious when looking at a group of leaves together.

Leaves grow in shapes and positions that maximize their exposure to sunlight. In open settings with direct sunlight leaves tend to hang down. In the understory of a forest where sunlight is more limited leaves tend to be held in well-defined horizontal planes to capture as much sunlight as possible. The length and position of the leafstalks and, over the years the length and shape of branches, grow to put the leaves in the brightest possible location.

Maple branches in sunlight (top) develop leaves arrayed around the twig, often drooping. Shaded branches (bottom), in contrast, hold leaves in a horizontal plane with leaves of different sizes and very different stalk lengths arranged for maximum light-gathering.

Alternate versus opposite is just one small aspect of the broad category of leaf arrangement. Leaves can be clustered or dispersed, on long stalks or short, held stiffly upright or flexible and drooping, arranged in organized rows all facing the same direction, or sticking out at all angles. For example, leaves of Eastern White Oak are stiff and stick out at rigid angles from the tip of the twig, while leaves of Northern Red Oak and Eastern Black Oak are more flexible, drooping gracefully and swaying in the breeze. Leaves of Swamp Cottonwood tend to droop from the twigs, unlike the leaves of Eastern Cottonwood, which tend to stick out and flutter at all angles.

Leaves often twist and bend to find sunlight, for example the apparently two-ranked needles on lower branches of the true firs are actually attached to the twig in a spiral arrangement; they are curved so that they appear two-ranked in a single plane.

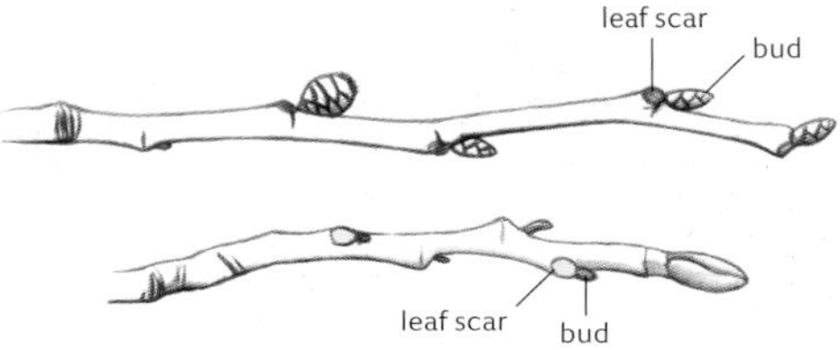
leaf scar
bud
leaf scar
bud

The buds and leaf scars of American Elm (top) are two-ranked, appearing only on two sides of the twig, while on Tuliptree (bottom) the buds and leaf scars are arranged all around the twig.

FOLIAGE TEXTURE

Differences in leaf size, shape, color, and and arrangement all contribute to an overall pattern that can be described as the "texture" of the foliage of a tree. This can be evident at a distance and is often helpful in identifying trees or at least picking out a tree that is different. The dense crown of Southern Magnolia, with dark glossy leaves standing upright and stiff, and some showing the rusty underleaf, is utterly unlike the sparse and pale green crown of the Quaking Aspen, with small rounded leaves hanging loosely and fluttering in the breeze. All of these things and more contribute to an overall texture. Motion also plays a role, as wind lifts leaves to show flickering undersides or glossy flashes; some leaves flutter, some wave gently, some are held stiffly. This is all very difficult to capture in a small image, and is not emphasized explicitly in this guide, but by watching for these overall "gestalt" differences you will learn to identify more trees more quickly.

LEAF COLOR

Healthy mature leaves are always some shade of green. Average colors differ slightly among species and can be useful for identification. However, these differences are subtle, and are usually overshadowed by variation within each species. Differences in other non-color aspects of leaf appearance such as transparency or glossiness can also be seen, and contribute to an overall perception of leaf color. The color and contrast of leaf veins is also a useful, and little-studied, identification clue.

One important source of color variation is the age of an individual leaf. Leaf color changes throughout the growing season, with tender new leaves in spring a brighter yellow-green, while older leaves in summer are darker, often more bluish green, and with more blemishes from insect and other damage. By late summer, deciduous leaves show indications of the fall colors to come. All of these changes occur slowly and gradually over the course of the year, so leaf color is most useful for identification when compared directly with adjacent trees on the same date.

Cultivated trees show a much wider range of leaf color than wild trees. Purple-leaved cultivars have been developed in plums, smoketree, Norway and Sycamore Maples, and a few other species. Variegated leaves, green with white or yellow patches, are seen on some cultivars including Boxelder, Norway Maple and English Holly. Some individual trees in the wild show bright reddish colors on their emerging leaves in spring and cultivars of many species have been developed to enhance this display of spring color (see Golden Honeylocust, page 123).

Leaf color also reflects the health of the tree, and a tree that is in poor health or growing in poor soil will develop leaves that are off-color, for example pale yellow-green, or that turn yellow or brown early in fall.

Leaf color can be useful for picking out an individual tree that is different or unusual. With practice in your local area, in combination with foliage texture and leaf arrangement, leaf color may be quite helpful for identifying species.

UNDERLEAF

The underside of a leaf is always paler green than the uppersurface, and often hairy or fuzzy, never glossy. Some species have a whitish underleaf, and a few brownish, due to minute hairs or scales. Confirming the presence or absence of hair on the underleaf may require very close views and magnification, but differences in overall color can be obvious and useful at a distance.

FALL LEAF COLOR

The brilliant colors of the autumn forest are among the most striking and most viewed spectacles in nature. Nearly all broadleaf trees develop some amount of yellow or red color before they drop their leaves in the fall. Yellow pigments are already present in the leaves, masked by green chlorophyll, and are simply revealed when the tree begins to withdraw resources from the leaf and the chlorophyll breaks down. Red pigments, shown by fewer trees, are synthesized by the tree just before leaves drop.

By combining just a few pigments—green, brown, yellow, and red—trees produce the entire range of fall colors. The clarity and extent of these colors is variable from year-to-year depending on weather. For example, more red is produced in leaves on bright sunny days.

Color is controlled at least partly by genetics, some individual trees and cultivars are consistently bright or drab, and trees of the same species growing side-by-side can show very different colors. Color also depends to some extent on the species. Birches are always yellow, for example, and all maples tend to show clear red and yellow fall colors, while the oaks tend to show murky maroon and yellow-brown colors.

Each species or genus also often shows a particular pattern of color. Aspens are famous for their dramatic show of golden-yellow color as all the leaves change simultaneously, while birches tend to show a mixture of fully yellow leaves among fully green leaves. Sugar Maple shows red on the outermost leaves, blending to pale yellow and a luminous yellow-green center. Sweetgum trees in the fall are distinctive for having scattered purple, red, yellow, and green leaves all simultaneously on a single tree, even on the same branch.

Flowers

Even though present only on mature trees and generally only briefly, flowers provide some of the most distinctive characteristics for identifying trees. Microscopic differences in flower anatomy are important to botanists in distinguishing genera and families. Even when viewed from a distance there are many obvious differences in flower color, structure, placement on the tree, and timing of flowering, which provide helpful and conspicuous clues for identification.

FLOWER STRUCTURE

The flower is the reproductive organ of the plant. A greatly simplified "average" flower can be thought of as concentric rings beginning with the female pistil in the center—the ovary at the base with extended style and the stigma at the tip. Surrounding that are the male stamens—long filaments each tipped with a pollen-bearing anther. Surrounding that are the petals, modified leaves that are usually showy and colorful and form the corolla. Surrounding the petals are the sepals, modified leaves, usually green and smaller than the petals, forming the calyx.

The ovary needs to be fertilized by pollen from the anthers for reproduction. This pollen may be carried on the wind or on the body of a pollinator, such as an insect. Once pollen contacts the stigma, it travels through a pollen tube to the ovary, where the ovules are fertilized and development of seeds and fruit begins. The strategies that plants have evolved to get the pollen to the ovary are extremely diverse, and those strategies have a lot to do with the appearance of the flower.

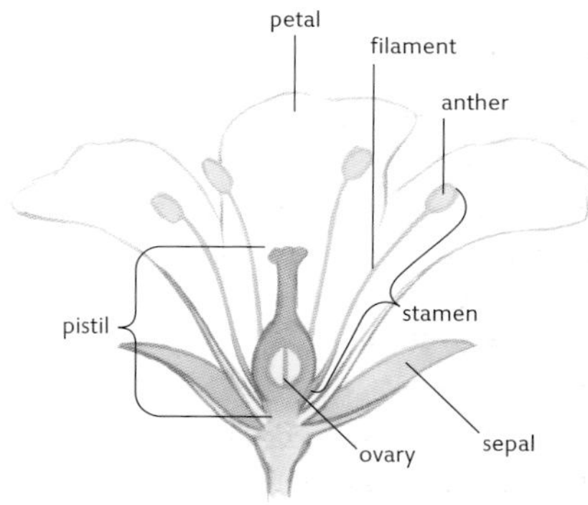
petal
filament
anther
pistil
stamen
ovary
sepal

The female parts at the center of a flower are collectively referred to as the pistil with the ovary at the base. The male parts of the flower are called stamens; they have a long fine filament tipped with a pollen-bearing anther. Surrounding the stamens and pistil is a ring of petals and below that a ring of sepals.

Petals are typically colorful, while sepals are usually smaller and green. In the magnolias these parts are not differentiated and are called tepals.

Some flowers or flower clusters appear on a stalk from a modified leaf called a bract. Flowering Dogwood technically has a cluster of flowers surrounded by several large showy bracts. The flowers and fruit of lindens are on a slender stalk arising from a long narrow bract.

Many species simply cast their pollen out into the wind to land on another plant. All gymnosperms use this strategy, as do elms, oaks, birches, and some others. As a general rule the trees that are wind-pollinated have inconspicuous small greenish flowers that appear before the leaves (most of the earliest-flowering trees each spring are wind-pollinated), so that the pollen disperses more easily through the open canopy.

Many species are insect-pollinated, and produce showy flowers with colors and odors that attract insects. These flowers also have shapes designed to deposit pollen on a consistent part of the insect so that it can be transferred to the next flower.

FLOWER CLUSTERS

Any cluster of flowers is called an inflorescence, and the shape of the entire cluster can be distinctive. Most such clusters are clearly a collection of individual flowers arising from a main stalk. In some cases (e.g. Flowering Dogwood) the cluster takes on the appearance of an individual flower, with showy bracts surrounding a cluster of tiny flowers.

Precise distinctions of branching patterns within an inflorescence have given rise to several botanical terms, such as umbel, corymb, raceme, panicle, and others but distinctions can be subtle and difficult to determine. In this guide, non-technical terms such as "long, narrow spike" or "broad, flat-topped cluster" are used to describe the exterior appearance of the cluster without relying on detailed examination of the branching patterns within.

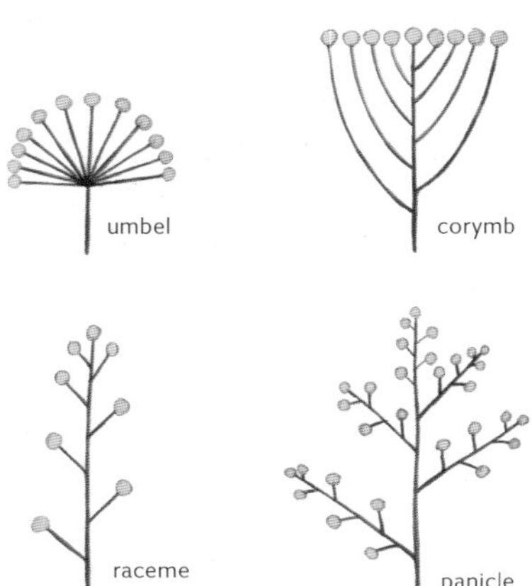
umbel
corymb
raceme
panicle

Flowers generally grow in characteristic arrangements and hoticulturalists and botanists have special terms they use to name specific patterns.

Flowers and flower clusters may be terminal (at the tip of a twig or spur branch) or axillary (emerging from the axil where each leaf meets the twig).

Flowers and flower clusters growing from the junction of the leafstalk and the twig are called axillary flowers.

MALE AND FEMALE FLOWERS

Flowers with functional male and female parts are called perfect flowers. Many species of plants have separate male and female flowers. In this case male flowers (with functioning stamens) are called staminate flowers, and female flowers are called pistillate or carpellate flowers. When a tree has separate male and female flowers on the same tree, it is called monoecious (e.g. the birches). When separate male and female flowers are found on separate trees, the tree is called dioecious (e.g. American Holly, Ginkgo, willows, etc.). Only female flowers will produce fruit. In some species, perfect and imperfect flowers can be mixed on a single plant, and plants can be monoecious or dioecious.

PHENOLOGY

Phenology is the timing of natural events, and the seasonal cycles of trees provide many clues to their identification. Major events such as the emergence of leaves are very noticeable, and certain species consistently leaf out earlier or later than other trees. Bigtooth Aspen is one of the last trees to leaf out within its range, and in addition its leaves emerge covered with silky white fuzz, which is very conspicuous among the well-developed green leaves of almost every other tree around it. Catalpas leaf out late in spring, and then retain the bright yellow-green color of fresh young leaves well into the summer, after most other species have become dark green.

The relative time of flowering can also be a very useful clue for identifying trees. This can be measured relative to other events like leaf emergence, or relative to other species in the area. In many species the text mentions whether the flowers appear before, with, or after the leaves, and this relative timing is fairly consistent within a species. For example all native magnolias flower after the leaves emerge, making their flowers less conspicuous, while the cultivated Asian species flower in early spring before the leaves emerge, when their large showy flowers are very conspicuous with no leaves to obscure them. Most of the plums, cherries, crabapples, and pears flower just before or as their leaves emerge, while most hawthorns flower later, after their leaves have emerged.

Few species of trees flower in summer, and these are mostly insect-pollinated with showy and fragrant flowers. Even fewer species flower in fall.

Timing of the emergence of cones or flowers varies up to several weeks each year in response to local conditions. Studies of Noble Fir at three locations found that cone emergence spreads uphill at about 50 to 100 feet in elevation each day. Similarly, Red Maple trees in Georgia flower in early February, while the same species in New England flowers two months later in April. It has been calculated that flowering moves north at about seventeen miles a day. A study of pines in Alabama found that the average cone emergence time of each species varied by up to forty-five days from year to year. However, in all of these cases the relative time of flowering or cone emergence of different species remains consistent—if it is a late spring it seems to be late for all species more or less equally.

Timing varies from year to year, but there is also a genetic component, so that trees transplanted from one region to another may not fully adjust to their new climate. In New England some cultivated Red Maples flower early in spring and retain bright foliage in fall for up to two months after the truly native local trees have dropped all of their leaves. Watching for these differences in timing can be very useful.

Fruit

Fruit refers generally to the seed and the entire structure around the seed. It develops directly from the female parts of the flower. Most species flower in spring or summer and their fruit ripens a few months later during the same growing season. In a few genera, such as most pines and oaks of the red oak group, cones or fruit do not ripen until the second growing season.

Fruit is extremely useful for identification, as it tends to be distinctive for each species and is generally present for a longer time than flowers, often year-round. Even if the fruit itself disappears, it may leave behind a distinctive fruiting structure, such as a stalk or woody capsule. Old fruit or fruit parts might also be found on the ground below a tree, and can be very helpful for identification (as long as you can be sure which tree the fruit came from).

Because fruit develops directly from the ovary of the flowers, the arrangement of fruit will always match the arrangement of female flowers. That is, if flowers are axillary in branched clusters, fruit will also be axillary in branched clusters. Fruit becomes much larger and may develop elongated stalks as it ripens, but its position on the tree and relative to other fruits will not change.

The wide range of fruiting structures on plants is classified by botanists into different categories based on how each one develops from the parts of the flower. The fruit of the walnut tree is not considered a true nut because the hard bony shell is enclosed in a fleshy husk, and it is better-described as a "nut-like drupe." These technical terms and the close examination they require are critical to any serious study of botany, but in this guide the fruits are described simply by superficial aspects of their shape, arrangement, and color.

Some fruit (and leaves) and twigs are blue-green and may be covered in a whitish waxy powder—this is often described as glaucous.

GYMNOSPERM CONES

Gymnosperm means "naked seed" and the trees in this diverse group do not have "true" flowers or fruit like the fleshy surrounding pulp of many familiar trees in the angiosperm group. The conspicuous cones on gymnosperms are female or "seed cones." Male cones are inconspicuous and produce pollen in spring, falling soon after.

Yews produce a seed surrounded by a berry-like cup called the "aril."

Pines produce woody cones covered in scales. The base of each scale has ovules that when fertilized develop into seeds. The tip of pine cone scales has sharp prickles.

On Douglas-firs, each scale hides a single seed with a long papery bract that projects beyond the scale edge.

Cypress cones have tighly packed scales in a soccer ball shape.

Juniper fruit is a small cone with a fleshy covering (making it berry-like); each cone holds one to several seeds.

ANGIOSPERM FRUIT

Angiosperms have encased ovaries that produce seeds. This differs from the "naked seeds" produced by the gymnosperms. Angiosperms produce an amazing variety of fruits, some of which can be very useful for identfying certain groups of trees. Some of the basic types of fruits covered in this guide are listed below. See the group introductions for more information about the types of fruit produced by particular genera of trees.

Some trees produce a multi-seeded berry on a single stalk, such as the Persimmon (left). Other trees produce multiple individual berries on a single stalk that contain seeds, such as the mulberries (right).

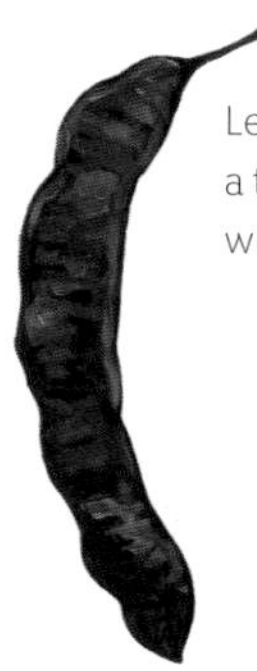

Legumes produce a two-parted pod with multiple seeds.

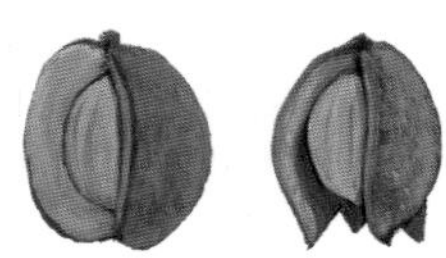

The fruit of hickories and walnuts is hard, woody and nut-like surrounded by a leathery husk. Because of the way the husk develops, this does not meet the botanical definition of a nut.

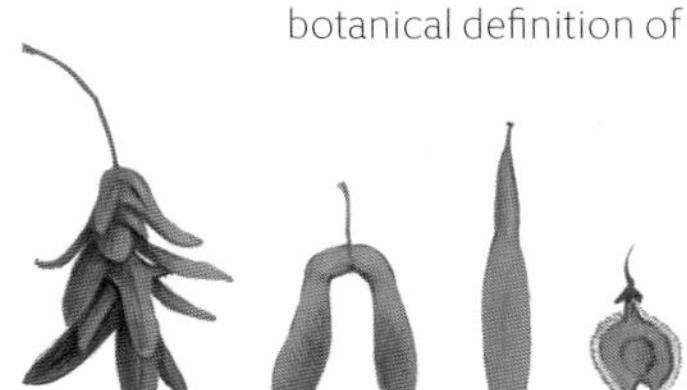

The winged fruit of hornbeams, maples, ashes, elms, and others is called a samara or "key." The base of the wing contains a covered seed. When the fruit falls, the "wing" helps disperse the seed in the wind.

Beeches (left) and chestnuts have seeds encased in a thorny capsule. Sweetgum fruit (right) is a ball formed of many small capsules.

The fruit of cercocarpus trees (top) is a small woody capsule with a twisted feathery plume that helps it catch the wind. The unusual fruit of the Osage-orange (bottom) is an aggregate fruit containing hundreds of seeds.

The familiar plum, cherry, apricot, and peach have an outer skin that encases fleshy fruit. Inside the hardened pit or stone contains a single seed. Birds and other animals widely disperse the seeds of sweet-fruited trees. This type of fruit is sometimes called a drupe.

Apple and pears have a fleshy exterior that covers multiple seeds in thin cases.

Some trees, such as magnolias, produce a woody collection of fruits called a follicle. The follicle contains multiple capsules with individual berries. The capsules split to reveal covered seeds. Some are brightly colored and attract birds and other animals for dispersal.

Twigs

Although the differences between twigs and buds of different species can be quite subtle, they still offer surprisingly useful clues for identification. From a distance, the shape and thickness of twigs gives a winter tree its "texture." Everything from the color and thickness to the branching angles and the prominence of buds all contribute to the subtly distinctive appearance of different species' twigs.

Twigs (defined as the growth of the most recent growing season) are distinct from branchlets (previous season's growth). Branchlets can develop corky wings on a few species, twigs do not. Branchlets are almost invariably gray-brown. Twigs usually emerge bright green as new growth in the spring, and turn brownish during the summer (often with colorful green, yellow, or red tones through their first winter), finally turning gray-brown as they mature in a year or two. Twigs of some species become more colorful in the weeks before buds open in the spring.

Color of twigs and branchlets is variable and is most often shades of gray-brown, but twig color is usually consistent enough in a species so that those with colorful twigs (such as obviously greenish, yellowish or reddish twigs) can be identified. At close range, many different details of twigs can be helpful.

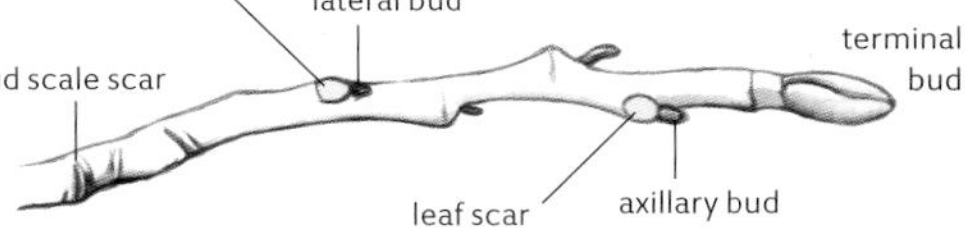
leaf scar
lateral bud
terminal bud
bud scale scar
leaf scar
axillary bud

A typical winter twig of a deciduous tree (Tuliptree) is shown here. The terminal bud is largest, at the tip of the twig and lateral or axillary buds are shown along the side of the twig, alternating sides in this species, as it is a species with alternate leaves. Just below each bud is the leaf scar, a rounded smooth area where the previous season's leaf was attached. A ring of scale scars is left by the bud scales of last year's terminal bud, and marks the boundary between the most recent season's growth and the previous season's growth.

Opposite leaves are associated with opposite branching, which can be seen in the twigs of species like ashes and maples. Beware that twigs often die and fall away, leaving a twig on just one side of the branch, and this can result in an apparently alternate arrangement. In general the twigs of species with opposite branching are straight, while alternate leaves and buds cause the twigs to zigzag.

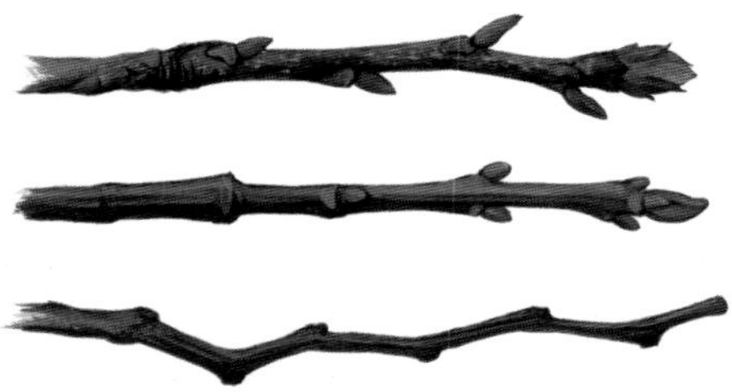

Hickories (top) and ashes (middle) have stout twigs. Hickory twigs are crooked and zigzag with enlarged buds at the tips, while ash twigs are straight and orderly without prominent enlarged buds. Locust twigs (bottom) are more slender, tapered, and zigzag.

Some species have hairy or velvety twigs, which can be helpful for identification but often require a very close examination or magnification to see clearly. Hairs wear off over time.

Small pale spots along the twigs, known as lenticels, are actually pores used for gas exchange ("breathing") and are conspicuous in some species. In a few species these persist even on older branches and trunks. In some trees, notably birches and cherries, the lenticels are expanded into horizontal lines or bands. Both lenticels and small resin blisters along twigs may be raised and create a rough texture on some species.

The pith at the center of the twig or branchlet is usually solid, but can have hollow chambers in a few genera, such as walnuts. Also, the shape of the pith in cross section differs between species, but requires cutting open the twig and is not covered in this guide.

Spur twigs are short, side twigs that never grow very long and give rise to a cluster of buds and then of leaves, flowers, and/or fruit. These are conspicuous in many species in the rose family as well as Ginkgo, birches, Osage Orange, and a few others.

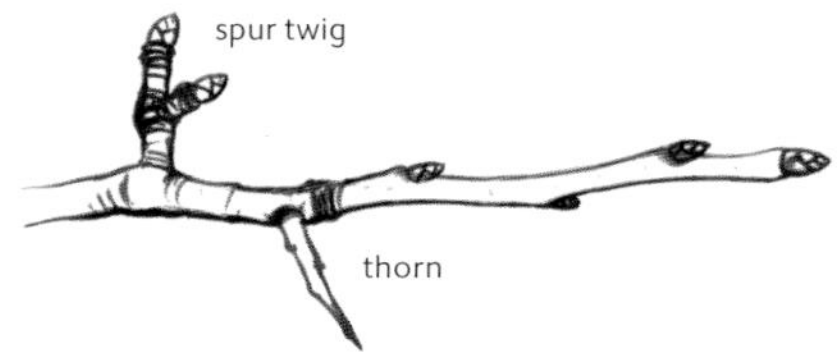
spur twig
thorn

Apples and many other trees in the rose family develop short, slow-growing spur twigs, which often have clustered flower buds.

Buds

Buds are formed during the summer growing season, and are then present throughout the fall and winter, providing useful identification clues almost year-round. Buds hold the embryonic leaves and flowers that will emerge at the beginning of the new growing season. In most species, each bud is protected by bud scales, and both the size and shape of the bud as well as the shape, arrangement, and color of the bud scales provide identification clues. Many of these clues require magnification to see clearly and are beyond the scope of this guide, but the general size, shape, and color of the buds can be seen at a distance and are very useful for identification.

For example, the large silky white buds of Eastern Black Oak instantly distinguish this species (even at some distance) from Northern Red Oak. The opposite clustered flower buds of Red and Silver Maples in winter create an appearance unique to those two species. The large silky white buds of Austrian Pine and Longleaf Pine are distinct from the smaller brownish buds of similar pines.

Buds of Eastern Black Oak (top) are larger than those of Northern Red Oak (bottom) and covered with silvery hairs

Terminal buds grow at the end of the twig and are generally the largest of the buds on the twig. Lateral or axillary buds grow along the side of the twig in the axil just above the base of each leaf or (after the leaves fall) the leaf scar.

Buds that will produce leaves differ in shape and size from those that will produce flowers. In general leaf buds are smaller, more slender, and less conspicuous, while flower buds are larger, more spherical, and more conspicuous.

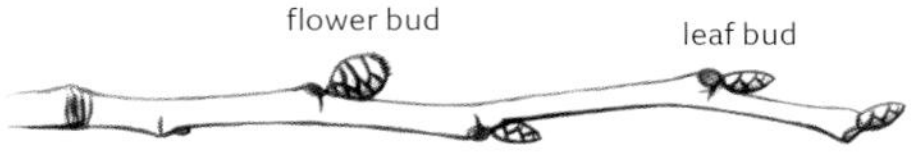
flower bud
leaf bud

The flower bud of this American Elm twig is much larger and more spherical than the slender leaf buds.

The Tuliptree has only two bud scales which meet at the edges but do not overlap. This arrangement is called valvate bud scales, and the bud appears smooth. American Elm has the more common arrangement of bud scales, called imbricate, with many scales overlapping like roof shingles.

Scales of the terminal buds fall away after the bud opens, leaving a complete ring of scars, known as scale scars, that mark the boundary of each season's growth.

A distinctive modified bud shown by all species in the birch family (except hornbeams and Seaside Alder) is a miniature finger-like catkin called an ament. This is the male flower bud, preformed in the fall and present at the tips of the twigs all winter.

Bark

Bark is a protective woody or corky layer produced on the surface of the branches and trunk. On twigs this is a single smooth layer. A new layer is added to the inside of the bark each year (except in palms and Saguaro), so the bark builds in thickness over time, and on larger branches and the trunk, the outermost layers often crack or peel in distinctive patterns as a tree ages. While bark can be helpful for identification, bark patterns are also extremely variable depending on the age of the tree and the environmental conditions of the location.

In general older trees have thicker bark and therefore deeper furrows and higher ridges, and also show more variation in appearance. Bark texture continues to change as a tree increases in size. Most of the images of "mature bark" in this guide represent the typical appearance of a tree about 18 inches in diameter (or less in smaller species). Trees that grow much larger will develop different-looking bark, and some of these variations are rarely seen now that most old-growth forests are gone.

In addition to the bark itself, some trees grow certain lichens—Kentucky Yellowwood and beech have similar smooth gray bark, but Kentucky Yellowwood supports lichens on the trunk, while beech is usually without lichens. With experience you will develop a sense of the subtle variations in the patterns and textures, and bark will become one of the more important clues for identifying trees.

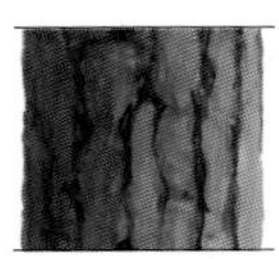

Ponderosa Pine (rectangular flat plates and darker furrows)

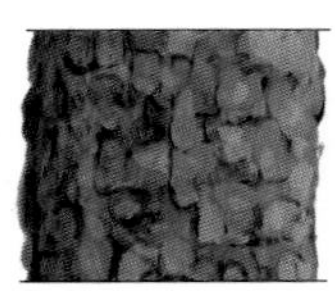

Blue Spruce (scaly)

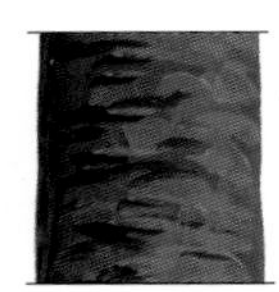

Balsam Fir (smooth)

Dawn Redwood (fibrous and shredding)

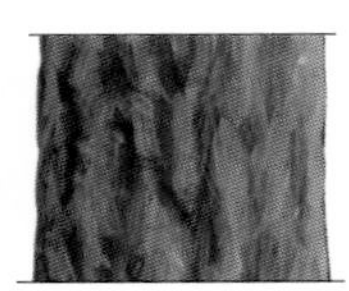

Common Douglas-fir (furrowed and corky)

The bark of gymnosperms shows a range of variation similar to angiosperms. With smooth, scaly, and furrowed bark, they are all very similar to the bark of some angiosperm species, but variation within each genus is relatively small. The broad plates shown by Ponderosa and other pines are found only among the pines. The fibrous shredding bark of Dawn Redwood is shared by a few other species in the cypress family, but not by any angiosperm.

Tree bark can be an important identification feature for many groups of trees. Especially when mature (as shown here), many species develop characteristics that are easily recognized amid mixed groups of species. Some of the terms used to describe bark in this guide are illustrated here.

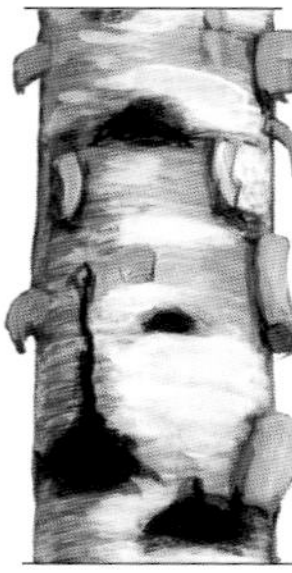

Paper Birch has thin smooth bark that often peels in horizontal bands. Similar horizontally peeling bark is shown by some other birches and by a few species of cherries, as well as Paperbark Maple.

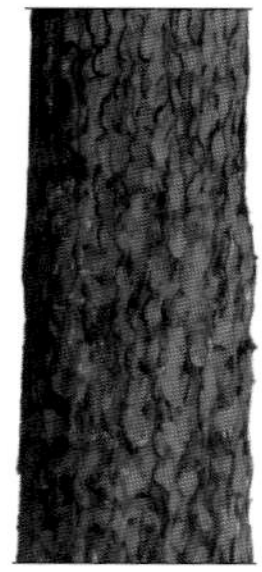

Eastern Redbud has thin bark that flakes off in small scales without clear ridges, similar to Black Cherry, most spruces, and many other species. The size, color, and looseness of the scales can be helpful distinctions.

Red Alder has relatively thin smooth bark. Similar bark is shown by beeches, Kentucky Yellowwood, and others.

American Elm has bark in narrow ridges, each comprised of small scales that flake off, the ridges intertwining in irregular patterns.

Chestnut Oak has thick bark that forms rugged ridges. Other species with very thick ridged bark include the cottonwoods, older trees of Northern Red Oak, Sassafras, and Black Locust.

Lyontree has shaggy bark in long strips that peel from the ends, in this case (as in madrones) revealing smooth reddish inner bark. Similar peeling strips are shown by Shagbark Hickory and to a lesser extent by few other species.

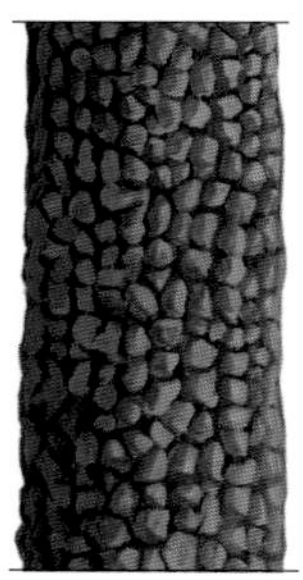

Common Persimmon has thick bark divided into small blocks not arranged into obvious ridges. Similar blocky bark is shown by Flowering Dogwood, Alligator Juniper, among others.

White Ash has a very regular pattern of interlaced small ridges, forming diamond-shaped furrows. Similar tightly-furrowed bark is shown by several other large ashes, some hickories, and Norway Maple.

On most species of trees, the bark seems to pass through three fairly distinct stages of development. On River Birch, these three stages are dramatically different. Like most birches, saplings have smooth reddish bark with obvious pale horizontal lenticels ("breathing pores"). As the trunk expands the thin bark peels in sheets that become loose and shaggy, revealing smooth reddish layers of new bark below. Eventually, the bark stops peeling, and mature trunks instead show an irregular pattern of flaky gray scales.

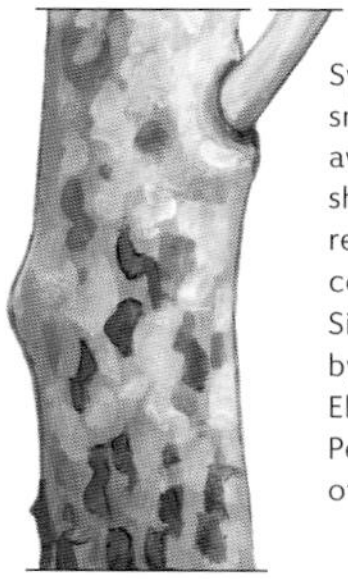

Sycamore has thin smooth bark that falls away in irregularly shaped scales revealing differently colored inner bark. Similar bark is shared by the exotic Chinese Elm, Lacebark Pine, Persian Parrottia, and others.

A few species found in very harsh climates, such as the aspens and paloverdes (Blue Paloverde shown), have thin, greenish bark where photosynthesis occurs, a process usually restricted to leaves.

The Sibley Guide to Trees

Yew Family

The yew family (Taxaceae) includes about twenty species of evergreen shrubs and trees worldwide in five genera. Two genera, *Taxus* and *Torreya*, are native to North America, and one species from each genus is covered here.

Yews and torreyas are superficially similar, but yews have shorter leaves that are soft and blunt-tipped (vs. stiff and sharp), alternate leaves and branches (vs. nearly opposite), seeds ripens in a single growing season, and thin, purplish red bark.

The leaves, bark, and seeds of some yews are poisonous, but the fleshy red fruit covering of the seed (called the "aril") is not. Birds consume them and disperse the seeds in droppings.

Species of yews are so similar to one another that identification often relies on geography, rather than physical characteristics. Some botanists have classified all yew species as subspecies of one single worldwide species, but more study is needed. Specialists distinguish yew species by microscopic study of leaf cells.

The native species in most of eastern North America, Canada Yew (*Taxus canadensis*), is a sprawling shrub. Any other yew in that region with upright stems can only be an exotic species. Another native species, Florida Yew (*Taxus floridana*), can be a small tree, but is very rare and local along the Appalachicola River in northern Florida.

Most tree-like yews encountered in North America are hybrids of English Yew (*Taxus baccata*) native to Europe, and Japanese Yew (*Taxus cuspidata*) native to Japan. These two nonnative species and hybrids between them are often tree-like, commonly cultivated, and locally naturalized (zones 4–7). Distinguishing these species and hybrids from each other, and from tree-like specimens of Pacific Yew, is difficult or impossible.

Pacific Yew

Taxus brevifolia

Evergreen. Shrub or small tree usually under 25' tall, (max. 75'). Very slow-growing; trunk straight to contorted, fluted, and crown open-conical. Branches horizontal to drooping.

leaves 1", bright green, shiny; usually somewhat curved
underleaf paler green

pollen cones round, yellowish

underside of needles fairly bright yellow-green, not whitened

seed surrounded by berry-like red cup

twigs green, becoming reddish-brown after a year
leaves appear 2-ranked, spreading horizontally from twig

bark reddish brown with green and purple highlights, peeling in small rectangular scales

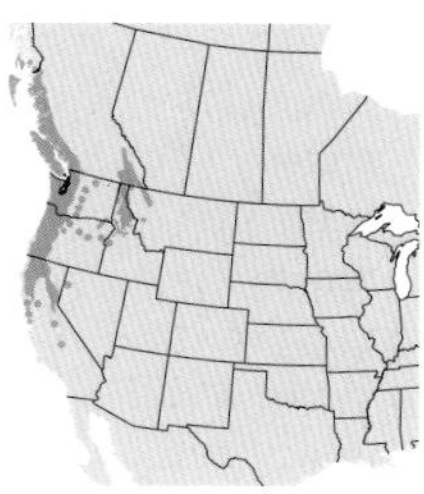

Uncommon in forests, especially in moist shaded sites. Threatened by overharvesting of wood for woodworking and of bark for medicinal uses. Rarely cultivated.

California Torreya

Torreya californica

CALIFORNIA NUTMEG TREE, STINKING CEDAR

Evergreen. Shrub or small to medium tree usually 15–45' tall (max. 141'); luxurious and droopy, crown conic becoming round-topped on old trees. Needles stink when crushed, leading to the alternate common name "Stinking-cedar."

bark with thin scaly ridges, dark

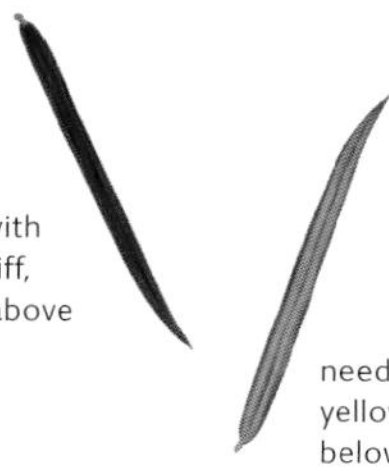

needles 2", very sharp with spiny tips, stiff, dark green above

needles paler yellow-green below

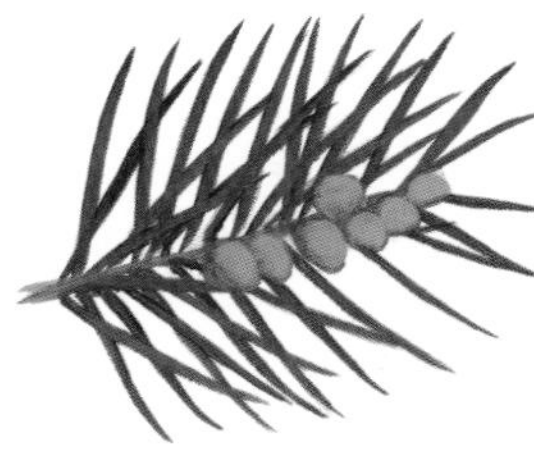

pollen cones whitish (Mar–Apr)

aril 1¼", oval, light green or streaked purple (ripe in second fall), seed dark

twigs green becoming reddish-brown after one year

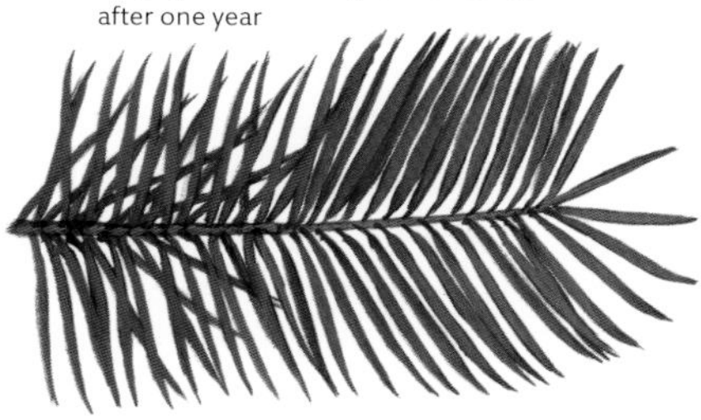

underside of needles pale yellow-green, unlike firs

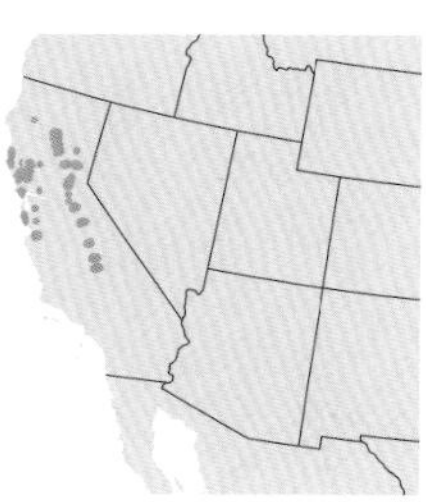

Rare and local along mountain streams, protected slopes, creek bottoms, and moist canyons within its limited range. Very rarely cultivated mostly within native range.

Florida Torreya

Torreya taxifolia

STINKING-CEDAR, GOPHERWOOD

Evergreen. Shrub or small tree, similar to California Torreya but with shorter leaves, darker green aril, pale yellowish-gray branchlets. Has upper surface of leaf rounded (vs. flattened) and underside of leaf with tiny shallow grayish pits (vs. deep whitish pits). Rare and local in the wild and found in only a few locations on bluffs and ravines along the Appalachicola River, Florida.

The Florida Torreya is an endangered species of tree, and efforts are ongoing to rescue it. Already rare with a very small population, all trees in the wild have been afflicted by a fungal disease since the 1950s. Currently, only sprouts survive, but full-size trees grow in gardens, where the species is occasionally cultivated (zones 6–9).

Pine Family

The pine family (Pinaceae) includes about 250 species of mostly evergreen trees in eleven genera. The pines in the genus *Pinus* are introduced here and covered in the pages that immediately follow. (See page 36 for the introduction to the other six genera in the pine family covered in this guide).

The pines (genus *Pinus*) are about 115 species of trees (occasionally shrubs) found mainly in northern temperate regions. Forty-one species are native to North America and are illustrated here along with seventeen additional species that are commonly cultivated.

Pines are distinguished from other genera in the pine family by having relatively long needles in bundles or clusters of two to five and joined at the base, and woody cones with scales thickened at the tip.

Needles persist for anywhere from two to thirty or more years, after which they turn brown and fall in the late summer.

All pines produce cones. Cones of most species mature at the end of their second growing season (some species require three growing seasons to mature). All other trees in the pine family have cones that mature in a single growing season. The familiar pine cone is typically egg-shaped, with many woody scales arranged in a spiral pattern, and each scale protects two seeds.

As in other gymnosperms, pines do not have true flowers. Pollen is produced in small male cones appearing at the base of new growth in spring. They may be purple, pink, red, orange, or greenish, but all turn yellow as they release pollen and then pale orange-brown as they dry, falling soon after. Female cones with developing seeds are small and scaly, usually near the tips of new growth in the spring. They are varied colors, as in the male cones, but all become green or purple as the cones grow, and eventually turn brown when fully mature, and grayish several years after maturity. There is variation within each species, but differences in color can still be useful for identification, as long as cones of similar age are being compared.

Like many other trees, pines produce large crops of fruit at irregular intervals, often about every three to seven years. This is thought to be a strategy to reduce seed predation by squirrels, birds, and other animals. By providing only a limited supply of seeds for several years, they support only a small population of seed-eating animals. When the trees produce a much larger crop of seeds, the supply exceeds the demand, increasing the chances that seeds will be left uneaten and have a chance to germinate.

Cones may fall quickly after maturity, or persist for many years. In a few species, cones may persist so long that they are enveloped by the growing trunk. Several species have serotinous cones—they open only when heated by fire. This characteristic is more common in some regions, and varies between individual trees of the same species, so that one tree might have its branches festooned with old cones, while a neighboring tree of the same species might have cones that release seeds and fall soon after maturity.

In serotinous species, the seeds remain viable inside the closed cones for decades. The cones protect the seeds from fire, and sufficient heat causes the cones to open. After the fire has passed, seeds are released onto a fertile and sunny bed of ash. Lodgepole Pine is one such species, and can quickly reseed a

new growth in spring forms slender upright "candles"; timing and thickness of candles helpful for distinguishing species

female cones purplish

male pollen cones yellow

White Pine Group	Yellow Pine Group
needles usually in bundles of 5, slender and flexible	needles usually in bundles of 2 or 3, thicker and stiffer

needle sheath sheds soon after needles full grown	needle sheath persistent
twigs smooth after needles fall	twigs usually remain rough after needles fall

 cones often narrow, with thin flexible scales and no prickles cones often stalked	 cones often broader, with thick woody scales and small to large prickles cones usually not stalked
bark tends to be thin, scaly, dark	bark often with broad orange plates
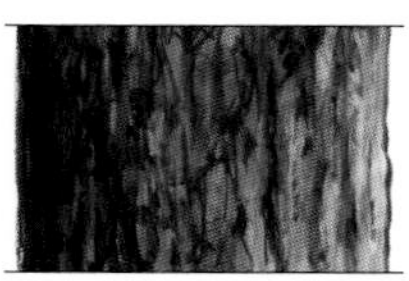	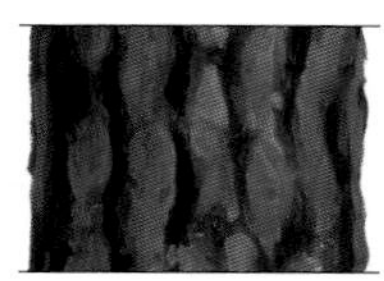

burned area, forming pure stands, and sometimes sprouting so densely that the small trees are stunted by competition with their peers.

All pines have whorled branches, usually producing a single "layer" of branches from the trunk, all on the same level each year. Leaves emerge spirally, all around the twig. Only a few species, e.g., Bristlecone Pine, have curved-up leaves.

The genus *Pinus* is separated broadly into two groups (see table above): the white pine group and yellow pine group. Named for the color of their wood, they differ in many details. The two groups are also sometimes called soft pines and hard pines, respectively, again referring to properties of the wood. The Pinyon, Foxtail, and Lacebark Pines are sometimes included in the white pine group, but tend to have stouter needles, often less than five in a bundle, and share some features of cone scales and seeds with the yellow pines. They can be separated as a third group, intermediate between the other two.

In economic value, pines rank among the most important groups of trees. They are harvested from the wild and grown commercially worldwide for lumber and for pulp. Pine sap also provides turpentine, and was formerly an important source of pitch and resin, but similar products are now derived mainly from petroleum. Pines are a dominant plant in a variety of ecosystems across North America, and many other species of plants and animals depend on pines for food and shelter.

Eastern White Pine

Pinus strobus

WEYMOUTH PINE, PUMPKIN PINE

Evergreen. Tall, often over 100' (max. 220'), or a low-creeping shrub at timberline. The only native white pine in its range. Easily identified by large size, irregular crown, long horizontal branches, slender needles in bundles of 5, and slender, stalked cones that lack prickles. One of the most important lumber trees in the East.

bark on young trunks pale gray-green and smooth

bark on mature trunks dark gray, often tinged with purple; sightly to conspicuously furrowed

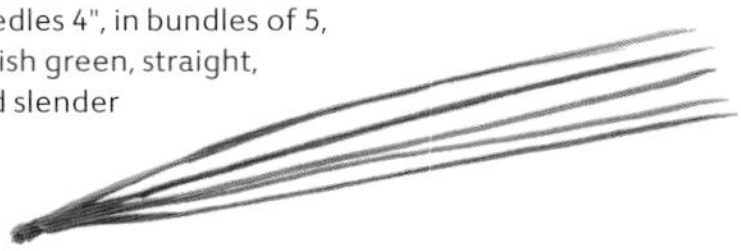

needles 4", in bundles of 5, bluish green, straight, and slender

mature cones 5½", relatively slender, with relatively long stalk and thin scales often dotted with sap; not persistent

needles form triangular clusters angled toward branch tips

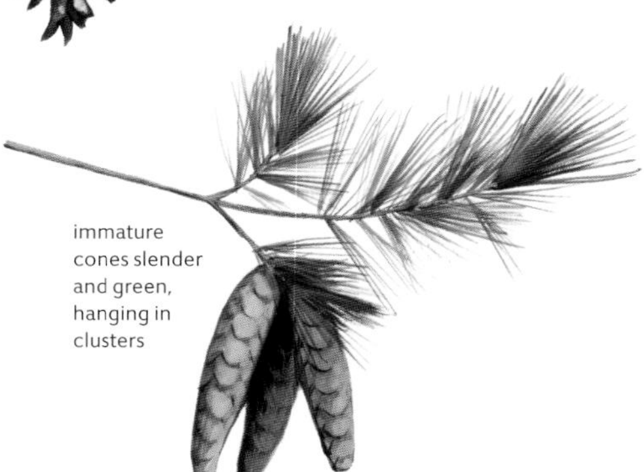

immature cones slender and green, hanging in clusters

graceful, long horizontal branches; irregular outline

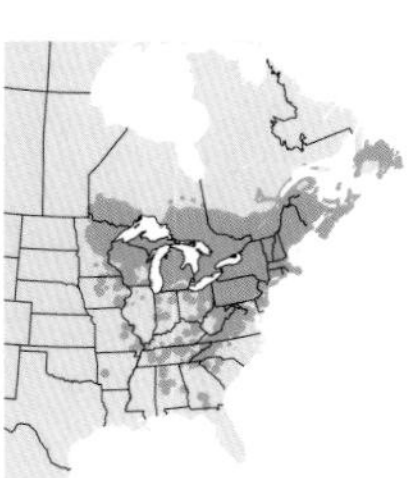

Common and widespread in rich, well-drained soils. Many cultivars, including dwarf and weeping forms, and very commonly cultivated (zones 3–7); often planted in public parks.

Western White Pine

Pinus monticola

MOUNTAIN WHITE PINE, SILVER PINE

Evergreen. Tall, often to 100' (max. 225'). Closely related and very similar to Eastern White Pine, but no natural range overlap. Distinguished from other pines in its range by tall, narrow form, dense clusters of bluish needles, and slender, hanging cones. A commercially important species, the source of most wooden matchsticks.

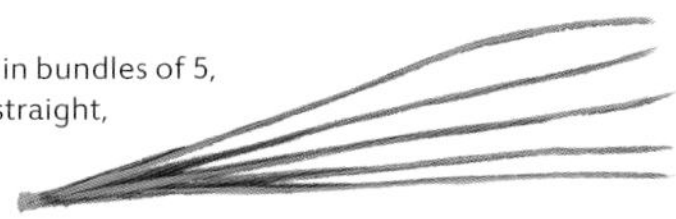

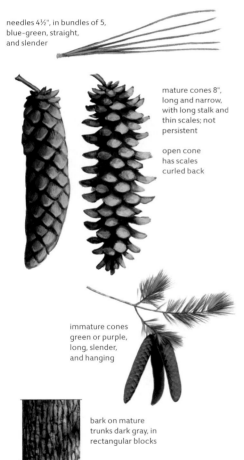

needles 4½", in bundles of 5, blue-green, straight, and slender

mature cones 8", long and narrow, with long stalk and thin scales; not persistent

open cone has scales curled back

immature cones green or purple, long, slender, and hanging

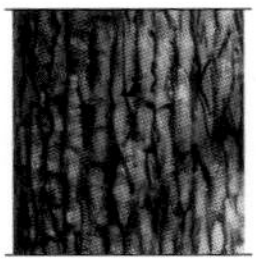

bark on mature trunks dark gray, in rectangular blocks

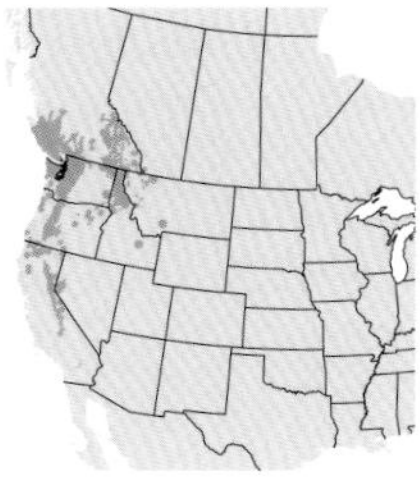

Widespread but scattered in moist forests from sea level to 10,000'. Rarely cultivated.

Sugar Pine

Pinus lambertiana

BIG PINE

Evergreen. Tall, often over 100' (max. 270'). North America's largest pine, identified by large size, very long cones (longest of any pine) at branch tips, and long, irregular branches. Named for its sweet-smelling resin, which exudes from freshly cut wood.

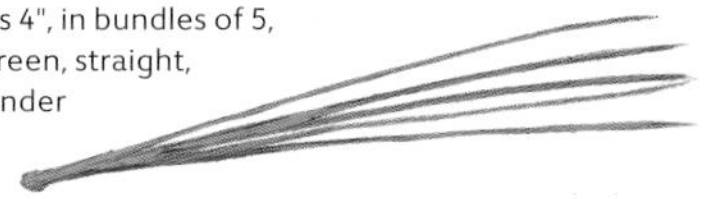

needles 4", in bundles of 5, blue-green, straight, and slender

long horizontal branches lined with clusters of needles; often weighed down at tips by large cones

mature cones huge, 14", with long stalk and thick scales; usually persistent through winter

immature cones usually purplish, very long, slender, and hanging

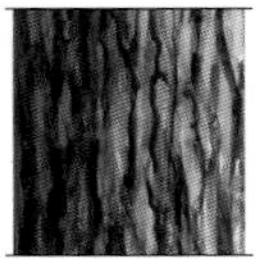

bark on mature trunks orange and gray, conspicuously furrowed

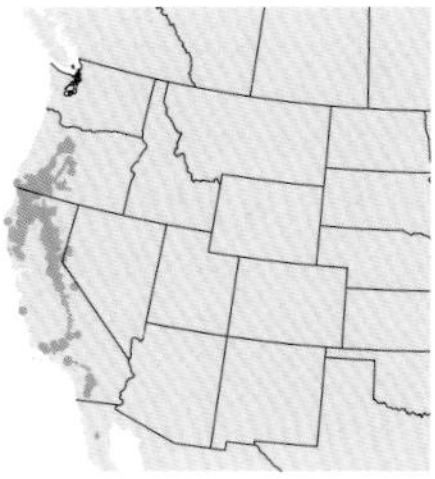

Uncommon and scattered on dry mountain slopes, mainly at 3,000–7,000' elevation. Very rarely cultivated.

Limber Pine

Pinus flexilis

ROCKY MOUNTAIN WHITE PINE, WHITE PINE, SQUIRREL PINE

Evergreen. Small to large tree usually 35–50' tall (max. 80'). Trunk straight to contorted, crown conic, becoming rounded or flat-topped. Branches often persistent to trunk base. Named for very flexible branches. Very similar to Southwestern White Pine and apparently hybridizes where range overlaps.

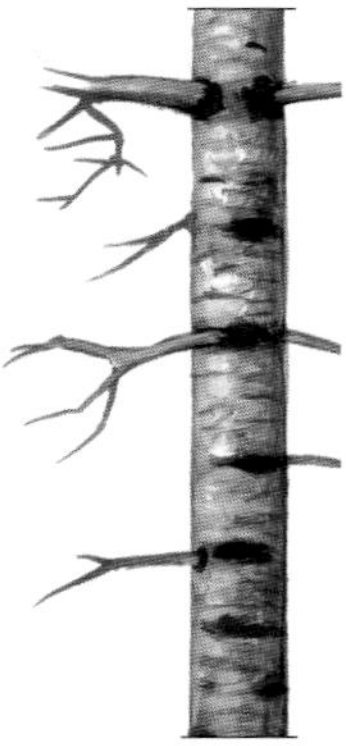

bark on young trunks pale gray, nearly smooth

older trunks gray with thin scaly plates and ridges

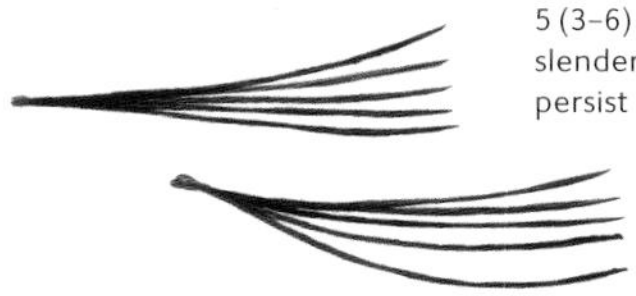

5 (3–6) needles, slender, curved, 2¼"; persist 5–6 years

cones 5", bright green when immature, with thick scales; not persistent

tall and straight-trunked in forests

in the open, a small bushy tree, with branches nearly to the ground

needles dense, dark green, crowded at ends of long, pale, curving branches

White Pine blister rust, a lethal fungal disease introduced from Asia, produces yellow cankers on bark, eventually girdling and killing the tree. All species in the white pine group are susceptible. The disease is most prevalent in regions where late summers are cool and damp; it has killed large numbers of pines and is of great concern, especially in the West, where it threatens to wipe out entire populations of Limber and Whitebark Pines.

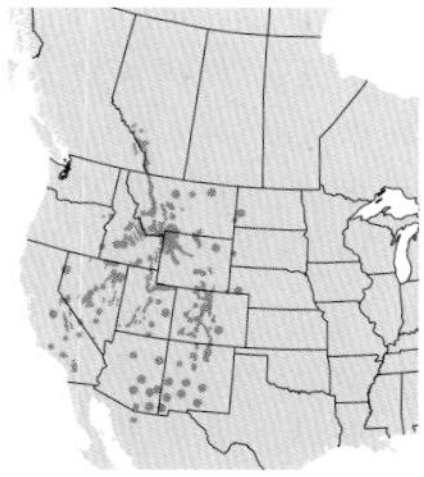

Common in high montane forests, rocky slopes, often at edges of forest or at timberline. Commonly cultivated (zones 4–7). Several cultivars vary in growth habit and needle color.

Southwestern White Pine

Pinus strobiformis

MEXICAN WHITE PINE, BORDER LIMBER PINE

Evergreen. Medium to large tree usually 60–80' tall (max. 111'); slender, straight. Differs from Limber only in larger cones, with narrower scale tips, and lacks white lines on needle backs. Intermediate trees, possibly hybrids, are found where range overlaps with Limber.

5 (2–4) needles, 3½", average longer and thinner than Limber; persist 3–5 years

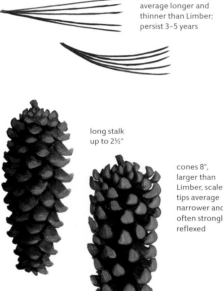

long stalk up to 2½"

cones 8", larger than Limber, scale tips average narrower and often strongly reflexed

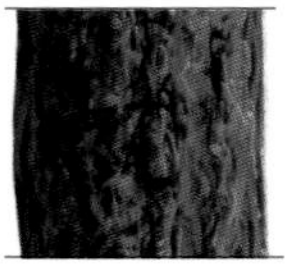

bark gray, scaly, like Limber

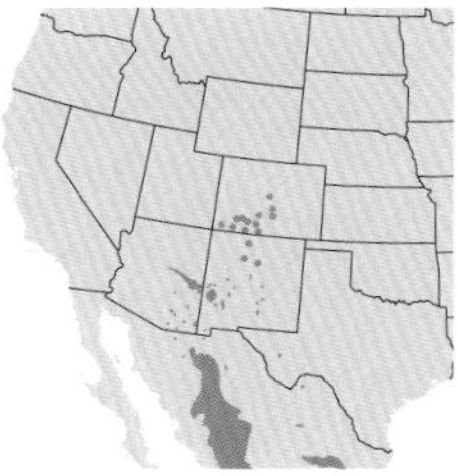

Common in arid to moist montane forests. Uncommonly but widely cultivated (zones 6–7).

Whitebark Pine

Pinus albicaulis

SCRUB PINE, WHITE PINE, NORTHERN NUT PINE

Evergreen. Small to medium tree usually 15–30' tall (max. 90'); relatively straight and tall when growing in forest, but low, twisted and contorted in typical harsh, alpine habitat. Cones remain tightly closed until opened by animals, especially squirrels, Grizzly Bears, and Clark's Nutcrackers.

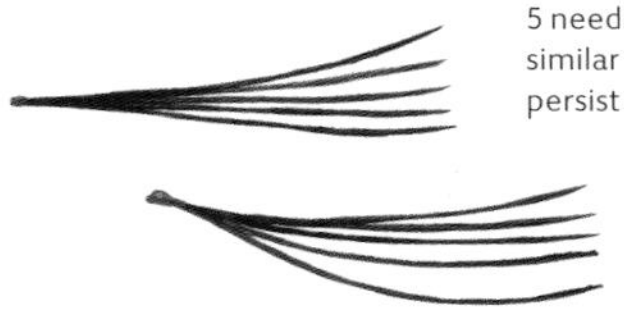

5 needles, 2½", very similar to Limber; persist 5–8 years

cones 2½", dark reddish to gray-purple, remain closed

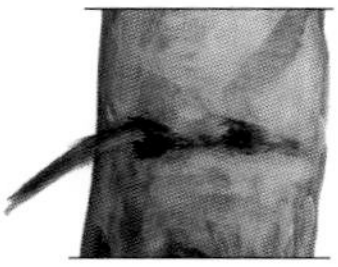

bark whitish or scaly and gray similar to Limber, but averages paler

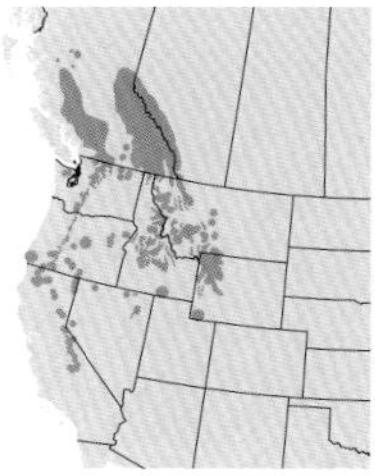

Thin, rocky, cold soils at or near timberline, montane forests. Very rarely cultivated (zones 3–5).

Colorado Bristlecone Pine

Pinus aristata

FOXTAIL PINE, HICKORY PINE, PRICKLECONE PINE, ROCKY MOUNTAIN BRISTLECONE PINE

Evergreen. Small tree usually 10–30' tall (max. 76'); slow-growing, bushy, with dense dark needles; trunk strongly tapering, leaning, twisted, with irregular crown often wind-sheared.

bark on young trunks pale gray

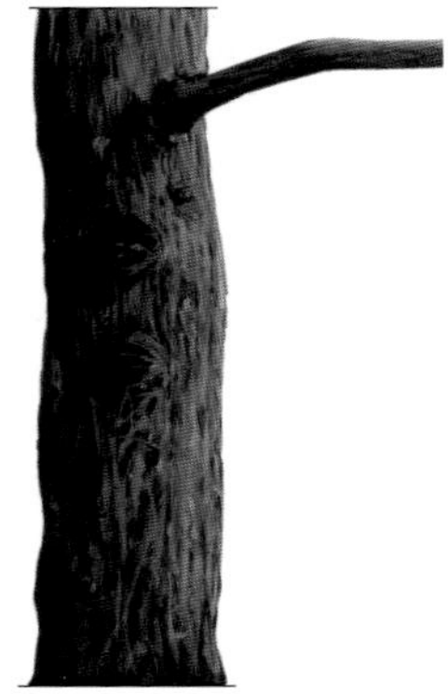

bark gray to red-brown, shallowly fissured, with long, flat, irregular ridges

5 short needles, 1½", dark blue-green, upcurved; persisting 10–17 years

branches resemble bottlebrushes because of persistent needles

needles often "dusted" with tiny white resin dots, unlike other foxtail pines

Colorado Bristlecone Pine is very similar to Intermountain Bristlecone Pine and Foxtail Pine. These three species do not overlap in range, but distinguishing them by an other means is very difficult. Intermountain Bristlecone is distinguished from Foxtail Pine by cones with a rounded base (vs. tapered), and cone scales with small, but distinct, prickles. It is distinguished from Colorado Bristlecone Pine by cones averaging slightly larger, needles averaging shorter and stouter, with blunter tip.

cones 2½", cylindrical and blunt-tipped, short delicate prickles; not persistent

young female cones blue to purple

male pollen cones reddish

old trees become gnarled and contorted in harsh, alpine habitat

Uncommon and local on barren windswept rocky slopes on scattered mountaintops at or near timberline. Commonly cultivated (zones 4–7).

Most pines have small lightweight seeds with long papery wings and are dispersed by the wind. The Foxtail pines and Pinyon pines, along with Whitebark and Limber pines, all have larger, heavier seeds with rudimentary wings and are dispersed by animals and birds.

Intermountain Bristlecone Pine

Pinus longaeva

GREAT BASIN BRISTLECONE PINE, ANCIENT PINE

Evergreen. Small tree usually 15–40' tall (max. 47'). Strongly tapering, crown rounded, flattened (sheared), or irregular. Branches contorted, pendent. Often considered a subspecies of Colorado Bristlecone Pine.

5 (3–4) needles, short, 1"

cones 3¼", with small, slender prickles

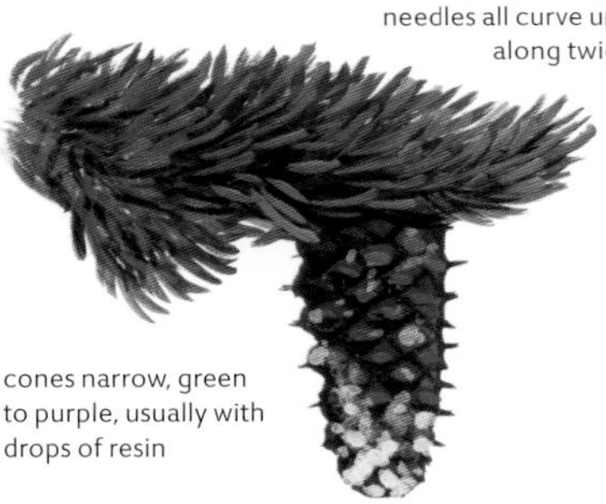
needles all curve up along twig
cones narrow, green to purple, usually with drops of resin

An Intermountain Bristlecone Pine is often reported to be the oldest living thing on Earth. A well-documented individual tree in eastern Nevada is over 4,800 years old, with several other trees known to be over 4,000 years old. In the harsh alpine environment, where these trees live, they grow very slowly, about an inch in diameter every 100 years.

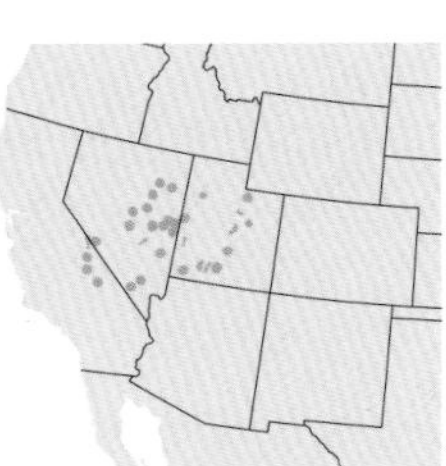

Uncommon and local on rocky slopes near or at timberline. Very rarely cultivated.

Foxtail Pine

Pinus balfouriana

Evergreen. Small to medium tree usually 20–40' tall (max. 76'); erect or leaning with irregular crown of contorted branches.

needles like Intermountain, 1", average shorter, stouter, and blunter than Colorado Bristlecone

cones 3¼", cylindrical, base strongly tapered, purple to red-brown, prickles minute or absent; not persistent

needles persist 10–30 years
cones like bristlecone pines, but with tapered base and depressed centers of scales with virtually no prickles

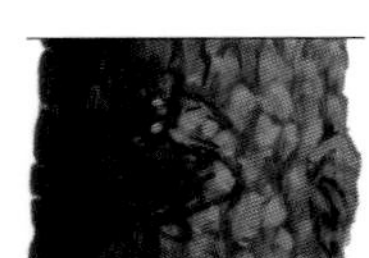
bark tends towards blocky plates

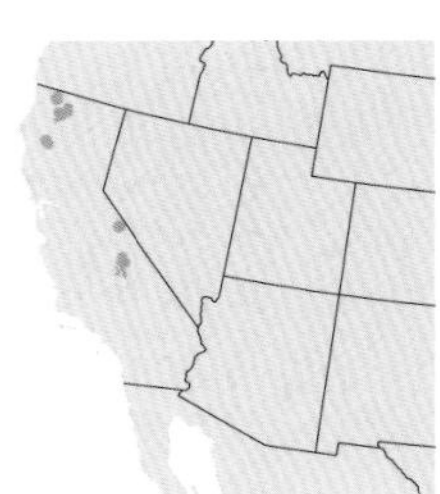

Rare and local at timberline and in alpine meadows; of conservation concern. Very rarely cultivated.

Two-needle Pinyon

Pinus edulis

PINYON PINE, NUT PINE, PIÑON PINE, COLORADO PINYON, ROCKY MOUNTAIN PINYON

Evergreen. Shrub or small tree usually 10–20' (max. 69'). Easily recognized by small size, short needles, and small, round cones. Seeds of this species, harvested from wild trees, are the commercial pine nuts (pignolis), of great importance to wildlife and humans.

bark on mature trunks dark gray-brown, often with reddish patches; furrowed, with broad, scaly ridges

2 (1–3) needles, short, 1¼", stiff, bright green or blue-green, upcurved

dense, rounded crown; branches persistent to near base

immature cones green, knobby, and nearly round

mature cones 1¾", with thick scales that lack prickles

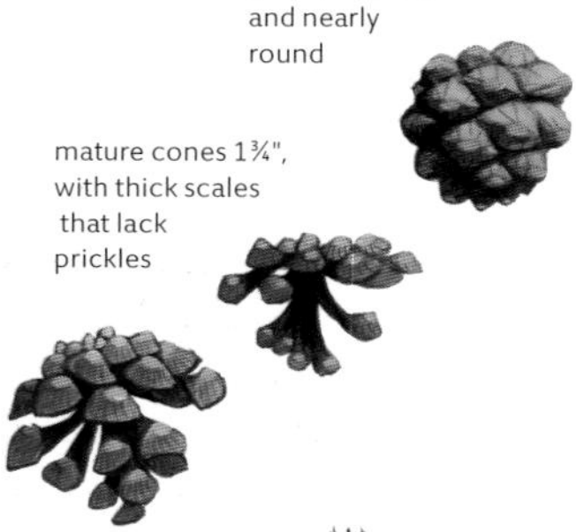

old cones sometimes persist for several years

needles persist 4–6 years

older trees develop taller trunk, more irregular crown

Across much of its range in the Southwest, large numbers of Pinyon Pine have died in recent years as a result of drought, which weakens trees and makes them more susceptible to insect pests and diseases.

Common on dry, rocky soils of slopes and mesas, usually in well-spaced groves; often mixed with juniper. Uncommonly cultivated (zones 4–5).

Similar species of pinyon pines differ in the number of needles in a bundle. All species hybridize where ranges overlap, and taxonomy and identification is complex. All have similar habit, overall size, cone features, bark, and needle length. These species are all in similar rocky, arid habitats, and are rarely cultivated.

Mexican Pinyon

Pinus cembroides

A small tree with needles in bundles of 3 (occasionally 2 or 4). Needles average slightly longer, 1½", persist 3–4 years. Cones are very small, 1"; nuts are widely collected for food in Mexico.

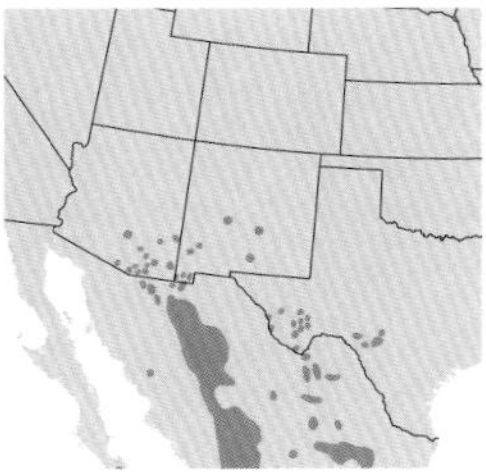

usually 3 needles, 1½"

Singleleaf Pinyon

Pinus monophylla

Unique among pines in having single needles, not divided into a cluster. Stout curved needles create a sparse, coarse appearance. Needles often bluish, persist 4–6 years; cones large, 2".

1 needle, 1"

Parry Pinyon

Pinus quadrifolia

The scarcest pinyon in North America. Usually bundles of 4 needles (sometimes 3 or 5), needles short, 1", persist 3–4 years; cones large 2¼".

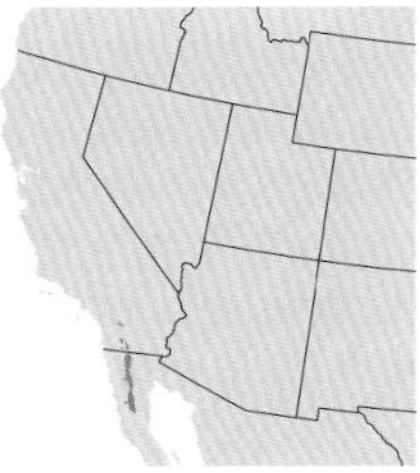

usually 4 needles, 1"

Papershell Pinyon

Pinus remota

TEXAS PINYON

An uncommon and local small tree closely related to Two-needle Pinyon. It has needles mostly in bundles of 2 (sometimes 3). Thin seed shell, like Two-needle, and raised knobs on cone scales smaller than other pinyons.

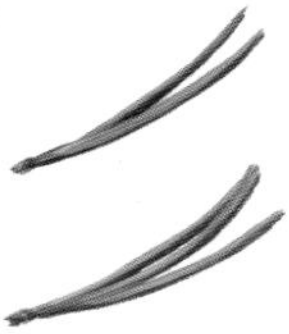

2–3 needles, 1½"

Border Pinyon

Pinus discolor

JOHANN'S PINYON

Usually a shrub under 15' tall. Similar to Mexican Pinyon, but with usually 3–4 needles. Cones have thinner scales; "flowers" 1–2 months later (mid-summer). Native to southeastern Arizona and southwestern New Mexico and south into Sierra Madres at medium to high altitudes. Found in dry, cool forests and scrub. Rarely cultivated.

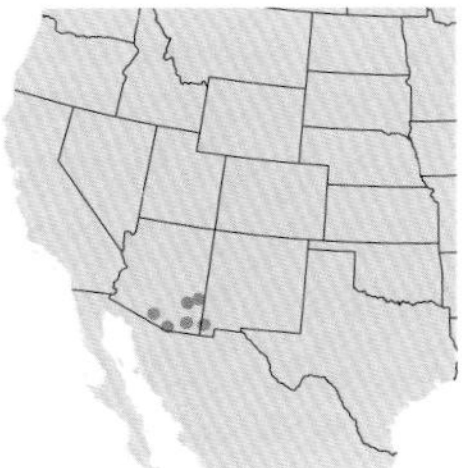

3–4 needles, 1½"

Pinyons set large numbers of cones about every six years following a winter and spring of abundant rainfall. The cones ripen in the second autumn, and open to release the large nutritious seeds known as "pine nuts." The seeds are a favorite food of many birds and animals, especially the aptly named Pinyon Jay, which depends on pinyons for a large part of its diet. When seeds are abundant, the jays cache them for later consumption. The trees benefit when forgotten or unused seeds are able to germinate.

Bhutan Pine

Pinus wallichiana

HIMALAYAN PINE, BLUE PINE

Evergreen. Medium to large tree usually 30–60' tall (max. 99'). Similar to Eastern White Pine, but branches more spreading, sparser, and needles drooping.

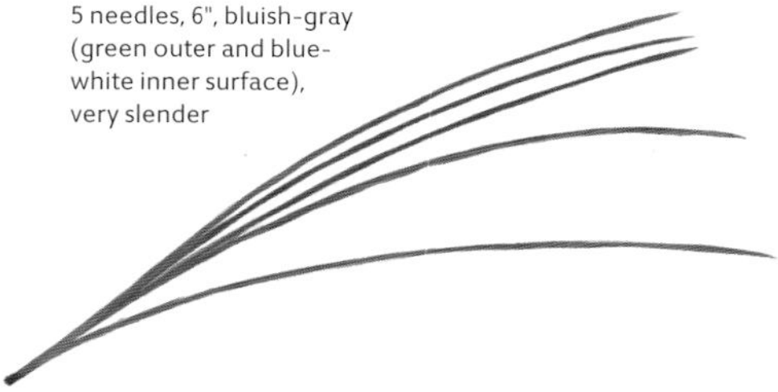

5 needles, 6", bluish-gray (green outer and blue-white inner surface), very slender

needles pointing forward and more or less drooping; persist 3–4 years

cones very large, 9", slender, curved, stalked

Many other cultivated pine species and forms may be encounterd in addition to the species illustrated here. In particular, a hybrid of Bhutan x Japanese White Pine has been commonly cultivated in recent years. Such hybrids, and other cultivars, can make the identification of cultivated pines very complex.

Native to southern Asia; uncommonly, but widely cultivated and locally naturalized (zones 5–7).

Macedonian Pine

Pinus peuce

GREEK STONE PINE, BALKAN PINE

Evergreen. Medium tree often 30–50' tall (max. 67'). Relatively narrow, old trees resemble Eastern White Pine. Native to southeastern Europe; uncommon in cultivation (zones 4–7).

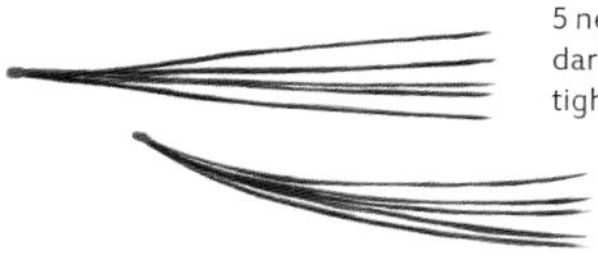

5 needles, 3½", stiff, dark gray-green, in tight clusters

cones 4½", scales tend to curve in

Korean White Pine

Pinus koraiensis

KOREAN NUT PINE, MANCHURIAN WHITE PINE

Evergreen. Medium to large tree usually 30–40' tall in cultivation (max. 72'). Similar to Swiss Stone and Whitebark Pines. Native to northeastern Asia. Uncommon in cultivation (zones 4–7).

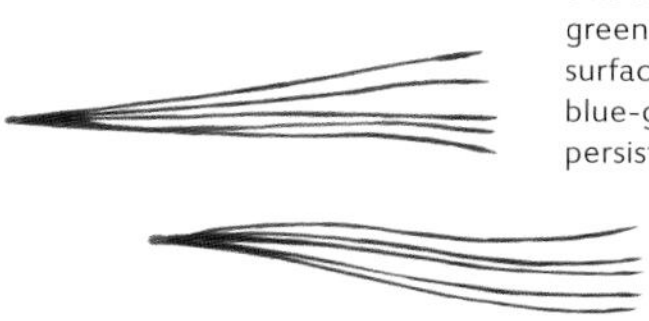

5 needles, 3½", dark green with whitish inner surface giving overall blue-green color; persist 3 years

cones 4½", heavy, blunt-tipped, short-stalked; not persistent

Japanese White Pine

Pinus parviflora

Evergreen. Large shrub or small tree to 25' tall (max. 59'). In the wild, a medium tree with typical white-pine form, but cultivated plants almost always dwarf and shrubby, with dense blue-green foliage. Native to Japan; shrubby forms are commonly cultivated, many cultivars (zones 4–7).

5 needles; 2", slender, often curving or twisted, dark green or blue-green; persist 3–4 years

cones smaller than other white pines, 2½"; persistent

Lacebark Pine

Pinus bungeana

BUNGE'S PINE

Evergreen. Small to medium tree usually 30–50' tall (max. 65'); often bushy with multiple leaning trunks. Pale mottled bark, irregularly curved trunk, and open crown of sparse needles easily recognizable. Native to northern China; uncommonly cultivated (zones 5–7).

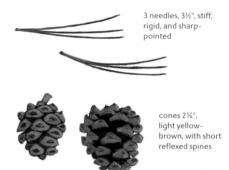

3 needles, 3½", stiff, rigid, and sharp-pointed

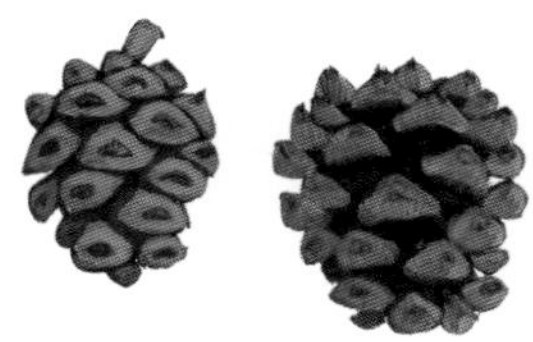

cones 2¼", light yellow-brown, with short reflexed spines

Swiss Stone Pine

Pinus cembra

AROLLA PINE, RUSSIAN CEDAR

Evergreen. Medium tree usually 30–40' tall (max. 59'); often a dense, garden shrub. Short level branches turning up at ends retained to ground level. Native to mountains of central Europe and western Asia. Uncommonly cultivated in North America (zones 3–7).

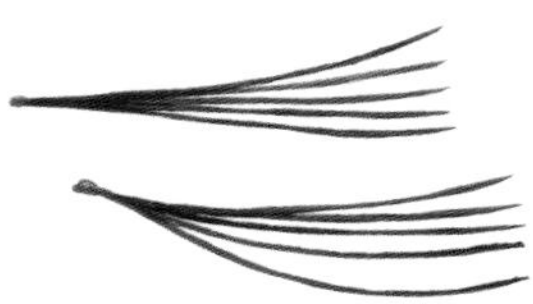

5 needles, 3", blue-green, curved and held close to twigs; persist 4–5 years

cone 3" long, rounded, blue to purple, remaining closed like Whitebark

needles sparse and widely spaced, lacy appearance; persist 3–4 years

bark exfoliates in rounded whitish to gray-green flakes, sycamore-like

The Lacebark Pine has two close relatives near its native range in central Asia, but its closest relatives in North America are the pinyons and foxtail pines. It has long been considered a part of the white pine group, but differs in having only three needles in a bundle, shorter cones with very thick scales, and with other details of cone scales and seeds similar to trees in the yellow pine group. Along with pinyon and foxtail pines, it is often classified in a separate section of the genus *Pinus*.

Italian Stone Pine

Pinus pinea

MEDITERRANEAN STONE PINE, UMBRELLA PINE, PARASOL PINE

Evergreen. Medium to large tree often 50' tall (max. 95'). Strongly umbrella-shaped crown is distinctive; Not related to Swiss Stone Pine.

2 (3) needles, 4½", fairly stout, often twisted, fairly sparse

cones 4½", nearly round, scales smooth with no prickles

broad, flat crown, like an umbrella, trunk short or long

Native to Mediterranean region. Commonly cultivated along Pacific Coast, but rarely elsewhere (zones 7–11).

Aleppo Pine

Pinus halepensis

JERUSALEM PINE

Evergreen. Medium to large tree, usually 40–70' tall (max. 144'). Twisting branches and mass of fine twigs with old cones retained, open crown. Aleppo is closely related to Maritime and Chir Pines. Together with Italian Stone Pine, these form a group of species native to the Mediterranean region.

2 (3) needles, 3¼", slender, sparse, shining bright green

cone 3", reddish, angled back along twigs, persistent

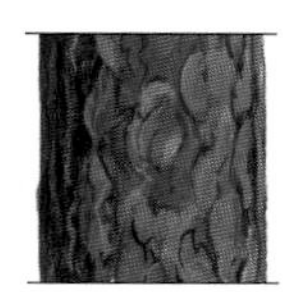

bark with gray ridges and scales flaking off to reveal orange inner bark

The very similar Brutian or Calabrian Pine (*Pinus brutia*) of southeastern Europe and the Middle East is also cultivated to some extent. More cold-hardy, it averages longer stiffer needles, and larger stouter cones not angled back along the twigs.

Native to Mediterranean region. Commonly cultivated in southwest and California (zones 9–10).

Bosnian Pine

Pinus leucodermis

SNAKESKIN PINE, GRAYBARK PINE, BALKAN PINE

Evergreen. Small to medium tree usually 25–35' tall (max. 45'); strongly upright. Similar to Austrian Pine but more closely-related to Maritime and Italian Stone Pines. Native to southeastern Europe. Commonly cultivated since 1970s (zones 5–6+).

2 needles, 3¼", stiff, dark green; persist 5–6 years

cones 3" long, dark purple or blue when young

Heldreich Pine (*Pinus heldreichii*), native to Greece, is very similar to Bosnian Pine. It is variously considered a full species, a subspecies of Bosnian Pine, or a hybrid of Austrian × Bosnian Pine. Rarely cultivated.

Japanese Red Pine

Pinus densiflora

Evergreen. Medium to large tree usually 40–60' tall (max. 71'); multiple crooked trunks with orange bark. Native to northeastern China and Japan. Commonly cultivated (zones 3–7) and several cultivars.

2 needles, 4", slender, twisted, soft; persist 3 years; needles appear in clumps or tufts

cones 2", sometimes in very large clusters; persist up to 3 years

Mugo Pine

Pinus mugo

SWISS MOUNTAIN PINE, DWARF MOUNTAIN PINE, KNEE PINE

Evergreen. Shrub to medium tree (max. 62'). Most planted cultivars short and bushy to about 20'. Related to Scotch and Japanese Red Pines, but with short, stiff, sharp needles.

2 needles, 2", dark green, stiff; persist 5 years or longer

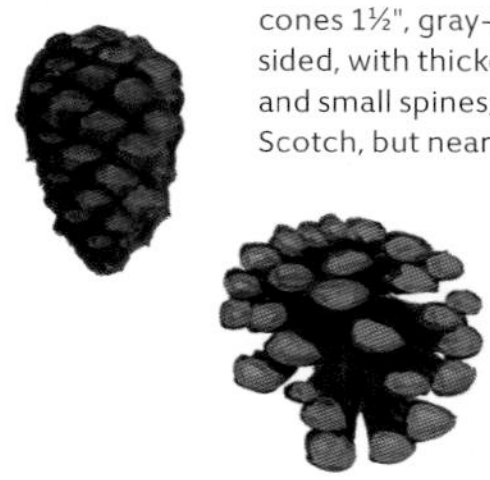

cones 1½", gray-brown, lopsided, with thickened scales and small spines; similar to Scotch, but nearly stalkless

bark brownish gray, rather smooth but splitting vertically and horizontally

Mugo Pines with tree-like stature are sometimes separated as the species Mountain Pine (*Pinus uncinata*). Often 50' tall, this form is much less commonly cultivated in North America.

Native to Europe. Commonly and widely cultivated; rarely escaped in New England (zones 3–7).

Patula Pine

Pinus patula

JELECOTE PINE, MEXICAN WEEPING PINE, MEXICAN YELLOW PINE

Evergreen. Medium to large tree (max. 86'); slender and tall with graceful weeping foliage and reddish bark. Related to Slash and Longleaf Pines. Native to Mexico. Uncommonly cultivated, almost exclusively in warmer parts of California (zones 9–10).

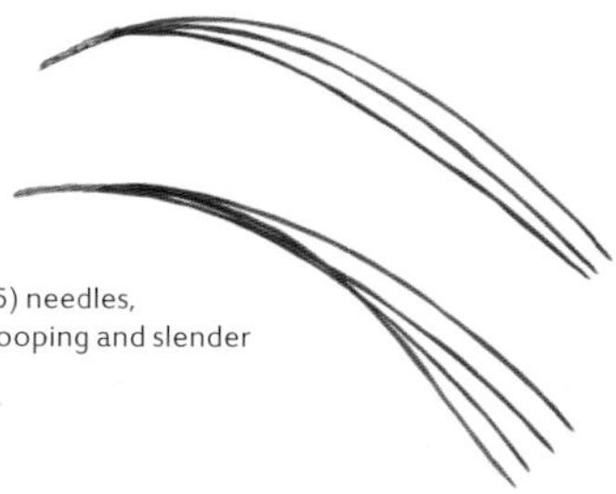

3 (4–5) needles, 8", drooping and slender

cones narrow, 4"

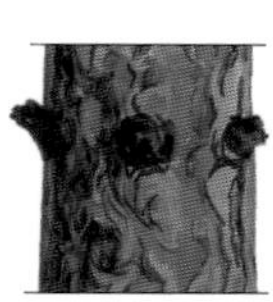

bark reddish

Maritime Pine

Pinus pinaster

SEASIDE PINE, CLUSTER PINE

Evergreen. Medium to large tree (max. 88'); long, leaning reddish trunk with irregular dark crown. Tolerant of sandy soil and seaside conditions. Native to southwestern Europe, northwestern Africa. Commonly cultivated along Pacific Coast, rare elsewhere (zone 8–9).

2 (3) needles, 7½"

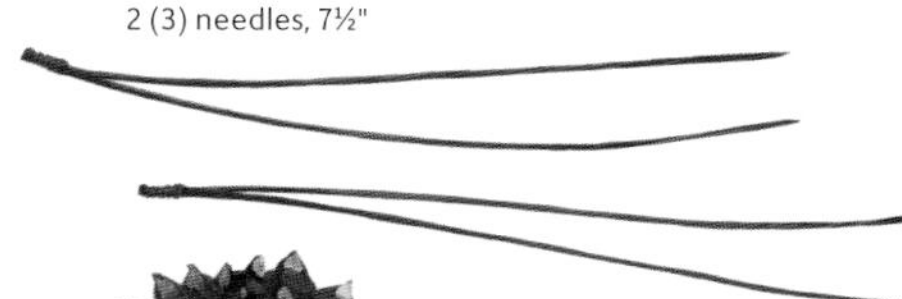

cones 6", reddish when mature, in large clusters

Chir Pine

Pinus roxburghii

EMODI PINE

Evergreen. Medium to large tree usually 40–70' tall (max. 102'). Native to southern Himalayan region; occasionally cultivated in warmer parts of California (zones 9–10).

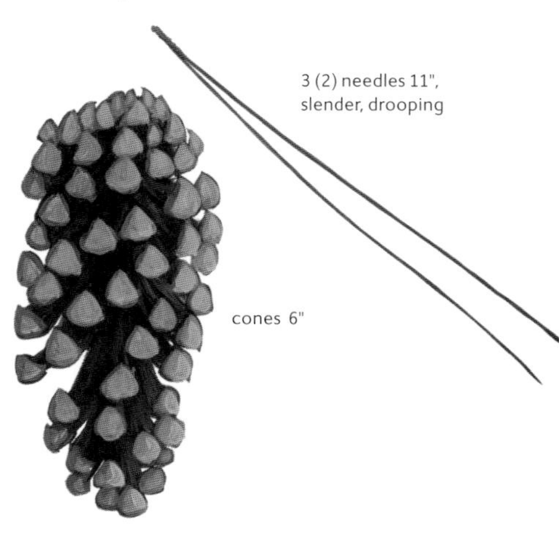

3 (2) needles 11", slender, drooping

cones 6"

Lodgepole Pine

Pinus contorta var. *latifolia*

TAMARACK PINE, SCRUB PINE

Evergreen. Medium to large tree, often to 80' (max. 150'). Over most of range, a very straight-trunked, slender pine; note short needles and small cones. A fire successional tree dominant on millions of acres, often forming dense single-species stands. Closely related to Jack Pine; the two hybridize where ranges overlap.

very straight-growing, with ascending upper branches

2 needles 2½", yellow-green, curved, and thick

mature cones 1½", broadly oval and slightly prickly

mature cones often persist several years, opening only after fire
immature cones green, small, and egg-shaped

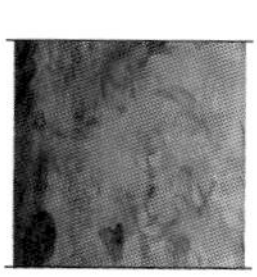
bark on mature trunks gray to pale orange; relatively smooth with thin scales

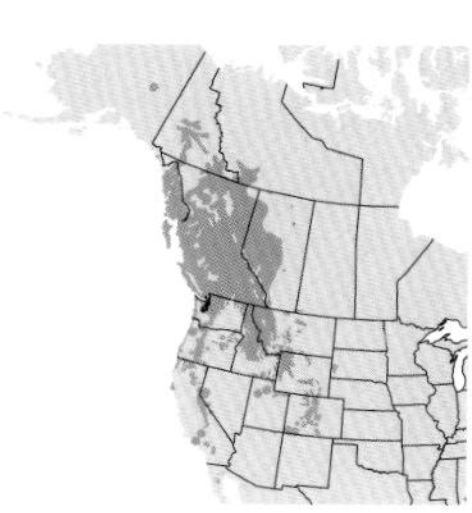

Common in forests from sea level to timberline (where reduced to shrub form). Rarely cultivated, except for Shore Pine.

'Shore' Lodgepole Pine

Pinus contorta var. *contorta*

Evergreen. Smaller (30', max. 123') crooked variety of Lodgepole. Common in coastal forests from sea level to 1,800'. Found in a variety of habitats, from bogs to dry foothills, but typically in low, wet areas. Commonly cultivated in the West (zone 5).

needles darker, more slender, and slightly shorter

mature cones more recurved and asymmetrical

crooked, more irregular habit, often shaped by wind

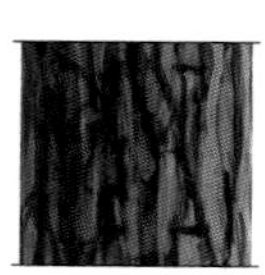
bark darker and more furrowed

Jack Pine

Pinus banksiana

SCRUB PINE, GRAY PINE, BLACK PINE

Evergreen. Small to medium tree usually 20–40' tall (max. 97', smaller to East); usually crooked, leaning, gaunt and yellow-green with abundant retained cones, crown irregular, often flat-topped. No other eastern pine has such short needles or curved cones.

bark orange- to
red-brown, scaly

2 needles, very short,
1¼", yellow-green,
stiff, divergent
and twisted; persist
2–4 years

short yellow-green
needles relatively
sparse

closed cones
sickly gray-white,
persistent
cones 2",
curved and
pointing towards
tip of twig

The close association between the endangered Kirtland's Warbler and this tree in Michigan is as obligatory as any bird/tree relationship. The warbler nests only in open scrubby Jack Pine stands of a certain age and density, which occur naturally after fires, but now must be maintained by controlled burning.

on some trees
most cones open,
on others, cones
remain closed until
fire event

usually a
crooked,
irregular tree with
short needles,
jutting branches,
and many persistent
small cones

Closely related to Lodgepole Pine, and the two species hybridize over a broad area of western Alberta and northeastern British Columbia, where their ranges overlap. Also closely related and similar to Virginia and Sand Pines.

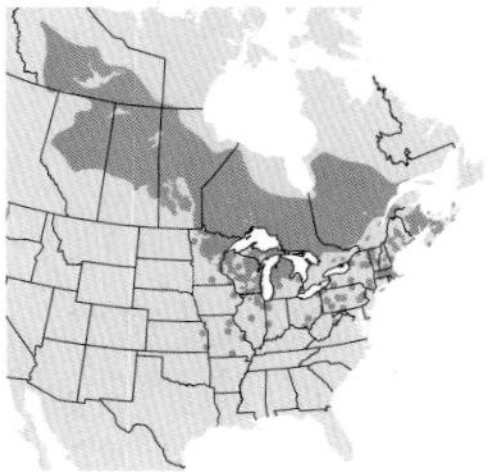

Fire successional in boreal forests, tundra transition, in dry sandy or rocky, barren soil. Commonly cultivated (zones 2–6).

Virginia Pine

Pinus virginiana

JERSEY PINE, SCRUB PINE

Evergreen. Small tree usually 20–40' tall (max. 120'). Somewhat scrubby and scraggly; crown irregularly rounded or flattened, often filled with retained small cones. Weedy and fire successional, often forms large stands.

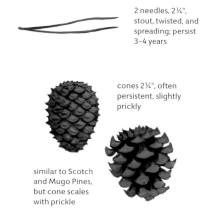

2 needles, 2¼", stout, twisted, and spreading; persist 3–4 years

cones 2¼", often persistent, slightly prickly

similar to Scotch and Mugo Pines, but cone scales with prickle

relatively short needles, about as long as cones

bark gray-brown with irregular, scaly-plated ridges; on upper sections of trunk reddish, scaly

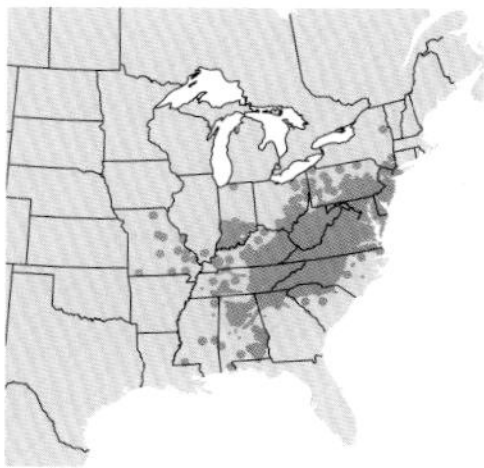

Common in dry uplands, sterile sandy barrens, old fields. Uncommonly cultivated mainly within native range (zones 4–8).

Sand Pine

Pinus clausa

SCRUB PINE, SPRUCE PINE

Evergreen. Small to medium tree usually 20–35' tall (max. 100'), straight and erect to leaning and crooked, much branched; crown mostly rounded or irregular.

2 needles 2¾" long, slightly twisted, rich green

cones 2½" long, slightly prickly; persistent, open at maturity in some populations, open only by fire in others

old cones persist for years

bark relatively smooth, scaly, grayish to reddish

Similar to Spruce Pine but occurs naturally only in deep coastal sands and along inland dune ridges. Also distinguished by under surface of cone scales tipped with dark brown band.

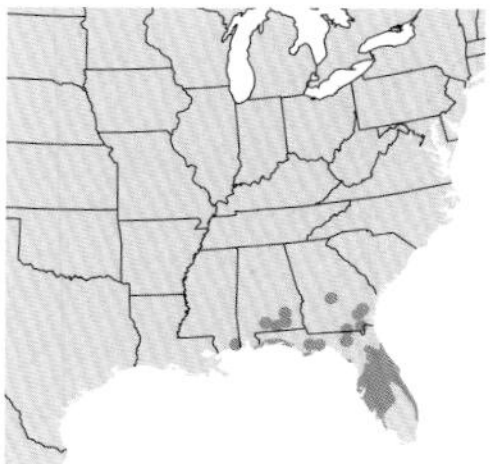

Common locally in deep sandy soil; Fire successional and rapidly recolonizes after fires. Planted widely for wood pulp, rarely cultivated for ornament (zones 8–9).

Scotch Pine

Pinus sylvestris

SCOTS PINE, SCOTCH FIR, NORTHERN PINE

Evergreen. Small to medium tree usually 25–50' tall (max. 106'). Trunk usually curved, with few long branches. Distinctive orange bark of upper trunk and branches, short blue-green needles, and small cones without prickles.

bark on upper trunk and branches of mature tree smooth, bright rusty-orange
bark of main trunk gray with thin scaly ridges

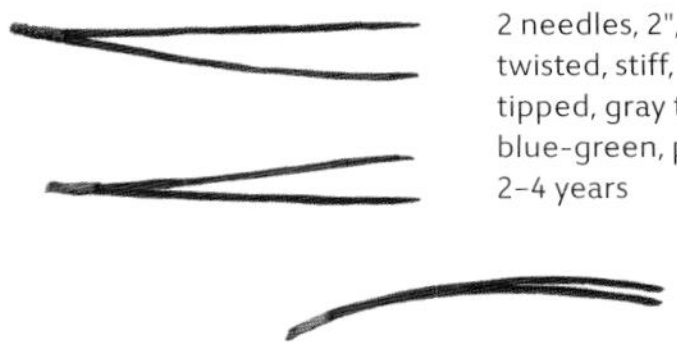
2 needles, 2", twisted, stiff, blunt-tipped, gray to blue-green, persist 2–4 years

curved orange trunk and irregular crown
most cultivated and escaped trees, shorter, curved

cones 2", not prickly, open when ripe and sometimes persistent

twigs slender
needles twisted; cones point back along twig

Native to Eurasia. Very commonly cultivated and widely naturalized in abandoned fields, fencerows, and woods (zones 3–7).

some varieties tall and straight; valuable lumber trees

Spruce Pine

Pinus glabra

CEDAR PINE, WALTER PINE, BOTTOM WHITE PINE

Evergreen. Medium tree usually 40–60' tall (max. 156'). Related and similar to Shortleaf Pine, but with less prickly cones and deeper green leaves, and underside of cone scales lack dark tips.

2 needles, 2½", twisted; persist 2–3 years

cones small, 2¼", with minute prickles; sometimes persistent

twigs slender, aging gray, smooth; the only other hard pine with similarly smooth twigs is Sand Pine

The Spruce Pine is unusual among pines in that it occurs mainly as scattered individual trees in mixed hardwood forest. Most pines are not shade-tolerant and cannot sprout and grow in the understory of a hardwood forest, but Spruce Pine thrives in these areas.

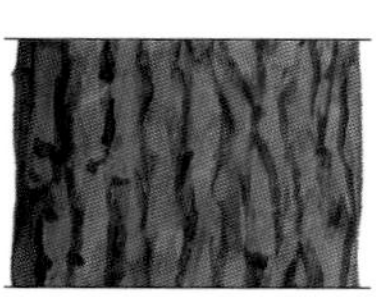

bark gray, tightly furrowed, with small scales, more like a hardwood than a pine

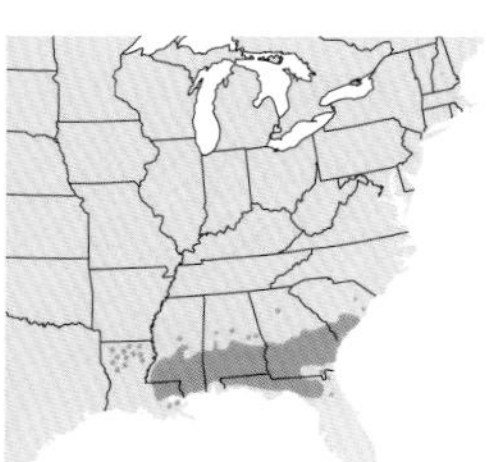

Uncommon and scattered in sandy or rich bottomland forest, tolerates shade and brief inundation. Rarely cultivated (zones 8–9).

Table Mountain Pine

Pinus pungens

MOUNTAIN PINE, HICKORY PINE, PRICKLY PINE

Evergreen. Small to medium tree usually 30–50' tall (max. 97'); straight to crooked, erect to leaning, crown irregularly rounded or flattened. No other eastern pine has such sharp-tipped needles or long-spined cones.

2 (3) needles, 2", twisted, yellow-green, sharp-pointed; persist 3 years

cones 3", pale yellow-brown, heavy with obvious curved hooks; persistent for years

stout pale cones in clusters of 2–3

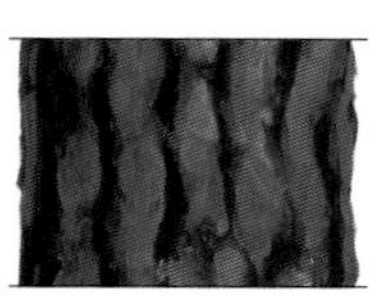

bark red- to gray-brown, irregularly checked into scaly plates

Uncommon in scattered locations in dry, mostly sandy or shaly uplands of Appalachians and associated Piedmont slopes. Rarely cultivated.

Pitch Pine

Pinus rigida

NORTHERN PITCH PINE, TORCH PINE, SAP PINE

Evergreen. Small to medium tree usually 40–60' tall (max. 101'). Straight or crooked, commonly with tufts of needles along trunk; crown rounded or irregular. Known to hybridize naturally with Shortleaf Pine, and very closely related to and intergrading with Pond Pine.

tufts of needles often sprout directly from trunk, a habit shared only with Pond Pine
bark red-brown, deeply and irregularly furrowed, with long, rectangular plates

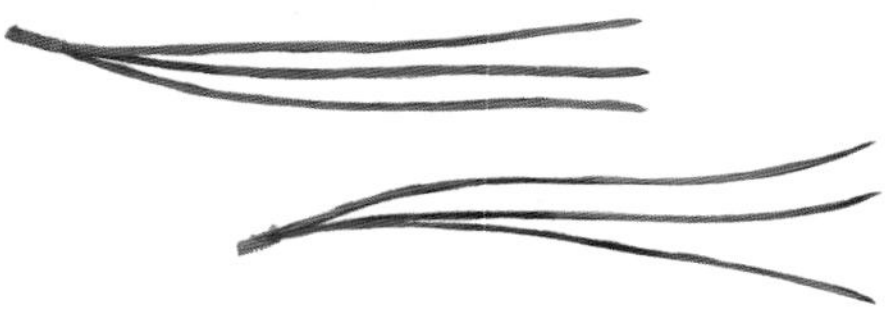
3 (4–5) needles, 3¼", yellow-green, stiff, spreading, somewhat curved and twisted; persist 2–3 years

Twigs are fibrous and do not snap cleanly when bent; the only 3-needle pine with fibrous twigs (Virginia and Table Mountain Pines both 2-needled with fibrous twigs).

cones 2½", flat at base, very prickly; often persistent

irregular branches and clumps of foliage create relatively smooth rounded crown

cones often in clusters of 2–3
long, stiff needles clumped at twig tips

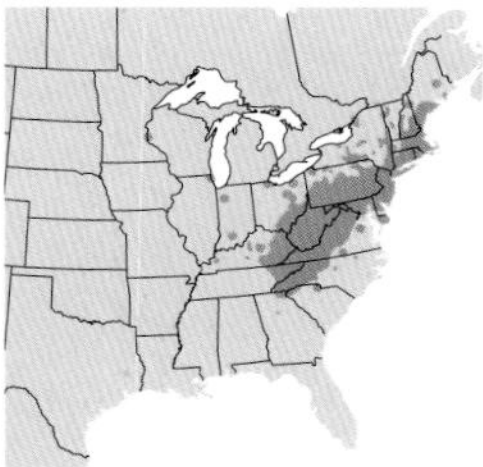

Common and widespread, especially in dry sandy "pine barrens" or rocky soil, but also in damp soils in swamp margins. Fairly commonly cultivated (zones 4–7).

In spring, the timing of the emergence of seed cones and pollen cones can be helpful for identifying similar species of pines in any locale. In one Alabama study, Slash Pine "flowered" first, followed about 30 days later by Loblolly and Longleaf Pines (Loblolly averaged about a week earlier than Longleaf, but with much overlap).Shortleaf Pine "flowered" about 20 days after Longleaf. The date varied by up to 40 days from year to year, but the relative time of the emergence of cones of these species was consistent.

Pond Pine

Pinus serotina

SWAMP PINE, MARSH PINE, POCOSIN PINE

Evergreen. Medium to large tree usually 40–60' tall (max. 120'); straight or more often crooked. Very similar to Pitch and Loblolly Pines. Distinguished from Pitch by longer needles and less prickly cones; from Loblolly by smaller, less prickly, and more persistent cones, and by needles sprouting from trunk.

3 (2–5) needles, 7"

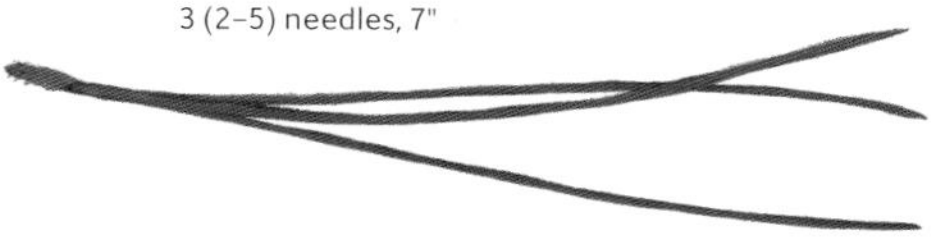

cones 2½", slightly or not prickly, persistent

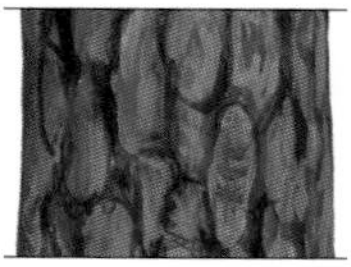

bark red-brown, irregularly furrowed and cross-checked into rectangular, flat, scaly plates

Most of the southeastern pines are known to hybridize, in particular, Pitch, Pond, Loblolly, Longleaf, and Shortleaf Pines. Species that occur in close proximity and have similar cone emergence times can be expected to hybridize.

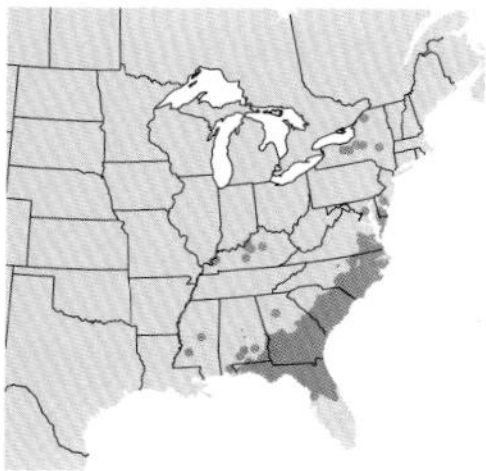

Common in flatwoods, bogs, savannahs, and barrens. Fire successional and sprouts from trunk after fires. Increasingly harvested for pulpwood; rarely cultivated as ornamental (zones 7–9).

Loblolly Pine

Pinus taeda

OLDFIELD PINE, SHORTLEAF PINE, NORTH CAROLINA PINE

Evergreen. Large tree usually 60–90' tall (max. 182'); usually straight, crown broadly conic to rounded. Similar to Slash Pine but needles usually in threes. Similar to Longleaf Pine, but shorter needles, shorter cones, and lacks silvery terminal buds.

3(2–5) needles, 7", slender, bright green; persist 2–3 years

cones 3½", stout prickles; usually not persistent

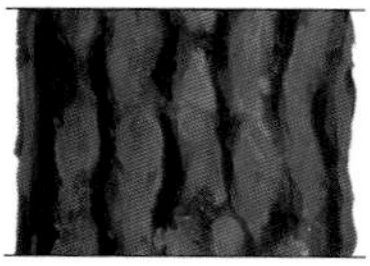

bark red-brown, deeply furrowed forming large rectangular, scaly plates

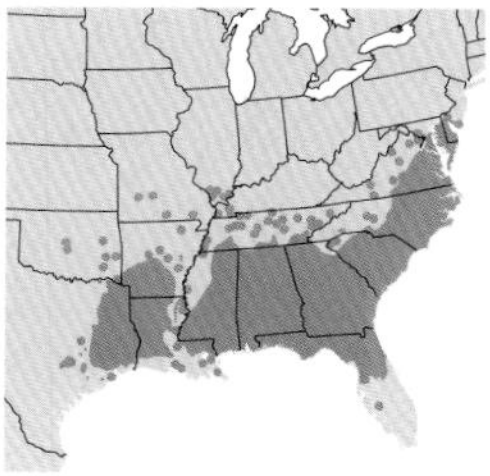

Common in damp lowlands and swamp borders to dry uplands, old fields. Commonly cultivated for lumber, rarely cultivated for ornament (zones 6–9).

Longleaf Pine

Pinus palustris

SOUTHERN YELLOW PINE, LONGSTRAW PINE, HILL PINE, PITCH PINE, HARD PINE, HEART PINE

Evergreen. Large tree usually 60–70' tall (max. 150'); crown rounded, branches curved up at tips.

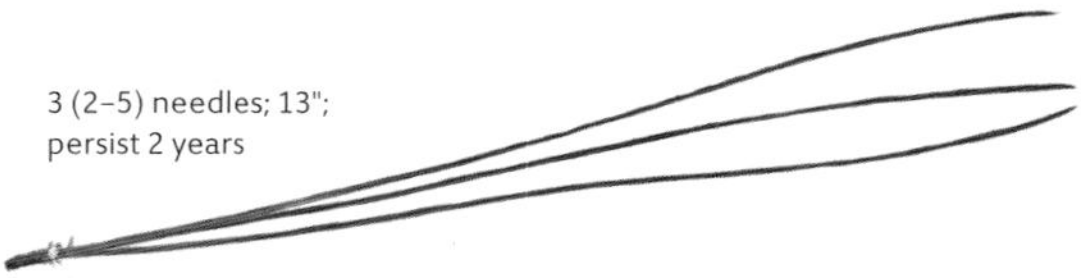

3 (2–5) needles; 13"; persist 2 years

bark orange-brown, with coarse, rectangular, scaly plates

cone 8", wide-based, open at maturity, with short prickles; not persistent

needles form large round clusters at branch tips

twigs stout (to almost 1"), orange-brown, rough

This species formerly covered millions of acres of a unique habitat known as Longleaf Pine savannah. Ninety-five percent of this savannah is now gone, due in part to overharvesting, but mainly because other species (especially Slash Pine) respond better to commercial forestry practices. Longleaf Pines were important producers of naval stores, such as, tar, pitch, turpentine, and valued for lumber. Several species of birds prefer this habitat, including Bachman's Sparrow and the critically endangered Red-cockaded Woodpecker, and it is hypothesized that the habitat might have been important for the Ivory-billed Woodpecker.

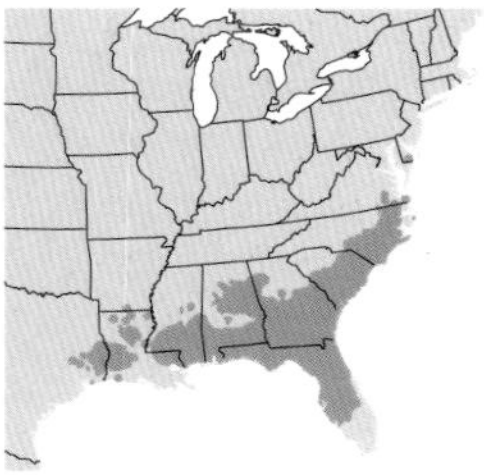

Dry sandy uplands, sandhills, and flatwoods. Commonly cultivated for ornament, mainly in and near native range (zones 7–10).

tall straight tree with sparse branches and needles in large round tufts at branch tips

Slash Pine

Pinus elliottii

YELLOW SLASH PINE, SWAMP PINE, PITCH PINE

Evergreen. Medium to large tree usually 60–80' tall (max. 144'). Straight to contorted; crown conic, becoming rounded or flattened. Similar to Loblolly Pine, but often has two needles per bundle.

2–3 needles; 7", glossy dark green; persist 2 years

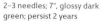

cones 5½", stalked; rich brown, short stout prickle on each scale

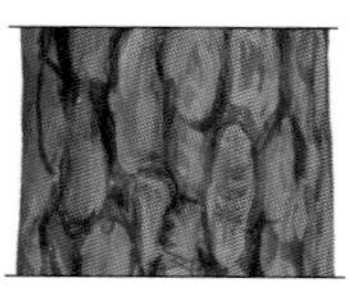

bark orange- to purple-brown, irregularly furrowed and cross-checked into large, irregularly rectangular, papery-scaly plates; similar to Shortleaf Pine

Slash Pines in southern Florida (*Pinus elliottii* var. *densa*) differ from northern trees in having usually 2 needles, broader crown, and heavier wood.

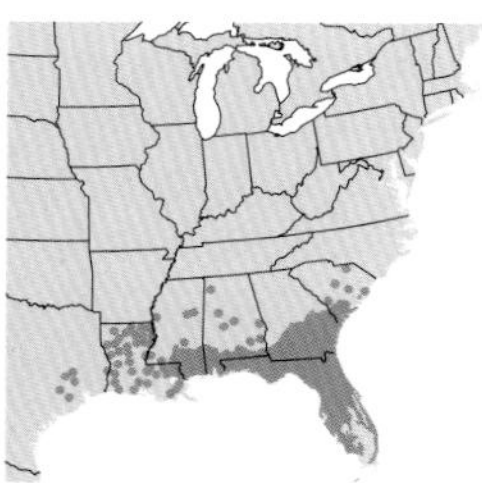

Found on moist to dry soils, especially in wet flatwoods. Commonly cultivated for lumber in warm climates worldwide, rarely cultivated for ornament (zones 8–10).

Shortleaf Pine

Pinus echinata

YELLOW PINE, SHORTSTRAW PINE, ARKANSAS PINE, ROSEMARY PINE, LONG-TAG PINE

Evergreen. Medium to large tree often 80–100' tall (max. 146'); crown rounded to conic. Leaves are short only in comparison to other southern pines. Branches contorted, curving, unlike Loblolly Pine, which can grow in same area.

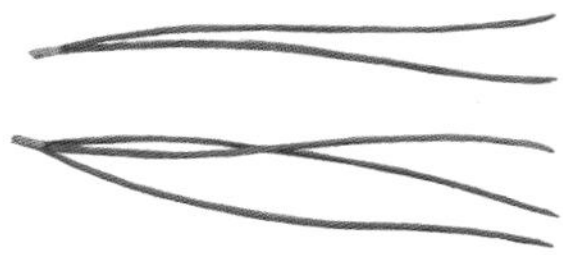

2 (3) needles, 3 ½", slightly twisted, slender and flexible, dark blue-green; persist 2–4 years

cones 2", prickly; can persist several years

underside of cone scales with dark border, unlike similar species

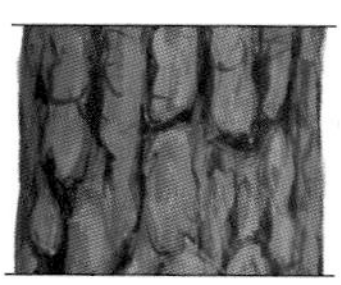

bark red-brown, often in large plates; smoother and redder than Loblolly, with gray, ridged, furrowed bark

Hybridizes with Loblolly Pine, Spruce Pine, and several other species.

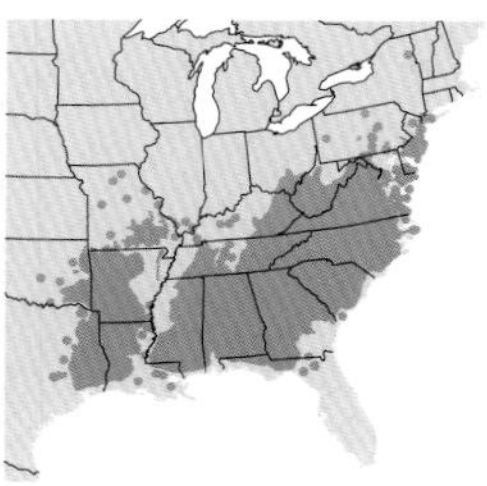

Uplands, dry forests. Commonly cultivated for lumber and uncommonly for ornament (zones 6–9).

Red Pine

Pinus resinosa

NORWAY PINE

Evergreen. Medium to large tree usually 50–80' tall (max. 154'); crown narrowly rounded. Red Pine was once the most important timber pine in the Great Lakes region.

bark pale silvery red-brown, furrowed into irregular scaly ridges

2 (3) needles; 5", rigid and straight, often yellow-green; persist 2–4 years

cones small, 2", not prickly

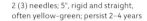

needles densely tufted at branch tips

twigs fairly stout, rough

cones very small among long needles

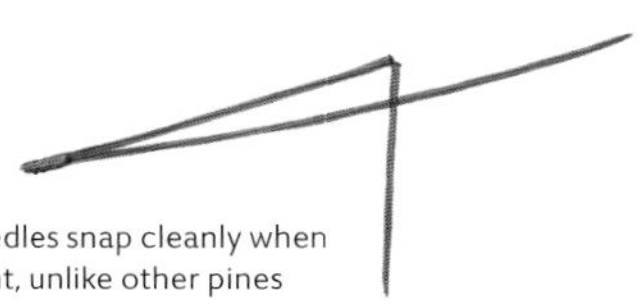

needles snap cleanly when bent, unlike other pines

trunk straight, pale silvery and reddish; oval crown with tufts of dark needles, stout twigs

Red Pine is intermediate between Eastern White and Jack Pines in habitat requirements. As Red Pine forests in the Great Lakes regions were logged and burned, the depleted sandy soils and open areas were colonized by Jack Pine, while farther east, Red Pine was able to grow in areas formerly covered by Eastern White Pine forests.

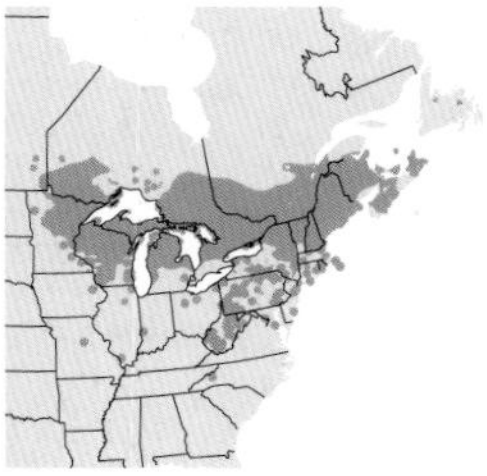

Common in dry woodlands, sandy soils, eastern boreal forests. Very commonly cultivated and naturalized, most trees seen are planted (zones 2–5).

Red Pine is similar to Austrian and Japanese Black Pines, two commonly cultivated and naturalized species. Red Pine is distinguished by thinner, silvery-red bark, long straight trunk, brittle needles, red-brown winter buds (vs. pale silvery winter buds), and non-prickly cones.

Austrian Pine

Pinus nigra

EUROPEAN BLACK PINE, COMMON BLACK PINE

Evergreen. Medium to large tree usually 50–60' tall (max. 93'). Dark, dense, sturdy-looking tree, broad and conical with short trunk and strong branches.

2 needles, 4", very dense; persist 4–8 years

cones 3", pale yellow-brown becoming dark brown; often prickly

needles stouter than Red Pine, retained on twigs 3+ years (vs. 2) resulting in bushier crown; leaves stiff

buds large ½–1", silky whitish

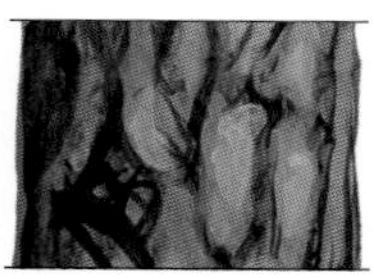

mature trunks with distinctive broad pale ridges of grayish-yellow plates

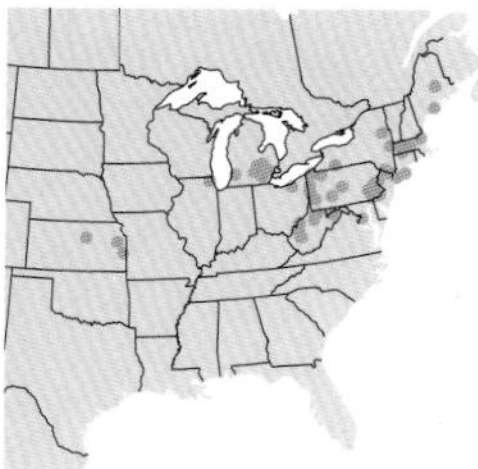

Native to southern Europe and Asia Minor. Very commonly cultivated and widely naturalized (zones 3–7). Several subspecies and many cultivars differ in growth form and foliage.

Japanese Black Pine

Pinus thunbergii

PINUS THUNBERGIANA

Evergreen. Typically a small to medium tree 20–40' tall, with multiple leaning and curving trunks, but can be taller (max. 90'). Similar to Austrian Pine, but usually a smaller tree, cones stalked with base less rounded.

2 needles, 3¼" long; dark green, rigid, thick, sharply pointed, twisted and spreading; persist 3–5 years

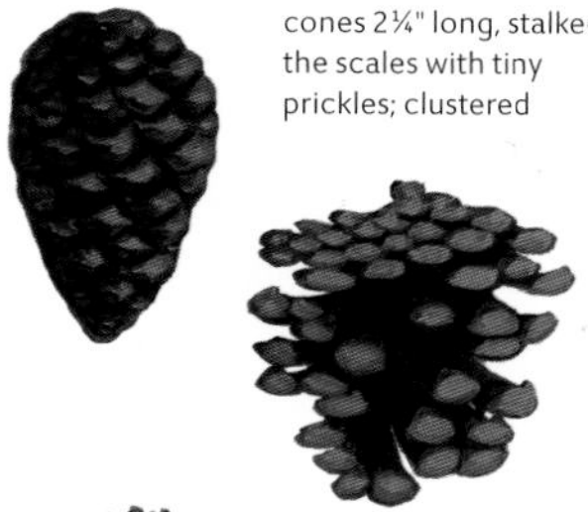

cones 2¼" long, stalked, the scales with tiny prickles; clustered

small, leaning tree, with dense dark needles

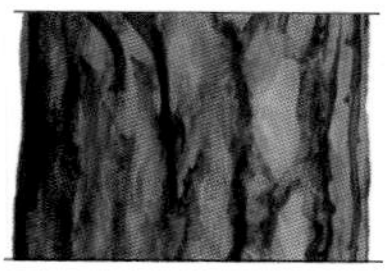

mature trunks with broad grayish yellow plates, similar to Austrian Pine

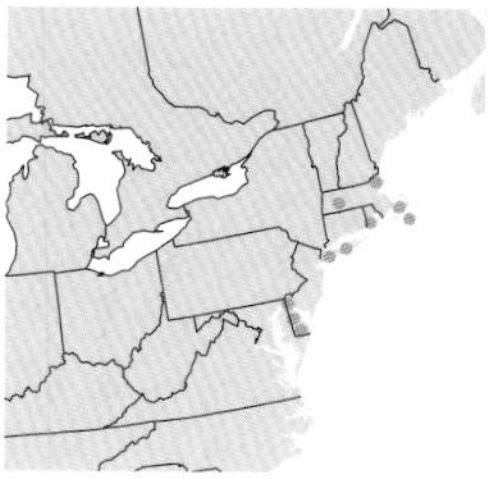

Native to Japan and Korea. Commonly cultivated and locally naturalized (zones 6–8). Recently afflicted by diseases and many plantings have declined or disappeared.

Ponderosa Pine

Pinus ponderosa

WESTERN YELLOW PINE, YELLOW PINE, PONDOSA PINE, BLACKJACK PINE, BULL PINE, ROCK PINE, WESTERN RED PINE

Evergreen. Large tree often 60–130' tall (max. 262'). Majestic with long clear trunk and open, broadly conic to rounded crown. Most economically important western yellow pine; wood is more similar in character to the white pines, and it is often referred to as white pine.

bark on young trunks dark gray with small scales

older trunks with large rectangular flat plates orange to reddish and darker furrows

3 (2–5) needles, 7", flexible, clustered at branch tips; persist 4–6 years

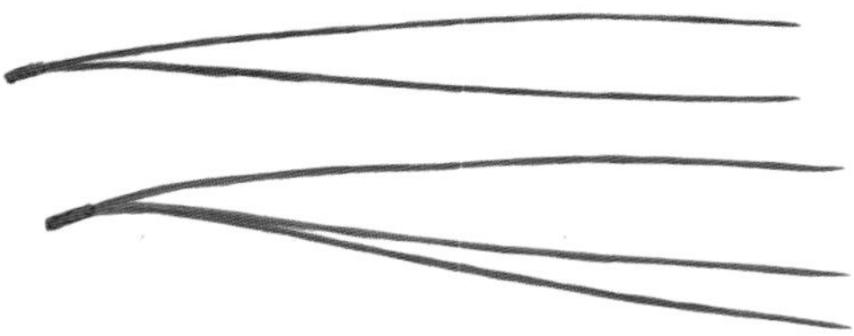

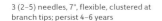

cones 4½", shiny reddish brown, stout recurved prickles; not persistent but often leave rosette of scales on branch

twigs stout (to 1"), orange-brown, rough

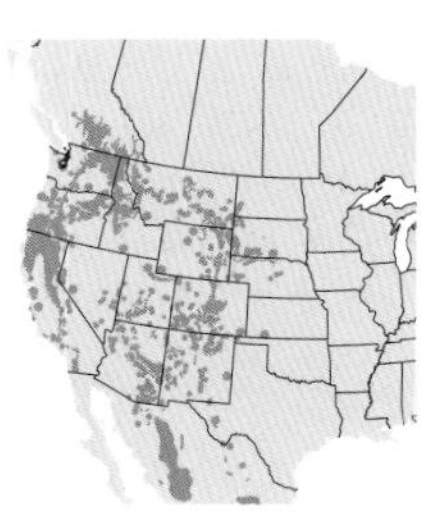

Common in a variety of habitats from moist, rich valley to dry, rocky slopes. Commonly cultivated (zones 3–6).

Arizona Pine

Pinus arizonica

ARIZONA YELLOW PINE

Evergreen. Large tree often 70–90' tall (max. 120'). Sometimes considered a subspecies of Ponderosa, but differs in having needles in bundles of 4–5, cones smaller, less prickly and often lopsided, and twigs usually glaucous.

4–5 (3) needles, 7", very slender

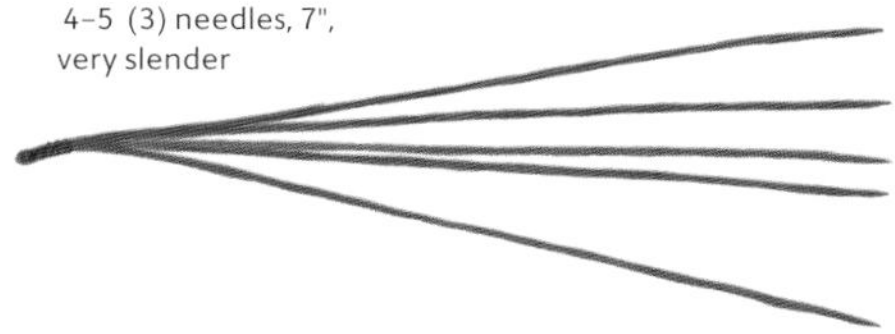

cones 2½", often lopsided, scales raised, less prickly than Ponderosa

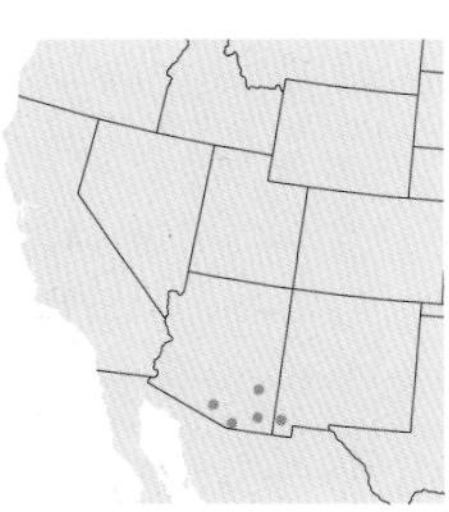

Locally common on canyon slopes at 6,000–8,000' elevation. Rarely cultivated.

Washoe Pine

Pinus washoensis

Evergreen. Medium tree usually 40–50' tall (max. 150'); straight; crown pyramidal. Very similar to Ponderosa and Jeffrey Pines, and sometimes considered the same species.

3 (2) needles, 5", gray-green, slightly twisted; persist 4–6 years

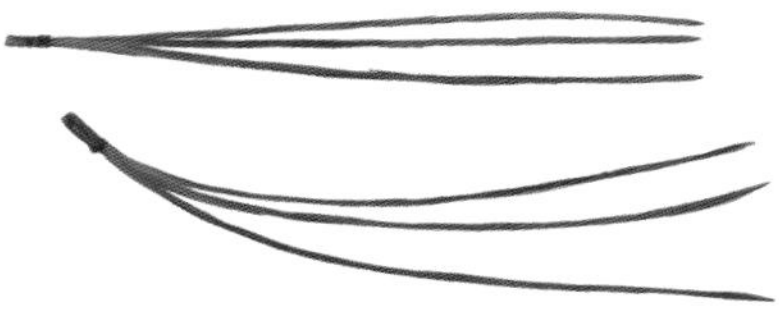

cones 3½", with small prickles; not persistent

contrastingly dark underside of cone scales unlike Jeffrey Pine

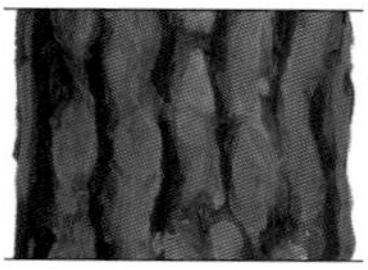

bark yellow-brown to reddish, fissured, plates scaly

Although Washoe Pine is considered closely related to the Ponderosa Pine complex, and is very similar to Jeffrey Pine, no natural hybrids have been found. Other hybrids within this complex do occur, and all species hybridize readily in cultivation. The taxonomy of these forms is still unresolved.

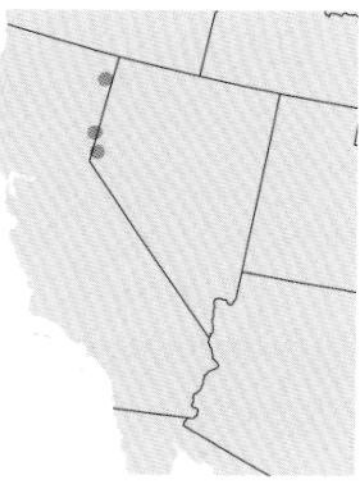

Common but very local in dry montane forests; often occurs in large stands in its limited range. Not cultivated.

Jeffrey Pine

Pinus jeffreyi

WESTERN YELLOW PINE, BULL PINE, BLACK PINE, PONDEROSA PINE

Evergreen. Large tree often 100–130' tall (max. 197', historically reported at 300'). Where the two occur together,very similar to Ponderosa, but averages smaller, with larger cones, and sweet-scented wood.

3 needles, 7", gray-green to yellow-green, twisted; persist 4–6 years

cones 9", large but not heavy, short recurved prickles; open and fall at maturity

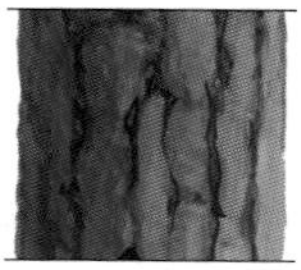

bark like Ponderosa, but may average darker, more purplish

The resin chemistry of Jeffrey and Ponderosa Pines is significantly different and the two can be distinguished by smelling the bark crevices. Jeffrey Pine smells sweet, like pineapple or vanilla, quite different from the more turpentine-like odor of Ponderosa Pine.

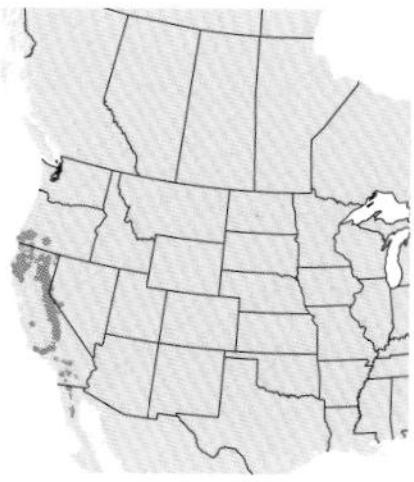

Common in high, dry montane forests mostly at higher elevations than Ponderosa Pine. Uncommonly or rarely cultivated (zone 5).

Chihuahua Pine

Pinus leiophylla

YELLOW PINE, PINO REAL

Evergreen. Medium tree usually 35–50' tall (max. 87'). Slender, crown conic, becoming rounded; one of the few pines that produce sprouts from stumps. Member of the Yellow Pine group, but with needle sheath not persistent.

3 (2–4) needles, 3", slender, straight, gray-green; persist 2 years

cones mature in three years (unlike most other pines) and persist for many years
cones short, 1 ¾", nearly round when open, scales slightly thickened and sometimes with short prickle

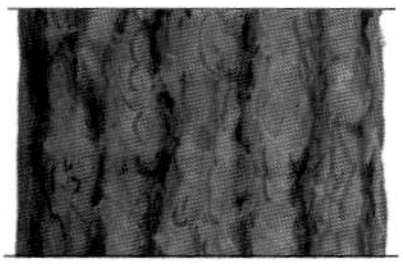
bark gray, scaly, with deep fissures

This pine (with one other Mexican species) is classified in a separate group within the yellow pines. It differs from other yellow pines in having cones that mature in three growing seasons (not two), and the sheath at the base of the needles falls away (like white pines). It can resprout from the stump (like Pitch Pine), presumably an adaptation to fire.

Common on dry rocky slopes and plateaus, often with pinyon and oaks. Not cultivated.

Apache Pine

Pinus engelmannii

ARIZONA LONGLEAF PINE

Evergreen. Medium tree usually 50–60' tall (max. 98'); straight; crown irregularly rounded, rather sparse. Hybridizes with Ponderosa Pine. Similar to Longleaf Pine but needles drooping, no range overlap.

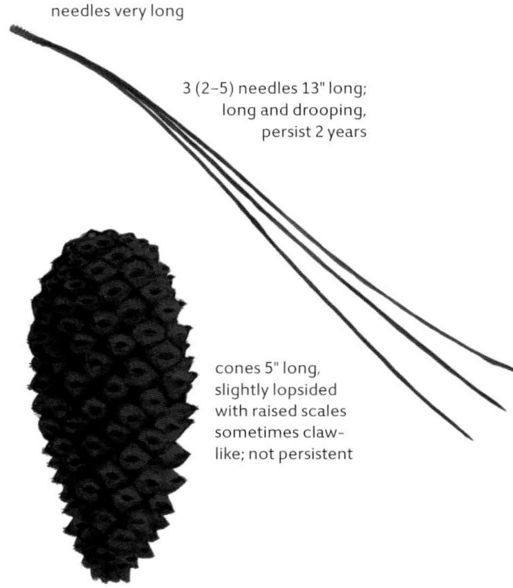
sheath at base of needles very long
3 (2–5) needles 13" long; long and drooping, persist 2 years
cones 5" long, slightly lopsided with raised scales sometimes claw-like; not persistent

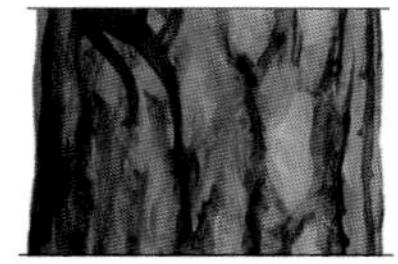
bark dark brown, at maturity deeply furrowed, ridges becoming yellowish, of narrow, elongate, scaly plates

Native to Mexico, this tree just barely enters our region in a few isolated mountain ranges in southeastern Arizona and southwestern New Mexico. If you see Apache Pines, you might also see Buff-breasted Flycatcher, Mexican Chickadee, Grace's Warbler, and other exotic birds, that barely reach the United States.

Locally common on high and dry ridges, slopes, and plateaus. Very rarely cultivated.

Coulter Pine

Pinus coulteri

BIGCONE PINE, PITCH PINE

Evergreen. Medium to large tree usually 40–60' tall (max. 144'). Crown broad, sparse, irregular; huge and heavy cones weigh as much as 8 pounds!

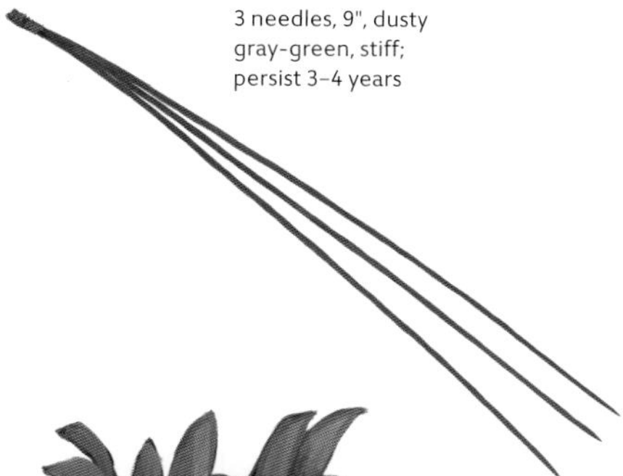

3 needles, 9", dusty gray-green, stiff; persist 3–4 years

massive cones 11", pale yellow-brown with strong recurved claws; persistent

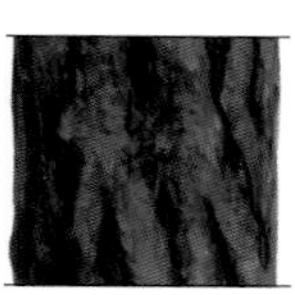

bark dark gray-brown to near black, deeply furrowed, with rounded ridges

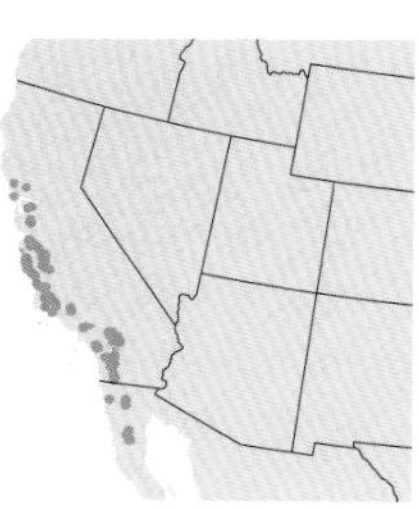

Uncommon and local on dry rocky slopes, flats, ridges, and chaparral, transitional to oak-pine woodland. Uncommonly cultivated and only near native range.

Gray Pine

Pinus sabiniana

DIGGER PINE, BULL PINE, FOOTHILL PINE, GHOST PINE

Evergreen. Medium to large tree usually 40–50' tall (max. 161'). Often forked; crown foliage sparse, grayish, drooping; bark dark.

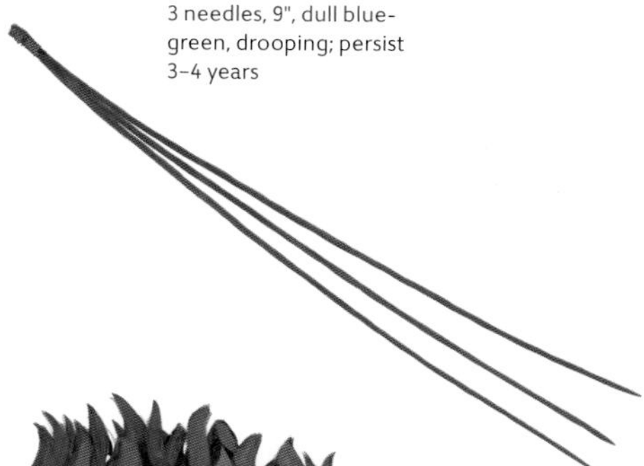

3 needles, 9", dull blue-green, drooping; persist 3–4 years

cones stout, 8" on stalk to 2", dull brown, massive with large recurved claws like Coulter; persistent

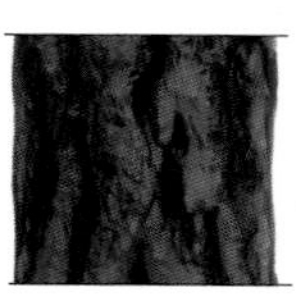

bark dark, deeply furrowed, with blocky ridges and orange inner bark

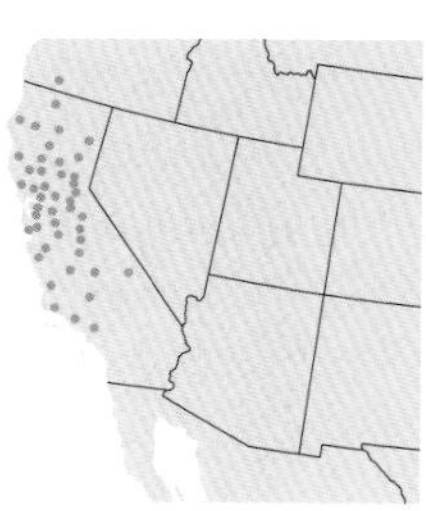

Uncommon and local on dry foothill slopes; nearly ringing the Central Valley of California. Rarely cultivated, only near native range.

Torrey Pine

Pinus torreyana

DEL MAR PINE, SOLEDAD PINE

Evergreen. Small to medium tree usually 20–30' tall in the wild, much larger in cultivation (max. 133'). Often twisted and stunted by ocean winds, crown rounded to flattened or irregular. Two different subspecies: Mainland Torrey Pine (*P. t. torreyana*) averages taller with smaller cones than Island Torrey Pine (*P. t. insularis*), found on Santa Rosa Island, California.

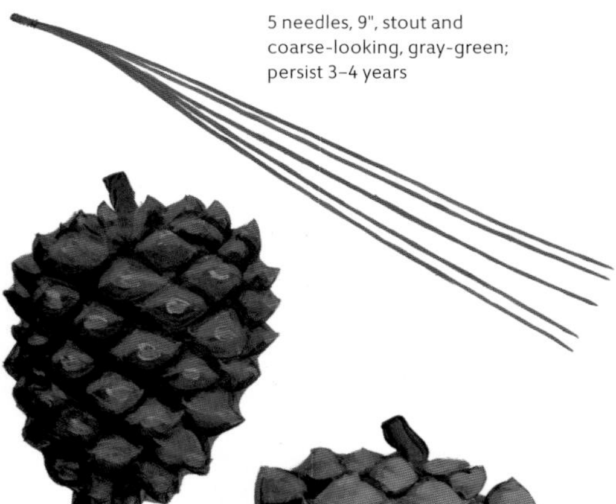

5 needles, 9", stout and coarse-looking, gray-green; persist 3–4 years

cones 5", nearly round, massive, orange-brown, scales raised, but not prickly, mature in 3 years; persistent

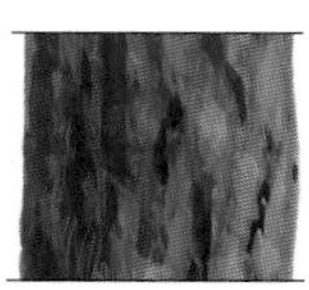

bark reddish, deeply furrowed

This species and Arizona Pine are the only yellow pines with five needles per bundle.

The rarest North American pine, found in the wild in only two locations in coastal southern California. Uncommonly cultivated, only in California.

Monterey Pine

Pinus radiata

INSIGNIS PINE, RADIATA PINE

Evergreen. Medium to large tree usually 40–70' tall (max. 165'). Contorted to straight; crown broadly conic, becoming rounded to flattened. Hybridizes naturally with Knobcone Pine.

3 (2–4) needles; 5" long, bright green, slightly twisted; persist 3–4 years

cones 4½", very lopsided, slightly prickly, glossy brown; often closed and long-persistent

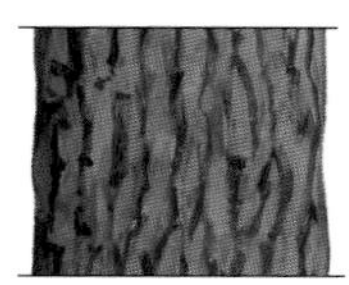

bark gray, with deep reddish furrows

Although this species is rare and local in the wild in California, and mostly a small, windswept tree there, it grows very quickly and well in other settings, becoming a taller and better-formed tree than in the wild. It grows even better in other parts of the world, and has become one of the most important commercial lumber trees in the southern hemisphere, achieving its record height in New Zealand (211').

Rare in the wild; found at only three sites on central California coast. Commonly cultivated and naturalized along Pacific Coast north to Oregon.

Bishop Pine

Pinus muricata

PRICKLECONE PINE, SANTA CRUZ ISLAND PINE

Evergreen. Small to medium tree 40–60' tall (max. 121'). Straight to contorted, crown becoming rounded, flattened, or irregular. Irregular crown with strong twisted branches, obvious cones. Southern trees average smoother bark, thinner twigs, and thicker, sparser, greener (less bluish) needles than northern, but no subspecies are named.

2 needles, 5", dark green, slightly twisted; persist 2–3 years

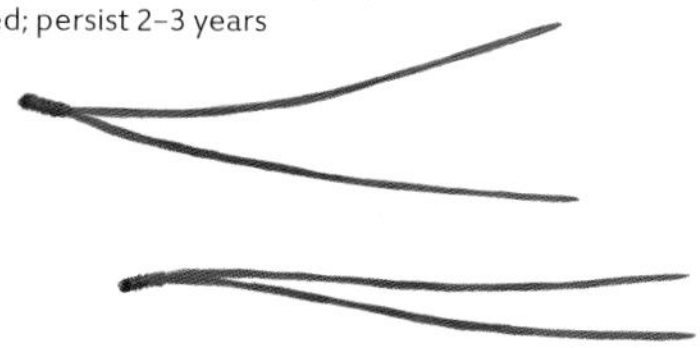

cones 3", red-brown, lopsided with stout prickles, mature in 3 years; long persistent

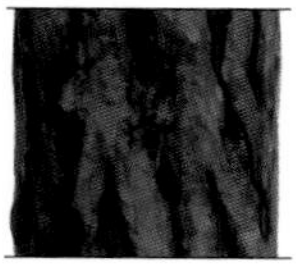

bark dark gray, deeply furrowed; orange on smaller branches

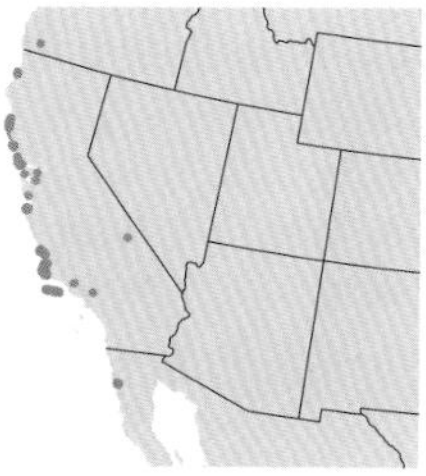

Uncommon and local on dry ridges or around bogs in coastal forests; very tolerant of salt and seaside conditions. Uncommonly cultivated, only in California.

Knobcone Pine

Pinus attenuata

Evergreen. Shrubs or trees usually 20–60' tall (max. 117'). Usually straight, crown mostly narrowly to broadly conic. Hybridizes with Bishop and Monterey Pines. Cones persist for long periods and may become embedded in trunk.

3 (2) needles, 5" yellow-green, twisted; persist 4–5 years

cones 5", curved, yellow-brown, heavy and hard with obvious knobby scales rising to blunt point; long-persistent, opened by fire

bark purple-brown to dark brown, shallowly and narrowly fissured, with irregular, flat, loose-scaly plates

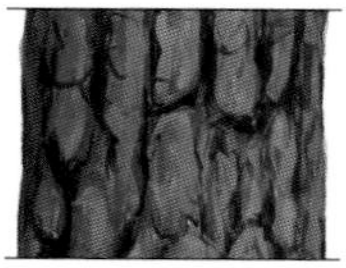

Fairly common in chaparral on dry slopes and foothills of Sierra Nevada and the Cascade and Coast ranges. Rarely cultivated.

Pine Family: Other Genera

Six additional genera are included in the pine family. Five are native to North America (*Larix, Tsuga, Picea, Pseudotsuga,* and *Abies*) and one is cultivated and naturalized here (*Cedrus*). The six genera are broadly distinguished by the features outlined here.

True Cedars (genus *Cedrus*)	needles short, clustered 	cones upright 
Larches (genus *Larix*)	needles soft, clustered; only genus with deciduous needles 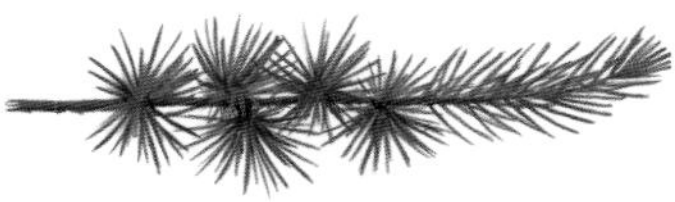	cones small, upright 
Hemlocks (genus *Tsuga*)	needles very short, flattened; twigs very slender, rough 	cones small, pendent 
Spruces (genus *Picea*)	needles short, stiff, often prickly; twigs rough 	cones pendent, with thin papery scales 
Douglas-Firs (genus *Pseudotsuga)*	needles short, soft; twigs smooth 	cones pendent, with seed bracts projecting 
True Firs (genus *Abies*)	needles short, blunt-tipped; twigs smooth 	cones upright 

Pine Family: True Cedars

The true cedars (genus *Cedrus*) include three species from the Himalayan and Mediterranean regions, all cultivated and one naturalized in North America. They are not related to other trees called cedars, which are all in the cypress family.

Deodar Cedar

Cedrus deodara

HIMALAYAN CEDAR, INDIAN CEDAR

Evergreen. Medium to large tree often 50–60' tall (max. 114'). Differs from other cedars in its longer needles, larger cones, and drooping branchlets.

needles variable in length mainly from 1–2"

cones upright 4", green then gray-brown, like firs but stouter

cones disintegrate over winter, leaving upright central spike

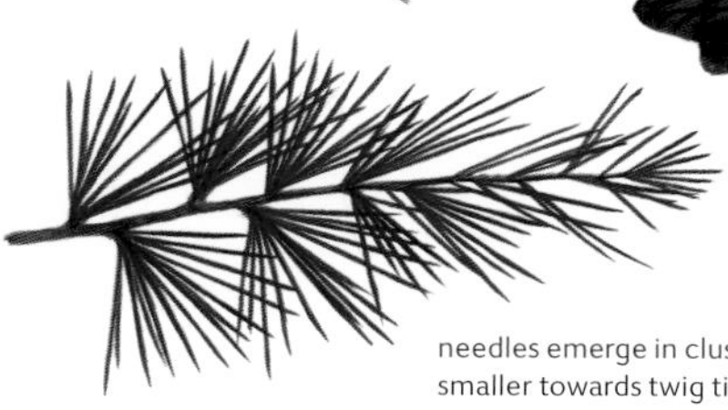

needles emerge in clusters, smaller towards twig tips

Native to the Himalayan region. Commonly cultivated and locally naturalized (zones 7–9), the least cold-hardy of the genus.

Atlas Cedar

Cedrus atlantica

MOUNT ATLAS CEDAR, NORTH AFRICAN CEDAR, ALGERIAN CEDAR

Evergreen. Small to large tree often 30-50' tall (max. 125'). Branchlets not drooping; variable in form with some resembling the broad layered form of Lebanon. Cones and needles shorter than Deodar. Native to North Africa. Commonly cultivated (zones 6–9). Several cultivars, one with pale bluish needles is the most common.

twigs hairy

needles ¾", olive-green to bluish

Lebanon Cedar

Cedrus libani

CEDAR OF LEBANON

Evergreen. Medium to large tree often 40–60' tall (max. 101'). Cones and needles intermediate in size between Deodar and Atlas; branches level, usually forming broad horizontal layers. Native to Turkey, Syria, and Lebanon. Uncommon in cultivation but the most cold-hardy of the cedars (zones 5–7).

needles 1", medium length, dark green, sharp

all cedar bark is gray, developing rough cracks and furrows

Pine Family: Larches

The larches (genus *Larix*) are ten species of tall slender trees found around the colder parts of the northern hemisphere. Three species are native to North America, and are covered here along with two Old World species that are commonly cultivated.

Larches are the only deciduous members of the pine family, losing their needles each winter. Needles are short and soft, growing singly along new growth, but clustered together, tuft-like on short spur twigs along older growth. Cones are small and held upright along branchlets. They mature in a single growing season and persist several years.

Pale green in spring and yellow in fall, with thin gauzy foliage, larches make attractive landscape trees. Larches are fast-growing, but little-used commercially. With a high resin content, the hard and heavy wood is decay resistant and useful for railroad ties, utility poles, flooring, and cabinetry, but is unsuitable for pulp.

Western Larch typically tall, narrow tree with remarkably straight, clear trunk and small, narrow crown

Western Larch

Larix occidentalis

WESTERN TAMARACK, MONTANA LARCH

Deciduous. Large tree often over 100' tall (max. 192'). Straight trunk with short branches only near top, creating unusually small, narrow crown. One of the most valuable timber-producing species in western North America.

needles 1½", pale green

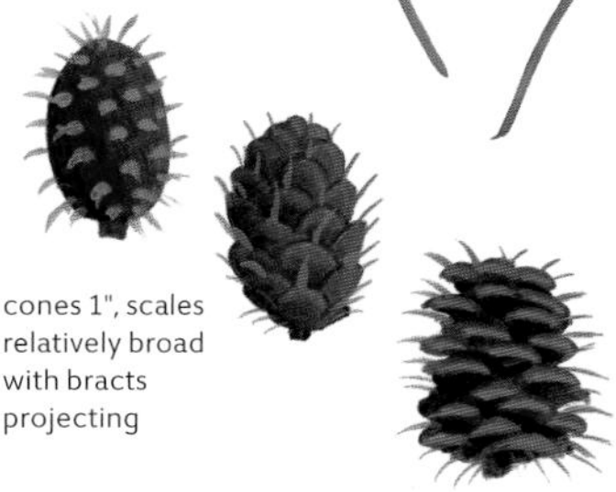

cones 1", scales relatively broad with bracts projecting

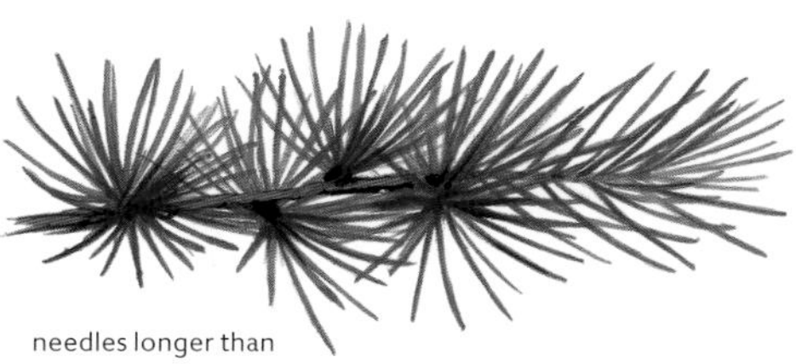

needles longer than American Larch, bright green

twigs orange-brown, hairy when new

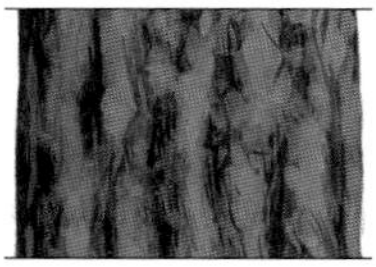

bark reddish brown, scaly, with deep furrows between flat, flaky, cinnamon-colored plates

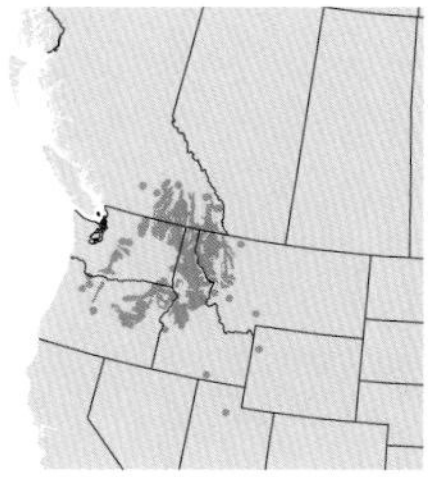

Common and a dominant forest tree in montane valleys and lower slopes, often in pure stands. Rarely cultivated.

American Larch

Larix laricina

TAMARACK, HACKMATACK, BLACK LARCH

Deciduous. Medium to large tree usually 40–80' tall (max. 125'), but in harsh conditions a ground-hugging shrub. Crown narrow, with sparse, irregular branches.

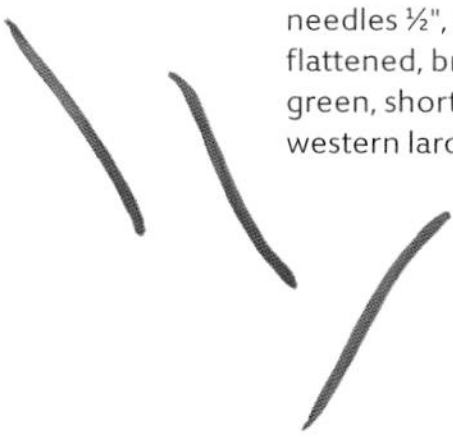

needles ½", soft, flattened, bright green, shorter than western larches

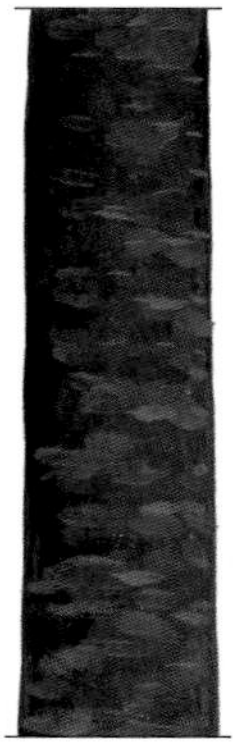

bark of young trees gray, smooth

older trunks reddish brown and scaly, inner layer red-purple; bark tight-fitting, brown to reddish, with small rounded scales

cones ½", inconspicuous, stand up along twigs, with 4–5 rows of scales

scales relatively narrow, dark reddish turning yellow-brown

young female cones pinkish, upright

female and male cones emerge early spring with leaves (Mar–Apr)

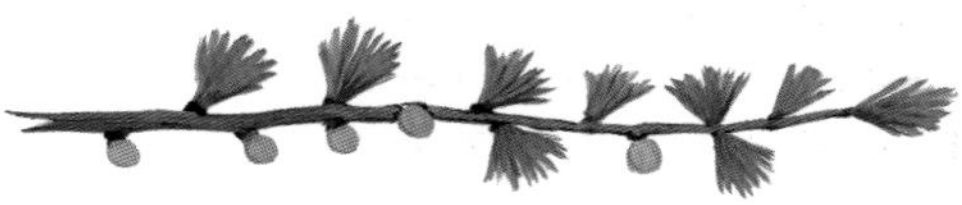

male pollen cones yellow, below twigs

needles grow in clusters radiating from short spur twigs

fall color pale yellow

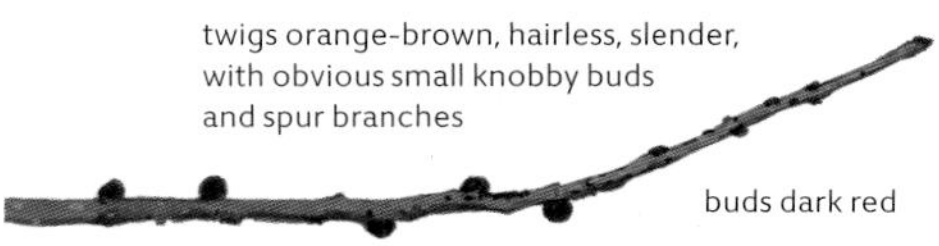

twigs orange-brown, hairless, slender, with obvious small knobby buds and spur branches

buds dark red

winter tree like dead spruce, but with long branches at erratic angles, haze of small yellowish twigs

Common in boreal forests in wet, poorly drained bogs and swamps, also on moist upland soils. Rarely cultivated.

Subalpine Larch

Larix lyallii

ALPINE LARCH, MOUNTAIN LARCH, TIMBERLINE LARCH, WOOLY LARCH

Deciduous. Small to medium tree 25–50' tall (max. 101'); usually stunted in harsh timberline sites. Similar and related to Western Larch, distinguished by woolly twigs, slightly shorter and plumper needles, and smaller overall size.

needles 1¼", less flattened than other larches

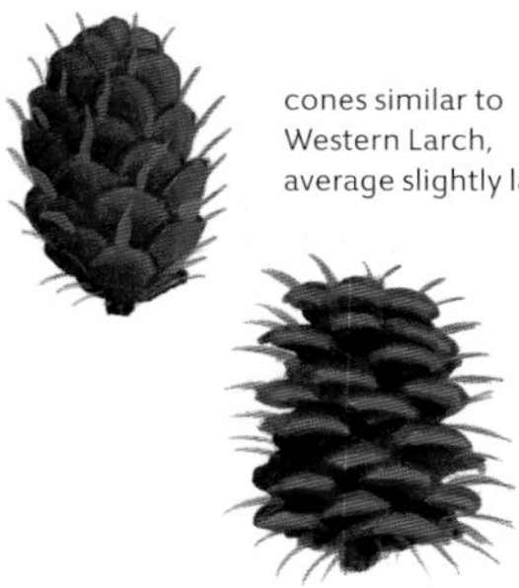

cones similar to Western Larch, average slightly larger

needles average shorter and drabber than Western Larch

twigs pinkish or yellow, covered with pale wool, especially when new

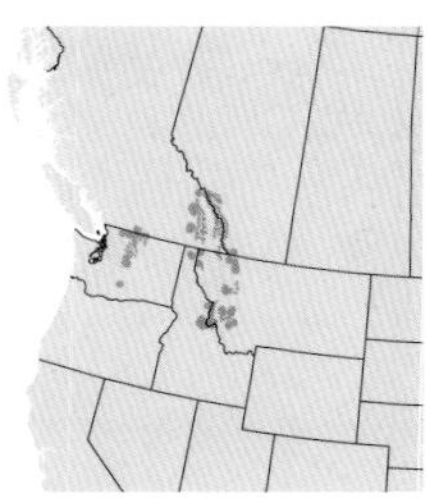

Locally common on rocky slopes near timberline, usually found 500–1,000' higher than Western Larch. Very rarely cultivated.

European Larch

Larix decidua

COMMON LARCH

Deciduous. Medium to large tree usually 50–70' tall (max. 109'); similar to American, but longer needles and cones, often drooping branchlets, and bark with larger plates.

needles 1¼"

cones 1½", orange brown, with 8–10 rows of scales, much larger than cones of American Larch; persistent

Native to Europe. Commonly cultivated (zones 2–6).

Japanese Larch

Larix kaempferi

Deciduous. Medium to large tree often 60–80' tall (max. 103'), similar to European Larch but cones smaller with recurved scales, needles relatively broad and bluish.

cones 1¼", nearly round

twigs reddish (vs. straw-colored or gold in other species)

Native to Japan. Commonly cultivated (zones 4–7).

Pine Family: Hemlocks

There are eight to ten species of hemlocks (genus *Tsuga*) worldwide, all of which are trees. The four species native to North America are covered here. At least two additional species are occasionally cultivated in North America, but are not illustrated.

All hemlocks have short flat needles, small pendent cones, and drooping twig tips.

Hemlock bark was formerly an important source of tannin. Only Western Hemlock is common enough to support a significant commercial harvest, and it is a major source of pulpwood.

bark on young trunks dark gray-brown, peeling in rectangular scales

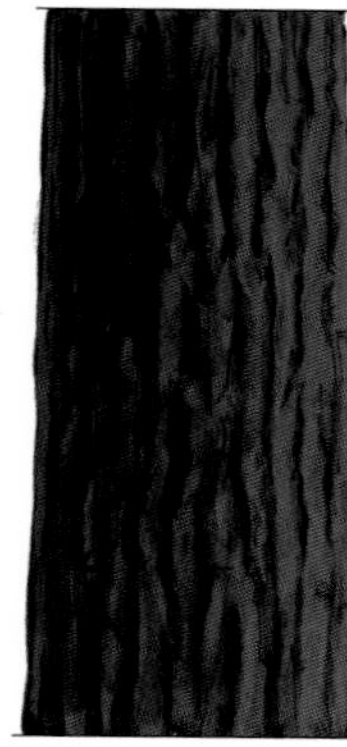
bark on old trunks dark gray, ridged and furrowed

male pollen cones small, yellow below twig, female flowers in a tiny green or purplish cone at twig tip

all new growth drooping gracefully at tips of branches

branch infected with Hemlock Wooly Adelgid

usually broader than spruces and firs, with fine lacy twigs with gracefully drooping tips

Hemlocks in the East have recently been threatened by the Hemlock Woolly Adelgid, an aphid-like insect introduced from Asia. Infested trees often die within a few years, and can only be saved by aggressive use of pesticides to kill the insects. Adelgids do not survive very cold winters. Eastern Hemlock is less resistant than other species and groves from southern New England south are severely threatened. Hemlocks tend to grow in cool shady ravines and north-facing hillsides, and their dense foliage maintains a cool and moist microclimate below. These groves are favored by many species of birds, such as Blackburnian and Black-throated Green Warblers, as well as a variety of other animals and plants. The loss of these southern hemlock groves would also mean the loss of a unique ecosystem.

Eastern Hemlock

Tsuga canadensis

CANADIAN HEMLOCK, HEMLOCK SPRUCE

Evergreen. Medium to large tree often 60–70' tall (max. 159'). Needles and cones shorter than other hemlocks.

needles ½", flattened, blunt; persist 2 years
underleaf silvery
cones ¾"
needles strongly 2-ranked
twigs yellow-brown, densely hairy
needles pale silvery below

Numerous cultivars of Eastern Hemlock have been developed, including compact shrubs, dwarfs, and larger, more graceful trees.

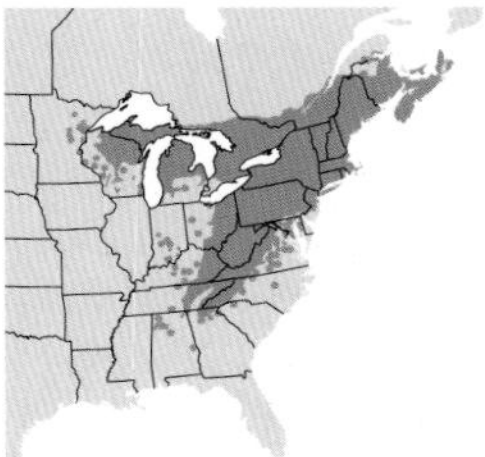

Common but local in moist rocky ridges, steep ravine slopes, cool wet swales. Very commonly cultivated (zones 3–7).

Carolina Hemlock

Tsuga caroliniana

Evergreen. Medium to large tree (max. 140'). Similar to Eastern Hemlock, but needles average slightly longer and not in flat sprays, cones slightly longer, and smaller range.

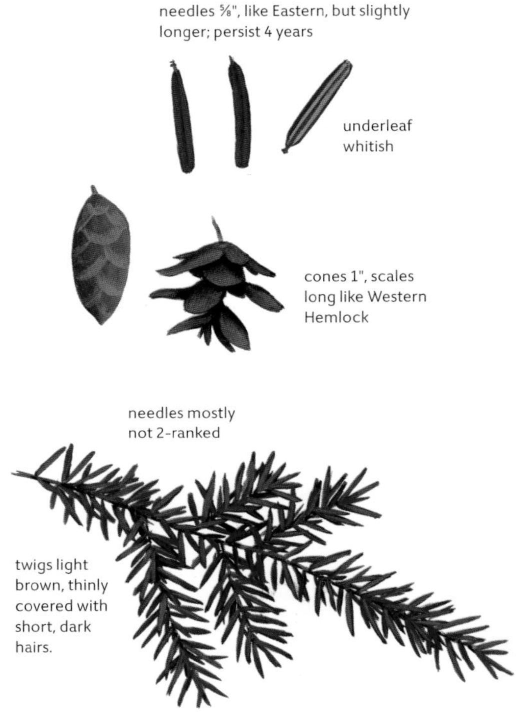
needles ⅝", like Eastern, but slightly longer; persist 4 years
underleaf whitish
cones 1", scales long like Western Hemlock
needles mostly not 2-ranked
twigs light brown, thinly covered with short, dark hairs.

It has been suggested that this species is more closely related to some Asian hemlocks than it is to Eastern Hemlock. Two other species of hemlocks native to Japan are occasionally cultivated in North America.

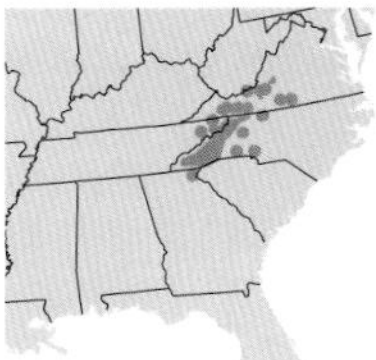

Uncommon and local on rocky montane slopes. Commonly cultivated (zones 4–7), many cultivars.

Western Hemlock

Tsuga heterophylla

PACIFIC HEMLOCK

Evergreen. Medium to large tree often 75–120' tall (max. 259'); the tallest hemlock, slender and elegant. Very important commercial tree for lumber and pulpwood.

needles ½"; persist 4–7 years
underleaf whitish

cones ¾", scales rounded to pointed

needles mostly 2-ranked
twigs yellow-brown, finely hairy

At high elevations and when stressed, Western Hemlock tends to develop characteristics similar to Mountain Hemlock, with leaves more evenly distributed around twigs, and less conspicuous pale bands on the underleaf. This may account for reports of hybridization between the two species, which rarely or never occurs.

Common and widespread in coastal to midmontane forests; a dominant species over much of its broad range. Rarely cultivated mainly within native range (zones 6–7).

Mountain Hemlock

Tsuga mertensia

ALPINE HEMLOCK

Evergreen. Small to large tree usually 30–100' tall (max. 194'); often growing stunted at timberline. Differs from all other hemlocks in larger cones, longer needles, not two-ranked, and not flattened.

needles ¾", green to gray-blue, curved toward twig tip, less flattened than other hemlocks; persist 2–3 years
underleaf same color as upper

cones large for a hemlock, 2", scales broad

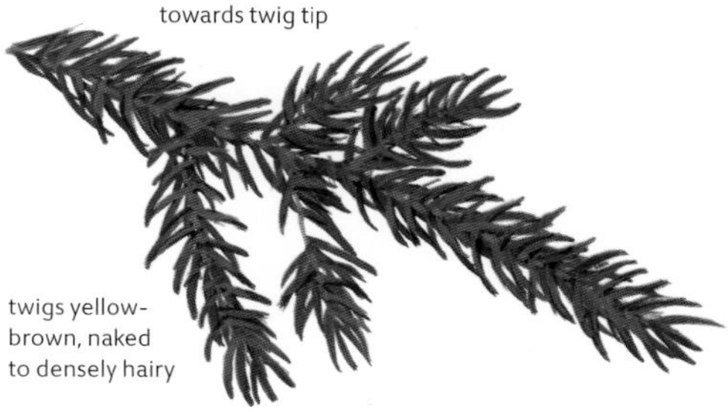
needles mostly not 2-ranked; curved towards twig tip
twigs yellow-brown, naked to densely hairy

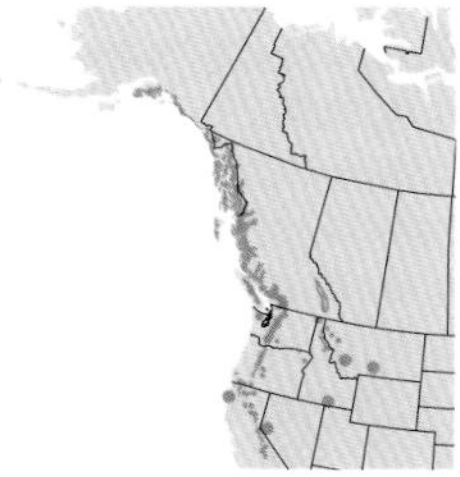

Coastal and montane forests to alpine slopes (where it occurs in low, matted form); adaptable to a wide variety of climatic conditions. cultivated only rarely within native range.

Pine Family: Spruces

The spruces (genus *Picea*) include about thirty-five species of trees worldwide. Seven are native to North America, and are covered here along with three commonly cultivated exotics (one of which is naturalized).

Spruces differ from all other conifers in having single, pointed, and usually prickly needles that leave a raised leaf scar on the twig when they fall. Spruce cones hang down from the branches, have relatively thin papery scales, and trees usually have a narrow conical form.

Spruce wood is a very important source of lumber for construction and for more specialized uses, such as piano sounding boards, and is used extensively for paper pulp.

Blue Spruce has broad conical shape and branches to ground in open-grown trees

The Blue Spruce is celebrated for its blue foliage, which is a prominent feature of many cultivated trees. Bluish trees are rare in the wild, where most have a more ordinary bluish green color, and similarly bluish foliage occurs in many other species of spruces and in Douglas-Fir.

Blue Spruce

Picea pungens

COLORADO SPRUCE

Evergreen. Medium to large tree often 80–100' tall (max. 148'); crown broadly conic, branches slightly to strongly drooping. Told from similar species by longer cones and very prickly needles.

needles 1", relatively stout and very prickly, sometimes pale blue-green; 4-angled

cones 3", pinkish turning pale yellow-brown, scale tips narrow, wavy

needles relatively long, stiff, very prickly

twigs stout, yellow-brown

bark gray-brown and pale orange, scaly

Common in midmontane forests. Commonly cultivated and locally naturalized (zones 3–7). Many cultivars.

White Spruce

Picea glauca

SKUNK SPRUCE, CAT SPRUCE

Evergreen. Medium to large tree usually 50–60' tall in the East, 70–90' tall in the West (max. 184'); a low creeping form is found at treeline. Crown broadly conic to spirelike, branches slightly drooping. Alternate names refer to the pungent smell of crushed needles.

bark gray-brown, scaly

needles ½", usually pale grayish blue-green, slightly prickly, not flattened

twigs rather slender, pinkish brown

cones 1¾", scales broad, flat-tipped

often very narrow conical form, twigs drooping or not; needles dark green to bluish

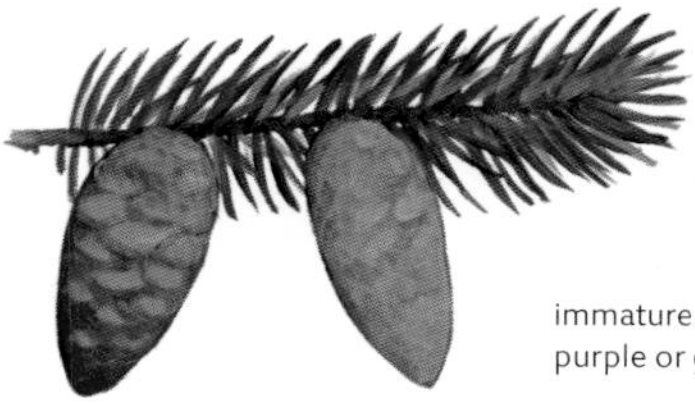
immature cones purple or green

mature cones red-brown

young female cones upright, red to purple

Variation has led to recognition of several subspecies, but all variation could be the result of environmental influences and hybridization with Engelmann Spruce (page 46).

Common and widespread in muskegs, bogs, and river banks to montane slopes. Commonly cultivated (zones 2–6). Several cultivars.

male pollen cones yellowish, mostly below branches, in early spring

Engelmann Spruce

Picea engelmannii

ENGELMANN BLUE SPRUCE, ROCKY MOUNTAIN WHITE SPRUCE

Evergreen. Medium to large tree often 80–120' tall (max. 238'); crown narrowly conic, branches spreading horizontally to somewhat drooping. Closely related to and hybridizes with White Spruce in the North and Blue Spruce in the South.

needles ¾", gray-green, rigid and prickly, not flattened

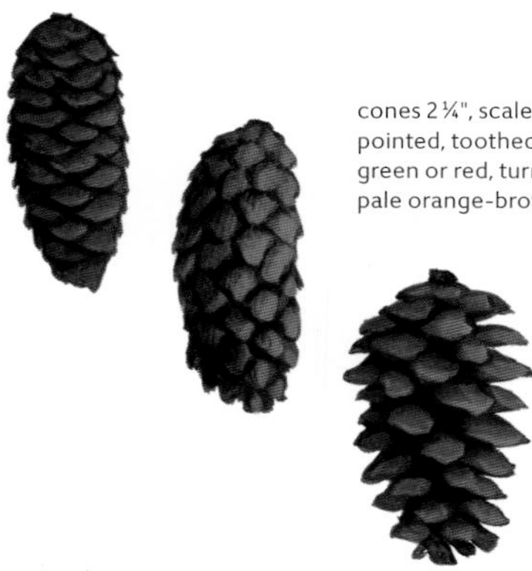

cones 2¼", scales pointed, toothed, green or red, turning pale orange-brown

twigs rather stout, yellow-brown

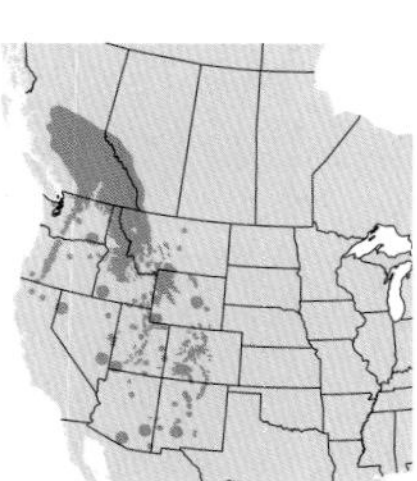

Common in montane and subalpine forests. Commonly cultivated but less so than Blue Spruce. (zones 3–5).

Sitka Spruce

Picea sitchensis

WESTERN SPRUCE, TIDELAND SPRUCE, ALASKA SPRUCE

Evergreen. Very large tree often 100–160' tall (max. 314'), but shrubby at northern limits of range; the largest spruce with relatively broad crown. Very important for lumber (was preferred for early airplanes).

needles ⅞", blue-green to yellow-green, sharp-pointed; flattened, underside with white bands

cones 3", scales pointed, toothed, green to reddish

twigs not pendent, rather stout, pinkish brown

Intergrades extensively with White Spruce in the river valleys of north coastal British Columbia and coastal Alaska.

Common in coastal temperate rainforest of Pacific coast. Uncommonly cultivated (zones 5–8).

Brewer Spruce

Picea brewerana

WEEPING SPRUCE, SISKIYOU SPRUCE

Evergreen. Medium to large tree often 80–100' tall (max. 200'); strongly drooping twigs, gray-green needles. The only native species with strongly drooping twigs and (with Sitka) the only native species with flattened and white-striped needles.

needles ¾", flat, grayish or bluish with white bands below, not prickly

cones 4", scales rounded

needles relatively long and sparse
twigs pendent, slender, gray-brown

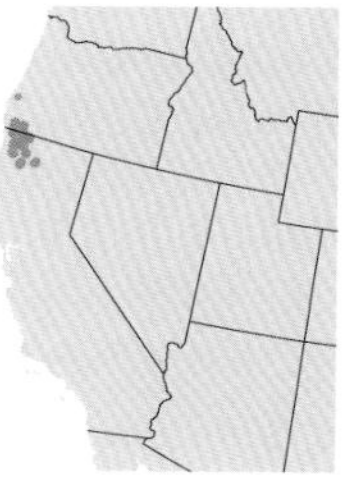

Fairly common in mixed conifer forests of the Siskiyou Mountains. Uncommonly cultivated (zone 5).

Red Spruce

Picea rubens

YELLOW SPRUCE, HE BALSAM

Evergreen. Medium to large tree often 60–70' tall (max. 162'); crown narrowly conic. Branches horizontally spreading, twigs not pendent.

needles ⅝", green, not flattened

cones 1½", reddish brown; scales broad, rounded

immature cones short, dark bluish

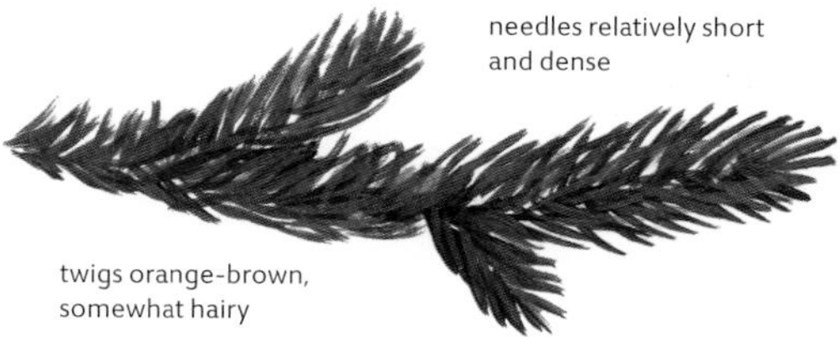
needles relatively short and dense
twigs orange-brown, somewhat hairy

In the Appalachians, this species has been growing poorly in its mountaintop habitat, possibly due to acid rain or other environmental pollution.

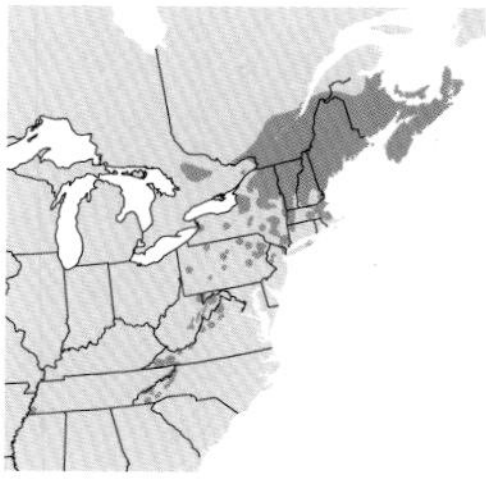

Common in upper montane to subalpine forests. Rarely cultivated (zones 3–5).

Black Spruce

Picea mariana

DOUBLE SPRUCE, SWAMP SPRUCE, GUM SPRUCE

Evergreen. Small to medium tree usually 25–30' tall (max. 100'). The smallest spruce, often very slender with irregular crown; low mat-like form found at treeline. Hybridizes to a limited extent with Red Spruce on disturbed sites in eastern Canada. Hybridization with White Spruce is not confirmed.

often very narrow form with short, layered branches and dense clumps of twigs at top

needles very short, ½", not flattened, soft

cones small, 1", scales broad, rounded
cones long-persistent, unusual for a spruce

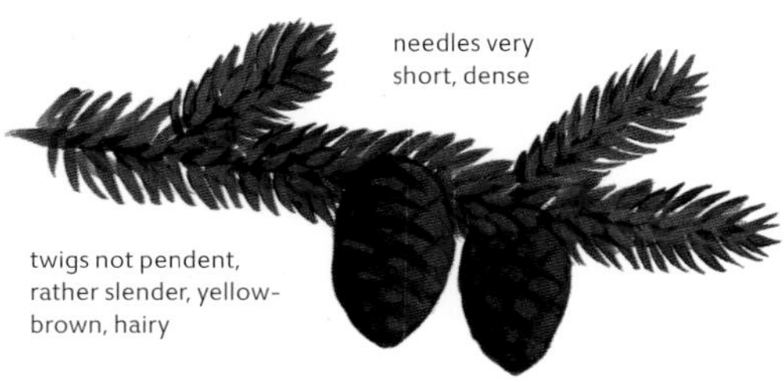
needles very short, dense
twigs not pendent, rather slender, yellow-brown, hairy

young female cones red, nearly round, male cones small, yellow

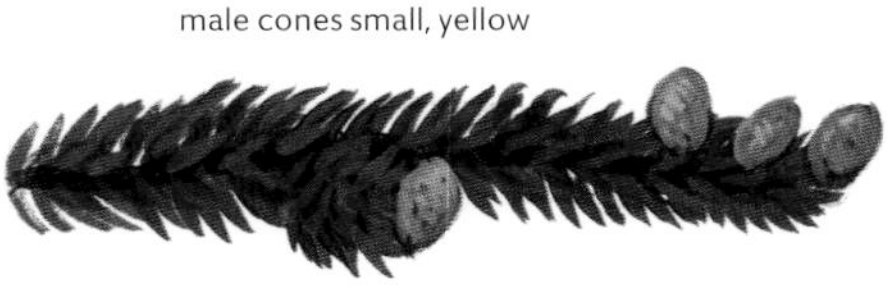

Common in muskegs, bogs, bottomlands, dry peatlands. Uncommonly cultivated (zones 3–5).

This species grows in many habitats and can grow into a well-formed, narrow tree. It can be difficult to distinguish from Red Spruce, but it is characteristically associated with more extreme conditions and is a pioneer tree at the margins of bogs and at timberline. In Alaska, with White Spruce and American Larch, it marks the northern limit of tree growth. In one location, a Black Spruce with a trunk diameter of 1" was 128 years old!

This species often pioneers on floating mats of decomposing plants at the edges of ponds, which are becoming bogs. Trees in these settings grow slowly and poorly with narrow, sparse, and irregular crowns. Some trees in bogs propagate by "layering," when the lowest branches become embedded in sphagnum, and sprout, eventually forming a ring of new trees, which continue to grow even after the original central trunk has died.

Norway Spruce

Picea abies

FINNISH SPRUCE, SPRUCE FIR

Evergreen. Medium to large tree usually 50–80' tall (max. 124'). The largest spruce in much of the East, further distinguished by drooping twigs and long cones.

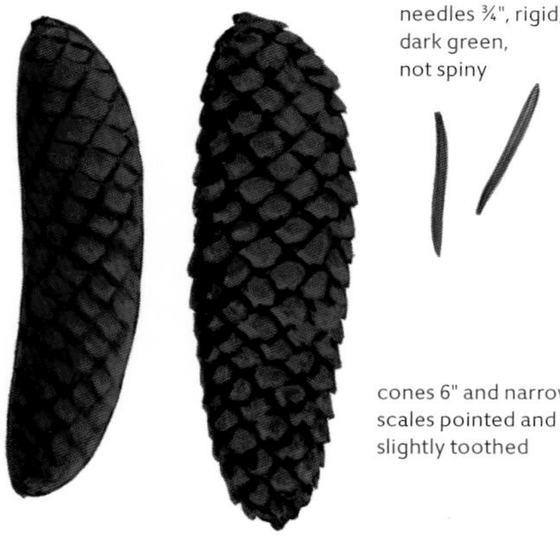
needles ¾", rigid, dark green, not spiny
cones 6" and narrow; scales pointed and slightly toothed

twigs stout, orange brown, usually naked

ascending branches with drooping twigs; other spruces usually without drooping twigs

Native to Europe. Very commonly cultivated and locally naturalized (zones 3–7). Many cultivars.

Serbian Spruce

Picea omorika

SERVIAN SPRUCE

Evergreen. Medium to large tree often 80' tall in the wild (max. 61'); narrow and stately with short branches swept up at the tips and retained to ground. Native to a very small area straddlng the border of Serbia and Bosnia. Commonly cultivated (zones 4–7).

needles ½", flat, bicolored
underleaf with 2 white lines
cone 2", purple turning red-brown

needles relatively sparse, often recurved

Oriental Spruce

Picea orientalis

CAUCASIAN SPRUCE, EASTERN SPRUCE

Evergreen. Medium to large tree often 100' tall in the wild (max. 85'); slender, dense, and elegant. Native to Caucasus and Asia Minor. Commonly cultivated, tolerates drier climate than Norway Spruce (zones 4–7).

needles short, ⅜", dark green, soft
cones 3", purple turning red brown

needles very short and dense

Pine Family: Douglas-firs

The Douglas-firs (genus *Pseudotsuga*) include five species of trees worldwide, two North American natives, one in Mexico, and two in eastern Asia. They show a mixture of characteristics of several other genera, and have at times been classified as spruces, firs, or hemlocks before being classified in their own genus.

The Common Douglas-fir is one of the most important commercial trees in North America, for lumber and for pulp—it grows quickly and to large size, and the wood is light but strong. This species is also widely grown on tree farms for Christmas trees.

male cones small, yellow
young female cones shaggy, reddish, at twig tips

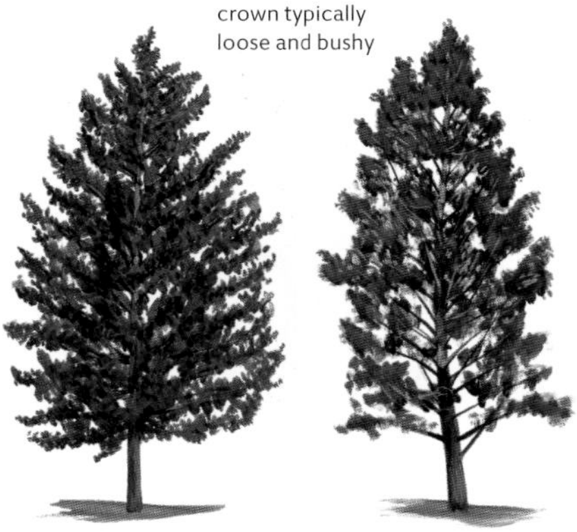
crown typically loose and bushy

crown can also be dense and conical (left), or sparse and rigid (right)

Bigcone Douglas-fir

Pseudotsuga macrocarpa

Evergreen. Small to medium tree usually 40–50' tall (max. 173'). Very similar to Common Douglas-fir (no range overlap), but needles and cones average longer.

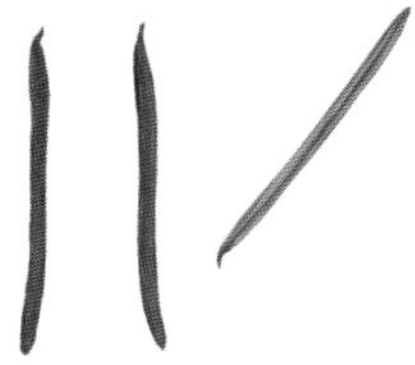
needles 1¼", average slightly longer than Comon and often roughly 2-ranked

cones 5½", larger than Common, with shorter bracts (and wider scales)

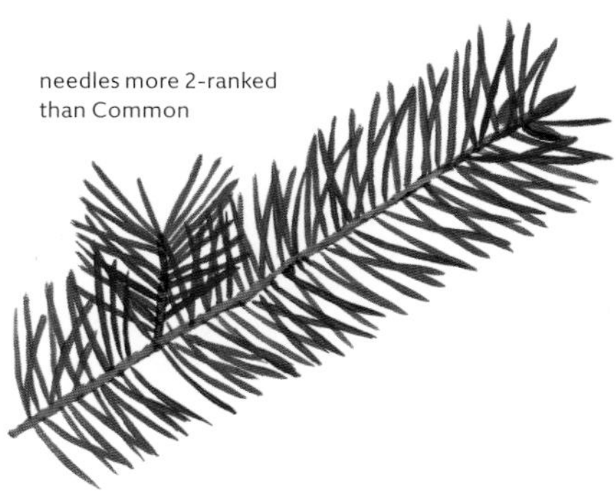
needles more 2-ranked than Common

Uncommon and local on slopes, cliffs, and canyons, in chaparral and mixed coniferous forests in its limited range. Very rarely cultivated.

Common Douglas-fir

Pseudotsuga menziesii

DOUGLAS FIR

Evergreen. Medium to very large tree often 80–120' tall (max. 326'). Pendent cones, like spruces, but with seed bracts projecting beyond cone scales, thicker bark, and softer needles with usually bushier crown.

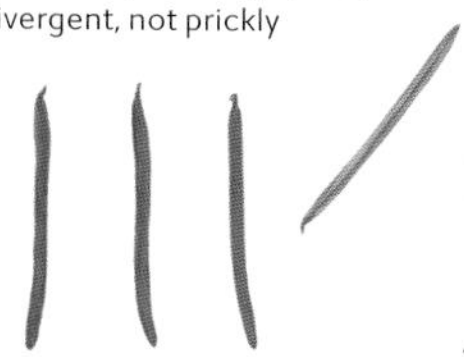

needles 1", relatively sparse, divergent, not prickly

needle color variable, dark green, yellow-green, or blue-green

cones 3", pale brown with long bracts projecting beyond scales

twigs slender

buds pointed, orange-brown

softer-looking needles and more "relaxed" branching than spruces or firs

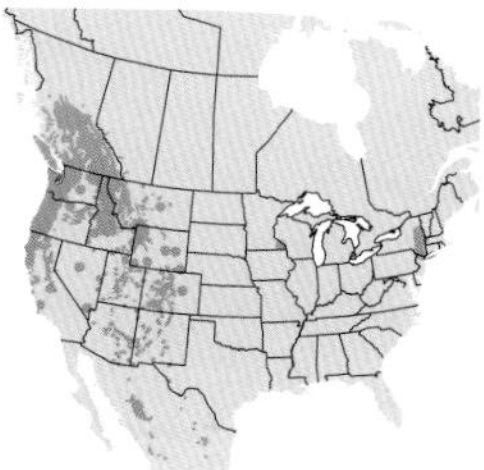

Common and widespread, a principal component of coniferous forests in many regions. Commonly cultivated (zones 4–6).

bark of young trunks smooth pale gray

bark on old trees deeply-furrowed, corky

'Rocky Mountain' Common Douglas-fir

Pseudotsuga menziesii var. *glauca*

Typically a smaller tree than Pacific form, with needles more frequently bluish or grayish, and cones smaller. Best distinguished by seed bracts reflexed or spreading, not straight. Intergrades with Pacific form where range meets in southern British Columbia and northeast Washington.

cones with reflexed seed bracts

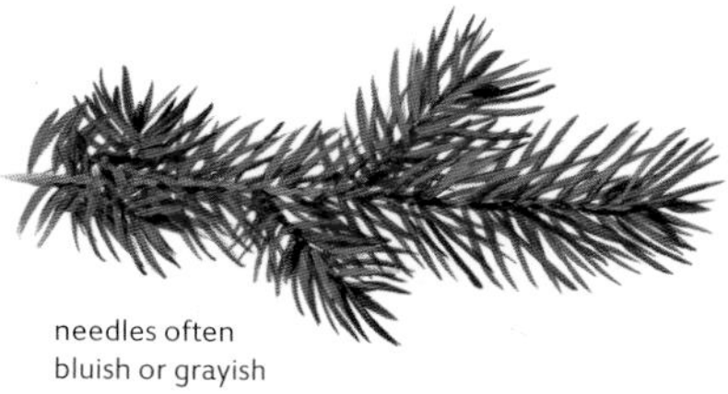

needles often bluish or grayish

Pine Family: True Firs

The true firs (genus *Abies*) includes about fifty species of trees found in cool moist climates around the northern hemisphere. Eleven species are native to North America and are covered here along with three species of introduced firs. All firs are characterized by short needles, mostly soft and blunt-tipped, that do not leave a raised scar on the twig (unlike spruces); cones are upright and limited to the highest branches on the tree, and cone scales fall individually during the fall, leaving only a central spike. Firs tend to have very narrow shape and rigid upright or horizontal branching, never drooping as on some spruces. Bark is smooth and pale gray with resin blisters on young trunks, becoming thicker and cracking into broad ridges on older trunks, but not scaly like spruces. Identification of species depends on careful examination of needles, cones, and range.

Fir needles are dimorphic, with fertile branches having short needles that curve up around the twig. Lower branches have longer straighter needles that spread in two ranks on either side of twig.

Firs are generally not important for lumber, but several species (especially Fraser and Noble Firs) are very popular as Christmas trees. Aromatic and resinous sap, especially from Balsam Fir, has been used for a variety of products.

young female cones upright green to purple, only on highest branches

male pollen cones yellow to red

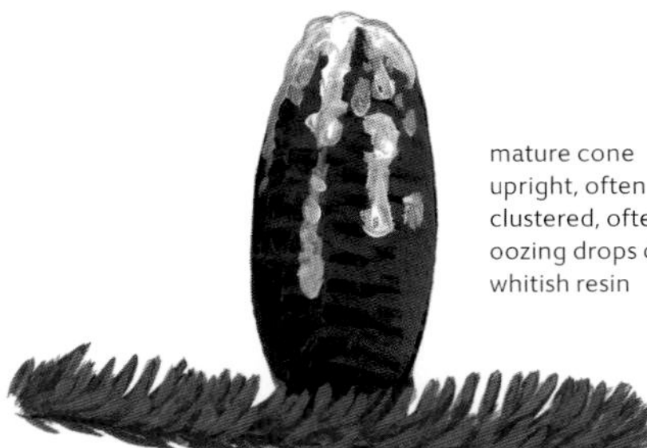

mature cone upright, often clustered, often oozing drops of whitish resin

cone scales fall away leaving upright central spike

firs typically very narrow, with rigid ascending branches and very orderly branching pattern, never with drooping twigs

needles curved up on branches with male or female cones, higher on tree

longer, more sparse, needles in 2-ranked arrangement on twigs lower on tree, in shade, and without male or female cones

Balsam Fir

Abies balsamea

BALM-OF-GILEAD, BALSAM

Evergreen. Small to medium tree often 40–60' tall (max. 125'). Spicy-scented resin that exudes from the bark of this tree has been used for medicine, fragrance, glue, varnish, and other purposes.

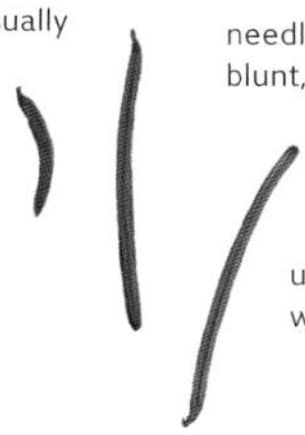
flattened, notched or rounded at tip; usually not 2-ranked
needles ¾", short, blunt, blue-green
underleaf pale with a few lines

cones 3" long; grayish-purple or purplish-green; bracts sometimes projecting and reflexed, especially closer to range of Fraser Fir

needles sometimes 2-ranked along twigs; like all firs needles often longest in middle of twig

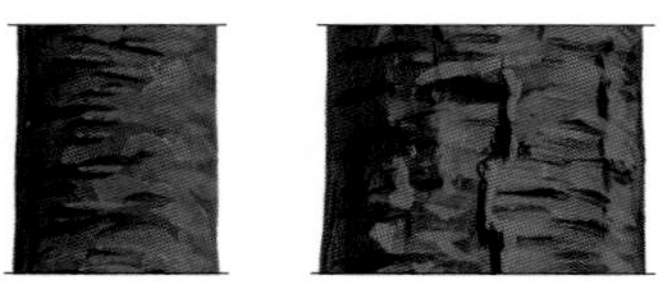

bark gray, thin, smooth, in age often becoming broken into irregular brownish scales

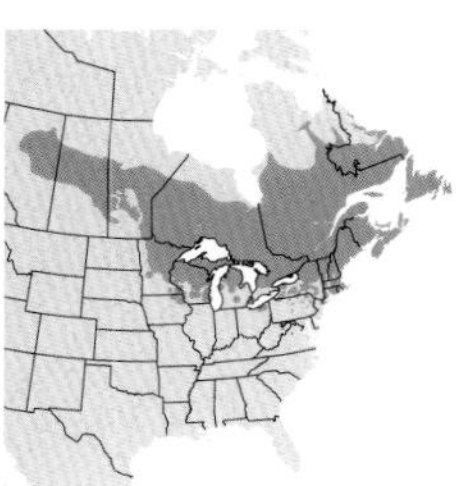

Common and widespread in moist woodlands and swamps in the boreal forests. Commonly cultivated for ornament (zones 3–5).

Fraser Fir

Abies fraseri

SOUTHERN BALSAM FIR, MOUNTAIN BALSAM FIR, SHE BALSAM

Evergreen. Small to medium tree usually 30–60' tall (max. 94'). Very similar to Balsam and sometimes considered a subspecies, but range does not overlap, and Fraser has longer, projecting bracts on cones.

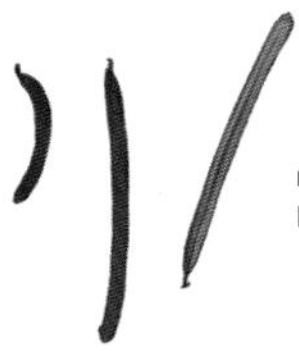
needles like Balsam

cones 2", purple with obvious pale green bracts

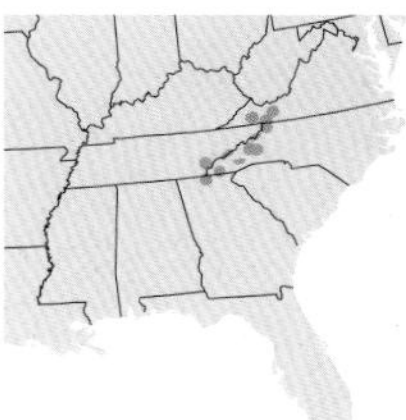

Rare, local, and declining in the wild in mountaintop forests. Rarely cultivated for ornament, but commonly grown for commercial Christmas tree market.

Compared to spruces, firs have longer needles, which are straighter and more perpendicular to the twig. Fir needles are also a darker richer green vs. the duller, moss green color of spruces. Fir buds burst earlier in spring and their odor is stronger and sweeter vs. the weaker and slightly peppery odor of spruce buds. Fir twigs are pale gray vs. orange in spruces and fir bark is smooth with nodules, whereas spruce bark is flaky. Firs have shorter needles that make branches appear more "ropy" and their branching pattern is more conspicuous.

Subalpine Fir

Abies lasiocarpa

ALPINE FIR, WESTERN BALSAM FIR

Evergreen. Small to large tree usually 30–60' tall (max. 172'); closely related to Balsam Fir, most easily distinguished by range. Odor sharp.

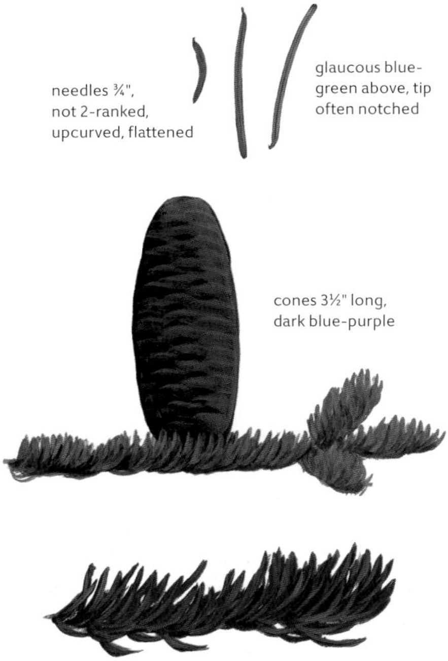
needles ¾", not 2-ranked, upcurved, flattened
glaucous blue-green above, tip often notched
cones 3½" long, dark blue-purple

firs often have "split" top

Rocky Mountain Alpine Fir

Abies bifolia

ROCKY MOUNTAIN SUBALPINE FIR, CORKBARK FIR, ABIES SUBALPINA

Evergreen. Small to medium tree usually 30–60' tall; essentially the inland counterpart of Subalpine Fir, from Alaska to Arizona. Combined species ranges on map below.

Common in a wide variety of habitats from coastal to subalpine coniferous forests; usually in small stands at high elevations. Uncommonly cultivated (zones 5–6).

Subalpine Fir and Rocky Mountain Alpine Fir are often considered parts of the same species, but recent studies have documented many chemical differences, so most botanists now consider them separate species. Visually, they can be distinguished by the color of the inner bark (red in Subalpine, light brown in Rocky Mountain Alpine) and the shape of the basal bud scales (broader and toothed in Subalpine). Rocky Mountain Alpine Fir tends to have shorter leaves on average, and fewer leaves with notched tips than Subalpine Fir. But in a broad region extending from south-central Yukon to northern Washington, all trees are intermediate between the two types.

A distinctive population, separated as Corkbark Fir (*Abies arizonica*), is found in the southern Rocky Mountains from Colorado to New Mexico and Arizona. Compared to Rocky Mountain Alpine Fir, this tree tends to have more bluish needles, smaller cones, and paler, thick and corky bark. Chemical studies suggest that it is distinct, and is more closely allied with Subalpine Fir. An isolated population (as-yet unnamed) in coastal Alaska differs in chemistry and may also be distinct.

Noble Fir

Abies procera

FEATHERCONE FIR, OREGON LARCH

Evergreen. Large to very large tree often 150–200' tall (max. 295'); closely related to Red Fir, very narrow pointed crown, stiff branches horizontal. Odor pungent, slightly turpentine-like.

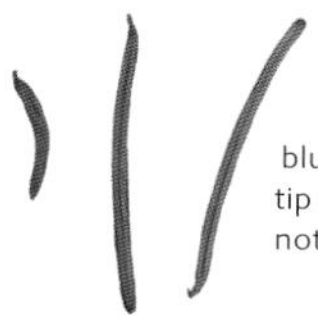

needles ¾", not 2-ranked, flattened

blue-green, tip rounded to notched

cones 5", green, red, or purple with obvious green bracts reflexed

needles on fertile branches 4-sided

bark on mature trunk thin, scaly

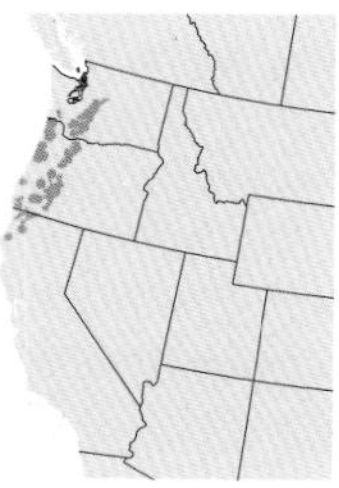

Common in mixed coniferous forest, especially in Cascade Mountains of Washington. Uncommonly cultivated (zones 5–6).

California Red Fir

Abies magnifica

SHASTA RED FIR

Evergreen. Medium to very large tree, often 80–120' tall (max. 252'); closely related to Noble Fir, but bracts do not project beyond cone scales. Odor camphor-like.

needles 1", not 2-ranked, flattened,

blue-green, tip pointed to rounded

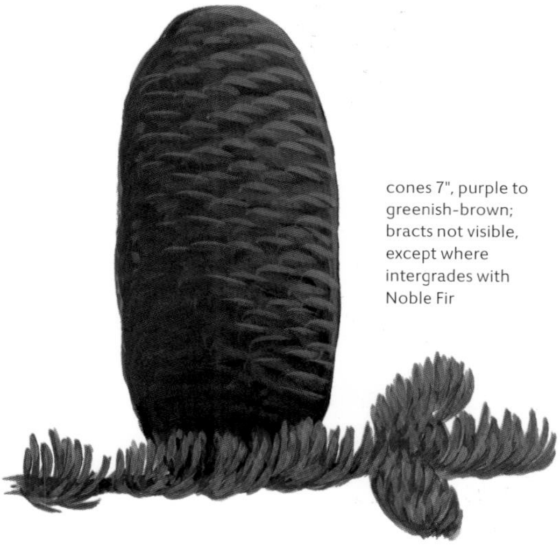

cones 7", purple to greenish-brown; bracts not visible, except where intergrades with Noble Fir

Populations in northern California, known as "Shasta Red Fir," are intermediate between California Red and Noble Firs.

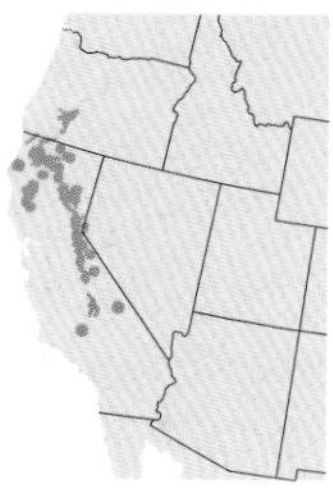

Common in mixed coniferous forests, often in large stands at high elevation. Uncommonly cultivated, popular for Christmas trees (zone 5–7).

Colorado White Fir

Abies concolor

COLORADO FIR

Evergreen. Medium to large tree often 60–90' tall (max. 110'); a relatively long-needled fir, usually pale gray-green in color.

bark on mature trunk thick with rough gray ridges

needles 2", curved, flattened

usually glaucous gray-green above and below; rounded tip

mature trees develop irregular or flat-topped crown, drooping branches

cones 4", olive green or purple

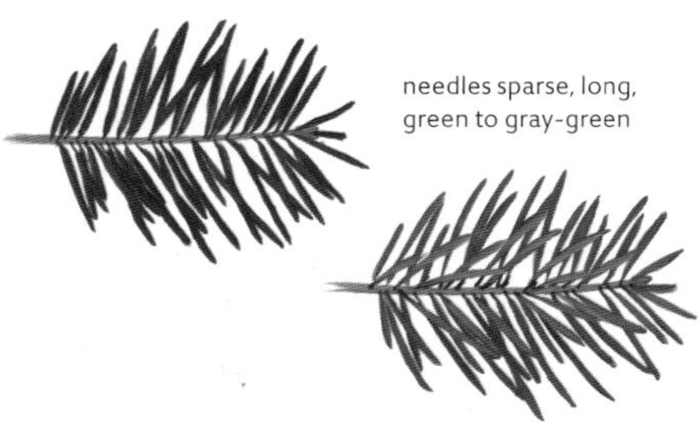

needles sparse, long, green to gray-green

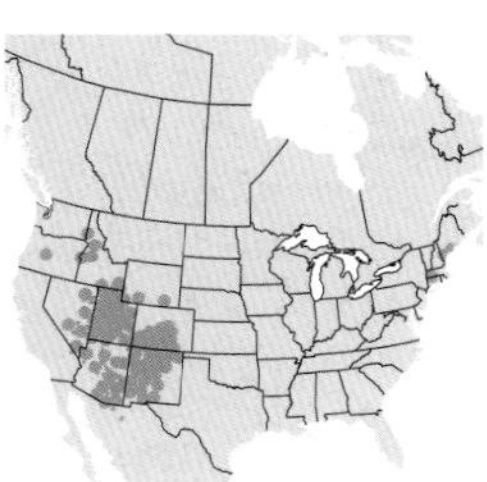

Common in coniferous forests; Commonly cultivated and rarely naturalized in northeast (zones 4–7).

This species is comprised of at least five distinguishable populations of trees in different western regions, all with green cones and glaucous needles. These forms differ mainly in details of needles and chemistry. Sierra White Fir, currently treated as a species (page 57), is a part of this "white fir complex."

Sierra White Fir

Abies lowiana

PACIFIC WHITE FIR, CALIFORNIA WHITE FIR

Evergreen. Medium to very large tree often over 100' tall (max. 246'). Very similar to and sometimes considered a subspecies of Colorado White Fir, but has needles shorter, less glaucous, more two-ranked, with notched tip. Odor pine-like.

needles 1¼", somewhat glaucous greenish
tip notched, mostly 2-ranked, flattened

cones 3½" long, olive green

needles long, 2-ranked, glaucous green

Sierra White Fir differs from Colorado White in having shorter needles 1¼" long, less glaucous above, with tip weakly notched, and more strongly 2-ranked; cones average slightly smaller. It is also a larger tree than Colorado White Fir, but apparently intergrades, where range overlaps in southern and northern California.

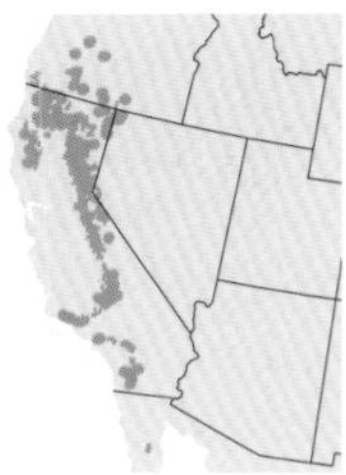

Common in mixed montane coniferous forests. Rarely cultivated.

Grand Fir

Abies grandis

GIANT FIR, LOWLAND WHITE FIR, YELLOW FIR

Evergreen. Medium to large tree often 150–200' tall (max. 267'); older trees round-topped.

needles 1¾", strongly 2-ranked (one-ranked on higher branches)
notched at tip

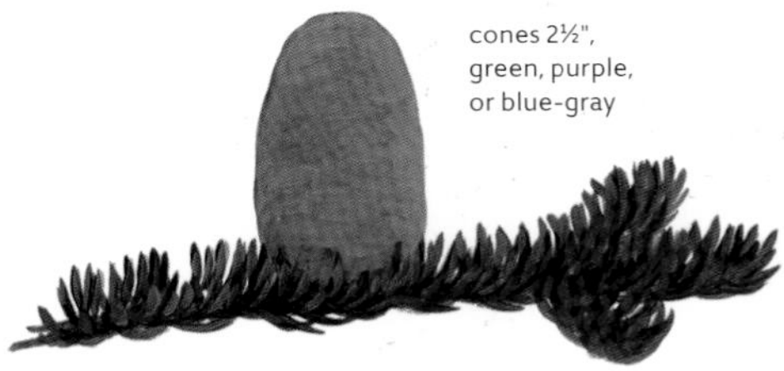
cones 2½", green, purple, or blue-gray

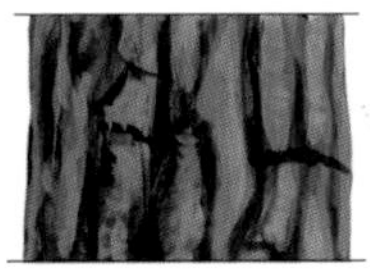
bark on mature trunk divided into thick, flat-topped ridges

Intergrades with Colorado White Fir where range overlaps in southern Oregon and northern California. In that region, most can be distinguished by habitat, with Colorado White Fir in higher and drier areas, and Grand Fir in lower, wetter areas. Grand Fir also has more reddish inner bark (vs. yellowish); smaller cones and notched needles.

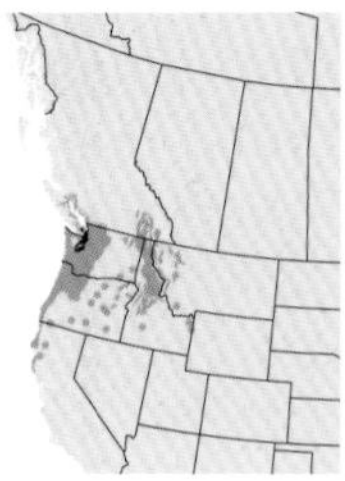

Common, mainly in lowlands of moist, coastal coniferous forests and lower mountain slopes. Uncommonly cultivated (zones 4–7).

Pacific Silver Fir

Abies amabilis

SILVER FIR, CASCADES FIR, BEAUTIFUL FIR

Evergreen. Large tree often 60–90' tall (max. 245'); dense and dark green with slender pointed crown, short stiff branches horizontal.

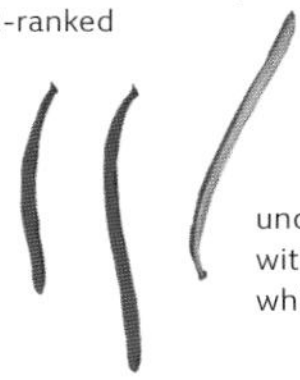
needles ¾", mostly 2-ranked
notched at tip, flattened, dark green above
underleaf pale with many whitish bands

cones 4", broad, purplish; mature in fall, relatively early

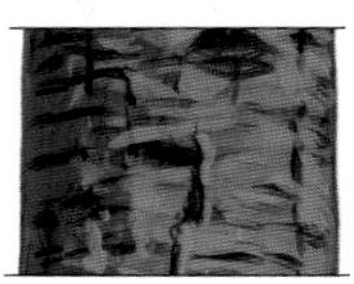
bark on mature trunk smooth, thin, gray

The rigid upright crown, horizontal branches, and paler, smooth trunk indicate a fir, and distinguish this species from its common associates Common Douglas-fir, Western and Mountain Hemlocks.

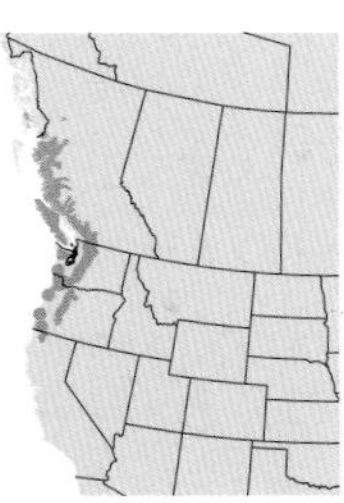

Common in moist, coastal coniferous forests. Uncommonly cultivated, mostly within native range (zones 5–6).

Bristlecone Fir

Abies bracteata

SANTA LUCIA FIR

Evergreen. Small to medium tree often 50–80' tall (max 182'); narrow, pointed crown and horizontal branches like other firs but longer, pointed needles and bristly cones unique.

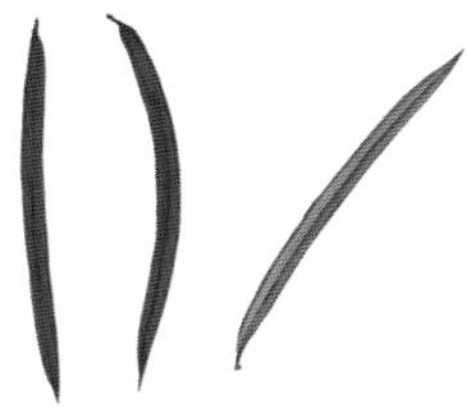
needles 1½", flattened
sharply pointed, dark green above

cones 3½", short oval, purplish-brown, with 2" slender bracts bristling out and curving down

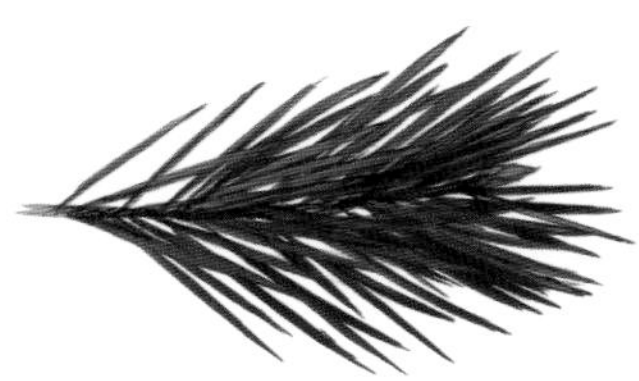
buds ¾", much larger and more pointed than other firs

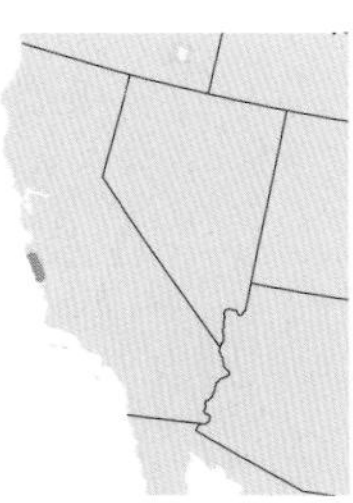

Rare and local in moist canyon bottoms in the Santa Lucia Mountains. Cultivated only rarely, only near natural range.

European Silver Fir

Abies alba

COMMON SILVER FIR

Evergreen. Medium to large tree often 50–70' tall (max. about 100'). Tall and narrow, but older trees can become irregularly flat-topped. Distinguished from native firs by fairly short needles with white bands below, narrow cones with bracts projecting.

leaves ¾",
base twisted
underleaf
whitish
cones 5", green
turning red-brown;
bracts project
about ¼" beyond
cone scales

Although these three species are the most commonly cultivated exotic firs in North America, at least 16 other species are reportedly cultivated here. Most are large trees suitable only for parks and arboreta, but in those settings observers should bear in mind that many other species of firs might be planted.

Native to central and southeastern Europe. Uncommon in cultivation and naturalized in North Carolina (zones 4–6).

Nikko Fir

Abies homolepis

Evergreen. Medium to large tree often 40–70' tall (max. 91'); dense branches, relatively broad shape for a fir. Native to Japan. Fairly commonly cultivated, the most frequently cultivated exotic fir in North America, naturalized in New York (zones 4–6).

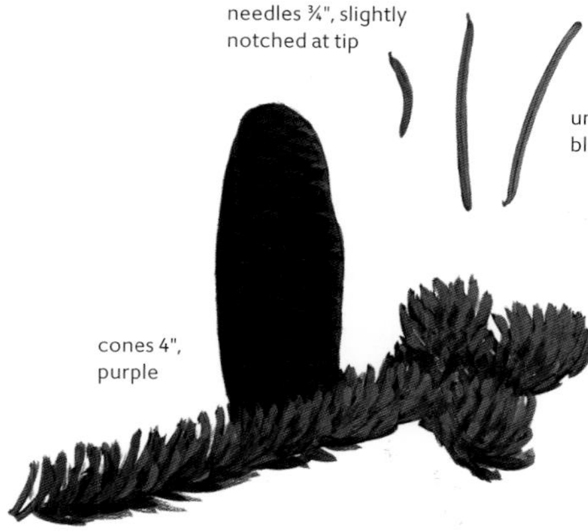
needles ¾", slightly
notched at tip
underleaf
bluish-white
cones 4",
purple

Caucasian Fir

Abies nordmanniana

NORDMANN FIR, CRIMEAN FIR

Evergreen. Medium to large tree often 50–70' tall (max. 93'); very similar to European Silver Fir but tends to have leaves less two-ranked. Native to Caucasus region. Commonly cultivated in North America (zones 4–6).

needles 1"
underleaf with
two white bands
cones 5½", reddish-brown
with reflexed bracts

Cypress Family

The cypress family (Cupressaceae) includes about 120 species worldwide in twenty to thirty genera. Thirty species in nine genera are native to North America and trees in four additional genera are commonly cultivated.

A few genera have feathery pinnate leaves (Bald-cypress, Dawn Redwood, Giant Sequoia, and Redwood, sometimes separated as the family Taxodiaceae), while all the others have small scale-like leaves pressed close to the twigs, giving the twig a cord-like appearance.

This table compares the cones, branchlet arrangement, and leaf arrangement of five native genera of scale-leaved conifers.

Cypress	cones large, round, woody 	branchlets radiate in all directions 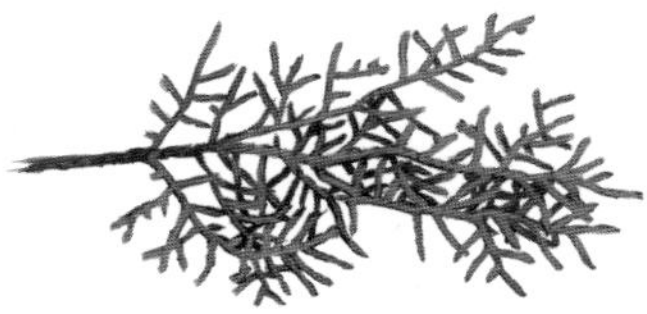	leaves in alternating pairs all equal size 
Juniper	cones small, fleshy, berry-like 	like cypress 	leaves in alternating pairs or whorls of three all equal size 
False-Cypress	cones like Cypress but smaller 	branchlets 2-ranked forming flattened spray 	leaves in alternating pairs all equal size, twigs not flattened 
Arborvitae	cones upright with several pairs of elongated scales 	like false-cypress 	leaves in opposite pairs alternating small and large, twigs flattened 
Incense-Cedar	cones pendent with one main pair of elongated scales 	like false-cypress 	leaves in whorls of four 

Cypress Family: Cypresses

The cypresses (genus *Cupressus*) are ten to twenty-six species of shrubs or small trees worldwide, all very similar in appearance. With many isolated local populations, as many as fifteen species have been recognized in North America, most with a very limited natural range. Seven native species are covered here, along with one commonly cultivated European species.

Cypress species are distinguished by minute details of leaf color and size, appearance of leaf glands, cone color and size, growth habit, and bark. Hybridization and variation complicates identification.

male cones
tiny, yellow

young female
cones tiny,
spiky

mature cones persist
for years in small
clusters

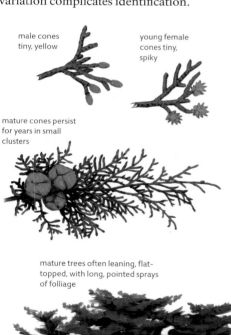

mature trees often leaning, flat-
topped, with long, pointed sprays
of folliage

Monterey Cypress

Cupressus macrocarpa

Evergreen. Medium tree often 40–70' tall (max. 103'). Crown generally broadly spreading, fairly sparse, often just a few major limbs from near ground, more upright in sheltered locations.

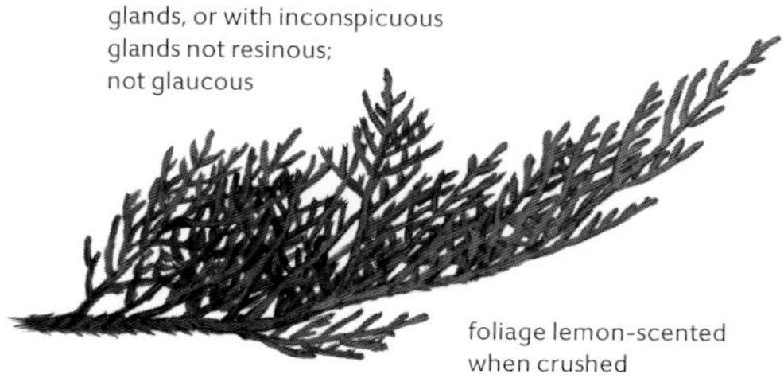
leaves rich green, without
glands, or with inconspicuous
glands not resinous;
not glaucous
foliage lemon-scented
when crushed

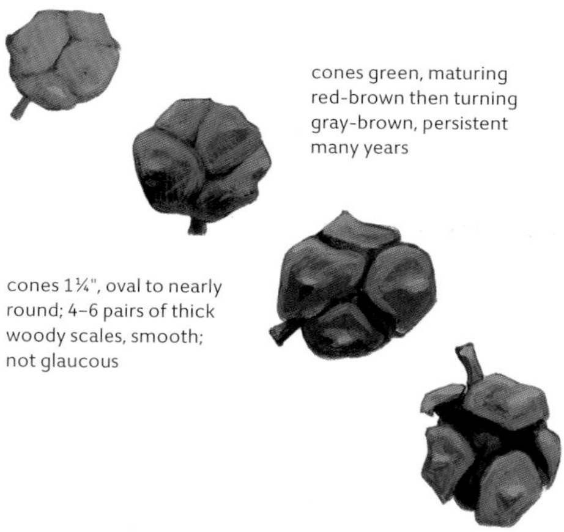
cones green, maturing
red-brown then turning
gray-brown, persistent
many years
cones 1¼", oval to nearly
round; 4–6 pairs of thick
woody scales, smooth;
not glaucous

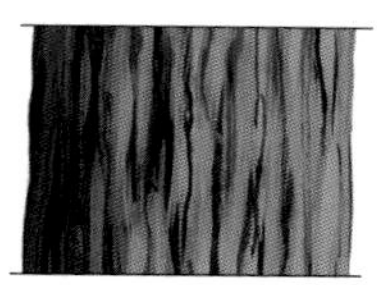
bark rough, fibrous

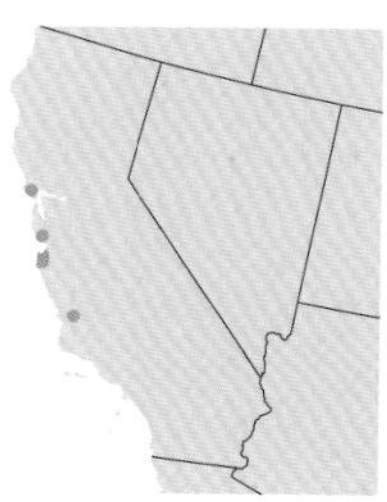

Very rare and local in the wild (only two groves near Monterey California). Commonly cultivated and now naturalized widely along Pacific Coast and beyond (zones 7–9).

Arizona Cypress

Cupressus arizonica

ARIZONA SMOOTH CYPRESS, CUYAMACA CYPRESS, PIUTE CYPRESS

Evergreen. Medium to large tree often 40–60' tall (max. 112'); the most widely-distributed native cypress, often with pale blue-green foliage.

leaves often strongly glaucous; usually with conspicuous glands that produce drop of resin

cones 1"

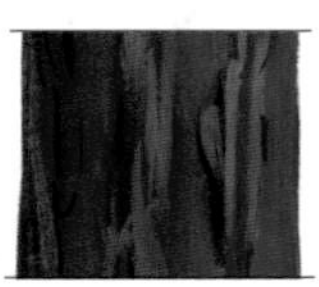

bark on young and many old trunks smooth, reddish

This species varies regionally, with five named varieties (four in North America), sometimes treated as species. They differ in leaf details, and some develop furrowed bark on mature trunks. The Smooth Arizona Cypress (*C. a.* var. *glabra*) of central Arizona often has glaucous blue-gray leaves and is the most commonly cultivated form.

Uncommon in canyon bottoms, pinyon-juniper woodland, chaparral. Uncommonly cultivated (zones 7–9).

Baker Cypress

Cupressus bakeri

MODOC CYPRESS

Evergreen. Small to medium tree, often 30–80' tall (max. 129'); flaking reddish-purple bark and gray-green foliage like Arizona, but cones smaller.

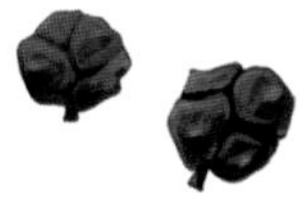

cones ½"

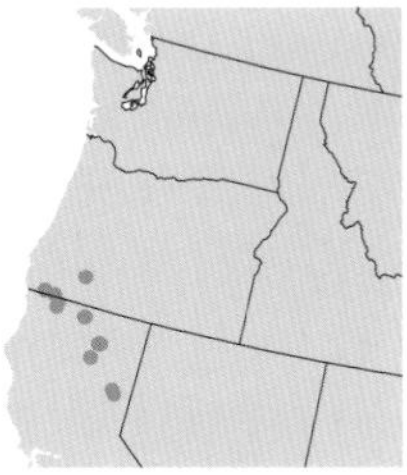

Rare and local in mixed evergreen forests. Very rarely cultivated but hardy to Massachusetts (zones 5–8).

Gowen Cypress

Cupressus goveniana

GOWEN CYPRESS, MENDOCINO CYPRESS, SANTA CRUZ CYPRESS

Evergreen. Small tree usually 15–25' tall (max. 75'); bark usually rough, furrowed, foliage dark green usually without glands, cones dark and smooth. Varieties are recognized in Northern California and on Santa Cruz Island that are sometimes considered separate species.

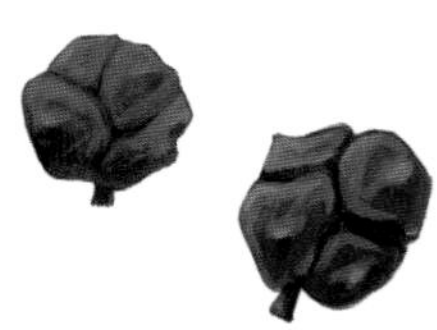

cones ¾", smooth, dark

Rare and local in coastal pine forests, especially on poor soils. Uncommonly cultivated (zones 7–9).

Tecate Cypress

Cupressus forbesii

Evergreen. Small to medium tree often 20–30' tall (max. 71'); bark smooth, reddish, foliage dark green usually without glands, cones large and smooth.

cones 1¼", smooth, dark

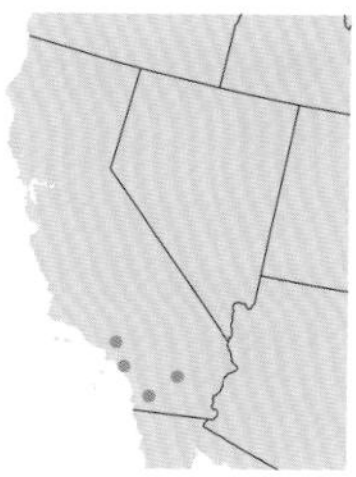

Uncommon and local in chaparral. Not cultivated.

Sargent Cypress

Cupressus sargentii

Evergreen. Shrub or small tree usually 15–30' tall (max 50'); broad and spreading with bark rough, furrowed, foliage often glaucous with inconspicuous glands.

cones 1", smooth or slightly lumpy, dark and glaucous

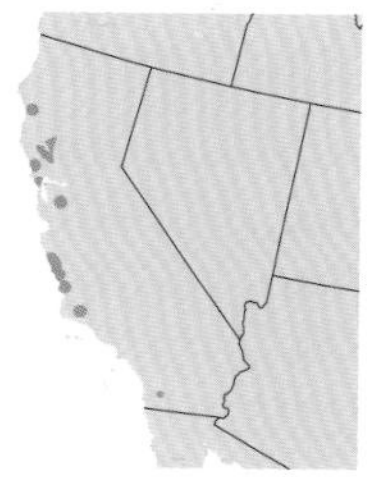

Uncommon and local in chaparral, foothill woodland, and lower montane forests, on serpentine. Very rarely cultivated.

MacNab Cypress

Cupressus macnabiana

Evergreen. Shrub or occasionally a small tree 20–30' tall (max. 55'); crown broadly conical, dense. Bark rough, furrowed, foliage sometimes pale glaucous, with glands. Twigs are arranged in flattened sprays, like Alaska-cedar, but unlike other cypresses.

cones ¾", lumpy, pale brown

Uncommon and local in chaparral and foothill woodland, often on serpentine. Rarely cultivated.

Italian Cypress

Cupressus sempervirens

COMMON CYPRESS, MEDITERRANEAN CYPRESS

Evergreen. Small to large tree often 30–50' tall (max. 94'). Form usually columnar, often very narrow and tapering; some are broader and spreading. Native to southern Europe, north Africa, southwest Asia. Commonly cultivated, especially in California, but apparently not naturalized (zones 7–11).

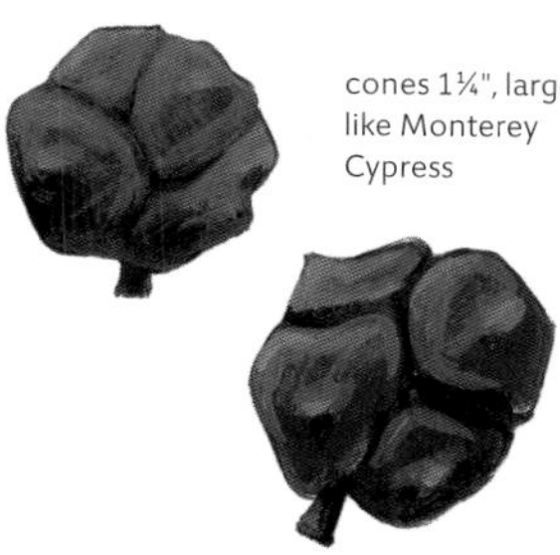

cones 1¼", large, like Monterey Cypress

usually a narrow columnar form in cultivation

Cypress Family: Junipers

The junipers (genus *Juniperus*) are about sixty species of shrubs and small trees worldwide with thirteen species native to North America. Eleven are often tree-like, and are covered here along with several commonly cultivated exotic species.

All junipers have tiny, scale-like leaves (juvenile-form leaves on vigorous growth are longer and spiny). Seeds are in a cone, but with a complete fleshy, berry-like covering. Most juniper species in North America are found in the arid West, where they are a prominent feature of plant communities in the transition between low-elevation desert or grassland and higher oak and pine forests. Pinyon-juniper woodlands cover much of the Great Basin region, and oak-juniper woodlands are extensive from Texas to Washington. In these settings, junipers are often merely shrubs, branching low and spreading into a rounded form.

Identifying species of junipers can be extremely difficult, and is sometimes impossible without chemical tests. Field identification must rely on range and details of cones.

Most junipers do not grow large enough to be commercially important for lumber, but the wood is very durable and may be used locally for fence posts or firewood. The aromatic wood has also been widely used to build insect-repellent storage for clothing (and incorrectly called "cedar"), while the fibrous bark was used for weaving mats and cloth (and is commonly used by birds for nest material). Juniper berries are used as flavoring in foods and in alcoholic beverages (especially gin).

juvenile-type leaves long, sharp, stick out from twigs, very prickly

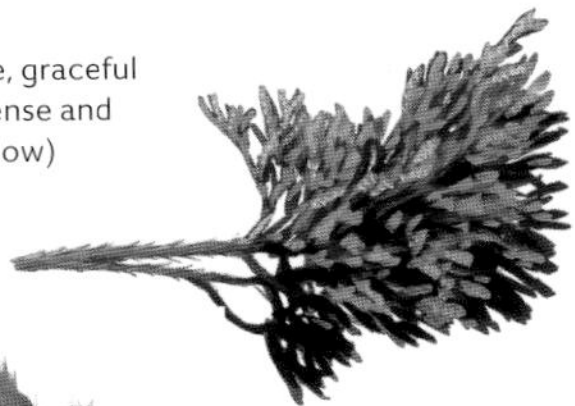

foliage sparse, graceful (above) or dense and clumped (below)

most junipers low, bushy, especially in open western habitats, such as pinyon-juniper woodlands

old trees gnarled, twisted, with clumped foliage

occasionally tall, relatively narrow tree, with clumped foliage

Eastern Redcedar

Juniperus virginiana

EASTERN REDCEDAR, PENCIL CEDAR

Evergreen. Small to medium tree often 20–50' tall (max. 81'); dense, usually single-stemmed. The only native juniper that is commonly upright and columnar, but many plants broad, rounded, and bushy.

bark exfoliating in thin strips

male cones tiny, yellowish, often profuse

leaves greenish, with inconspicuous glands
young female cones tiny, round, greenish

seed cones 1/8", round, bluish, glaucous, berrylike; maturing in 1 year

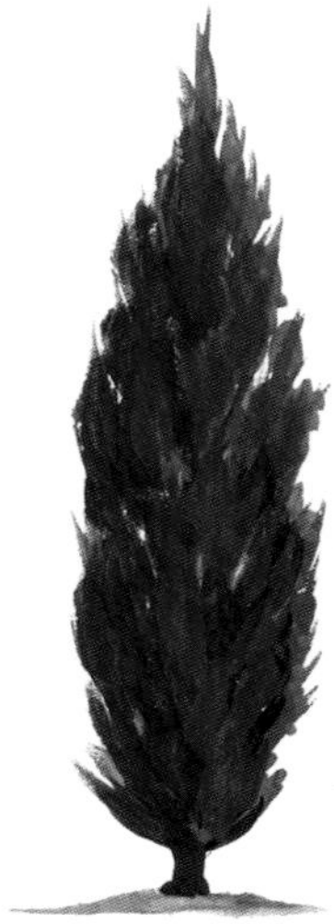
often narrowly upright, but can be low, rounded bush

leaves green, but sometimes reddish brown in winter

Coastal southern populations are sometimes considered a separate species, Southern Redcedar (*Juniperus silicicola*). Reported to have more slender twigs, smaller fruit, and a less upright form than typical Eastern Redcedar. It is found in the coastal plain from North Carolina to Florida.

Eastern Redcedar often hybridizes with Rocky Mountain Juniper across a broad area, where range overlaps. Eastern has more slender leafy twigs, and cones ripen in one year (vs. 2).

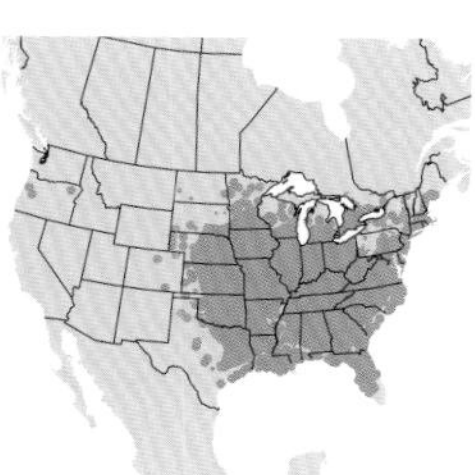

Common in overgrown pastures, roadsides, dry open woodlands and hillsides, barrens. Commonly cultivated (zones 3–9) and many cultivars.

Rocky Mountain Juniper

Juniperus scopulorum

ROCKY MOUNTAIN REDCEDAR, COLORADO JUNIPER

Evergreen. Shrub or small tree often 15–30' tall (max. 70'). Single-stemmed (rarely multi-stemmed), crown conical to occasionally rounded. Closely related to Eastern Redcedar.

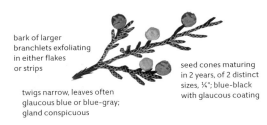

bark of larger branchlets exfoliating in either flakes or strips
seed cones maturing in 2 years, of 2 distinct sizes, ¼"; blue-black with glaucous coating
twigs narrow, leaves often glaucous blue or blue-gray; gland conspicuous

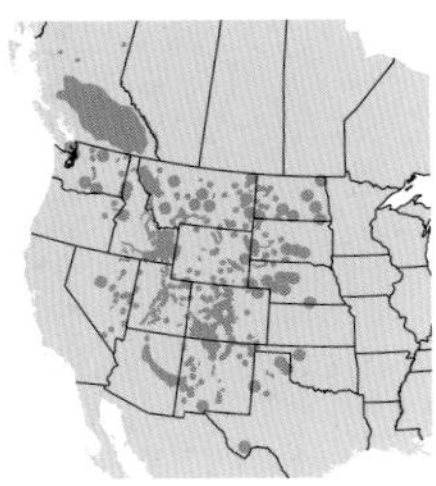

Common on rocky soils, slopes, and eroded hillsides. Commonly cultivated (zones 3–7), many cultivars.

Western Juniper

Juniperus occidentalis

SIERRA JUNIPER, WESTERN REDCEDAR

Evergreen. Shrub or small tree often 10–25' tall (max. 86'); usually single-trunked with more grayish green foliage than other junipers.

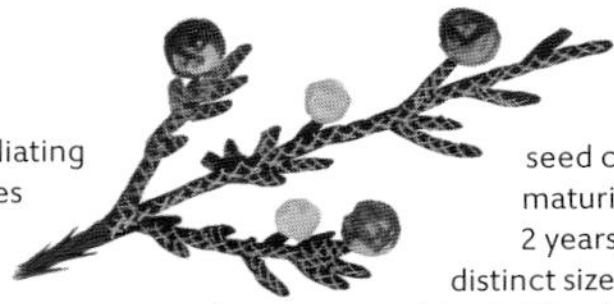
bark of larger branchlets exfoliating in scales or flakes
seed cones maturing in 2 years, of 2 distinct sizes, ¼", blue to blue-black, glaucous
leaves green, with conspicuous glands

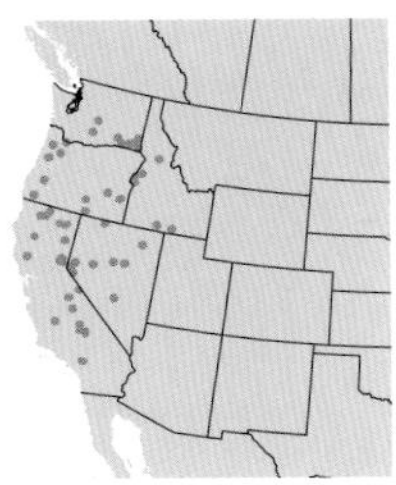

Common on dry rocky slopes. Rarely cultivated, but several cultivars developed.

Utah Juniper

Juniperus osteosperma

Evergreen. Shrub or small tree usually 15–20' tall (max. 40'); multi- or single-stemmed, crown rounded.

bark of larger branchlets smooth
seed cones maturing in 1–2 years, of 1–2 sizes, ⅓", bluish brown to tan, glaucous
leaves light yellow-green, glands inconspicuous

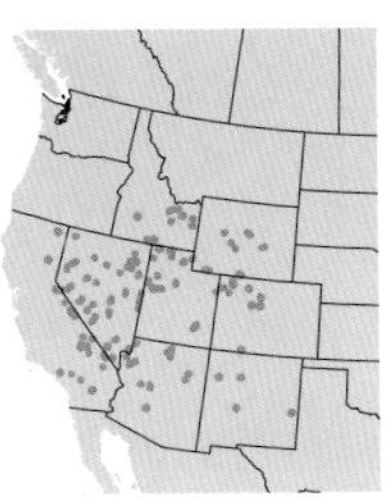

Common on dry, rocky soil and slopes; the most common juniper of Utah. Rarely cultivated.

California Juniper

Juniperus californica

SWEET-BERRIED JUNIPER, DESERT WHITE CEDAR

Evergreen. Shrub or small tree usually 10–20' tall (max. 25'); usually multistemmed.

bark of larger branchlets smooth
seed cones maturing in 1 year, of 1 size, ⅓", bluish brown, glaucous
leaves light green, glands conspicuous

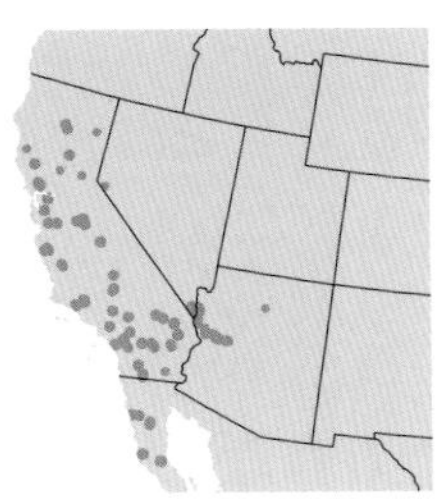

Common on dry, rocky slopes and flats. Very rarely cultivated.

Ashe Juniper

Juniperus ashei

MOUNTAIN-CEDAR

Evergreen. Small tree usually 15–30' tall (max. 41'); occasionally branching at base. Used locally for fenceposts and "cedarwood oil."

bark of larger branchlets exfoliating in strips
leaves dark green, glands inconspicuous
seed cones maturing in 1 year, of 1 size, ¼", dark blue, glaucous

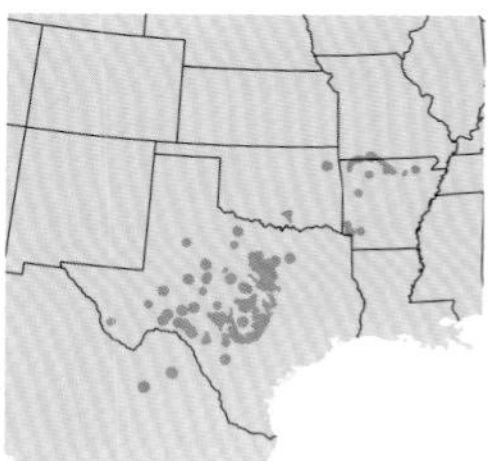

Common on limestone hills and bluffs. Rarely cultivated.

Oneseed Juniper

Juniperus monosperma

Evergreen. Shrub or small tree often 10–20' tall (max. 28'); usually branching near base, crown rounded to flattened.

branchlets erect, 4–6-sided
bark of larger branchlets exfoliating in either flakes or in strips.
leaves green to dark green, glands white-dotted
seed cones maturing in 1 year, of 1 size, ¼", reddish blue to brownish blue, glaucous

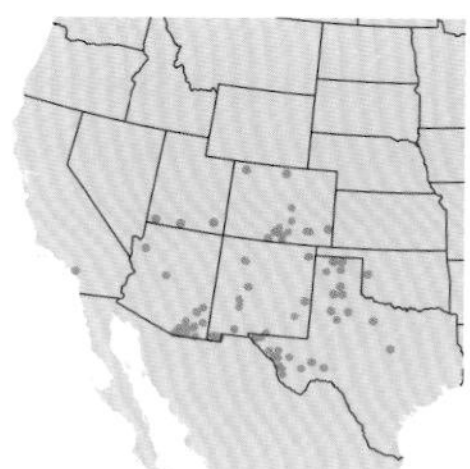

Common on dry, rocky soils and slopes. Rarely cultivated.

Drooping Juniper

Juniperus flaccida

Evergreen. Shrub or small tree often 15–25' tall (max. 35'); usually single-stemmed, crown rounded, branches drooping.

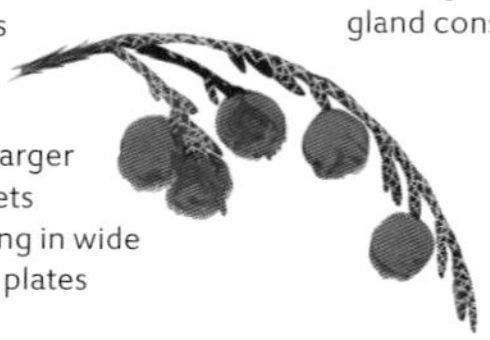
seed cones maturing in 1 year, of 1 size, large, ½", tan-brown to brownish purple when mature, glaucous
leaves green, gland conspicuous
bark of larger branchlets exfoliating in wide strips or plates

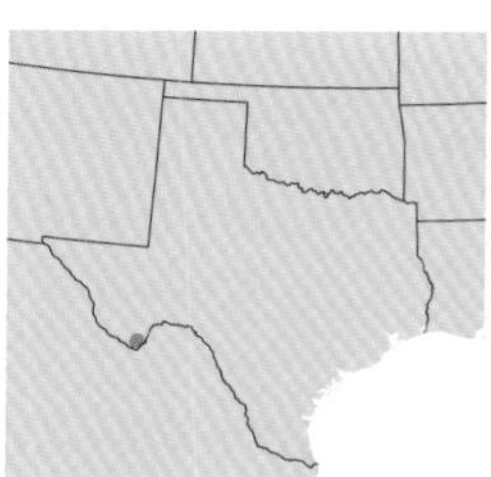

Local and uncommon in rocky soils and slopes. Very rarely cultivated.

Alligator Juniper

Juniperus deppeana

CHECKERBARK JUNIPER, THICKBARK JUNIPER, MOUNTAIN CEDAR

Evergreen. Small to medium tree often 20–40' tall (max. 71'); single-stemmed, crown rounded. Named for unique checkerboard bark, like alligator skin.

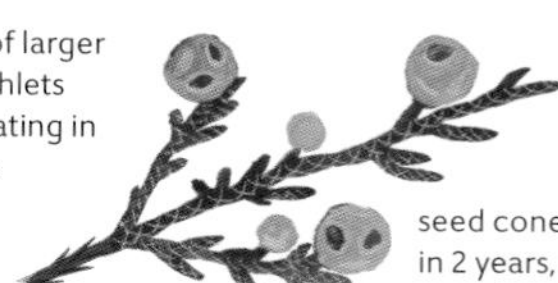
bark of larger branchlets exfoliating in plates
seed cones maturing in 2 years, of 2 distinct sizes, large, ⅜", reddish tan to dark reddish brown, glaucous
leaves green, to silvery glaucous, glands conspicuous

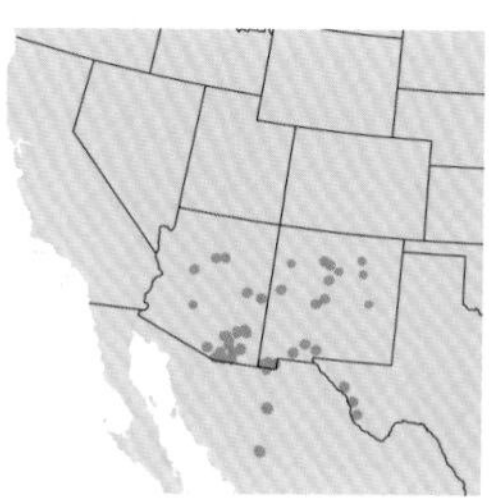

Common in rocky soils, in mountains; at higher elevations than other junipers, often scattered in oak woodlands. Very rarely cultivated.

Redberry Juniper

Juniperus coahuilensis

Evergreen. Shrub or small tree often 10–20' tall; single-stemmed or branched at base. Unusual in that it sprouts from the stump after burning or cutting. Formerly considered part of Pinchot Juniper.

bark of larger branchlets exfoliating in strips, or occasionally in flakes
leaves green to light green, glands sometimes have white dots
seed cones maturing in 1 year, of 1 size, ¼", red to pink with glaucous coating

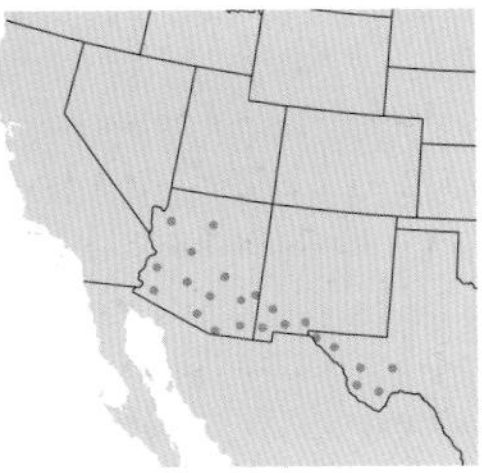

Uncommon and local on grasslands and adjacent rocky slopes. Not cultivated.

Several other species of exotic junipers are commonly cultivated (zones 4–9), including Common Juniper (*Juniperus communis*), Chinese Juniper (*Juniperus chinensis*) and Flaky Juniper (*Juniperus squamata*). These cultivated junipers are shrubs or small trees, and most of the tree-like cultivars have an upright columnar form like Italian Cypress. They all retain spiny juvenile foliage, with sharp pointed leaves up to ½" long, and most cultivars have gray-green or bluish foliage. Identification is very complex, with many hybrids and a wide array of cultivars.

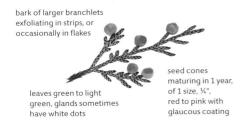

Flaky Juniper, and several other cultivated species, have spiny gray-green leaves up to ½", like a miniature spruce

Pinchot Juniper

Juniperus pinchotii

Evergreen. Shrub or small tree usually under 20' tall (max. 28'); usually multistemmed. Seed cone relatively sweet and juicy, like Redberry but unlike other junipers.

bark of larger branchlets exfoliating in strips or sometimes in flakes
leaves yellow-green, glands often whitish
seed cones maturing in 1 year, of 1 size, ¼", copper to copper-red, not glaucous

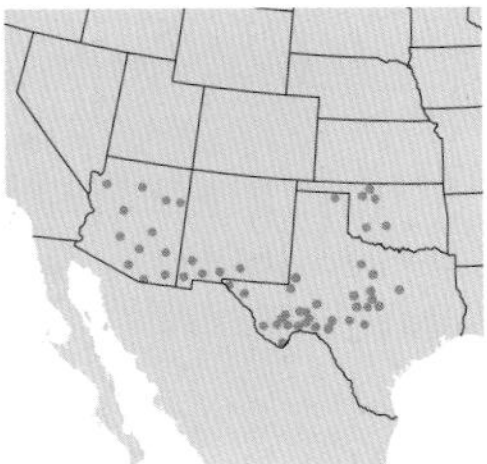

Locally common on gravelly soils on rolling hills and in ravines. Rarely cultivated.

White Cypress-pine

Callitris columellaris

Evergreen. Shrub or small tree usually under 30' tall; usually branching low, into irregular crown like shrubby forms of junipers. Juniper-like, but a member of a distinct subfamily native to Australasia.

seed cones oval, ½" long, dark brown; on short stalk
leaves tiny, scale-like, in whorls of 3, usually glaucous

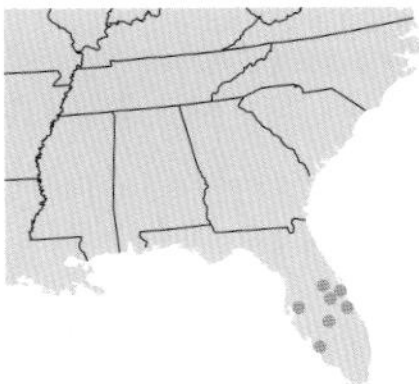

Native to Australia. Commonly cultivated and locally naturalized in Sand Pine scrub and thickets in Florida (zone 9).

Japanese-cedar

Cryptomeria japonica

JAPANESE CRYPTOMERIA, JAPANESE REDWOOD, PEACOCK PINE

Evergreen. Small to medium tree often 30–50' tall (max. 93'); narrow crown, finer branches drooping. Related to Baldcypress, but native to China and Japan. Commonly and widely cultivated, many cultivars (zones 5–6).

seed cones ¾", reddish brown, sharp-pointed scales, spiky

leaves short, ⅓", divergent, curved and prickly

Chinese-fir

Cunninghamia lanceolata

CHINA FIR

Evergreen. Medium tree often 30–50' tall (max. 95'); often multi-trunked, broad and spreading. In its own subfamily, distinct from all others in cypress family. Native to China. Commonly cultivated (zones 7–9).

cones 1½", upright, nearly round, prickly

needles 1¾" long, broad, flat, very sharp-pointed

Other cypresses

The following four pages cover six native species in the cypress family. All have similar scale-like leaves, but differ in details of leaf arrangement, and are best distinguished by the shape and structure of the small woody cones. Most of these species are important commercially for their strong rot-resistant wood used for shingles, fences, and other outdoor applications.

Despite the fact that botanists classify the wild forms as species in different genera, identification of cultivated trees is very challenging, where a mixture of hybrids and cultivars tends to obscure the relatively small differences between species.

ARBORVITAES (genus *Thuja*) include five species of evergreen trees worldwide, (two native). They have upright woody cones opening slightly like small flowers, and flattened twigs, often forming flat fan-shaped sprays.

INCENSE-CEDARS (genus *Calocedrus*) include three species worldwide (one native). They are similar to the arborvitaes, but with slender cones hanging down, and longer leaves arranged in groups of four.

FALSE-CYPRESSES (genus *Chamaecyparis*) include five or six species worldwide (two native). They differ from the true cypresses in having twigs arranged in flattened sprays, and smaller cones, maturing in a single growing season.

ALASKA-CEDAR (genus *Callitropsis*) has been considered a false-cypress, but pointed knobs on cone scales, cones maturing in second growing season, and recent genetic evidence confirms a close relationship to true cypresses and junipers.

Northern White-cedar

Thuja occidentalis

AMERICAN ARBORVITAE, TREE OF LIFE

Evergreen. Small to medium tree often 30–45' tall (max. 125'). Trunk sometimes divides, crown narrow, tapered; can sprout from fallen trunk.

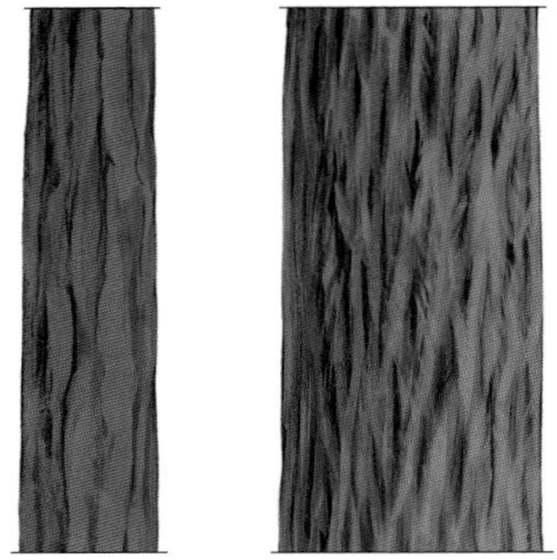

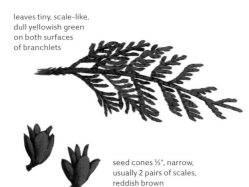

bark reddish brown or grayish brown, thin, fibrous, fissured

leaves tiny, scale-like, dull yellowish green on both surfaces of branchlets

seed cones ½", narrow, usually 2 pairs of scales, reddish brown

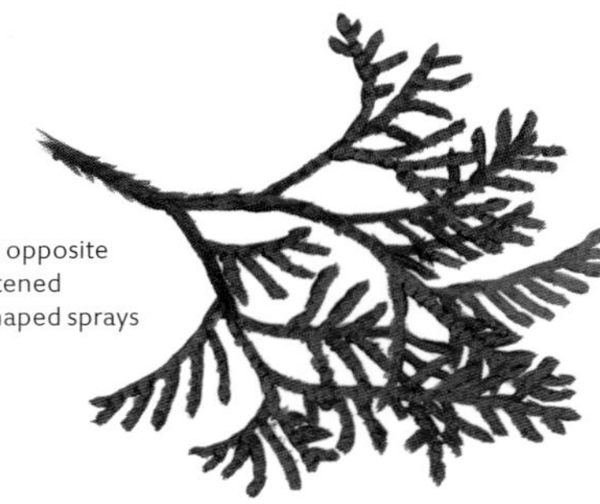

leaves opposite in flattened fan-shaped sprays

immature seed cones yellow-green in late summer

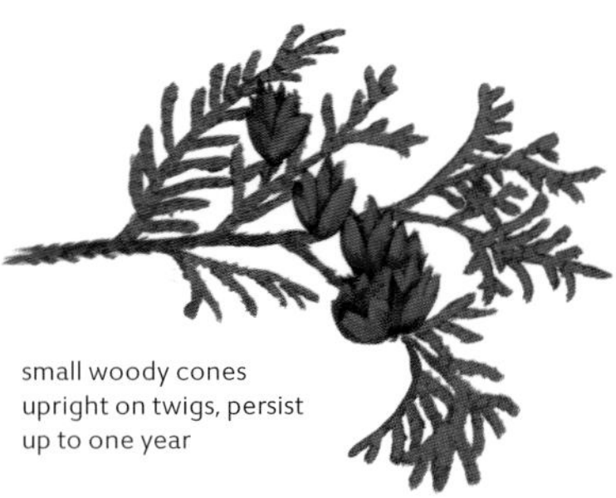

small woody cones upright on twigs, persist up to one year

usually compact, dense, with conspicuous flat fans of foliage

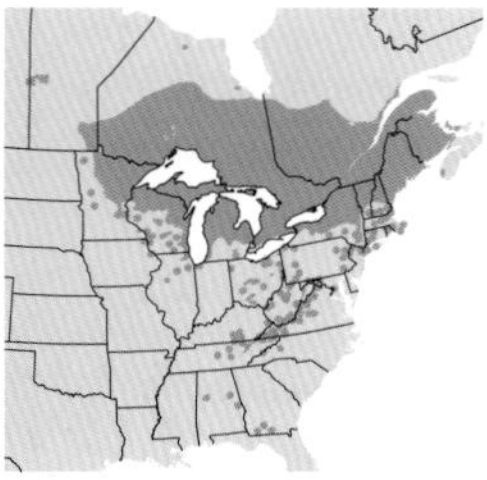

Uncommon and local in scattered locations in swamps, streamsides, lake shores, also uplands. Commonly cultivated as an ornamental and hedge plant (zones 3–7).

Western Redcedar

Thuja plicata

PACIFIC REDCEDAR, GIANT ARBORVITAE, SHINGLE CEDAR

Evergreen. Medium to large tree often 60–130' tall (max. 277'). Sometimes stunted in harsh environments; often buttressed at base, crown conical, and branches arching.

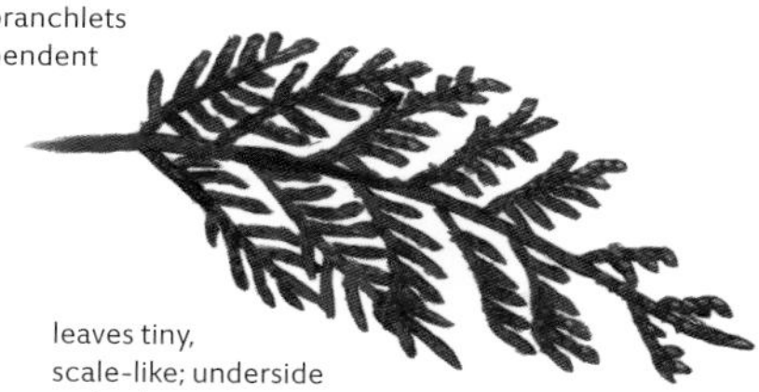
branchlets pendent
leaves tiny, scale-like; underside with white marks
crushed foliage has sweeter, fruitier smell than Northern White-cedar

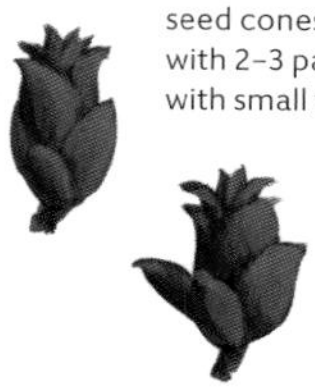
seed cones ⅓", narrow, with 2–3 pairs of scales, each with small tooth near tip

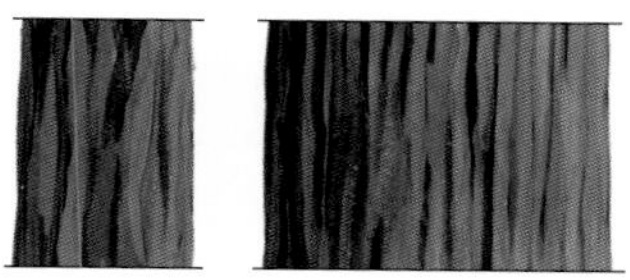
bark reddish, fibrous

This species is one of the most useful and important trees in the Northwest. Some Native American tribes were reportedly called "people of the redcedar" for their use of the tree. Wood was used for dugout canoes and functional or decorative items from totem poles to tools. The fibrous bark was woven into baskets, mats, clothing, and other items.

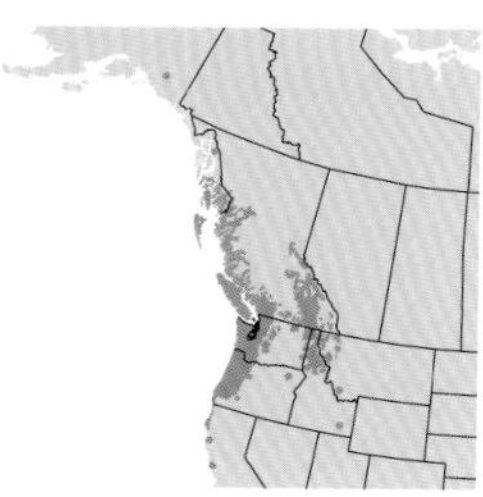

Common in a variety of habitats but especially moist soils in mixed coniferous forest. Commonly cultivated for ornament (zones 5–7), several cultivars.

Incense-cedar

Calocedrus decurrens

Evergreen. Large tree often 60–100' tall (max. 229'); usually tall, narrow, columnar, with bright green foliage. Named for the incense-like odor of its sap, and important for lumber, particularly for pencils.

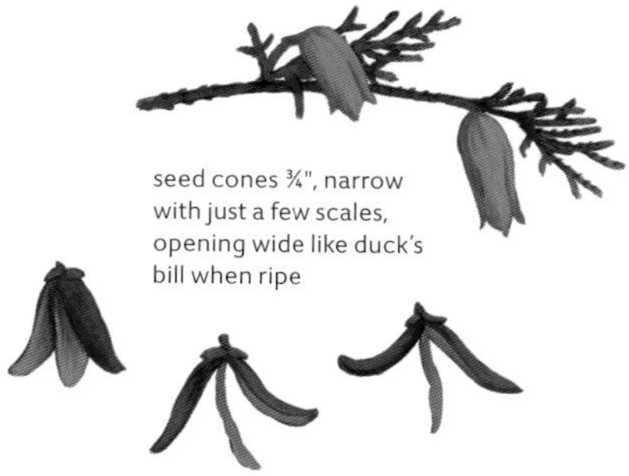
seed cones ¾", narrow with just a few scales, opening wide like duck's bill when ripe

leaves in whorls of 4
leaves tiny, scale-like, bright green
twigs in flattened sprays

pollen cones tiny, greenish yellow.

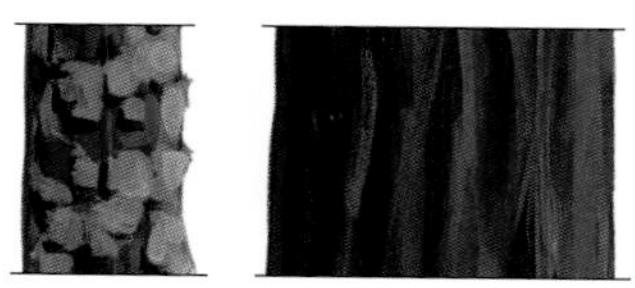
bark cinnamon brown, fibrous, furrowed and ridged

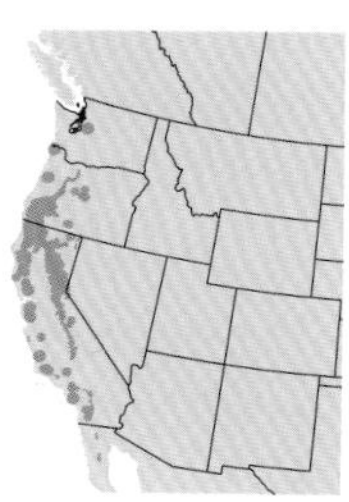

Common in montane forests. Fairly commonly cultivated (zones 5–8).

Port Orford-cedar

Chamaecyparis lawsoniana

LAWSON CYPRESS, OREGON CEDAR, GINGER-PINE

Evergreen. Medium to large tree often 110–150' tall (max. 224'); cultivated into many forms of color and shape.

seed cones ⅜", reddish brown, mature in first growing season

foliage sprays fan-shaped

bark reddish brown, with broad, rounded ridges

This native reportedly has at least fifty cultivars planted in North America. Seeds were cultivated beginning in the 1850s and propagated in many locations worldwide. The cultivars vary in leaf color (whitish to yellow to bluish), leaf shape (scale-like to needle-like), and habit (bushy to columnar to weeping).

Common in forests of the Coast Ranges. Commonly cultivated (zones 5–7); many cultivars.

Atlantic White-cedar

Chamaecyparis thyoides

SOUTHERN WHITE-CEDAR, COAST WHITE CEDAR, WHITE CYPRESS

Evergreen. Small to medium tree often 30–50' tall (max. 87'); relatively narrow and upright, with dense dark crown. Similar to Northern White-cedar, but is distinguished by twigs not flattened and cones rounded.

seed cones ¼", lumpy, pale brown

immature fruit green in summer

leaves in opposite pairs, twigs not flattened

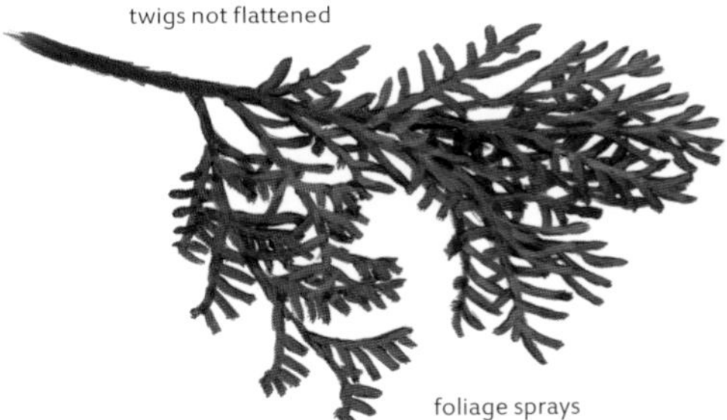

foliage sprays fan-shaped

bark dark brownish red, irregularly furrowed and ridged

Common locally in swamps and bogs, in wet woodlands and along streams; mostly in coastal plain. Rarely cultivated.

Alaska-cedar

Callitropsis nootkatensis

YELLOW-CYPRESS, STINKING CYPRESS, NOOTKA CYPRESS

Evergreen. Medium to large tree often 50–100' tall (max. 189'), or dwarfed at high elevations.

seed cones ¼", glaucous, bluish to purple

leaves sometimes glaucous, with conspicuous glands that produce drop of resin

foliage sprays drooping

bark rough, furrowed, fibrous

Common in wet coastal mountain forests. Commonly and widely cultivated (zones 4–7).

Cultivated species and hybrids

Alaska-cedar is known to hybridize with Sargent Cypress in the wild, and domestic hybrids with Monterey Cypress are commonly cultivated as 'Leyland Cypress' ('× *Cupressocyparis leylandi*'). This is often used as a hedge plant (like several species described below), but can be a large tree to 80' tall. Form varies from more cypress-like to more Alaska-cedar-like.

HINOKI-CYPRESS (*Chamaecyparis obtusa*) and SAWARA-CYPRESS (*C. pisifera*), both native to Japan, are commonly cultivated and reportedly locally naturalized in North America (zones 4–8). Both are similar to Atlantic White-cedar, and superficial differences between cultivars are much more obvious than the differences between species.

ORIENTAL ARBORVITAE (*Platycladus orientalis*) is a shrub or small tree native to China and related to the arborvitaes. It is commonly cultivated here (zones 6–11). It differs from arborvitaes in having cones with ragged scales that open wide, and foliage with almost no scent.

JAPANESE ARBORVITAE (*Thuja standishii*) and in a closely related genus the Hiba Arborvitae (*Thujopsis dolobrata*) are shrubs or small trees native to Japan and uncommonly cultivated (zones 5–7).

The fundamental similarity of these species to the native false-cypresses or arborvitaes, their ability to hybridize, and the deliberate cultivation of varied forms, makes identification extremely difficult. Despite the fact that botanists classify the wild forms as species, gardeners often make no real distinction, and the result is a diverse mixture of strikingly different cultivars, with genetic backgrounds that are nearly impossible to discern.

Baldcypress

Taxodium distichum

DECIDUOUS CYPRESS, SWAMP CYPRESS, SABINO TREE

Deciduous. Medium to large tree often 80–100' tall (max. 146'). Stately and picturesque with soft pale green foliage; crown conical when young, becoming irregular and flat-topped with age. Wood extremely durable and rot-resistant.

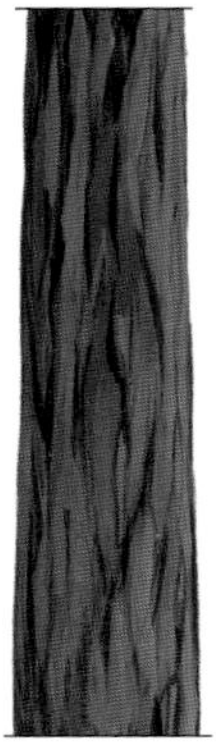

young trunk dark red-brown, but soon becoming gray with fibrous bark

bark reddish to gray, with fibrous ridges

cones 1", round, with few woody scales

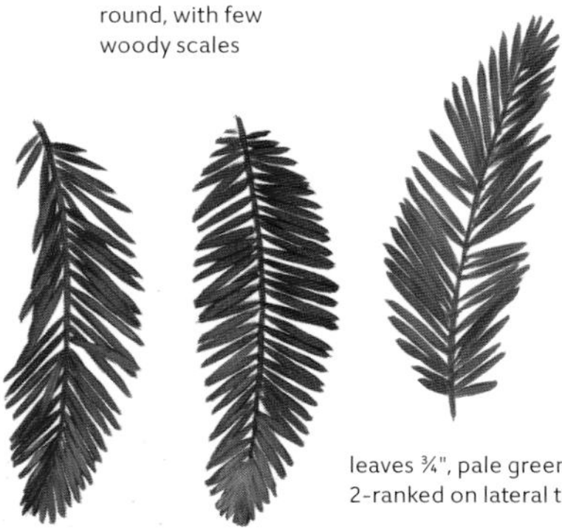

leaves ¾", pale green, 2-ranked on lateral twigs

fall color golden to purplish, late in fall

many small leaves create feather-like deciduous lateral branchlet

young female cones small, spiky, inconspicuous

twigs slender, green, turning light brown

pollen cones reddish-brown in dangling catkins, 7", early spring before leaves (Feb–Apr)

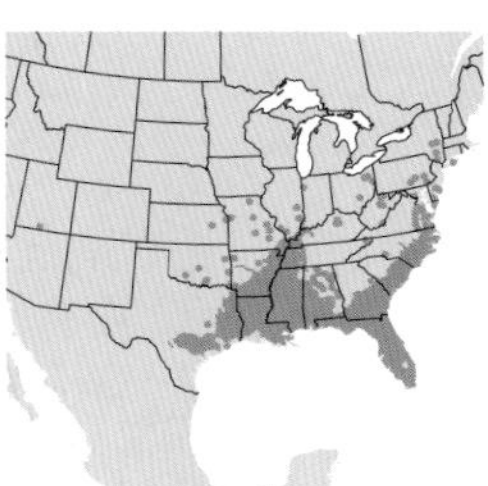

Common in wet swampy habitat where inundated for at least part of the year. Uncommonly cultivated, and grows in relatively dry settings well beyond native range (zones 4–11).

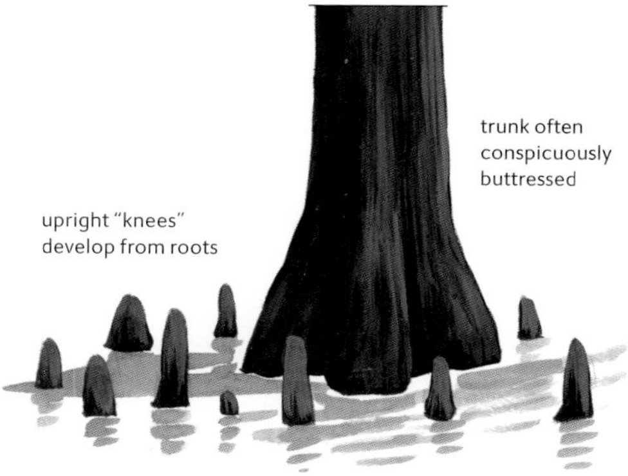
trunk often conspicuously buttressed
upright "knees" develop from roots

'Pondcypress'

Taxodium distichum var. *imbricarium*

Deciduous. Small to medium tree (max. 135'), usually not as large as typical Baldcypress. Differs from Baldcypress in twigs upright along branchlets, with tiny leaves pressed close to twigs (not feathery); rarely produces 'knees.' Sometimes considered a distinct species, but intergrades with Baldcypress. Common in still water (ponds, marsh edges, and wet depressions); typical Baldcypress is found in slow-moving water, such as river swamps. Rarely cultivated.

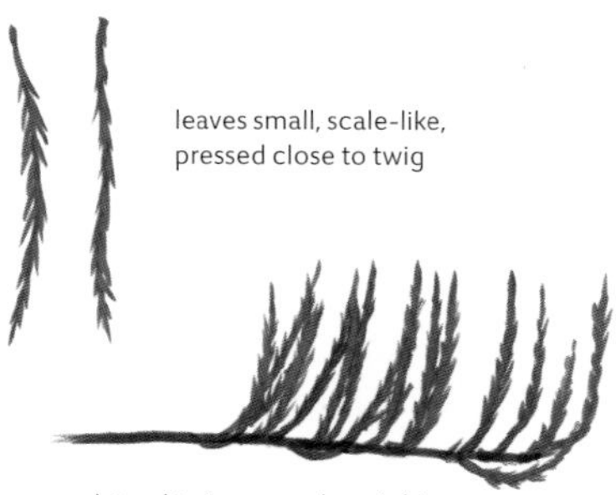
leaves small, scale-like, pressed close to twig
lateral twigs curved, upright

'Montezuma' Baldcypress

Taxodium distichum var. *mucronatum*

Very similar to typical Baldcypress, but foliage sub-evergreen or briefly deciduous (in dry season). Needles shorter, cones slightly larger to 1½", branches often strongly pendant, flowers in fall (not spring). Less cold-hardy. Rare in cultivation, mostly in Texas, but some in California.

Dawn Redwood

Metasequoia glyptostroboides

CHINESE REDWOOD, DECIDUOUS REDWOOD

Deciduous. Medium to large tree often 30–50' tall (max. 104'); conical, with straight trunk and branches to ground. This species, previously known only from fossils, was thought to be extinct until the rediscovery of a small grove in 1944 in China. Native to west central China. Commonly and widely cultivated but not known to escape (zones 5–8).

cones 1" long, on long stem; round; mature in December

leaves opposite, linear, 1" long, green to yellow-green, generally 2-ranked in feather-like sprays

short twigs deciduous (like Baldcypress), 3½" long with many small leaves
leafy twigs broader and more arched than Bald Cypress

twigs slender, light reddish-brown, with short, yellowish buds

bark fibrous, stringy, red-brown to gray

Redwood

Sequoia sempervirens

CALIFORNIA REDWOOD

Evergreen. Large to giant trees often 150–250' tall (max. 379'). The tallest living thing on Earth and among the oldest at over 2,000 years. Crown relatively narrow, pointed, branches often angled up; often suckers from base.

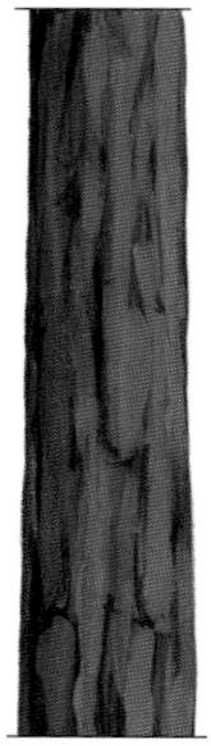

young trunk, with scaly ridges of cinnamon and gray

bark reddish brown, fibrous, ridged and furrowed to about 12" thick

needles up to 1", short and wide in dense flat sprays, reminiscent of yews

underleaf with whitish bands

pollen cones tiny, yellowish, clustered at twig tips

cones 1", mature in one season

leaves on vigorous or fertile shoots small, scale-like

tall, stately tree with pointed crown, ascending branches of feathery foliage

Fast-growing, relatively easy to propagate, and with extremely durable wood, the Redwood is an important source of lumber. Many young trees are harvested each year on plantations.

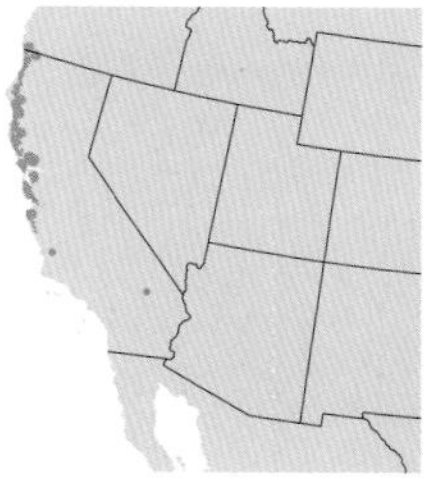

Locally common in protected valleys in coastal fog belt. Uncommonly but widely cultivated (zones 7–9). Several cultivars include varied growth forms and pale bluish needles.

Giant Sequoia

Sequoiadendron giganteum

BIGTREE, SIERRA REDWOOD, WELLINGTONIA

Evergreen. Large to giant tree often 100–250' tall (max. 290'). Crown narrow and pointed on young trees, becoming irregularly rounded in age. Branches often angled down with upswept tips; does not sucker. By volume, the largest living thing on Earth. Closely related to Redwood and sometimes placed in the same genus.

bark reddish brown, fibrous, ridged and furrowed, up to 24" thick

leaves small, scale-like, sharp, bluish-green

The Giant Sequoia grows in drier regions than the Redwood and is more reliant on fire. The very thick bark and high crown allows trees to survive fires that burn the entire understory. After a fire, the sunny, ash-covered ground provides an ideal bed for seeds, which are released from the cones following the heat of fire. Due to fire suppression, livestock grazing, and other land-use changes, very few new sequoia trees have sprouted in the past 100 years. Changes in fire policy on preserved land where Giant Sequoias grow will hopefully lead to more reproduction.

cones 2½", larger than Redwood, persistent; mature in second growing season

twigs lined with tiny leaves, cord-like

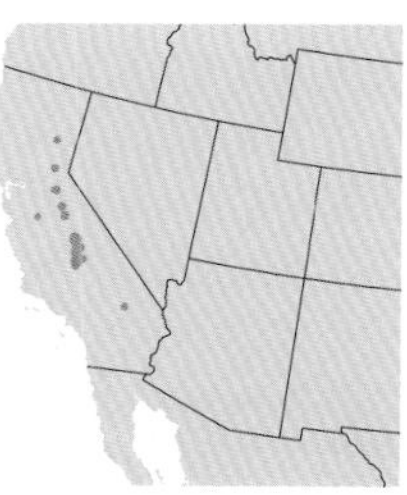

Uncommon and very local in dry montane forest in isolated groves on the w slopes of the Sierra Nevada, California. Uncommonly but widely cultivated (zones 6–8).

tall and massive tree, foliage tends to form more rounded clumps than Redwood

Exotic Gymnosperms

The three types of trees detailed here are all exotic gymnosperms commonly cultivated in North America, and each represents a distinctive family with no close relatives among our native species.

MONKEY PUZZLE FAMILY

One of only three genera in the family Araucariaceae, the genus *Araucaria* includes nineteen species of evergreen trees native to the southern hemisphere (mostly New Caledonia). All are remarkable-looking trees with short leaves arranged in dense whorls around branches. In addition to Monkey-puzzle Tree, at least two other species are cultivated in warmer parts of North America.

UMBRELLA-PINE FAMILY

The Japanese Umbrella-pine is the only species in the family Sciadopityaceae. It is a primitive species, known from fossils as much as 230 million years old. It lacks true leaves, the flat and flexible green "needles" are composed of stem tissue and are essentially modified green twigs (known as cladophylls).

PODOCARP FAMILY

One of about eighteen genera in the family Podocarpaceae, the genus *Podocarpus* includes about 100 species of evergreen shrubs or trees with narrow willow-like or sickle-shaped leaves. They are almost all found in the southern hemisphere and are thought to have originated as part of the Antarctic flora on the supercontinent Gondwana 50 to 100 million years ago.

Monkey-puzzle Tree

Araucaria araucana

MONKEY-TAIL TREE, CHILEAN PINE

Evergreen. Medium tree often 30–50' tall (max. 77'). Named for the viciously spiny leaves covering the branches, which would "puzzle" a monkey to climb. Native to Chile. Commonly cultivated in Pacific Northwest, less often elsewhere (zones 7–10).

leaves 1½", triangular, stiff and sharp
leaves overlap like shingles, covering stout twigs

upright female seed cones 7"

straight trunk with small, rounded crown of thick green twigs

Japanese Umbrella-pine

Sciadopitys verticillata

PARASOL PINE

Evergreen. Small to medium tree often 25–40' tall (max. 54'); often multi-trunked, dense, dark green and conical with foliage to ground. Native to Japan. Commonly cultivated (zones 5–7).

"needles" 4½", broad, flat, flexible, clustered at twig tips in umbrella-like whorls

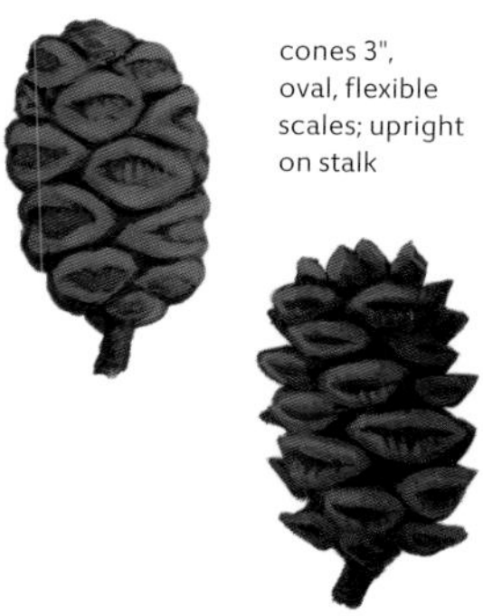

cones 3", oval, flexible scales; upright on stalk

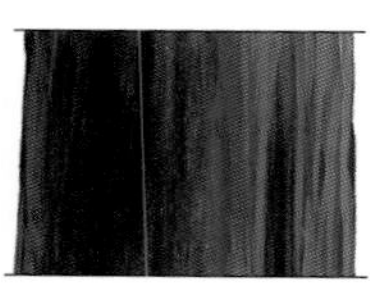

bark reddish-brown, fibrous

Bigleaf Podocarp

Podocarpus macrophyllus

JAPANESE YEW, YEW PINE

Evergreen. Shrub or sometimes a small tree usually 20–30' tall (max. 40'); usually a large dense shrub.

leaves 5½", narrow, willow-like

seed cones ¼", blue, berry-like on bright red stalks; ripe Oct–Nov

leaves bunch at tips of branches with vigorous growth

Several other species of podocarps are cultivated in warmer parts of North America.

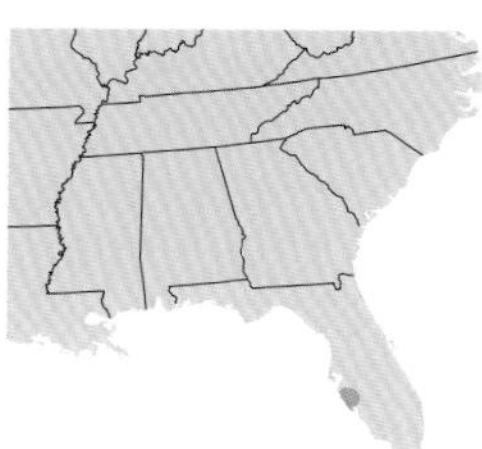

Native to China and southern Japan. Commonly cultivated; naturalized in central Florida (zones 7–9).

Ginkgo Family

The Ginkgo is truly a living fossil and one of the most unusual trees in the world. The genus is known from fossils that date back 270 million years and are nearly identical to present-day trees. Only a few species of ginkgos have ever been identified in the fossil record, and only a single species is extant.

The Ginkgo is classified not just in its own family, but in a separate division of the kingdom Plantae. Of the trees covered in this guide, all that precede Ginkgo are in the division Pinophyta; all species that follow Ginkgo are in the division Magnoliophyta, and only the Ginkgo is in the division Ginkgophyta. The exact relationship of Ginkgo to other living plants is uncertain.

The fruit produced by female Ginkgo trees is technically a naked seed with a fleshy outer coat (somewhat like yews) suggesting a relationship with the gymnosperms. The leaves, however, are unique among modern trees: similar to ferns with a fan-like vein pattern that simply forks repeatedly and never develops the net-like veins of broadleaf trees. Ginkgo seeds are fertilized by motile sperm, as in cycads, ferns, mosses, and algae.

Ginkgos disappear from the fossil record about 2 million years ago, but have long been cultivated in Asia, and are now cultivated worldwide.

Extracts of Ginkgo leaves have long been used medicinally, and some modern studies suggests they may have a few potentially beneficial effects, such as improving blood flow. However, the most broadly-advertised claims—that Ginkgo extract enhances memory and prevents dementia—have not been confirmed by research. The wood of ginkgos has never been used commercially, but the seeds are a popular specialty food item in Asia. The species is important as an ornamental tree with a very high tolerance for the confined spaces and pollution of cities. Four Ginkgo trees about a mile from the 1945 atomic blast at Hiroshima, Japan, were among the very few living things that survived, and soon regained their full health.

Ginkgo

Ginkgo biloba

MAIDENHAIR TREE, GOLDEN FOSSIL TREE, STINKBOMB TREE

Deciduous. Medium to large tree often 40–70' tall (max. 128'). Crown oval to conical, often lopsided with long straight branches jutting out. Alternate names refer to the resemblance of the leaves to maidenhair fern, the bright golden fall color, and the pungent smell of the fruit.

leaves fan-shaped
3", all veins radiating
from base

fruit slightly oval,
1", on long stalk;
yellow to orange;
ripe in fall (Aug–Nov)

Native to China, but nearly or entirely extinct in the wild. Commonly cultivated as an ornamental yard and street tree, but very rarely naturalized (zones 4–8); many cultivars.

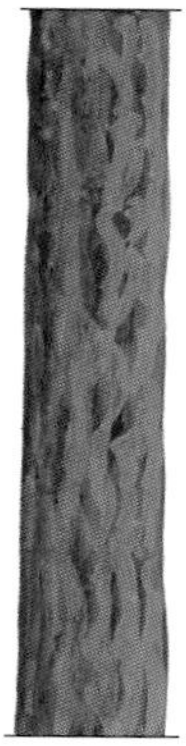

bark on young trunk rough, gray

mature bark pale gray, furrowed, with flattened ridges

flowers in catkin-like clusters, early spring with leaves (Mar–May)

many spur twigs thick, knobby

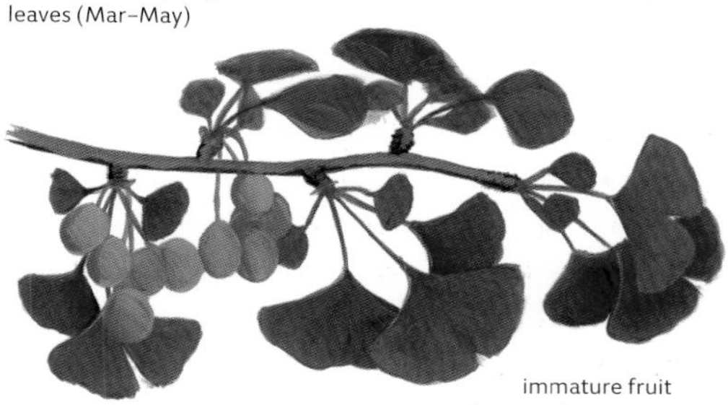

immature fruit pale green in summer

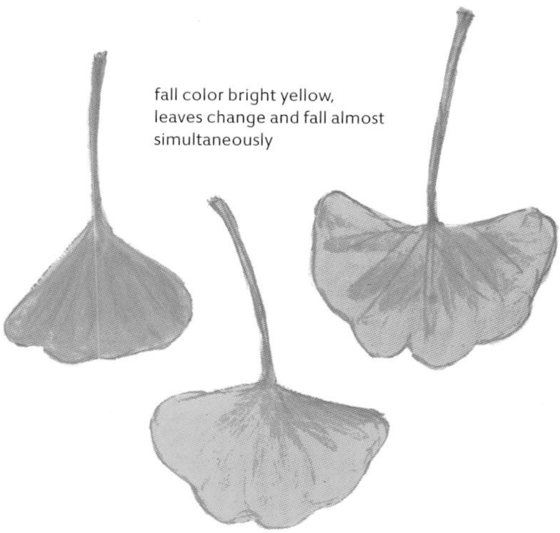

fall color bright yellow, leaves change and fall almost simultaneously

No definite wild population of Ginkgo trees is known to exist. Two small groves in China appear to be wild, but may have been planted by Chinese monks about 1,000 years ago.

winter tree gaunt and irregular with sparse straight branches

sparse, tapered winter twigs covered with knobby spur twigs

Palm Family

The palm family (Arecaceae) includes about 2,500 mostly tropical species of trees, shrubs, and vines. Of the twenty-nine species native to North America, only four are tree-like and cold-hardy enough to grow in the region covered by this book. Four native species and six other cold-hardy exotics are illustrated here. Dozens of other species are commonly cultivated in frost-free regions.

Palms are tremendously important to humans in the tropics, providing a variety of foods, fibers, and oils. In North America, some palms are grown commercially for their fruit (dates), but palms grown here are mostly ornamental.

Rio Grande Palmetto

Sabal mexicana

MEXICAN CABBAGE PALM, TEXAS SABAL PALM

Very similar to Cabbage Palmetto; may average shorter with flower stalk shorter than leaves, fruit brown (vs. blackish). Formerly common in southern Texas along lower Rio Grande Valley, now rare and local, but still commonly cultivated near native range.

may retain
dead leaves
along trunk

Cabbage Palmetto

Sabal palmetto

CABBAGE PALM, CAROLINA PALMETTO

Evergreen. Small to medium tree often 40' tall (max. 90'). Flower stalk as long as leaves (mainly Jun–Aug), fruit black. The state tree of Florida and South Carolina; our most cold-hardy native palm tree.

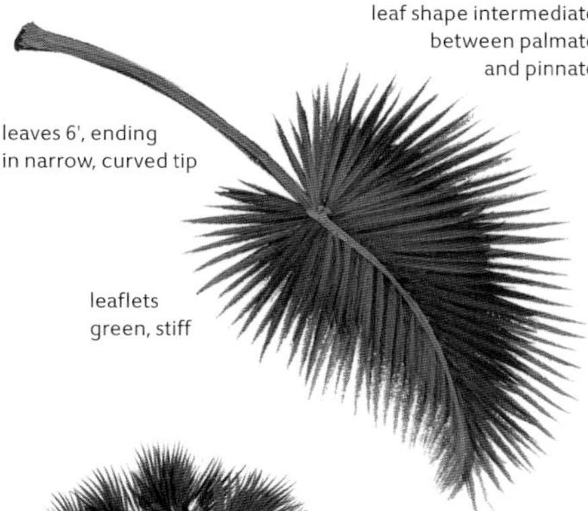
leaf shape intermediate
between palmate
and pinnate
leaves 6', ending
in narrow, curved tip
leaflets
green, stiff

trunk may retain
dead leaves,
but most shed
old leaves
older trunks,
smooth, gray

Common along coastal plain in maritime dune forests, flatwoods, brackish edges; commonly cultivated, and highly tolerant of wind and salt (zones 8–10).

California Fan Palm

Washingtonia filiferia

DESERT FAN PALM, CALIFORNIA WASHINGTONIA, PETTICOAT PALM

Evergreen. Medium to large tree to 60' tall (max. 101'); rounded crown on tall, thick trunk. Old leaves persist along trunk, but are usually trimmed from cultivated trees.

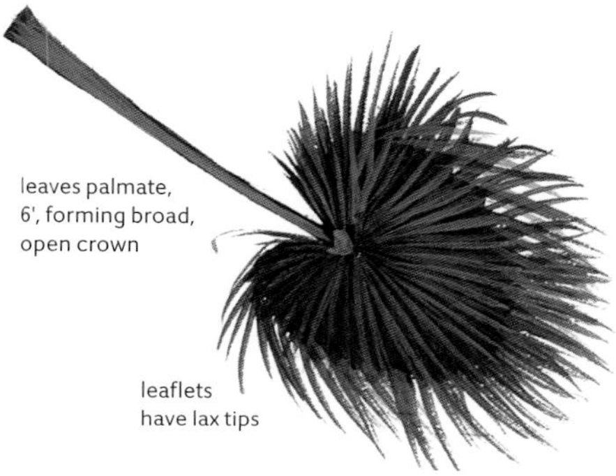
leaves palmate, 6', forming broad, open crown
leaflets have lax tips

flower cluster on stalk much longer than leaves, 10'
fruit black to brown

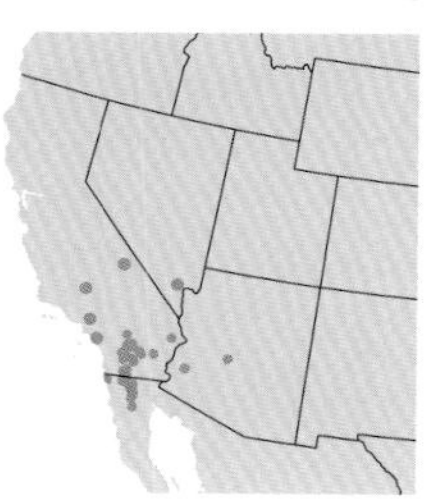

Native to northwestern Mexico and southern California; commonly cultivated near its native range. Slightly more cold-hardy than Mexican Fan Palm (zones 8–11).

Mexican Fan Palm

Washingtonia robusta

WASHINGTON PALM

Evergreen. Native to Mexico and commonly cultivated in Florida, less in California (zones 8–11). Very similar to California Fan, but tends to be taller, with denser crown and stiffer leaflets. Hybrids occur and identification can be difficult.

Palms are easily recognized, and differ from other trees in several fundamental ways. Their trunks are an undifferentiated bundle of fibers and they do not grow annual layers of new wood. Trunks do not grow thicker each year, only taller. Virtually all palms have a single unbranched stem, with new leaves growing at the tip of the stem.

Saw-Palmetto

Serenoa repens

Evergreen. Sprawling shrub or occasionally a small tree to 20' tall (max. 25'); slender trunk, leaning and curving, with relatively small crown; most often tree-like in coastal hammocks.

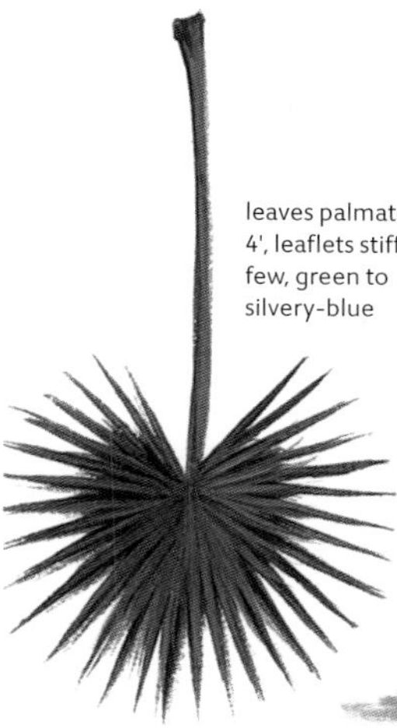
leaves palmate, 4', leaflets stiff, few, green to silvery-blue

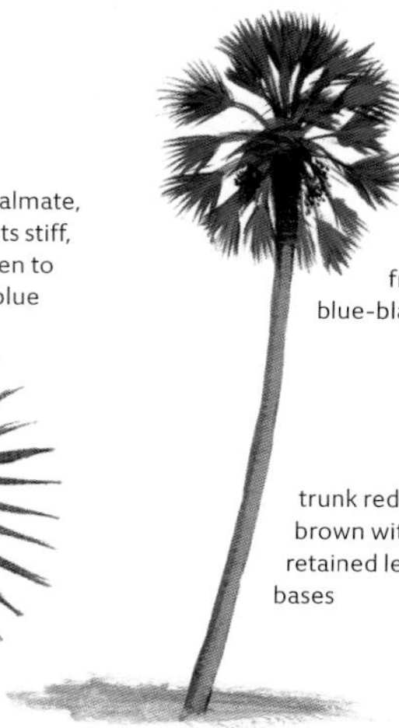
fruit blue-black
trunk reddish brown with retained leaf bases

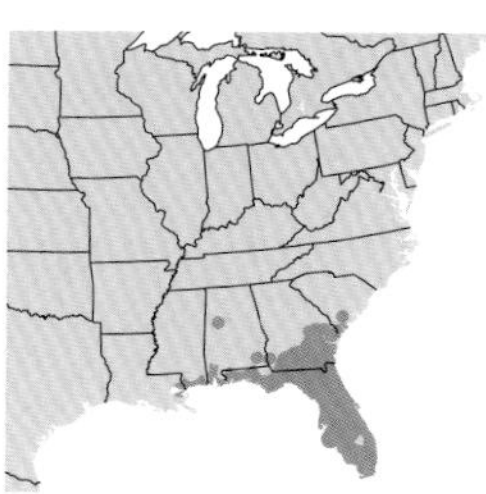

Common in maritime forests and pine flatwoods. Occasionally cultivated within native range (zones 8–10).

Canary Island Date Palm

Phoenix canariensis

PINEAPPLE PALM

Evergreen. Medium tree often 40' tall (max. about 60'); an imposing tree with stout trunk and very long feathery leaves.

leaves pinnate, huge, 15', stiff, gray-green with many short leaflets

flower stalks 3', orange; fruit yellow
trunk rough, often wider near crown

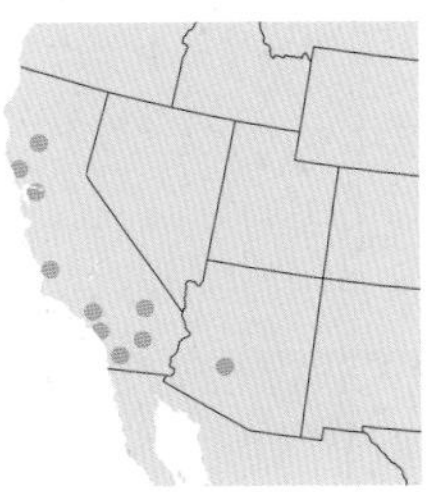

Native to Canary Islands. Commonly cultivated as a street and park tree in well-drained soil in dry or humid climates (zones 9–11).

Seventeen species of date palms are native across Tropical Africa and Asia. At least six of these are cultivated in North America, but all hybridize freely when grown together (e.g. in cultivation) and identification to species is often impossible. Canary Island Date Palm is the most numerous as a landscape tree, while a similar species, Date Palm (*Phoenix dactylifera*) is grown commercially in California and Arizona for its fruit. The Senegal Date Palm (*Phoenix reclinata*) is a small, multi-trunked date palm cultivated in zones 9–11.

Jelly Palm

Butia capitata

PINDO PALM, BRAZILIAN BUTIA, BECCARI

Evergreen. Small tree usually under 20' tall (max. 28') with short, stout trunk. Similar to date palms, but smaller, with much smaller leaves. Native to eastern Brazil. Tolerant of heat, drought, and salt; commonly cultivated and locally naturalized along coastal plain from Florida to North Carolina (zones 8–11).

leaves 6', arched, pinnate, blue-green

flower clusters relatively short, yellow to pinkish
fruit 1", yellow to orange, sweet and edible in large heavy clusters
stout trunk, rough, with retained leaves near crown

Mazari Palm

Nannorrhops ritchiana

MEZRI PALM

Occasionally a small tree to 20' tall (max. about 25'); low-growing, sprawling, and multi-trunked. Native to Asia. Occasionally cultivated (zones 8–11).

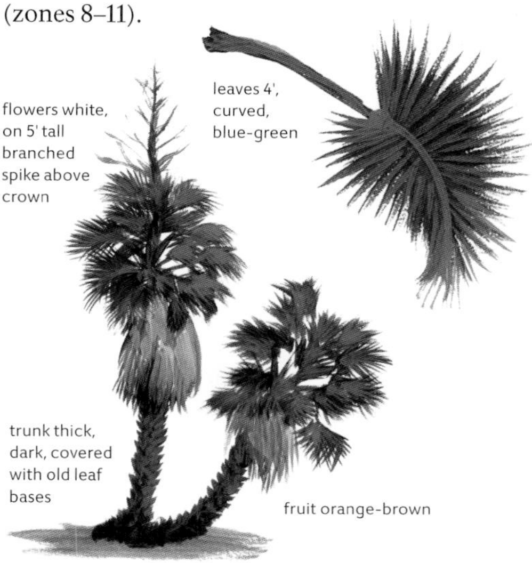
flowers white, on 5' tall branched spike above crown
leaves 4', curved, blue-green
trunk thick, dark, covered with old leaf bases
fruit orange-brown

Chilean Wine Palm

Jubaea chilensis

COQUITO PALM, HONEY PALM

Medium to large tree often 30–50' tall (max. about 80'); massive with thick trunk and broad gray-green crown. Native to Chile. Commonly cultivated and fairly cold-hardy (zones 8–10).

leaves 14', bright green above, gray-green below; pinnate like date palms
fruit orange-brown
flowers purple, on 4' stalks hidden among leaves
sweet sap collected to make syrup or wine

Chinese Windmill Palm

Trachycarpus fortunei

CHINESE FAN PALM, CHUSAN PALM

Evergreen. Small tree usually 10–20' tall (max. about 40'). Native to Asia. Commonly cultivated and locally naturalized in Seattle (zones 7–10); our most cold-hardy palm.

leaves palmate, circular, 2½' across; relatively short-stalked with broad and blunt-tipped leaflets
fruit bluish
flowerstalk short
trunk usually rough with ragged leaf bases

European Fan Palm

Chamaerops humilis

DWARF FAN PALM, HAIR PALM

Evergreen. Small tree to 20' tall (max. 40'). Cold-hardy; only palm native to Europe. Commonly cultivated in California and Southeast, rare farther north (zones 8–10).

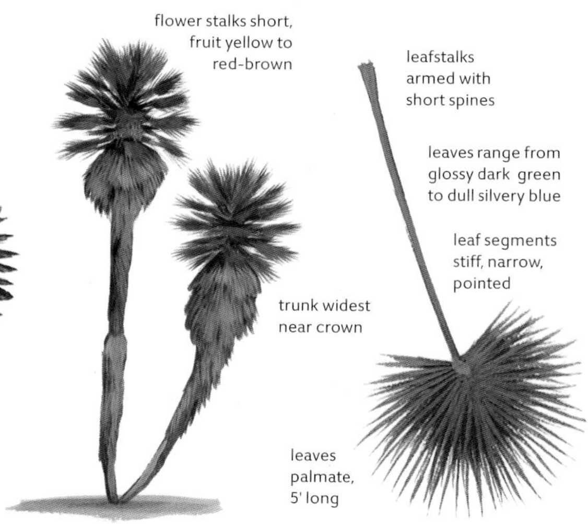
flower stalks short, fruit yellow to red-brown
leafstalks armed with short spines
leaves range from glossy dark green to dull silvery blue
leaf segments stiff, narrow, pointed
trunk widest near crown
leaves palmate, 5' long

Joshua Tree

Yucca brevifolia

YUCCA PALM, PALM TREE YUCCA

Evergreen. Shrub or small tree often 20' tall (max. 48'). Very distinctive, odd form with few contorted branches, each ending in a spiky cluster of leaves. Several other species of yuccas can occasionally grow to small tree size and appear similar to Joshua Tree.

leaves slender stiff spikes 12" long, shorter than most yuccas
flowers, greenish-white, in clusters 20" long (Feb–Apr)
trunk shaggy with old leaves

Yuccas are in the Agave family (Agavaceae). There are about 40 species of yuccas worldwide, with about 25 native to North America, 11 of which are reported to reach tree size. All are very similar in appearance, and only the Joshua Tree is commonly tree-like.

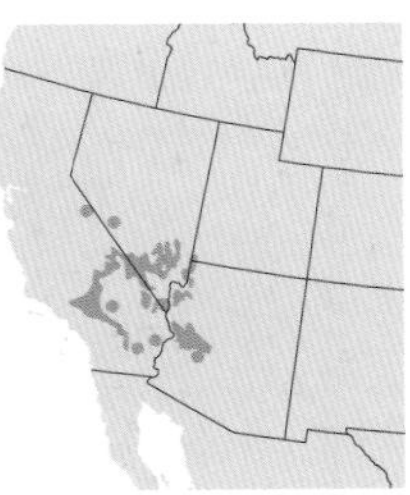

Common locally in its very limited range in sandy and rocky desert flats. Uncommonly cultivated near native range (zones 7–10).

Saguaro

Cereus giganteus

Columnar cactus, often 20' tall (max. 50'); sharp, densely packed spines on ridges of trunk and branches. This species technically qualifies as a tree, with its height and a single trunk, but lacks typical leaves, bark, and twigs; unlike any other tree and identification is simply not an issue.

large white flowers at branch tips develop oval red fruit
spiny "leaves" along trunk and branches
trunk green, "pleated"

The Saguaro (family Cactaceae), is not closely related to palms, but to Tamarisk, a cedar-like tree (p. 108). The Saguaro shares native habitats in the Sonoran Desert with the Joshua Tree, Yellow Paloverde (p. 120), and Desert Ironwood (p. 124).

Locally common in Sonoran desert, especially on rocky slopes and ridges. Commonly cultivated in and near native range.

Laurel Family

The laurels (family Lauraceae) include about 2,500 mostly tropical species of shrubs and trees worldwide. In North America, twelve species are native. Five native and one cultivated species in four genera are tree-like and cold-hardy in the region covered by this book.

Many species have aromatic oils used in a diverse range of spices and perfumes. Cinnamon, camphor, bay leaves, and root beer are some of the products derived from trees of the laurel family. Commercial bay leaves come from the Bay Laurel (*Laurus nobilis*) native to Europe, which is occasionally cultivated in North America. Leaves of Red Bay are similarly aromatic and can be used like typical bay leaves to season food. Leaves of California Laurel can also be used, but have a much stronger flavor.

The related Avocado (*Persea americana*) is commonly cultivated and locally naturalized in the southern United States, but is not cold-hardy, so it is rarely grown elsewhere.

In marshy areas in the southeastern states, small "islands" of trees with a high concentration of bay trees, called bay heads, are a distinctive ecosystem. They are formed when underlying peat builds up in one area to allow the growth of plants that prefer slightly higher ground.

A fungal disease, known as Laurel Wilt, has spread recently through the southeastern states, attacking bay heads with many Red Bay and related trees. The nonnative Asian Ambrosia Beetle introduces the fungus into trees to provide food for its wood-boring larvae. The growth of the fungus, similar to Dutch Elm Disease, disrupts the tree's sap flow and causes a fatal wilting. Foresters are concerned not only for the future of Red Bay and other bays, but also for other species in the Laurel family, including Sassafras, California Laurel, and the commercially-grown Avocado. Efforts to control the disease are ongoing.

Camphor-Tree

Cinnamomum camphora

CAMPHOR LAUREL

Evergreen. Medium to large tree usually under 50' tall (max. 67'); spreading with elegant drooping twigs and dense rounded crown, but can also form thickets. This species is the source of commercial camphor, and leaves are very aromatic.

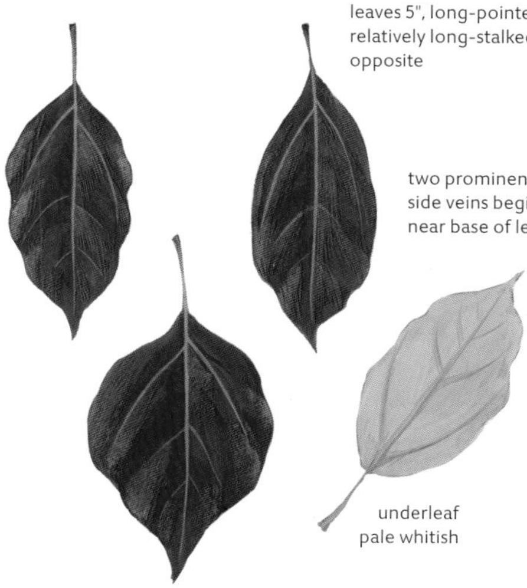
leaves 5", long-pointed, relatively long-stalked, opposite
two prominent side veins begin near base of leaf
underleaf pale whitish

tiny, fragrant, whitish flowers (May) become small, ⅓" blackish berries, ripe in summer
leaves glossy green with wavy edges

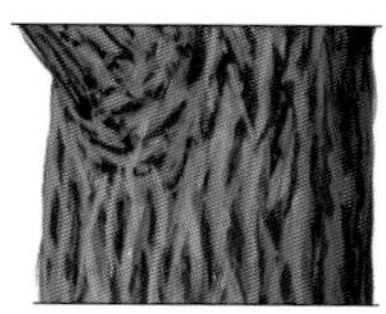
bark gray-brown, furrowed, clean

Native to Japan, China. Commonly cultivated as an ornamental and for commercial camphor, and widely naturalized (zones 9–11)

California Laurel

Umbellularia californica

OREGON MYRTLE, CALIFORNIA BAY, PEPPERWOOD

Evergreen. Small to large tree, usually under 70' tall (max. 150'); rounded crown, dense and dark green, often multi-trunked, many upright branches. Leaf scent among the strongest of any tree, perfuming the air over a large area.

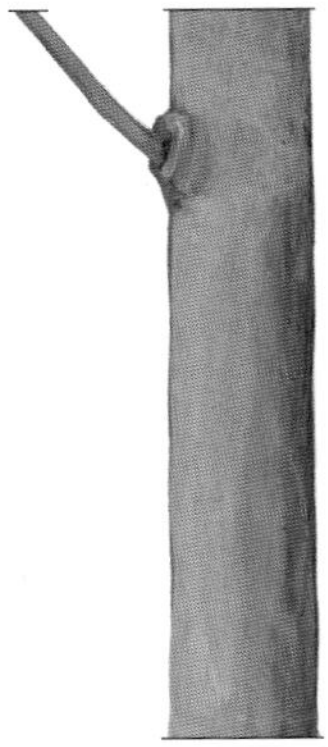
bark of young
trunks smooth gray

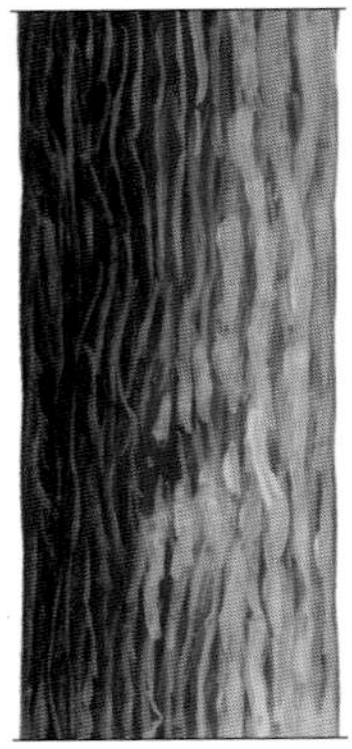
bark on mature trunks
relatively smooth with
many pale low ridges

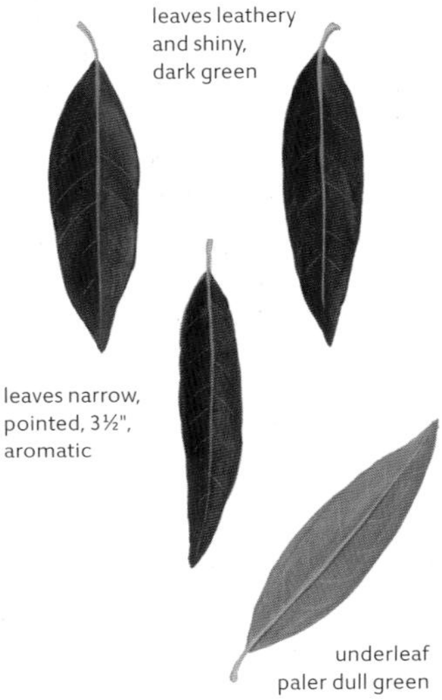
leaves leathery
and shiny,
dark green
leaves narrow,
pointed, 3½",
aromatic
underleaf
paler dull green

usually multi-trunked
and rounded with dense
dark green foliage

flowers tiny,
in yellowish clusters
(Jan–Mar), before
new leaves

fruit olive-like 1", round,
greenish to purple,
ripe in late fall

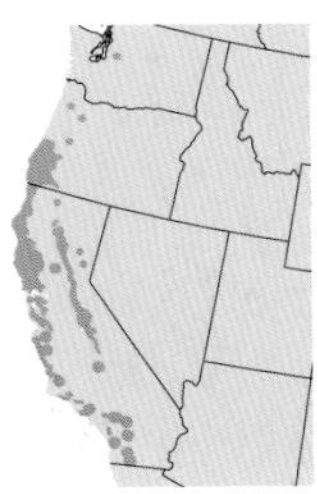

Common in mixed forests in moist soils; coastal foothill canyons, on slopes and along streams. Commonly cultivated along streets and parks in Pacific states (zones 8–10).

Bay Laurel

Laurus nobilis

TRUE LAUREL, SWEET LAUREL, ROYAL BAY

Evergreen. Shrub or small tree often 20–30' tall (max. 62'). Compact, dense, dark tree in warmer regions; shrubby farther north. This species is the source of commercial bay leaves, similar to the related California Laurel, but leaves broader with distinctive crinkled margins, fruit smaller (about ½") and blackish. Native to the Mediterranean region. Commonly cultivated and locally escaped (zones 8–10).

Sassafras

Sassafras albidum

WHITE SASSAFRAS, CINNAMON WOOD, MITTENLEAF

Deciduous. Small to medium tree often 40' tall (max. 130') with many stout, contorted, spreading branches. Often spreads by root suckers, forming thickets with domed crown.

bark of young trunks soon develops ridges; saplings and branches green to reddish

bark on mature trunks rough, deeply furrowed

leaves 5" with three main veins from base
leaves can be unlobed, 2-lobed, or 3-lobed (all on the same tree)
underleaf drab green

fall color bright yellow to red

fruit ⅓", dark blue berry on red stalk

flowers small, yellow-green, in loose clusters appearing with leaves in spring
flowers droop as leaves emerge

twigs bright green, turning reddish where exposed to sunlight
buds large, greenish

Aromatic oils in the roots and bark of this tree have been used in many medicinal and cosmetic products. Sassafras roots provided the original flavoring for root beer, and were used until 1960, when certain compounds in the roots were found to be carcinogenic. Root beer is now flavored artificially.

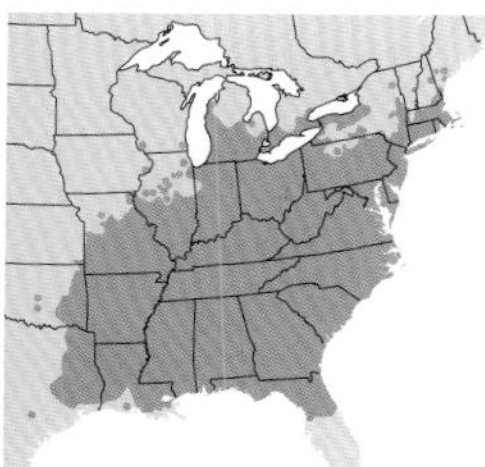

Common in sparse woods or edges, hedgerows, or old fields. Occasionally cultivated (zones 4–9).

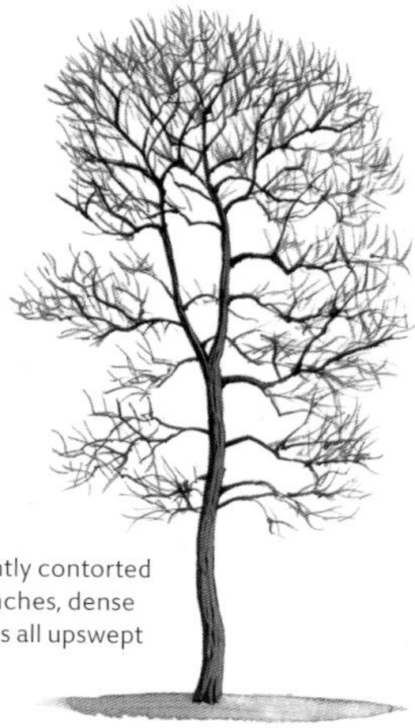
slightly contorted branches, dense twigs all upswept

Red Bay

Persea borbonia

SHOREBAY

Evergreen. Large shrub or small tree usually under 30' tall (max. 77') with dense rounded crown. Many other southeastern trees with similar leaf shape, such as hollies and Sweetbay, have smooth gray bark.

leaves 4½", narrow, short-stalked, shiny dark green
underleaf silky whitish or light brown

fruit oval, ½", blue-black, shiny on short red stem (autumn)

flowers tiny, long-stalked, in axillary clusters, creamy-white (Apr–May)

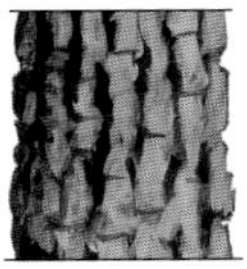
bark dark, deeply grooved and checkered

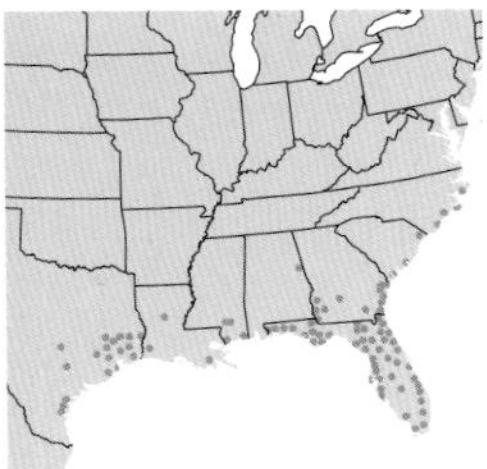

Uncommon to rare, mostly in sandy, well-drained lowland soils such as pine-oak scrub or dune forests. Rarely cultivated (zones 8–9).

Silk Bay

Persea humilis

SCRUB-BAY

Evergreen. Shrub, or sometimes a small tree to 20' tall (max. 41'). Often considered a variety of Red Bay, but differs consistently in microscopic leaf hairs. Rare, found only in central Florida. Not cultivated.

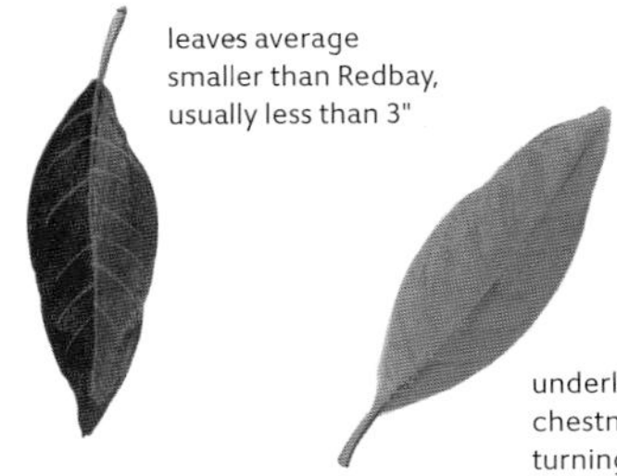
leaves average smaller than Redbay, usually less than 3"
underleaf silky chestnut-brown, turning dark gray

fruit like Red Bay, but longer stalk

Swamp Bay

Persea palustris

SWAMP REDBAY, SWEETBAY

Evergreen. Slender tree occasionally 30' tall (max. 83'). Very similar to Red Bay, but with densely hairy twig (vs. smooth), and found in wetter habitat.

underleaf with brownish fuzz

fruit like Red Bay, but slightly smaller and much longer-stalked

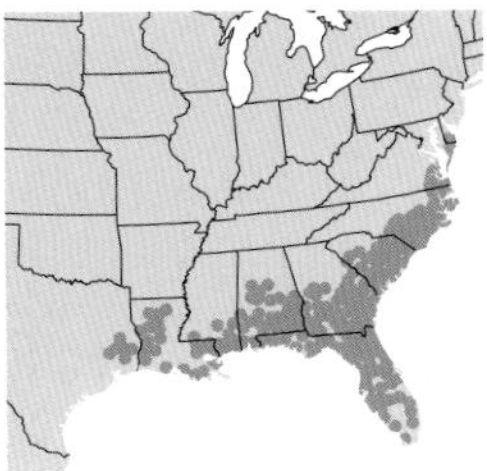

Common in moist to wet soils, swales, less often in drier soils. Rarely cultivated (zones 7–9).

Common Pawpaw

Asimina triloba

CUSTARD APPLE, FALSE-BANANA

Deciduous. Large shrub or small tree usually under 25' tall (max. 60'); often forming thickets, wide-topped with sparse, straight branches, distinctive flowers and fruit. The northernmost representative of the tropical Custard-Apples (family Annonaceae).

bark thin smooth,
gray to dark brown

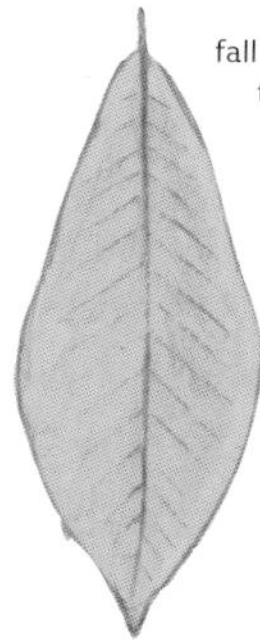
fall color yellow
to cinnamon

many straight
parallel veins
leaves large 9",
narrow base,
short-pointed
underleaf
paler green

fruit lumpy, oblong
4" long, yellow to dark brown
edible with sweet banana-like flavor and
soft texture; ripe in autumn after leaf fall

Up to 8 species of pawpaws are recognized in North America. Only the Common Pawpaw is regularly tree-sized; the others are small to large shrubs (two species are rarely tree-like reaching 20' tall). All are generally similar to Common Pawpaw but with smaller leaves and flowers.

flowers 2", dark purple, bell-like,
hanging below twigs in spring
with new leaves
(Mar–Jun)

twig pale brown
buds dark brown,
without scales

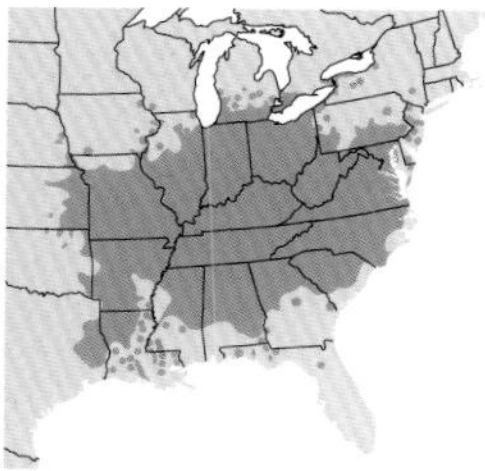

Uncommon in rich mesic soils in hardwood forests, bottomlands. Uncommonly cultivated, mostly within native range (zones 5–8).

small tree with
sparse, straight
branches

Magnolia Family

The magnolias (family Magnoliaceae) includes about 100 species in ten genera worldwide. In North America, eight species in the genus *Magnolia* and one in the genus *Liriodendron* (Tuliptree) are native. All are tree-like. These nine species and two additional Asian species that are commonly cultivated are included in this guide.

The magnolias are an ancient lineage of trees and are considered "primitive" by botanists. Most other plants with showy flowers have large and colorful petals backed by smaller, leaf-like sepals. On magnolias, these two parts are not differentiated, and the flower is composed simply of some number of "tepals," intermediate between petals and sepals. Magnolia flowers are pollinated mostly by beetles, considered primitive, given the relatively recent evolution of bees.

Magnolia flowers are large and showy, white in nearly all species, but yellowish-green in Cucumbertree and pink in some Asian hybrids.

Magnolia fruits develop in an upright aggregate cluster at the tip of the twig. When ripe, the individual capsules split open and a small (usually red) berry-like fruit is released dangling from a silky stalk. Birds are the main consumers of these fruits, and disperse the seeds widely.

Leaves of most magnolias are large and relatively floppy, remaining pale, translucent green, with wavy or rolled edges, for weeks after they emerge. Fall color of most species is yellowish to pale brown.

The wood of magnolias is little used, with most species being too small or too scarce for commerce. The primary economic value of the genus is ornamental, and the magnolias are very popular planted trees in yards and parks.

The bark of at least some magnolias has long been used in traditional medicine in China and Japan. Certain compounds found in the bark have shown some promise for treating a variety of conditions, from anxiety to allergies to periodontal disease.

The Tuliptree is a very distinctive member of the magnolia family, with very different leaf shape, bark, and growing habit. Its flowers share some fundamental similarities with magnolias, and the fruit is also an upright cluster, but in the Tuliptree, each seed has a long papery wing, and these fall individually through the winter.

leaf color in fall varies by species, some yellow to maroon, others pale yellow to ash-brown

berry-like fruit ranges from smooth to hairy

flowers usually white tepals (petals and sepals not differentiated)

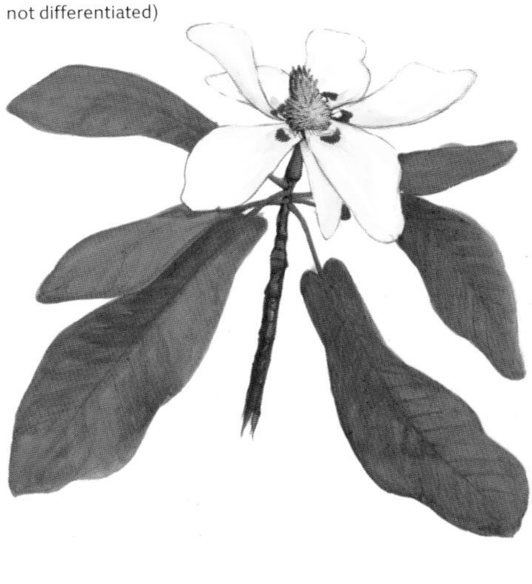

Cucumbertree

Magnolia acuminata

MOUNTAIN MAGNOLIA, INDIAN-BITTER

Deciduous. Medium tree often 50–80' tall (max. 125') with straight trunk; pyramidal when young but spreading in maturity. Fall leaf color ranges from maroon to rich yellow. The only magnolia with furrowed bark, yellow-green flowers.

bark furrowed with straight, flat-topped ridges; gray-brown

leaves large, 8", pointed tip and wavy edge, yellow-green

underleaf pale green

opening flower green with pale papery bud scales

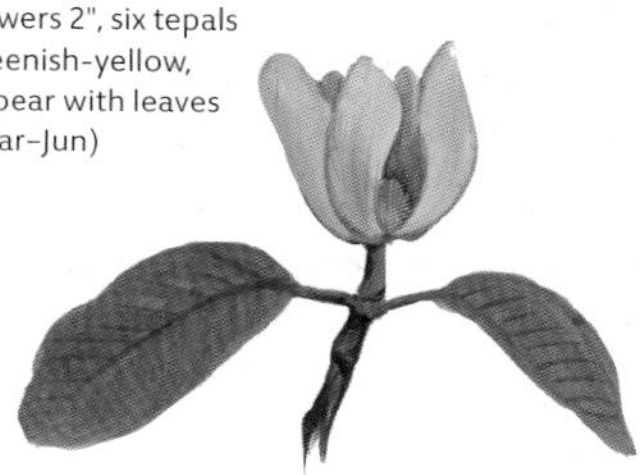

flowers 2", six tepals greenish-yellow, appear with leaves (Mar–Jun)

fruit 2½", irregular, red-brown, not hairy

buds large, blunt-tipped, often silky gray

straight central trunk; note straight vertical shoots from branches

Yellow Cucumbertree (var. *cordata*) has smaller and broader leaves, smaller and more yellow flowers , and hairy twigs Rare in the wild and uncommon in cultivation (zones 5–8)

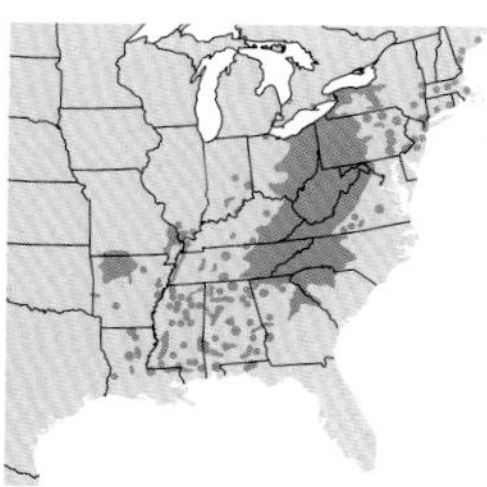

Common in rich woods, coves, streamsides. Commonly cultivated as a large and attractive shade tree, many cultivars including yellow-flowered varieties; zones 4–8.

Fraser Magnolia

Magnolia fraseri

EARLEAF MAGNOLIA, MOUNTAIN MAGNOLIA

Deciduous. Small to medium tree, often 40' tall (max. 110'); large, diamond-shaped leaves, green below (very similar to Pyramid Magnolia).

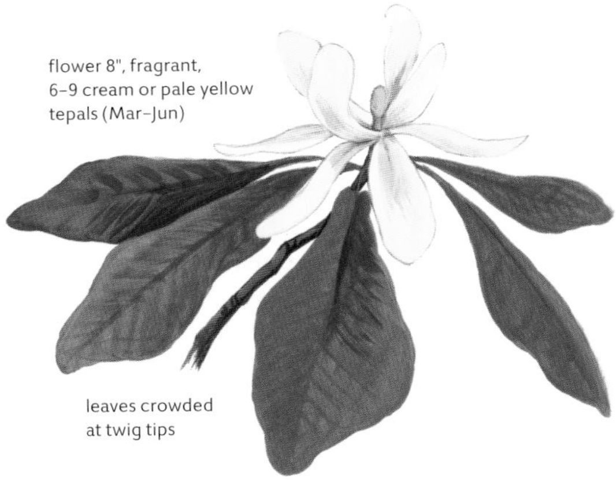
flower 8", fragrant,
6–9 cream or pale yellow
tepals (Mar–Jun)
leaves crowded
at twig tips

long petiole
about 3", often
reddish
leaves 10", diamond-shaped,
smaller than Bigleaf and Ashe,
widest above middle

underleaf
greenish
conspicuously
lobed at base

fruit 3½",
rose red,
not hairy

twigs bright red-brown
flower buds
smooth, purple-green

Common in rich woods in mountain valleys and slopes. Rarely cultivated, (zones 5–8).

Pyramid Magnolia

Magnolia pyramidata

SOUTHERN CUCUMBERTREE, MOUNTAIN MAGNOLIA

Deciduous. Usually a shrub or small tree under 30' tall, (max. 98'). Very similar to Fraser, but leaves smaller, flowers half as large (4" across vs. 9") with shorter stamens, fruit averages smaller, native range does not overlap.

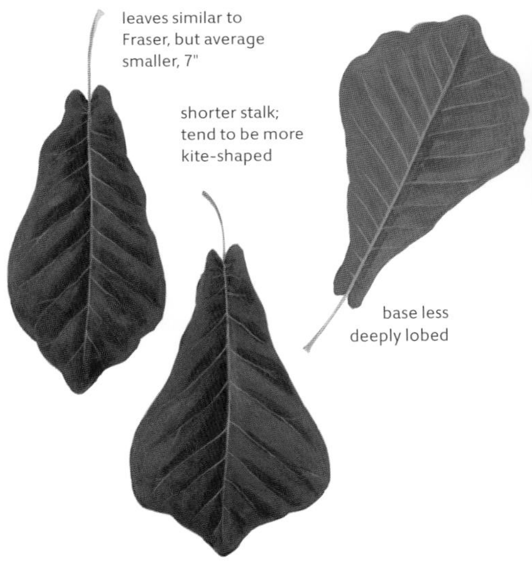
leaves similar to
Fraser, but average
smaller, 7"
shorter stalk;
tend to be more
kite-shaped
base less
deeply lobed

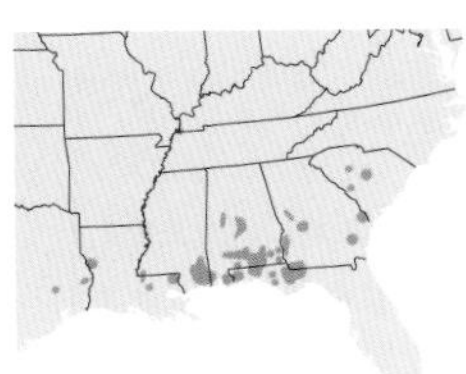

Rare in rich upland woods. Rarely cultivated (zones 6–9).

Bigleaf Magnolia

Magnolia macrophylla

SILVERLEAF MAGNOLIA, WHITE CUCUMBERTREE

Deciduous. Small tree with straight upright trunk, often 30–40' tall (max. 108'); round-topped, broad. Huge leaves, silvery-white below, striking (very similar to Ashe Magnolia).

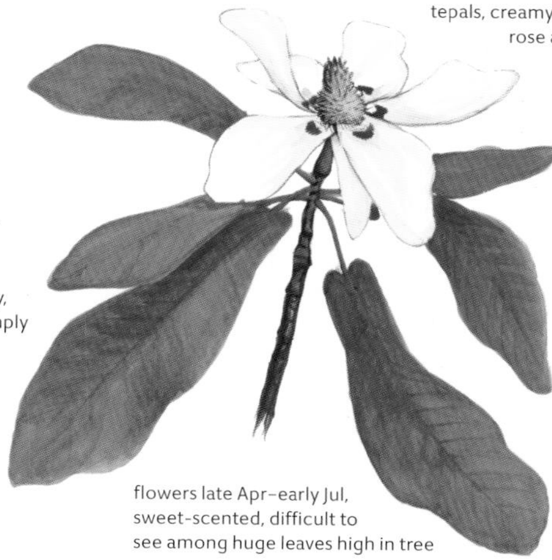
flowers 11" across, 6 (sometimes 9) tepals, creamy white, rose at base
leaves floppy, drooping limply from midrib
flowers late Apr–early Jul, sweet-scented, difficult to see among huge leaves high in tree

leaf huge, 25" (max. 42")
base shallowly lobed
often widest above middle, rounded or blunt-pointed

underleaf silver-white

fruit 3½", rounded, rose-red, hairy

flower buds and new twigs silky whitish

A closely related species native of Mexico, *Magnolia dealbata*, is occasionally cultivated in California and Texas (zone 8–10).

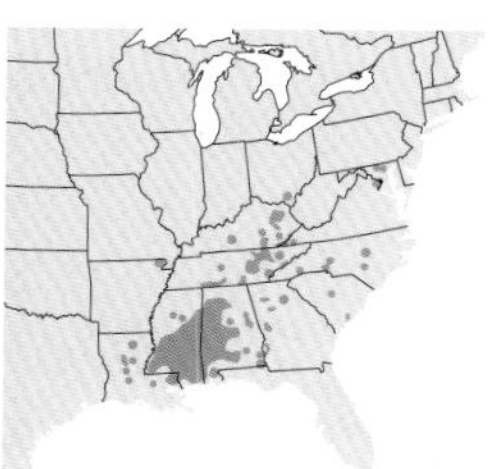

Uncommon and local in rich moist woods from bottomlands to slopes, infrequently cultivated (zones 5–8).

Ashe Magnolia

Magnolia ashei

SANDHILL MAGNOLIA, DWARF BIGLEAF MAGNOLIA

Deciduous. Shrub or occasionally a small tree to 30' tall (max. 52'), with leaning trunk and low branches. Very similar to Bigleaf; distinguished by range and by slightly smaller flower (9" vs. 11") with fewer stamens (about 200 vs. about 500).

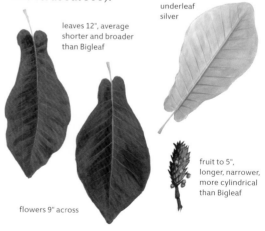

leaves 12", average shorter and broader than Bigleaf

underleaf silver

fruit to 5", longer, narrower, more cylindrical than Bigleaf

flowers 9" across

Rare and local in rich woods, found only in northwest Florida. Rarely cultivated (zones 6–9).

Umbrella Magnolia

Magnolia tripetala

ELKWOOD

Deciduous. Large shrub or small tree typically 15–30' tall, (max. 80'); usually multi-trunked and broad-spreading, somewhere between tree and shrub. Name refers to large leaves clustered at branch tips (a habit shared with other large-leaved magnolias).

bark gray-brown,
smooth

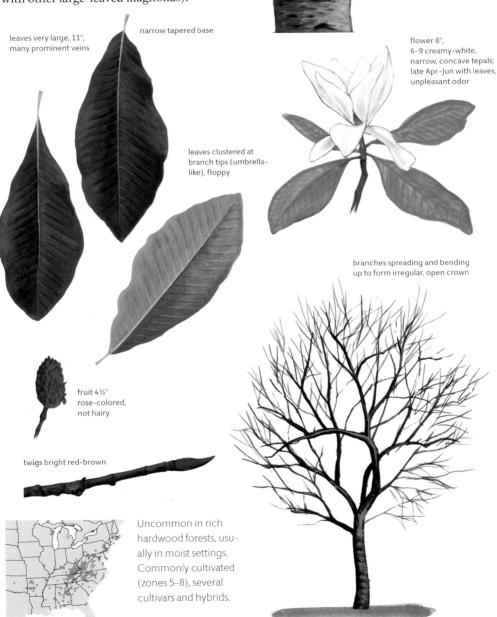

leaves very large, 11",
many prominent veins
narrow tapered base
leaves clustered at
branch tips (umbrella-
like), floppy

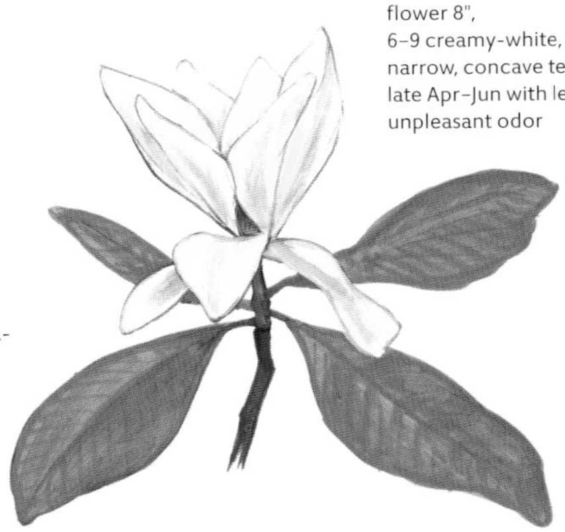
flower 8",
6–9 creamy-white,
narrow, concave tepals;
late Apr–Jun with leaves,
unpleasant odor

branches spreading and bending
up to form irregular, open crown

fruit 4½"
rose-colored,
not hairy

twigs bright red-brown

Uncommon in rich hardwood forests, usually in moist settings. Commonly cultivated (zones 5–8), several cultivars and hybrids.

Southern Magnolia

Magnolia grandiflora

EVERGREEN MAGNOLIA,
GREAT FLOWERED MAGNOLIA, BULL BAY

Evergreen. Small to medium tree, often 50' tall, (max. 98'), generally pyramidal. Shares leathery leaves and chambered pith with Sweetbay, distinguished by larger leaves, reddish below.

bark gray-brown,
smooth; developing
some scales with age

leaves 6"
shiny dark green,
very thick, stiff,
leathery
base usually
rounded
underleaf
usually pale
green, but rusty haired
in some cultivars

flower 8" across; 6–12
creamy-white tepals, fragrant;
appear in late spring and
occasionally
in fall

fruit oval

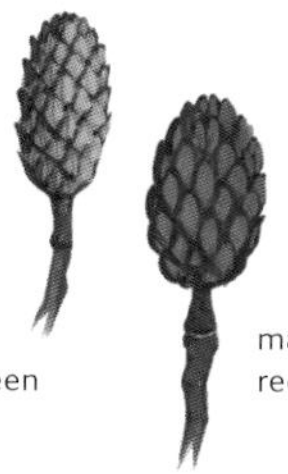
developing
fruit pale green
mature fruit 3½",
red-rusty, hairy

buds and young
twigs rusty-hairy

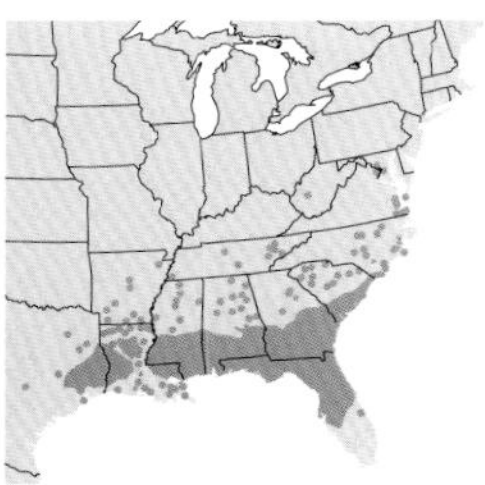

Common in a variety of wooded habitats from damp lowlands to dunes. Very commonly cultivated and escaped north of native range (zones 7–9); many cultivars.

usually pyramidal shape
with low branches; dense
dark foliage with
rusty underleaf
showing

Sweetbay

Magnolia virginiana

SWAMP BAY, LAUREL MAGNOLIA

Tardily deciduous or semi-evergreen. Shrub or small tree often 40' (max. 70'). Usually shrubby and deciduous in the North, tree-like and evergreen in the South. All parts of the tree are aromatic, hence the name, Sweetbay.

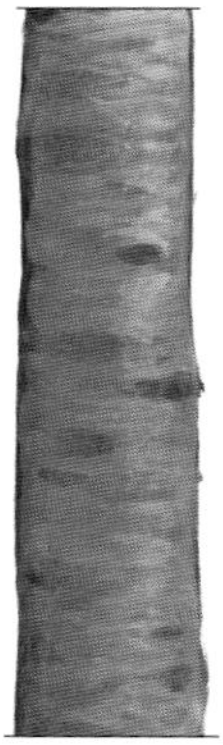

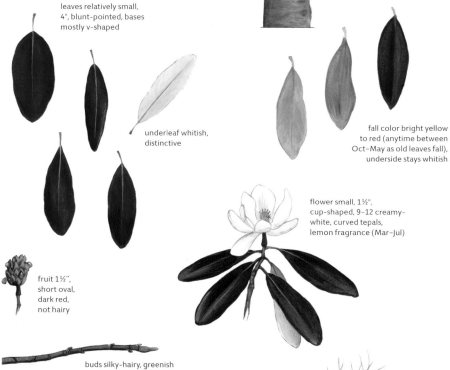

bark light gray-brown, smooth to scaly

leaves relatively small, 4", blunt-pointed, bases mostly v-shaped

underleaf whitish, distinctive

fall color bright yellow to red (anytime between Oct–May as old leaves fall), underside stays whitish

flower small, 1½", cup-shaped, 9–12 creamy-white, curved tepals, lemon fragrance (Mar–Jul)

fruit 1½", short oval, dark red, not hairy

buds silky-hairy, greenish

Nominally evergreen in the South, Sweetbay drops leaves in spring after one year. Old leaves are dull dark green, turning gray-brown or red before falling. The mixture of dark green, grayish and red alongside the bright yellow-green of new growth is distinctive in spring.

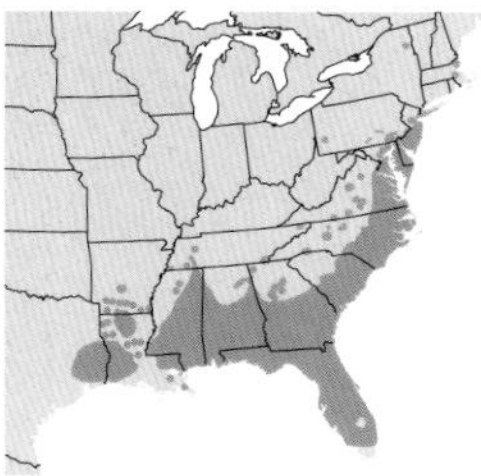

Common in wet soil, in swamps or along streams in lowlands; often with Sweetgum; commonly cultivated (zones 5–9).

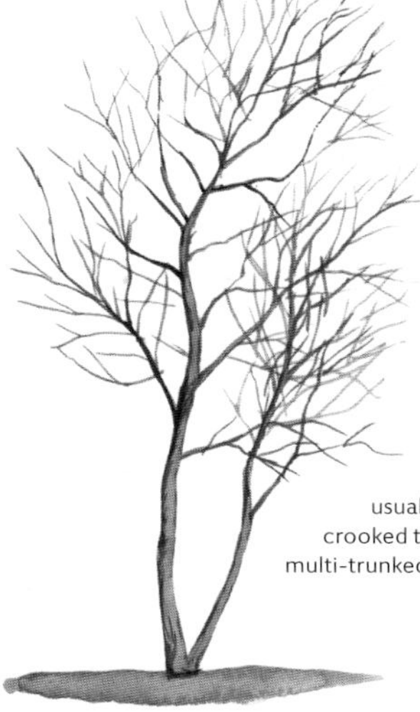

usually a small, crooked tree, often multi-trunked, shrubby

'Saucer' Magnolia

Magnolia '× soulangiana'

COMMON MAGNOLIA, LILY TREE

Deciduous. A small bushy tree commonly 20–30' tall. Short-trunked with spreading branches, large whitish buds. Pink flowers in spring appear slightly later than other Asian magnolias.

Many species, hybrids, and cultivars of Asian magnolias are grown for ornament. As a rule, they flower in early spring before their leaves emerge and before the native magnolias. While most native species have creamy-white to pale greenish flowers, the most popular Asian cultivars have profuse flowers of bright white or rosy-pink, making for a spectacular floral display against the gray backdrop of early spring.

leaves 5", dark green, stiff with wavy edge
underleaf paler green

leaves dark green, stiff, arched

flowers 7½", white, pink, or purple, 9 tepals (Mar–Apr) before leaves

buds large, 1", silky gray-white, blunt

tree in full flower is spectacular pale pink

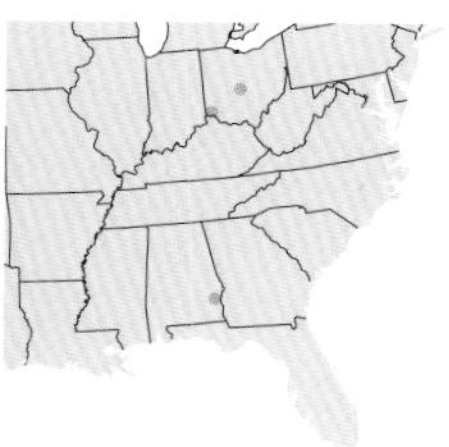

The most commonly cultivated magnolia (zones 4–9); many cultivars. Garden hybrid of 2 Chinese species, *M. denudata × liliiflora.*

Star Magnolia

Magnolia stellata

Deciduous. Shrub or small tree usually under 20' tall. Similar to 'Saucer' Magnolia, but with smaller buds and leaves, white flowers with more tepals that flop loosely. Native to Japan. Very commonly cultivated (zones 4–8), many cultivars.

leaves oval, small, 3"

fruit a small irregular cluster

flowers white, 3½", 12–18 tepals, (late Feb–Apr)

buds oval, silky gray-white

Tuliptree

Liriodendron tulipifera

YELLOW-POPLAR, WHITE-POPLAR

Deciduous. Medium to large tree, often 90' tall (max. 200'). One of the largest hardwood trees in North America, with clear straight trunk. Leaf shape is unique, as are tulip-like flowers. Only one other species in the genus, native to Asia.

young bark smooth, faintly striped or speckled with dark chevrons at branch sites

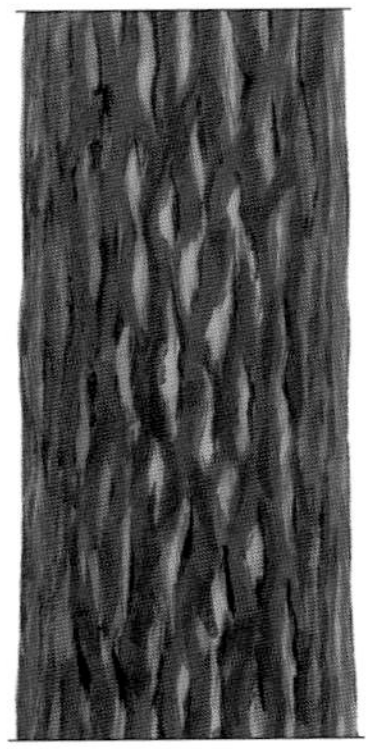

mature trunk has distinct chiseled ridges with paler furrows

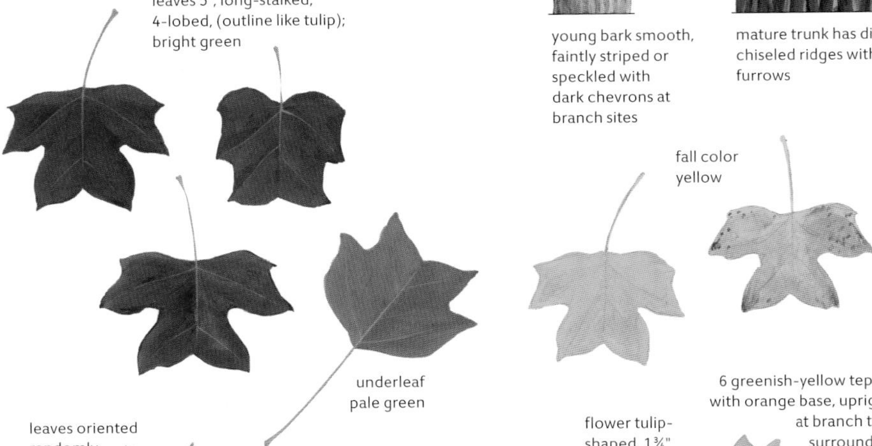

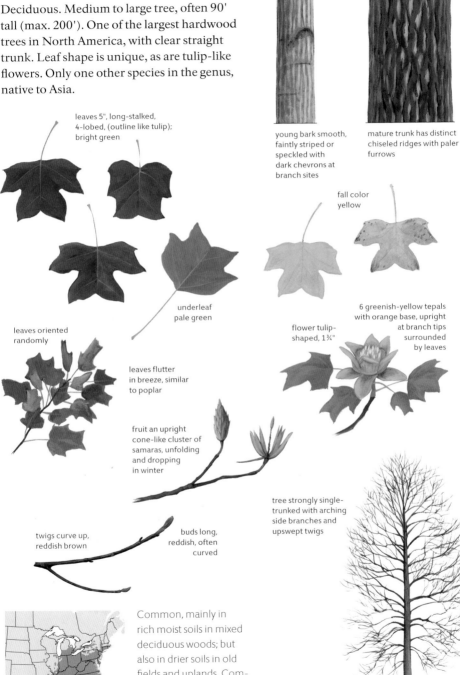

leaves 5", long-stalked, 4-lobed, (outline like tulip); bright green

underleaf pale green

fall color yellow

leaves oriented randomly

leaves flutter in breeze, similar to poplar

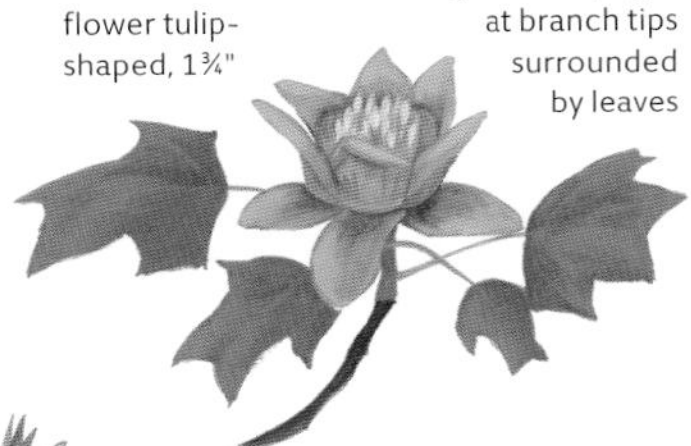

flower tulip-shaped, 1¾"

6 greenish-yellow tepals with orange base, upright at branch tips surrounded by leaves

fruit an upright cone-like cluster of samaras, unfolding and dropping in winter

twigs curve up, reddish brown

buds long, reddish, often curved

tree strongly single-trunked with arching side branches and upswept twigs

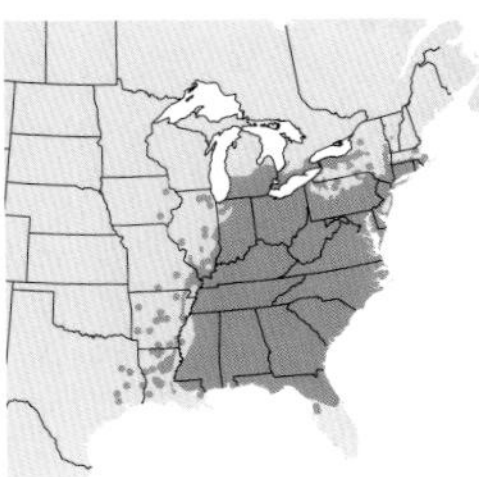

Common, mainly in rich moist soils in mixed deciduous woods; but also in drier soils in old fields and uplands. Commonly cultivated (zones 4–9), many cultivars.

Katsura Family

The Katsura Tree is one of only two species in the family Cercidiphyllaceae, both native to Japan and China. Its closest relatives in North America are the witch-hazels and Sweetgum. Thought to represent the last relicts of an ancient group of trees, katsuras have opposite leaves, soft wood like conifers, and unusual, tiny flowers.

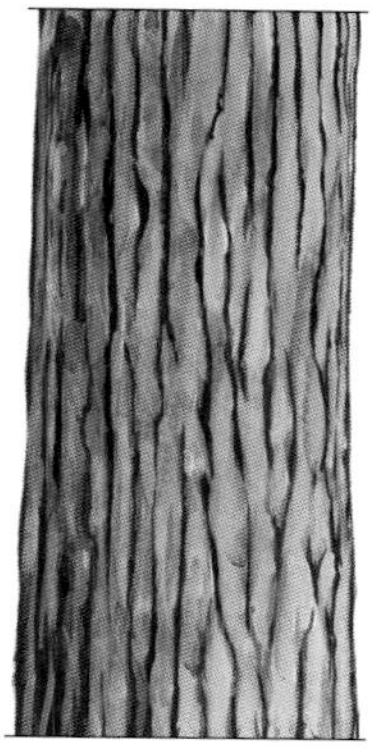
bark splits into narrow strips, pale gray

Katsura Tree

Cercidiphyllum japonicum

Deciduous. Medium tree with dense pyramidal to spreading shape, often 40' tall (max. 100'), often branching low like giant shrub. The largest broadleaf tree in Asia.

fall color scarlet, gold, pink, or mottled

leaves 3", nearly round or heart-shaped, blunt-toothed
3 main veins from base of leaf
underleaf green

twigs slender, reddish brown with pale lenticels
buds small, reddish, curved in towards twig

flowers like small red tufts in leaf axils, in early spring (Mar) before leaves
male flowers smaller than female; sexes on separate trees, wind-pollinated

fruit small, ¾" pods in clusters of 2–4 on short spur along twigs; open in October to release seeds

Native to Japan and China. Commonly cultivated as an ornamental yard and street tree and locally escaped (zones 4–8); several cultivars.

Sycamore Family

The sycamore family (Platanaceae) includes a single genus of tree (*Platanus*) with about ten species of trees worldwide. In North America, three species are native, and one exotic hybrid is commonly cultivated. Sycamores are large and statuesque, with very distinctive smooth, pale, and mottled bark, broad palmate leaves, and seeds clustered in balls that hang on long stalks. Although they grow quickly and large, the wood of sycamores is little-used.

'London Planetree'

Platanus '× *acerifolia*'

HYBRID PLANETREE, LONDON PLANE

Deciduous. Large tree often 70' tall (max. 150'); variable and difficult to distinguish from American Sycamore, but with two or more fruit balls on each stalk, and on average has smaller and more deeply-lobed leaves.

leaves average smaller than American Sycamore, with deeper lobes and fewer teeth
usually 2 (up to 6) fruit balls per stalk, fruit smaller than American with shorter stalk

A cultivated hybrid originating in Europe. Common in cultivation (zones 5–8) as it is tolerant of pollution and poor soil and thrives in cities.

American Sycamore

Platanus occidentalis

BUTTONBALL-TREE, AMERICAN PLANETREE

Deciduous. Large tree often 80' tall (max. 176'); the most massive tree east of Rockies. Large size, pale mottled bark, ball-like fruit, and large, maple-like leaves make sycamores, as a group, instantly recognizable.

leaves oddly floppy, with assorted sizes and angles, some even twisted upside down showing different colors
leaves very large and broad, 7", 3- to 5-lobed with many teeth, drab green
leaves maple-like, but with shorter stalks
underleaf pale green
fruit 1¼" balls, hang singly on 5" stalk; rarely double, ripe in fall, persist all winter
twigs relatively slender, zigzag
buds short, stout, entirely covered by leafstalk in summer

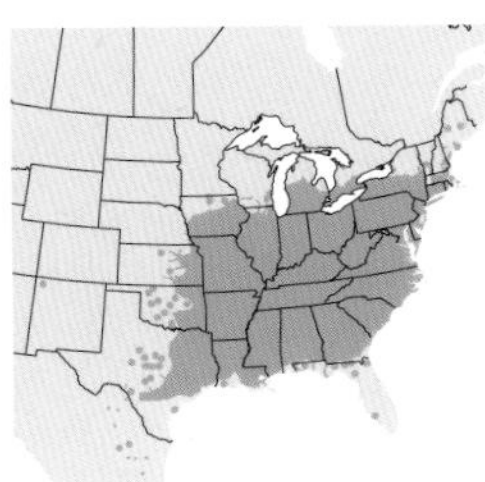

Common in wet soils such as stream banks and bottomlands. Commonly cultivated (zones 4–9), although 'London Planetree' is reportedly more numerous in cities.

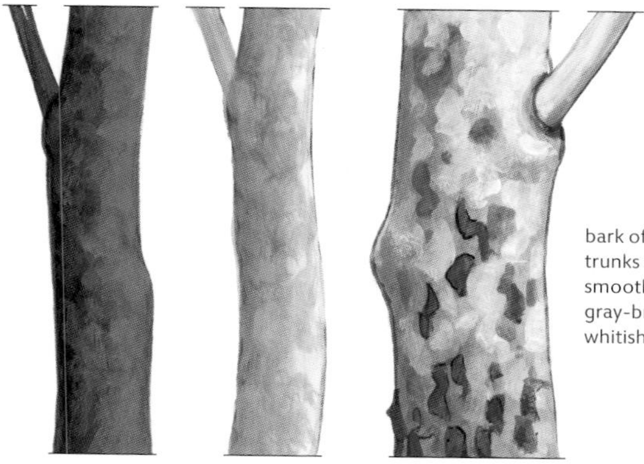

bark of young trunks and branches smooth pale green, gray-brown, cream, or whitish, or mottled

mature trunks with rough gray scales at base

fall color dusty green turning yellow and orange-brown

male flowers small red balls, 1/3", on long stalk, appear with leaves (Mar–Jun)

female flowers in balls on long stalk

pale trunk and massive contorted side branches; dense clusters of twigs

twigs long, tapered, zigzag

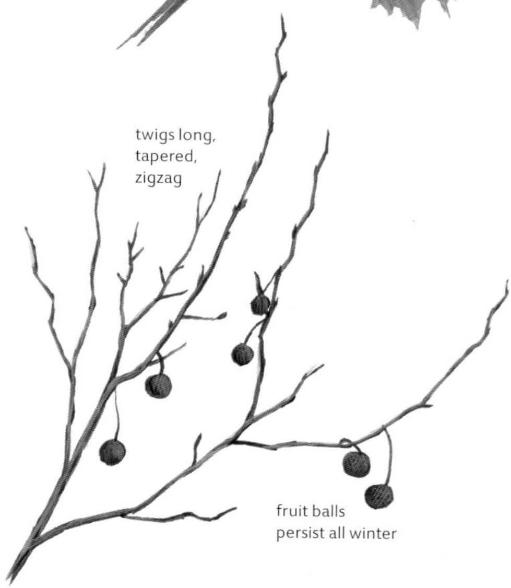

fruit balls persist all winter

California Sycamore

Platanus racemosa

WESTERN SYCAMORE, CALIFORNIA PLANETREE

Deciduous. Medium to large tree, often 60' tall (max. 116'). Distinguished from 'London Planetree' by more deeply-lobed leaves with few teeth, shorter stalks.

leaves 6", few or no teeth, 3–5 long narrow lobes, short stalk
underleaf pale green, hairy
several flower balls on each stalk
fruit balls bristly, 2–7 per stalk, relatively small, about 1" wide

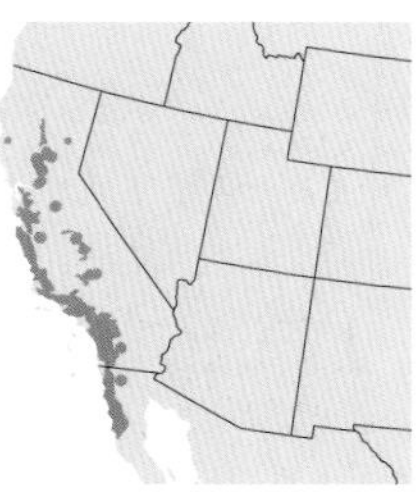

Common in valleys and canyons. Commonly cultivated in California and nearby states (zones 7–9).

Arizona Sycamore

Platanus wrightii

ARIZONA PLANETREE, ALAMO

Deciduous. Large tree often 60' tall (max. 120'). Similar to California and sometimes considered the same species, differs in details of leaf shape and fruit.

leaves 6", few or no teeth, 5–7 very long, narrow lobes
leaves often hang down
underleaf pale green, less hairy than California
fruit relatively smooth, not bristly, 2–5 per stalk

This large tree provides habitat and nesting sites for several species of birds from Mexico in their limited range in the United States, including Elegant Trogon, Sulphur-bellied Flycatcher, Violet-crowned Hummingbird, and others.

Locally common along permanent streams in mountain canyons. Uncommonly cultivated (zones 7–9).

Witch-hazel Family

The witch-hazel family (Hamamelidaceae) includes about eighty species of shrubs and small trees in twenty-seven genera worldwide. Two species in the genus *Hamamelis* are native to North America and are, at least sometimes, tree-like. One related Asian species is commonly cultivated in North America. The genus *Fothergilla* includes several species of shrubs native to the Southeast.

The witch-hazels have yellow flowers with long delicate petals, unusual in their winter emergence. The fruit is a two-parted capsule holding two seeds, which splits open explosively in the late summer after flowering, forcefully ejecting the seeds and throwing them as much as thirty feet away from the tree!

Sweetgum Family

The sweetgum family (Altingiaceae) was considered part of the Witch-hazel family until very recently. As a separate family it includes only fifteen species of trees, one of which is native to North America. The rest are found in Asia.

Sweetgum is one of the most common and widespread trees in the southeastern United States, especially common on fertile flood-plain soils, but found in many other settings, and quick to colonize open areas. The wood is used for furniture, cabinetry, veneer, and many other products, and is one of the most important commercial hardwoods.

A fragrant resinous gum can be obtained from this tree. In the past it was used medicinally and for chewing gum. A similar resin from the Oriental Sweetgum (*Liquidambar orientalis*), known as storax, is an ingredient in perfumes, incense, and other products.

Persian Ironwood

Parrottia persica

PARROTTIA, PERSIAN WITCH-HAZEL

Deciduous. Large shrub or often tree-like to 25' tall (max. 60'), branching low, often multi-trunked, with rounded crown. Attractive mottled bark and unusual winter flowers are distinctive. Native to Iran. Commonly cultivated and locally escaped (zones 5–9).

leaves 3½", oval, dark green, wavy or toothed edges
leafstalk short
fruit ½", dry, woody capsule
twigs slender
flowers tiny, red, in dense clusters in late winter long before leaves (Jan–Mar)
fall color yellow, orange, or maroon
bark thin, peeling in scales, reveal patches of whitish, green, and gray

American Witch-hazel

Hamamelis virginiana

SOUTHERN WITCH-HAZEL, WINTERBLOOM

Deciduous. Usually a shrub, but can be a small tree to 20' tall (max. 35'), typically with several trunks and spreading, crooked branches. Unusual for flowering in fall or winter.

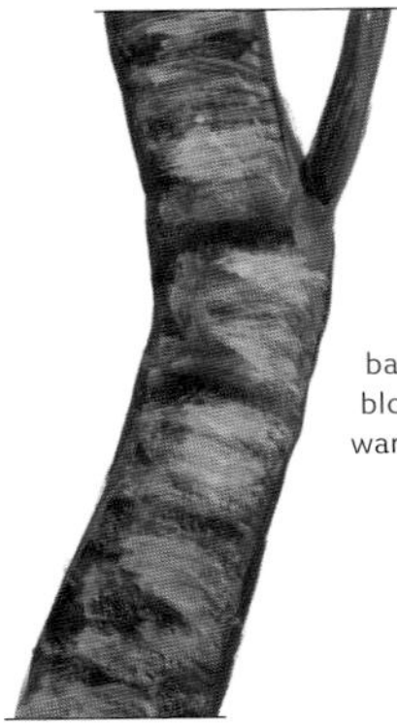

bark thin, smooth and blotchy, large oval warty lenticels

leaves 4", widest above middle, few shallow rounded teeth, lopsided base, dull green

underleaf pale green

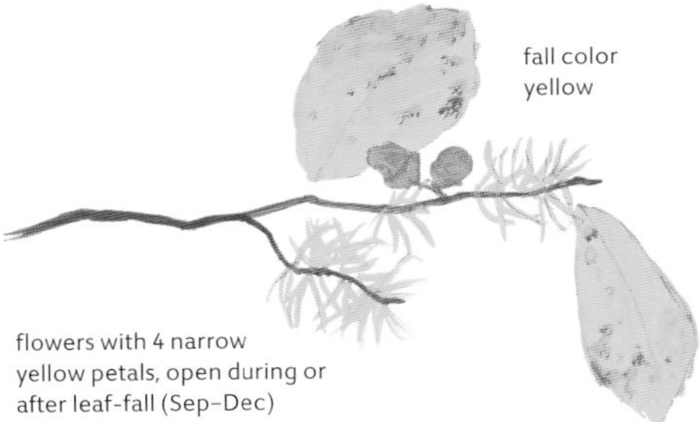

fall color yellow

flowers with 4 narrow yellow petals, open during or after leaf-fall (Sep–Dec)

small tree, often strongly leaning, with irregular crown of ascending branches

fruit ½", 2-beaked woody capsule, splits open when mature (Oct–Jan), forcefully ejects seeds

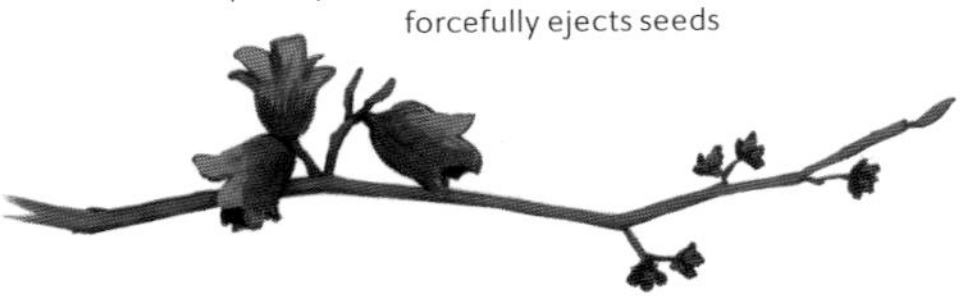

twigs zigzag

buds long, fuzzy

Common understory tree in a variety of habitats from rich shaded streambanks to dry rocky slopes. Fairly commonly cultivated (zones 3–8), but usually a shrub in cultivation.

Springtime Witch-hazel (*Hamamelis vernalis*) is sometimes considered a distinct species, flowering January to April with smaller and more orange-yellow flowers, narrower leaves, tardily deciduous, and rarely tree-like. It is found mainly west of the Mississippi River, but plants with these characteristics (or mixed) are also found in East to Georgia.

Note that cultivated Witch-hazels (nearly always large broad shrubs) are as likely to be one of several Asian species and their hybrids. Some flower in late winter.

Sweetgum

Liquidambar styraciflua

REDGUM, STARLEAF-GUM

Deciduous. Medium to large tree often 60–75' tall (max. 96'); neatly conical when young, becoming rounded with age. One of the characteristic trees of the South, easily recognized by star-shaped leaves and dangling seed balls.

some young trunks
smooth silvery gray
soon becoming rough

bark usually dull
gray-brown, ridged

leaves 5", distinctive
star-shape, 5–7 lobes,
finely-toothed
fall color yellow,
orange, red,
maroon, even
on a single tree
leaves variable,
some strongly
maple-like

fruit 1", long-
stalked woody
ball of pointed
capsules, ripe in
fall, persistent
through winter

female flowers
solitary ½" ball
on 2" stalk
male flowers
in 3" terminal
spikes

branchlets often with
corky wings
twigs
reddish brown

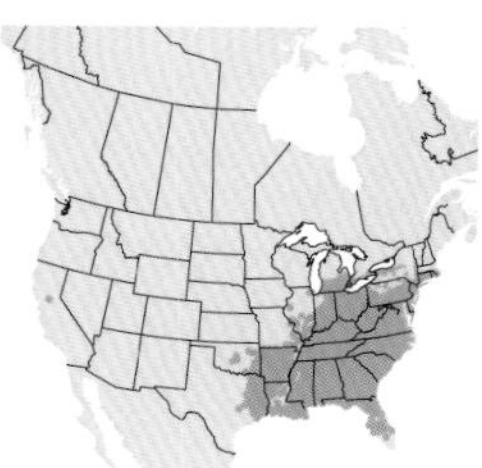

Common in rich soils of higher bottomlands. Also invades abandoned fields. Commonly and widely cultivated as a street tree (zones 5–9); many cultivars.

winged branchlets and
persistent fruit balls
conspicuous
in winter
conical shape in
younger trees, with
straight central trunk

Tamarisk Family

The genus *Tamarix* (family Tamaricaceae) is distantly related to cacti and to some small trees of southern Florida. The genus includes about fifty species of shrubs or small trees, all native to arid climates in Eurasia and North Africa, very tolerant of saline and alkaline soils, and all very similar in appearance. Identification of species often requires examination of the leaves and flowers under magnification.

At least eight species of tamarisk are reportedly naturalized in North America. Until the mid-1900s, tamarisks were promoted for windbreaks and erosion prevention in the arid West, but are now naturalized and displacing native willows and cottonwoods along thousands of miles of watercourses. By accumulating salt from ground-water in their leaves, which fall and increase the salinity of the nearby soil, tamarisks prevent the growth of less salt-tolerant species of plants.

Tamarisk

Tamarix species

SALT CEDAR

Evergreen. Shrub or small tree usually 10–20' tall (max 40'); short, crooked, multiple trunks with ragged oval crown of slender drooping twigs.

bark of small trunks smooth, dark gray with pale lenticels

bark of mature trunks rough, gray to reddish, shredding into long scaly strips

twigs and leaves like junipers, more or less lax and drooping

twigs very slender, red-brown

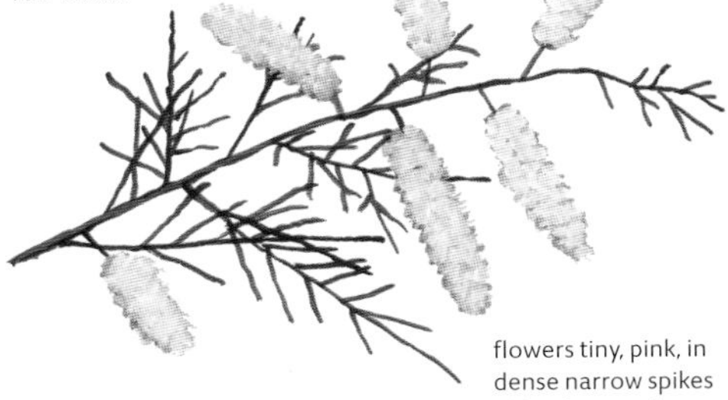

flowers tiny, pink, in dense narrow spikes 2½", often profuse (Apr–Sep)

leaves tiny, scale-like, pale green to bluish

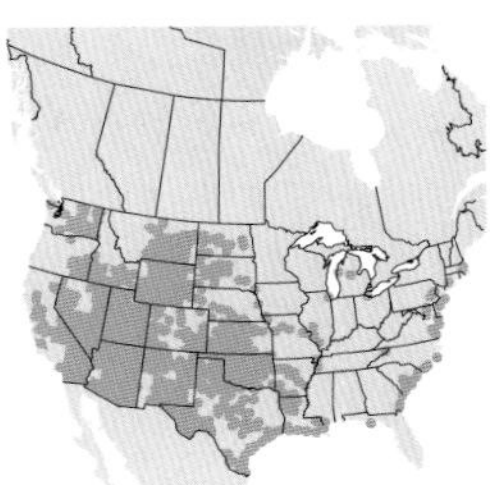

Eight species are known to be escaped, all combined on this map (zones 2–9, but tree-like only in zones 7–9).

tree often lopsided, with haze of very fine twigs, pale, dusty-looking

Myrtle Family

The genus *Eucalyptus*, part of the myrtle family (Myrtaceae), includes about 700 species, nearly all trees, native to Australia and adjacent regions. Most are evergreen (a few are drought-deciduous) with long narrow leaves and high concentrations of aromatic oils. Dozens of *Eucalyptus* species are cultivated (and many escaped) in the warmer parts of North America. Only three of the most cold-hardy species are illustrated here.

Extensively planted worldwide for ornament, for their wood and oils, and for windbreaks and erosion control, eucalypts have often become naturalized and invasive, as they are in California.

Longbeak Eucalyptus

Eucalyptus camaldulensis

RIVER RED GUM

Evergreen. Medium to large tree often 80' tall, twigs drooping.

leafstalk red
leaves 6", very slender, often silvery
fruit small, clustered on short stalk

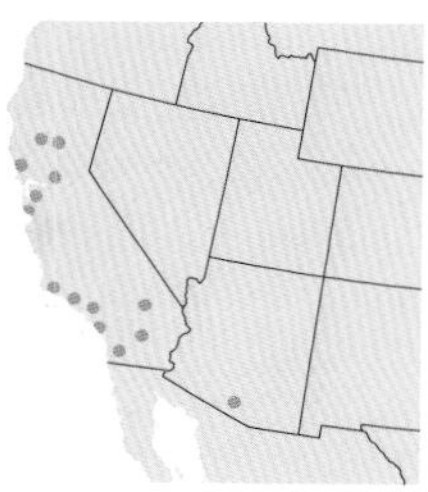

Native to Australia. Commonly cultivated throughout desert Southwest and naturalized locally (zones 9–10).

Cider Gum

Eucalyptus gunnii

Evergreen. Medium tree usually 30–50' tall (max. 62'). Native to Tasmania. Commonly and widely cultivated, more cold-hardy and tolerant of wet soils than other eucalypts, but tree-like only in warmer areas (zones 7–10).

leaves 4", relatively short and broad, gray-green

juvenile leaves small, round, silver-blue; opposite and clasping stem

fruit very small, clustered on stalk

Eucalypts have strikingly different adult and juvenile foliage. Juvenile leaves of many species are nearly circular, pale bluish-white, opposite and with base growing around or "clasping" the twig. In contrast, adult leaves of the same tree are narrow, sickle-shaped, dark green, and alternate. This juvenile growth is the "silver-dollar-tree" popular in flower arrangements, and such leaves are produced by many different species of eucalypts.

Bluegum Eucalyptus

Eucalyptus globulus

TASMANIAN BLUE GUM, FEVER TREE

Evergreen. Large tree often 80' tall (max. 165'). Tall with irregular rounded crown. Very large leaves, solitary whitish flowers, and peeling bark distinguish this species from most other eucalypts.

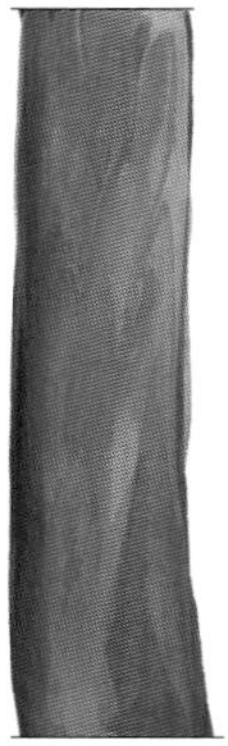

bark smooth brown

older bark peels in long sheets and strips to reveal pale whitish trunk

leaves large, 10"; sickle-shaped, hang down from twigs

underleaf green like upperleaf

juvenile leaves 4"; much broader, paler blue-green

flowers creamy-white in 'powder-puff' cluster, solitary

fruit an urn-shaped capsule 1" across, glaucous blue-green turning brown

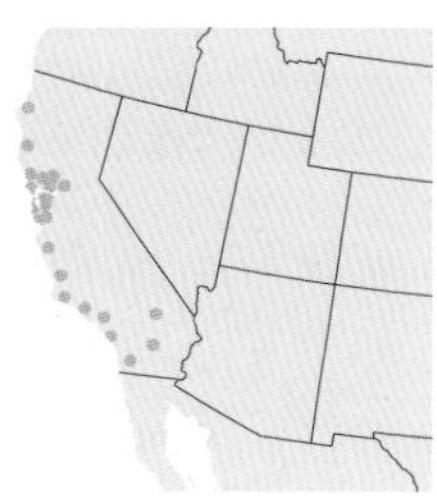

Native to Tasmania and southern Australia. Very commonly cultivated and naturalized, the most common species of *Eucalyptus* in California (zone 10).

tree usually tall with often crooked trunk, few ascending branches leading to dense clumps of hanging leaves in crown

Crape-myrtle

Lagerstroemia indica

LADIES' STREAMER, LILAC OF THE SOUTH

Deciduous. Shrub or small tree usually 15–25' tall (max. 60'); often multi-trunked and often has leaves restricted to tips of branches. Small size, spectacular floral display, and attractive bark make this a very popular ornamental plant.

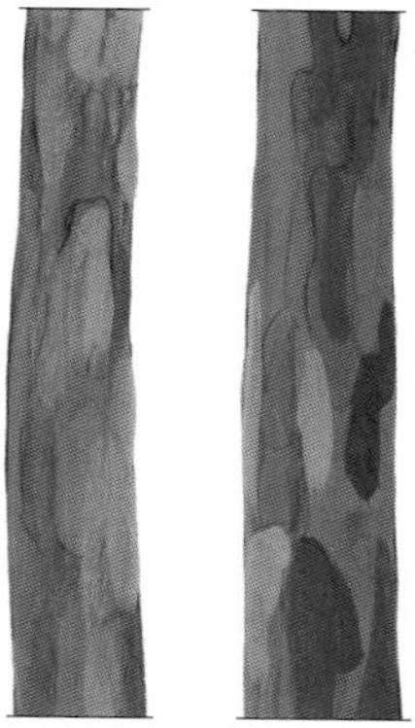
bark pale brown peeling
to reveal various shades of
orange to greenish

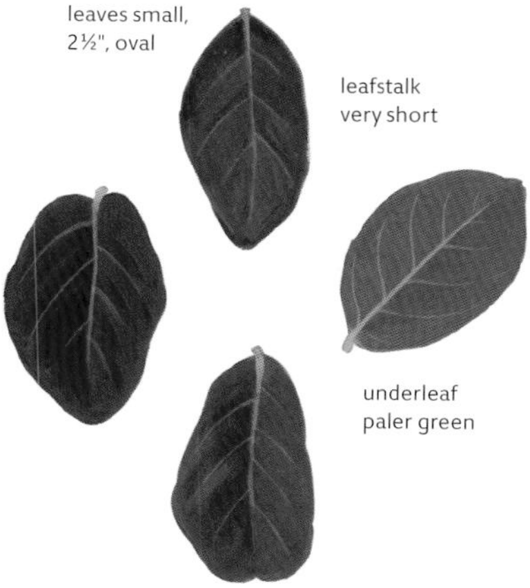
leaves small,
2½", oval
leafstalk
very short
underleaf
paler green

fall color
yellow to red

fruit small oval
capsules,
in terminal
clusters;
persistent all
winter

flower color varies
with cultivar: white,
pink, red, or
dark purple

twig slender, 4-angled or winged,
green to red

flowers in large
showy terminal
clusters 10"
(Jun–Oct)

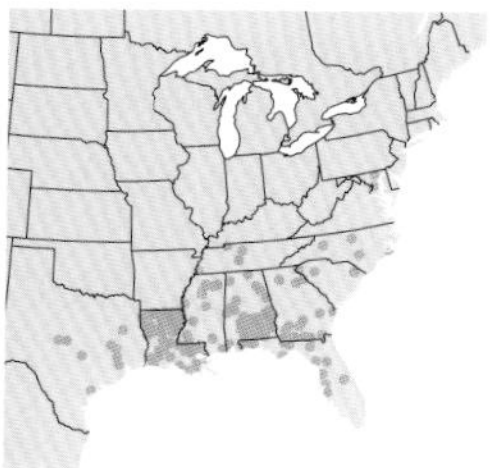

Native to east Asia. Very commonly cultivated in yards, parks, and streets, and locally naturalized. Thrives in hot, moderately dry climate (zones 7–9).

Legume Family

The legumes or beans (family Fabaceae) include nearly 20,000 species worldwide, making it the third largest family of flowering plants. In North America, forty-four native species are sometimes tree-like, but many are tropical and some are usually shrubs. Many exotic species are commonly cultivated in North America and have escaped and now grow in the wild.

A total of thirty-five species in eighteen genera are tree-like and cold-hardy enough to be covered in this guide. This includes twenty-three native species, along with twelve commonly cultivated exotics.

Trees in this family share certain characteristics in common:

- All have alternate leaves, and nearly all have pinnately compound leaves. The only species without compound leaves are the redbuds and some Australian acacias.
- Many have thorny twigs, often small single or paired thorns arising next to each leaf bud on the twig.
- Buds are small and inconspicuous.
- All have seeds enclosed in pods. These pods may be slender or wide, flattened or plump, constricted between seeds or uniform in width, and all of these features are helpful for identification. The only other trees with pod-like fruit are the catalpas (page 388) and Desert-willow (page 387).

The legume family is often divided into three subfamilies, grouped by aspects of their flowers.

The redbuds would be placed in the Faboideae subfamily, based simply on flowers, but with unique leaf shape and other differences they are sometimes placed in their own subfamily and may be a sister group to the entire legume family.

CAESALPINIOIDEAE: Honeylocust, paloverdes, coffeetree. These species have flowers with petals (variably conspicuous).

MIMOSOIDEAE: *Acacia*, Silktree, Ebony Blackbead, *Leucaena*, mesquite. These species have tiny flowers, with long projecting stamens, clustered tightly in a fuzzy ball or spike.

FABOIDEAE: Scholartree, yellowwood, locusts, *Olneya*, *Laburnum*, *Maackia*. These species have showy pea-like flowers.

The legume family is extremely important worldwide as a food source—beans, peas, lentils, etc. all come from plants in the legume family. Popular ornamental legumes include many of the trees shown in this guide, as well as lupine, broom, and wisteria. In the desert Southwest, mesquite is economically important. Its wood is widely used for charcoal, the flowers are attractive to bees and the source of mesquite honey and, along with several other southwestern species, it provides shade and forage for livestock, and lumber for fenceposts, where no other trees are available.

Honey Mesquite

Prosopis glandulosa

MESQUITE, TORREY MESQUITE

Deciduous. Shrub or small tree to 20' tall (max. 55'). Across much of its range, the largest tree; a very important component of open woodland sites in the desert grasslands. Wood is valued for fuel, and nectar for honeybees.

bark of mature trunks dark gray and reddish with very coarse, ragged ridges

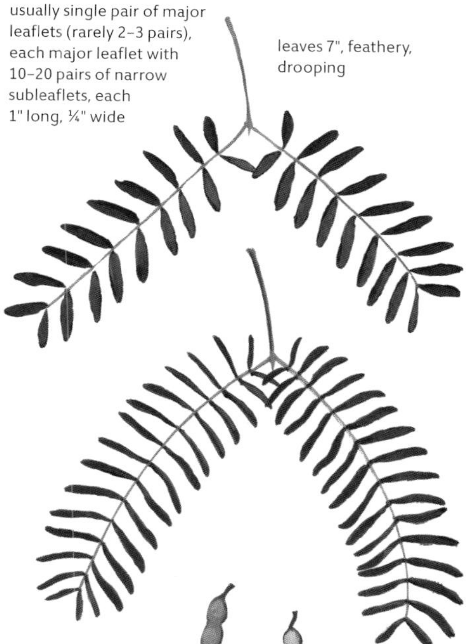

usually single pair of major leaflets (rarely 2–3 pairs), each major leaflet with 10–20 pairs of narrow subleaflets, each 1" long, ¼" wide

leaves 7", feathery, drooping

Two named varieties are known: Honey Mesquite (var. *glandulosa)* typical in Texas and eastward and Western Honey Mesquite (var. *torreyana*), but differences are very slight.

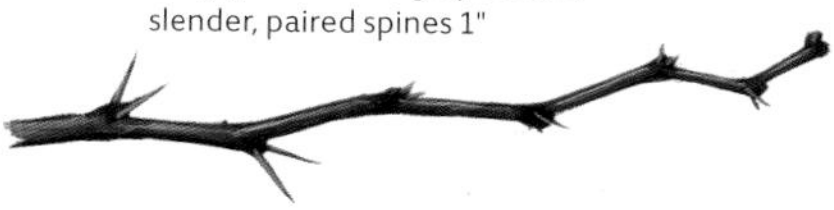

twigs yellowish or gray-brown, slender, paired spines 1"

flowers tiny, white to pale yellow, in slender 2" spikes in leaf axils (Apr–Jul)

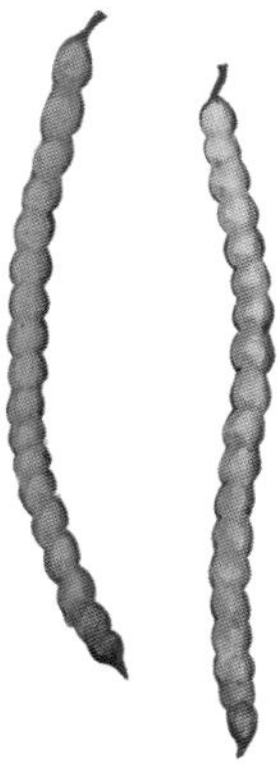

fruit pods 7", cylindrical (not flattened), pale brown

winter twigs zigzag, tapered with knobby spur branches and retained leaf stalks

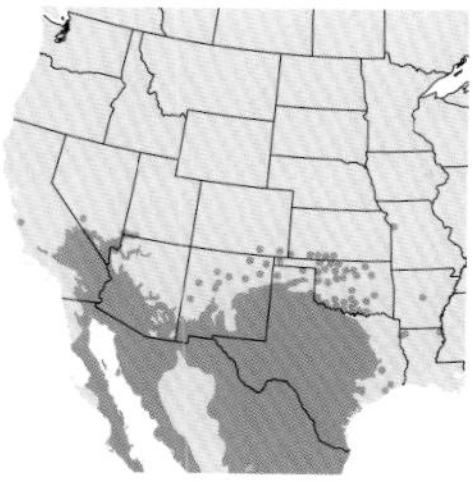

Common on arid rangeland, largest and most common along desert washes. Commonly cultivated in and near native range; naturalized well beyond native range (zones 7–9).

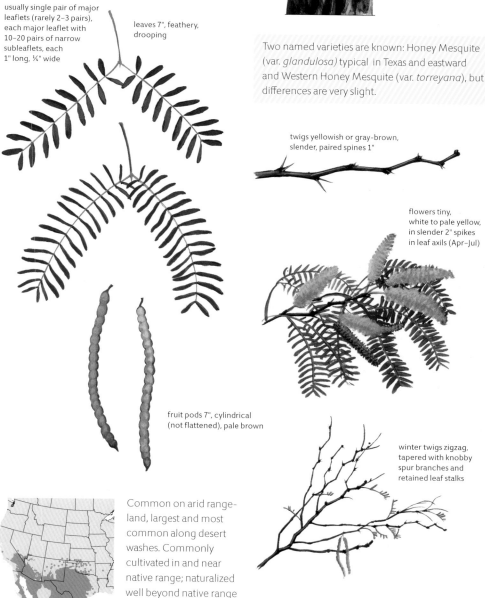

Screwbean Mesquite

Prosopis pubescens

SCREWBEAN, TORNILLO

Deciduous. Shrub or small tree to 20' tall (max. about 25'). Spreading, thorny tree, like Honey Mesquite, but smaller, with much smaller leaves and very distinctive fruit.

leaves small, 2",
5–9 pairs of
tiny subleaflets

fruit pods 1½",
pale tan, form
tight spiral;
not persistent

Several other species of mesquites are native, usually shrubs, in the arid Southwest. Two South American species are commonly cultivated in the Southwest (zones 8–9). Chilean Mesquite (*Prosopis chilensis*) and Argentine Mesquite (*Prosopis alba*) are both small trees, often 30' tall, similar to Honey Mesquite, but usually less wide-spreading, leaves often persist through winter, with slight differences in leaves and fruit. All species of mesquites interbreed, producing an array of hybrids, and many cultivated trees are apparently hybrids between South American species and Honey Mesquite. Identification can be very challenging.

Common along streams, desert washes. ravines, sandy and gravelly soils with access to some water. Uncommonly cultivated (zones 7–9).

Velvet Mesquite

Prosopis velutina

MESQUITE

Deciduous. Shrub or small tree to 20' tall (max. about 50'); usually multi-trunked and spreading. Closely related to Honey Mesquite and sometimes considered the same species, differs mainly in downy (velvety) leaves and fruit.

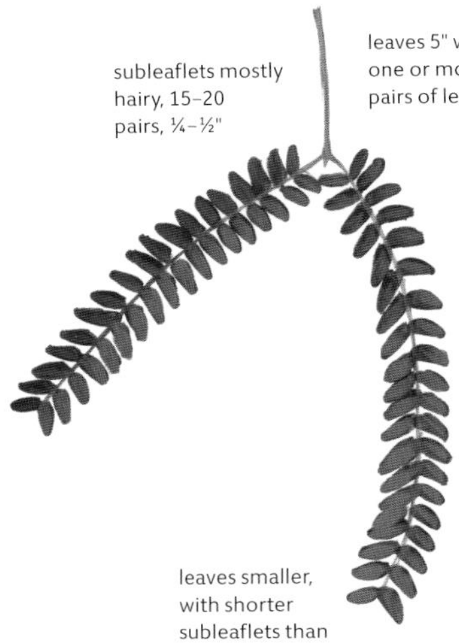
subleaflets mostly
hairy, 15–20
pairs, ¼–½"
leaves 5" with
one or more
pairs of leaflets
leaves smaller,
with shorter
subleaflets than
Honey Mesquite

fruit 6", narrow,
slightly flattened
and constricted
between seeds

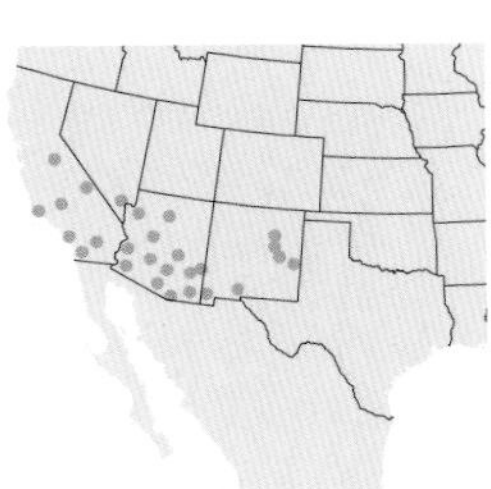

Common along streambeds and ravines or slopes and uplands where deep soil and some moisture is found. Uncommonly cultivated (zones 7–9).

Littleleaf Leucaena

Leucaena retusa

GOLDENBALL LEADTREE, LITTLELEAF LEADTREE

Deciduous. Usually a shrub, occasionally a small tree to 20' tall (max. about 25') with low, spreading crown. Bark smooth and grayish.

leaves small, 3½", 2–3 pairs of leaflets each with 6–10 pairs of tiny oval subleaflets

fruit 8" slender, flattened pod

tiny pale yellow flowers in dense balls (continuously Apr–Oct), especially after rain

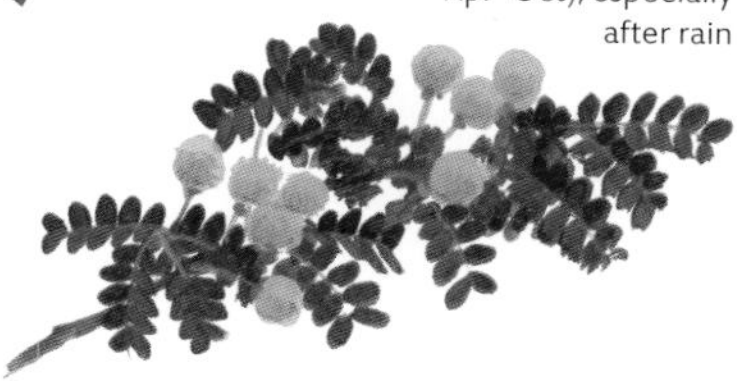

The genus *Leucaena* differs from most southwestern legumes in its thornless twigs. In extreme southern Texas, the Great Leadtree (*Leucaena pulverulenta*) can be 60' tall.

Locally common on steep rocky hillsides and limestone bluffs. Uncommonly cultivated (zones 7–9).

Tenaza

Havardia pallens

APE'S-EARRING, HUAJILLO, GUAJILLA, MIMOSA BUSH

Evergreen or drought-deciduous. Shrub or small tree often 20–30' tall (max. 41'). Long upright branches give relatively upright growth form; feathery leaves and fragrant white flowers attractive to bees and birds make this a desirable landscape plant.

leaves 4", gray-green, feathery, 6–10 pairs of leaflets, each with 30–40 subleaflets; similar to Huisache

fruit 5", flat, straight pod, long, velvety-hairy

flowers white, in ball-shaped clusters to 1", fragrant (Mar–Apr)

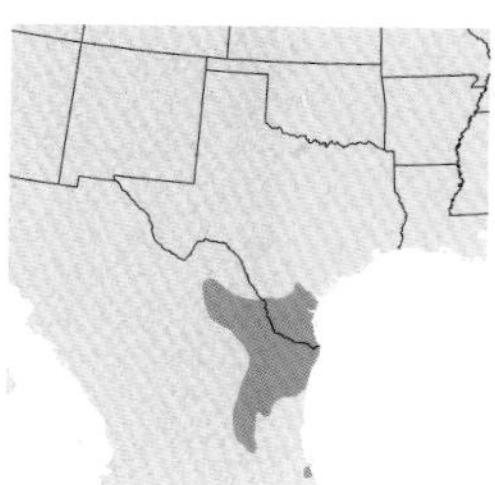

Common within its limited range in arid grasslands, pastures. Uncommonly cultivated in arid Southwest.

Ebony Blackbead

Ebenopsis ebano

TEXAS-EBONY, PITHECELLOBIUM FLEXICAULE

Evergreen to semi-evergreen. Shrub or small broad tree 15–30' tall (max. 50'). Often multi-trunked, usually branching low, with dense dark green foliage.

bark very rough
and dark

leaves small, 2",
dark green,
leathery
leaves bipinnately
compound, alternate,
tiny round subleaflets

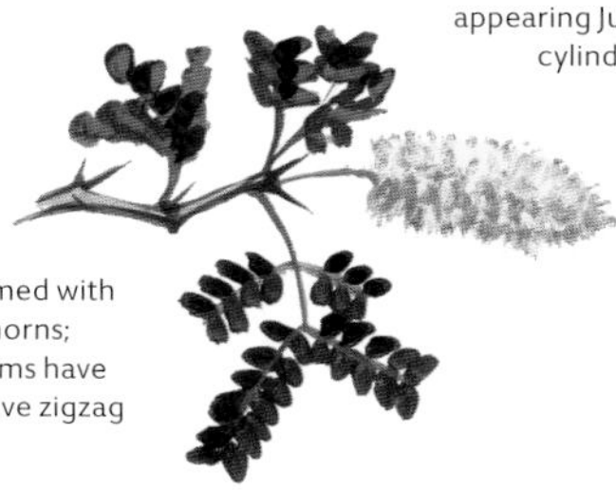
flowers 2", light yellow
or cream, very fragrant,
appearing Jun–Aug in
cylindric spikes
well-armed with
many thorns;
gray stems have
distinctive zigzag
jointing

fruit 5", thick curved
pod, ripe in autumn;
persistent until after
flowering the next year

stiff irregular
twigs, clumps of
small dark leaves,
and large, curved
pods distinctive

Tenaza and Ebony Blackbead were formerly both in the genus *Pithecellobium* and are related to Silktree. Littleleaf Leucaena is more closely related to mesquites.

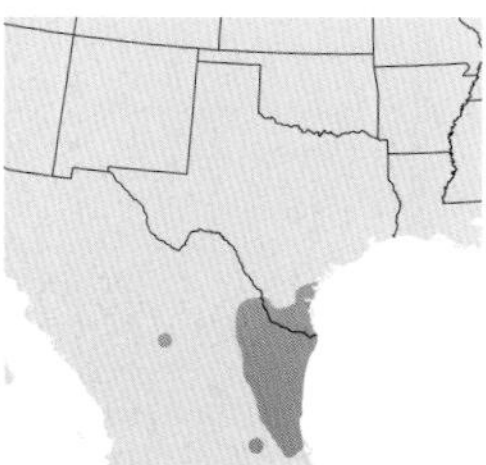

Common in limited United States range. Commonly cultivated only within native range (zones 8–11).

The arid Southwest is home to many species of shrubs and small trees in the legume family, which create important habitat for wildlife. The foliage provides much-needed shade in a region with few other trees, while the protein-rich leaves and seeds are eaten by many species of animals.

Huisache

Acacia farnesiana

SWEET ACACIA, TEXAS HUISACHE, CASSIE

Deciduous. Shrub or small tree often 20' tall (max. 29'); thicket-forming, with straight trunk and many long, pendulous branches. Cultivated in Europe for its fragrant flowers, used as a base for perfumes.

bark of young trunk brown with many pale lenticels

bark of mature trunk splits into thin gray strips

leaves 3" with 3–5 pairs of feathery leaflets

flowers bright yellow, very fragrant, open early spring

fruit 2", dark brown to black, thick oblong pods

In addition to the three species of native acacias shown here, four species are at least sometimes tree-like in southern and western Texas. Huisachillo (*Acacia tortuosa*) is similar to Huisache, but smaller, with smaller leaves and flowers and longer, narrower fruit pods. Guajillo (*Acacia berlandieri*) has short curved thorns like catclaws, but larger feathery leaves, like Silktree, and white flowers in round clusters. Two other species in the catclaw group are similar to Wright and Gregg Catclaws.

twigs zigzag, orange-brown, paired whitish spines

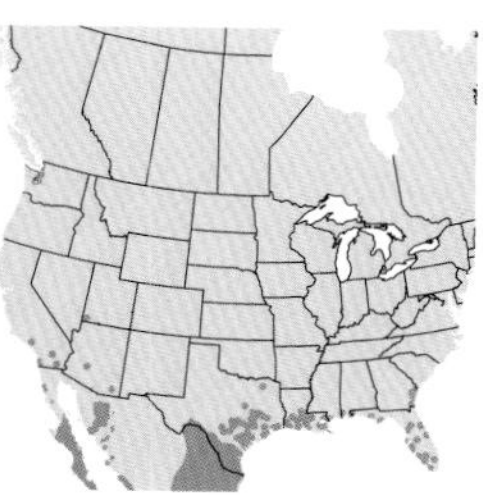

Common in arid grasslands in Texas, invasive in sandy soils in open woods and rangeland. Widely cultivated and naturalized beyond native range (zones 8–11).

low spreading tree, very showy in full bloom, twigs drooping

Gregg Catclaw

Acacia greggii

CATCLAW ACACIA, DEVIL'S CLAW, PARADISE FLOWER, WAIT-A-MINUTE TREE

Deciduous (often leafless most of year). Shrub or small tree usually under 20' tall (max. about 30'), multi-trunked, with spread greater than height. The only catclaw found west of Texas.

bark gray-brown,
scaly to slightly furrowed

compound leaves
1½", 1–3 pairs of leaflets,
each with 4–6 pairs
of subleaflets

flowers fragrant,
bright creamy yellow in
dense oblong spikes
(Mar–May)
leaves densely
clumped on twigs

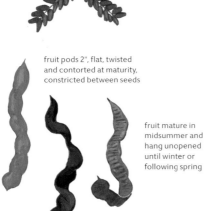

fruit pods 2", flat, twisted
and contorted at maturity,
constricted between seeds
fruit mature in
midsummer and
hang unopened
until winter or
following spring

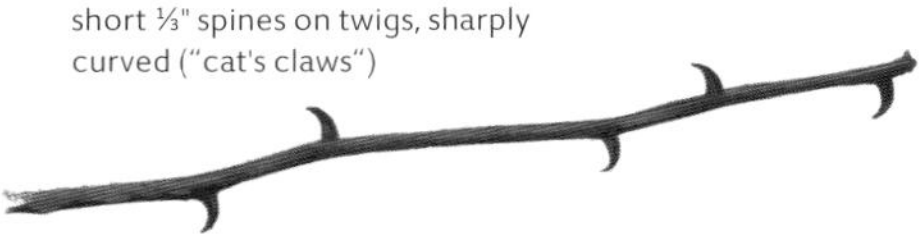
short ⅓" spines on twigs, sharply
curved ("cat's claws")

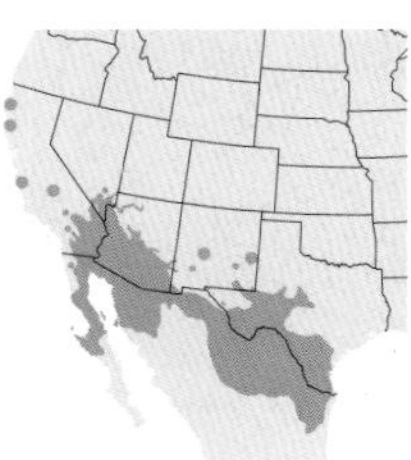

Common in desert washes and other sites with some moisture. Infrequently cultivated (zones 7–9).

Wright Catclaw

Acacia wrightii

TEXAS CATCLAW, WRIGHT ACACIA, UNA DE GATO

Deciduous. Shrub or small tree occasionally 30' tall (max. 33'); very similar to Gregg, but fruit wider and not contorted at maturity.

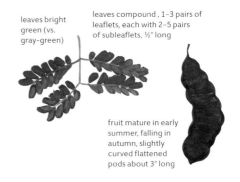

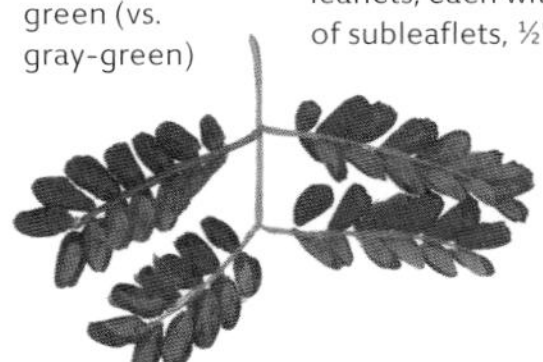
leaves bright
green (vs.
gray-green)
leaves compound, 1–3 pairs of
leaflets, each with 2–5 pairs
of subleaflets, ½" long

fruit mature in early
summer, falling in
autumn, slightly
curved flattened
pods about 3" long

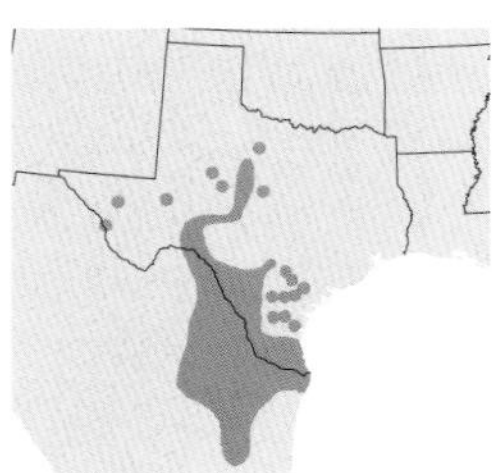

Common in desert washes. Largest and most abundant south of Rio Grande. Infrequently cultivated.

Silver Wattle

Acacia dealbata

GOLDEN MIMOSA

Evergreen. Medium tree often 50' tall, (max. 70'); leaves bipinnate.

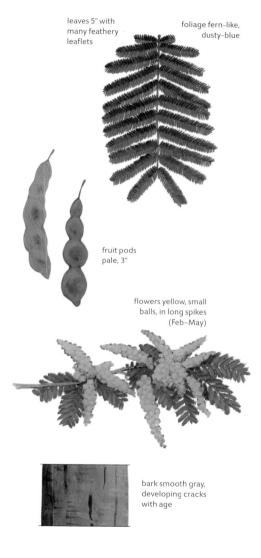

leaves 5" with many feathery leaflets

foliage fern-like, dusty-blue

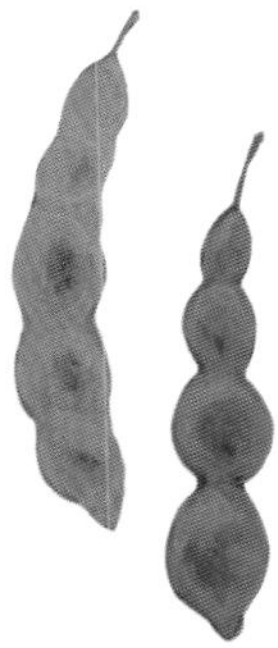

fruit pods pale, 3"

flowers yellow, small balls, in long spikes (Feb–May)

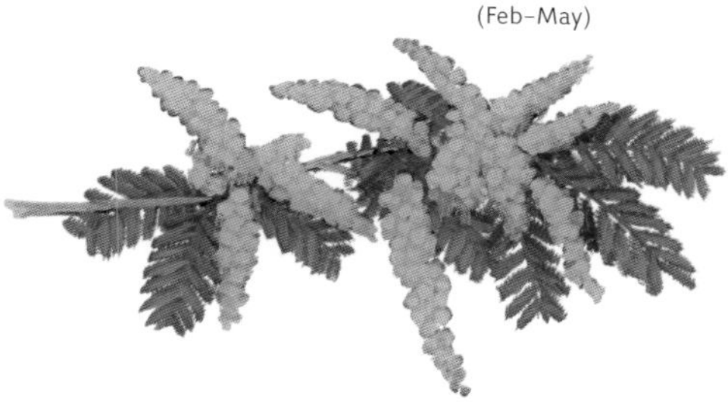

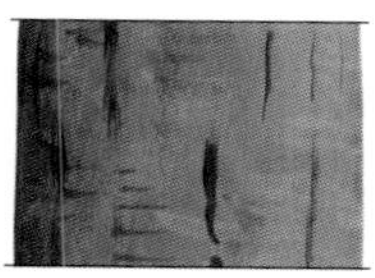

bark smooth gray, developing cracks with age

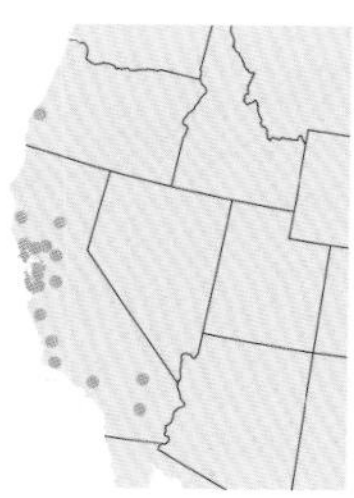

Native to Australia. Commonly cultivated and naturalized in California. The most hardy of all cultivated acacias (zones 9–11).

Australian Blackwood

Acacia melanoxylon

TASMANIAN BLACKWOOD

Evergreen. Small to medium tree usually 25–40' tall (max. 70'); relatively narrow, with dense foliage and short gray trunk with shaggy bark. Differs from Silver Wattle in usually simple leaves and solitary balls of whitish flowers. Similar to several other species of Australian acacias cultivated in California.

leaves 4", narrow, straight or slightly curved, gray-green to dark green

A few species of Australian acacias have the bipinnate leaves typical of the genus reduced to "phyllodia" (wide flattened leafstalks) that resemble simple leaves. Foliage on young trees and vigorous shoots can be compound or odd combinations of pinnate and simple.

wide, flattened leafstalk (called "phyllodia")

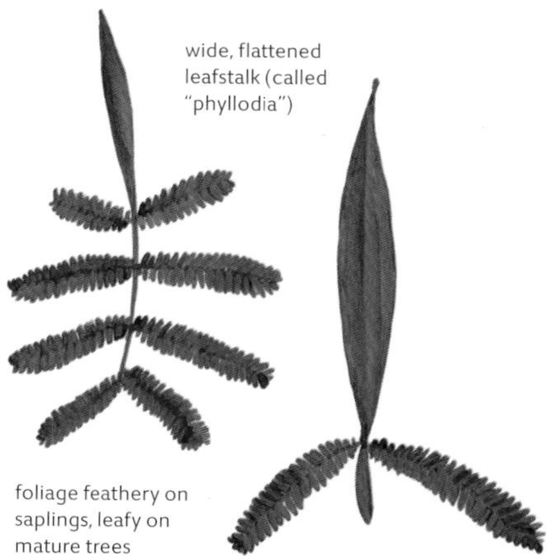

foliage feathery on saplings, leafy on mature trees

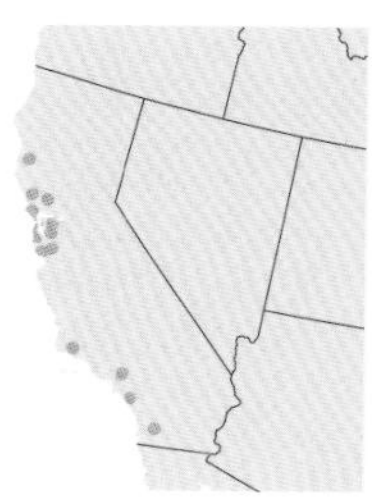

Native to eastern Australia. Commonly cultivated and naturalized in California (zones 9–11).

Blue Paloverde

Parkinsonia florida

PALOVERDE, GREEN-BARKED ACACIA

Deciduous. Usually a large shrub, sometimes tree-like 15–25' tall (max. 40'), with low spreading crown arching to the ground, and short crooked trunk. Usually appears as an irregular gauzy mound of slender blue-green twigs. Conserves water with tiny leaves that grow briefly and die away (photosynthesis occurs mostly in the green bark).

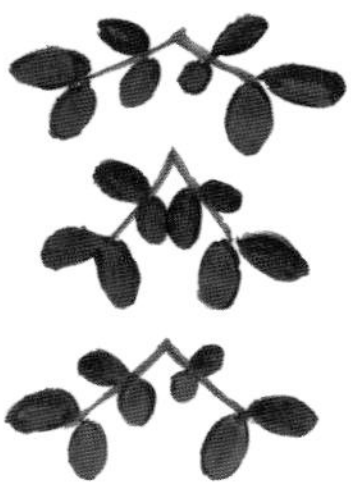
leaves tiny, compound, 1¼", 2 pairs of leaflets, each with 2–3 pairs of dull green subleaflets ⅓"

fruit pods flat, yellow-brown, 2½"

flowers bright yellow, ¾" across, in clusters 3" long, covering entire tree (Mar–Jun, sometimes in fall)
twigs blue-green with small spines in leaf axils

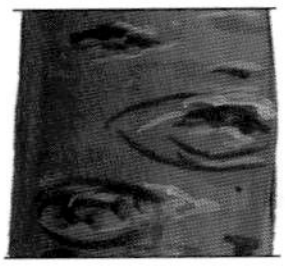
bark smooth blue-green becoming scaly and gray on older trunks

Fairly common in arid rocky or sandy desert mostly along washes and ravines. Fairly commonly cultivated within native range (zones 9–10).

Yellow Paloverde

Parkinsonia microphylla

FOOTHILL PALOVERDE, LITTLELEAF PALOVERDE, LITTLELEAF HORSEBEAN

Deciduous. Shrub or small tree occasionally 25' tall (max. 29'). Leaves emerge in spring after rain and fall very shortly after fully grown.

leaves persist only briefly
leaves small, 1", with 2 leaflets, each with 4–7 pairs of tiny oval leaflets, fall early

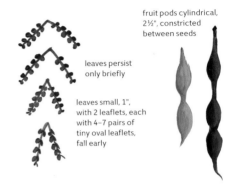

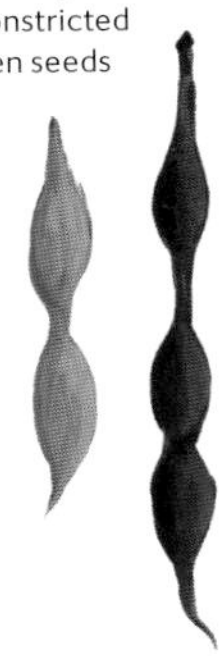
fruit pods cylindrical, 2½", constricted between seeds

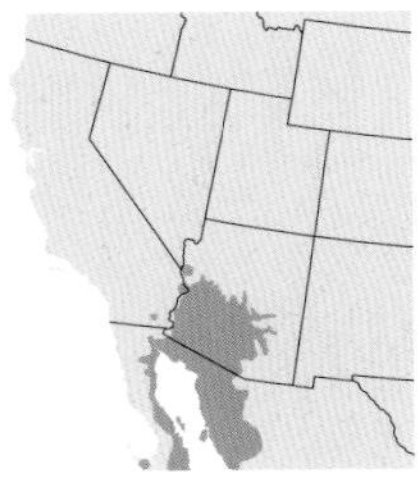

Common but treelike only around Wickenburg, Arizona; in arid rocky or sandy soils, not restricted to washes. Uncommonly cultivated within native range (zones 9–10).

Jerusalem Thorn

Parkinsoniana aculeata

RETAMA, PALOVERDE

Deciduous. Shrub or small tree usually under 30' tall (max. about 40'); usually low and rounded with drooping twigs. Long slender grass-like leaves very distinctive. Common in moist soils along streams and rivers from Texas to Arizona. Commonly cultivated and naturalized outside native range (zones 8–10).

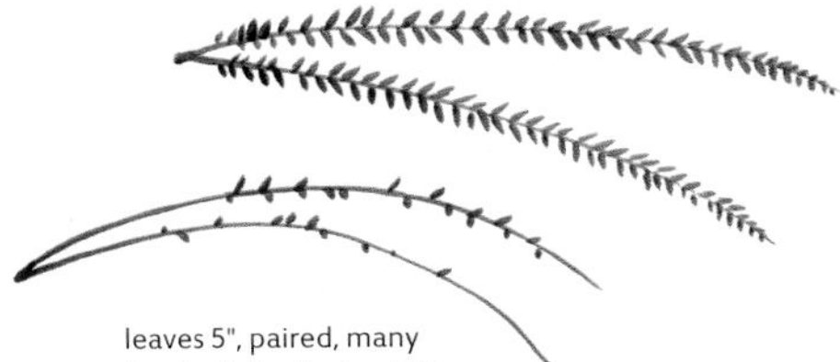
leaves 5", paired, many tiny leaflets, shed quickly, leaving long grass-like leaf stalks

Kentucky Coffeetree

Gymnocladus dioicus

KENTUCKY MAHOGANY, COFFEE-NUT TREE, STUMP TREE, LUCK BEAN

Deciduous. Medium to large tree often 60' tall (max 135'). Seeds were sometimes roasted and used as a coffee substitute.

bark of young trunks pale gray, breaking into long shallow ridges with orange furrows

older trunks have long, narrow scaly ridges, small curled scales

leaves huge, 30", bipinnately compound, 5–9 pairs of leaflets, each with 6–14 oval, pointed subleaflets 2¼"

leaves develop late and drop early

underleaf pale green

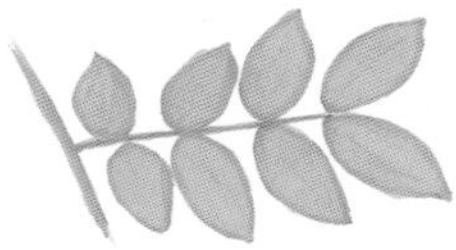

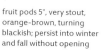

fall color yellow

flowers small, whitish, clustered on 4" spikes at twig tips in early spring (Apr–Jun); male and female on separate trees

fruit pods 5", very stout, orange-brown, turning blackish; persist into winter and fall without opening

twigs very stout, greenish to orange, buds tiny

winter twigs stout, untidy, upright, some retain slender curved stalks and oval fruit pods

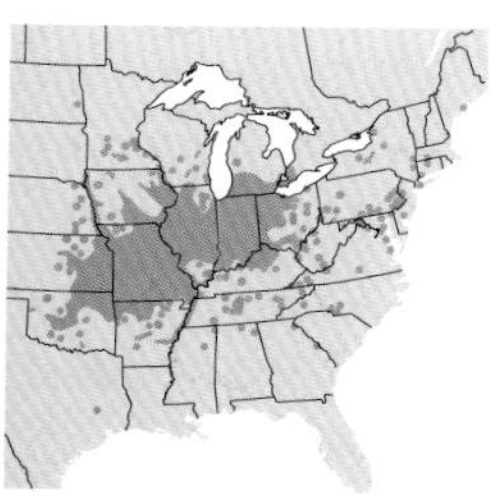

Common in deep rich soils in bottomlands. Uncommonly cultivated and occasionally naturalized (zones 3–8).

Honeylocust

Gleditsia triacanthos

Deciduous. Medium to large tree often 70' tall (max. 116'); usually short trunk and oval crown. Presumably named for the sweetish pulp found in the pod surrounding the seeds.

bark dark gray-brown, often with reddish or orange tone, smooth with pale horizontal lenticels

older trunks with broad ridges peeling from sides

leaves 6", usually pinnately compound, 15–30 leaflets, each 1"

leaves dark green, form arched cluster at twig tips

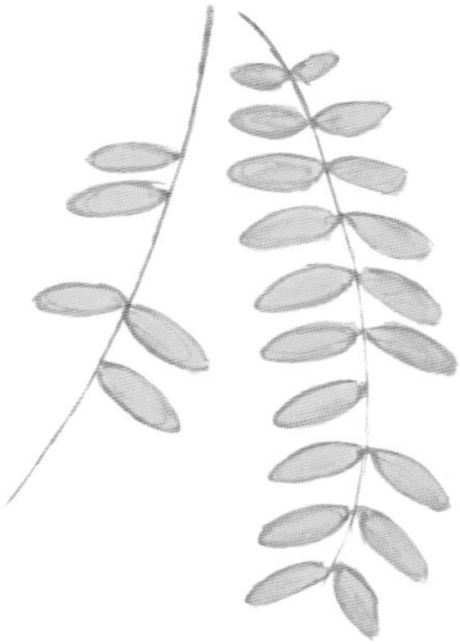

fall color pale to golden yellow, but leaves frequently dry, orange-brown in late summer

fruit pods 8", broad, flat, dark red-brown, slightly contorted

mature in late summer/early fall, persist into winter

twigs stout, zigzag, tapered

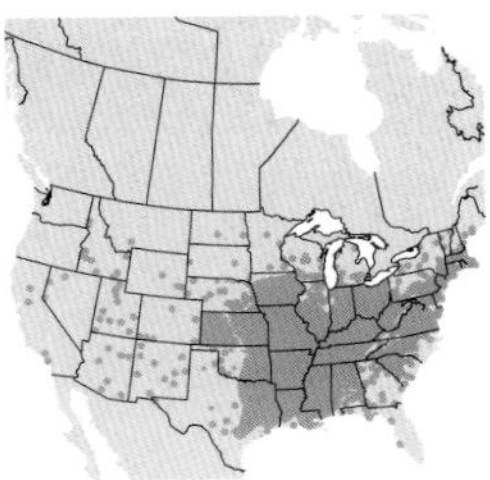

Common in rich moist soils of lowlands, but grows well in many habitats. Very commonly cultivated and widely naturalized beyond native range (zones 4–9).

distinctive long twigs spreading horizontally from crown

spines, up to 3", grow from trunks and branches, often profusely, spines often branched

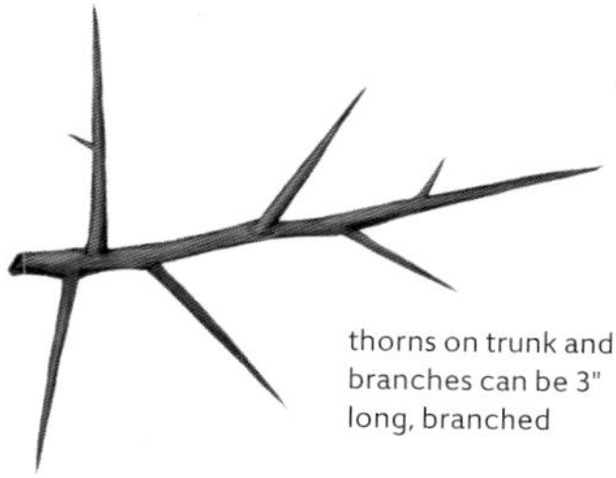
thorns on trunk and
branches can be 3"
long, branched

male and female flowers
on separate trees

flowers inconspicuous
yellow-greenish in
short spikes, 3", in
spring with leaves

occasional scattered
leaves are bipinnately
compound, many tiny
subleaflets

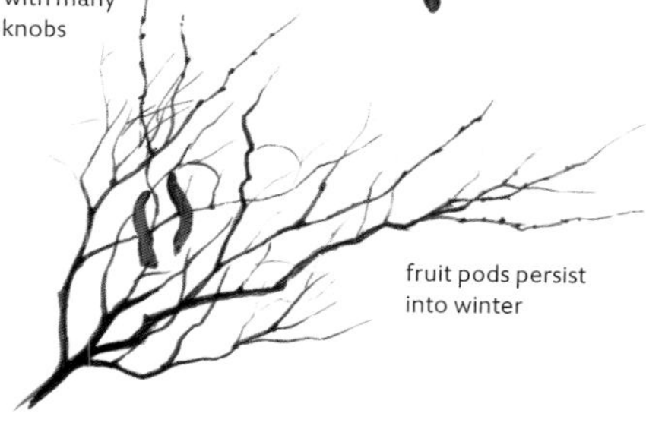
tapered, zigzag
twigs with many
small knobs
fruit pods persist
into winter

leaves in arched
clusters at branch tips

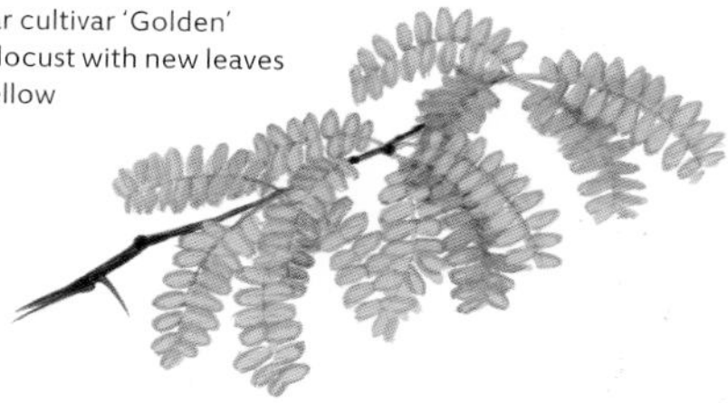
popular cultivar 'Golden'
Honeylocust with new leaves
pale yellow

Waterlocust

Gleditsia aquatica

Deciduous. Small to medium tree usually under 60' tall (max. about 80'). Very similar to Honey Locust and reliably distinguished only by very short fruit pods with 1 (occasionally 2 or 3) seeds. Trees intermediate between Waterlocust and Honey Locust found in the lower Mississippi Valley are sometimes named Texas Honeylocust.

short pod 3",
each with only
1–3 seeds

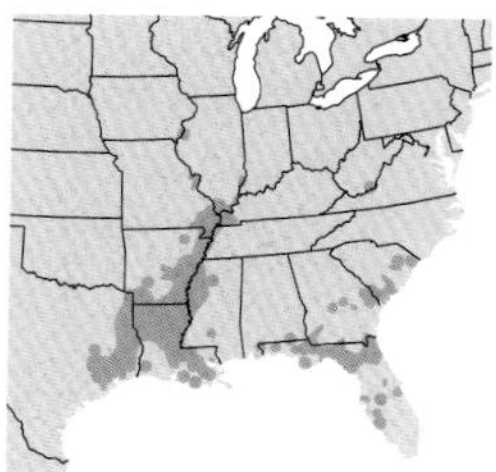

Common in bottomlands, in same habitat as Honey Locust. Not cultivated.

Desert Ironwood

Olneya tesota

TESOTA, PALO-DE-FIERRO

Semi-evergreen or drought-deciduous. Shrub or small tree usually under 25' tall (max. 33'), usually multi-trunked and spreading, with relatively dense foliage. One of the heaviest of all North American woods (does not float in water); makes very good fuel and used for specialized purposes.

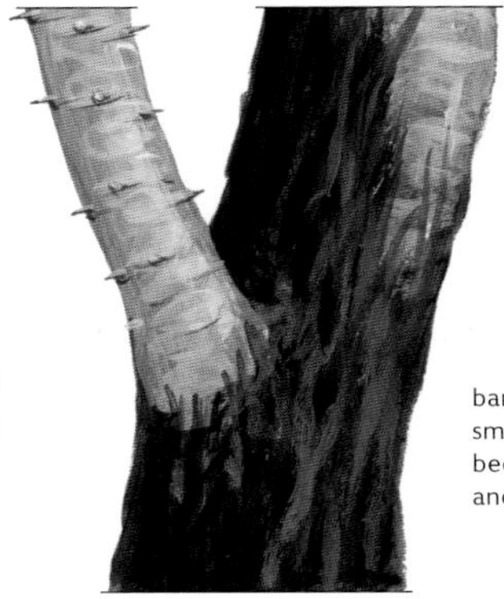
bark on young trunk smooth gray-green, becoming rough, shreddy, and gray on older trunks

leaves small, about 2", 6–9 leaflets each about ¾"

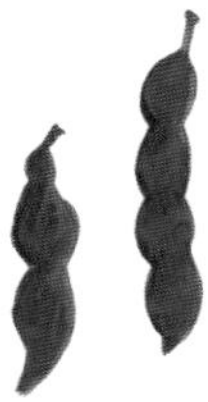
fruit pod 2–3", ripe in late summer

leaves a more solid mass of gray-green foliage than other species in its habitat
flowers white to pink, in curved clusters at twig tips (Apr–Jun), just before new leaves emerge

Desert Ironwood is sometimes referred to as a "nurse plant." Low branches, relatively dense foliage, thorny twigs, and leaf litter under the tree provide a favorable microclimate for the seeds of other desert plants to grow. Desert Ironwood is extremely long-lived (to 1,500 years) and it is common to see Saguaro cacti growing up through the branches of the Desert Ironwood. Many other plants and animals also depend on the shelter provided by this unique tree.

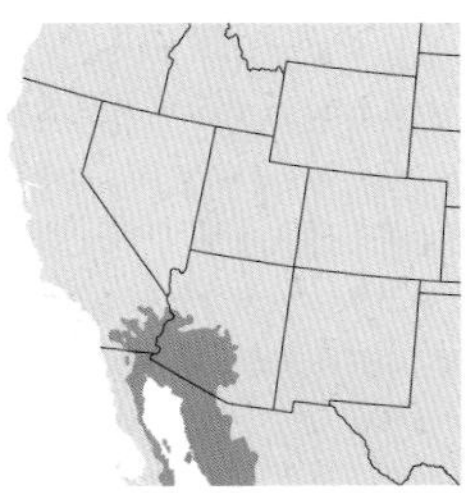

Locally common in sandy washes in Sonoran desert, with at least some access to water. Uncommonly cultivated (zone 10).

Smokethorn

Psorothamnus spinosus

SMOKE TREE

Deciduous. Shrub or occasionally a small tree to about 25' tall; a mass of spiny gray twigs (appearing smoky) with few leaves. Fruit a tiny pod holding a single seed.

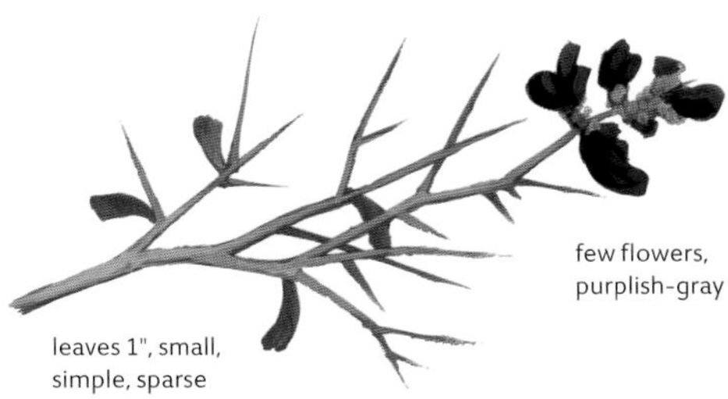
few flowers, purplish-gray
leaves 1", small, simple, sparse

Locally common in desert washes and river valleys. Occasionally cultivated near native range (zones 9–11).

Mescalbean

Sophora secundiflora

CORALBEAN, TEXAS MOUNTAIN-LAUREL

Evergreen. Shrub or small tree often 25' tall (max. 35'), usually multi-stemmed, with dense crown of dark leathery leaves. Flowers spectacular, with strong fragrance like grape soda, but brief.

leaves 5", glossy, hairy, compound, 7–9 leaflets, each 2"

underleaf pale whitish

seeds scarlet, contain a poisonous alkaloid

fruit pod hairy, green to tan, 5", constricted between seeds

flowers 1", fragrant, blue to violet, on drooping racemes 4" (spring)

white-flowered trees rare

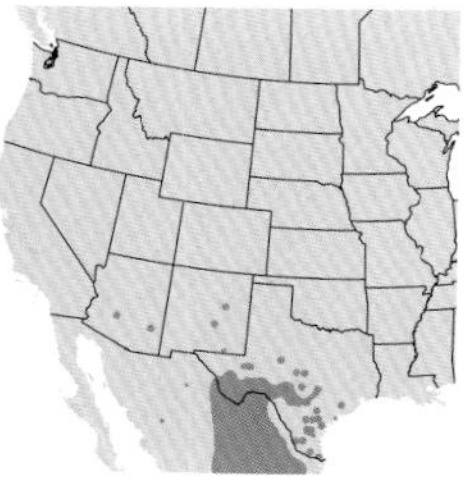

Common, especially riparian deciduous forests, still common but more scattered in less arid parts of oak-juniper or mesquite savanna. Uncommonly cultivated (zones 7–10).

Eve's Necklace

Styphnolobium affine

CORALBEAN, PINK SOPHORA, TEXAS SOPHORA

Deciduous. Shrub or small tree usually 15–30' tall (max. 41'), usually upright irregular crown, sparsely-branched with twigs more or less drooping; can be vine-like in shaded understory. Flowers like Mescalbean, but white and pink, not violet.

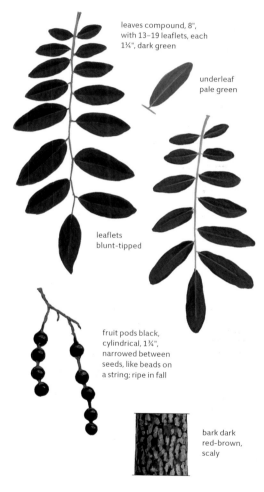

leaves compound, 8", with 13–19 leaflets, each 1¼", dark green

underleaf pale green

leaflets blunt-tipped

fruit pods black, cylindrical, 1¾", narrowed between seeds, like beads on a string; ripe in fall

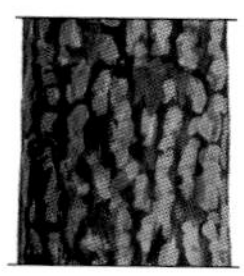

bark dark red-brown, scaly

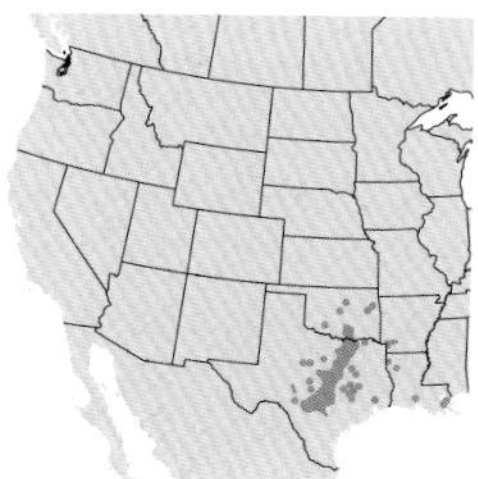

Uncommon and local in limestone soils along streams of central Texas. Uncommonly cultivated (zones 7–9).

Pagoda Tree

Styphnolobium japonicum

CHINESE SCHOLARTREE, JAPANESE PAGODA TREE, SOPHORA JAPONICA

Deciduous. Small to medium tree often 50' tall (max. 90'). Rounded crown, profuse whitish flowers, later in summer than any other ornamental flowering tree in temperate climates.

bark gray with
shallow scaly
ridges

leaves compound
8", 7–19 oval leaflets

fall color yellow

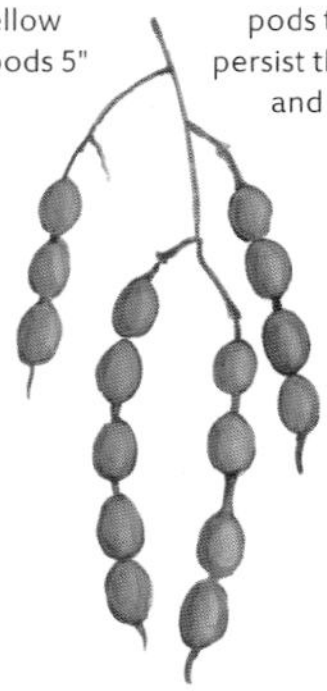
dull yellow
seed pods 5"
pods turn black and
persist through winter
and drop in spring
pods hang in tangled
clusters from yellowish
twigs, constricted
between seeds like
necklace

profuse clusters
of small creamy-
white flowers
in late summer

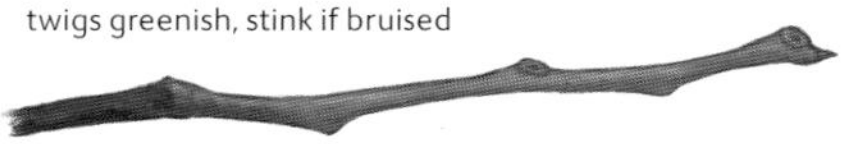
twigs greenish, stink if bruised

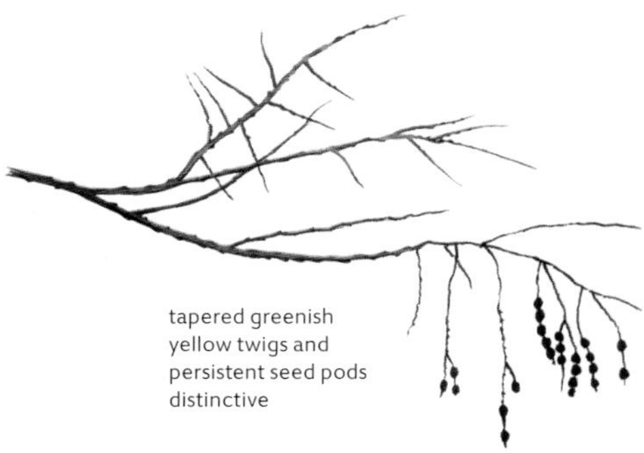
tapered greenish
yellow twigs and
persistent seed pods
distinctive

Native to China, Korea, and Vietnam. Commonly cultivated and locally naturalized (zones 4–7).

Black Locust

Robinia pseudoacacia

YELLOW LOCUST, LOCUST

Deciduous. Medium or large tree often 40–60' tall (max. 96'). Relatively tall and narrow with upper trunk and branches curved and contorted; often suckers to form pure stands.

bark on young trunks soon develops scaly ridges

bark on mature trunks extremely rugged with deep furrows and interlacing ridges

leaves compound 11", with 7–19 leaflets each 1½"

leaves often dull blue- or gray-green

underleaf paler green

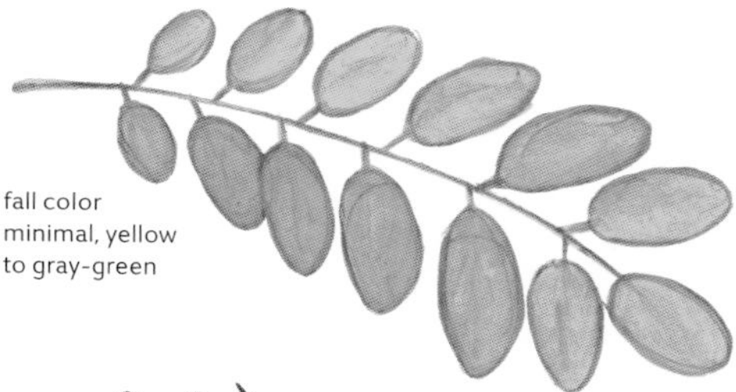

fall color minimal, yellow to gray-green

flowers showy, pea-like, white, in hanging clusters, 6", after leaves in late spring (May–Jul)

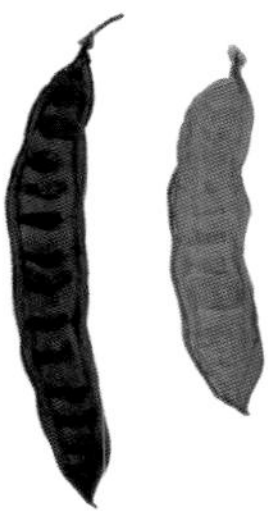

fruit pods 3", flattened, dark brown, ripe in fall; some persist into winter, some open to show whitish interior

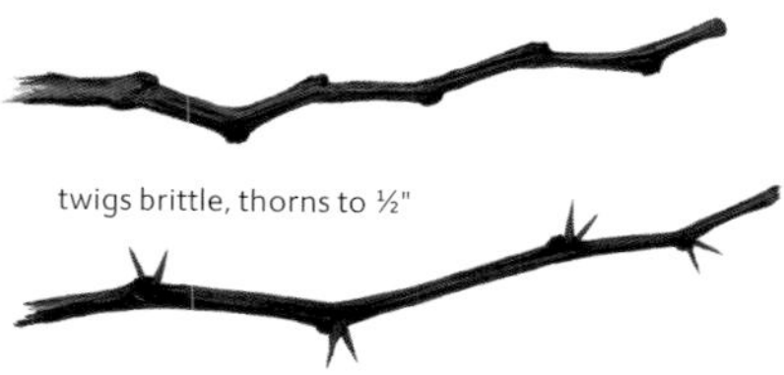

twigs brittle, thorns to ½"

twigs zigzag, twisted; seed pods often persist into winter

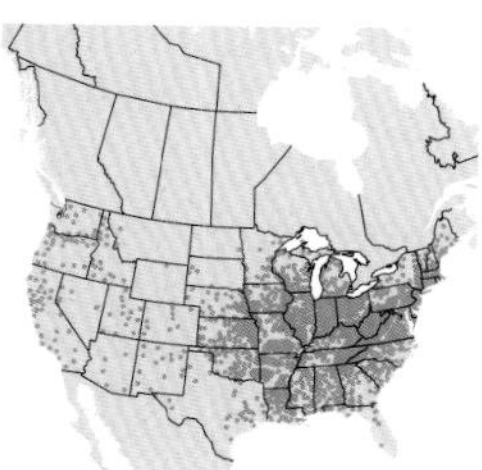

Common in old fields, roadsides, disturbed woods. Commonly cultivated and widely naturalized and invasive beyond native range (zones 3–8).

Several popular cultivars include tree with leaves emerging bright golden-yellow, and several with pink flowers, presumably representing hybrids with other species of locusts.

New Mexico Locust

Robinia neomexicana

Shrub or small tree to 25' (reported max. 76'), but larger trees may be hybrids with Black Locust. Differs from Black Locust in purple-pink flowers and bristly hairs on seed pods.

flowers purple-pink in hanging clusters

fruit pods 3", flattened like Black Locust, but covered with bristly hairs

twigs like Black Locust

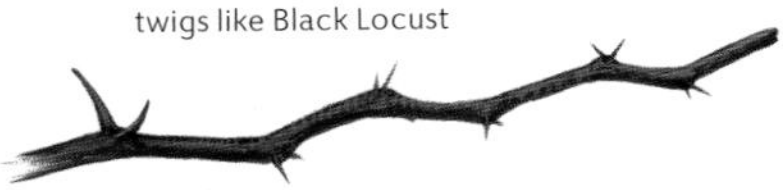

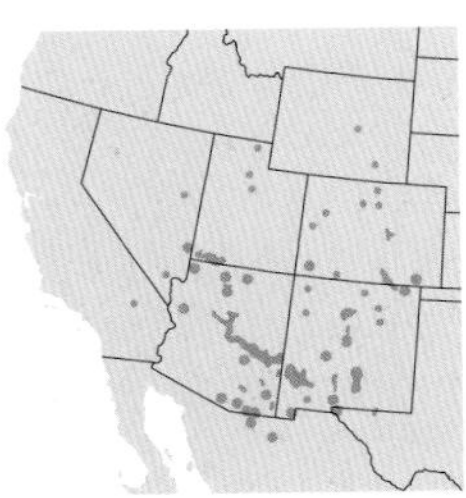

Common in canyons and moist slopes, occasionally cultivated.

Some botanists have recognized as many as twenty species in the exclusively North American genus *Robinia*. The more common treatment now is to recognize five variable species. Distinguishing species, varieties, and hybrids is challenging. Black Locust is the largest and most consistently tree-like, and the only species with white flowers. Other species are usually shrubs or small trees, and tend to have larger flowers than Black Locust, and flowers pink to purplish, not white. Hybrid Black × Clammy Locust with pink to purplish flowers is very popular and commonly cultivated.

Clammy Locust

Robinia viscosa

Deciduous. Large shrub or small tree usually under 20' tall (max. 23'). Differs from all other locusts in sticky glands on twigs, leafstalks, fruit; flowers pink, rarely white, may be later than Black Locust.

Rare in wild, found in thin woods, roadsides and thickets. Formerly commonly cultivated, now rare; often hybridizes (zones 5–8).

Bristly Locust

Robinia hispida

Deciduous. Shrub or occasionally a small tree to about 18'. Very similar to other locusts, and identification is difficult. Pink flowers and bristly pods like New Mexico, lacks sticky glands of Clammy Locust.

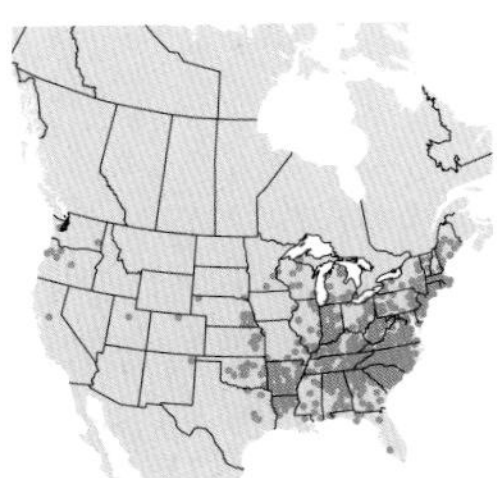

Rare in the wild. Occasionally cultivated, mainly as cultivars and hybrids (zones 5–8).

Kentucky Yellowwood

Cladrastis kentukea

AMERICAN YELLOWWOOD, YELLOW ASH, YELLOW LOCUST

Deciduous. Medium to large tree usually 30–50' tall (max. 73'). Often multi-trunked or low-branched, with broad, rounded crown of angular, thick-jointed twigs. Named for the yellow heartwood.

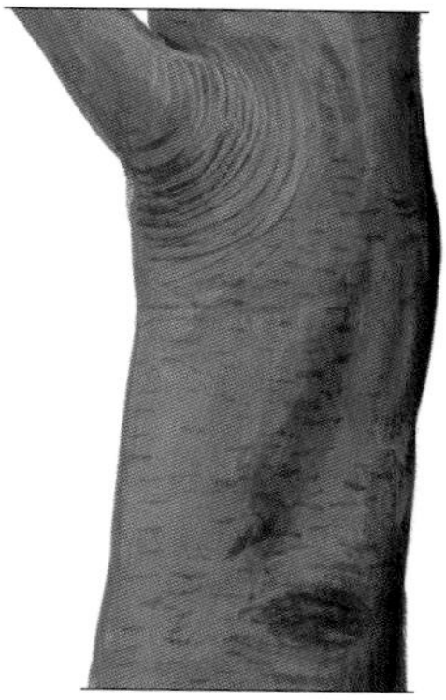

bark thin, smooth, pale gray, like beech, but often with lichens and mosses (unlike beech)

leafstalks often persist through winter

leaves compound, 10", 5–11 oval leaflets, each 3"

leaves relatively pale green, or slightly bluish

fall color yellow to gold

flowers white, in terminal hanging clusters, 10", late spring after leaves (Apr–Jun)

fruit pod 3", flattened, green turning brown, ripe in fall and sometimes persist into winter

twigs stout, zigzag

buds small, hairy, naked, covered by leafstalks

irregular tapered twigs, seed pods persist into winter, dangling in clusters at twig tips

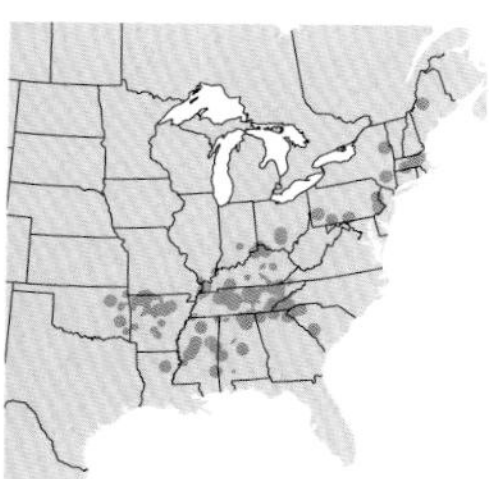

Rare and local in the wild in rich rocky coves, limestone cliffs, rich hardwood forests. Commonly cultivated (zones 4–8) several cultivars including one with pink flowers.

Japanese Yellowwood (*Cladrastis platycarpa*), native to Japan and uncommonly cultivated (zones 5–7). Differs from Kentucky Yellowwood in having flowers in upright clusters, later in Jun–Jul, average more leaflets (7–15), and leaves more hairy. Another Asian species, Chinese Yellowwood (*Cladrastis sinensis*), is rarely cultivated.

Common Laburnum

Laburnum anagyroides

GOLDEN CHAIN-TREE, GOLDEN RAIN TREE

Deciduous. Shrub or wide bushy tree usually 15–20' tall (max. about 35'). All parts of the plant contain a highly toxic alkaloid and may be fatal if eaten.

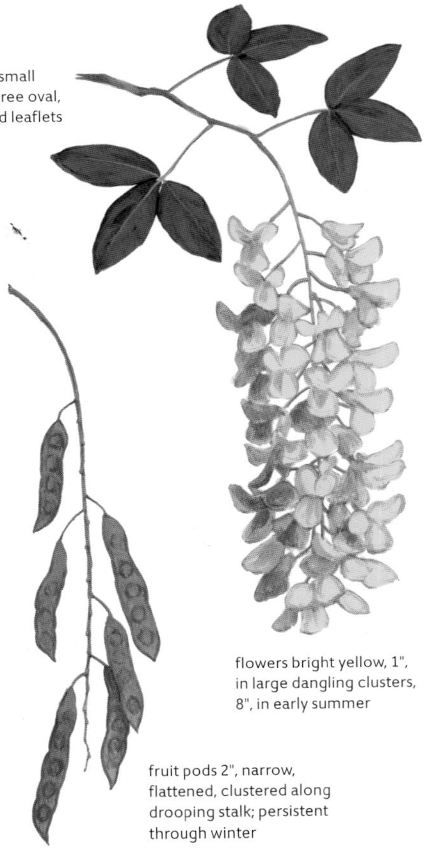
leaves small 2¼", three oval, pointed leaflets
flowers bright yellow, 1", in large dangling clusters, 8", in early summer
fruit pods 2", narrow, flattened, clustered along drooping stalk; persistent through winter

Scotch Laburnum (*Laburnum alpinum*), larger and more often tree-like (max. 40') with later blooms, is uncommonly cultivated (zones 4–7). Hybrids with larger flower clusters are cultivated as Voss's Golden Rain Tree (*Laburnum* × *watereri*), reportedly naturalized in Maine.

Native from Europe to Asia Minor. Commonly cultivated and occasionally naturalized to forest edges, roadsides and fields (zones 5–7).

Amur Maackia

Maackia amurensis

MANCHURIAN MAACKIA

Deciduous. Shrub or small tree often 25' tall (max 49'), low with rounded crown. Leaves resemble Kentucky Yellowwood, but peeling orange bark, upright clusters of small flowers, and lack of fall color distinctive. Native to Japan and Korea; uncommonly cultivated (zones 4–7).

leaves 10", compound with 7–11 broad oval leaflets each 2½", often gray-green
flowers dull greenish-white in erect spikes 5" (Jun–Jul)
seed pods flat, tapered, 2½", scattered along stiff stalk
twig grayish
buds small, rounded, brown

Eastern Redbud

Cercis canadensis

RED-BUD, JUDAS TREE

Deciduous. Small tree usually less than 30' tall (max. 66'). Short trunk and rounded crown; renowned for its spectacular display of bright pink flowers in early spring before the leaves.

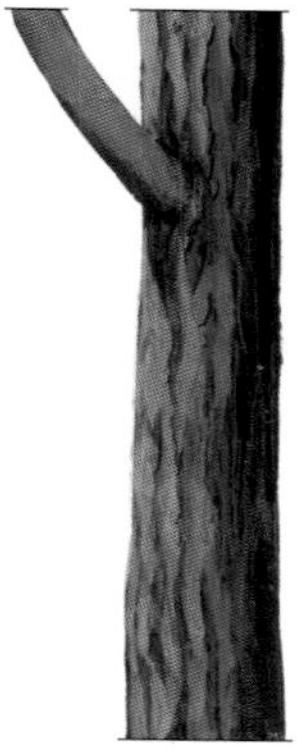
bark of young trunks
gray, developing
orange furrows

older trunks with small
scales, gray to red-brown

emerging leaves
often distinctive
golden-green
leaves 4", round
to heart-shaped,
hanging down

fall color
golden-yellow

flowers small,
purple/pink, pea-like; profuse
along branches (even trunk)
in small clusters in early spring
before leaves

flowers
occasionally white

fruit pods 2½",
flattened, green
or red turning dark
reddish-brown;
mature in summer

fruit pods may persist
through winter, hanging in
bunches from branches

twigs dark reddish with many
white lenticels
leaf buds
inconspicuous
flower buds larger,
clustered on older branchlets

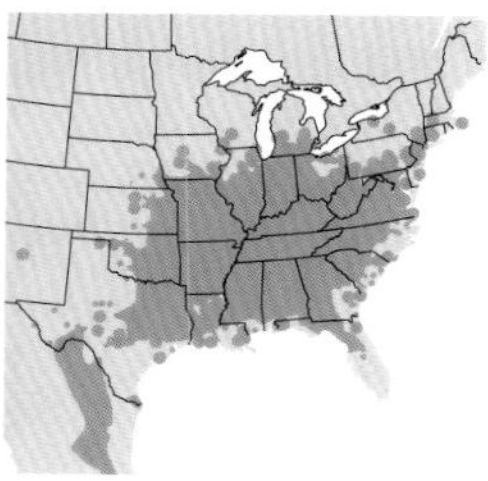

Common understory tree in rich, well-watered forest. Commonly and widely cultivated (zones 4–9).

spreading
rounded crown
of slender zigzag twigs

Bright pink flowers all along the branches and trunk of the Eastern Redbud are spectacular in early spring.

California Redbud

Cercis occidentalis

ARIZONA REDBUD, WESTERN REDBUD

Deciduous. Shrub or occasionally a small tree to 20' tall (max. 32'); usually spreading, multi-trunked. Leaves smaller than Eastern, more leathery, with shorter stalk and lacking pointed tip.

leaves 3½", heart-shaped to nearly round
leafstalks mostly less than 1"

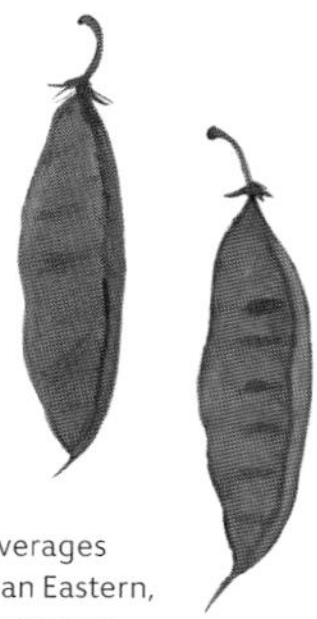
fruits pea-pod shape, 2½", brown when mature (Jul–Aug+)
fruit pod averages broader than Eastern, often paler orange-brown, rather than reddish

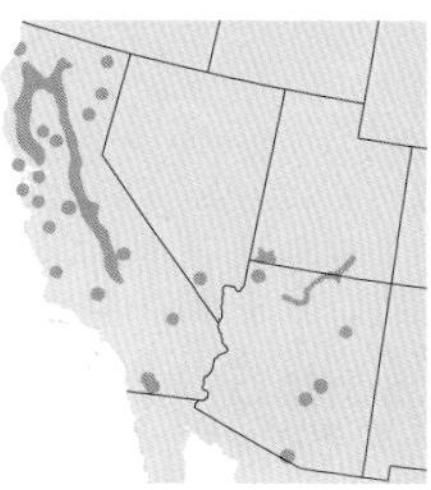

Locally common in foothills, canyons and slopes to 6,000' elevation. Commonly cultivated within its range (zones 7–9).

'Texas' Eastern Redbud

Cercis canadensis var. *texensis*

Subspecies of Eastern Redbud from southern Oklahoma to central Texas. Glossy, bluish, leathery leaves without long pointed tip, like California, but narrow pods like Eastern. Farther west the 'Mexican' Eastern Redbud (*C. c. mexicanus*) similar to Texas, but twigs and leafstalks hairy (Trans Pecos to New Mexico, and Mexico). Grows alongside Eastern in Texas.

leaves leathery, 3½", heart-shaped, similar to California Redbud

Cultivated forms include white-flowered trees, which have yellow-green new growth vs. reddish on pink-flowered trees, and purple-leaved cultivars, both uncommon in cultivation. Natural variation is rare in the wild.

Silktree

Albizia julibrissin

MIMOSA, SILKY ACACIA

Deciduous. Small to medium tree often 20–30' tall, taller in the South (max. 60'); spreading flat top, umbrella-like shape, large lacy leaves, and pink flowers distinctive.

bark thin, but coarse-textured, gray, not ridged

leaves large, 7", lacy, 8–16 leaflets, each with many tiny, narrow subleaflets
leaves fold up at night
fall color absent

flowers large, pale pink powder puffs (Apr–Aug)

fruit pods flat, 5", cross-banded

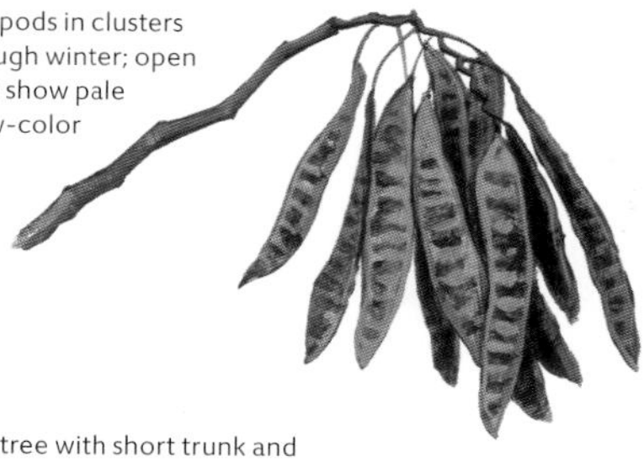
fruit pods in clusters through winter; open pods show pale straw-color

twig fairly stout, greenish to red-brown
buds tiny

low tree with short trunk and broad, umbrella-like crown of lacy leaves

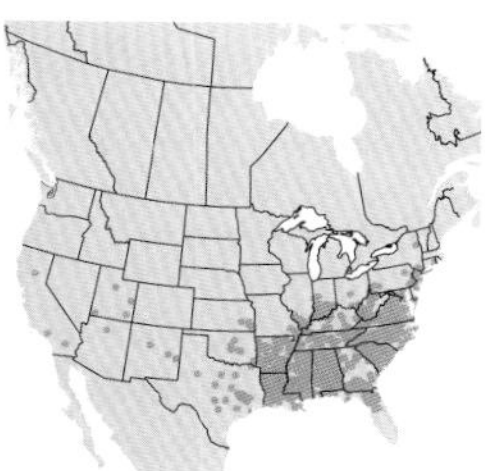

Native to southern Asia from Iran to Japan. Commonly cultivated in sunny yards and parks, widely naturalized and invasive (zones 6–9). Several cultivars differ in flower color and size.

Bayberry Family: Bayberries

There are over thirty species of bayberries (family Myricaceae) in the genus *Morella* worldwide. Five species are native to North America, three of which are sometimes tree-like.

A whitish waxy coating, usually present on the bayberry fruit, has long been used to make candles with the distinctive bayberry fragrance. Only a few species of birds can digest this waxy coating (notably Yellow-rumped Warbler and Tree Swallow) and the berries are a staple food for the birds in late fall.

Odorless Bayberry

Morella inodora

ODORLESS WAX-MYRTLE

Evergreen. Usually shrubby, occasionally tree-like, 15–20' tall, wide-spreading. Very similar to other bayberries; distinguished by broader leaves and sparser, larger fruit, which lacks the characteristic bayberry scent.

leaves broader than Southern, smooth margins curled under, no odor

fruit ¼", oval; on stalk to ½", single or in sparse clusters

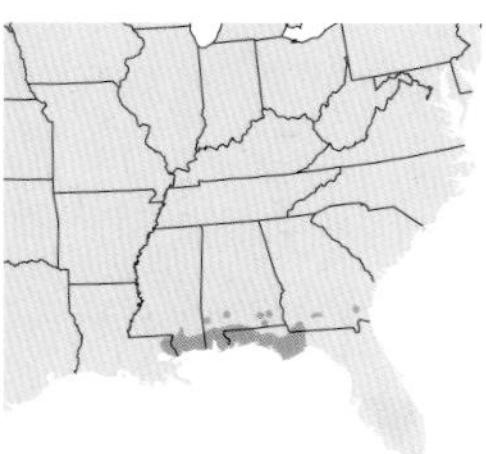

Rare in wet soils of coastal pine forests, swamps, bogs, ponds. Rarely cultivated (zones 8–9).

Southern Bayberry

Morella cerifera

COMMON WAX-MYRTLE

Evergreen. Small tree or shrub usually under 20' tall (max 28'); often in dense thickets. Cultivated plants are sometimes trimmed to expose trunk, making them appear more tree-like.

leaves narrow, 3", tapered base and toothed tip, very fragrant
underleaf pale yellow-green

fruit tiny, ⅛", ripe in Sep–Oct; persistent through winter

This species shows two main variants depending on habitat type. In moist swampy soils, plants tend to be solitary and larger, often tree-like, with larger leaves. On drier sites, plants are smaller with smaller leaves and tend to be clumped in shrubby thickets. Whether these are separate species, subspecies, or merely ecological variants is still debated.

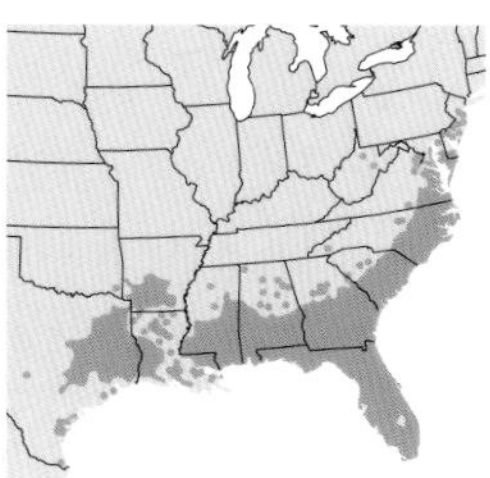

Common in a variety of habitats including moist swampy woods, drier sandy woods, or open fields. Commonly cultivated (zones 8–11) with several cultivars.

Pacific Bayberry

Morella californica

CALIFORNIA WAX-MYRTLE

Evergreen. Shrub or occasionally a small tree 20–30' tall (max. 38'). Smaller at northern and southern edges of range; usually multi-trunked, leaning, and crooked. Unlike other bayberries, this species has male and female flowers on the same plant.

bark smooth pale gray
with paler blotches

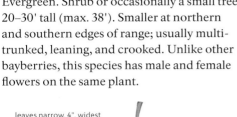

leaves narrow, 4", widest
with irregular teeth towards
tip, somewhat fragrant
when crushed; leaves
smaller at tips of twigs
underleaf
paler green

flowers tiny,
inconspicuous catkins
in leaf axils (spring
to early summer)

fruit in small
clusters
along twig

fruit ¼", small waxy berries
in tight clusters, pale bluish
or black; ripe in early autumn
and drop during winter

twig red-brown

small crooked tree with
dense dark foliage
and pale trunk

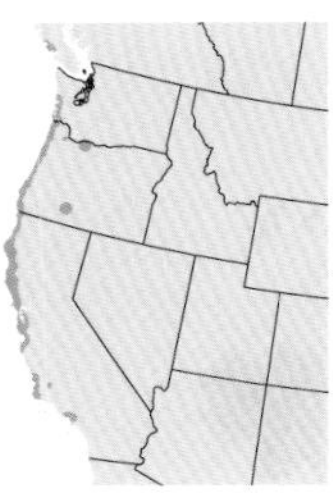

Common in moist soils from foothill slopes and canyons to coastal dunes; adaptable to a wide variety of habitats. Occasionally cultivated within natural range.

Walnut Family

The walnut family (Juglandaceae) with about seventy species of trees worldwide, includes the walnuts, the hickories (see page 142), and the wingnuts (see page 149). Walnuts (genus *Juglans*) include about twenty species worldwide, with six native and two exotic cultivated species in North America.

All walnuts have large pinnately compound leaves and produce robust, edible nuts, rich in fats and protein. Hickories are similar, but walnuts have single flower catkins, usually larger leaves with more leaflets, and larger, rounder fruit with a husk that does not split.

Walnuts may be subdivided into four subgroups:

BLACK WALNUT GROUP includes five of our natives; all have rounded fruit and oval buds and are very similar and closely related.

BUTTERNUT GROUP includes our other native walnut. Compared to Black Walnut, it has more cylindrical nuts (vs. round), rust-colored hairs on twigs and fruit, longer, flattened buds, and multiple fruits on a stalk.

ASIAN BUTTERNUT GROUP includes the Japanese Walnut.

ENGLISH WALNUT is the only species in its group and differs from all American species in having fewer, rounded leaflets without teeth, and large nuts with husks that often split.

Relatively slow-growing, walnuts have long been cultivated for their high-quality wood and nuts, and only incidentally for shade or ornament. The ground beneath walnut trees is often relatively open, due to a chemical produced by the tree inhibiting growth of other plants.

Walnuts are a favorite of squirrels and other animals. Native walnut species have relatively small, bitter and/or thick-shelled nuts. The familiar commercial walnuts are derived from the English Walnut.

Walnut wood is hard and durable with beautiful grain, but walnuts grow too slowly to be farmed commercially, so wood comes from individual trees harvested wherever they can be found.

Identification of walnut species can be very difficult. Each species is variable, and differences between species are small. Hybridization occurs wherever ranges overlap, and cultivated species and hybrids add further complexity. The introduction of Black Walnut in California has led to hybridization with Northern California Walnut and others. Most commercially-grown walnuts in California are now grafted to rootstocks of hybrid Northern California × English Walnut, and those trees might also be locally naturalized.

flowers April–May, with emerging leaves

male flowers in stout dangling catkins, 4" when open

female flowers small, green, at tip of developing shoot

all parts have distinctive odor

on all walnuts, leaves yellow in fall; fruit at tips of stout twigs usually fall with leaves

Black Walnut

Juglans nigra

Deciduous. Large tree often 50–75' tall, (max. 132'), with clear straight trunk. Slow-growing, with flavorful and hard-to-extract nut meats, not grown commercially. Beautiful wood is in very high demand, and individual trees are harvested for veneer and other applications.

bark of smaller branches and trunks peeling in thin long scales

bark dark, roughly furrowed in diamond pattern

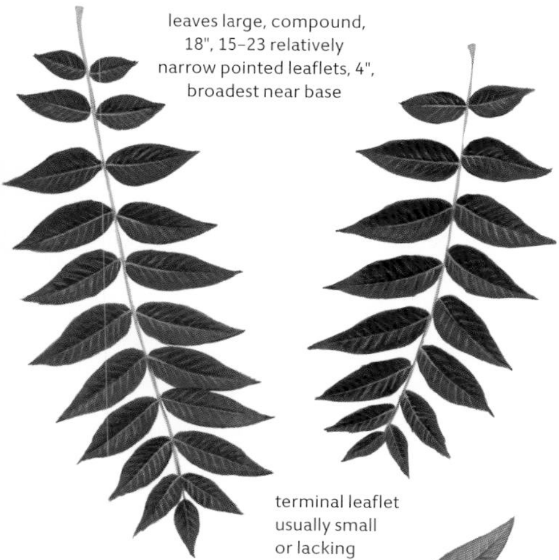

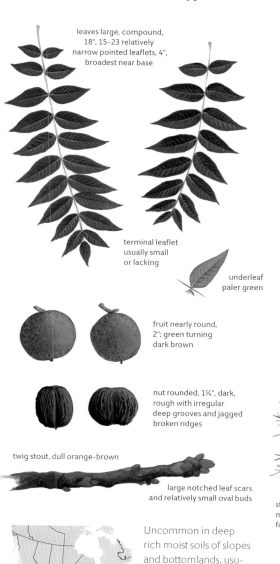

leaves large, compound, 18", 15–23 relatively narrow pointed leaflets, 4", broadest near base

terminal leaflet usually small or lacking

underleaf paler green

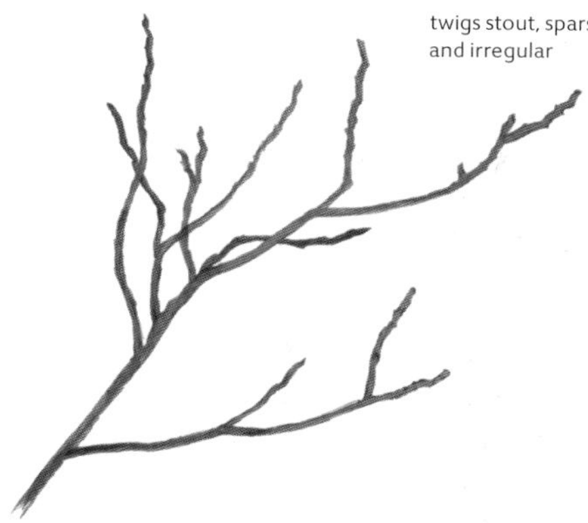

twigs stout, sparse and irregular

fruit nearly round, 2"; green turning dark brown

nut rounded, 1¼", dark, rough with irregular deep grooves and jagged broken ridges

twig stout, dull orange-brown

large notched leaf scars and relatively small oval buds

stout trunk with several main lateral branches forming open, broad crown

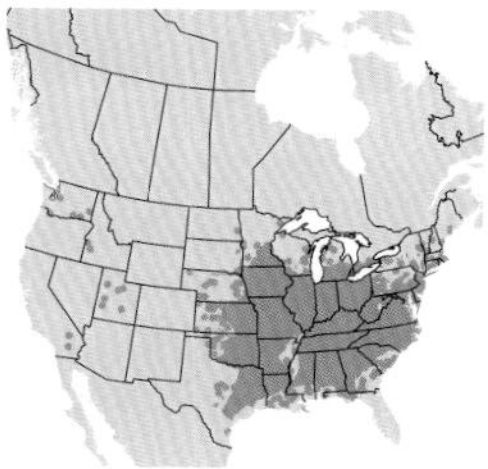

Uncommon in deep rich moist soils of slopes and bottomlands, usually in open deciduous woods or along edges. Commonly cultivated (zones 4–9).

Arizona Walnut

Juglans major

ARIZONA BLACK WALNUT, NOGAL

Deciduous. Shrub or small tree to 30–50' tall; overall a small version of Black Walnut. Intergrades with Little Walnut and sometimes considered the same species, also intergrades with Black Walnut in Texas and Oklahoma.

leaves 10",
9–15 narrow leaflets
leaflets coarsely-
toothed, blunt

underleaf
paler green

fruit round 1½", thin,
brown-haired husk
nuts oval, 1",
deep grooves, but
smooth ridges

twigs red-brown, hairy

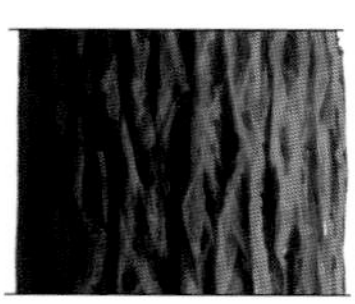
bark similar to
Black Walnut

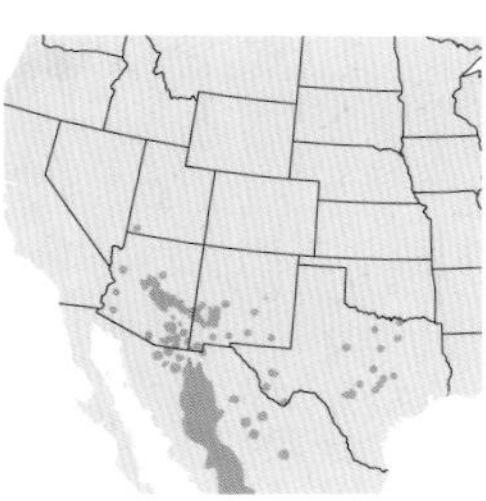

Uncommon and local along streams and in rocky canyons. Very rarely cultivated.

Little Walnut

Juglans microcarpa

TEXAS WALNUT, RIVER WALNUT

Deciduous. Shrub or small tree often 20' tall (max. 59'), with short leaning trunk; small leaves and fruit. Intergrades with Arizona and Black Walnut and sometimes considered a variety rather than a separate species.

leaves relatively small, 8",
17–25 narrow leaflets;
terminal leaflet usually small

underleaf
paler green

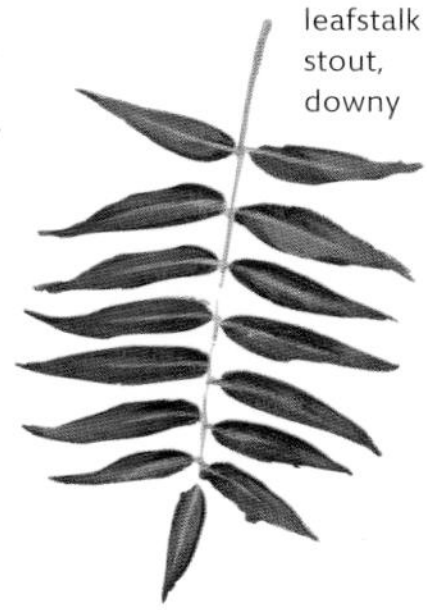
leafstalk
stout,
downy

fruit small, oval, 1",
smooth husk
nuts small, ¾",
round, grooved,
with smooth ridges

twigs orange-red, downy

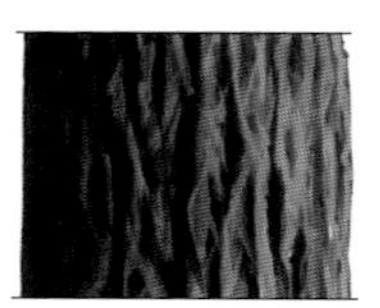
bark similar to
Black Walnut

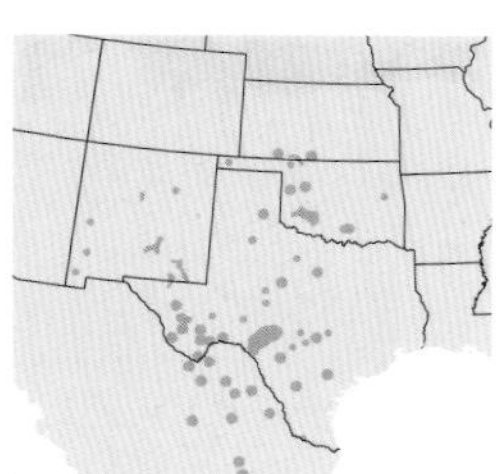

Uncommon and local along streams and rivers. Very rare in cultivation.

Northern California Walnut

Juglans hindsii

HINDS'S BLACK WALNUT, CALIFORNIA BLACK WALNUT

Deciduous. Small to medium tree often 50–75' tall (max. 115'); trunk often clear for 10–20'. Hybridizes with Black and English Walnut.

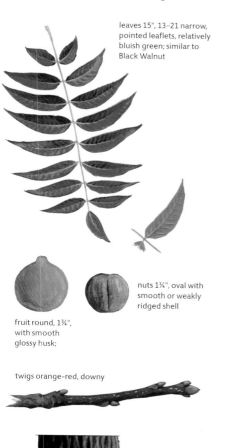

leaves 15", 13–21 narrow, pointed leaflets, relatively bluish green; similar to Black Walnut

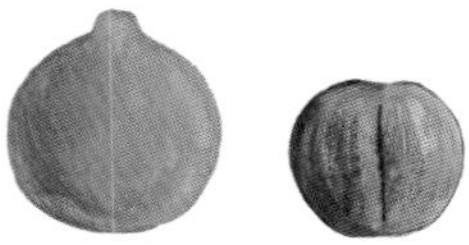

nuts 1¼", oval with smooth or weakly ridged shell

fruit round, 1¾", with smooth glossy husk;

twigs orange-red, downy

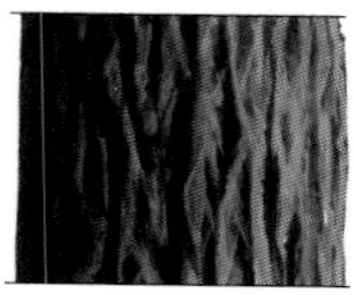

bark similar to Black Walnut

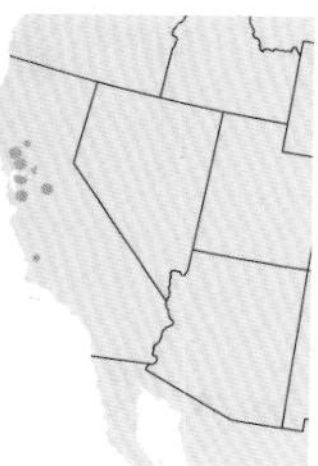

Rare in the wild, grows naturally in only a few locations along foothill streams. Commonly cultivated and used as rootstock for commercial plantings of English Walnut and now locally naturalized in California.

Southern California Walnut

Juglans californica

CALIFORNIA BLACK WALNUT

Deciduous. Shrub or short-trunked small tree usually under 30' tall (reports to 116' tall may be hybrids). The most distinctive western walnut, but the small leaves with oval leaflets are sometimes matched by early-season leaves of other species.

leaflets distinctively small and rounded

compound leaves small, 8", 11–15 oval leaflets, 3" each

fruit small, nearly round, 1¼"

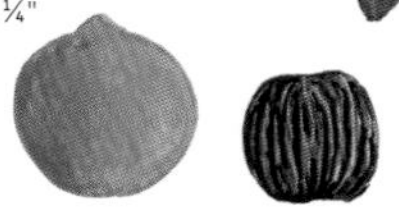

nuts small, 1", shallowly grooved, ridges smooth

twigs orange-red, downy

bark similar to Black Walnut

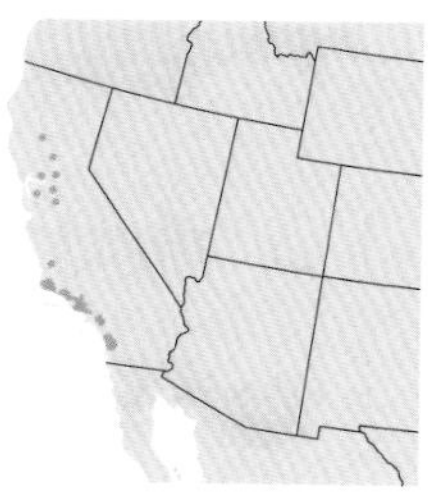

Uncommon and local in moist soil along streams in canyons and hillsides. Extremely rare in cultivation.

Butternut

Juglans cinerea

WHITE WALNUT, OILNUT

Deciduous. Medium tree commonly 60' tall (max. 88'); usually with short crooked or forked trunk. Named for the rich oil found in the nuts. Wood is prized for woodworking, and nut husks can be used to produce a yellow-brown dye.

bark of young trunks smooth pale gray, soon developing ridges

bark light gray with broad, smooth ridges

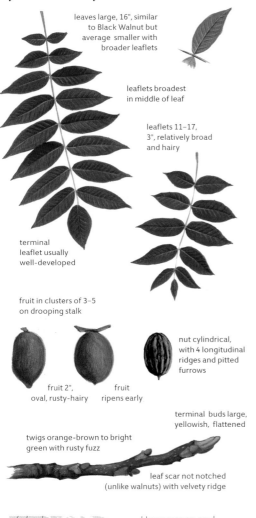

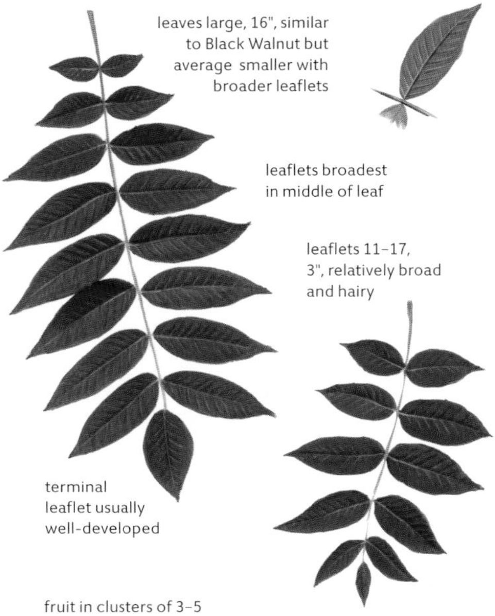
leaves large, 16", similar to Black Walnut but average smaller with broader leaflets
leaflets broadest in middle of leaf
leaflets 11–17, 3", relatively broad and hairy
terminal leaflet usually well-developed

Butternut canker is a disease caused by a fungus, first discovered in Wisconsin in 1967. Presumably from Asia, it has since spread virtually throughout the range of Butternut, with over ninety percent of trees infected in some regions. The fungus produces large cankers on the bark, and is usually fatal, although a few cases of long-term survival of trees have been reported. Few other walnuts are infected, and Asian species are most resistant. Efforts to develop a resistant Butternut tree are ongoing.

fruit in clusters of 3–5 on drooping stalk
fruit 2", oval, rusty-hairy
fruit ripens early
nut cylindrical, with 4 longitudinal ridges and pitted furrows

terminal buds large, yellowish, flattened
twigs orange-brown to bright green with rusty fuzz
leaf scar not notched (unlike walnuts) with velvety ridge

like Black Walnut, sheds leaflets early fall, leafstalks remain
pale trunk forks into "bouquet-shape," like some elms

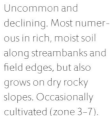

Uncommon and declining. Most numerous in rich, moist soil along streambanks and field edges, but also grows on dry rocky slopes. Occasionally cultivated (zone 3–7).

Japanese Walnut

Juglans ailantifolia

HEARTNUT

Deciduous. Large broad tree often 50' tall (max. 75'). Related to Butternut, with similar bark and oval fruit, but leaf scars notched, female flowers bright red on tall spike, and fruit in long, hanging clusters of 4–10.

leaves 20", blunt-tipped
leaflets, usually 11–17

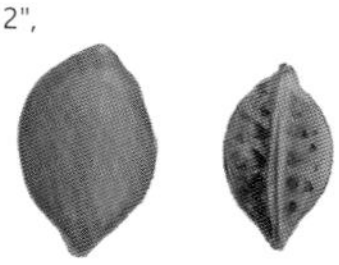
fruit 2",
oval
nut 1½",
smoothish or
weakly pitted
fruit in clusters of 4–10
on dangling stalk

twig gray-brown
buds pointed

The very similar Manchurian Walnut (*Juglans mandshurica*), native to northern China and Siberia, is sometimes cultivated, mainly in the northern Great Plains. It is more cold-tolerant than other species of walnuts.

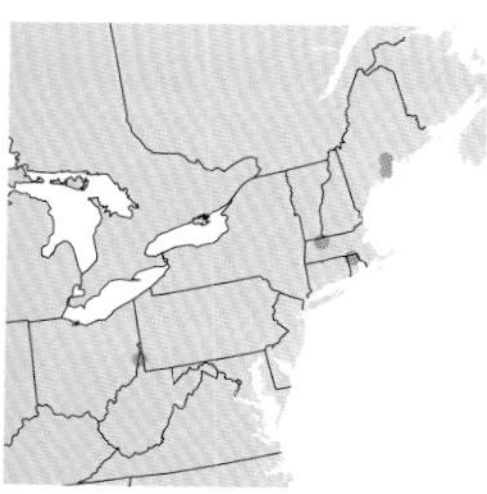

Native to Japan. Commonly cultivated, rarely escaped in New England (zones 4–9).

English Walnut

Juglans regia

PERSIAN WALNUT, MADEIRA NUT

Deciduous. Medium to large tree often 40–60' (max. 76'), broad-spreading crown. Long cultivated in Britain and Europe for ornament and nuts; this is the species that produces all commercial walnuts. Toothless leaves, and thin, smooth nut shell set this species apart from all other walnuts.

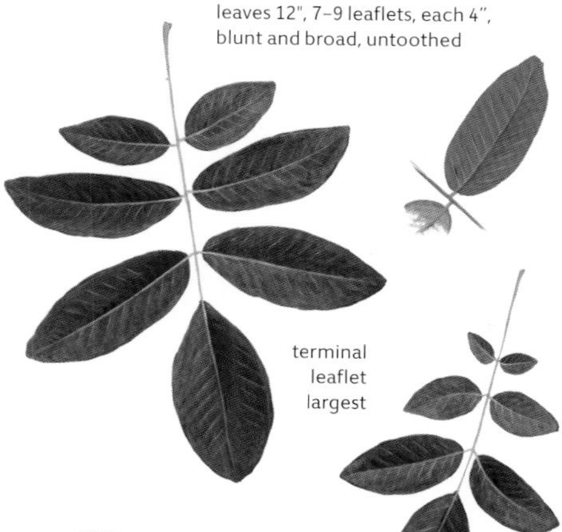
leaves 12", 7–9 leaflets, each 4",
blunt and broad, untoothed
terminal
leaflet
largest

fruit 2½", smooth, glossy;
husk splits partway unlike
all other walnuts

nut oval,
with smoothly
rounded ridges.

twig stout, greenish-brown
buds grayish

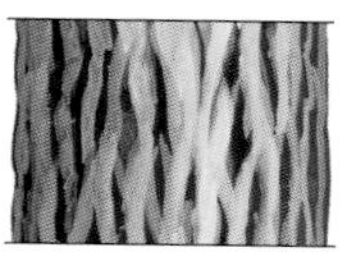
bark with smooth
silvery gray ridges interlacing;
young bark resembles aspen

Native to southeastern Europe, India, China. Planted for shade and nuts; locally naturalized in Pacific coast and Northeast (zones 5–9).

Walnut Family: Hickories

all hickories have conspicuous, large, leafy bracts, pale yellow-green to reddish, hanging at base of new growth in spring

Eleven hickory species are native to North America with about twenty-five total species worldwide. Hickories, like walnuts, have nutritious nuts enclosed in a tough husk, and alternate, pinnately compound leaves.Hickories differ from walnuts in having branched flower catkins, smaller nuts with husks that split, and generally fewer and larger leaflets. Hickories are superficially similar to ash, but are easily distinguished by their alternate leaves and branches, more crooked twigs, and very different flowers and fruit.

Hickories may be divided into three subgroups:

SHAGBARK GROUP (three species) has stout twigs and large buds, fruit with very thick husks, and five to nine large leaflets with a noticeably larger terminal leaflet. Two species, Shagbark and Shellbark, have very shaggy bark.

PIGNUT GROUP (four species) differs from the shagbarks in having more slender twigs, smaller buds, fruit with thinner husks, and three to seven smaller leaflets, all about the same size; they rarely have shaggy bark.

PECAN GROUP (four species) is distinguished by relatively slender, flattened buds, fruit with a very thin husk, and seven to seventeen slender leaflets. Nutmeg Hickory combines features of the pecan and pignut groups.

Hickory wood is valued for its strength and durability. The wood burns hot and is highly valued for fuel. Because hickories are slow-growing, sparsely-distributed, and very difficult to transplant, hickory wood is not widely available commercially. Hickory nuts are an important food for wildlife and are still consumed by humans, although only Pecans are grown commercially in large quantities.

male flowers hang in triple catkins below umbrella-like dome of emerging leaves

all hickories have fruit at twig tips, usually in clusters of 2 or 3, surrounded by unkempt cluster of leaves

fall color of all hickories ranges from golden yellow to orange-brown

twigs stout, stiff, crooked

Shagbark Hickory

Carya ovata

Deciduous. Medium to large tree often 70–90' tall (max. 153'). Named for its very shaggy bark, matched only by related Shellbark. Also distinguished by large buds and fruit, thick fruit husk, usually only 5 leaflets, and a conspicuously large terminal leaflet. Unique among hickories in having hairy leaflet edges, especially on new leaves.

young bark smooth, gray, striped

mature bark very shaggy, in long, curling strips

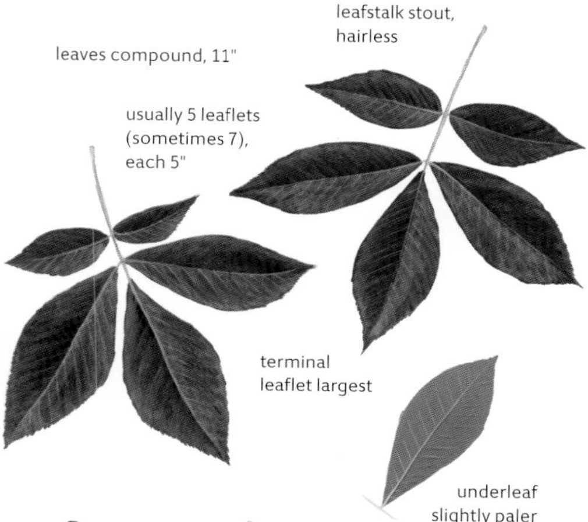

leaves compound, 11"

leafstalk stout, hairless

usually 5 leaflets (sometimes 7), each 5"

terminal leaflet largest

underleaf slightly paler

fruit large, 1¾", nearly round

husk thick, green, splits to base

nut 4-ribbed

branches dark, stout; trunk pale gray, contorted

lower branches arch and droop

In the Southeast, trees with narrower leaflets and smaller fruit (averaging 1") are considered either a variety (var. *australis*), or a separate species, *Carya carolinae-septentrionalis*.

twigs stout, usually hairless

buds large and dark; slightly more elongated than Mockernut

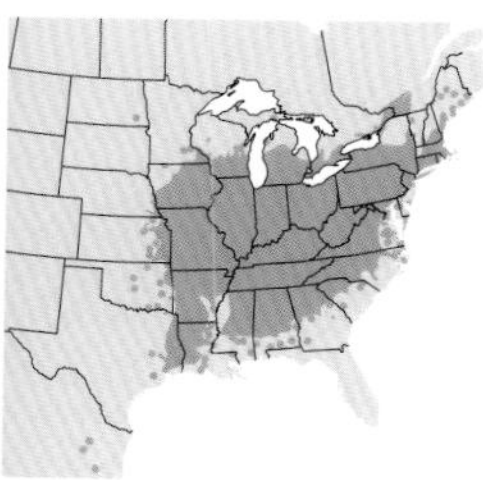

Common on relatively dry upland slopes in northern areas, well-drained rich lowlands in South. Often cultivated (zones 4–8) as single trees in farmyards for shade and nuts.

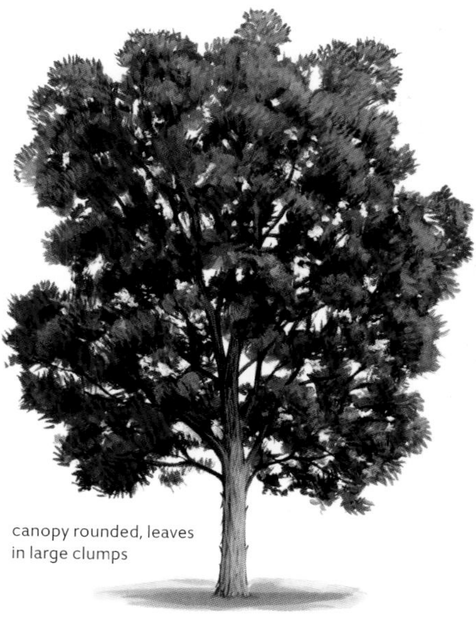

canopy rounded, leaves in large clumps

Shellbark Hickory

Carya laciniosa

BIGLEAF SHAGBARK

Deciduous. Medium to large tree often 70–90' tall (max. 139'). Very similar to Shagbark, but in wetter soils. Distinguished by smaller size, larger buds, hairy, orange twigs, larger fruit with a thicker husk, and usually more leaflets.

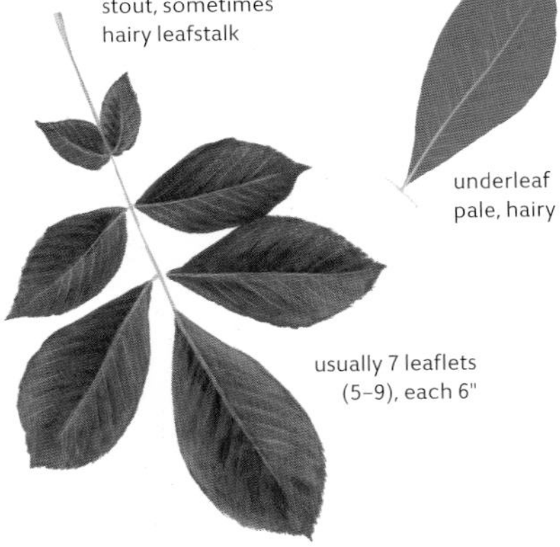
leaves compound,
large, 16"
stout, sometimes
hairy leafstalk
underleaf
pale, hairy
usually 7 leaflets
(5–9), each 6"

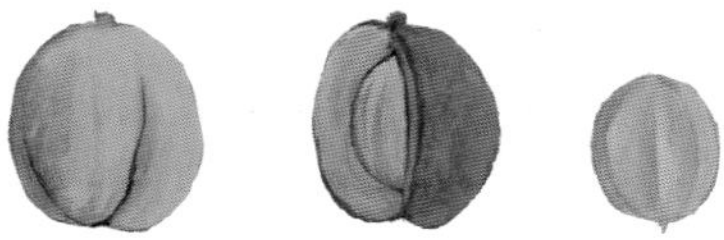
fruit very large, 2",
round and somewhat flattened
green husk
very thick,
splits to base
nut large, thick-shelled, flattened,
4-angled

buds very large,
brown
twigs light orange, stout,
usually hairy

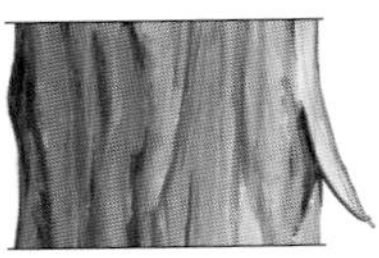
bark shaggy,
similar to Shagbark

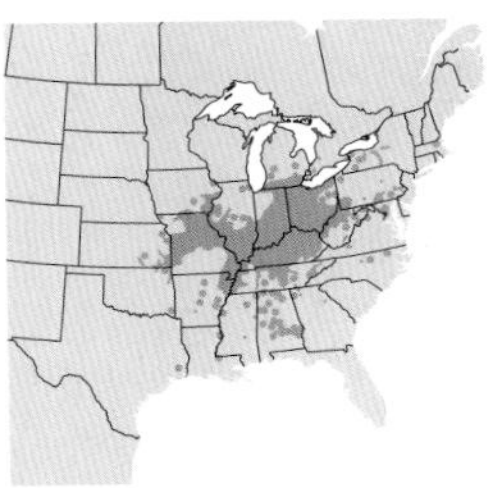

Uncommon in rich moist soils, including in bottomlands, even where inundated for short periods. Rarely cultivated.

Mockernut Hickory

Carya tomentosa

WHITE HICKORY, BULLNUT HICKORY

Deciduous. Medium to large tree often 50–70' tall (max. 156'). Similar to Shagbark and Shellbark Hickories in stout twigs, large buds and fruit, and large leaves; differs in tight bark, thinner fruit husk, hairy leafstalk, and stout, whitish winter buds.

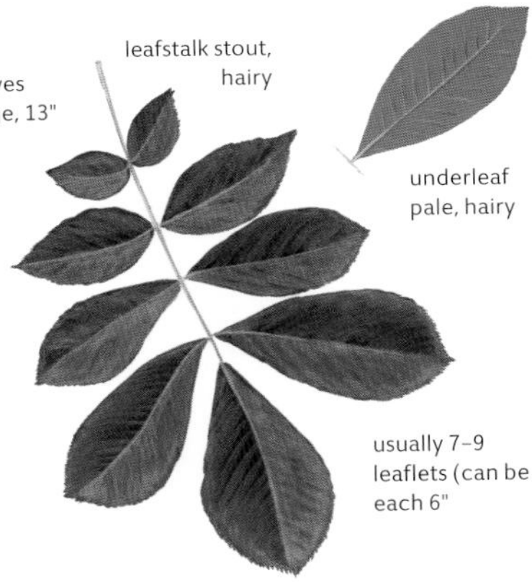
leafstalk stout,
hairy
leaves
large, 13"
underleaf
pale, hairy
usually 7–9
leaflets (can be 5),
each 6"

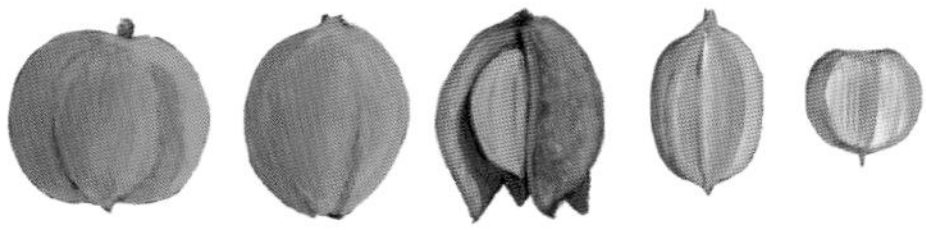
fruit large, 1¾";
oval to pear-shaped
husk, splits
to base
nut thick-shelled,
4-ribbed
green husk thinner than
Shagbark and Shellbark

twigs orange-brown,
stout, and hairy
buds large, long,
and stout
buds smooth and whitish
after dark outer scales shed in autumn

bark tight (never shaggy),
in smooth, round-topped ridges
that interlace in diamond pattern

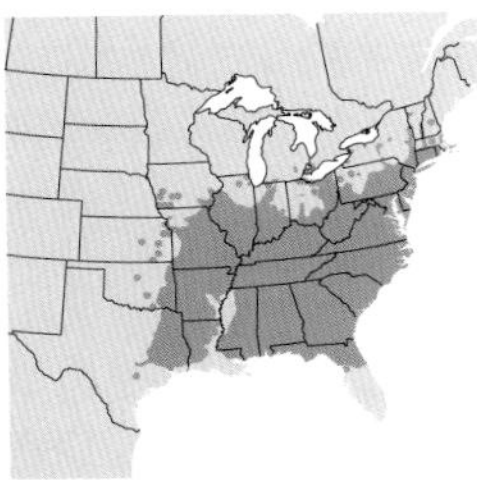

Common in Ohio Valley and South. Found from moist lowlands to dry slopes and ridges, but grows best in well-drained, moist soils. Rarely cultivated.

Pignut Hickory

Carya glabra

RED HICKORY, SWAMP HICKORY

Deciduous. Medium tree often 40–60' tall (max. 95'). Regionally variable, but usually differs from others in pignut group by 5 leaflets and fruit husk splitting only partway to base. Distinguished from shagbark group by tight bark, smaller leaves with generally smaller, more uniform leaflets, smaller fruit with thinner husk, usually more slender twigs, and smaller buds.

This species is variable across its range. Trees along the Gulf Coast (var. *megacarpa* or *C. leiodermis*) have tight bark and large, pear-shaped fruit. Many in the North (var. *odorata* or *C. ovalis*) have slightly shaggy bark, reddish leafstalk, smaller, oval fruit with the husk splitting to base, and often 7 leaflets (can be 5–9). Identification is further complicated by hybridization with Black, Sand, and Scrub Hickories, and also reportedly Bitternut Hickory, where range overlaps.

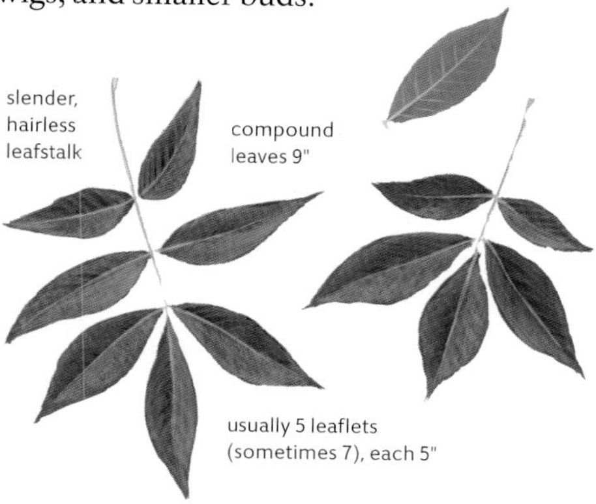
slender, hairless leafstalk
compound leaves 9"
usually 5 leaflets (sometimes 7), each 5"

relatively narrow habit in middle-aged trees, slightly contorted trunk and branches, and drooping lower branches

fruit 1½"; oval to slightly pear-shaped
husk usually lacks wings, usually splits only partway to base
thin husk; green to tan maturing to dark brown
unribbed nut

twigs reddish brown, usually relatively slender, and hairless
buds small, light brown and oval

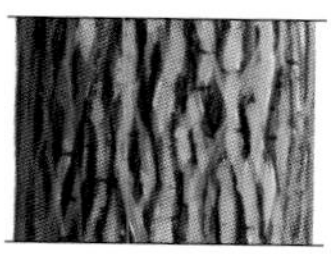
bark thin and tight, in smooth, interlacing ridges

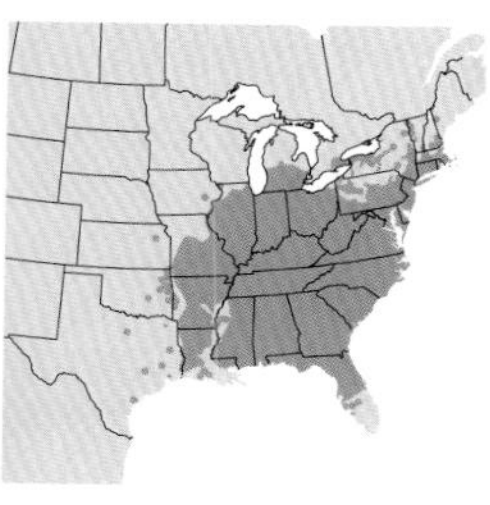

Common on mesic soils, especially rich soils on drier hillsides and ridges. Very common in southern Appalachians. Rarely cultivated.

Scrub Hickory

Carya floridana

Deciduous. Shrub or small tree to about 20' tall (max. about 80'); usually multi-trunked or thicket-forming. Closely related to Sweet Pignut, intermediates occur where range and habitat overlap. Uncommon in pine-scrub habitats of dry sand ridges in central Florida.

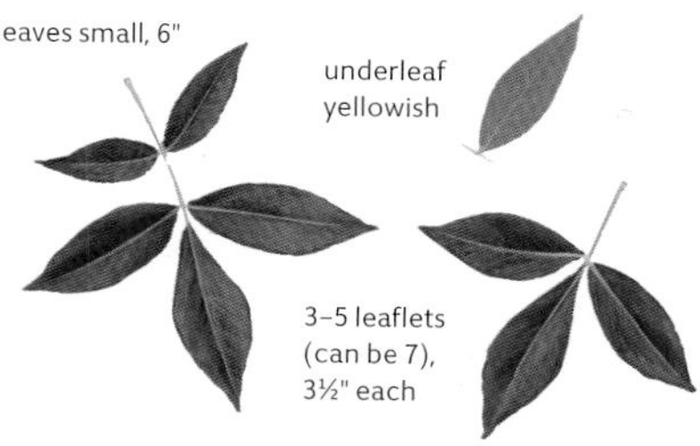
leaves small, 6"
underleaf yellowish
3–5 leaflets (can be 7), 3½" each

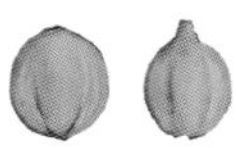
fruit slightly smaller than Sweet Pignut, 1"

twigs rusty-hairy

Black Hickory

Carya texana

BUCKLEY HICKORY

Deciduous. Small to medium tree usually under 50' tall (max. 90'). The only hickory with tufted, rust-colored hairs on twigs, buds, leafstalk, and underleaf, although most hairs lost in late summer. Closely related to Pignut.

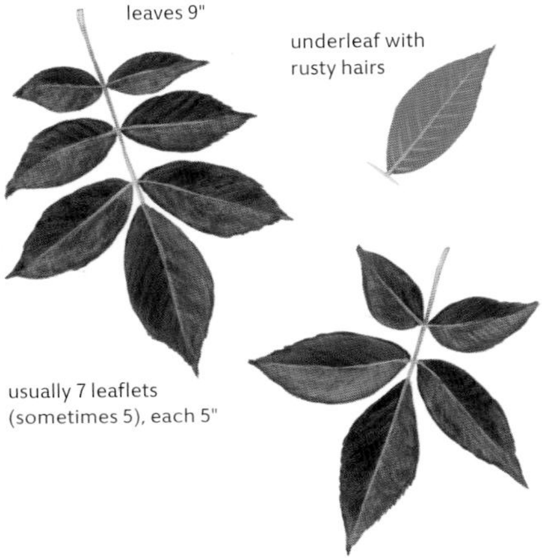
leaves 9"
underleaf with rusty hairs
usually 7 leaflets (sometimes 5), each 5"

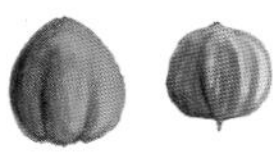
fruit 1¼", oval
husk very similar to Sweet Pignut, but often partly winged and splits to base
nut ribbed

twigs slender with rust-colored hairs
buds small, oval, and rusty brown

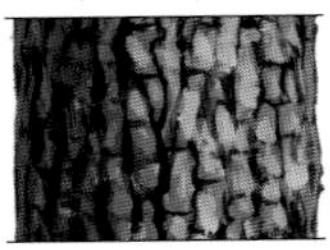
bark tight and rough, in irregular blocky ridges

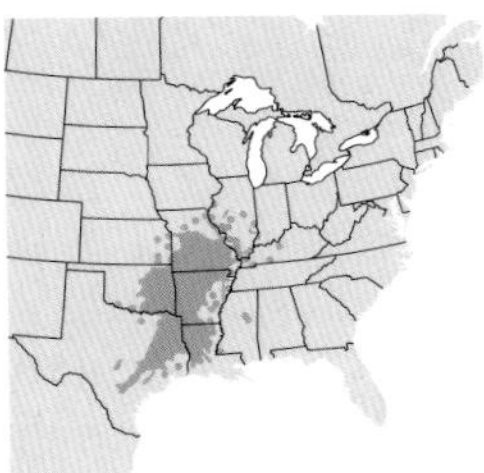

Uncommon in dry woods, sandy soils, and dry, rocky slopes and ridges. Often associated with Blackjack and Post Oaks. Not cultivated.

Sand Hickory

Carya pallida

PALE HICKORY, PALLID HICKORY

Deciduous. Medium tree often 50' tall (max. 110'). Similar to Pignut, distinguished by usually 7 leaflets, hairy leafstalk, and silvery scales on underleaf and leafstalk.

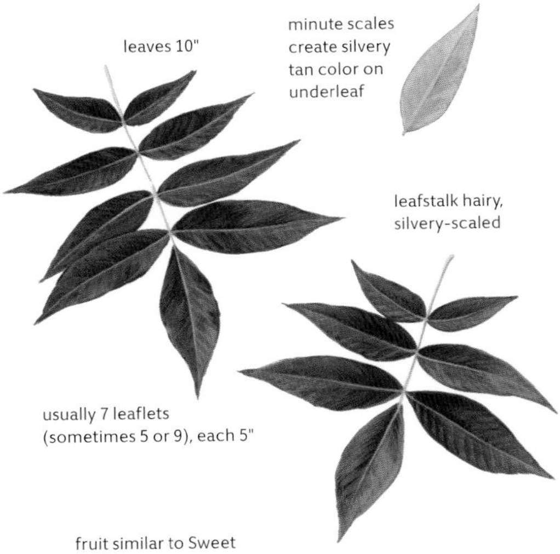
leaves 10"
minute scales create silvery tan color on underleaf
leafstalk hairy, silvery-scaled
usually 7 leaflets (sometimes 5 or 9), each 5"

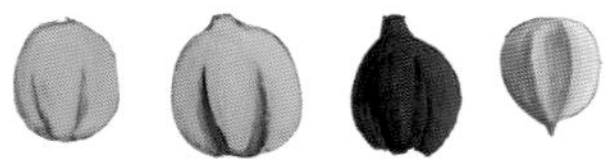
fruit similar to Sweet Pignut, but smaller, 1"
nut relatively thin-shelled, angled
husk lacks wings, splits to base

twigs similar to Sweet Pignut, but sometimes hairy or scaly
buds oval and reddish brown; partly covered with whitish or yellowish hairs

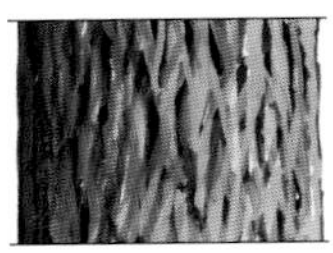
bark can be tight with interlacing ridges or somewhat shaggy

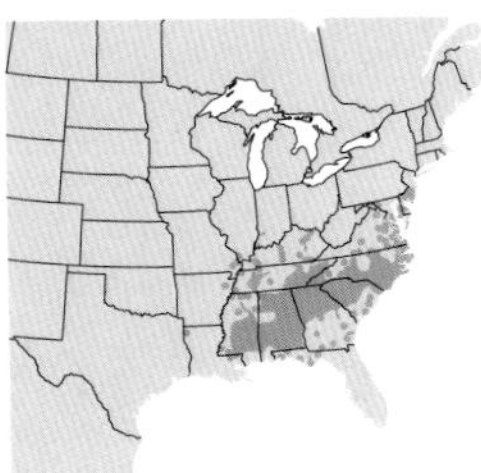

Uncommon in dry, sandy or gravelly soils. Not cultivated.

Pecan

Carya illinoinensis

SOFTSHELL HICKORY

Deciduous. Large tree often to 70' tall, taller in cultivation (max. 175'). Largest hickory and one of the most familiar trees in the South; distinguished by massive size, feathery leaves, and oblong fruit. One of the last trees to leaf out in spring, and leaves stay green into late fall.

bark on young trees gray-brown and smooth
bark on large trunks gray-brown, in thin, ragged, scaly ridges

leaves large, 16"
underleaf slightly paler green
leaflets often recurved, asymmetrical
usually 11–17 leaflets, each 5"

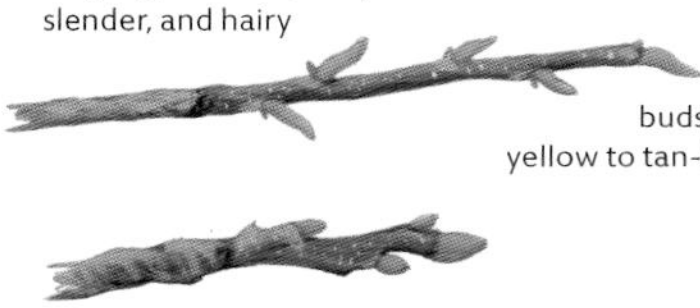
twigs light brown, fairly slender, and hairy
buds small; yellow to tan-brown

Slow-growing twigs, as on any tree species, can be much stouter than typical twigs and with buds more closely spaced.

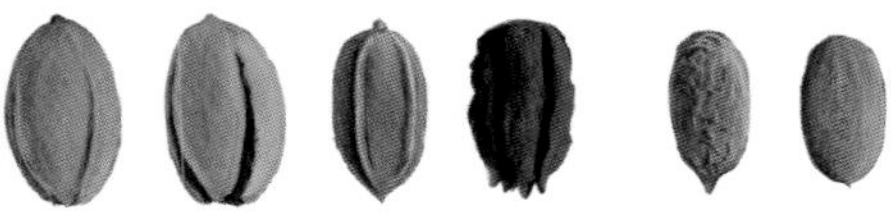
fruit 1½", oblong, not flattened
husk 4-winged, splits nearly to base
nut smooth, cylindrical light brown with stripes
husk very thin, green to orange-brown, maturing to blackish
nut of cultivated trees smooth, dark brown, and very thin-shelled

male flower catkins longer than on shagbark and pignut groups

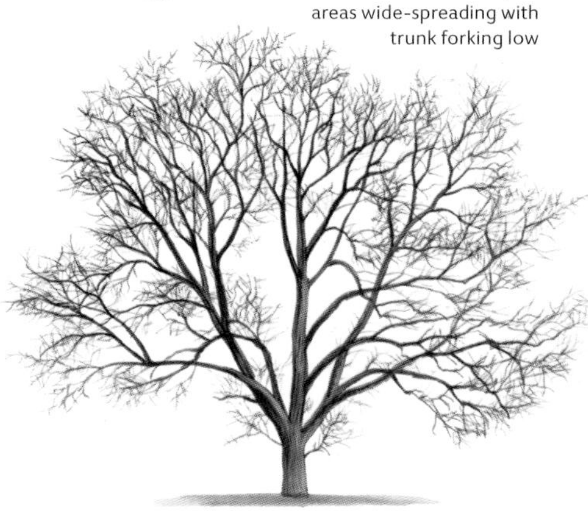
mature trees in open areas wide-spreading with trunk forking low

Artificial crosses of Pecan with several species of hickory are sold for nut production as *Carya* 'Hican'. A single tree can produce more than 1,000 pounds of nuts in a season.

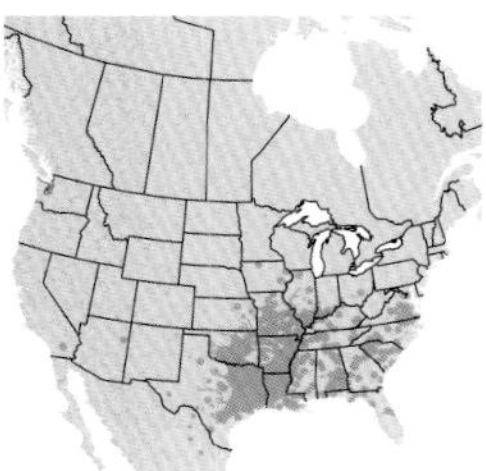

Common in many habitats; mostly in rich lowlands, including well-drained soils in floodplains. Commonly cultivated (zones 5–9) as a shade tree and for commercial use.

Water Hickory

Carya aquatica

BITTER PECAN

Deciduous. Medium to large tree often 70' tall (max. 143'). Distinguished from Pecan by fewer leaflets, flattened fruit, rough, angular nut, smaller overall size, and thin, unridged bark. Like Pecan, leaves emerge late.

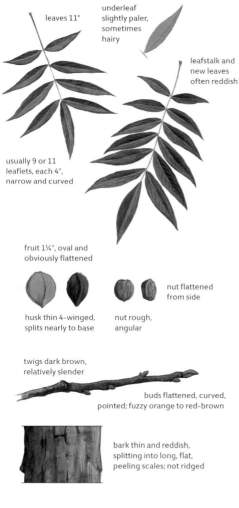

leaves 11"
underleaf slightly paler, sometimes hairy
leafstalk and new leaves often reddish
usually 9 or 11 leaflets, each 4", narrow and curved

fruit 1¼", oval and obviously flattened

nut flattened from side
husk thin 4-winged, splits nearly to base
nut rough, angular

twigs dark brown, relatively slender

buds flattened, curved, pointed; fuzzy orange to red-brown

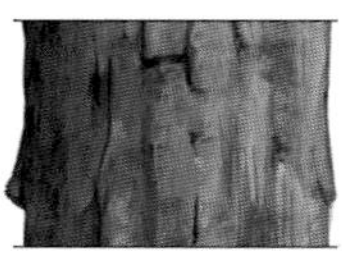
bark thin and reddish, splitting into long, flat, peeling scales; not ridged

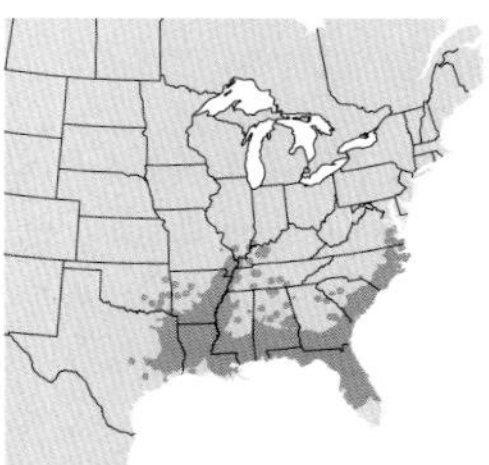

Common in wet, poorly drained, or flooded (and often inundated) bottomlands. Not cultivated.

Bitternut Hickory

Carya cordiformis

SWAMP HICKORY, PIGNUT

Deciduous. Medium tree often 60' tall (max. 153'). One of the most common and widespread hickories, particularly in Midwest. Note small, rounded, thin-husked fruit; small leaves with fewer leaflets than others in pecan group; yellow buds; and thin bark. Nuts are so bitter even squirrels usually avoid them. Like Pecan, leaves emerge relatively late.

underleaf slightly hairy and pale
compound leaves small, 8"
leaflets can be narrow or broad
slender leafstalk
usually 7–11 leaflets, each 4"

fruit small, 1"; rounded and often slightly flattened

very thin, rough husk

nut small, thin-shelled, smooth; nearly round with pointed tip
4-winged, splits only to middle

twigs light brown and slender to relatively stout

buds long, 4-angled, and yellowish

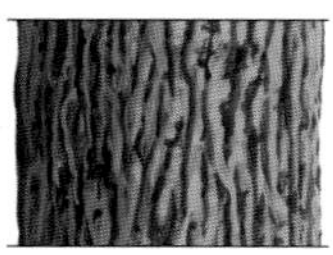
bark thin and tight, in shallow, interlacing ridges

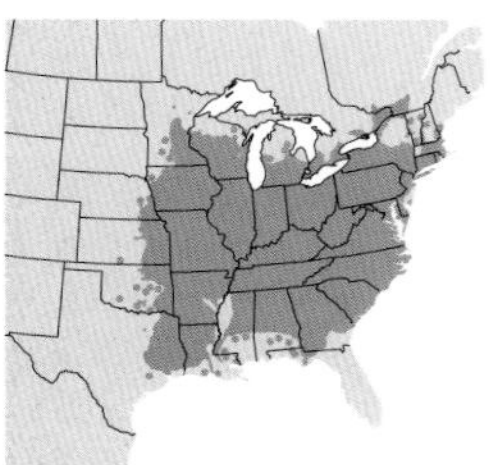

Common and widespread in a variety of habitats, from rich, moist lowlands (where most common) to drier uplands. Rarely cultivated.

Nutmeg Hickory

Carya myristiciformis

Deciduous. Medium to large tree often 70' tall (max. 145'). Whitish underleaf shared only with Sand Hickory. Similar to others in pecan group in bud details and winged fruit husk, but fewer leaflets, larger terminal leaflet, and slightly thicker fruit husk, more like pignut group.

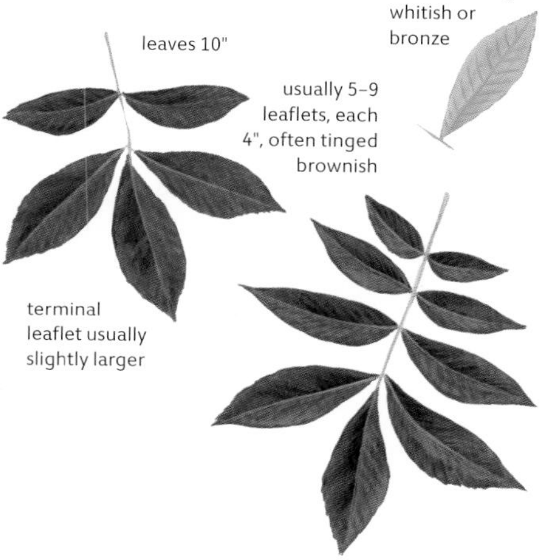
underleaf bright whitish or bronze
leaves 10"
usually 5–9 leaflets, each 4", often tinged brownish
terminal leaflet usually slightly larger

fruit 1¼", oval

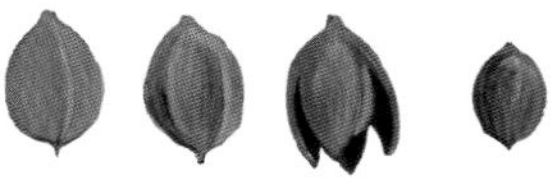
nut oval, smooth, thick-shelled

husk fairly thick, 4-winged, splits to base

twigs brownish, fairly slender

buds pale yellow to bronze, fairly slender

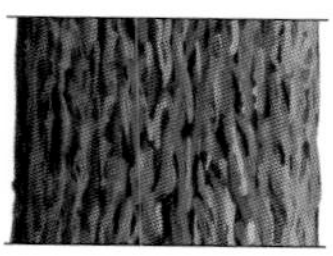

bark gray-brown to reddish, tight and scaly to slightly shaggy

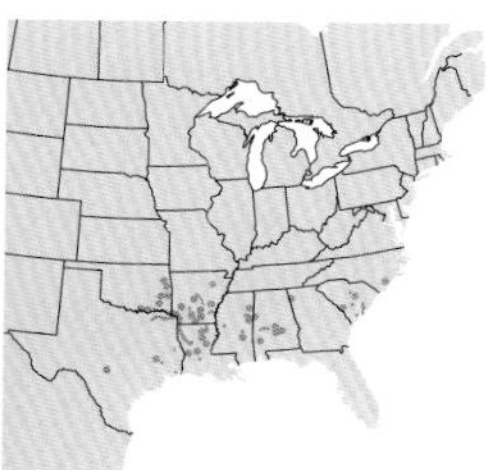

Rare and local in rich, moist soils of higher bottomlands, stream-banks, and poorly drained uplands. Not cultivated.

The nut meat of Shagbark Hickory is sweet-tasting and said to be the best of all hickories. Pecan produces a much more important commercial nut crop, but Shagbark Hickory provides most "wild" hickory nuts. Most other species in the genus also have sweet-tasting nut meat, the only exceptions, with bitter-tasting fruit, being Bitternut, Water, and sometimes Pignut Hickory.

Hickory Family: Wingnut

The wingnuts (genus *Platycarya*) include about ten species of trees native to Asia. They are related to walnuts and hickories, with similar compound leaves, but the fruit is a dangling string of small seeds each with a narrow papery wing.

Chinese Wingnut

Pterocarya stenoptera

Deciduous. Medium to large spreading tree often 50' tall (max. 98'); often multi-trunked. Leaves are similar to those of walnuts, but fruit is very different; fall color absent. Native to China. Rarely cultivated, this is the most frequent of several species of wingnuts in cultivation. Naturalized in Louisiana (zones 6–8).

leaves large, 12", 11–25 leaflets, central stalk winged

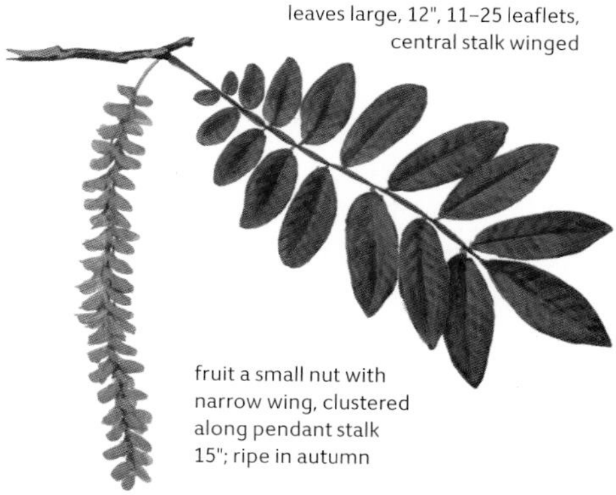
fruit a small nut with narrow wing, clustered along pendant stalk 15"; ripe in autumn

Birch Family: Birches

About thirty-five species of birches occur around the colder regions of the northern hemisphere, with about eighteen species native to North America. Seven are only small shrubs, but eleven native species and two cultivated species are tree-like and are covered here. All birches have more or less oval, toothed leaves, slender and graceful twigs, conspicuous male flower catkins in early spring, tiny papery seeds in a cone-like structure, and thin colorful bark. The birches can be divided into two groups:

> WHITE BIRCH GROUP includes seven native and two cultivated species with white or bronze-red bark that often peels in papery sheets. They have longer leafstalks and pendent fruiting catkins on long stalks.
>
> SWEET BIRCH GROUP includes five species characterized by darker and rougher bark, short leafstalks, upright fruiting catkins on very short stalks. Their bark is never white. Bruised twigs have a strong wintergreen or root beer odor.

An important but minute feature for identifying some species of birch is the shape of the seed wings. Each fruiting catkin is densely packed with tiny seeds, and each has a small papery, three-lobed wing about $1/10$" wide. The exact shape of the lobes differs between species.

Most birch trees are too small to be useful for lumber, but the wood of large trees (especially Yellow Birch) finds many uses in carpentry, furniture, plywood, and veneer.

Birch bark is highly resinous, slow to rot, and quick to burn, making it one of the most useful natural materials in the forest. Note that peeling the bark from a live tree will kill it. The tiny seeds are a favorite food of small finches, such as redpolls, and the trees themselves are important ecologically as pioneers, quick to colonize disturbed areas.

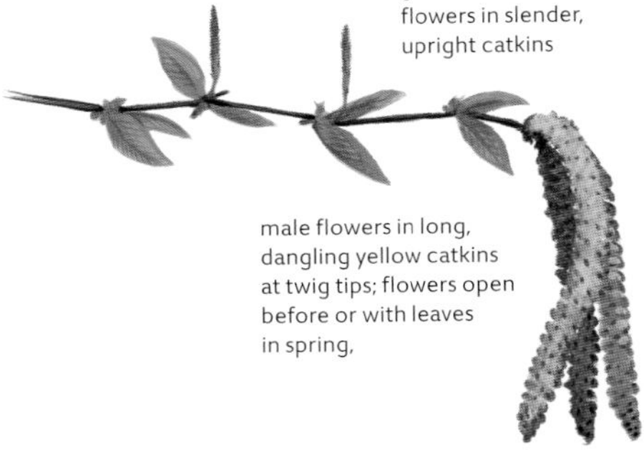

green or red female flowers in slender, upright catkins

male flowers in long, dangling yellow catkins at twig tips; flowers open before or with leaves in spring,

fruiting catkins hang among leaves in late summer

fall color generally clear yellow; fruiting catkins turn brown and may persist through winter

Paper Birch, typical of white birch group, with longer leafstalks and less oval leaves, slender dangling fruit catkins

Yellow Birch, typical of sweet birch group, with short leafstalks on oval leaves, stout upright fruit catkins

Paper Birch

Betula papyrifera

CANOE BIRCH, WHITE BIRCH, SILVER BIRCH

Deciduous. Medium tree, often 70' tall (max. 120'); usually single-trunked, with relatively narrow crown. The most widespread and familiar birch in North America—its peeling white bark is an icon of the northern woods. Distinguished from similar birches by large size, oval leaves, and long-stalked fruit.

bark of saplings dark reddish brown with pale lenticels

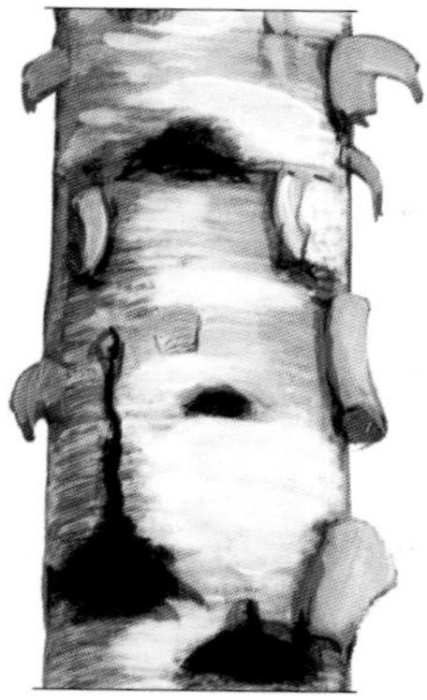

bark becomes white and peeling at varying ages

leaves 3½"; coarsely double-toothed
more or less oval, fairly short stalk
underleaf paler green, as in most birches

The bark color of Paper Birch is variable. Older trees are typically whitish, but some trees retain dark or reddish, unpeeling bark, a variation that is more frequent in the West.

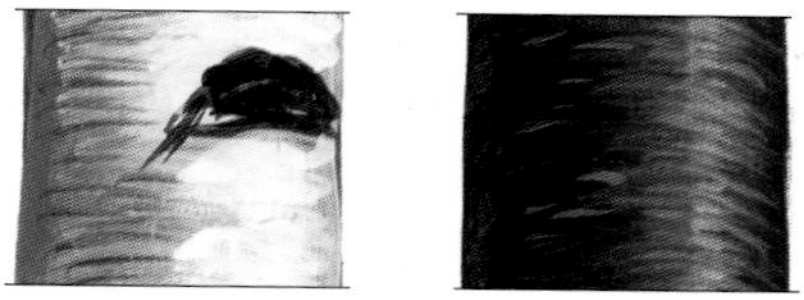

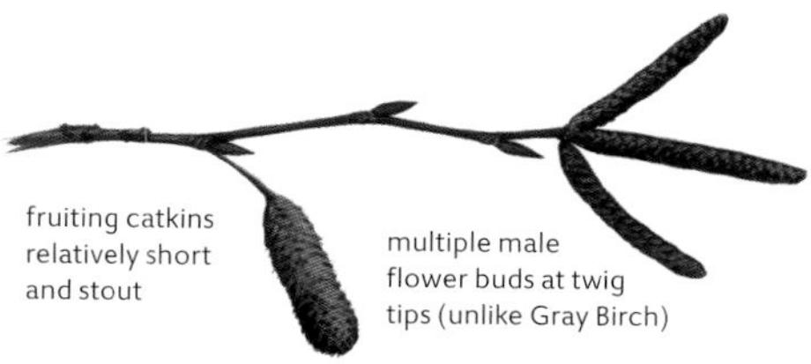

fruiting catkins relatively short and stout
multiple male flower buds at twig tips (unlike Gray Birch)

twigs stout for a birch
buds relatively large and divergent

mature tree has oval habit, few strong branches, clumps of fine twigs in crown
branches begin lower on trunk than in aspens; more graceful, ascending, and regular with slender, straight twigs

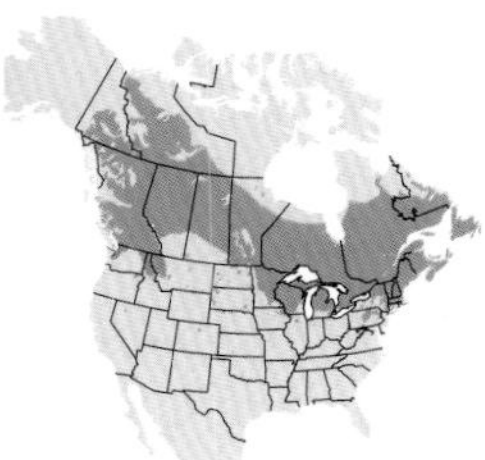

Common in rich upland soils, generally in open woods or wood edges. Commonly cultivated (zones 2–6).

Heartleaf Birch

Betula cordifolia

MOUNTAIN WHITE BIRCH

Deciduous. Shrub to medium tree, usually under 40' tall (max. 67'). Very similar to Paper Birch; distinguished primarily by heart-shaped leaves with more veins, and usually pale reddish or bronze bark.

leaves 4", double-toothed and distinctively heart-shaped; 9–12 pairs of veins (9 or fewer on Paper)

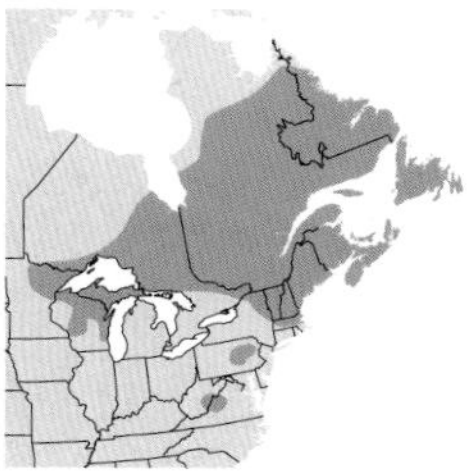

Common, farther north and at higher elevations (e.g., above 2,500' in Adirondacks) than Paper Birch. Not cultivated.

Kenai Birch

Betula kenaica

PAPER BIRCH, BLACK BIRCH, RED BIRCH

Deciduous. Small tree, usually under 30' (max. about 40'). Distinguished from Paper Birch by smaller size, often reddish trunk, and smaller leaves with blunter tip and coarser, more regular teeth.

leaves small, 2½", coarsely double-toothed and more or less triangular; only 2–6 pairs of veins

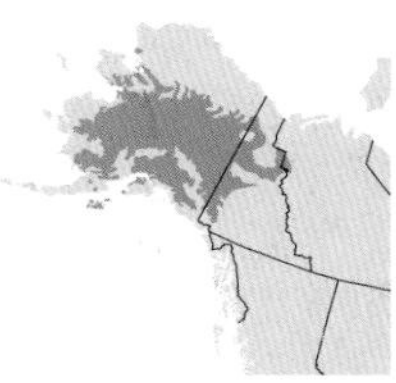

Common in bog margins and rocky slopes near treeline. Not cultivated.

Resin Birch

Betula neoalaskana

PAPER BIRCH, ALASKA PAPER BIRCH

Deciduous. Small to medium tree often 40' tall (max. about 75'). Distinguished from Paper Birch and Kenai Birch by longer leafstalk and rough twigs. Bark of mature trunks varies from bright white to reddish-brown. Hybridizes with Paper Birch, but apparently more closely related to Gray Birch.

leaf stalk longer than Paper Birch

leaves small, 2½", double-toothed and somewhat triangular

twigs rough, covered with bumpy resin gland

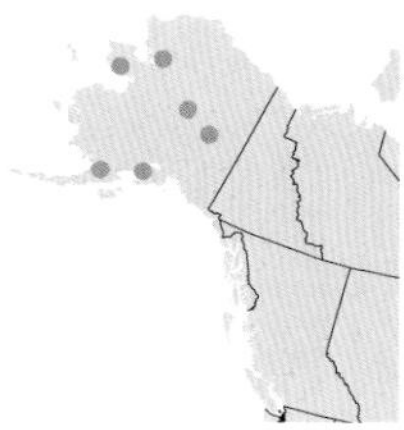

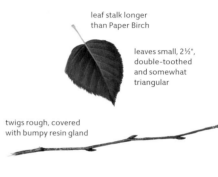

Common and widespread, especially in poorly-drained soils such as bogs and streamsides. Not cultivated.

The taxonomy of birches in general, and Paper Birch in particular, is complex and confusing. Species are variable, and hybridization is common with related shrubby species, making it very difficult to define populations. Heartleaf Birch and Kenai Birch, often considered subspecies of Paper Birch, are treated here as species. Paper Birch trees with dark, non-peeling bark occur sporadically, especially in the West. These have been named as var. *commutata*, but apparently reflect merely individual or environmental variation. Paper Birch trees in the northern Rocky Mountains tend to have broader leaves and are sometimes separated as *Betula subcordata*, but more likely are simply a minor regional variation.

Gray Birch

Betula populifolia

WHITE BIRCH, WIRE BIRCH, OLDFIELD BIRCH

Deciduous. Small tree, usually under 30' (max. 80'); often with multiple, leaning trunks and narrow crowns. Distinguished from similar white-barked species by long-pointed triangular leaves, usually solitary male catkins, and nonpeeling bark. Superficially similar to Paper Birch, but more closely-related to Resin Birch, European Weeping Birch, and several Asian species.

bark of young trunks reddish brown with pale lenticels

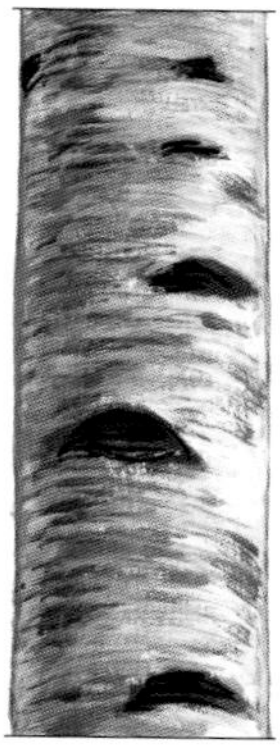

bark of mature trunks grayish white, nonpeeling

long stalk causes leaves to flutter like poplar leaves

leaves 3½", coarsely double-toothed and glossy above

triangular and long-pointed

fruiting catkins relatively short and short-stalked with small scales

male flower buds usually solitary at twig tips (compare Paper Birch)

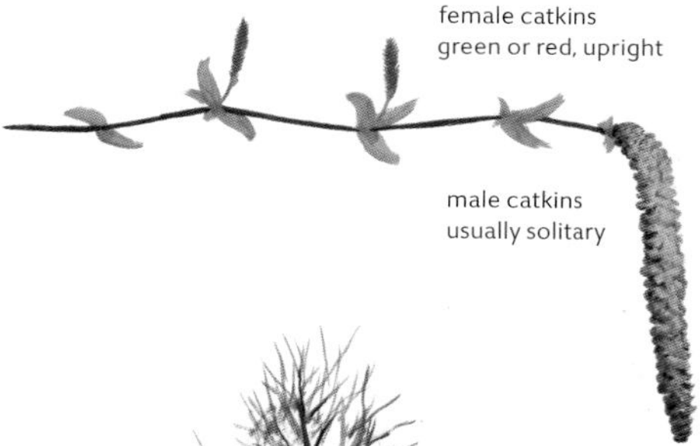

female catkins green or red, upright

male catkins usually solitary

twigs slender and rough

buds small

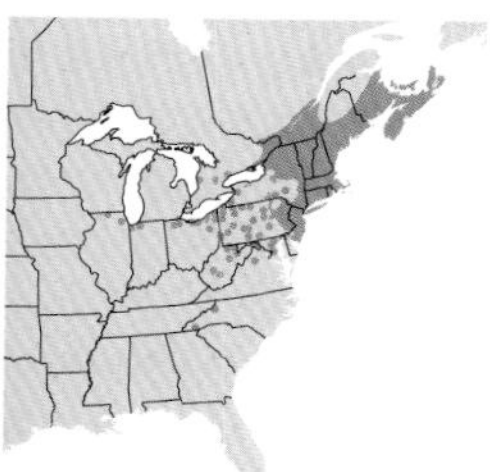

A common pioneer species in disturbed soils, especially on well-drained hillsides, roadsides, and sandy or rocky sites. Once commonly cultivated (zones 3–6), now infrequently.

typically leaning, crooked trunks and narrow crowns

European Weeping Birch

Betula pendula

WEEPING BIRCH, EUROPEAN WHITE BIRCH

Deciduous. Medium tree, often 50' tall (max. 107'); often multi-trunked, with broad crowns of slender, weeping twigs. Closely related and similar to Gray Birch. Distinguished from all other white-barked birches by weeping twigs, black diamonds near trunk base, and leaf details.

bark on mature trunks white and slightly peeling with rough, diamond-shaped black furrows near base

leaves fairly small, 3", double-toothed
relatively long stalk
triangular, shorter-tipped than Gray Birch
one common cultivar has deeply divided leaves

weeping twigs distinctive among birches

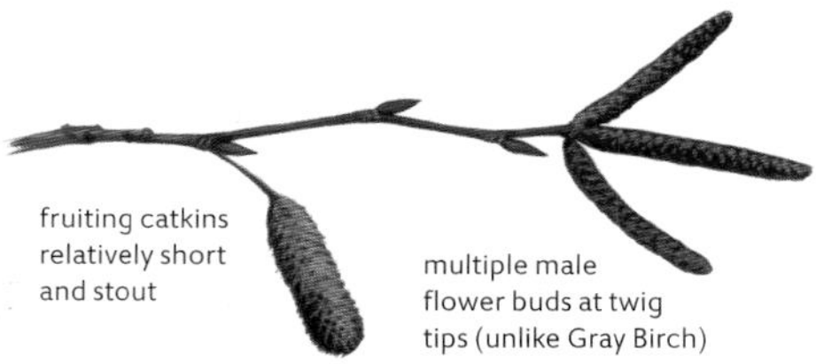
fruiting catkins relatively short and stout
multiple male flower buds at twig tips (unlike Gray Birch)

twigs slender and rough like Gray Birch
buds slender, larger than Gray Birch

Native to Europe. The most commonly cultivated birch in North America, particularly from Anchorage, Alaska, to the Midwest (zones 2–6); naturalized locally.

Manchurian Birch

Betula platyphylla

Deciduous. Small, single-trunked tree, closely related to European Weeping Silver, Gray, and Resin Birches. Distinguished by a narrow crown, dark, glossy leaves, and white, nonpeeling bark. Native to Japan and China. Commonly cultivated, especially in northern North America (zones 4–7). Grows in upland edges and clearings and is locally naturalized in Massachusetts.

leaves 3½", double-toothed
triangular like Gray Birch, but larger, broader, and often darker

Downy Birch

Betula pubescens

EUROPEAN WHITE BIRCH, HAIRY BIRCH

Deciduous. Small to medium tree, usually under 50' tall (max. 67'); usually single-trunked, with narrow crown. Often confused with European Weeping Birch. Distinguished by small, single-toothed leaves, smooth, downy twigs, and grayer, usually nonpeeling bark.

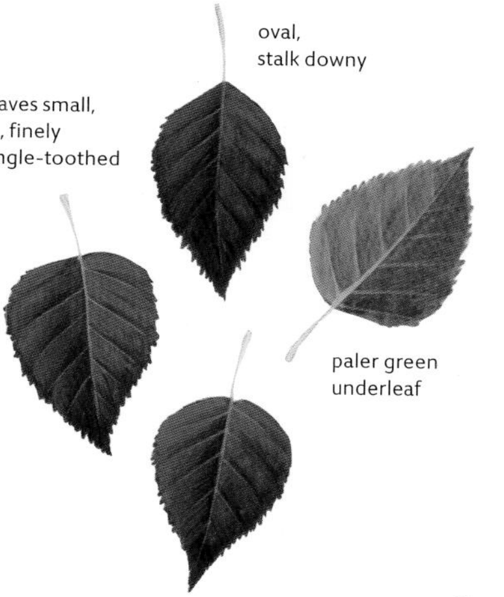
oval,
stalk downy
leaves small,
2", finely
single-toothed
paler green
underleaf

fruiting
catkins
short

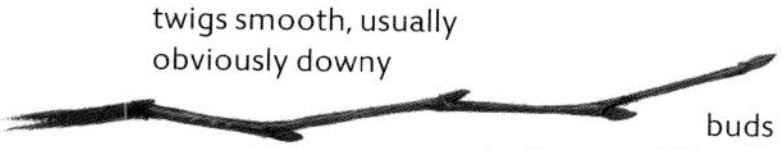
twigs smooth, usually
obviously downy
buds similar
to European Weeping Birch

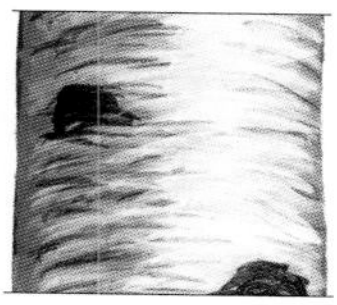
bark on mature trunks remains
smooth, pale brown to whitish,
usually nonpeeling

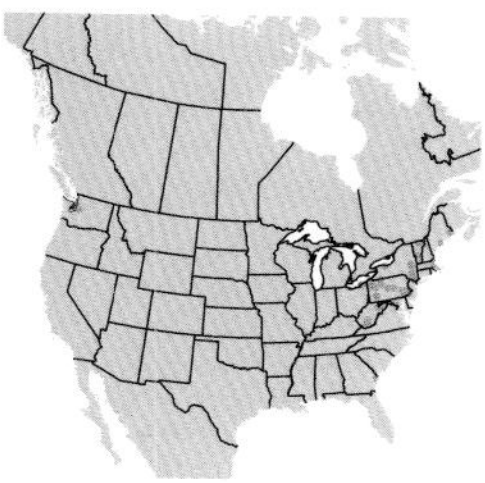

Native to Europe and Greenland. Mainly on poorly drained wet soils. Commonly cultivated (zones 2–6) and locally naturalized along roadsides and damp thickets.

Water Birch

Betula occidentalis

RED BIRCH, BLACK BIRCH, SPRING BIRCH

Deciduous. Usually shrubby, but can be a small multi-trunked tree to 25' tall (max. 55') with open, spreading crown. Distinguished from other birches by shrubby form and small, rounded leaves. The only birch species in much of the West. Commonly hybridizes with Paper Birch.

leaves small,
2", single- or
double-toothed
paler green
underleaf
nearly round
with only 2–6
pairs of veins

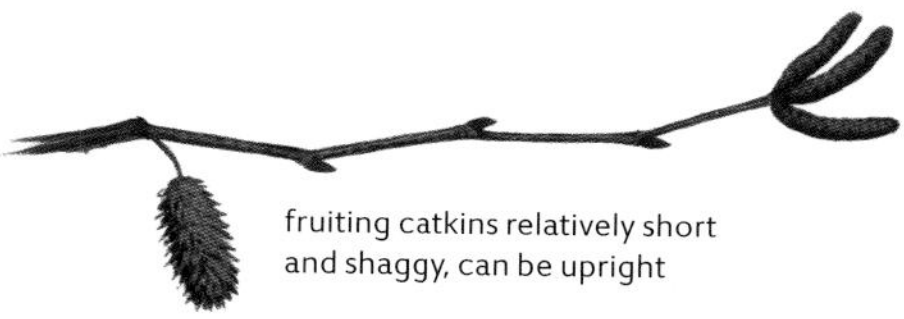
fruiting catkins relatively short
and shaggy, can be upright

twigs brownish and rough
buds small
and pointed

bark dark gray to shiny reddish,
with long, horizontal lenticels;
not peeling

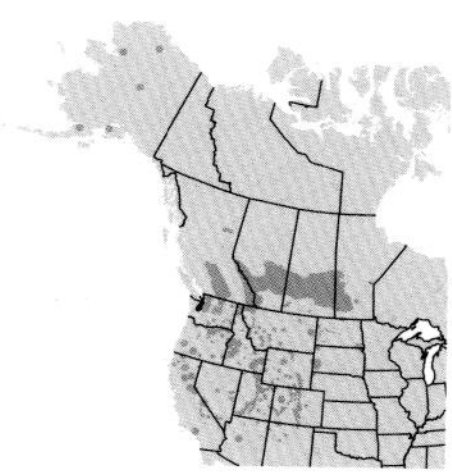

Common along streams and in other wet places. Uncommon in cultivation (zones 4–6), mainly in the West.

Yellow Birch

Betula alleghaniensis

GRAY BIRCH, SILVER BIRCH, SWAMP BIRCH

Deciduous. Medium to large tree often 60' tall (max. 100'). Single-trunked with rounded crown. Very similar to Sweet Birch; best distinguished by bark. Slow-growing species, but accounts for seventy-five percent of birch lumber in the United States.

bark of younger trunks pale golden bronze, peeling or not, with many gray lenticels

bark of older trunks often develops broad gray plates that peel from edges

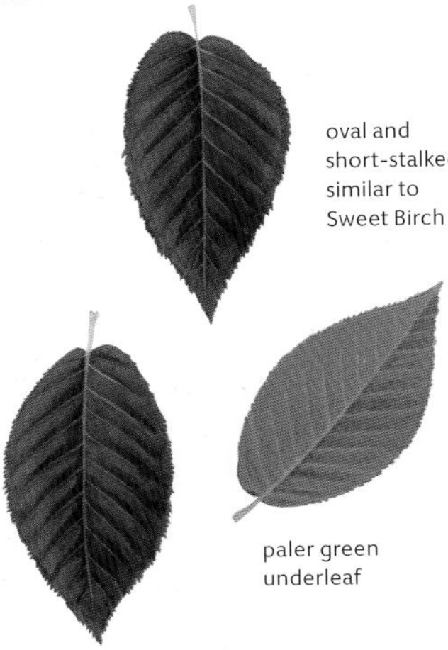
leaves large, 4", finely double-toothed
oval and short-stalked, similar to Sweet Birch
paler green underleaf

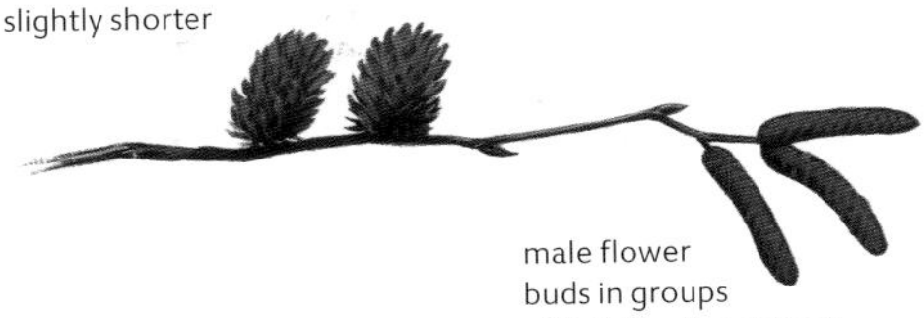
fruiting catkins similar to Sweet Birch, but average slightly shorter
male flower buds in groups of 3–6, like Sweet Birch

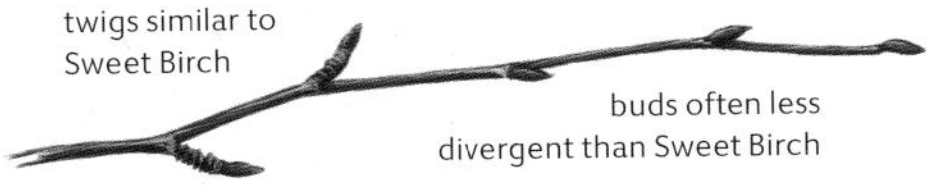
twigs similar to Sweet Birch
buds often less divergent than Sweet Birch

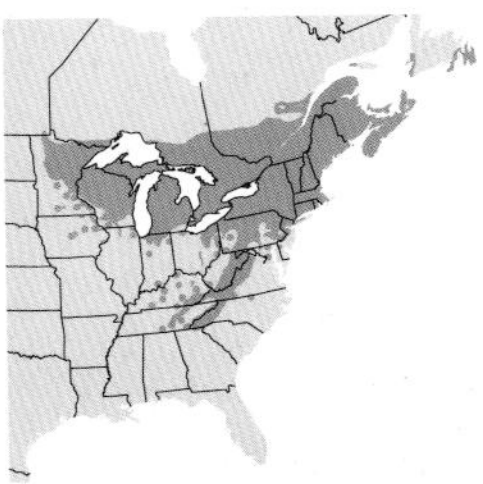

Common and characteristic tree of rich, moist soils in northern Appalachians and Great Lakes regions; generally grows in wetter settings than Sweet Birch. Rarely cultivated.

Murray's Birch

Betula murrayana

Small (to about 45'), multi-trunked tree, described in 1985 from two trees. Now only a single tree is known, found with shrubby Bog Birch (*B. pumila*) in a swampy forest of southeastern Michigan. Apparently derived from hybrids of Yellow Birch × Bog Birch.

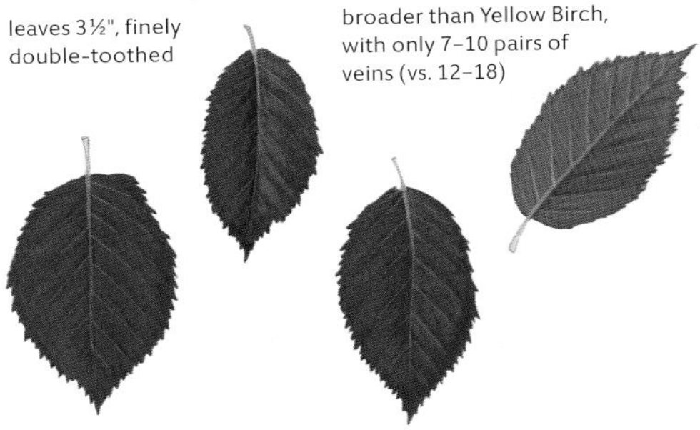
leaves 3½", finely double-toothed
broader than Yellow Birch, with only 7–10 pairs of veins (vs. 12–18)

Virginia Birch

Betula uber

Small deciduous tree to about 30' tall, slender, and single-trunked. Described in 1918 and rediscovered in 1974. Closely related to Sweet Birch and may be simply a mutant of that species. Known from 17 trees in Smyth County, Virginia.

leaves small, 1¾"
single- or double-toothed with only 2–6 pairs of veins

Sweet Birch

Betula lenta

CHERRY BIRCH, BLACK BIRCH

Deciduous. Medium to large tree, often 60' tall (max. 117'). Straight, single trunk, with spreading crown. Similar to Yellow Birch in large, oval leaves and wintergreen odor of twigs (the sap is extracted for birch beer); distinguished by dark gray bark.

bark on young trunks smooth and shiny gray with dark, horizontal lenticels

bark on older trunks dark gray, peeling in broad plates

large and oval

leaves 4", finely double-toothed

paler green underleaf

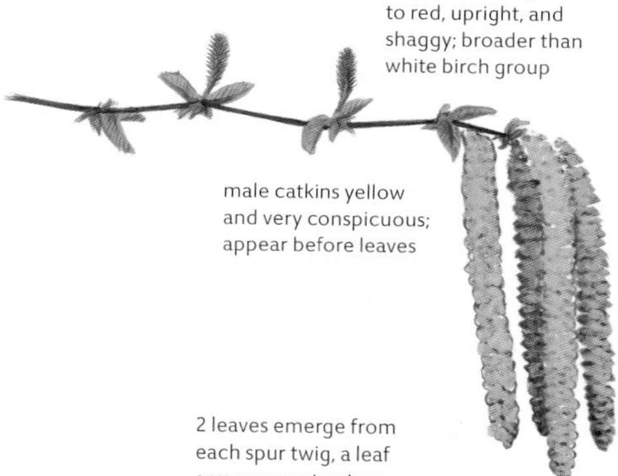

female catkins green to red, upright, and shaggy; broader than white birch group

male catkins yellow and very conspicuous; appear before leaves

fruiting catkins erect, shaggy, and stalkless

2 leaves emerge from each spur twig, a leaf arrangement unique to birches

twigs dark gray-brown and glossy; prominent spur twigs common

buds pointed and divergent

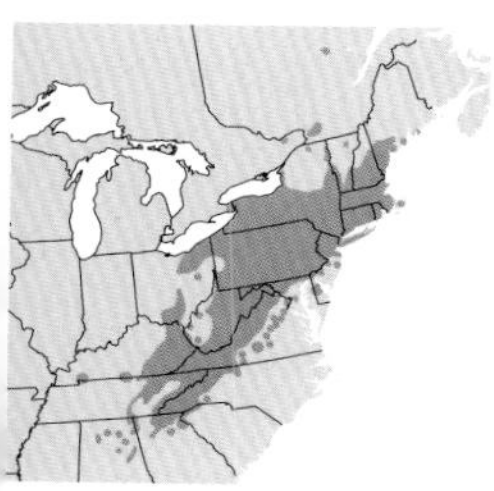

Common in forests with moist or mesic soils; more shade-tolerant than white birch group. A dominant species of northern hardwood forests. Rarely cultivated.

young trees upright with straight central trunk and ascending branches

older trees have more rounded crown with spreading branches

River Birch

Betula nigra

RED BIRCH, BLACK BIRCH, WATER BIRCH

Deciduous. Medium to large tree, usually under 60', but often to 80' in lower Mississippi valley (max. 120'); often multi-trunked. Note vase-shaped habit and rounded crown.

bark on young trunks variegated gray, reddish, and yellowish, peeling in ragged sheets

bark on mature trunks gray and rough, in poorly defined ridges and blocks

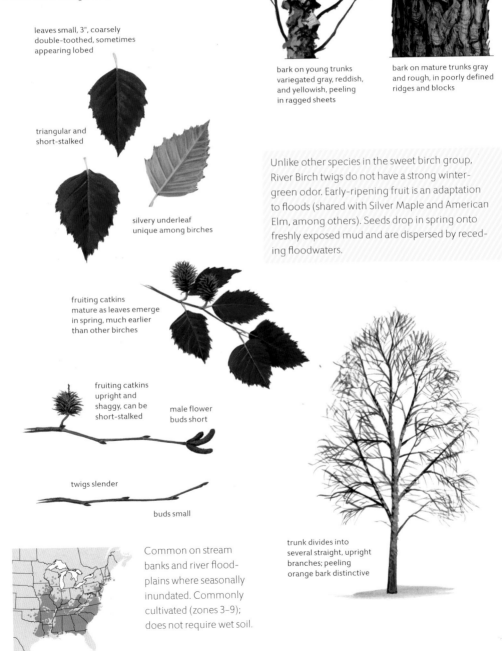

leaves small, 3", coarsely double-toothed, sometimes appearing lobed
triangular and short-stalked
silvery underleaf unique among birches

Unlike other species in the sweet birch group, River Birch twigs do not have a strong wintergreen odor. Early-ripening fruit is an adaptation to floods (shared with Silver Maple and American Elm, among others). Seeds drop in spring onto freshly exposed mud and are dispersed by receding floodwaters.

fruiting catkins mature as leaves emerge in spring, much earlier than other birches

fruiting catkins upright and shaggy, can be short-stalked
male flower buds short

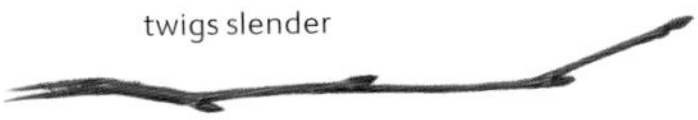
twigs slender
buds small

trunk divides into several straight, upright branches; peeling orange bark distinctive

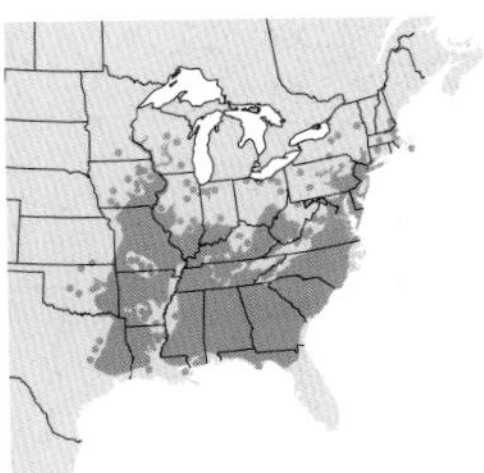

Common on stream banks and river floodplains where seasonally inundated. Commonly cultivated (zones 3–9); does not require wet soil.

Birch Family: Alders

There are about twenty-five species of alders around the northern hemisphere, with about seven native to North America. Our native species and two commonly cultivated species are covered here.

Alders are mostly shrubs and small trees of disturbed and wet areas, instantly recognizable by the small, woody, cone-like fruiting structures. These are persistent year-round and nearly always visible on any plant that has reached fruiting age.

Most alders flower very early in spring, well before the leaves emerge, with the exceptions of Green Alder and Seaside Alder. Green Alder flowers later in the spring, as the leaves open, and also has stalkless buds and other small differences. The Seaside Alder is one of our few native trees (and the only alder) that flowers in fall, and is distinctive in several other details.

Red Alder, unlike our other alders, is large enough to be commercialy important for lumber. Alders are most important to humans as pioneer species that stabilize and fertilize barren areas, such as strip mines, clear-cuts, rockslides, and riverbanks. Alders fix nitrogen from the air in a symbiotic relationship with bacteria in its root system, which nourishes the tree. As alder leaves fall, the nitrogen-rich litter quickly fertilizes barren ground. Conifers have been shown to grow better in areas where alders have preceded them, so alders are often planted as the first step in reforestation.

alders often have upright twigs and leaves pointing up

Smooth Alder

Alnus serrulata

HAZEL ALDER

Deciduous. Shrub or small tree, usually under 20' (max. 32'), multiple, crooked trunks and ragged crowns.

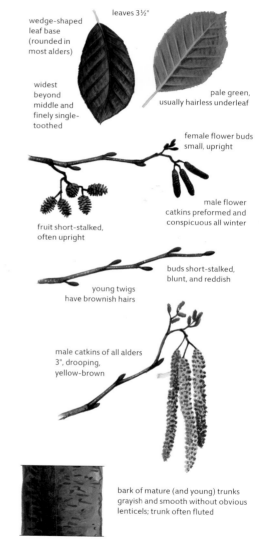

wedge-shaped leaf base (rounded in most alders)

leaves 3½"

widest beyond middle and finely single-toothed

pale green, usually hairless underleaf

female flower buds small, upright

male flower catkins preformed and conspicuous all winter

fruit short-stalked, often upright

buds short-stalked, blunt, and reddish

young twigs have brownish hairs

male catkins of all alders 3", drooping, yellow-brown

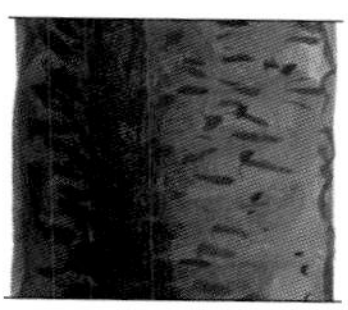

bark of mature (and young) trunks grayish and smooth without obvious lenticels; trunk often fluted

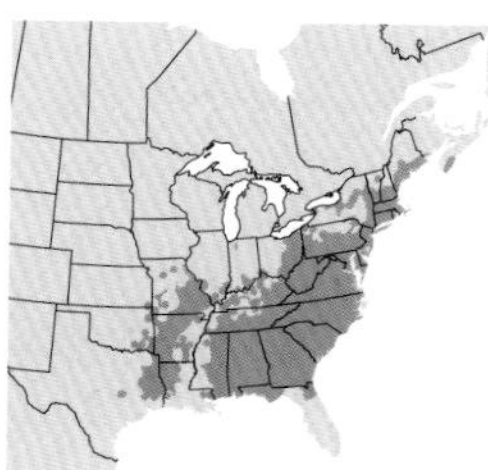

Common in wet soils, including pond and stream margins, swamps, and ditches. Not cultivated.

Red Alder

Alnus rubra

OREGON ALDER

Deciduous. Medium height to tall, to 60' (max. 136'); often multi-trunked, with narrow crowns. The tallest alder in North America. Note straight trunk and slender, drooping branches. Important source of lumber for furniture and paper pulp.

bark on young trees smooth and gray with inconspicuous lenticels

bark on mature trunks light gray with darker branch scars; base of trunk can be scaly

oval and double-toothed, with rounded teeth
leaves large, 4½", relatively thick
leaf edges curl under slightly (unlike other alders)
dark green and not shiny above
reddish hairs along veins of pale green underleaf

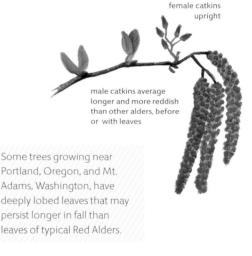

female catkins upright
male catkins average longer and more reddish than other alders, before or with leaves

Some trees growing near Portland, Oregon, and Mt. Adams, Washington, have deeply lobed leaves that may persist longer in fall than leaves of typical Red Alders.

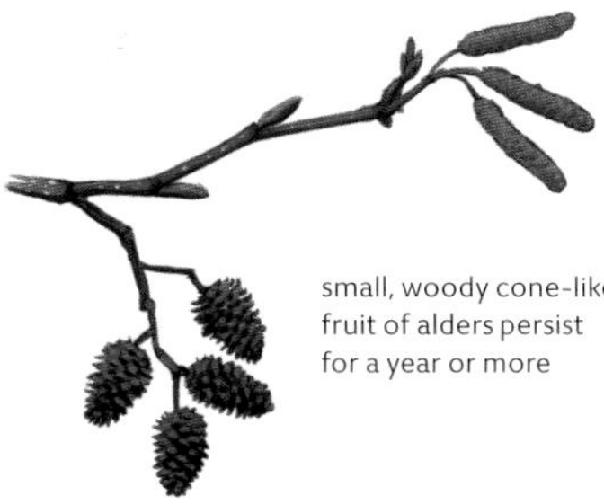
small, woody cone-like fruit of alders persist for a year or more

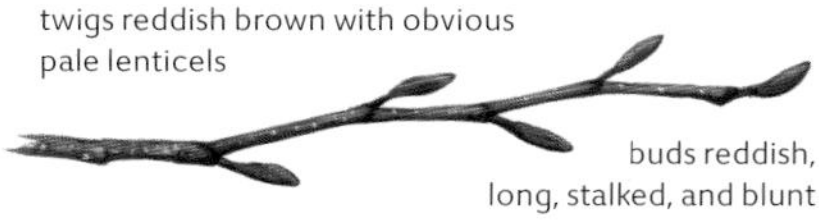
twigs reddish brown with obvious pale lenticels
buds reddish, long, stalked, and blunt

Common in moist soils along floodplains, lakeshores, and wet slopes from sea level up to 1,000'; often forms extensive stands. Rarely cultivated.

trunk forks low; branches spread or droop in horizontal layers
male flower buds give reddish tinge to branch tips through winter

White Alder

Alnus rhombifolia

CALIFORNIA ALDER

Deciduous. Small to medium height, usually under 50' (max. 115'). Often multi-trunked, with open, spreading crowns. The only western alder without obviously double-toothed leaves. Differs from Red Alder in leaf details, habitat, and bark.

leaves 3"
finely double-toothed, wavy borders
rounded tip
pale green, usually downy underleaf

female flower buds drooping

twigs smooth, reddish yellow with sparse pale lenticels
buds dull red with downy coating, stalked, and blunt

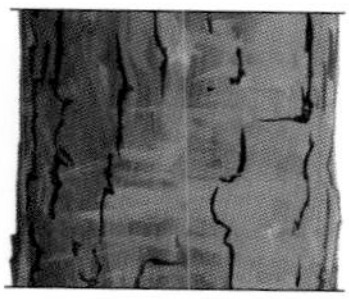
bark of mature trunks often darker, redder, and scalier than Red Alder

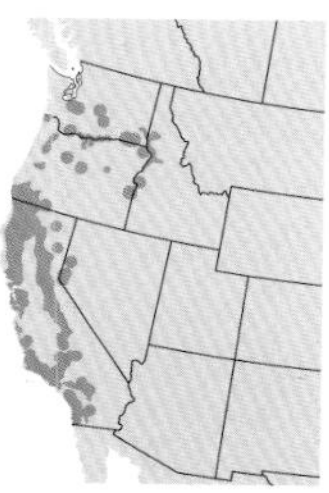

Locally common in dry, open rocky settings along permanent streams and adjacent slopes at 300–7,000'. Rarely cultivated, mainly in California (zone 6).

Arizona Alder

Alnus oblongifolia

NEW MEXICAN ALDER, ALISO

Deciduous. Medium height, often to 60' (max. 129'). Often multi-trunked, with spreading crowns. Range overlaps only with Thinleaf subspecies of Speckled Alder; Arizona Alder can grow much larger than Thinleaf and has narrower leaves and longer buds.

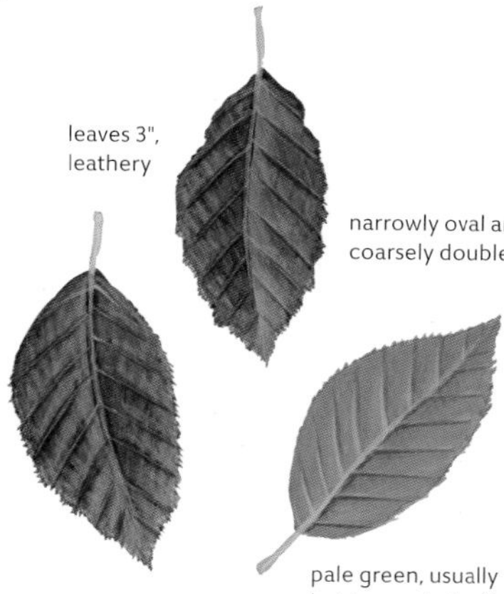
leaves 3", leathery
narrowly oval and coarsely double-toothed
pale green, usually hairless underleaf

female flower buds often upright

twigs reddish brown
buds dull red and downy, stalked and blunt

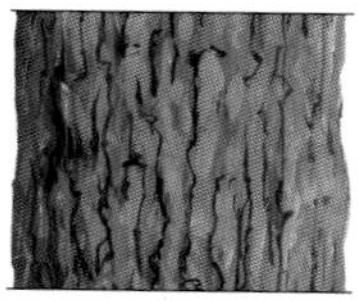
bark on mature trunks gray, becoming cracked and checkered

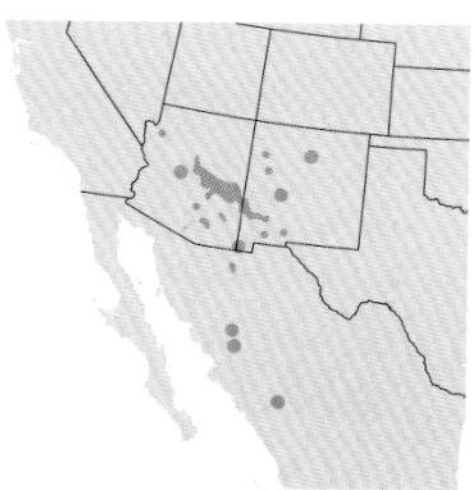

Common in scattered locations on sandy or rocky stream banks and moist slopes, typically in mountain canyons at 3,000–7,000'. Not cultivated.

Speckled Alder

Alnus incana

TAG ALDER, HOARY ALDER, GRAY ALDER

Deciduous. Shrub or small tree, usually under 20' (max. 66'). Often multi-trunked, with ragged, narrow crowns. Distinguished from Green and Smooth Alders by speckled bark, egg-shaped, double-toothed leaves and drooping female flowers.

bark on young trunks shiny brown or green with white lenticels

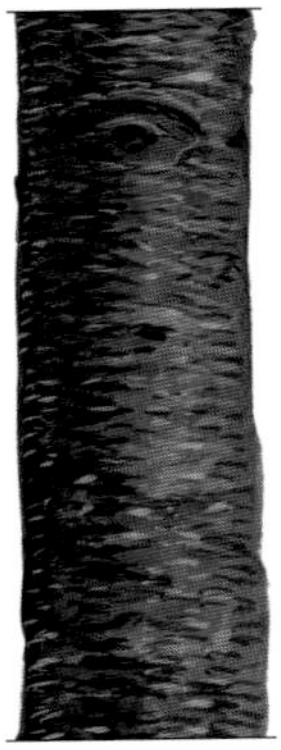

bark on mature trunks gray and profusely speckled with pale horizontal lenticels

leaves 3"

egg-shaped and coarsely double-toothed

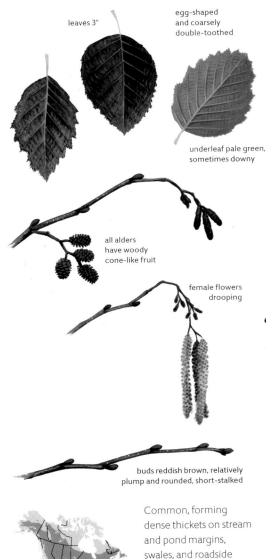

underleaf pale green, sometimes downy

all alders have woody cone-like fruit

trunks often lean and curve

often shrubby with multiple spreading trunks and sparse branches

female flowers drooping

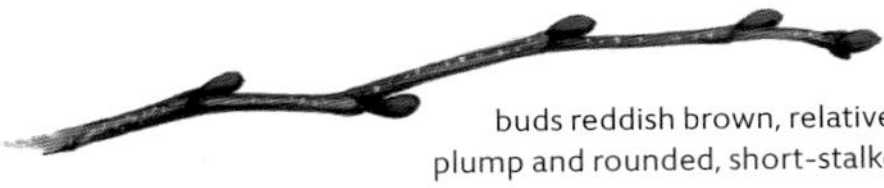

buds reddish brown, relatively plump and rounded, short-stalked

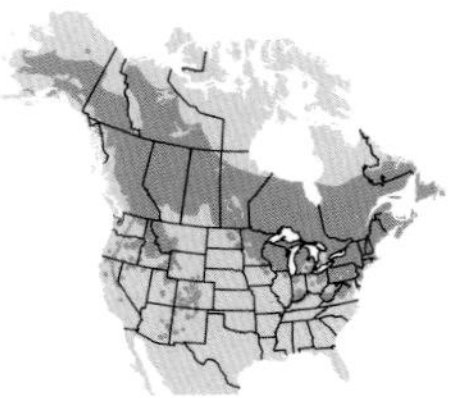

Common, forming dense thickets on stream and pond margins, swales, and roadside ditches. Closely associated with water. Rarely cultivated.

'Thinleaf' Speckled Alder

Alnus incana tenuifolia

Deciduous. Shrub or small tree; grows in Rocky Mountains and West. Sometimes considered a separate species; differs from Speckled in a somewhat more treelike form and details of leaf shape and leaf margins.

leaves average smaller, than Speckled, less pointed lobes, smaller teeth

Green Alder

Alnus viridis

MOUNTAIN ALDER, SITKA ALDER, SIBERIAN ALDER

Deciduous. Usually a multi-trunked, spreading shrub to 15', but sometimes can be a small tree to 30' (max. 37') in sheltered valleys. Differs from all other North American alders in unstalked buds, long-stalked fruit cones, and later flowering.

bark on very young trunks and small branches greenish with white lenticels

bark on mature trunks gray with large, pale, diamond-shaped lenticels in horizontal rows

leaves 2½"

relatively long, pointed teeth

yellow-green above, shiny on both sides

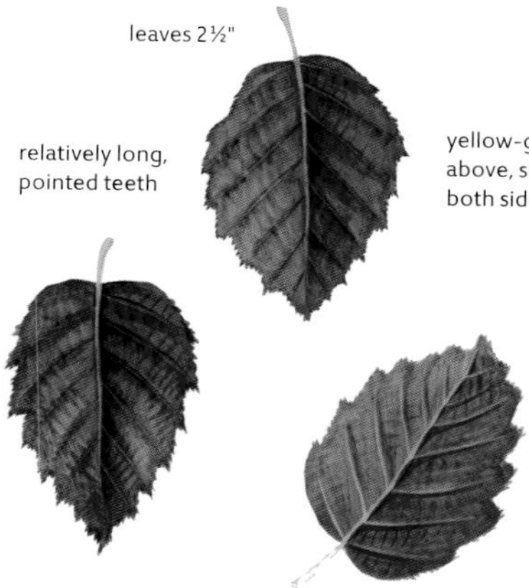

underleaf pale green, usually hairless

female catkins on upright shoot, remaining upright as fruit develops

flowers in spring with expanding leaves (most alders flower well before leaves, Seaside Alder flowers in fall)

Green Alder is a circumpolar species with three named subspecies in North America. The northwestern subspecies commonly called 'Sitka' Green Alder (*Alnus viridis sinuata*) is found from Alaska to Wyoming and California, and is the only form that is commonly tree-like. The leaves are coarsely double-toothed. Two other forms—'American' Green Alder (*A. v. crispa*) found from Alaska to Newfoundland and 'Siberian' Green Alder (*A. v. fruticosa*) ranging from Alaska to California—are shrubs under 12' tall. Both are rarely tree-like, and have more finely toothed leaves, single-toothed on 'American' Green Alder, and double-toothed on 'Siberian'.

male catkins upright in winter (female flowers enclosed in buds)

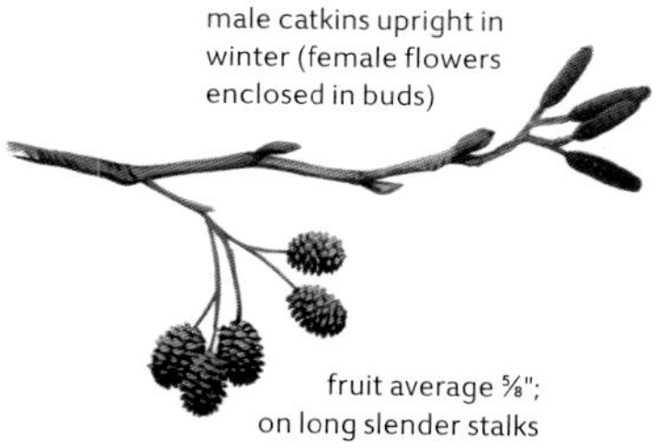

fruit average ⅝"; on long slender stalks (unlike other alders)

twigs hairy and grayish

buds pointed and unstalked

'American' Green Alder leaf, single-toothed

'Siberian' Alder leaf, double-toothed

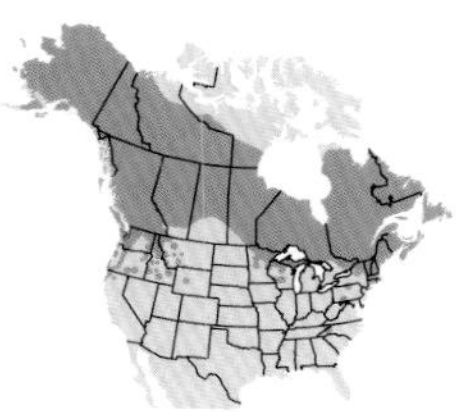

Common and widespread in moist sites, especially following disturbance. Pioneers often form dense strands on gravelley soils. Very rarely cultivated.

Seaside Alder

Alnus maritima

BROOK ALDER

Deciduous. Shrub or small tree, usually under 20' (max. 30'); usually with multiple spreading trunks and narrow crowns. Flowers in fall, unlike other alders, and lacks preformed flower buds through winter; also distinctive in solitary fruit cones.

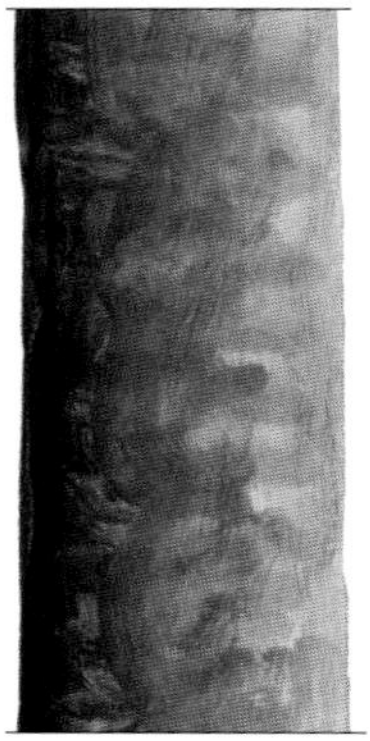
bark of mature (and young) trunks grayish and smooth without obvious lenticels

leaves 3", relatively narrow, sparse, small, single teeth
fewer, more curved leaf veins than other alders, not extending to edge

flowers in late summer or early fall (other alders flower in spring)

preformed flower buds absent
fruit solitary, on short stalk, mature in fall a year after flowers

buds short-stalked, blunt, and reddish

The closest relatives of Seaside Alder are two fall-flowering alders in southeast Asia. It is hypothesized that this species colonized North America via the Bering land bridge and was forced into these three relict populations by subsequent changes in climate and plant competition. The three disjunct populations of Seaside Alder are now considered three separate subspecies. The Georgia population has relatively broad, blunt-tipped leaves, long, narrow cones (nearly twice as long as wide) and is a large shrub or upright small tree with narrow crown. The Oklahoma population has relatively narrow, pointed leaves, cones slightly broader than in Georgia, and has a broad, spreading crown. The Atlantic coast population is shrubby, never tree-like, and has the broadest cones (nearly spherical) and broader leaves similar to the Georgia population.

Rare and local, growing in a few widely scattered sites. The most water-loving alder, often growing in standing water. Not cultivated.

European Alder

Alnus glutinosa

BLACK ALDER

Deciduous. Small to medium tree, often 50' tall (max. 87'). Often multi-trunked, with relatively tall, conical crown. Note distinctive, rounded or notched leaf tip. Several cultivars uncommon in North America have lobed to deeply dissected leaves.

leaves 4",
glossy and dark
double-toothed and
relatively broad
usually notched or
double-rounded at tip
paler green underleaf
with tufts of orange
fuzz along veins

female flower
buds upright
fruit on relatively
long, slender stalks

twigs green to brown,
sticky
buds long-stalked,
similar to Speckled

Native to Europe and Siberia. Grows in moist soils. Commonly cultivated and locally naturalized (zones 4-7), particularly in Northeast and Midwest.

Italian Alder

Alnus cordata

NEAPOLITAN ALDER

Deciduous. Small to medium tree, often 60' tall (max. 81'); single-trunked, with narrow, conical crown. Dark glossy leaves and neat oval shape reminiscent of Callery Pear.

leaves 3½", often
nearly round
glossy and finely
single-toothed
usually
heart-shaped
pale green underleaf,
often with tufts
of yellowish fuzz
along midvein

female flower
buds upright
fruit larger than
other alders, 1"

twigs often
reddish brown
buds long-stalked,
similar to Speckled

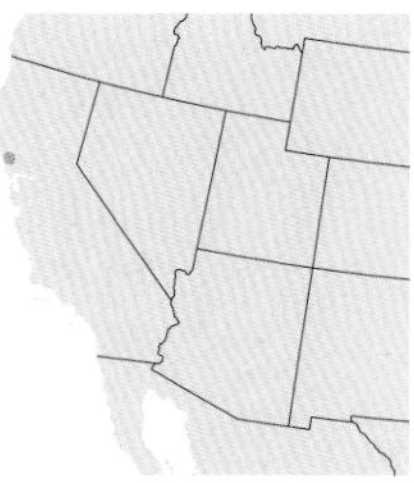

Native to Italy. Usually grows near water. Uncommonly cultivated and locally escaped, particularly in the Midwest (zones 5–7).

Birch Family: Hophornbeams

There are five species of hophornbeams worldwide, three of which are native to North America. They are closely-related to hornbeams with similar flowers, fruit, and leaves, but unlike hornbeams, the male catkins are preformed and exposed over the winter. Hophornbeam wood is heavy and was once widely used for sleigh runners, wheel rims, mallet heads, and for other items that required extreme durability and strength.

Chisos Hophornbeam

Ostrya chisosensis

Deciduous. Small tree usually under 25' tall (max. about 40'). Closely-related to Eastern with small fruit and small, curled, and hairy leaves, but leaves narrower and range does not overlap.

underleaf paler green, hairy
leaves 1½", similar to Knowlton, but narrower, less egg-shaped
fruit clusters 1"
fruit a small cluster at tip of twig, ripe in summer

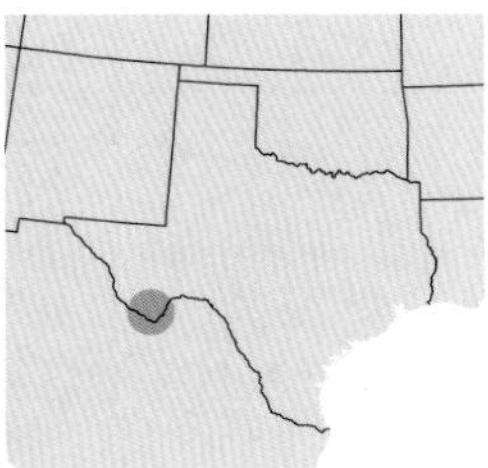

Uncommon and very local along streams and on moist slopes; known only from canyons in Chisos Mountains, Texas from 4,500–7,000' elevation.

Knowlton Hophornbeam

Ostrya knowltonii

WESTERN HOPHORNBEAM

Small tree usually under 20' tall (max 40'); generally smaller than Eastern and often multistemmed. Apparently more closely-related to Mexican species than to Eastern.

leaves small, curled
leaves 1¾", short-pointed, egg-shaped
underleaf hairy, especially on veins
fruit clusters 1"
twigs often hairy
male flower catkins short, about 1", brownish; flowers expand with leaves in April, later than Eastern

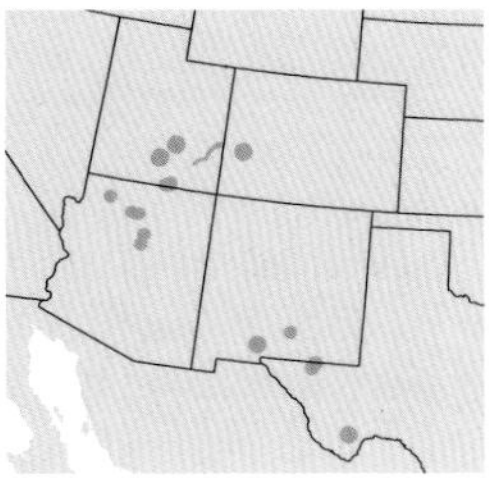

Uncommon and local in scattered locations along streams, wet seeps on rocky slopes, or in moist canyons from 3,500–7,000'; very rarely cultivated.

Eastern Hophornbeam

Ostrya virginiana

IRONWOOD

Deciduous. Small to medium tree, usually 25–40' tall (max 74'); slender and graceful with spreading branches. Distinguished from related Hornbeam by shaggy bark, different fruit, drier habitat. Wood very hard and heavy.

bark smooth on very young trunks and branches
mature bark brown in thick narrow scales loose at ends, shaggy

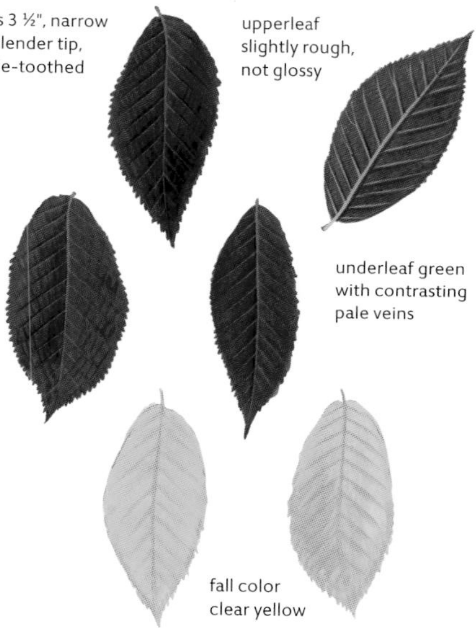
leaves 3 ½", narrow with slender tip, double-toothed
upperleaf slightly rough, not glossy
underleaf green with contrasting pale veins
fall color clear yellow

Populations on the Atlantic coastal plain (*O. virginiana* var. *lasia*) have smaller, blunter, often more downy leaves.

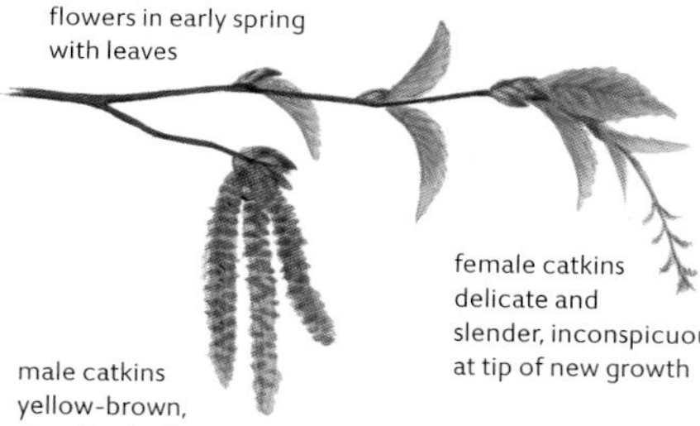
flowers in early spring with leaves
female catkins delicate and slender, inconspicuous, at tip of new growth
male catkins yellow-brown, dangling in clusters

fruit a hanging cluster of pointed papery bladders, each enclosing a seed; ripe in fall, drop with leaves

fruit clusters 2", hanging from twig tips

twigs extremely slender, male flower buds smaller than on birch

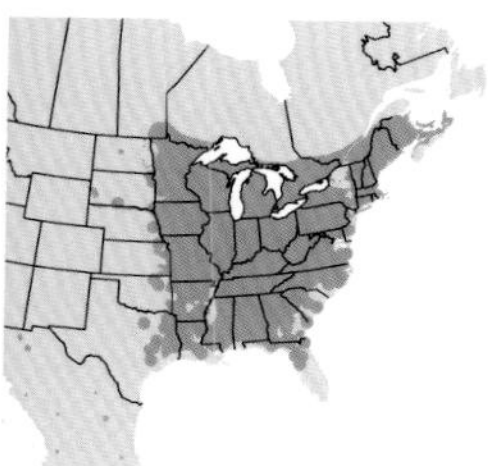

Fairly common understory tree with other deciduous species in relatively dry, fertile soils. Uncommon in cultivation (zones 3–9).

a small, slender tree with graceful spreading branches

Birch Family: Hornbeams

There are about twenty-five species of hornbeams worldwide, mainly in Asia, and only one species native to North America.

Hornbeams are closely related to birches and alders, but male flowers emerge from small lateral buds in spring (all other genera in the family Betulaceae have male flower aments exposed through the winter). The smooth gray bark and loosely clustered, three-lobed, papery fruits are also distinctive.

Hornbeam wood is very hard, and is used for some specialized purposes, but too scarce to be of much commercial importance.

Japanese Hornbeam

Carpinus japonica

Deciduous. Small spreading tree up to 20' tall. Differs from American in narrower leaves, unlobed fruit more densely clustered, mature bark furrowed and scaly. Native to Japan. Uncommon in cultivation (zones 5–7). Several other Asian species of hornbeams are also occasionally cultivated.

leaves dark, narrow, with many well-defined veins; no fall color

fruit not lobed, fruit clusters narrow

European Hornbeam

Carpinus betulus

HORNBEECH, YOKE ELM

Deciduous. Medium tree often 40–60' tall (max. 80'), broad rounded crown. Larger than American, distinguished by details of fruit and leaves, bark (furrowed in old age), winter buds (larger, not as divergent as American), and fall leaf color less bright.

leaves slightly larger, broader, duller green, more finely-toothed, than American

fruit bract larger than American, 1½", untoothed

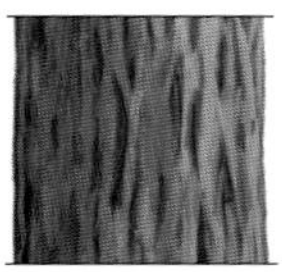

bark of mature trunk irregularly furrowed

Native to Europe, Asia Minor; Uncommon in cultivation and escaped in some locations (zones 4–7).

American Hornbeam

Carpinus caroliniana

BLUE BEECH, WATER BEECH, IRONWOOD

Deciduous. Small tree usually 20–30' tall (max. 69'); often branching low and spreading wider than tall. Smooth gray bark and clusters of papery fruit distinctive.

bark smooth, blue-gray, fluted, looking muscular

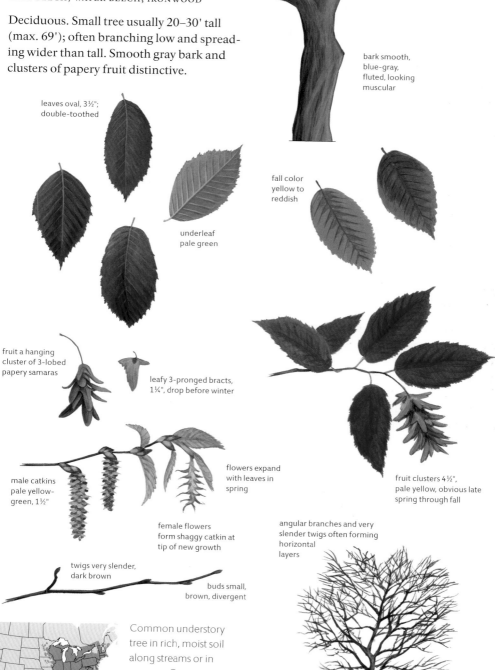

leaves oval, 3½"; double-toothed

underleaf pale green

fall color yellow to reddish

fruit clusters 4½", pale yellow, obvious late spring through fall

fruit a hanging cluster of 3-lobed papery samaras

leafy 3-pronged bracts, 1¼", drop before winter

male catkins pale yellow-green, 1½"

flowers expand with leaves in spring

female flowers form shaggy catkin at tip of new growth

twigs very slender, dark brown

buds small, brown, divergent

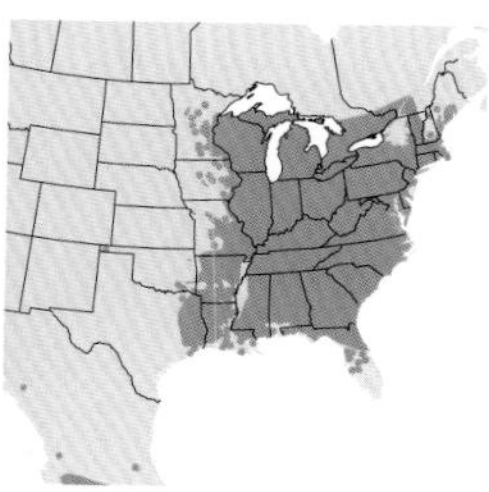

Common understory tree in rich, moist soil along streams or in swamps. Common in cultivation (zones 3–9).

angular branches and very slender twigs often forming horizontal layers

small tree, branching low and spreading

Birch Family: Hazels

The hazels (genus *Corylus*) include about twelve species of shrubs and trees worldwide. Two species (usually shrubs) are native to North America, and four exotic species are cultivated here. European species in this genus are the source of commercial hazelnuts (also known as filberts or cobnuts).

usually a multi-stemmed shrub or small tree with ascending twigs
bark light to dark brown, smooth

fall color drab yellow-green to dark red

The California subspecies of Beaked Hazel (illustrated here) is the only native hazel that is commonly tree-like. It is sometimes separated as a species, California Hazel (*Corylus californica*). Eastern populations of Beaked Hazel are rarely tree-like and average more distinctly pointed leaves and much longer "beak" on fruit (more than twice as long as nut). Another species of eastern North America, American Hazel (*Corylus americana*), is rarely tree-like (max 27'). It differs from Beaked Hazel in having the nut wrapped by two separate leafy bracts (vs. bracts fused into an unbroken husk with tubular "beak"), and male catkins often single (vs. 2–3 together on Beaked).

Beaked Hazel

Corylus cornuta

BEAKED HAZEL-NUT, BEAKED FILBERT

Deciduous. Shrub or (in the West) small tree to 25' tall (max. about 45'), usually multi-trunked with open, spreading crown.

leafstalk short
leaves 3½", rounded with irregular teeth, often blunt-tipped

female flowers tiny, red
male flowers in thick dangling yellow catkins 2", very early spring before leaves

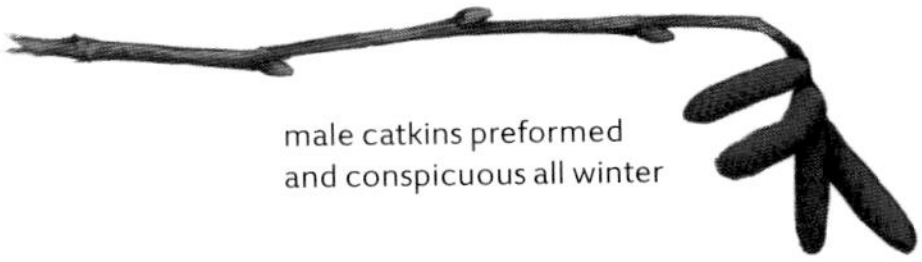
male catkins preformed and conspicuous all winter

nuts ½", round, wrapped in papery husk with long tube or "beak"

twig brownish
buds rounded, grayish to brown

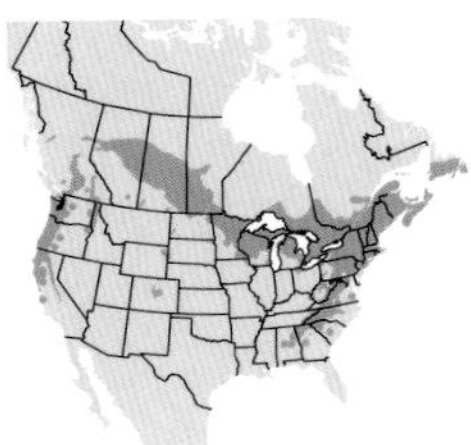

Common in damp to dry soils in forest edges, rocky slopes, streambanks, or as forest understory. Rarely cultivated (zones 4–8).

Turkish Hazel

Corylus colurna

CONSTANTINOPLE HAZEL, TREE HAZEL

Deciduous. Small to medium tree often 40' tall (max 70'), the largest hazel. Profuse yellow-brown male catkins appear very early in spring, long before leaves. Native to southeastern Europe and southwestern Asia. Uncommonly but increasingly cultivated (zones 4–7). Planted as an ornamental and as rootstock in commercial hazelnut orchards.

broadly conical shape, short trunk and branches nearly to ground

leaves 3½", rounded with coarse, irregular teeth

nuts ½", wrapped in papery husk with long shaggy fringe; ripe in fall

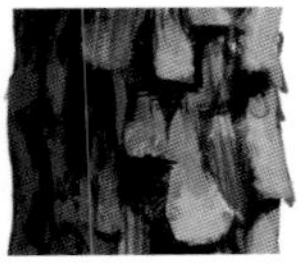
bark corky and scaly, peeling in short strips and square flakes, even on small branches

The European Hazel (*Corylus avellana*) is occasionally tree-like to 20' tall (max. 52'). It is the most commonly cultivated hazel and (as hybrids with Giant Hazel) the source of commercial hazelnuts and naturalized locally in the Pacific Northwest (zones 4–8). It differs from American Hazel in having shorter fruit husk barely extending beyond nut, and longer stalks on male catkins.

Asian Hazel (*Corylus heterophylla*), native to eastern Asia, is very similar to European Hazel, but with slightly more lobed leaves. It is uncommonly cultivated and reportedly escaped in Connecticut.

Giant Hazel

Corylus maxima

GIANT FILBERT

Deciduous. Shrub or small tree usually under 20' tall. Native to Europe; hybrid cultivars of this species with European Hazel produce all commercial hazelnuts (zones 4–8). Several common ornamental cultivars have reddish or purple leaves, catkins, and nut husks.

leaves 3½", similar to other hazels

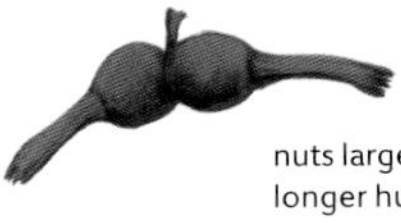
nuts larger, with longer husk than European

Beech Family: Beeches

There are eight to ten species of beeches (genus *Fagus*) worldwide with one naturalized and one native to North America. All species share smooth gray bark, very long pointed buds, and small nuts in prickly, four-parted husks. Beeches are generally short-trunked and spreading, even when forest-grown, and tend to form pure stands with little undergrowth. In these groves, the smooth gray trunks, open understory, and light filtering through the horizontal layers of pale green leaves, create a very distinctive environment.

Beech nuts are edible, and provide very important food for wildlife, including birds, rodents, deer, and bears. The nuts are little-used by people, but can be eaten and have been roasted and ground to brew a coffee substitute. Beech wood is hard and strong, but not very durable when exposed to weather. Beech trees grow slowly, so the wood is not important commercially.

male flowers
in inconspicuous green balls,
in spring with leaves
emerging leaves
hang limply, creased
along veins

small spiny fruit capsules
visible among leaves

European Beech

Fagus sylvatica

Deciduous. Large tree often 50–70' tall and wide-spreading with short trunk (max. 121'). Similar to American Beech, but leaves are smaller and wider, toothless with fewer veins; bark is slightly darker than American, prickles on fruit weaker and straighter.

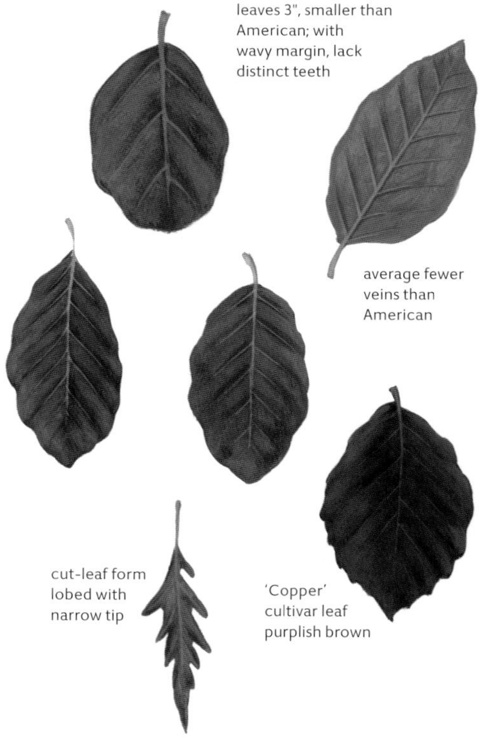
leaves 3", smaller than
American; with
wavy margin, lack
distinct teeth
average fewer
veins than
American
cut-leaf form
lobed with
narrow tip
'Copper'
cultivar leaf
purplish brown

Many beech cultivars are planted in North America, particularly 'Copper' (or 'Purple') Beech, tricolor-leaf, and cut-leaf forms. Other cultivars developed for growth habit include upright forms such as 'Dawyck' Beech and weeping forms, such as 'Weeping' Beech var. *pendula*.

Native to Europe. Commonly cultivated, and locally naturalized especially in eastern North America (zones 4–7); much more frequently cultivated than American Beech.

American Beech

Fagus grandifolia

Deciduous. Large tree, often 50–70' tall (max. 161'); spreading, short-trunked forest tree. Pale gray bark, toothed leaves, slender buds, and tendency to retain pale straw-colored leaves in winter easily recognizable.

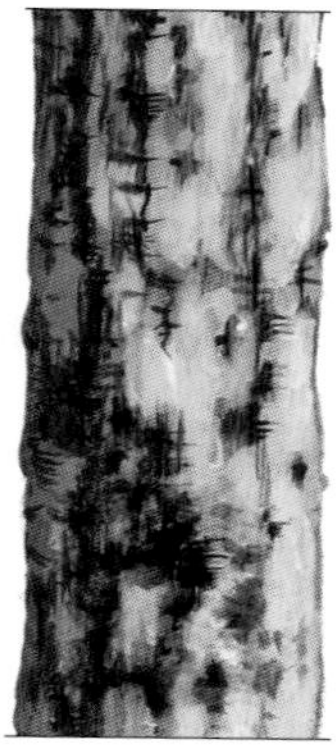

young tree infected with canker

bark gray, smooth, often defaced with carvings, never ridged or scaly

leaves 4", tip pointed; many straight parallel veins

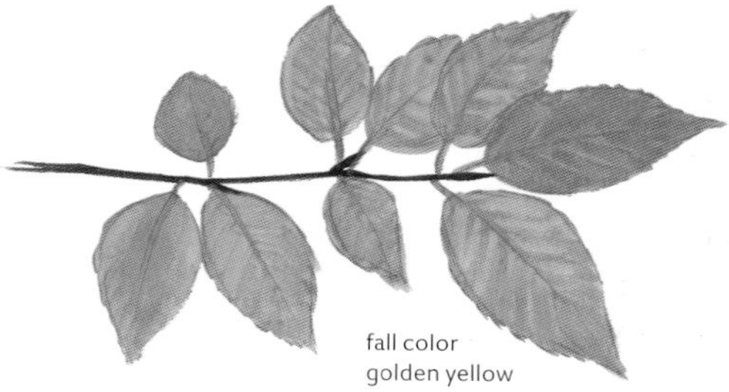

fall color golden yellow

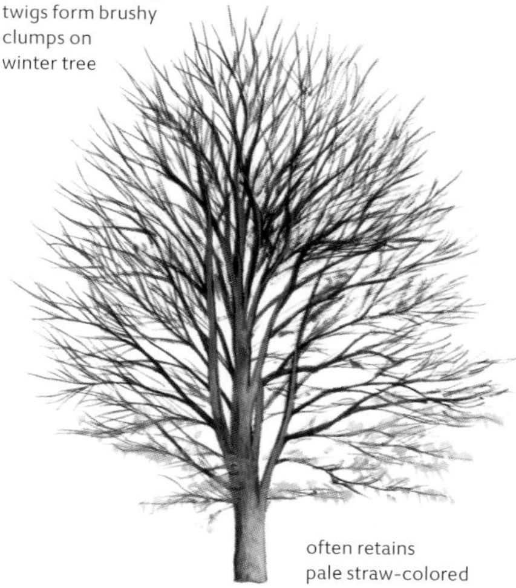

slender ascending twigs form brushy clumps on winter tree

often retains pale straw-colored leaves through winter

fruit a 4-part husk with hooked prickles, ¾", opening at maturity to reveal 1–3 small nuts

twigs slender and zigzag

strikingly slender pointed buds

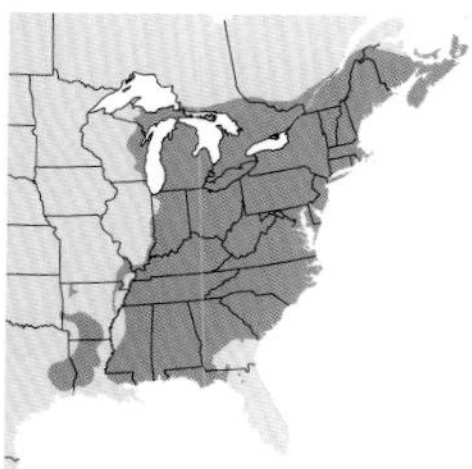

Common in rich well-drained upland soils, in deciduous forest and mixed broadleaf-conifer forest, often in relatively pure stands. Not often cultivated (zones 4–9).

Several subspecies of America Beech have been named. Northern trees on average have larger fruit with more and longer prickles, and narrower leaves with more pointed base than southern trees; in addition, forms with fuzzy leaves occur locally in north and south. But variation is clinal with extensive variation within each population.

Beech Family: Chestnuts

Eight to ten species of chestnuts are native worldwide in the the temperate northern hemisphere. Three species are native to North America (all tree-like) along with three commonly cultivated species.

All chestnuts share long narrow leaves with many parallel veins, each ending in a conspicuous tooth, large edible nuts enclosed in a spiny capsule, and male flowers in long slender spikes in early summer.

The chinkapins are two native species that differ from other chestnuts. Chinkapins are shorter with smaller leaves and nuts, which are usually single and enclosed in a capsule that splits into two parts (other chestnuts have several nuts in a capsule that splits into four parts). Chinkapins hybridize with American Chestnut and are considered part of the same genus.

Before 1930, American Chestnut was one of the most important forest trees. Its sweet edible nuts were consumed avidly by wild-life and humans, and it had light, strong, rot-resistant wood. Chestnut blight, a fungal disease introduced from Japan to New York, quickly spread throughout the eastern states and by 1930, it destroyed virtually all mature chestnut trees. Only a few isolated plantings in the West were spared, but most of those have since become infected. It has disappeared as a large tree, although infected trees continue to sprout from the roots as a fairly common understory shrub or small tree in many eastern forests. These plants rarely grow large enough to produce seeds. Related species such as Ozark Chinkapin, and even more distant relatives like Golden Chinkapin, are also susceptible to blight, while other species, notably Chinese Chestnut, are not. Efforts to develop a resistant strain of American Chestnut—mostly through hybridization with Chinese Chestnut and other resistant species—have shown promising results.

usually broad, spreading with short trunk; mature trees like this are almost always cultivated Eurasian species or hybrids.

male flowers pale whitish in slender spikes, 5", near twig tips; female flowers inconspicuous
flowers mid-summer (Jun–Jul)

new sprouts emerge from roots; older growth killed by chestnut blight

American Chestnut

Castanea dentata

Deciduous. Formerly a large, even massive, tree to 100' tall (max. claimed to 140'). Now rarely tree size, persisting mostly as multi-stemmed resprouts (infrequently to 30').

bark on young trunks brown with horizontal lenticels, soon developing furrows

bark on mature trunks gray with deep furrows

leaves long, 7", narrow
many sharp teeth
leaves often slightly curved
stalk short
underleaf green, hairless

long leaves of varying sizes usually 2-ranked along twig

fruit 4-parted capsule , 2", densely covered with spines, opening to expose (usually 3) nuts
fruit ripens and falls to ground Sep–Oct
nuts dark brown, ¾"

spiny fruit, 1–3, at twig tips, fall with leaves
fall color drab yellow

twig greenish-brown, hairless
buds blunt, brown

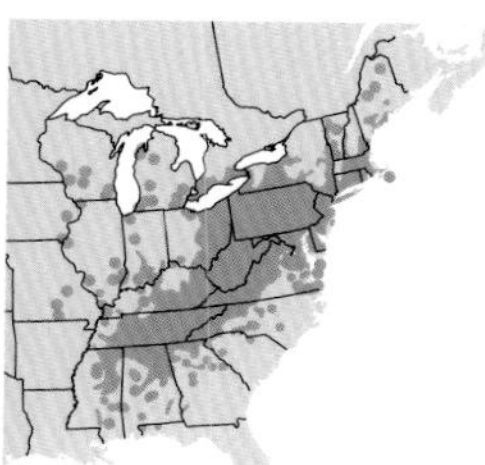

Previously common in rich well-drained soils with oaks and other trees; still locally common as an understory tree. Occasionally cultivated.

It is difficult to overstate the importance of American Chestnut trees in pre-1900 America. Fast-growing and abundant, it was one of the most common forest trees within its range, where fewer than 100 large trees survive today.

Allegheny Chinkapin

Castanea pumila

ALLEGHENY CHINQUAPIN, DWARF CHESTNUT

Deciduous. Shrubs or trees, usually under 30' tall, often thicket-forming (max. 65'). Usually smaller than Ozark Chinkapin with smaller leaves with white-woolly underside, and thinner twigs.

leaves small, 5", resembling beech; variable in shape
underleaf whitish-hairy
leaf tip pointed or rounded

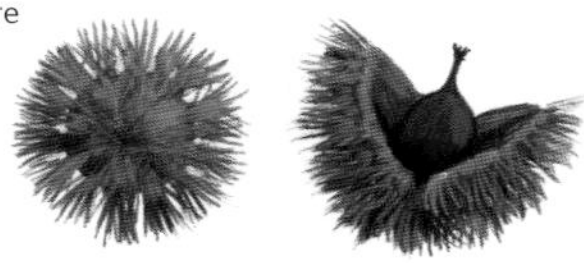
fruit 1½" with hairy spines (sparser in coastal plain form); husk splitting into two sections when mature
nut ¾", usually single

twig slender, whitish-fuzzy

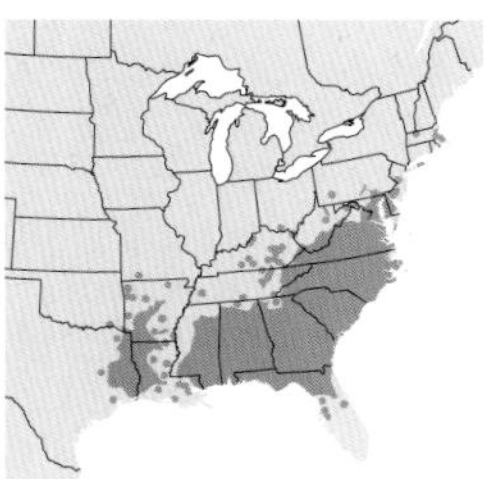

Common in open dry or rich woods or sandy ridges; blight resistant. Rarely cultivated (zones 5–9).

Several subspecies of Allegheny Chinkapin have been named, and are sometimes considered species, but variation is clinal and subtle. Plants in northern regions and at higher elevations tend to be larger and tree-like with pale-hairy underleaf, while coastal plain plants (sometimes separated as Florida Chinkapin, *Castanea alnifolia*) tend to be smaller with hairless underleaf, smaller leaves with more rounded tip, and less dense spines on the fruit husk. Allegheny Chinkapin apparently hybridizes with American Chestnut at scattered locations in the Mid-Atlantic region, but hybrids are very difficult to distinguish from either parent. Ozark Chinkapin, generally intermediate between Allegheny and American Chestnut, is sometimes considered part of Allegheny, as the two intergrade in the Ouachita Mountains in Arkansas.

Ozark Chinkapin

Castanea ozarkensis

OZARK CHESTNUT

Deciduous. Formerly a small to medium tree often 35' tall (max. 50'), but now devastated by blight and rarely tree-size; occurs as shrubby resprouts rarely over 30'. Smaller than American Chestnut with smaller fruit and usually single nut. Similar to Allegheny Chinkapin, but with leaves and twigs less hairy, leaves slightly larger.

leaves 6½", similar to other chestnuts but often broader with broad tip
underleaf pale

Uncommon on dry or well-drained soils in deciduous forest. Not cultivated.

Chinese Chestnut

Castanea mollissima

Deciduous, Small to medium, broad tree, rarely over 40' tall (max. 64'). Blight resistant and now the most common chestnut in North America.

leaves 6½", oval, smaller, wider, and more leathery than American
underleaf pale hairy, often whitish

fruit 2½", 2–3 nuts, each 1", similar to American Chestnut, but larger

twigs hairy pale brown

Differences between cultivated species of chestnuts are slight and most trees are cultivars (often hybrids) selected for certain characteristics. Chinese Chestnut is the most frequent, but Spanish and Japanese are also seen, as well as hybrids of these species and American Chestnut. Look at leaf and fruit characteristics, and do not expect to identify every chestnut tree to species.

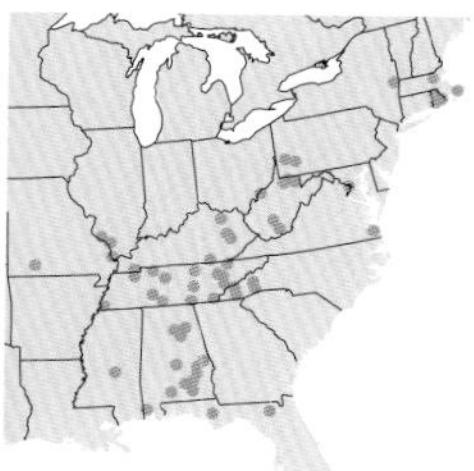

Native to China. Commonly cultivated and rarely escaped from cultivation (zones 4–8).

Japanese Chestnut

Castanea crenata

Deciduous. A small broad tree, rarely over 30' tall (max. 57'). Distinguished from native Chinkapins by much larger fruit and usually 3 nuts in each fruit (like Chinese); leaves relatively dark shiny green.

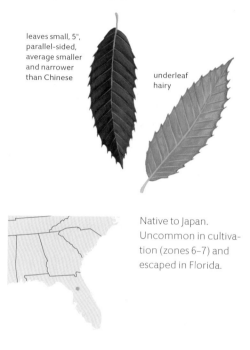

leaves small, 5", parallel-sided, average smaller and narrower than Chinese
underleaf hairy

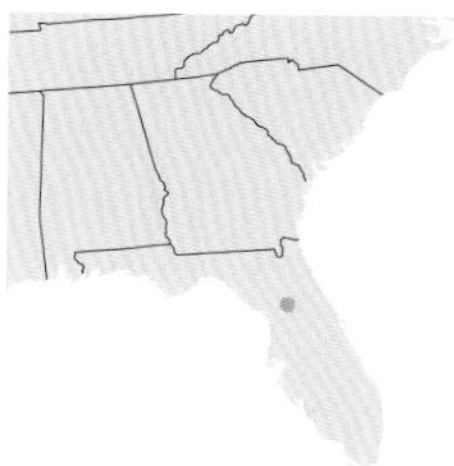

Native to Japan. Uncommon in cultivation (zones 6–7) and escaped in Florida.

European Chestnut

Castanea sativa

SPANISH CHESTNUT, SWEET CHESTNUT

Deciduous. Medium to large tree often 60' tall (max. 97'). Very similar to American Chestnut, but leaves average broader with more triangular teeth, not curving in at tips; nuts average larger. The source of most commercial chestnuts; less commonly grown as an ornamental.

Native to southern Europe, western Asia, northern Africa. Locally escaped in the Northeast and in Mississippi (zones 5–7).

Golden Chinkapin

Chrysolepis chrysophylla

GIANT CHINKAPIN, GOLDEN CHESTNUT

Evergreen. Shrub to large tree, often 50–80' tall (max. 127'). Distinctive with dense dark foliage, golden underleaf, spikes of pale flowers midsummer. Susceptible to Chestnut Blight. Leaves resemble California Laurel, but not aromatic.

young bark smooth, pale with lighter blotches

mature bark becoming thick, with broad pale or reddish-brown ridges

leaves 4", narrow, oval, pointed, with short stalk; yellow midvein; leathery; curled margins; dark glossy green

underleaf usually golden or brownish

older leaves pale yellow

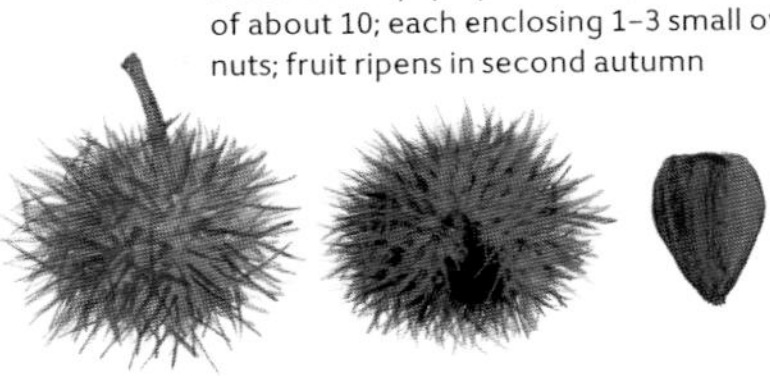

fruit a densely spiny husk 1½"; in clusters of about 10; each enclosing 1–3 small oval nuts; fruit ripens in second autumn

male flowers pale creamy-white in 2" spikes, upright, clustered at branch tips (Jul–Aug)

female flowers inconspicuous

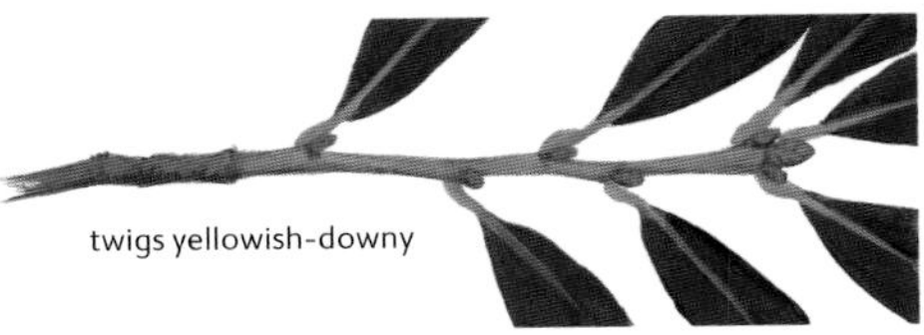

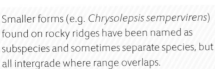

twigs yellowish-downy

Smaller forms (e.g. *Chrysolepsis sempervirens*) found on rocky ridges have been named as subspecies and sometimes separate species, but all intergrade where range overlaps.

dense conical crown

Locally common on mountain slopes and rocky ridges, rarely cultivated.

Tanoak

Lithocarpus densiflorus

TANBARK-OAK

Evergreen. Shrub to large tree often 50–75' tall, (max. 208'). Distinguished from Live Oaks by whitish-woolly underleaf, shaggy acorn cup, leaf edges curled down, and upright flower catkins. Similar to Golden Chinkapin, but leaves average broader and toothed with woolly underside; flower catkins are longer and fruit is very different.

bark pale gray
with irregular
narrow ridges

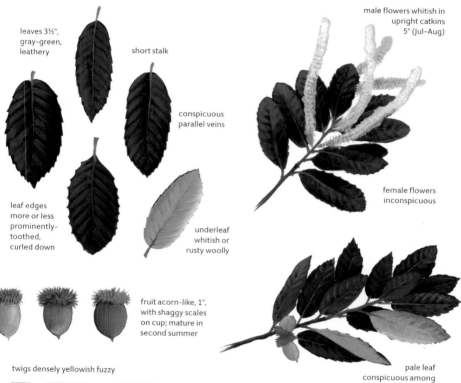

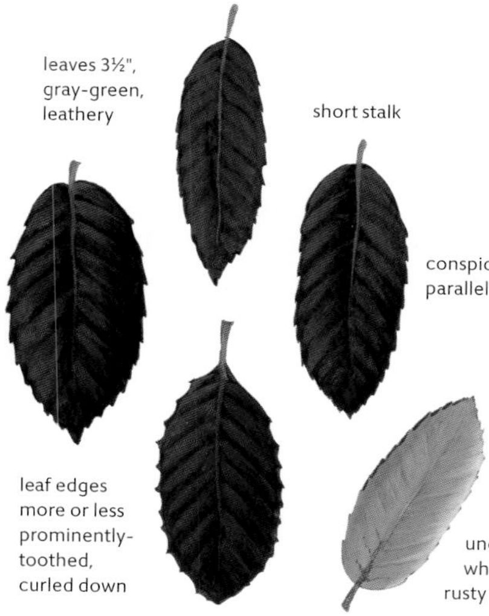
leaves 3½",
gray-green,
leathery
short stalk
conspicuous
parallel veins
leaf edges
more or less
prominently-
toothed,
curled down
underleaf
whitish or
rusty woolly

male flowers whitish in
upright catkins
5" (Jul–Aug)
female flowers
inconspicuous

fruit acorn-like, 1",
with shaggy scales
on cup; mature in
second summer

pale leaf
conspicuous among
dense, dark foliage

twigs densely yellowish fuzzy

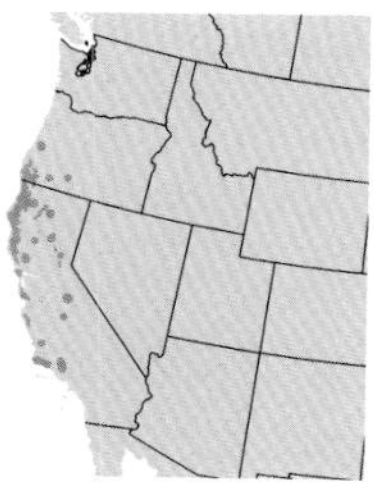

Common in mixed evergreen forest and redwood forest especially in coast ranges; rarely cultivated.

Tanoak (like Golden Chinkapin) is the only North American representative of its genus. Both have many related species native to Asia. In particular, Tanoak represents a link between chestnuts and oaks. Its flowers are similar to chestnuts, while the fruit is an acorn similar to oaks, but with a thicker woody shell and a spiny cup, reminiscent of the spiny husk of a chestnut. It is one of the species most susceptible to sudden oak death.

Beech Family: Oaks

The oaks are represented by about 400 species of trees and shrubs worldwide. In North America, about ninety species are recognized, and sixty-nine native species grow to tree size and are covered in this guide. Seven exotic species that are commonly cultivated or escaped are also included.

Oaks are widespread and dominant in many forest types, especially in the Southeast and Southwest. Most are deciduous, but a few species in warmer climates are evergreen. Most are medium to large trees, often with massive spreading branches; a few species are shrubby and thicket-forming, mostly in California and the arid Southwest, where they are a major component of chaparral and scrub plant communities.

All oaks have acorns (only the related Tanoak has a similar acorn-like fruit), and all have buds clustered at twig tips.

Oaks currently account for about half the annual production of hardwood in the United States, used mostly for furniture and other fine carpentry.

Acorns provide important food for wildlife and domesticated animals. Historically, acorns were important food for humans, but long preparation is required to reduce their strong bitter flavor, so acorns are rarely consumed by humans today.

Tannin in the bark of oaks was important for tanning leather. A yellow dye (quercitron) was produced from the inner bark of Eastern Black Oak.

Cork is harvested from the bark of the European Cork Oak. Several species are very popular ornamental and shade trees. The large oaks can live for centuries and grow into statuesque and venerable trees, often revered as symbols of strength and stability.

The native oaks can be subdivided into three groups, the red oaks, the white oaks, and the golden-cup oak group. They are all distinguished by several easily observed characteristics (see table), but more accurately by microscopic features of the wood.

Red Oak Group	White Oak Group
leaves bristle-tipped with pointed lobes 	leaves without bristle tips, usually with rounded lobes 
acorns mature in fall after second growing season; sprout in following spring acorn shells hairy inside acorn cup scales brownish and flat 	acorns mature in fall after one growing season; sprout mainly in fall acorn shells not hairy inside acorn cup scales paler and knobby 
buds of many species larger and more pointed 	buds of most species smaller and blunter than red oak 
bark tends to be dark, smooth or ridged, not peeling 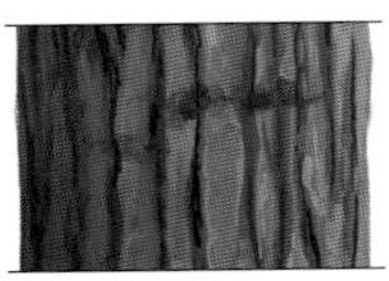	bark usually paler, blocky, scaly or peeling 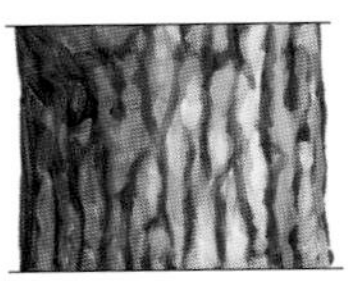

The red oak group is well-represented in the East and in the Southwest, while the white oak group is most diverse in the arid Southwest. The smaller golden-cup oak group is native in California and the Southwest. The golden-cup oak group with three species, is intermediate between red oaks and white oaks. In leaf, acorn, buds, and bark features, golden-cup oak group species are similar to trees in the white oak group, but their acorn cup scales are covered by a yellowish fuzz, unlike any other oaks. Details of their wood and chemistry also set them apart.

fully extended catkins hang down below developing leaves in long strands

TWIGS

All oaks have buds clustered at twig tips (shared by Golden Chinkapin, Pin Cherry, and Corkwood).

POLLINATION

All oaks are wind-pollinated with tiny yellow-green male flowers in dangling catkins that appear as the leaves unfold in early spring. Female flowers are tiny, greenish, and inconspicuous in the leaf axils. There are no consistent differences in flowers between species of oaks.

old flower catkins turn brown and dry before falling as leaves mature

emerging leaves may be green, red, or purple; variable from tree to tree

LEAF SHAPE

Leaf shape is particularly variable in oaks with single trees often showing a wide range of shapes. Much variation is accounted for by two tendencies: Leaves on young and vigorous shoots or stump sprouts tend to be leathery, large, and broad and either more lobed, or less lobed than the typical leaves (these leaves also often persist longer than typical leaves). Leaves from the canopy (sun leaves) tend to be smaller and more deeply lobed than shaded leaves.

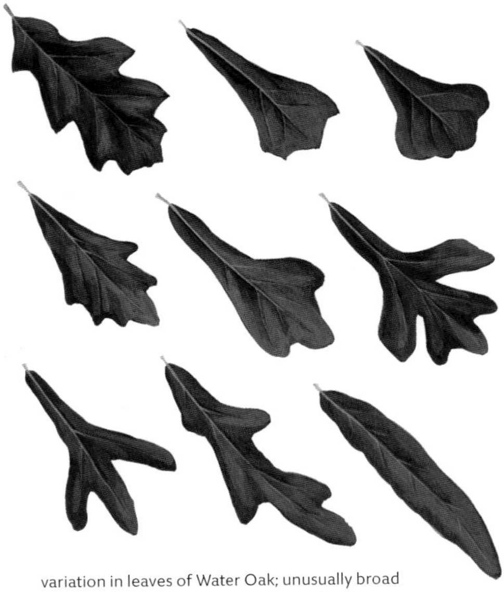

variation in leaves of Water Oak; unusually broad or narrow leaves appear on vigorous shoots

variation in leaves of Eastern Black Oak; more slender leaves grow in the treetops in full sun

HYBRIDIZATION

Hybridization is known between many species of oaks, and can be common locally, but recent studies have shown that many trees previously considered hybrids are instead merely individual variants. This makes identification especially challenging. When confronted by a confusing tree, consider the possibility that it is simply a variation of a common local species, and then the possibility of a hybrid of two species that are present in the immediate vicinity. Note that the genus is divided into three groups (red and white oaks, and Golden-cup Oak), and hybrids have been reported commonly *within* each of the groups of the genus, but never confirmed *between* groups. Finally, accept the fact that not all oak trees can be identified to species.

Willow Oak | Willow × Northern Red Oak | Northern Red Oak

DISEASES

Oaks have been relatively disease- and pest-free, but sudden oak death is a new and serious disease caused by a mold that enters the tree through the bark and attacks living tissue. First discovered in California in 1995, it has quickly spread, killing many oaks and other plants, especially Coast Live Oak, Shreve Oak, and the related Tanoak. It has also been found in over sixty other species of woody plants, infecting the leaves but not killing those species. Efforts are underway to find an effective treatment and to prevent further spread of the disease to other states, where it has the potential to kill millions of trees.

TREE SHAPE

Oak trees can be spreading or somewhat upright in shape, but all develop a broader crown with age. When growing in the open oaks can develop a very broad spreading crown with massive side branches.

FALL COLOR

Fall leaf color of most oaks is dull dark red, rusty orange, or drab golden yellow, usually mixed with green on each leaf. Oak leaves change color slowly and gradually. They are nearly always dark or drab, unlike the clear yellows or reds shown by, for example, birches or maples. Some oak species—including Northern Red, Scarlet, and Pin Oaks—can show relatively bright red leaves in fall, especially on cultivated trees, which are often planted for their fall colors.

fall leaf color yellow, orange, red, or purple, usually with drab or murky tone; leaves of white oak group (bottom right) often slightly more purplish or pinkish than red oak group

often retain orange-brown leaves through winter, particularly on young trees and lower branches

Northern Red Oak

Quercus rubra

RED OAK, GRAY OAK, EASTERN RED OAK

Deciduous. Medium to large tree often 90' tall (max. 165'). Often grows with similar species in the red oak group. Distinguished by shallow acorn cup, shallow pointed lobes, reddish buds, old trees with deeply ridged bark.

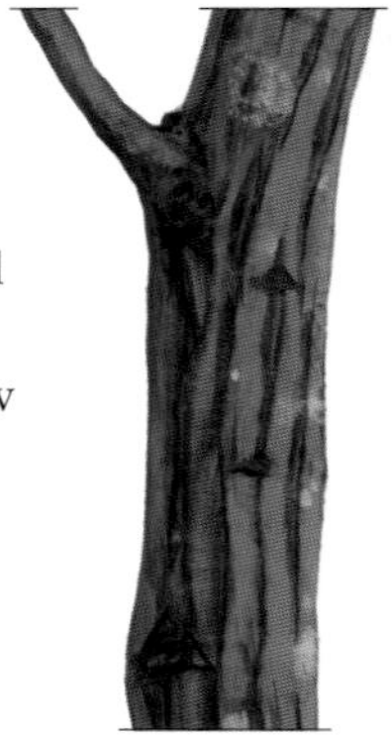

bark on young trunks dark grayish and smooth (like all red oaks)

bark on mature trunks forms long, broad, smooth ridges and shallow fissures

leaf stalk often red
leaves 7"
tapered, pointed, usually shallow lobes
smooth, green underleaf

leaves have long stalks and droop gracefully from twig tips, similar to closely related species

Two varieties are named: var. *borealis*, more common north, has a deeper acorn cup and more deeply lobed leaves than var. *rubra*; but these differences are not well defined and are overshadowed by individual and other variations.

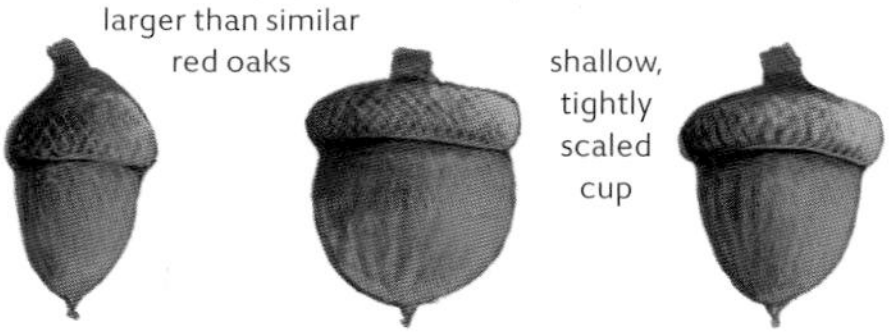
acorns 1", larger than similar red oaks
shallow, tightly scaled cup

buds and twigs reddish

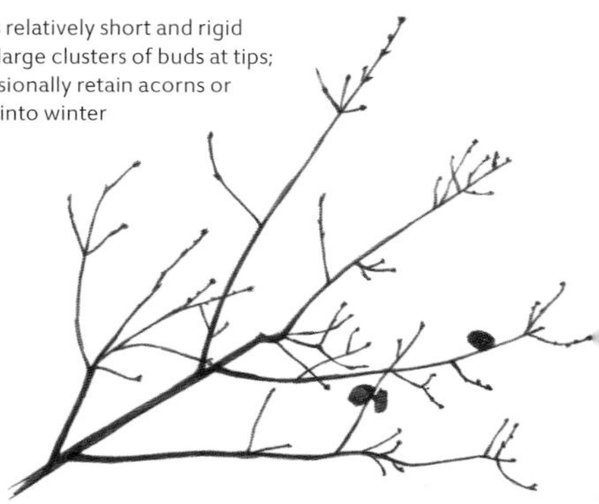
twigs relatively short and rigid with large clusters of buds at tips; occasionally retain acorns or cups into winter

Common and widespread, growing mainly on mesic uplands, occasionally in drier or wetter areas. A relatively fast-growing and stately oak, and very commonly cultivated (zones 3–7).

Eastern Black Oak

Quercus velutina

YELLOW OAK, QUERCITRON OAK

Deciduous. Medium to large tree often 80' tall (max. 131'). Distinguished from Northern Red and other oaks by coarser-looking foliage (created by large, dark leaves with broad lobes), leaves that are glossy above and slightly orange-tinged below, blocky bark, large, pale buds, and acorns with a relatively deep cup and slight fringe.

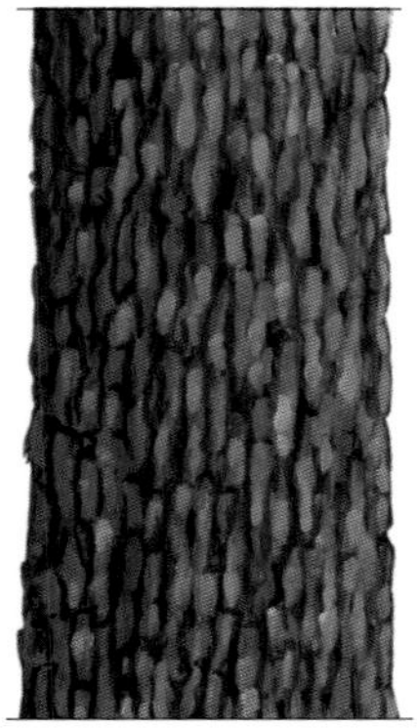
bark dark grayish, broken into irregular rectangular blocks (young/small trunks similar to Northern Red Oak)

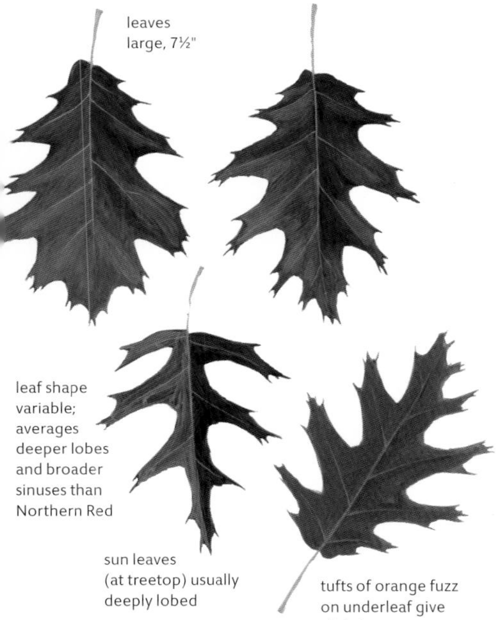
leaves large, 7½"
leaf shape variable; averages deeper lobes and broader sinuses than Northern Red
sun leaves (at treetop) usually deeply lobed
tufts of orange fuzz on underleaf give slightly orange tone

leaves droop gracefully, more so than Northern Red

On an individual oak tree, variation in leaf shape can be greater than the differences that distinguish species. In general, leaves that grow in sun are smaller and more deeply lobed and have less surface area, while leaves on shaded twigs are broader with shallower lobes and more surface area. This variation seems especially noticeable on Eastern Black Oak. Always check the whole tree to find the "average" leaf, rather than attempt to identify an oak from a single leaf or leaf cluster.

acorns ¾"
cup shaggy-fringed with loose scales, relatively deep

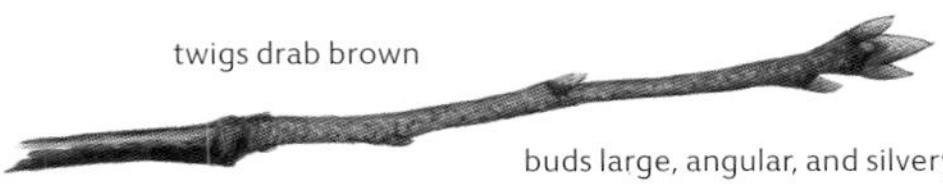
twigs drab brown
buds large, angular, and silvery

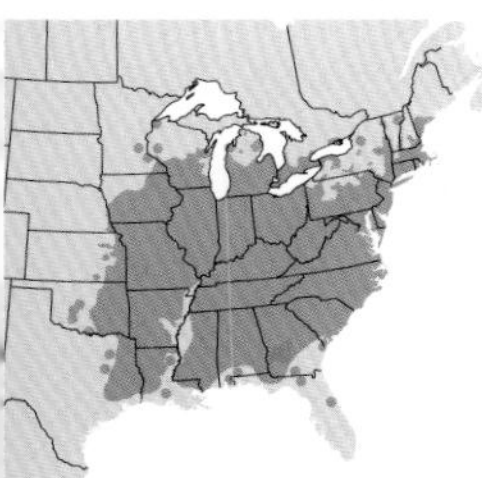

Common in well-drained moist soils or relatively dry, sandy upland sites, usually growing with other oaks. Uncommon in cultivation (zones 3–9).

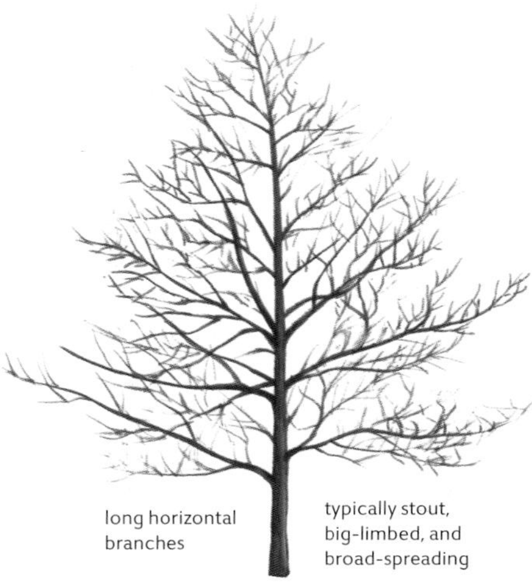
long horizontal branches
typically stout, big-limbed, and broad-spreading

Pin Oak

Quercus palustris

SWAMP OAK, WATER OAK, SPANISH OAK

Deciduous. Medium to large tree often 80' tall (max. 135'). Small, deeply lobed leaves give foliage a soft or fine look. Also note relatively smooth bark, drooping lower branches, small buds, and small acorns with a shallow cup. Fall color can be brighter red than on most oaks, especially in some cultivars.

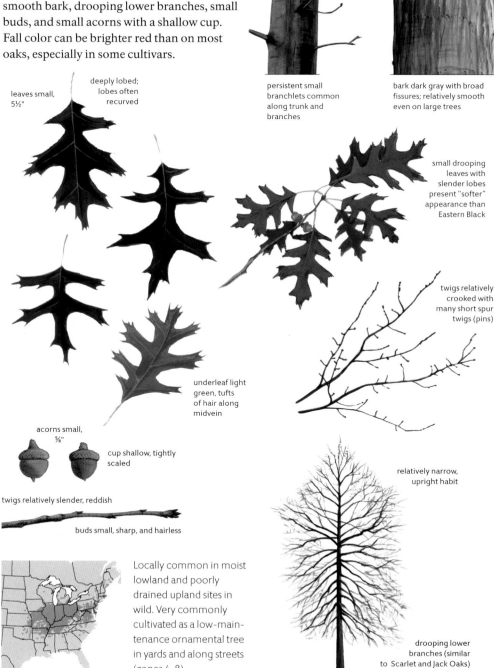

persistent small branchlets common along trunk and branches

bark dark gray with broad fissures; relatively smooth even on large trees

leaves small, 5½"
deeply lobed; lobes often recurved
underleaf light green, tufts of hair along midvein

small drooping leaves with slender lobes present "softer" appearance than Eastern Black

twigs relatively crooked with many short spur twigs (pins)

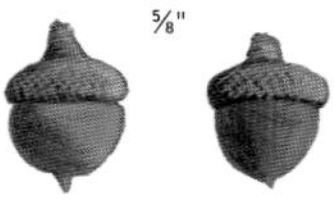

acorns small, ⅝"

cup shallow, tightly scaled

twigs relatively slender, reddish

buds small, sharp, and hairless

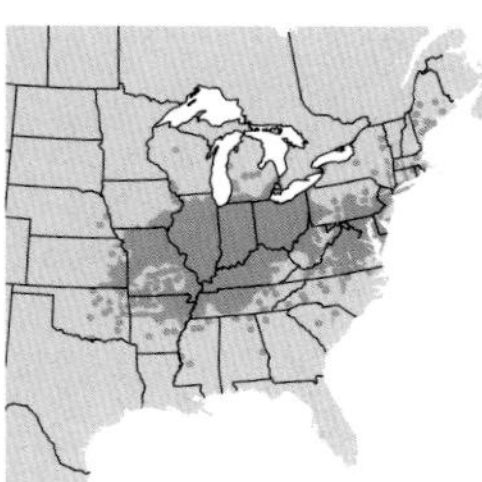

Locally common in moist lowland and poorly drained upland sites in wild. Very commonly cultivated as a low-maintenance ornamental tree in yards and along streets (zones 4–8).

relatively narrow, upright habit

drooping lower branches (similar to Scarlet and Jack Oaks)

Scarlet Oak

Quercus coccinea

BLACK OAK, SPANISH OAK

Deciduous. Medium to large tree often 80' tall (max. 181'). Differs from Eastern Black Oak in smaller, more deeply lobed leaves; also distinguished by buds that are pale only at tip, and a tightly scaled acorn cup. Distinguished from Pin Oak by drier habitat, a deeper acorn cup, hairy buds and rough bark. Fall color can be brighter red than on most oaks.

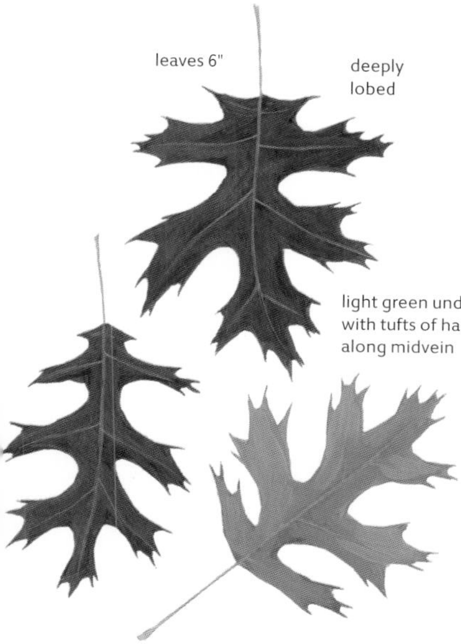
leaves 6"
deeply lobed
light green underleaf with tufts of hair along midvein

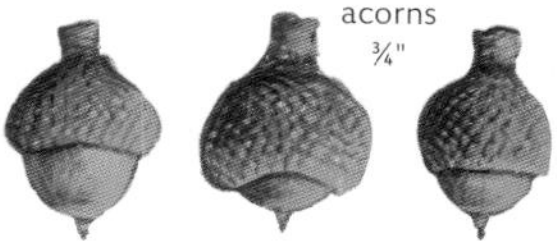
acorns ¾"
cup deep, tightly scaled
some trees (var. *tuberculata*) produce acorns with broad, warty cup scales

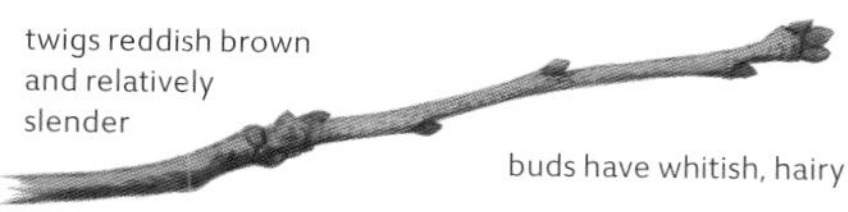
twigs reddish brown and relatively slender
buds have whitish, hairy tip

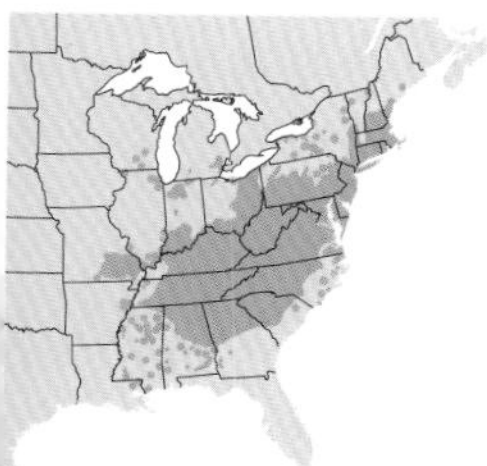

Locally fairly common in poor dry soils, dry slopes, and uplands. Uncommon in cultivation (zones 4–9); less tolerant than Pin or Northern Red Oaks.

Jack Oak

Quercus ellipsoidalis

NORTHERN PIN OAK, HILL'S OAK

Deciduous. Medium to large tree often 65' tall (max. 86'). Very similar to Pin and Scarlet Oaks; best distinguished by narrow acorns with a deep conical cup, and by habitat and range. Sometimes considered a variety of Scarlet Oak or a hybrid swarm derived from Pin Oak and Black Oak.

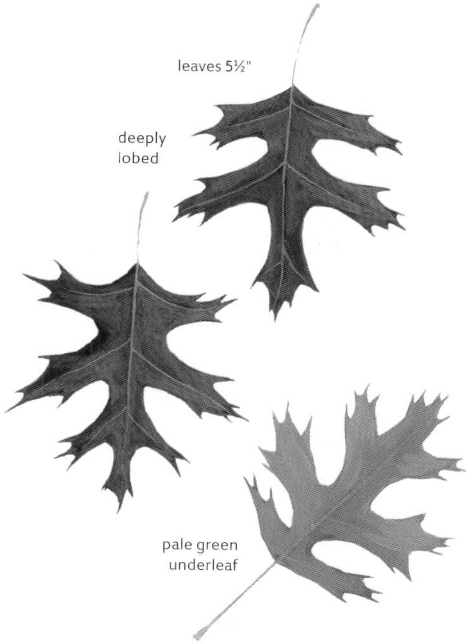
leaves 5½"
deeply lobed
pale green underleaf

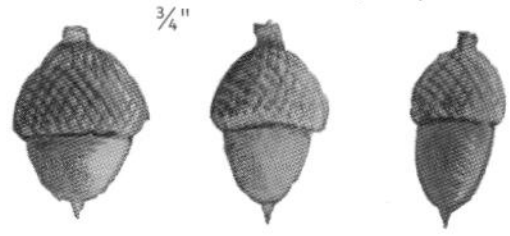
acorns ¾"
deep cup

twigs reddish brown
buds can be hairless, like Pin Oak, or with whitish, hairy tip, like Scarlet Oak

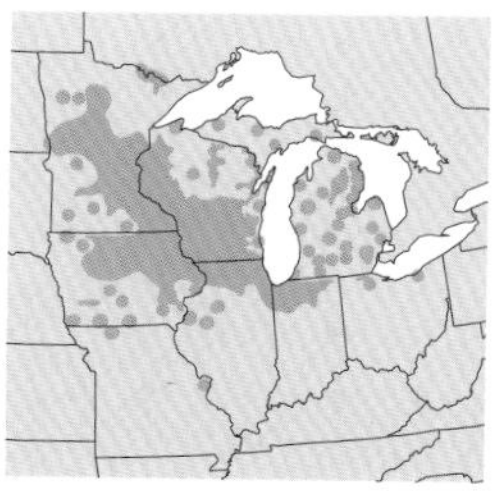

Locally fairly common on dry sandy soils in lowlands; rarely on mesic to dry uplands. Very rarely cultivated.

Shumard Oak

Quercus shumardii

LEOPARD OAK, SPOTTED OAK

Deciduous. Medium to large tree often 90' tall (max. 190'). Identified by broad, glossy leaves that have many lobes and bristles; also by relatively smooth bark, large buds, and large acorns with a shallow cup.

leaves large, 6½"
squarish lobes end in multiple bristles
shiny green above and below
usually orange, felty hairs in vein junctions of underleaf
acorns 1"
cup shallow, gray
twigs gray to light brown
end buds large, grayish or straw-colored, and hairless

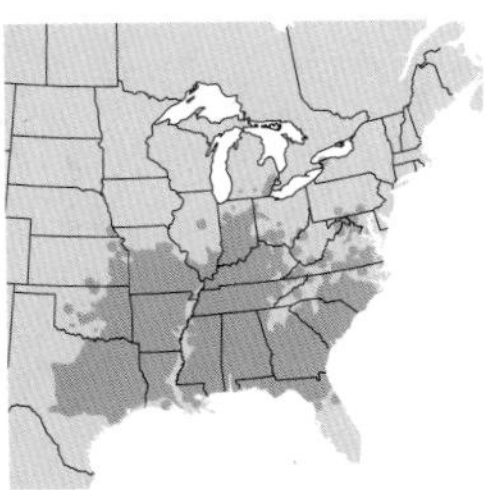

Fairly common in well-drained mesic soils near water or on poorly drained uplands. Generally uncommon in cultivation (zones 5–9).

Maple-leaf Oak

Quercus acerifolia

Deciduous. Large shrub or small tree usually under 30' tall (max. 50'); often with multiple trunks. Closely related to Shumard Oak and sometimes considered the same species; differs in leaf shape, smaller leaves and acorns, and usually brighter red fall foliage.

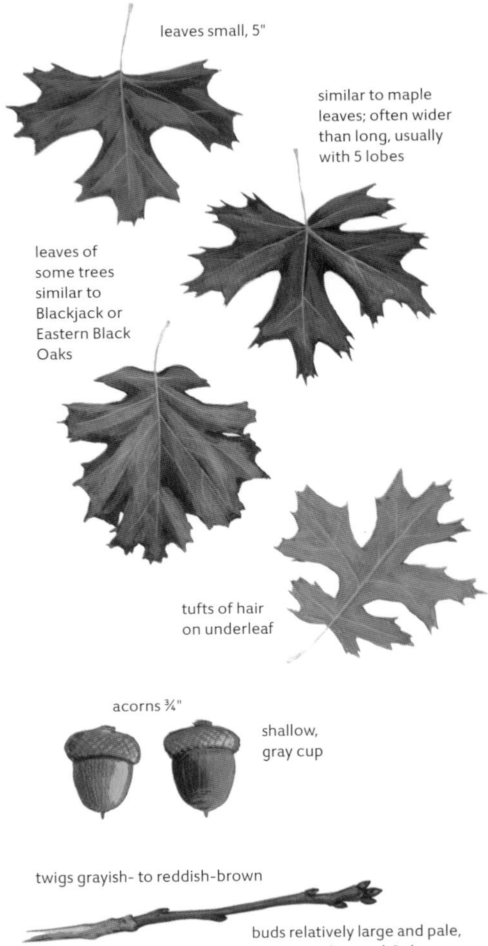
leaves small, 5"
similar to maple leaves; often wider than long, usually with 5 lobes
leaves of some trees similar to Blackjack or Eastern Black Oaks
tufts of hair on underleaf
acorns ¾"
shallow, gray cup
twigs grayish- to reddish-brown
buds relatively large and pale, similar to Shumard Oak

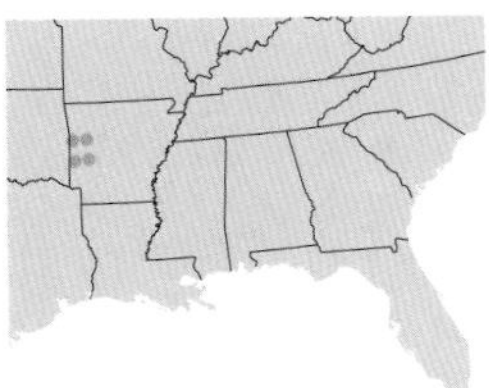

Rare and local; known only from four localities on dry slopes and ridgetops in Arkansas. Very rarely cultivated.

Southern Red Oak

Quercus falcata

TURKEYFOOT OAK, SPANISH OAK

Deciduous. Medium or large tree to 90' tall (max. 135'). Similar to Cherrybark, distinguished from other oaks by leaf shape, hairy underleaf. Compared to American Turkey Oak has less prominent 3-lobed leaf shape.

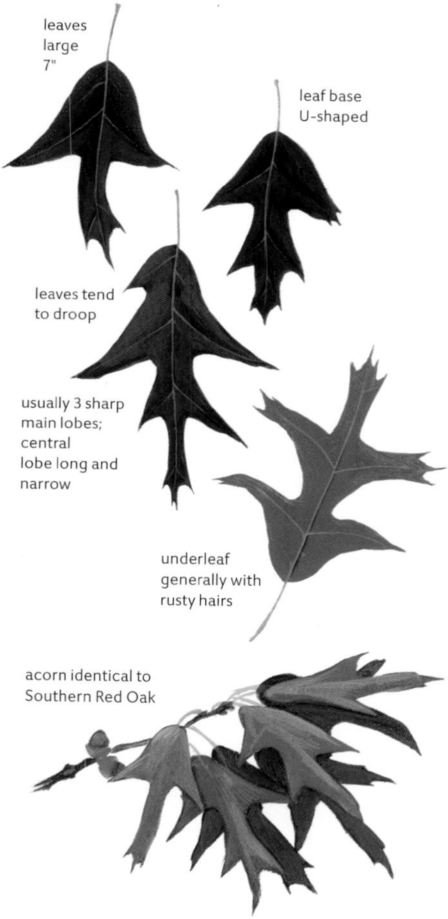
leaves large 7"
leaf base U-shaped
leaves tend to droop
usually 3 sharp main lobes; central lobe long and narrow
underleaf generally with rusty hairs
acorn identical to Southern Red Oak

twigs yellowish brown, hairy
buds reddish brown

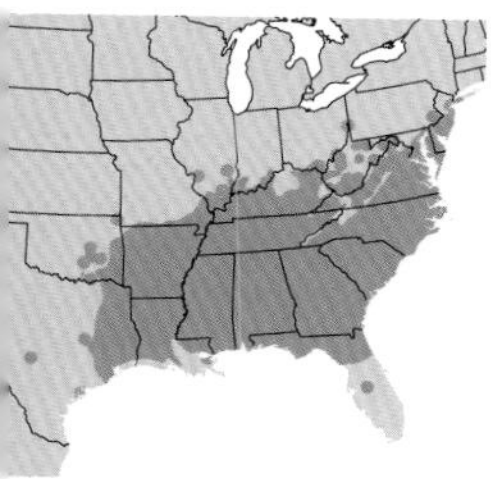

Common in dry to sandy uplands; not commonly cultivated (zones 7–9).

Cherrybark Oak

Quercus pagoda

PAGODA OAK, SWAMP RED OAK

Deciduous. Medium to large tree often 80' tall (max. 124'). Similar to Southern Red and the two were formerly considered a single species, but differs in leaf shape, underleaf color, and habitat. Named for dark scaly bark similar to Black Cherry.

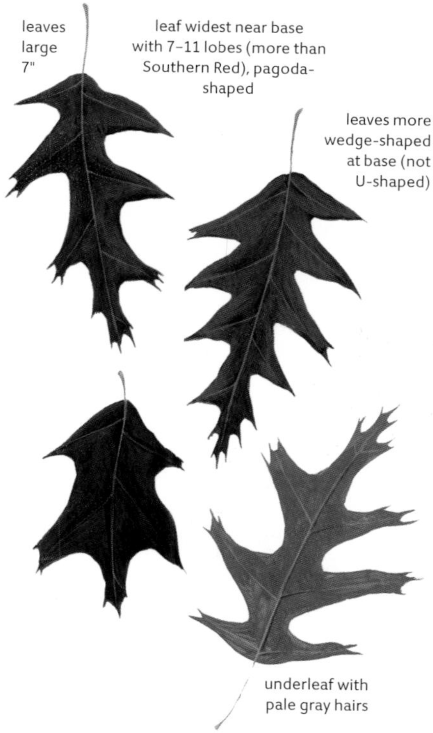
leaves large 7"
leaf widest near base with 7–11 lobes (more than Southern Red), pagoda-shaped
leaves more wedge-shaped at base (not U-shaped)
underleaf with pale gray hairs

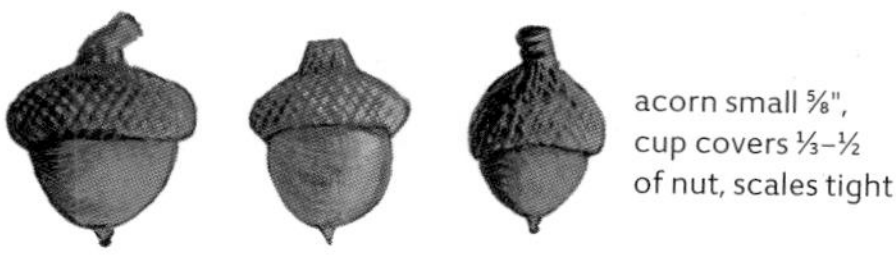
acorn small ⅝", cup covers ⅓–½ of nut, scales tight

twigs yellowish brown, hairy
buds reddish brown

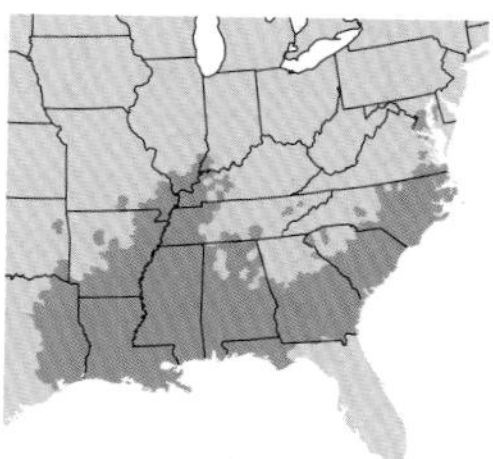

Common in well-drained soils in floodplain forests and riverbanks; not commonly cultivated (zones 7–9).

Buckley's Oak

Quercus buckleyi

TEXAS RED OAK

Deciduous. Shrub or small tree usually under 35' tall (max. 80'), often multi-trunked. Very similar to Texas Red and Shumard Oaks, but has smaller stature, leaves and acorns, and hairless underleaf.

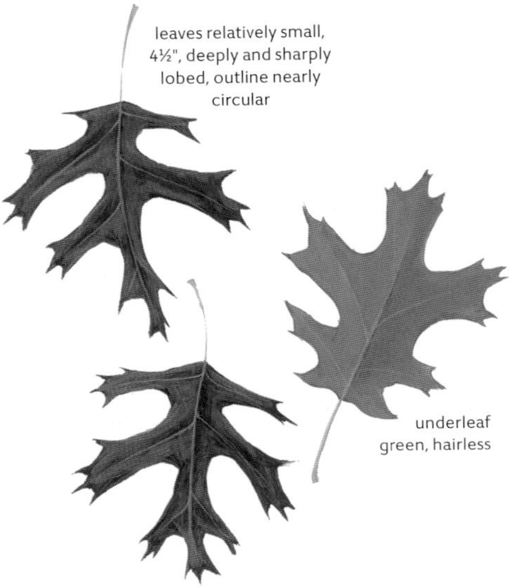
leaves relatively small, 4½", deeply and sharply lobed, outline nearly circular
underleaf green, hairless

acorn small ¾"; cup relatively deep covers ⅓–½ of nut, rarely shallow

twig reddish-brown

This species and Texas Red Oak are very closely related to each other and to Shumard Oak. In the past these have sometimes been considered subspecies and even part of Northern Red Oak, leading to a confusing history of names. Hybridizes with Shumard Oak where range overlaps across central Texas.

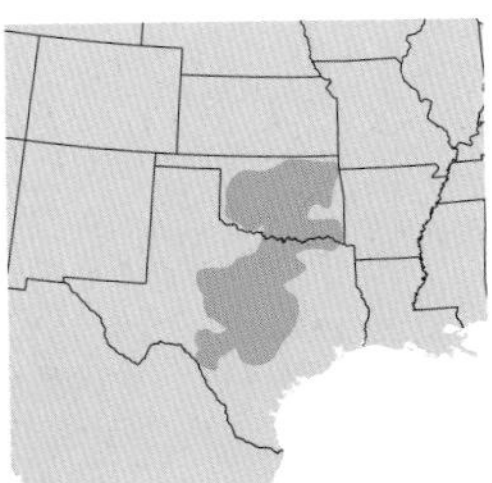

Common on well-drained sand or gravel soils, limestone ridges, creek bottoms. Uncommon in cultivation, mostly in Texas (zone 8).

Texas Red Oak

Quercus texana

NUTTALL OAK, RED RIVER OAK, SMOOTHBARK RED OAK

Deciduous. Medium or large tree to 75' tall (max. 118'). Similar to Shumard Oak, but acorn cup deeper and goblet-shaped. Distinguished from Buckley's Oak by larger size, slightly larger acorns with deeper cup (on average), and conspicuous hair tufts on underleaf.

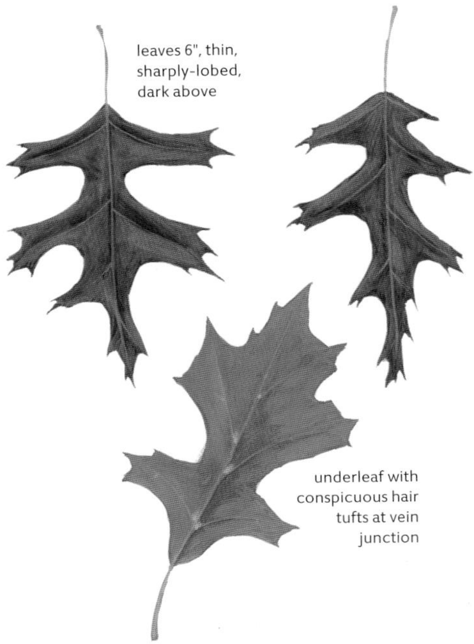
leaves 6", thin, sharply-lobed, dark above
underleaf with conspicuous hair tufts at vein junction

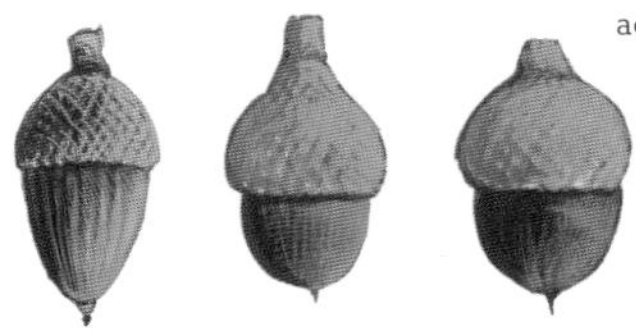
acorn medium-large, 1", cup deep goblet-shaped covers ⅓–½ of nut; scales tight

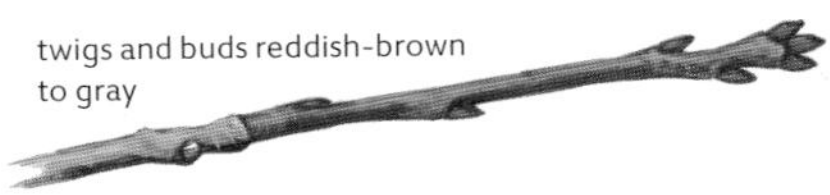
twigs and buds reddish-brown to gray

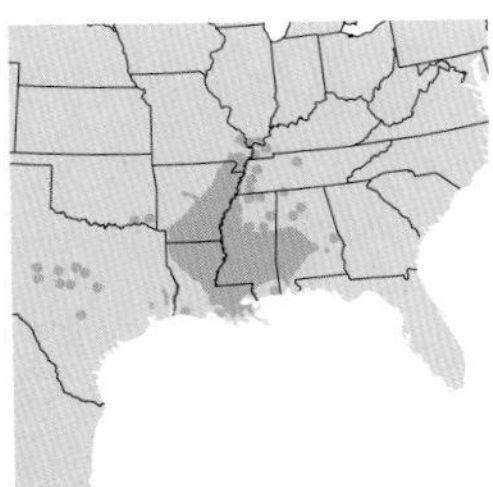

Common in floodplains and bottomlands. Uncommon but increasing in cultivation, particularly in warmer zones (zones 5–9).

American Turkey Oak

Quercus laevis

TURKEY OAK, CATESBY OAK, SCRUB OAK

Deciduous. Shrub or small tree usually under 30' tall (max. 60'), often thicket-forming. Leaf shape most like Southern Red, but leafstalk short and stiff (leaves less drooping), acorn larger with tightly rolled cup, buds larger.

bark dark gray,
deeply-furrowed

leaves 6", usually 3–5 slender pointed lobes, like a turkey foot
leafstalk short
underleaf occasionally orange-fuzzy

leaves held stiffly upright

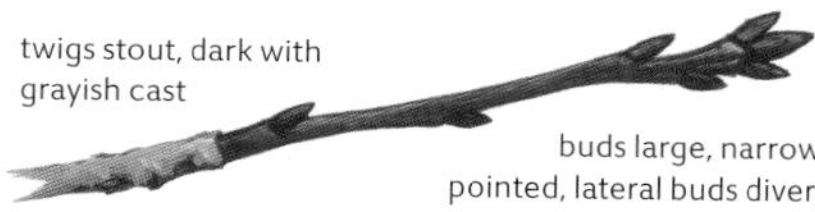
twigs stout, dark with grayish cast
buds large, narrow and pointed, lateral buds divergent

acorn large, 1", cup deep and goblet-shaped with scales rolled in tightly at edge

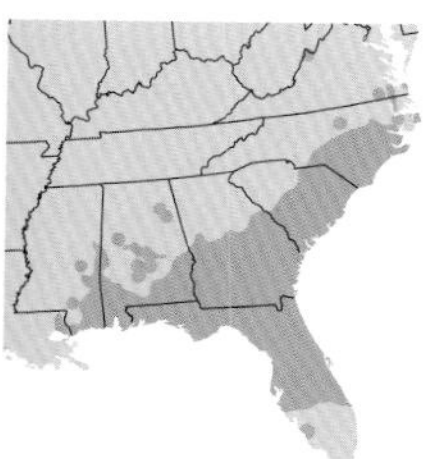

Common in pine-oak scrub in dry sandy soil, often with Bluejack and Sand Post Oaks. Not cultivated.

American Turkey Oak and the eleven preceding species (along with California Black Oak, page 197) all have very similar, deeply-lobed leaves. Although there are slight average differences between species in leaf shape and hairiness, identification must be confirmed by using other features. Bark is strongly ridged on a few species. Acorns have deep or shallow cups with loose scales (forming a small fringe) or tight scales, depending on species. Buds vary from small and dark to large and silvery. In any given region only a few species are likely to occur and several species are restricted to either drier or wetter habitats. Using all of these features in combination, it should be possible to identify most of these oaks with reasonable confidence.

Bear Oak

Quercus ilicifolia

SCRUB OAK

Deciduous. Shrub or small tree usually under 15' tall (max. 18'); often forming thickets. Recognized by small size and small leaves with whitish underleaf.

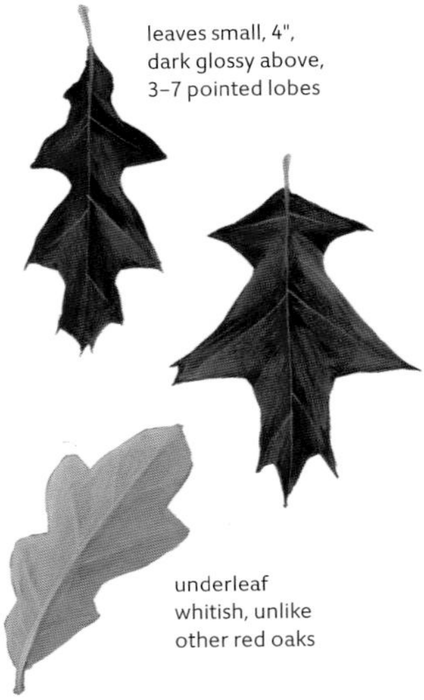
leaves small, 4",
dark glossy above,
3–7 pointed lobes
underleaf
whitish, unlike
other red oaks

acorn ¾",
cup fairly deep,
scales pointed, tight

twigs brown
to yellowish, downy
buds small,
blunt, dark reddish

Watch for Bear Oak as a small tree or shrub in sandy or poor soils in clearings, open ridgetops, or in the understory of open pine woods. Other oaks also take on small shrubby forms in the same locations, so identification must be based on details of foliage and fruit.

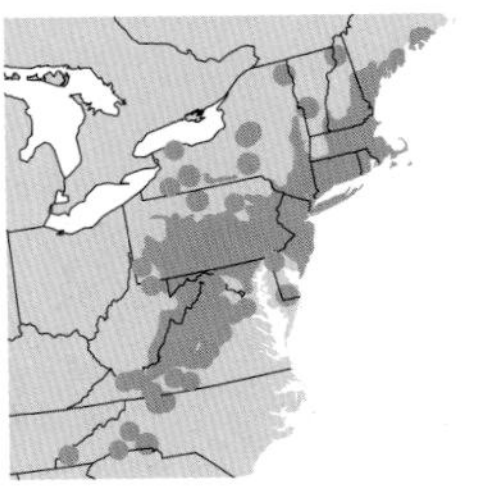

Locally common in poor soil in clearings and edges, dry sandy woods and barrens, rocky outcrops. Not cultivated.

Georgia Oak

Quercus georgiana

Deciduous. Small tree to 25' tall (max. 50'). Similar to Bear Oak, but leaves greenish below, no range overlap; also may have leaves glossier above and acorn cup may be shallower.

leaves small, 4",
3–5 broad lobes
underleaf
pale, hairless

acorn ¾",
cup shallow

twigs gray-pubescent

Georgia Oak is one of the rarest trees in the Southeast, considered threatened because it is found over such a small area in only a few locations.

Rare on rocky outcrops and ridges and dry slopes. Occasionally cultivated (zones 5–8).

Blackjack Oak

Quercus marilandica

BARREN OAK, BLACK OAK, JACK OAK

Deciduous. Small or medium tree usually under 50' tall (max. 90'); often scrubby with drooping branches. Large, mostly unlobed leathery leaves with tawny underleaf distinctive; appears dark overall with dark bark and dark glossy leaves.

bark dark in squarish blocks with deep fissures

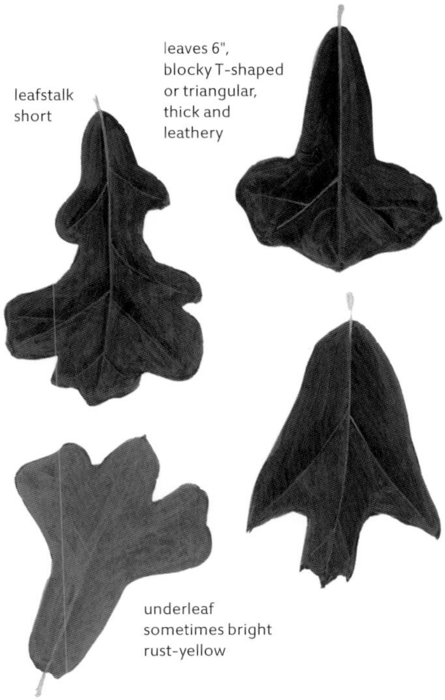
leafstalk short
leaves 6", blocky T-shaped or triangular, thick and leathery
underleaf sometimes bright rust-yellow

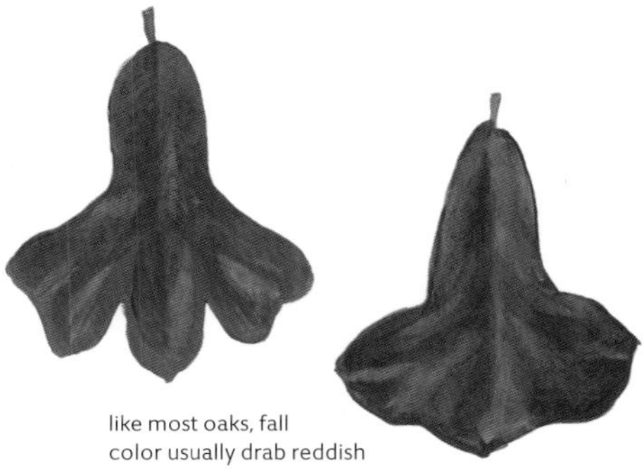
like most oaks, fall color usually drab reddish to orange brown

broad leathery leaves stand stiffly around twig tips

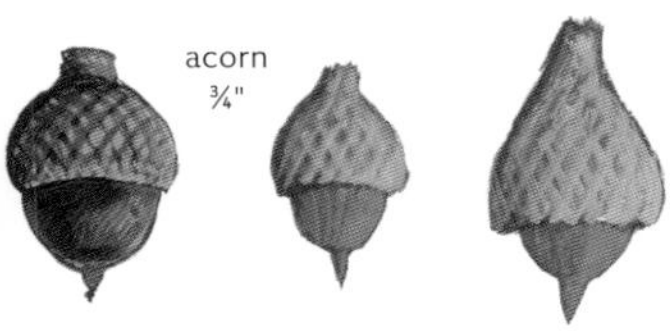
acorn ¾"
deep goblet-shaped cup, scales loose

twigs ashy brown, hairy
buds with tawny hairs

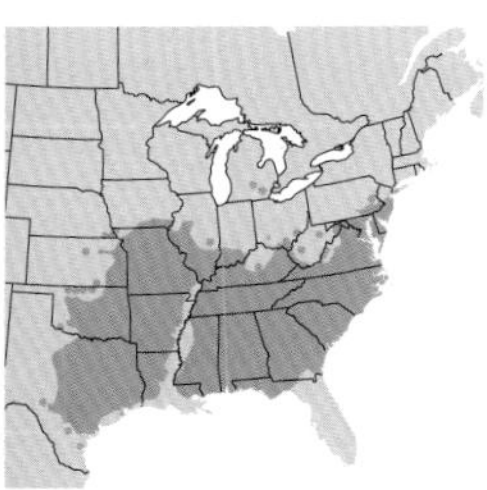

Locally common in poor, dry soils; dry ridges, barrens, disturbed fields. Often with Common Post Oak. Rarely cultivated.

This species is superficially similar to Common Post Oak (of the white oak group) and often found together. In Texas and Oklahoma, the two species are the primary trees in a distinct habitat called the "cross timbers" or post oak savannah, a transition between the forests of the East and prairie of the West. Trees in western areas, Texas and Oklahoma, have smaller leaves, 3" with gray fuzz in underleaf axils and are recognized as var. *ashei*.

Darlington Oak

Quercus hemisphaerica

LAUREL OAK

Semi-evergreen. Medium or large tree often 60' tall (max. 98'). Formerly considered a part of Swamp Laurel Oak, distinguished by leaf details, drier habitat, flowering two weeks later.

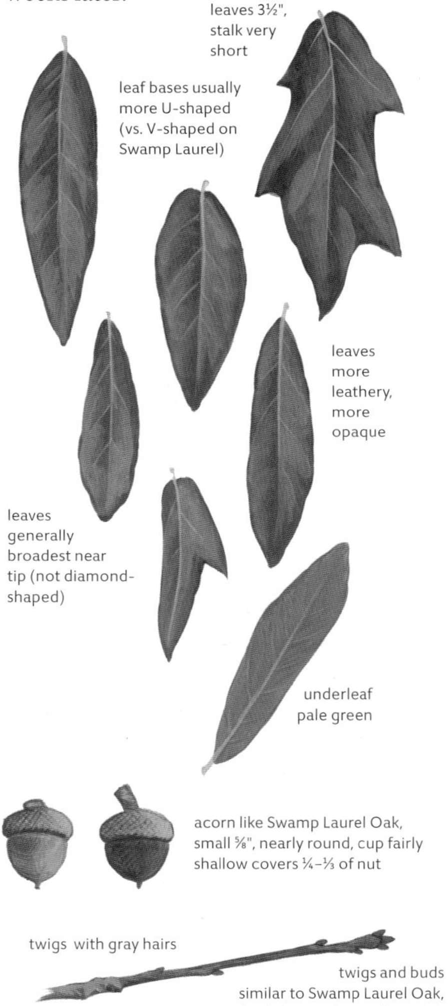
leaves 3½", stalk very short
leaf bases usually more U-shaped (vs. V-shaped on Swamp Laurel)
leaves more leathery, more opaque
leaves generally broadest near tip (not diamond-shaped)
underleaf pale green
acorn like Swamp Laurel Oak, small ⅝", nearly round, cup fairly shallow covers ¼–⅓ of nut
twigs with gray hairs
twigs and buds similar to Swamp Laurel Oak, buds larger than Willow Oak

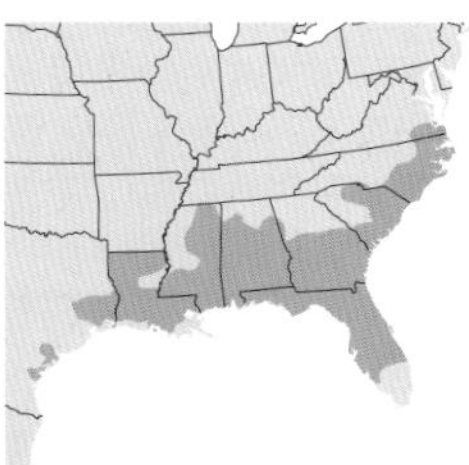

Common in fairly dry sandy soils of lowlands, stream terraces, occasionally hillsides; mixed open woods, hammocks; commonly cultivated (zones 6–9).

Swamp Laurel Oak

Quercus laurifolia

LAUREL-LEAF OAK, DIAMOND LEAF OAK, WATER OAK, OBTUSA OAK

Tardily deciduous. Medium to large tree usually under 60' tall (max. 148'); very similar to Willow Oak, but leaves average broader and more leathery, and persist most of winter. Even more similar to Darlington Oak.

leaves 3½", stalk very short
leaves on vigorous shoots often lobed; occasional leaves resemble Water Oak
leaves average slightly broader than Darlington
at least some leaves on each tree widest in middle (diamond shape)
underleaf pale green
leaves broader, less rigidly linear than Willow Oak
acorn small ⅝", cup shallow, scales tight, covers ¼–½ of nut

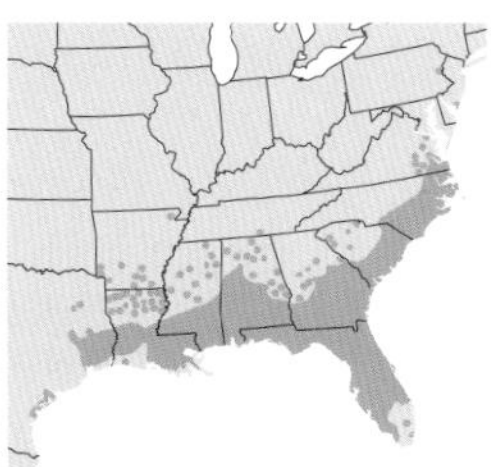

Uncommon and scattered in swamps, floodplains, wet hammocks; commonly cultivated (zones 6–9).

Willow Oak

Quercus phellos

PEACH OAK, PIN OAK, SWAMP WILLOW OAK

Deciduous. Large tree often 80' tall (max. 158'). Similar to Darlington and Swamp Laurel Oaks, but leaves deciduous, average narrower, and underleaf sometimes slightly hairy.

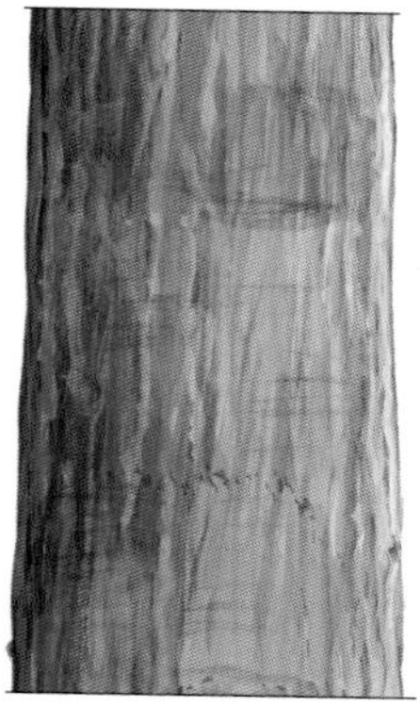
bark of mature
trunks smooth
with faint ridges

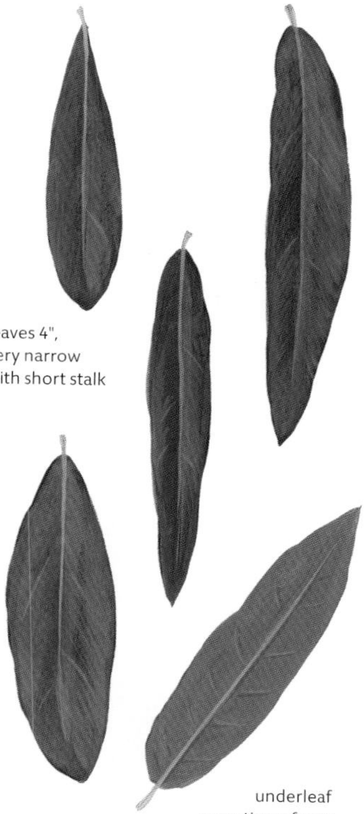
leaves 4",
very narrow
with short stalk
underleaf
sometimes fuzzy

fall color
yellow to pale
orange-brown

narrow leaves
stand out stiffly
all around twig

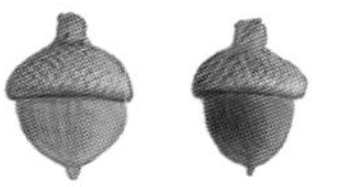
acorn small, ½", cup shallow
covers ¼–⅓ of nut with tight
grayish scales

twigs very slender for an oak
buds smaller
than on similar species

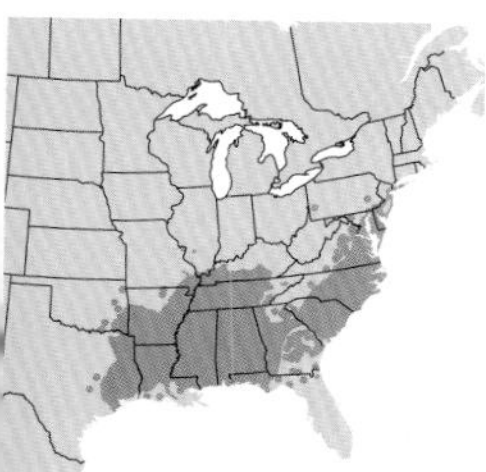

Common in bottomlands and other wet lowlands, occasionally on poorly-drained uplands. Commonly cultivated in yards and towns (zones 7–9).

The Willow Oak's relatively smooth bark without obvious ridges, even on large mature trunks, is shared by many other species in the red oak group. Pin, Jack, Shumard, Maple-leaf, Southern Red, Buckley's, Texas Red, Darlington, Swamp Laurel, and Water Oaks all have more or less similar bark. This unridged bark distinguishes all of these species from similar red oaks, such as Northern Red, Eastern Black, Scarlet, American Turkey, and Shingle Oaks, and from all trees of the white oak group. The bark of Cherrybark Oak is similar to Eastern Black with more obvious small scales making it somewhat reminiscent of Black Cherry.

Water Oak

Quercus nigra

POSSUM OAK, SPOTTED OAK

Tardily deciduous. Medium or large tree often 60' tall (max. 125'); narrow wedge-shaped leaves are distinctive, but leaf variation can cause confusion with other species such as Chapman Oak, Durand Oak, and others.

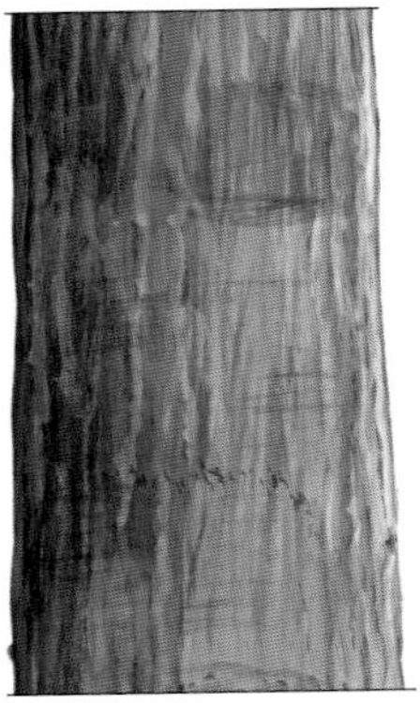

bark relatively smooth like Pin Oak, Willow Oak, and others

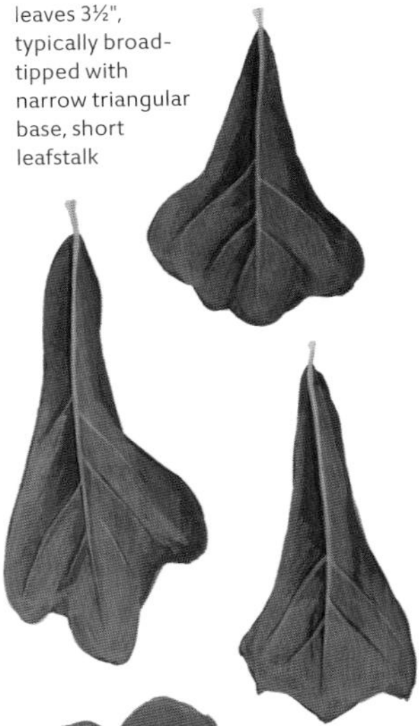

leaves 3½", typically broad-tipped with narrow triangular base, short leafstalk

leaves thick and leathery

underleaf hairless or with tufts of hairs in vein axils

broad leaf tips create "fan" shape at twig tips

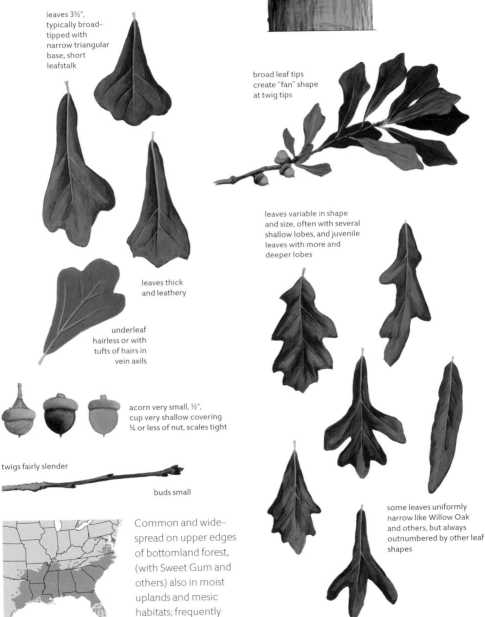

leaves variable in shape and size, often with several shallow lobes, and juvenile leaves with more and deeper lobes

some leaves uniformly narrow like Willow Oak and others, but always outnumbered by other leaf shapes

acorn very small, ½", cup very shallow covering ¼ or less of nut, scales tight

twigs fairly slender

buds small

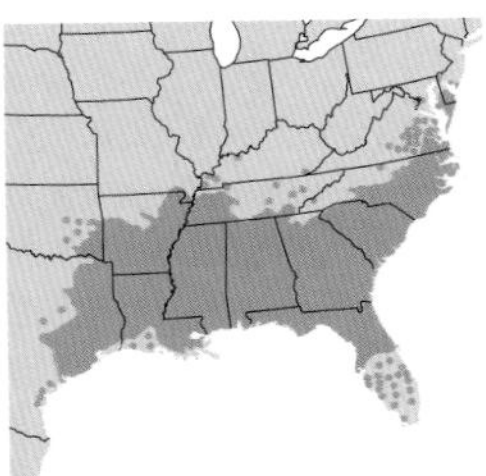

Common and widespread on upper edges of bottomland forest, (with Sweet Gum and others) also in moist uplands and mesic habitats; frequently cultivated (zones 6–9).

Shingle Oak

Quercus imbricaria

NORTHERN LAUREL OAK

Deciduous. Medium tree usually under 50' tall (max. 100'). Distinguished from similar species by leaves averaging larger and broader, pale hairy below, and less stiff, by bark that develops scaly ridges and furrows, and by relatively deep acorn cup.

leaves never lobed or toothed, 6", wider than most similar oaks
underleaf densely hairy
leaves droop gracefully (vs. stiffer leaves of Willow Oak)
acorn ¾", cup fairly deep similar to Eastern Black and Scarlet Oaks
twigs greenish to brown

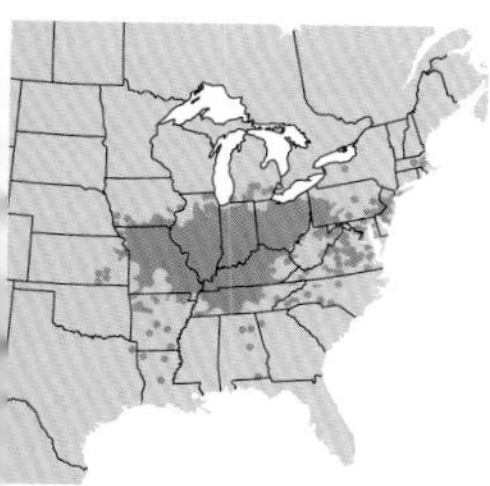

Common in rich moist soils in lowlands and along streams, but also found on drier hillsides; often with Pin Oak and Overcup Oak. Uncommon in cultivation (zones 4–8).

Arkansas Oak

Quercus arkansana

ARKANSAS WATER OAK, WATER OAK

Deciduous. Small understory tree usually under 50' tall. Similar to Blackjack Oak, but leaves more rounded, less leathery, and greenish below, acorn cup shallow. Closely-related to Water Oak (some hybrids known), but leaves broader, bark darker and rougher.

leaves 4½", small and broad with rounded base
underleaf paler green
acorn small, ⅝", with thin shallow cup
twigs with gray hairs

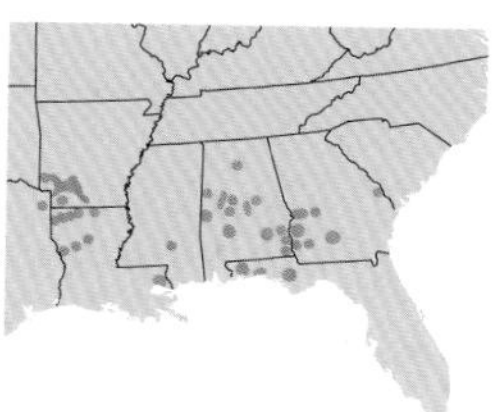

Rare and local in well-drained sandy soil, often in understory of hardwood forest; most numerous in south-western Arkansas. Not cultivated.

Bluejack Oak

Quercus incana

CINNAMON OAK, SANDJACK, SHIN OAK, TURKEY OAK, UPLAND WILLOW OAK

Tardily deciduous. Shrub or small tree usually under 25' (max. 68'), often forming thickets. Like Southern Live Oak (of white oak group), but leaves flat and bluish-gray, underleaf whitish.

leaves bluish
or ashy green
above
leafstalk
very short
leaves 3",
leathery
occasional
sprout leaves
with 2–3 lobes
leaf margins
flat, not
rolled under
underleaf
whitish
acorn small,
¾", cup shallow
twigs often hairy

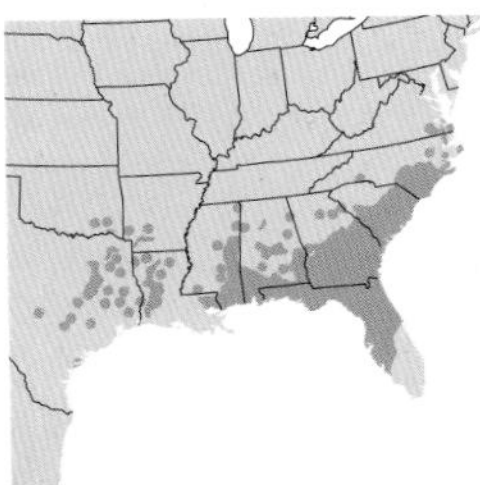

Common in well-drained sandy soils, dunes and ridges, associated with American Turkey Oak and Sand Post Oak. Not cultivated.

Myrtle Oak

Quercus myrtifolia

SCRUB OAK

Evergreen. Shrub or occasionally a small tree to 20' (max. 40'), usually forms thickets. Superficially similar small-leaved oaks (Chapman Oak, Sand Live Oak) are in white oak group; note Myrtle's mostly shiny underleaf (occasionally yellow-fuzzy).

leaves small, 1½", very short stalk,
leathery, edges rolled under,
oval to diamond-shaped,
hairless and shiny
underleaf
paler green
acorn ⅝", cup fairly
shallow covering ¼–⅓
of nut, scales tight
twigs and buds
dark reddish-brown

The common and scientific names of this species refer to the similarity of the small evergreen leaves to the Common Myrtle (*Myrtus communis*), an unrelated shrub native to the Mediterranean region and commonly cultivated in southern Florida.

Uncommon in dry sandy soil, particularly pine-oak scrub on coastal dunes. Rarely cultivated (zones 8–10).

California Black Oak

Quercus kelloggii

KELLOGG OAK, BLACK OAK

Deciduous. Large tree often 75' tall (max. 130'), shrubby at high elevations; crooked trunk. Only lobe-leaved red oak native to the West with larger acorns than similar species in the East.

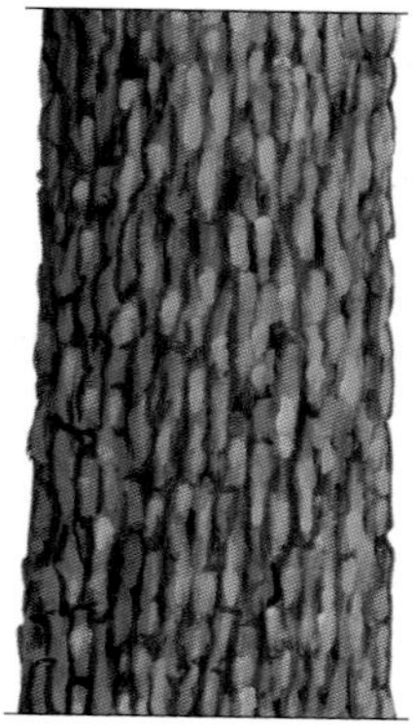

bark of mature trunks dark and deeply furrowed with broad irregular ridges

leaves 5½", thickish, glossy, deeply lobed

underleaf pale green

emerging leaves (Mar–Apr) reddish or purplish, like many eastern red oaks, but unlike other western species; new leaves and twigs covered by hoary whitish fuzz on smaller trees at higher elevations

acorn large, 1¼", with very deep cup often covering more than half of nut, cup scales thin, pointed, long and loose

California Black Oak reportedly hybridizes with Interior Live Oak and Coast Live Oak, producing a range of intermediate trees.

buds large, pale, pointed

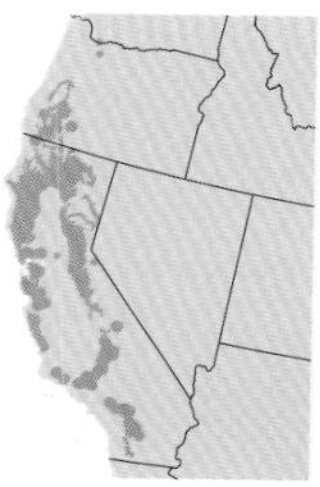

Common in sandy or gravelly soils of valleys and slopes; often in pure stands or mixed with conifers. Only occasionally cultivated within native range (zones 7–9).

when grown in the open, a large tree with broad crown

Silverleaf Oak

Quercus hypoleucoides

WHITE-LEAF OAK

Evergreen. Shrub or small tree often 30' tall (max. 60'). Usually a sparse tree with upswept branches; striking whitish underleaf distinctive. Foliage varies between trees, from larger sparser leaves to smaller and more densely clustered leaves.

leaves 3", narrow, usually untoothed, edges rolled under
leaves dark green above
underleaf striking white

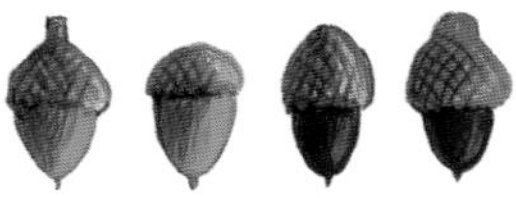
acorns mature in one or two growing seasons, small, ⅝", scales blunt, tight

Among the Red Oak group only three species—Coast Live Oak, Emory Oak, and Silverleaf Oak—have acorns that mature in one year like White Oaks.

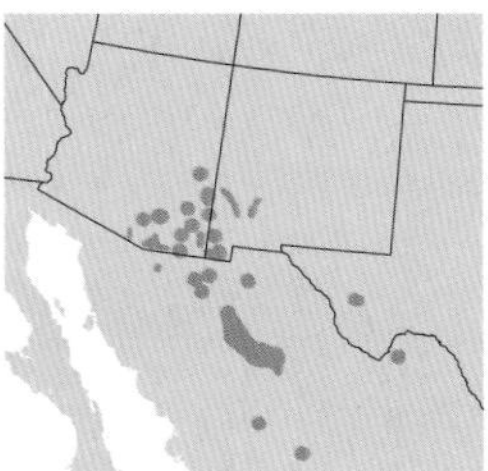

Common in less arid canyon sides and on ridges. Attractive and often used in landscaping near native range (zones 8–10).

Graves Oak

Quercus gravesii

CHISOS RED OAK

Deciduous. Small tree to 45'; small leaves with a few short lobes.

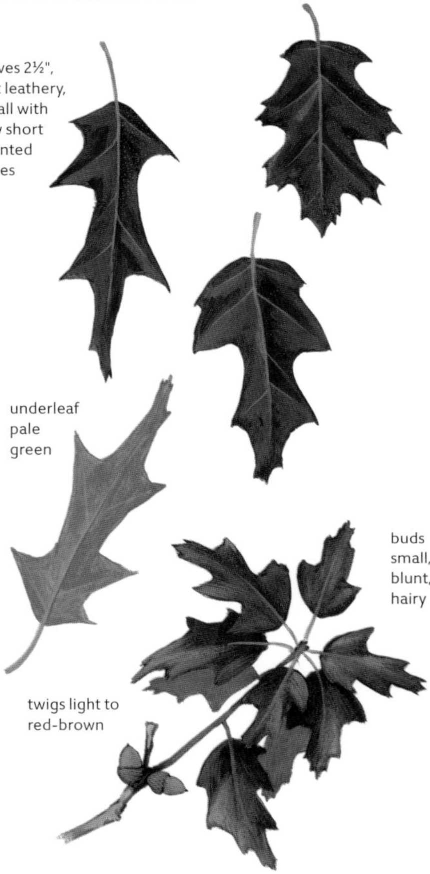
leaves 2½", not leathery, small with few short pointed lobes
underleaf pale green
buds small, blunt, hairy
twigs light to red-brown

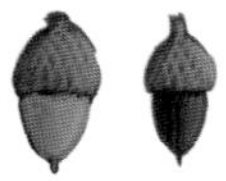
acorn small, 1", narrow with deep tapered cup, scales tight ½–⅞"

Related to Emory Oak, and on average differs in being deciduous with leaves more lobed and less leathery, but intermediate trees are not readily distinguished from Emory.

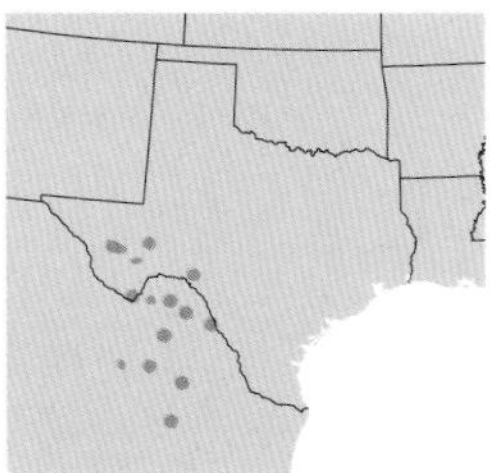

Locally common within very limited range in the Davis, Glass and Chisos Mountains. Not cultivated.

Emory Oak

Quercus emoryi

BLACK OAK, BLACKJACK OAK, BELLOTA

Evergreen. Small tree often 45' tall (max. 84'). Characteristic oak of Mexican border in Arizona and New Mexico. Closely related to Graves Oak.

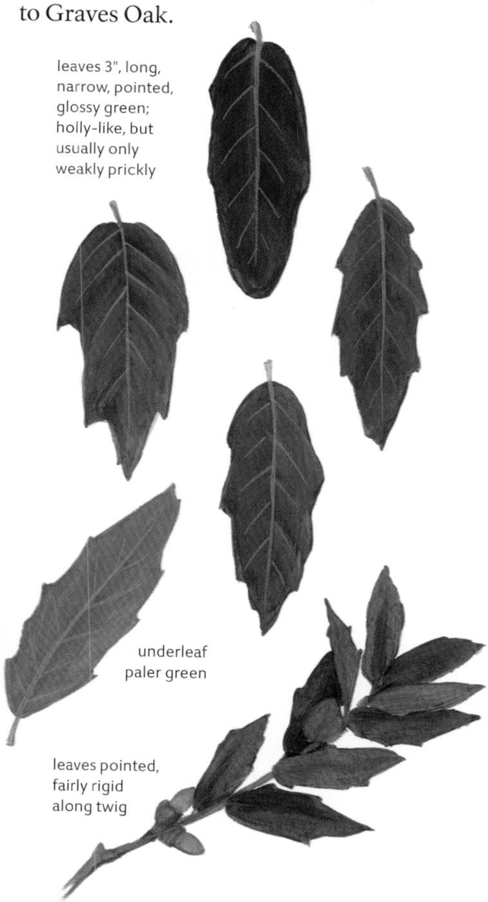
leaves 3", long, narrow, pointed, glossy green; holly-like, but usually only weakly prickly
underleaf paler green
leaves pointed, fairly rigid along twig

acorns ¾", long, ripe in a single growing season (unusual among red oaks)

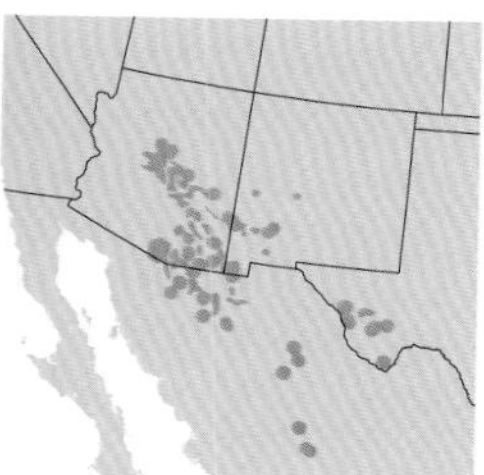

Common in foothills and slopes; rarely cultivated.

These four species, all shrubs or small trees, are very rare, local, and poorly known.

Slender Oak

Quercus graciliformis

CHISOS OAK

Tardily deciduous. Known only from a few dry rocky canyons in the Chisos Mountains of west Texas.

leaves 3½", narrow, drooping, smooth or with many teeth

Sonoran Oak

Quercus viminea

Evergreen or drought deciduous. Known in United States from a single specimen collected in Santa Cruz County, Arizona.

leaves 2", small, very narrow, base rounded, margins smooth or with small teeth

Robust Oak

Quercus robusta

Deciduous. Found only in a few moist wooded canyons in the Chisos Mountains of west Texas. Thought to be a hybrid of Emory and Graves Oaks.

leaves 4", usually with several large teeth, widest at base

Lateleaf Oak

Quercus tardifolia

CHISOS MOUNTAIN OAK

Evergreen. Known only from two small clumps in the Chisos Mountains, and may represent hybrids of Emory Oak with a Mexican species (*Quercus hypoxantha*).

leaves 3", fairly broad with few shallow lobes, base rounded, widest at middle, leathery and rough

Coast Live Oak

Quercus agrifolia

CALIFORNIA LIVE OAK, ENCINA

Evergreen. Medium tree normally 25–50' tall (max. 108'); very broad, up to 200' wide. Seen in the background of many early Hollywood movies. Short trunk and dense crown. Acorns mature in one growing season, unlike typical Red Oaks and unlike Interior Live Oak.

bark relatively smooth and pale, becoming thick, rough, dark with wide ridges

leaves 2½", broad, holly-like, cupped, stiff and brittle, smooth-edged, or with spiny teeth
underleaf pale green

acorns nearly as long as leaves

wide-spreading tree

acorns 1", slender, narrow cone-shape, deep cup with long-pointed scales

twigs hairy or not, buds blunt

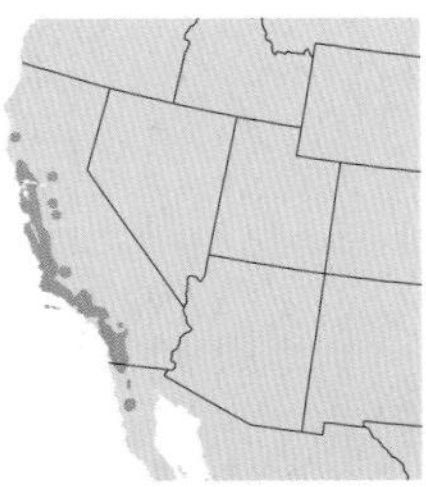

Common in moderately dry soils, forming park-like groves in foothills. Commonly cultivated near its native range (zones 8–9).

The name "live oak" is applied to several species of oaks, presumably because these species are evergreen, and therefore, look "alive" all year (but there are many other evergreen oaks that are not called live oaks). In fact, the various live oaks are unrelated and come from all three major groups of oaks. The Coast Live Oak and its close relatives are in the red oak group. The Canyon Live Oak, and its close relatives, are in the Golden-cup Oak group. The familiar Southern Live Oak and closely-related species in the Southeast are in the white oak group.

Interior Live Oak

Quercus wislizeni

SIERRA LIVE OAK, HIGHLAND LIVE OAK

Evergreen (leaves retained about two years). Shrub to medium tree often 30' tall (max. 89'). Usually short-trunked and broad-spreading, crown varies from dense to open and airy. A multi-trunked shrub in southern California.

small leaves, not much larger than large acorn

twigs usually hairy, buds pointed

leaves small, 1½", smooth-edged or spiny
underleaf shiny yellow-green

acorns, 1", usually stouter than Coast Live Oak, cup deep, scales loose

Very similar to Coast Live Oak and often found with it, but tends to have a narrower crown and smaller limbs, leaves thicker, leathery, flat (never curled); leaves retained about 2 years, begin falling in 2nd summer/fall (vs. leaves retained one year). Extensive hybrid swarms with Coast Live Oak and scrubby Shreve Oak in San Francisco Bay area where habitats meet. Small-leaved shrubby variants also exist; e.g. var. *frutescens* a shrub with leaves 1–1½". Also hybridizes with California Black Oak, the hybrids known as 'Morehus' Oak (*Quercus* '× *morehus*').

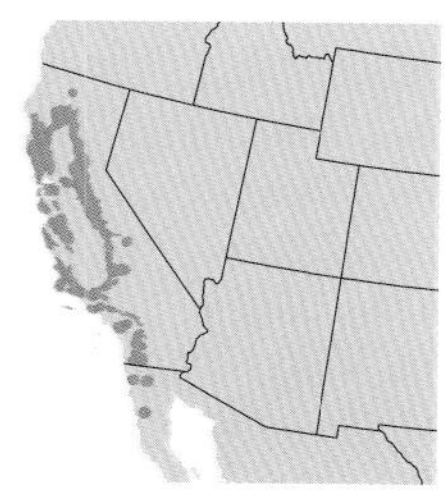

Common on dry slopes in foothill valleys, often with other oaks, especially Blue Oak. Uncommon in cultivation, only on West Coast (zones 8–9).

Shreve Oak

Quercus parvula

COAST OAK, SANTA CRUZ ISLAND OAK, TAMALPAIS OAK

Evergreen. Shrub or occasionally a small straight tree to 20' tall (max. about 55'); tree-like only along the central coast of California. Closely-related to Interior Live Oak, differs in details of bud, leaf, and acorn, but hybridizes extensively with both Interior and Coast Live Oaks.

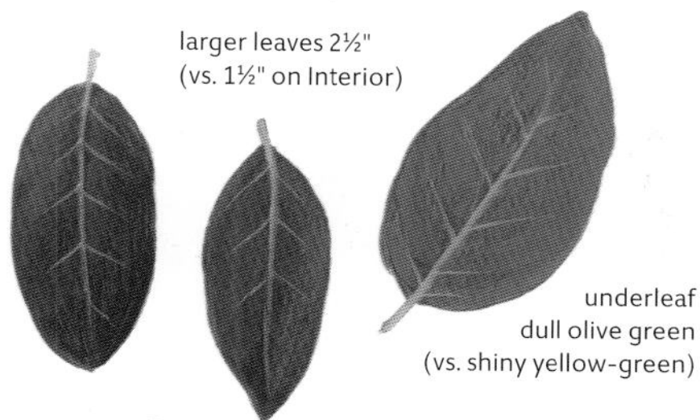
larger leaves 2½" (vs. 1½" on Interior)
underleaf dull olive green (vs. shiny yellow-green)

acorn, 1½", large and fairly stout, abruptly tapered at tip (vs. gradually tapered)

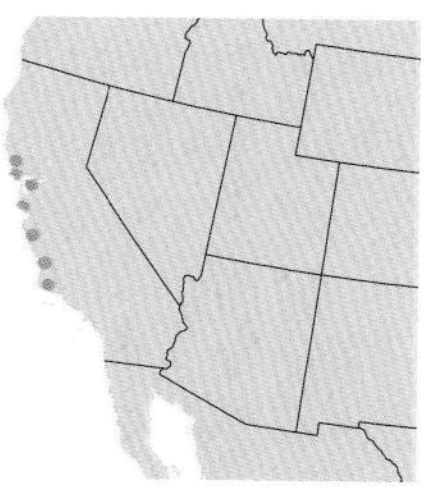

Locally common in relatively dry habitats, often on edges of coastal Redwood forest. Not cultivated.

Canyon Live Oak

Quercus chrysolepis

GOLDCUP OAK, MAUL OAK, IRON OAK

Evergreen (leaves persist 3–4 years). Shrub to medium tree typically under 40' tall (max. 110' tall or 130' wide). Wide-spreading with dense dark crown, taller and more upright in canyons.

bark in long narrow scales

leaves 2¼", pointed, oval, flat, leathery
leaves sometimes spiny-toothed (especially on juvenile growth, compare Palmer Oak)
underleaf yellowish-downy when fresh, later wearing to smooth pale bluish

leaves usually narrow, pointed (underleaf yellowish when fresh)

leaves on vigorous shoots often broader, spiny (underleaf bluish when worn)

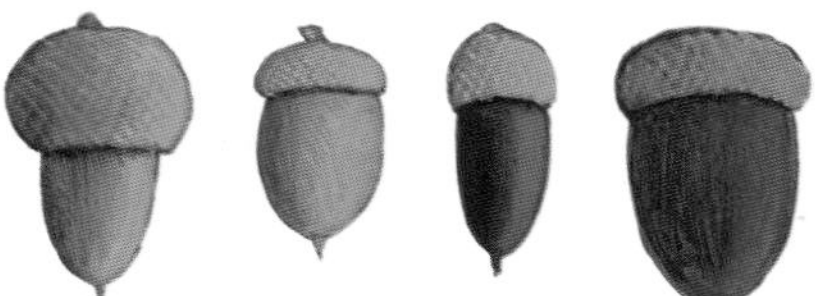

acorn 1", extremely variable, cup shallow, but often thickened and corky, covered with yellow-white wool

twigs golden-brown hairy to second year

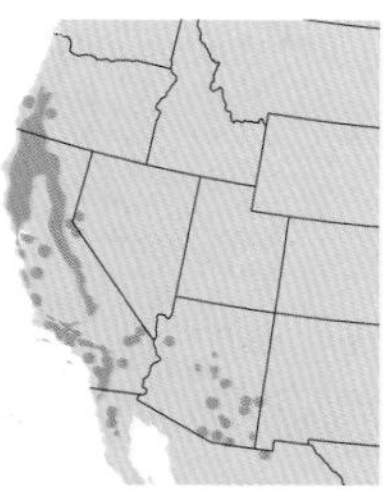

Common, especially in moist canyons and on north-facing slopes. Uncommon in cultivation in California, very rarely in Washington (zones 8–9).

The most commonly seen and most variable oak in California, and one of the most variable oaks in North America. Extremes resemble all other Golden-cup Oaks, but no recognizable forms. Also reportedly hybridizes locally with all other Golden-cup Oaks. A fourth species in the Golden-cup Oak group is Huckleberry Oak (*Quercus vaccinifolia*), a shrub to about 5' tall found in northern California.

The golden-cup oaks comprise three species found in California and the Southwest. They share most characteristics of the white oak group, but acorns mature in fall more than a year after the flowers (like red oak group) and the acorn cup scales are covered by a yellowish fuzz (unlike other oaks) and leaves persist up to four years. In general appearance, the trees and leaves are quite similar to the Coast Live Oak (which is in the red oak group).

Channel Island Oak

Quercus tomentella

ISLAND LIVE OAK, ISLAND OAK

Evergreen. Small tree often 30' tall (max. 65'), broad and rounded, may grow taller in cultivation. Resembles Canyon Live Oak in general form, but has larger, thicker leaves with more prominent teeth and somewhat corrugated leaf blade.

leaves 3½", leathery, brittle with rusty hairs
leaves wavy, strongly curled under, prominent parallel veins
underleaf brownish hairy
twigs hairy to 2nd year
acorn 1¼", cup shallow, pale woolly, solitary

Hybridizes with Canyon Live Oak on several islands (Canyon Live Oak absent on Santa Rosa), usually found at lower elevations in moist canyons, Canyon Live Oak higher.

Rare and local in lower parts of steep canyons; wild only on five southern Channel Islands. Very rare in cultivation, but cultivated trees can grow taller than in the wild.

Palmer Oak

Quercus palmeri

DUNN OAK

Evergreen. Shrub or small tree usually under 12' tall (max. about 15'), forms dense thickets, almost impenetrable due to rigid twigs and spiny leaves.

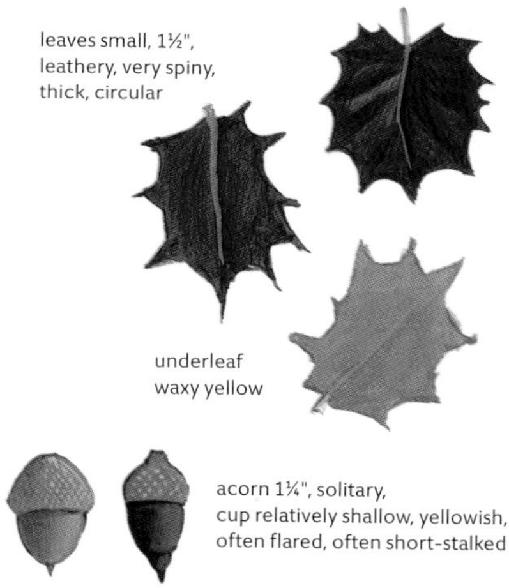
leaves small, 1½", leathery, very spiny, thick, circular
underleaf waxy yellow
acorn 1¼", solitary, cup relatively shallow, yellowish, often flared, often short-stalked

Hybridizes commonly with Canyon Live Oak where range overlaps. Plants across a wide area from southeastern Arizona to southwestern New Mexico show flatter leaves with fewer teeth than Palmer (more like Canyon) and are variously considered this species, Canyon Live Oak, or hybrids.

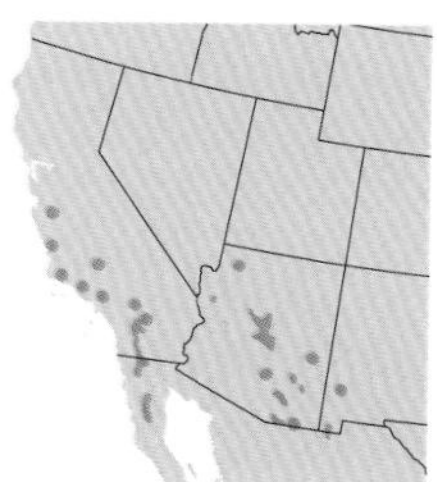

Uncommon and local in disjunct locations in canyons, thickets, margins of chaparral. Rare in California, more common in Arizona. Not cultivated.

Eastern White Oak

Quercus alba

STAVE OAK, FORKLEAF OAK, RIDGE WHITE OAK

Deciduous. Medium to large tree often 80' tall (max. 182'). Most widespread species of the white oak group, identified by short-stalked, evenly lobed leaves, pale ashy gray bark in strips or blocks, and acorns with a shallow cup. Majestic in old age with many famous and revered specimens.

bark on young/small trunks pale ashy gray, in long strips that typically peel from one side

bark on older/larger trunks forms long, peeling ridges or small blocks

sharply tapered base
leaf color generally more grayish or bluish than other oaks, not glossy
leaves 6½"
moderate to deep, rounded lobes
paler underleaf

mature leaves with short stalk
leaves stiff, do not droop or sway in breeze

twig formation appears stiffer than in red oak group

acorns ¾"
often short stalk
shallow cup

twigs greenish to purple-gray
buds small and blunt

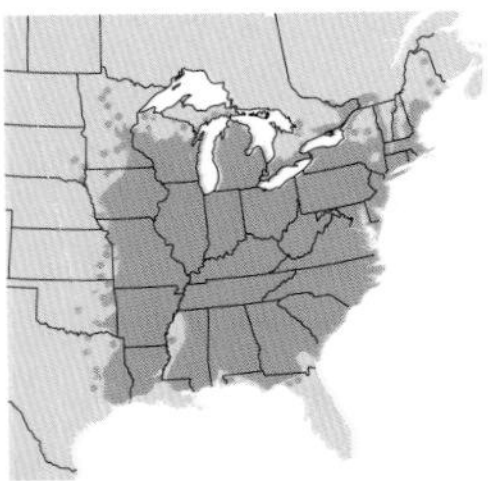

Widespread and common in rich, moist or dry soils; often on ridges and slopes. May be North America's most abundant native tree. Attractive and common in cultivation (zones 3–9).

Heavy crops of acorns appear every 4–7 years, but finding fallen intact acorns is uncommon. Less bitter tasting than acorns of the red oak group, they are avidly collected and consumed by wildlife. Most remaining acorns germinate soon after falling (acorns of red oak group germinate in spring after wintering on the ground).

Basket Oak

Quercus michauxii

SWAMP CHESTNUT OAK, COW OAK

Deciduous. Large tree often 90' tall (max. 200'). Very similar to Chestnut Oak, but acorn cup fringed with loose scales, bark pale, scaly, like Swamp White. Grows in wetter lowlands. Both this species and Chestnut Oak have been called *Quercus prinus*.

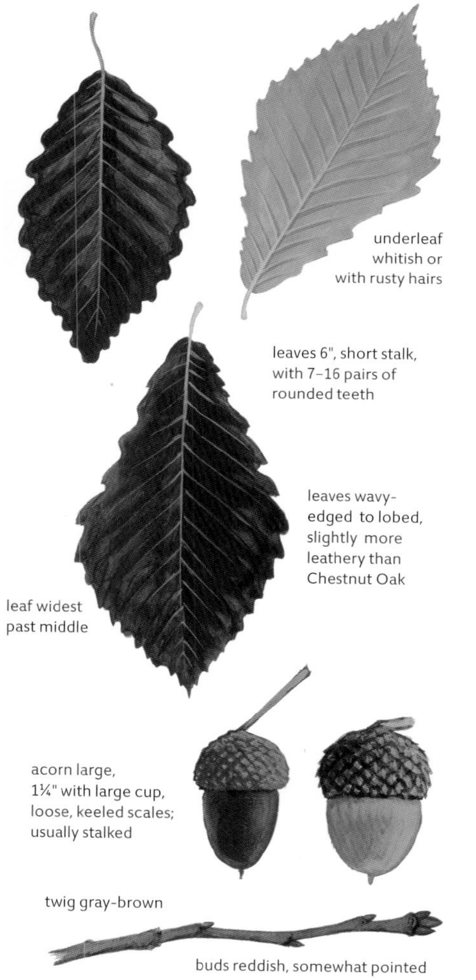
underleaf whitish or with rusty hairs
leaves 6", short stalk, with 7–16 pairs of rounded teeth
leaves wavy-edged to lobed, slightly more leathery than Chestnut Oak
leaf widest past middle
acorn large, 1¼" with large cup, loose, keeled scales; usually stalked
twig gray-brown
buds reddish, somewhat pointed

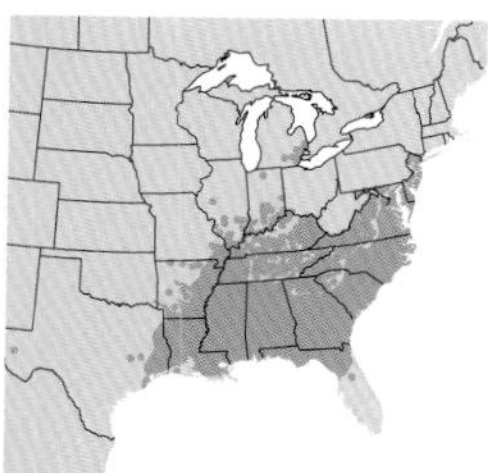

Common and widespread in coastal plain bottomlands; mixed hardwood. Rarely cultivated (zones 5–8).

Overcup Oak

Quercus lyrata

SWAMP POST OAK, SWAMP WHITE OAK, WATER WHITE OAK

Deciduous. Small to medium crooked tree usually under 60' tall (max. 156'); closely related to Burr Oak, but leaves more pointed, acorns almost completely covered by cup.

leaves 5½"; variable shape, often three equal squarish lobes at leaf tip, broad sinuses at midleaf; narrow base
underleaf whitish when young, becoming green, sometimes hairy
note that immature acorns of other oaks are enclosed by cup, but much smaller
acorn large 1", cup enclosing almost entire nut; stalk to 1½"; floats on water
twig gray-brown
buds small, grayish

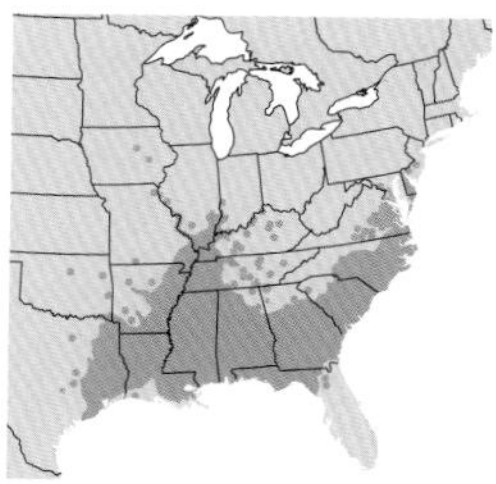

Common in swamp forests, periodically inundated, especially in bottomlands of lower Mississippi Valley; uncommon in cultivation (zones 5–9).

Swamp White Oak

Quercus bicolor

SWAMP OAK

Deciduous. Large tree often 70' tall (max. 108'); often with many dark twiggy tufts looking coarse and unkempt. Distinguished from similar species by sparsely-toothed leaves, small buds, scaly bark, and whitish underleaf.

bark in strips like Eastern White Oak but generally rougher; on older trunks furrowed and blocky

leaves 6½"
relatively few irregular teeth or sharp shallow lobes
underleaf whitish

Oaks have thick, stiff leaves that are slow to decompose, making fallen leaves available for identification throughout the winter. Searching the forest floor can reveal oak species that might otherwise be overlooked. Especially conspicuous among the leaf litter is the white underleaf of Swamp White Oak and a few other species.

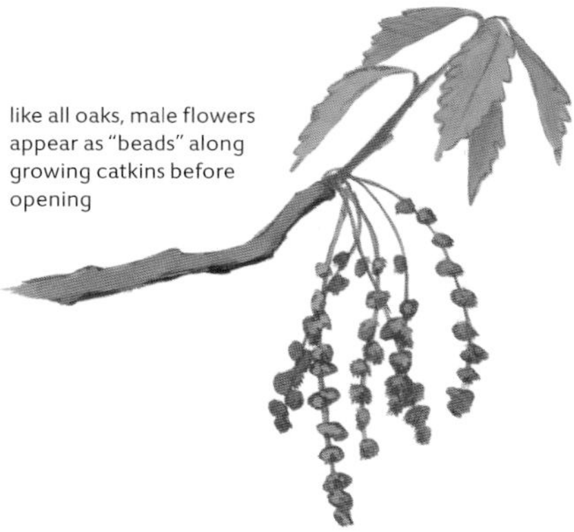
like all oaks, male flowers appear as "beads" along growing catkins before opening

acorn cup deep, slightly fringed, 1", on long thin stalk

Hybridizes commonly with Basket Oak where range overlaps. The hybrids tend to have more deeply lobed leaves and varying degrees of development of "awns" (fringe along the margin of the acorn cup). Such characteristics occur sporadically throughout many populations of Swamp White Oak; in some cases they may occur because of subtle introgression. Apparent hybrids × Burr Oak are also common in upper Midwest with intermediate leaf and acorn, but trees with similar characteristics can be found throughout range of Swamp White Oak.

buds relatively small, blunt, unlike Chestnut Oak or Basket Oak

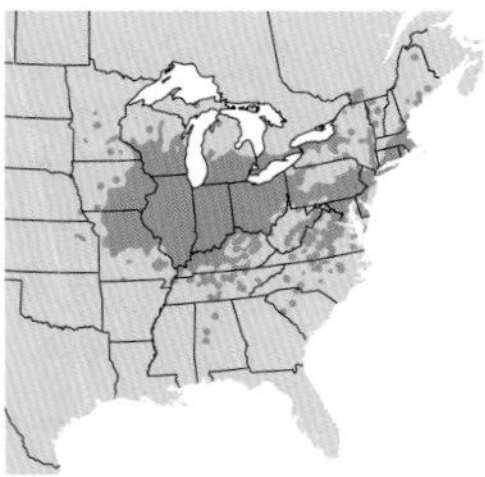

Common in wet woods and swamps, bottomlands, floodplains. Commonly cultivated (zones 4–8).

Burr Oak

Quercus macrocarpa

MOSSY-CUP OAK, BLUE OAK

Deciduous. Medium to large tree, often 80' tall (max. 165'); usually under 40' in northern and western range. Distinguished by fiddle-shaped leaves, corky wings on branchlets, and very large, shaggy-fringed acorns.

bark pale gray and
rugged, in long
rectangular blocks

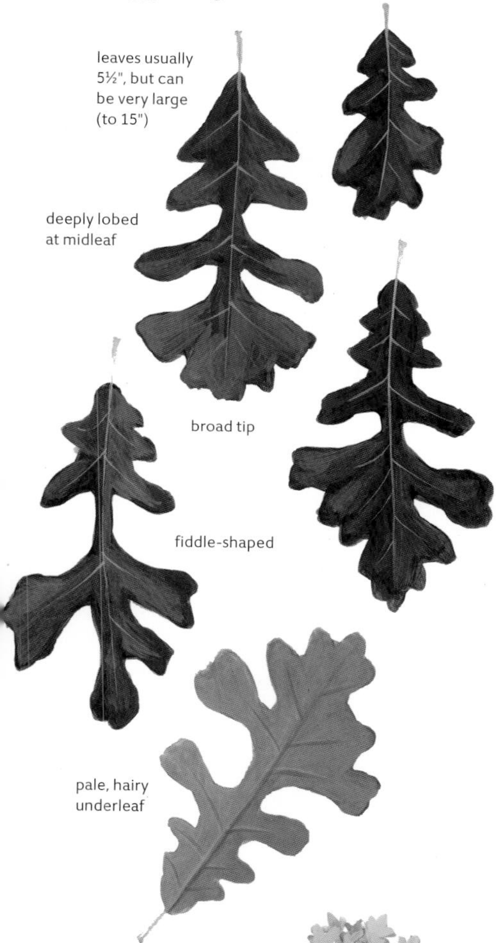
leaves usually
5½", but can
be very large
(to 15")
deeply lobed
at midleaf
broad tip
fiddle-shaped
pale, hairy
underleaf

As in most oaks, leaf size and shape are extremely variable, even on a single tree; notably small, unlobed leaves may be found on slow-growing twigs, while large and oddly shaped leaves often grow on vigorous shoots. Always check the whole tree to find the "average" leaf for identification.

acorns large, 2",
can be largest
of any
oak
very deep,
shaggy-
fringed
cup
stout stalk

Acorns largest and most prominently fringed on trees in South, becoming clinally smaller and less fringed northward. Smaller, more shrublike trees growing on bluffs and hillsides in northwestern parts of range sometimes considered a separate species (*Quercus mandanensis*).

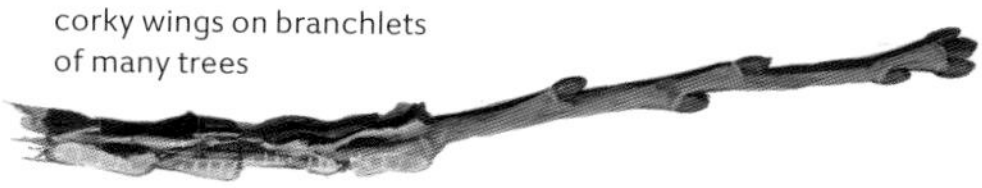
corky wings on branchlets
of many trees

twigs gray to reddish
buds hairy
and blunt

leaves of all
white oaks held
stiffly in bunches
at branch tips

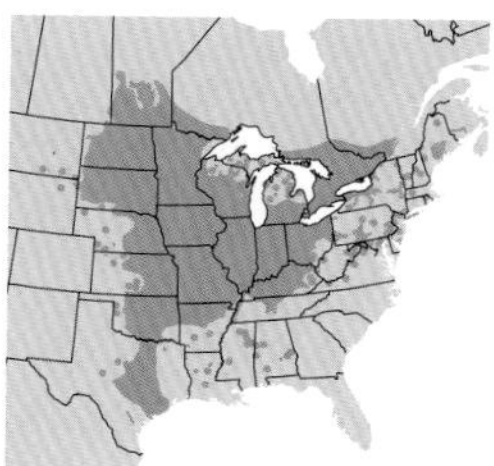

Common in a wide range of conditions, from wet bottomlands to dry, sandy ridges. Widely cultivated in cities and yards (zones 3–8).

Chestnut Oak

Quercus montana

MOUNTAIN CHESTNUT OAK, ROCK CHESTNUT OAK, ROCK OAK, TANBARK OAK

Deciduous. Large tree often 70' tall (max. 102'); bark and leaf similar to true chestnuts (genus *Castanea*), but note clustered end buds, less pointed leaf teeth.

rugged blocky ridges and deep furrows distinguish this oak from other chestnut-leaved oaks

leaves 6", with 7–16 pairs of usually rounded teeth
underleaf pale green, not whitish
acorn 1⅛", with fairly deep cup
buds dull orange-brown like Basket Oak but more pointed

Similar to Basket Oak, but Chestnut Oak has darker, deeply-ridged bark (unique in group), different habitat and range, and acorns average narrower with tight scales.

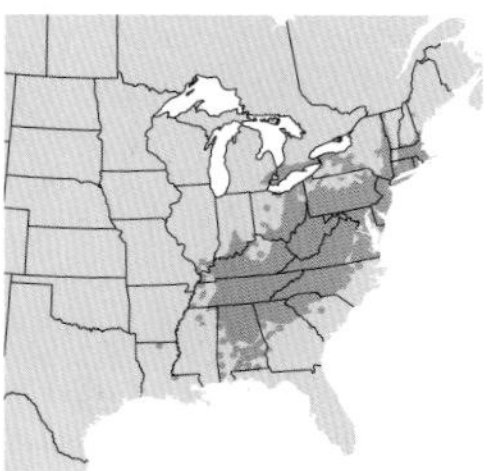

Common in uplands and dry woods, rocky slopes; uncommon in cultivation (zones 4–8).

Common Chinkapin Oak

Quercus muehlenbergii

CHESTNUT OAK, YELLOW OAK, CHINQUAPIN OAK

Deciduous. Small to medium tree often 50' tall (max. 160'). Distinguished from similar species by small stature, small leaves with coarse teeth and hairy underleaf, and small acorns. Very similar Dwarf Chinkapin Oak (*Quercus prinoides*) is rarely tree-like.

5", usually small, with jagged teeth, but some are indistinguishable from Basket or Chestnut Oaks
acorn relatively small, ¾", cup scales thin, tight, covering ⅓–½ of nut

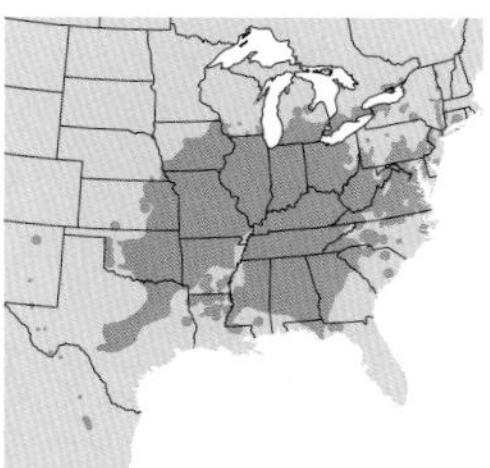

Uncommon and local in dry uplands; on clay or limestone soils on bluffs in Florida. Uncommonly cultivated but tolerant of varied settings (zones 5–7).

Oglethorpe Oak

Quercus oglethorpensis

Deciduous. Small to medium tree often 45' tall (max. 75'). Discovered relatively recently, in 1940; susceptible to chestnut blight. Identified by narrow oval leaves without bristle tip, small acorns.

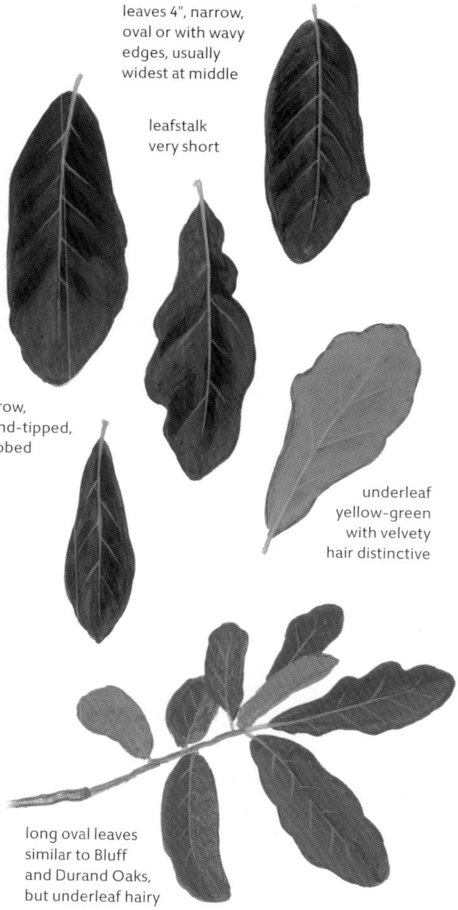
leaves 4", narrow, oval or with wavy edges, usually widest at middle
leafstalk very short
narrow, round-tipped, unlobed
underleaf yellow-green with velvety hair distinctive
long oval leaves similar to Bluff and Durand Oaks, but underleaf hairy

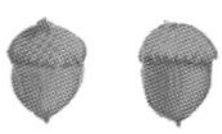
acorn tiny, ⅜", cup covers ⅓ or more

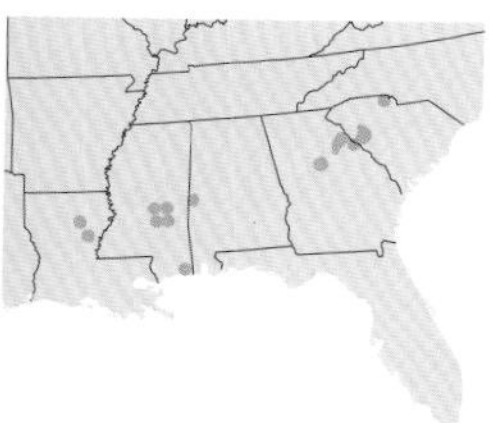

Rare and local in very small range, in drier bottomlands and seasonally wet poorly-drained sites; of conservation concern. Rarely cultivated (zones 6–9).

Chapman Oak

Quercus chapmanii

CHAPMAN WHITE OAK, SCRUB OAK

Semievergreen. Shrub or small tree to 25' tall (max. 45'); similar to Live Oak, Oglethorpe Oak, or Myrtle Oak.

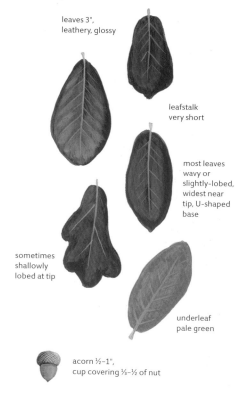

leaves 3", leathery, glossy
leafstalk very short
most leaves wavy or slightly-lobed, widest near tip, U-shaped base
sometimes shallowly lobed at tip
underleaf pale green

acorn ½–1", cup covering ⅓–½ of nut

This species is characteristic of the dry sandy soils of northern Florida, where it is found with several other species of shrubby oaks. It is most similar to Myrtle Oak (which is in the red oak group), but differs in having duller and paler green leaves (vs shiny and darker). It is also commonly found with Sand Live Oak, but tends to have leaves broadest near the tip, and paler bark with peeling scales like Eastern White Oak.

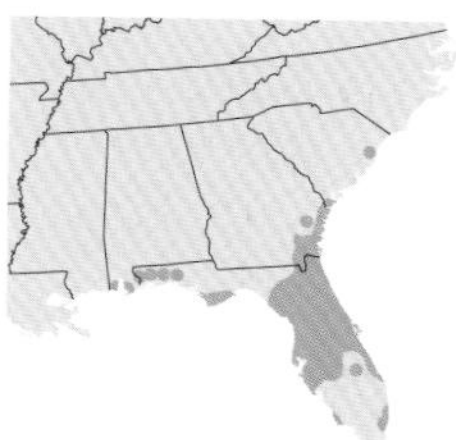

Uncommon in dry sandy soil, scrublands, open pine forests; in dunes or sand ridges with Sand Pine, Myrtle Oak and Sand Live Oak, but less common. Rarely cultivated.

Common Post Oak

Quercus stellata

IRON OAK, BOX WHITE OAK, ROUGH OAK

Deciduous. Shrub or small to medium tree usually under 40' tall (max. 108'). Characteristic tree of large areas of savannah in the long-grass prairie regions.

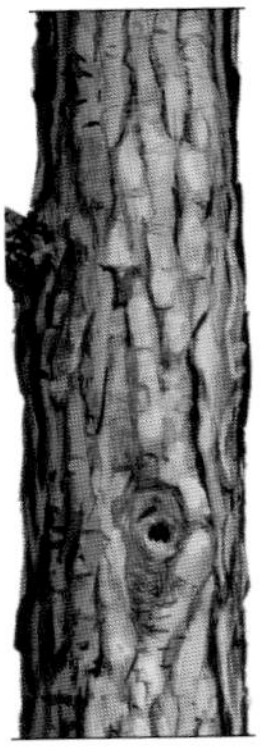

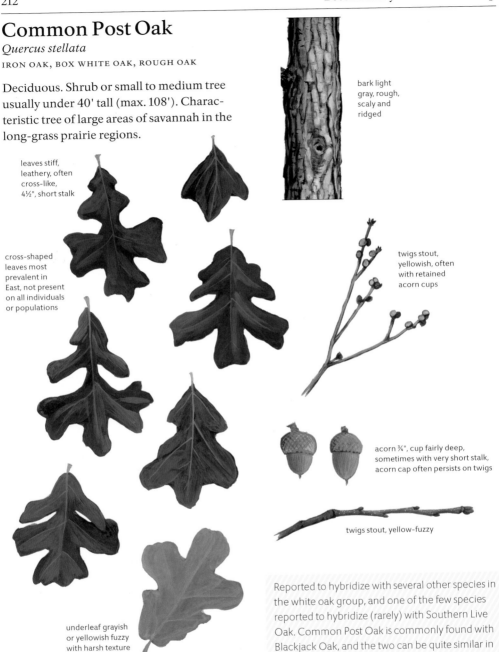

bark light gray, rough, scaly and ridged

leaves stiff, leathery, often cross-like, 4½", short stalk

cross-shaped leaves most prevalent in East, not present on all individuals or populations

underleaf grayish or yellowish fuzzy with harsh texture

twigs stout, yellowish, often with retained acorn cups

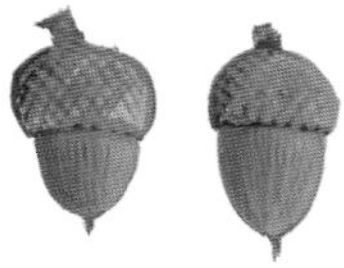

acorn ¾", cup fairly deep, sometimes with very short stalk, acorn cap often persists on twigs

twigs stout, yellow-fuzzy

Reported to hybridize with several other species in the white oak group, and one of the few species reported to hybridize (rarely) with Southern Live Oak. Common Post Oak is commonly found with Blackjack Oak, and the two can be quite similar in leaf shape. Blackjack Oak is in the red oak group, and differs in bark, acorns, and buds. In addition, Common Post Oak differs in having yellow-fuzzy twigs and underleaf.

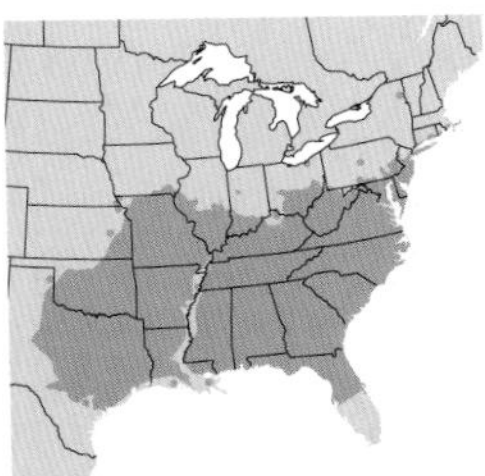

Common, especially on dry sites, ridges, prairies, open upland woods. Often with Mockernut Hickory, Southern Red Oak, Shortleaf and Loblolly Pines. Very rarely cultivated.

Sand Post Oak

Quercus margarettae

DWARF POST OAK, RUNNER OAK, SCRUBBY POST OAK

Deciduous. Shrub or sometimes a small scrubby tree to 25' (max. 40') in thickets. Very similar to Common Post Oak; distinguished by slender hairless twigs and smaller leaves less regularly cross-like with velvety-hairy underleaf.

leaves 3½", smaller than Common Post Oak
underleaf light green. velvety-hairy

twigs hairless, reddish-brown, (vs. hairy in Common Post Oak)

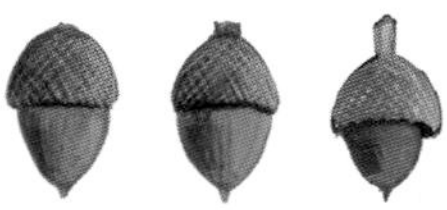
acorn ⅝", average smaller than Common Post Oak

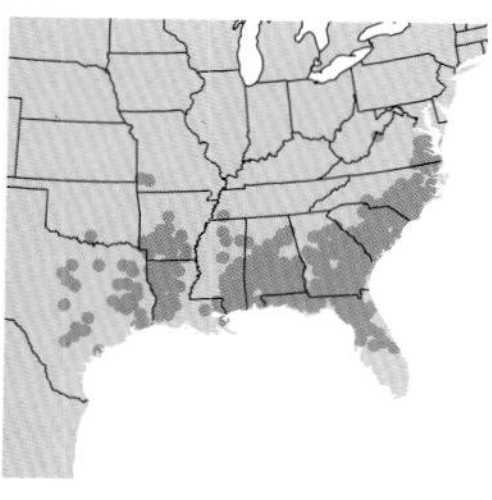

Common in well-drained or sandy soils; in dry pine-oak scrub or understory of dry woods. Not cultivated.

Swamp Post Oak

Quercus similis

DELTA POST OAK, BOTTOM-LAND POST OAK, MISSISSIPPI VALLEY OAK, YELLOW OAK

Deciduous. Shrub or small to medium tree to 80', single straight trunk. Related to Common Post Oak and only recently split; distinguished by slender twigs and leaves rarely cross-like with sparsely hairy underleaf.

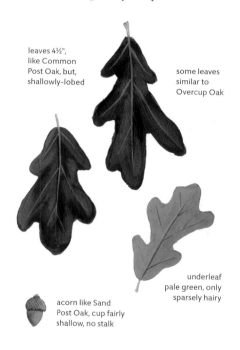

leaves 4½", like Common Post Oak, but, shallowly-lobed
some leaves similar to Overcup Oak
underleaf pale green, only sparsely hairy

acorn like Sand Post Oak, cup fairly shallow, no stalk

Swamp Post Oak is barely differentiated from Common Post Oak, and can only be identified by range and by careful study of twig and leaf features. Sand Post Oak is more distinctive with velvety-hairy underleaf, and hairless twigs that average more slender than Common Post Oak. Trees intermediate between Common Post Oak and Sand Post Oak can be found scattered throughout the range of both species, but occur consistently across a wide area in east Texas.

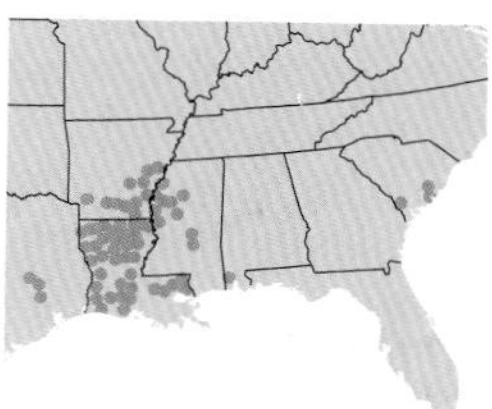

Uncommon in moist soils along streams and bottomlands. Not cultivated.

Scrub Oaks

Quercus species

About twenty species of native oaks are rarely or never tree-like and are collectively known as scrub oaks. Most grow in arid regions of the foothills of southwestern deserts and California, where they form chaparral or "shin-oak" habitat. About eight species are found in California, another eight to ten in the desert Southwest, and two in the Southeast.

In general, scrub oaks are evergreen, have small oval or slightly lobed or spiny leaves, and form dense thickets. Wherever these species occur, they often hybridize with each other and with related tree-like oaks. Consult a detailed regional guide for identification.

leaves range from ½–3" depending on species
some have leaves slightly lobed or spiny
underleaf whitish on some
leaves small, often in dense clusters
typical scrub oak acorns

Bluff Oak

Quercus austrina

BASTARD WHITE OAK

Deciduous. Medium tree often 40' tall (max. 80'); distinguished from Eastern White Oak by smaller leaves with fewer lobes and green underleaf. Water Oak (with similar leaf shape) is in the red oak group.

leaves 3½", often grayish-green, wedge-shaped or with few irregular shallow lobes
stalk very short
underleaf greenish, hairless
acorn ⅞", cup often deep, on stalk up to ⅝", scales thin

Related to and often confused with Durand Oak. It is distinguished from Durand by its larger, more acute buds, darker twigs, deeper, deeper acorn cups, and hairless leaves.

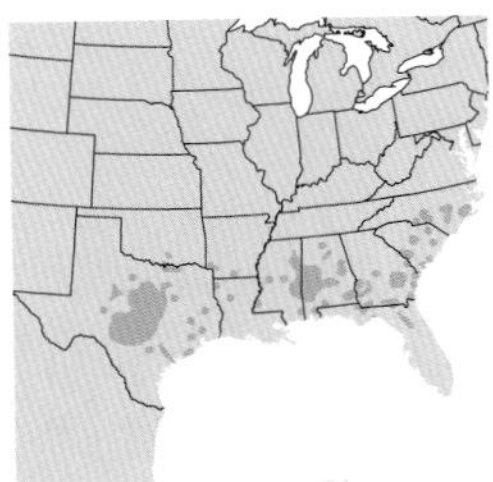

Rare and local in rich soils of uplands, bluffs, and well-drained sites in lowlands. Not cultivated.

These four species are all closely-related and barely tree-like, usually under 20–30' tall. Three are found only in central to west Texas.

Vasey Oak

Quercus vaseyana

Evergreen. Shrub or occasionally a small tree to 15' tall (max. 33'). Common in dry oak-juniper woodlands in central and west Texas.

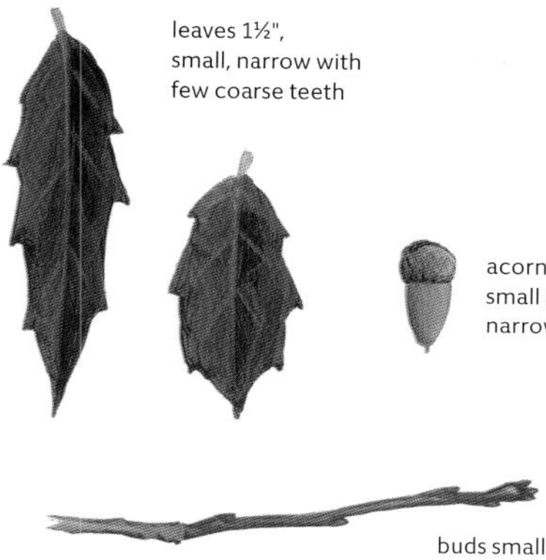
leaves 1½",
small, narrow with
few coarse teeth
acorn ½",
small and
narrow
buds small

Pungent Oak

Quercus pungens

SANDPAPER OAK

Evergreen. Shrub or occasionally a small tree to 15' tall (max. 18'). Closely-related to Vasey Oak and sometimes considered a subspecies. Locally common in dry oak-juniper woodlands from central Texas to southeastern New Mexico.

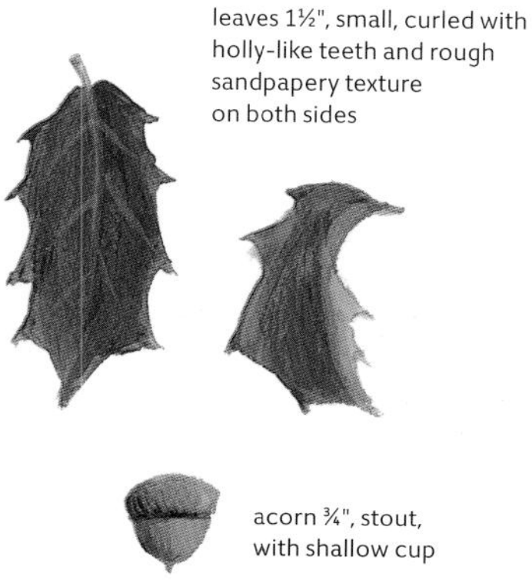
leaves 1½", small, curled with
holly-like teeth and rough
sandpapery texture
on both sides
acorn ¾", stout,
with shallow cup

Durand Oak

Quercus sinuata

BLUFF OAK, DURAND WHITE OAK, BIGELOW OAK, SCRUB OAK

Deciduous. Shrub or small tree usually under 30' tall (max. about 60'), sometimes multi-trunked. Uncommon in rich dry to mesic soils from North Carolina to Texas.

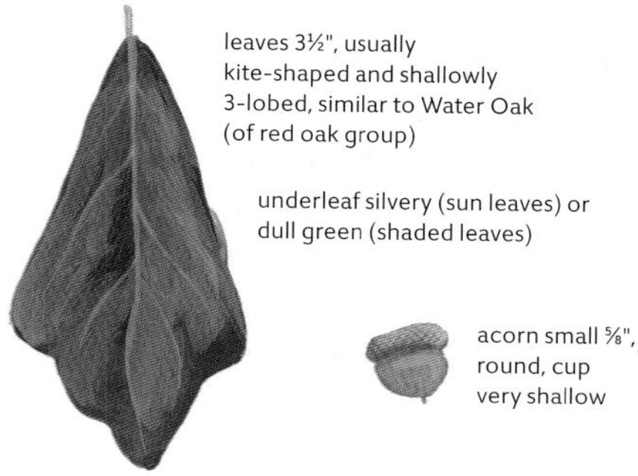
leaves 3½", usually
kite-shaped and shallowly
3-lobed, similar to Water Oak
(of red oak group)
underleaf silvery (sun leaves) or
dull green (shaded leaves)
acorn small ⅝",
round, cup
very shallow

Lacey Oak

Quercus laceyi

SMOKY OAK, CANYON OAK, TEXAS BLUE OAK

Deciduous. Shrub or sometimes a small tree to 25' tall (max. 58'). Locally common in mesic soils in west-central Texas. Occasionally cultivated near native range.

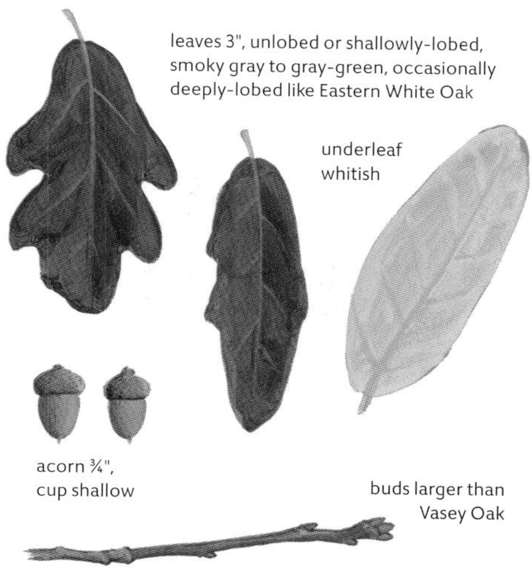
leaves 3", unlobed or shallowly-lobed,
smoky gray to gray-green, occasionally
deeply-lobed like Eastern White Oak
underleaf
whitish
acorn ¾",
cup shallow
buds larger than
Vasey Oak

Gambel Oak

Quercus gambelii

UTAH WHITE OAK, ROCKY MOUNTAIN WHITE OAK, ENCINO

Deciduous. Tall shrub or small to medium tree, usually under 30' tall (max. 47'). The common oak of the Rocky Mountains, and the only native oak in the southern Rockies with deeply-lobed leaves.

bark with rough gray ridges, branches often orange

leaves 4½", 4–6 lobed, leathery
underleaf pale green

acorn 1", oval with fairly deep, thick cup

buds fairly small, pointed

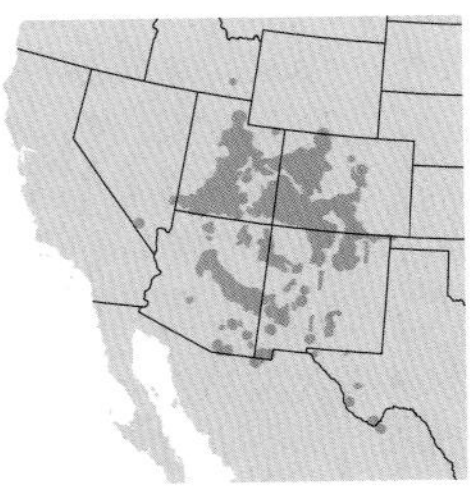

Common in montane woodlands and dry slopes to 10,500' elevation. Uncommon in cultivation (zones 3–9).

'Wavyleaf' Oak

Gambel Oak hybridizes with at least six other species to produce an array of hybrids, many of which have been called 'Wavyleaf' Oak (*Quercus 'undulata'*). The hybrids generally show shallow leaf lobes and are variable in size and shape of acorns, hairiness, leaf persistence, leaf texture, and other aspects.

Illustrated are hybrid Gambel × Common Chinkapin Oak and Gambel × Gray Oak. Others in this complex are Mohr Oak, Havard Oak, Arizona Oak, and Sonoran Scrub Oak. All produce similar hybrid leaf shapes, differing only in subtle ways, depending on parent species.

Gambel Oak
Gambel × Common Chinkapin hybrid Oak
Common Chinkapin Oak

Gambel Oak
Gambel × Gray hybrid Oak
Gray Oak

Sonoran Blue Oak

Quercus oblongifolia

MEXICAN BLUE OAK

Evergreen. Shrub or small tree usually under 25' tall (max. 65'). Small, mostly untoothed, blue-green leaves and pale checkered bark identify this species in its range.

leaves 1½", entire or sometimes toothed near tip, blunt
leaves oval with bluish cast
underleaf pale blue-gray

oval leaves often conspicuously bluish or pale gray-green

acorn ⅝", stout

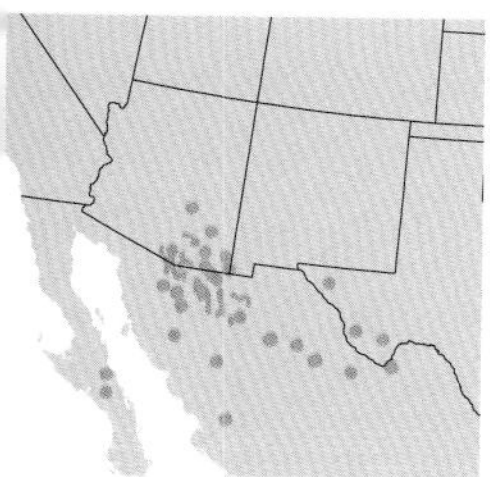

Rare and local in high grasslands and mid-elevation woodlands. Rarely cultivated (zone 7).

Engelmann Oak

Quercus engelmannii

MESA OAK, EVERGREEN WHITE OAK

Semi-evergreen. Shrub or small tree usually under 25' tall (max. 75'). Superficially similar to California Blue Oak in leaf color and habitat, but not closely related.

leaves 2", variable, usually narrow, blunt, untoothed or irregularly toothed
most leaves dull blue-green on both sides of leaf, not shiny, some are strikingly blue

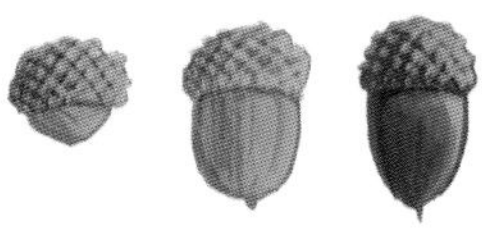
acorn 1", like Sonoran Blue Oak, but slightly larger with deeper cup and rougher scales

Closely similar to Sonoran Blue Oak and possibly the same species. Both are part of a well-marked subgenus of blue-leaved oaks found in southwestern United States and Mexico (in arid regions with profuse summer rains), also includes Arizona Oak, Gray Oak, and several scrub oak species.

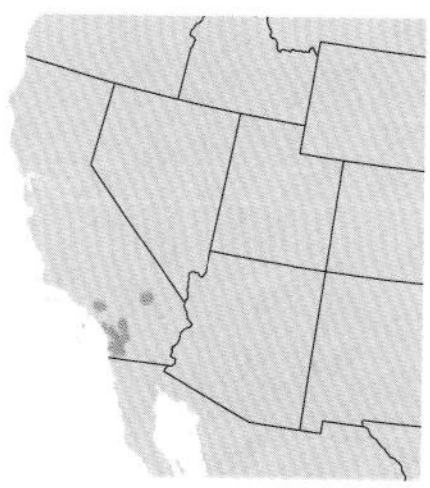

Common in open oak woodlands in interior foothills. Very rarely cultivated.

Arizona Oak

Quercus arizonica

ARIZONA LIVE OAK, ARIZONA WHITE OAK

Semievergreen. Small to medium tree usually under 30' tall (max. 42'). Similar to Emory Oak, but leaves dull (vs. shiny on both sides).

leaves 2½", oval, dull gray or blue-green above, weakly spine-toothed
underleaf pale yellow-gray, fuzzy with obvious veins
leaves usually narrow with few teeth
acorn small, ½", deep cup, sometimes on stalk to ¾"
twig pale brown, buds small and dark

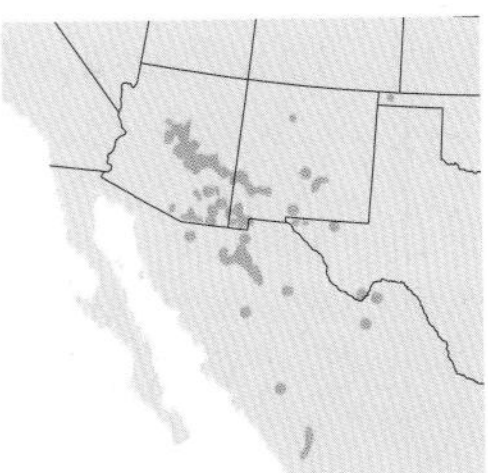

Common in mid-elevation dry woodlands. One of the largest southwestern oaks in canyons and other relatively moist sites; very rarely cultivated.

Gray Oak

Quercus grisea

SCRUB OAK, SHIN OAK

Tardily deciduous. Large shrub or small tree usually under 30' tall (max. 65'). Related to Mohr Oak, but most often confused with Arizona Oak, smaller with smaller, pointed leaves and more obvious veins.

leaves 2", flat, dull gray-green, U-shaped base, pointed tip, few or no teeth
underleaf fuzzy like upperleaf
acorn ¾", cup deep, stalk sometimes to 1¼"
twigs hairy

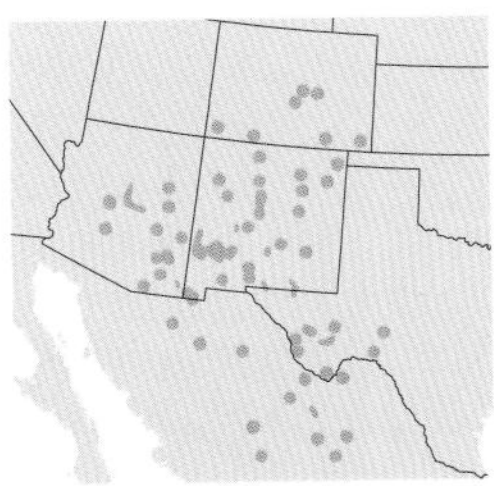

Common on igneous rocks and rocky slopes. Most common as a shrub in New Mexico, largest in moist canyons. Rarely cultivated.

Netleaf Oak

Quercus rugosa

Evergreen. Shrub or small tree usually under 20' tall (max. 42'). Distinctive with broad, wrinkled leaves and long-stalked acorns.

leaves 2", base rounded, widest above middle with coarse teeth
leaves droopy, thick, usually cupped with edges rolled, surface rough and veiny
underleaf whitish or golden hairy when new
leaves broad, usually dull green; acorn stalk very long
acorn ⅝", 2–6 on a slender stalk up to 5" long

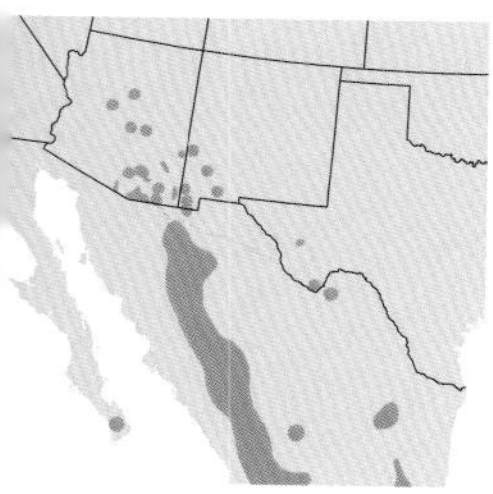

Uncommon on wooded slopes and canyons. Very rare in cultivation.

Mexican White Oak

Quercus polymorpha

NETLEAF WHITE OAK, MONTERREY OAK

Semi-evergreen. Shrub or small tree to 60' in cultivation with graceful form. A Mexican species recently discovered in a small grove in Val Verde County, Texas, where the tallest tree is 26'. Uncommonly, but increasingly, cultivated, especially in Texas (zones 7–8).

leaves 3½", long stalk; untoothed or with subtle teeth near tip, thick
underleaf pale
acorn ½", deep cup, on short stalk

Mexican Oak

Quercus carmenensis

Deciduous. Shrub or small tree usually under 20' tall. A Mexican species known in the United States from a single specimen found in the Chisos Mountains of Texas. Note small leaves, slender red twigs with tiny buds.

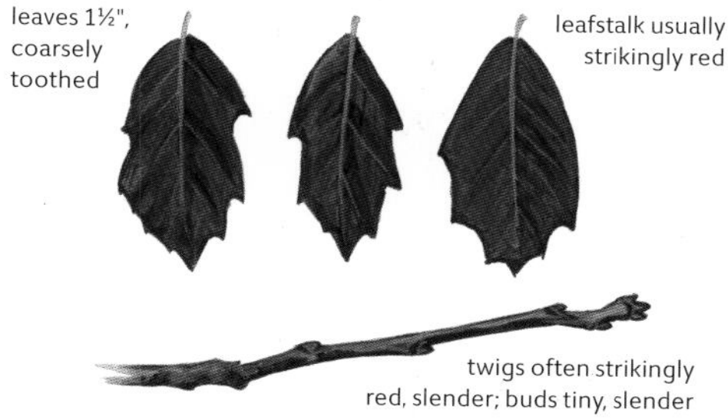
leaves 1½", coarsely toothed
leafstalk usually strikingly red
twigs often strikingly red, slender; buds tiny, slender

Chihuahua Oak

Quercus chihuahuensis

FELT OAK

Deciduous. Shrub or small tree usually under 20' tall. Rare and local in west Texas, apparently shows intergradation with Gray Oak and Arizona Oak.

leaves 2", sometimes toothed
upperleaf gray-green velvety, veins prominent
acorn ⅔", cup deep; on stalk up to 1½" long

Valley Oak

Quercus lobata

CALIFORNIA VALLEY OAK, CALIFORNIA WHITE OAK, WEEPING OAK, WATER OAK

Deciduous. Medium to large tree usually under 50' tall, but sometimes much larger (max. 178'). Relatively small leaves and drooping twigs give this oak a somewhat elm-like appearance.

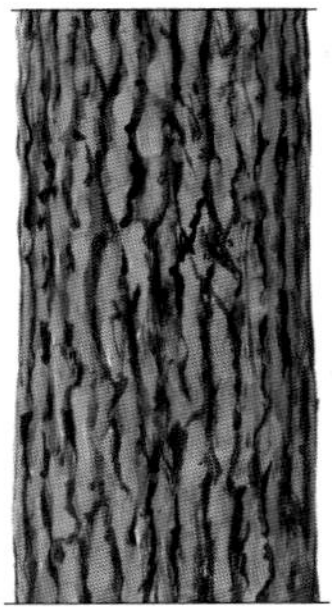
bark gray, scaly
older bark deeply checkered

leaves small, 3", average smaller and with more lobes than Oregon White
underleaf pale green

acorn large, 1½", sometimes bulbous, cup fairly deep

broad spreading tree with elm-like arching branches and often weeping twigs

twigs hairless and often drooping
buds ¼", pointed, often hairy

Common as widely-spaced trees on moist valley floors and moderate slopes, savannah. Occasionally cultivated in native range (zones 8-10).

Hybridizes with many other species of oaks, including extensive hybridization with Island Scrub Oak (*Quercus pacifica*) on Santa Cruz and Santa Catalina Islands, and with several other scrub oaks elsewhere in California. However, recent DNA studies have shown that at least some presumed hybrids with California Blue Oak are simply variants of pure Valley Oak.

Oregon White Oak

Quercus garryana

GARRY OAK, OREGON OAK, BREWER OAK, POST OAK

Deciduous. Medium to large tree usually under 60' tall (max. 90'). Only native oak in much of the Northwest, and the most important commercial oak in West. Told from Valley Oak by leaves larger, dark green, shiny, leathery, twigs not weeping, acorn smaller; similar to Gambel Oak.

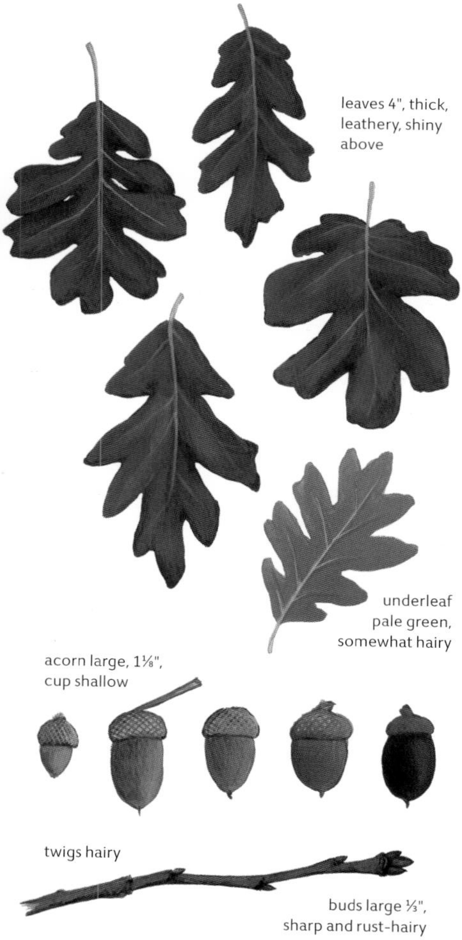
leaves 4", thick, leathery, shiny above
underleaf pale green, somewhat hairy
acorn large, 1⅛", cup shallow
twigs hairy
buds large ⅓", sharp and rust-hairy

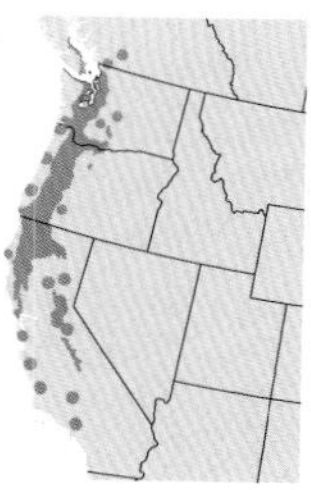

Common in mixed oak woodlands or mixed coniferous forest, in open woods or on edges. Rarely cultivated.

California Blue Oak

Quercus douglasii

BLUE OAK, IRON OAK, MOUNTAIN WHITE OAK

Tardily deciduous. Shrub or small tree usually under 30' tall (max. 90'); trunk leaning with short, thick, twisted branches, sometimes several trunks. Related to lobe-leaved Oregon White Oak and Valley Oak; not related to other western "blue oaks."

leaves 2", blue-green, shallow lobes or irregular teeth
underleaf pale bluish
twigs very brittle
acorn very long, relative to small bluish leaves
acorn 1", cup fairly deep; scales downy
at least some acorns "wrinkled"

Locally common on dry lower slopes, margins of chaparral, hot dry foothills. Rarely cultivated only within native range.

Southern Live Oak

Quercus virginiana

VIRGINIA LIVE OAK, ENCINO

Evergreen or deciduous. Small to large tree often 60' tall (max. 87' tall, 168' wide). Magnificently wide-spreading with massive horizontal branches, classically draped with Spanish Moss. Along with Southern Magnolia, the symbolic tree of the deep South.

bark dark, rough, blocky, easily distinguished from paler, smoother bark of red oak group

leaves 3", relatively small and narrow, stiff, may have rolled edges, shiny above, entire or some may be sharp-toothed
underleaf gray-white to pale green

picturesque and stately spreading tree

flowers in spring with new leaves

acorn relatively slender, ½", with fairly deep cup, usually on long stalk

twigs pale gray-brown, buds small

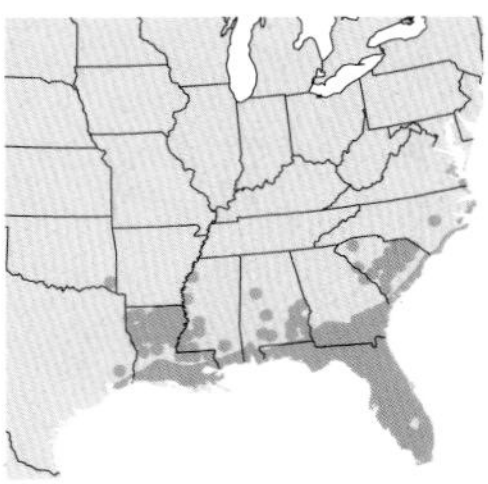

Common in many habitats from upland open woods to low wetland edges including salt marsh edges. Very common in cultivation (zones 8–10);

Some Southern Live Oaks drop old leaves during winter, appearing deciduous, as new leaves emerge from mostly bare twigs with flowers. Other trees are truly evergreen and retain old leaves through winter and for weeks or months after new leaves emerge. Vigorous shoots or young trees may retain leaves for up to two years.

Sand Live Oak

Quercus geminata

Evergreen. Shrub or small to medium tree often forming thickets, usually under 30' tall (max. about 50'). Similar to Southern Live Oak, but note smaller size, sandy habitat, leaves rough with edges rolled under, flowers 2–3 weeks later than Southern Live Oak.

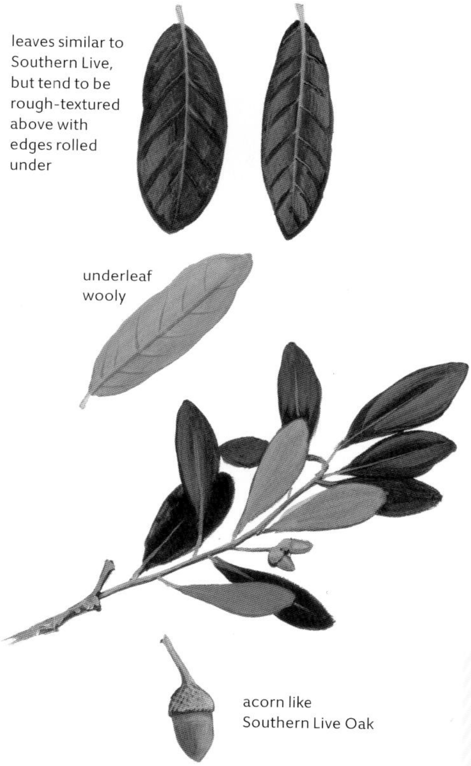
leaves similar to Southern Live, but tend to be rough-textured above with edges rolled under
underleaf wooly
acorn like Southern Live Oak

The small size is apparently a result of poor growing conditions in sandy soil where this species is found, as trees growing in better soil (including cultivated trees) grow quite large. Intergrades with Southern Live Oak are common along northern edges of range.

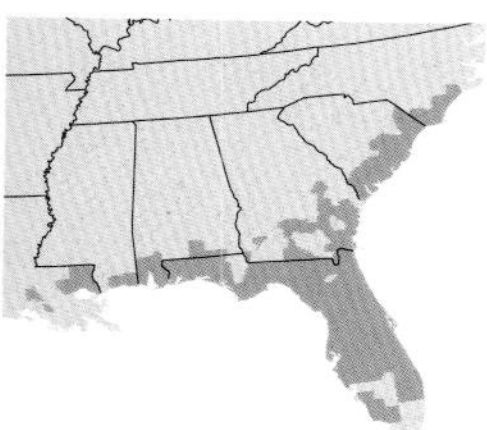

Most common tree of evergreen oak scrub in dunes and sand ridges near coast, often with pines. Commonly cultivated (zones 7–10).

Texas Live Oak

Quercus fusiformis

SCRUB LIVE OAK

Evergreen. Shrub or small to medium tree usually under 40' tall (max. 80'), sometimes forming thickets or "oak mottes." Very similar to Southern Live Oak and often considered a subspecies.

leaves like Southern Live Oak
acorn similar to Southern Live Oak

Difficult to distinguish from Southern Live Oak and perhaps best considered merely a subspecies or regional variety. Typical Southern extends west to Brazos River and Edwards plateau. To the west, trees are intermediate or more like Texas Live; on Edwards Plateau, mostly small thicket-forming trees with slender-pointed acorns. On deep sands in south, differ from typical Texas Live (of Mexico) in having broader, more rounded leaves, often with veins impressed, and relatively blunt, barrel-shaped acorns.

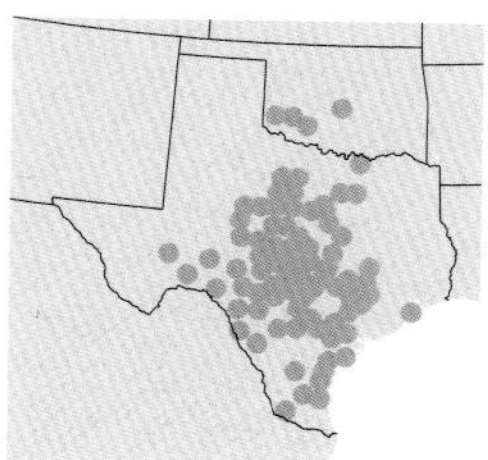

Common in grasslands, scrublands, open woods, sandstone ridges. Commonly cultivated within native range (zones 8–10).

English Oak

Quercus robur

PEDUNCULATE OAK, BRITISH OAK, TRUFFLE OAK

Deciduous. Medium tree often 60' tall (max. 102') usually a massive rounded tree with short trunk. Easily distinguished from Eastern White Oak by its very short leafstalks, "eared" leaf bases, and fruit on long thin stalks.

leaves fairly small, 4½", eared base, many rounded lobes
underleaf pale green

acorn ⅞", stout, on very thin stalk 2" long; cup small

twig stout, pale gray
buds large, brown, blunt

Native to Europe, northern Africa, Caucasus. Commonly cultivated and locally naturalized in woods edges, old homesites, roadsides (zones 4–8).

Holm Oak

Quercus ilex

HOLLY OAK

Evergreen. Small to medium tree often 40' tall (max. 104'). Large round crown. Bark gray, nearly smooth.

leaves leathery, stiff, variable, 2½"
juvenile leaves have holly-like teeth, crown leaves generally untoothed
very dark green above, sides often rolled under and tip curled down
underleaf more or less fuzzy and often gray

acorns 1" long, cup covers ½ of nut, thin and tight scales 1–4 on spike, large nipple-shaped tip

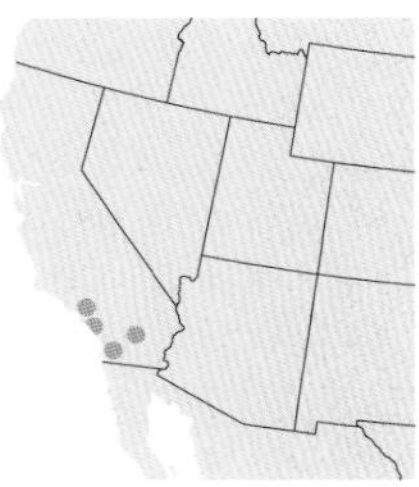

Native to southern Europe. Commonly cultivated, very hardy and salt-tolerant; naturalized in many locations along West Coast (zones 8–9).

European Turkey Oak

Quercus cerris

TURKISH OAK, TURKEY OAK, BITTER OAK

Deciduous. Medium to large and rugged tree often 60' tall (max. 107').

leaves average 4" long, coarsely toothed to pinnately lobed, leafstalk very short
leaves sharply toothed or shallowly lobed

acorn 1", cup large and deep with long, curved scales

Native to western Asia, southern Europe and now rarely cultivated and perhaps naturalized in some areas (zones 5–7).

Sawtooth Oak

Quercus acutissima

JAPANESE CHESTNUT OAK, BRISTLE-TIPPED OAK

Deciduous. Medium tree often 40' tall (max. 69'), usually broad-spreading. Leaves reminiscent of Chestnut (genus *Castanea*), bark like Chestnut Oak, buds like Eastern Black Oak, but acorns are distinctive.

leaves 5½", resembles chestnut leaf
long bristles at ends of leaf teeth

acorn 1", nearly round; cup covers about ⅔ of nut, thick cap of long curved scales looking hairy

A similar species of exotic oak, Oriental Oak (*Quercus variabilis*), also known as Chinese Cork Oak, is sometimes planted.

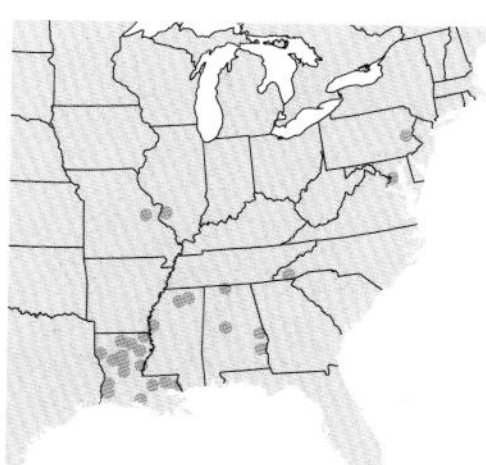

Native to eastern Asia and Japan. Widely and commonly cultivated and locally naturalized, especially in Southeast (zones 5–9).

Cork Oak

Quercus suber

CORK TREE

Evergreen. Small to medium tree often 35' tall (max. 85'). Bark of this species harvested for commercial cork in Europe, can be 12" thick on older trees. Leaves dull gray-green, dusty-looking.

leaves 3", usually with a few small prickly teeth, leathery
underleaf gray-fuzzy

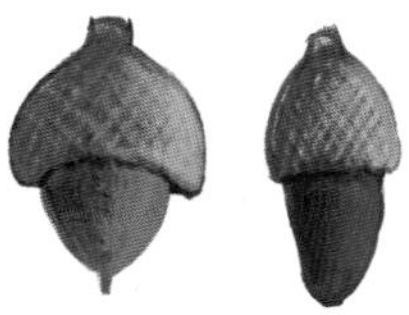
acorns 1" long, cup large and corky, covering ⅓–½ of nut

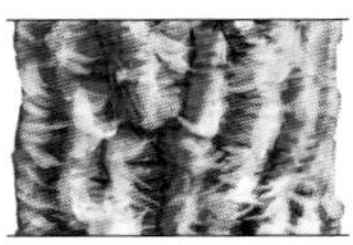
bark thick with ragged corky ridges

Native to western and central Mediterranean; Commonly cultivated in southeastern states and in parks in California (zones 8–9).

Chinese Evergreen Oak

Quercus myrsinifolia

BAMBOO-LEAVED OAK, JAPANESE LIVE OAK

Evergreen. Small rounded tree often 25' tall (max. 50'). Native to eastern Asia. Commonly cultivated in South (zones 7–9).

leaves 4", entire; long-pointed with small teeth towards tip, widely spaced on twigs
underleaf green

acorn ¾" long, cup with 3–6 conspicuous concentric rings, up to 4 together on stalk

Japanese Blue Oak

Quercus glauca

RING-CUPPED OAK

Evergreen. Large shrub or small upright tree often 20' tall (max. 25') often leafy to ground with upswept branches, drooping leaves. Native to eastern Asia. Uncommonly cultivated in Southeast (zones 8–9).

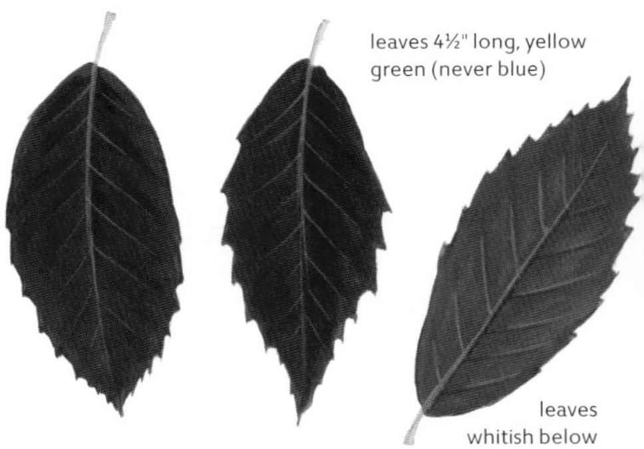
leaves 4½" long, yellow green (never blue)
leaves whitish below

Spurge Family

The spurges (family Euphorbiaceae) include about 7,000 species, mostly herbs found in tropical and subtropical regions. A few species are tree-like and two distantly-related Asian species are both tree-like and cold-hardy enough to grow in the region covered by this guide.

Tung-oil Tree

Vernicia fordii

TUNGTREE

Deciduous. Small tree usually 15–20' tall (max. about 40'), single-trunked with round spreading crown; large leaves and showy flowers in early spring.

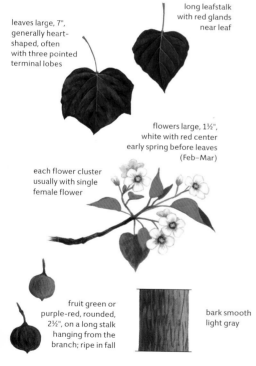

leaves large, 7", generally heart-shaped, often with three pointed terminal lobes
long leafstalk with red glands near leaf

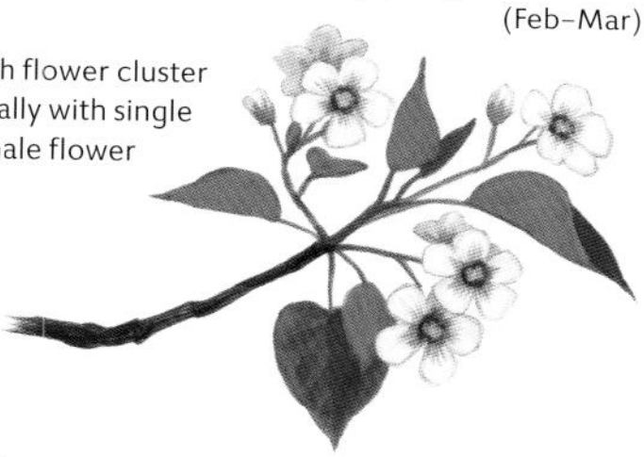
flowers large, 1½", white with red center early spring before leaves (Feb–Mar)
each flower cluster usually with single female flower

fruit green or purple-red, rounded, 2½", on a long stalk hanging from the branch; ripe in fall

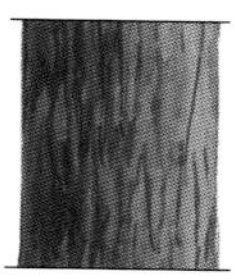
bark smooth light gray

Native to eastern Asia. Commonly cultivated for ornament and in commercial plantations for tung-oil; locally escaped to roadsides and other open or disturbed habitats (zones 8–10).

Chinese Tallowtree

Triadica sebifera

POPCORN TREE, CHINESE CANDLENUT TREE

Deciduous. Small to medium tree usually 25–40' tall (max. 56'), single-trunked with pyramidal crown. Milky sap is a skin irritant and poisonous if swallowed. Waxy seed coat is used in Asia for tallow in candles and soaps.

leaves 3", oval to diamond-shaped, long-pointed tip
fall color dark orange to red-purple

flowers in 3" upright spikes at twig tips, summer
leaves poplar-like, hang loosely in sun

fruit 3-parted capsules about ½", opening to reveal white seeds (hence "popcorn tree"); persist into winter

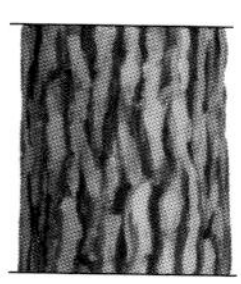
bark of mature trunks coarsely furrowed

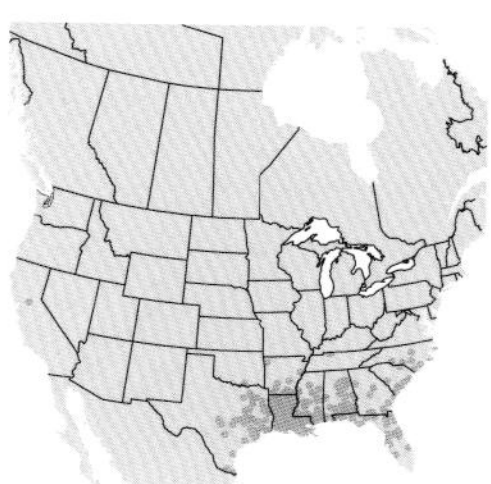

Native to China and Japan. Commonly cultivated in full sun, varied habitats, including wet places and suburban yards and now naturalized and invasive (zones 8–11).

Willow Family: Poplars

The poplars (genus *Populus*) include about thirty-five species of trees worldwide with eight species native to North America. Three exotic species are naturalized here and several additional cultivars are commonly planted and escaped.

Poplars are closely related to willows and all poplars are closely related to each other. Most species hybridize freely in the wild and in cultivation, leading to a confusing array of intermediate trees.

Poplars can be categorized into five groups of very closely related species, but hybridization occurs even between these groups.

WHITE POPLARS (White Poplar, other species in Eurasia): The leafstalk is short and not flattened, leaves are covered with white fuzz, and seed capsules are small and narrow. White Poplar is often included in the the aspen group, even though it looks very different.

ASPENS (Quaking, Large-toothed, and European Aspens): The leafstalk is long and flattened, leaves are relatively small and rounded, and seed capsules are small and narrow.

COTTONWOODS (Eastern and Fremont Cottonwoods, and European Black Poplar): The leafstalk is long and flattened, leaves are large and broadly triangular, and seed capsules are large and pointed.

BALSAM POPLARS (Balsam Poplar, Black and Narrowleaf Cottonwoods): The leafstalk is short and not flattened, leaves large, pointed, and dark, and seed capsules are large and round.

SWAMP COTTONWOOD (Swamp Cottonwood): The leafstalk is long and not flattened, leaves large and round-tipped, and seed capsules are sparse and narrow.

Poplars are among the most important commercial trees. Their very fast growth (up to 60' tall in twelve years) and ease of planting allows for mass-production. Huge "plantations" of poplars are grown and harvested for paper pulp, and the light, flexible (but not particularly strong) wood is used for applications, such as shipping pallets and plywood. Poplars are also popular ornamental trees, but they require large amounts of water and their roots, extending one-hundred feet or more from the tree, can damage water pipes and structures. Poplars are also very important ecologically with aspen groves in the western mountains and northern woods, riparian cottonwood groves in the West, and Black Cottonwood in the Northwest, each being the cornerstone of a unique ecosystem.

Quaking Aspen usually has a single main trunk continuing to the crown with small sparse leaves.

Quaking Aspen turns brilliant yellow or gold in fall.

White Poplar

Populus alba

SILVER POPLAR, SNOWY POPLAR, WOOLLY POPLAR, WHITE ASPEN

Deciduous. Medium tree often 50' tall (max. 125'); usually not large, trunk tends to lean and bend. Forms thickets.

young trunk pale greenish white with diamond-shaped marks
bark whitish, becoming blackish and furrowed on lower trunk

leaves 3", usually 3- to 5-lobed; wavy or coarsely-toothed, dark green above
leaf stalk short, not flattened, white
underleaf woolly white

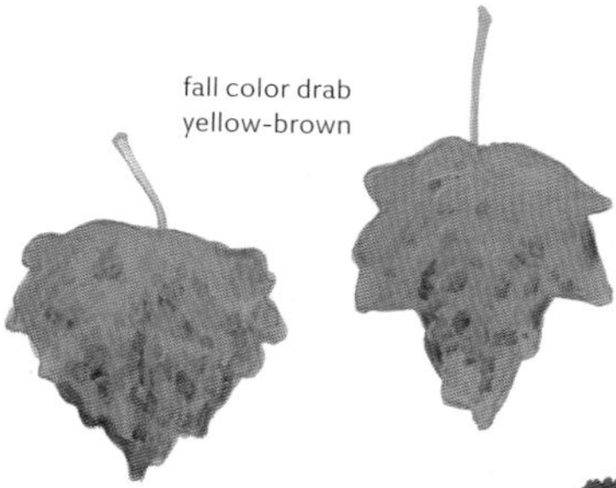
fall color drab yellow-brown

fruit capsules small, pointed, like aspens
leaves more deeply lobed on vigorous shoots

Many (if not most) of the trees in North America resembling White Poplar are, in fact, cultivars and hybrids. The most frequent are hybrids with European Aspen known as 'Gray' Poplar (*Populus* '× *canescens*'). These trees resemble true White Poplar, but generally have more rounded and less strongly-lobed leaves with less white woolly fuzz.

twig pale yellow-brown, covered with white fuzz when new
buds red-brown

Native to Eurasia. Widely planted and naturalized in North, often in poor, sandy soil along roadsides or waste places (zones 3–8). Rarely cultivated in its typical form.

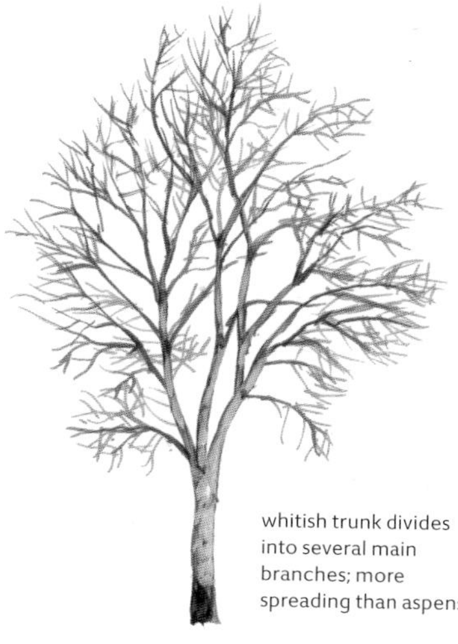
whitish trunk divides into several main branches; more spreading than aspens

Quaking Aspen

Populus tremuloides

TREMBLING ASPEN, POPPLE

Deciduous. Medium upright tree often 50' tall (max. 109'). The pale whitish trunks and fluttering green leaves of this species are an iconic feature of northern and montane forests.

bark color from white to greenish, grayish, or bronze

bark smooth, pale with dark scars that persist for many years; base of trunk becomes coarsely ridged gray on old trunks

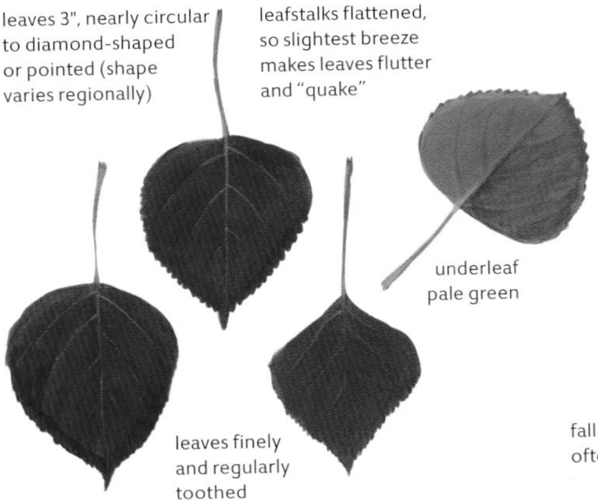

leaves 3", nearly circular to diamond-shaped or pointed (shape varies regionally)

leafstalks flattened, so slightest breeze makes leaves flutter and "quake"

underleaf pale green

leaves finely and regularly toothed

fall color yellow, often brilliant gold

flowers early spring before leaves (March–May)

catkins hairy

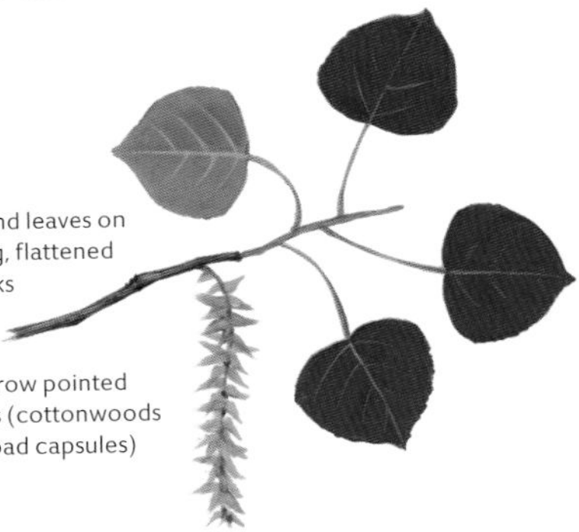

round leaves on long, flattened stalks

fruit narrow pointed capsules (cottonwoods have broad capsules)

Groves of Quaking Aspen can all be parts of a single plant, each stem connected to a common root system. These single organisms can cover many acres, and one in Utah is estimated to be 80,000 years old, possibly the oldest living thing on Earth. Adjacent colonies in the wild can often be distinguished by different timing of events like leaf-out, flowering or leaf-fall.

buds not resinous

Common in open woods, old fields, roadsides, cut over areas, or waste places, in dry to moist soil. Very widespread; commonly cultivated (zones 1–6).

single main trunk with relatively stout, jagged twigs (unlike more slender and graceful twigs of birches)

Bigtooth Aspen

Populus grandidentata

LARGE-TOOTHED ASPEN, CANADIAN ASPEN

Deciduous. Medium tree often 50' tall (max. 132'); tall, relatively straight trunk and sparse crown similar to Quaking Aspen. Distinguished from Quaking Aspen by toothed leaves, which emerge late in spring and are covered by silky white fuzz.

bark of all
aspens similar
mature trunks
become dark gray,
deeply furrowed
like cottonwood

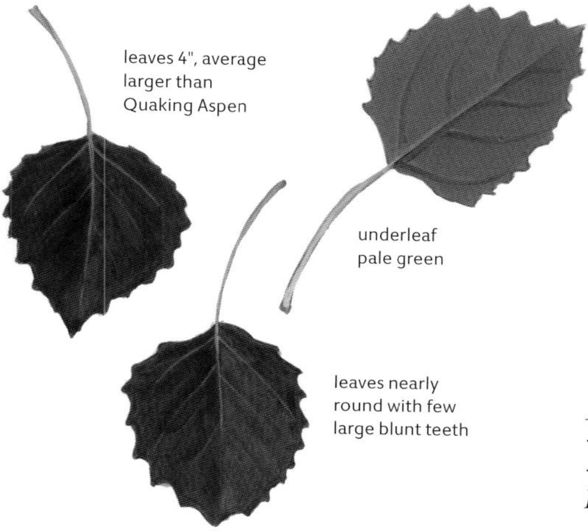
leaves 4", average
larger than
Quaking Aspen
underleaf
pale green
leaves nearly
round with few
large blunt teeth

leaves like
Quaking
Aspen, but
toothed

leaves emerge
late, silky-
whitish

fruit of all aspens
small, narrow
capsules densely
packed on catkin

twig similar to Quaking Aspen

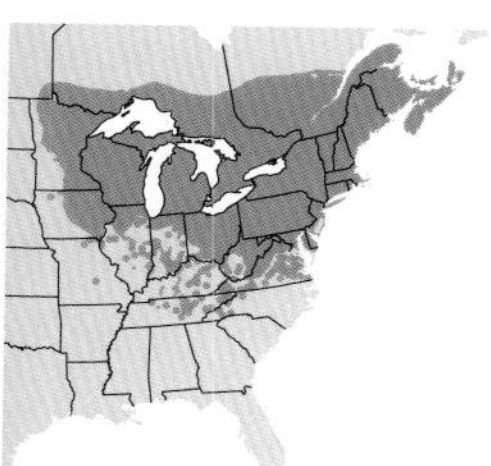

Common but scattered in dry woods, waste places, roadsides, in relatively dry infertile soil; rarely cultivated.

European Aspen

Populus tremula

Deciduous. Medium tree very similar to Quaking or Large-toothed Aspen, but with few irregular blunt teeth on leaf margins; leaf tip not as sharp or long-pointed. Bark may average darker and duller. One common cultivar is an upright form with emerging leaves reddish.

leaves 3",
rounded with
few blunt teeth

Native to Eurasia. Commonly cultivated and locally naturalized in North America (zones 2–5).

Eastern Cottonwood

Populus deltoides

SOUTHERN COTTONWOOD, NECKLACE POPLAR, CAROLINA POPLAR

Deciduous. Large tree often 60–90' tall (max. 170'). Young trees are slender and upright, but older trees fork low into massive side branches; imposing and ancient-looking at a relatively young age.

bark on young trunk
smooth greenish gray

mature trunk very deeply-
furrowed

leaves triangular,
5" with coarse
rounded teeth
flattened
leafstalk
underleaf
green, hairless
leaves in south
average larger
(5–9") than in
north (3–5")

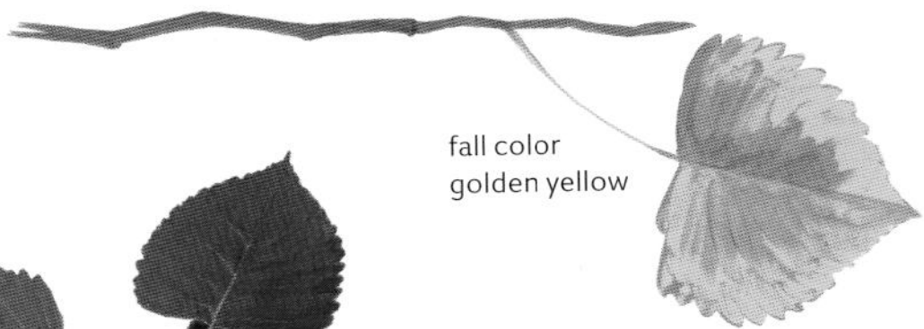
fall color
golden yellow

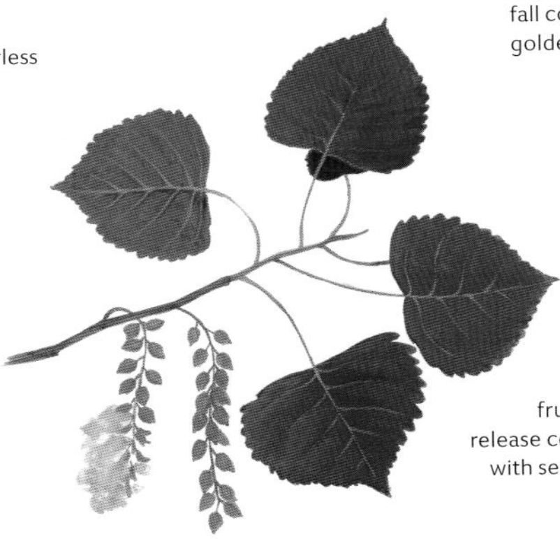
fruit capsules
release cottony fluff
with seeds in early
summer

fruit capsules
3- to 4-parted,
large and slightly
pointed

twig short with
large pointed buds

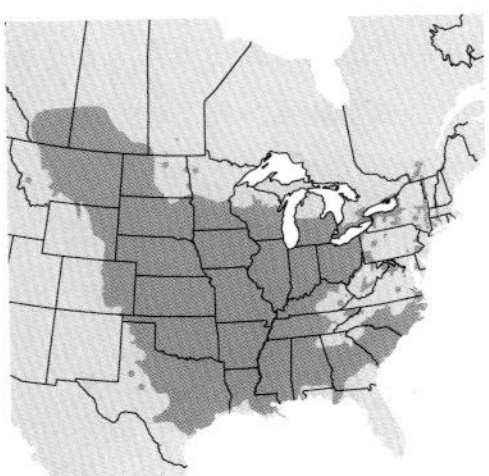

Common along river and stream courses in rich, moist woods, pond margins. Commonly cultivated and naturalized, especially in towns of the Great Plains (zones 3–9).

Cottonwood trees are the dominant structural feature of lowland riparian ecosystems throughout the Great Plains and the western states. These trees sprout along riverbanks and floodplains, and grow quickly into very large trees that provide food and shelter for a myriad of other plants and animals. The disruption of natural flood cycles in the West can make it impossible for young trees to become established, and grazing animals trample or consume sprouting trees, allowing non-native vegetation, such as Tamarisk, to become established. The result is that invasive species are encroaching along many western rivers, and where forests of old cottonwoods still exist, few young trees are growing up to replace them. Restoration projects in several states have been very successful at re-establishing normal flood cycles and protecting young trees so that the riparian cottonwood ecosystem can thrive.

Fremont Cottonwood

Populus fremontii

Deciduous. Medium to large tree often 50–70' tall (max. 92'); very similar to Eastern Cottonwood and most easily distinguished by range.

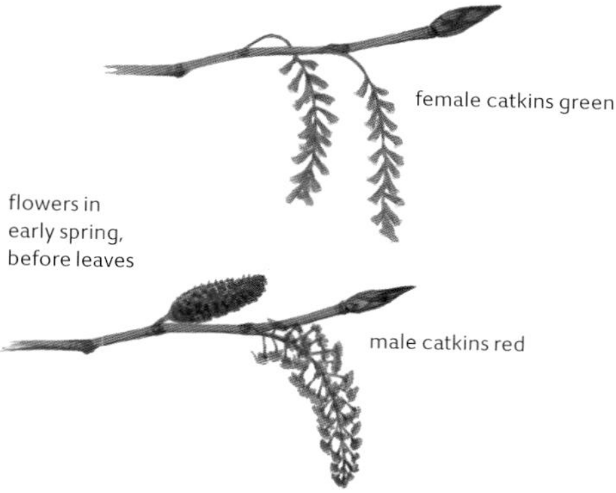
female catkins green
flowers in early spring, before leaves
male catkins red

leaves lack glands at base of stalk
leaves 5", average smaller and narrower than Eastern with longer tip
leaf shape varies regionally

leaves arranged loosely around twigs, at all angles; flutter in breeze

irregular crown with tangled twigs, massive contorted branches, rugged trunk forked low

In the past, the Eastern and Fremont Cottonwoods have been split into eight or more species, but differences are small, regional variations are not very well-defined, and all forms intergrade and are clearly very closely-related. Currently two species are recognized, but the average observer will distinguish them simply by range.

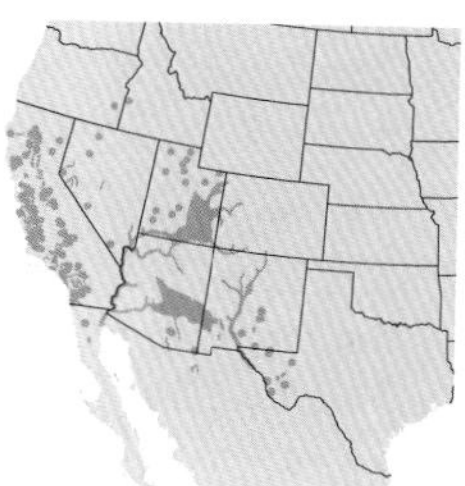

Common and widespread along watercourses in lowlands. Commonly cultivated and naturalized across native range (zones 3–9).

Black Poplar

Populus nigra

LOMBARDY POPLAR

Deciduous. Medium to large tree often 50' tall (max. 142'). Very closely-related to our native cottonwoods; the narrow upright form of the commonly planted cultivar is a familiar landscape tree.

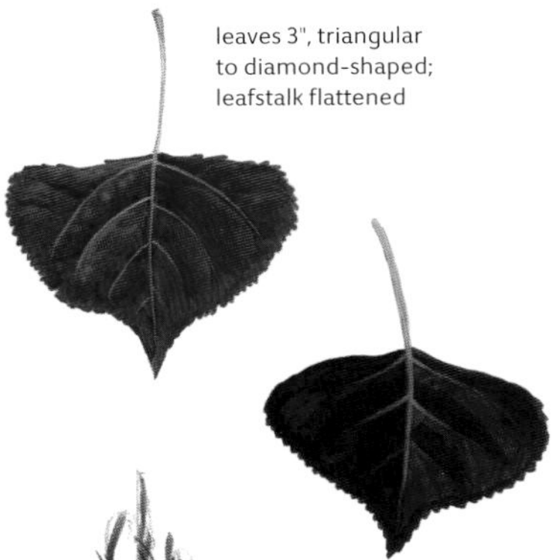

leaves 3", triangular to diamond-shaped; leafstalk flattened

most popular cultivar 'Lombardy' Poplar (var. *italica*) an extremely narrow upright form; several other cultivars and hybrids with similar form

Native to northwestern Africa, Europe, western Asia. Commonly and widely planted as an ornamental tree or as a windbreak (zones 2–9). Locally spreading by root sprouts.

'Carolina' Poplar

Populus '× *canadensis*'

HYBRID BLACK POPLAR

Deciduous. Hybrid of Eastern Cottonwood and Black Poplar; very similar to both with many different cultivars with same name. Commonly cultivated for commercial wood production, less often for ornament. Locally naturalized (zones 4–7).

leaves 4", intermediate between parent species and similar to both

'Balm-of-Gilead' Poplar

Populus '× *gileadensis*'

Deciduous. Origin unknown, possibly a hybrid Eastern Cottonwood × Balsam Poplar, or a variant of Balsam. Differs from Balsam in having broader, more hairy, heart-shaped leaves. Commonly cultivated and locally naturalized (zones 2–6).

leaves 4", similar to Balsam Poplar

Several other hybrid cultivars are more or less commonly cultivated and locally naturalized. Identification is complex. Planted poplars may not be identifiable except by a specialist.

Swamp Cottonwood

Populus heterophylla

RIVER COTTONWOD, BLACK COTTONWOOD, DOWNY POPLAR

Deciduous. Medium to large tree often 50–80' tall (max. 140'); differs from all other poplars in blunt-tipped oval leaves, scaly or shaggy bark.

bark reddish, strongly ridged like other cottonwoods, slightly scaly, or shaggy, like some hickories

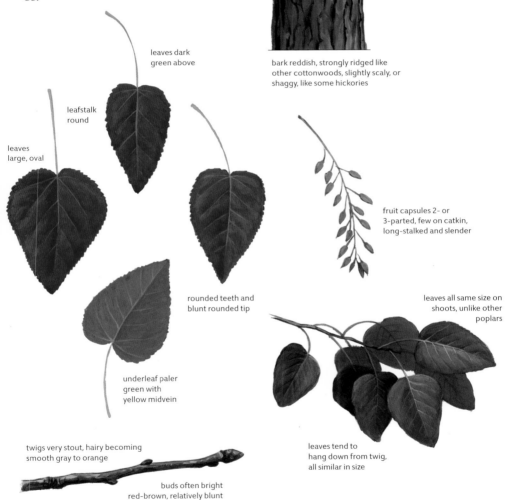

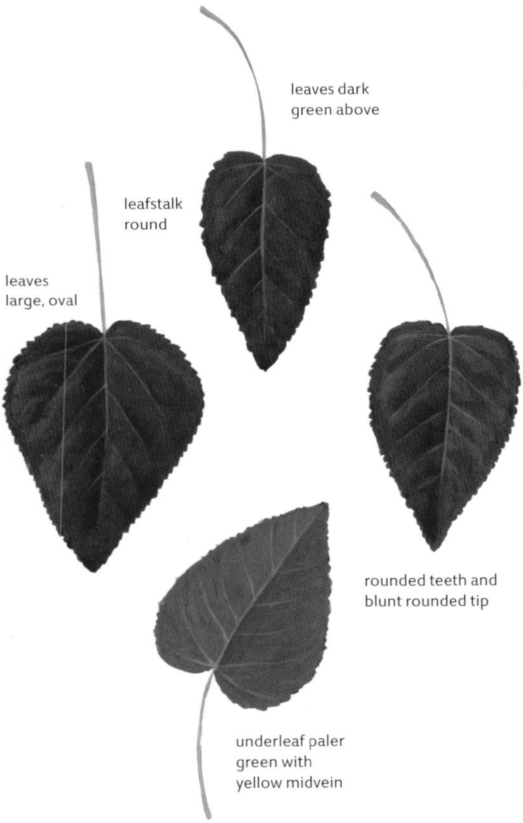
leaves dark green above
leafstalk round
leaves large, oval
rounded teeth and blunt rounded tip
underleaf paler green with yellow midvein

fruit capsules 2- or 3-parted, few on catkin, long-stalked and slender

leaves all same size on shoots, unlike other poplars

leaves tend to hang down from twig, all similar in size

twigs very stout, hairy becoming smooth gray to orange

buds often bright red-brown, relatively blunt

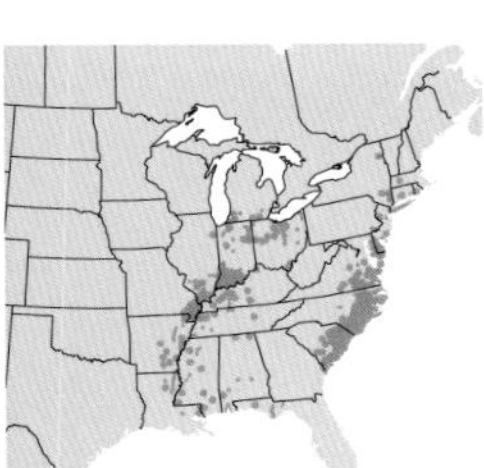

Uncommon or locally common in moist to wet soils of riverbottoms, swamps, or wet woods. Rarely cultivated.

With large buds, round leafstalks, and sometimes heart-shaped, large leaves, Swamp Cottonwood is most similar to Balsam Poplar. However, Swamp Cottonwood differs by having blunt-tipped leaves with coarser teeth, narrower fruit capsules, coarsely ridged bark, scentless buds, and little or no range overlap. This cottonwood is closely related to two Asian species, both of which are rarely cultivated here.

Balsam Poplar

Populus balsamifera

BALM-OF-GILEAD, TACAMAHAC

Deciduous. Medium to large tree often 60' tall (max. 138') with relatively straight trunk and narrow crown. The large leaves, dark above and pale below, and fragrant sticky buds are distinctive.

bark on young trunks smooth, pinkish to pale greenish

older trunks have rough gray ridges

leaves 5", shiny dark green above

underleaf pale green to whitish-rusty, not as pale as Black Cottonwood

leaves large, pointed, dark above and pale below

fruit capsules 2-parted, large, rounded

twig yellowish to red-brown

buds large, pointed, sticky, balsam odor when crushed

relatively narrow upright tree with irregular crown of short, stiff twigs

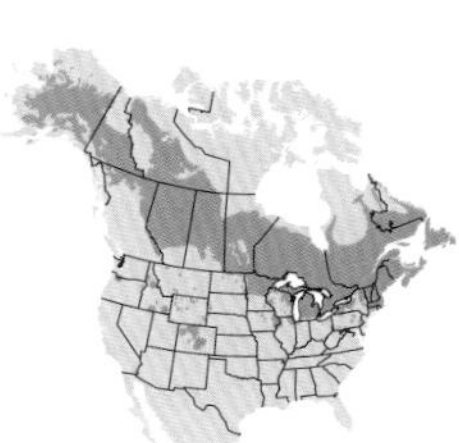

Common and widespread in mixed moist to dry woods; usually in clearings and edges, often along rivers. Seldom cultivated, but many similar species and hybrids are.

Black Cottonwood

Populus trichocarpa

WESTERN BALSAM POPLAR

Deciduous. Medium to large tree often 60–90' tall (max. 188'). The tallest poplar and largest broadleaf tree in the West, but trunk and branches never as massive as Eastern Cottonwood.

leaves 5", taper from broad base
leaves shiny dark green above
short, round leafstalk often bright red
small teeth on leaf margin

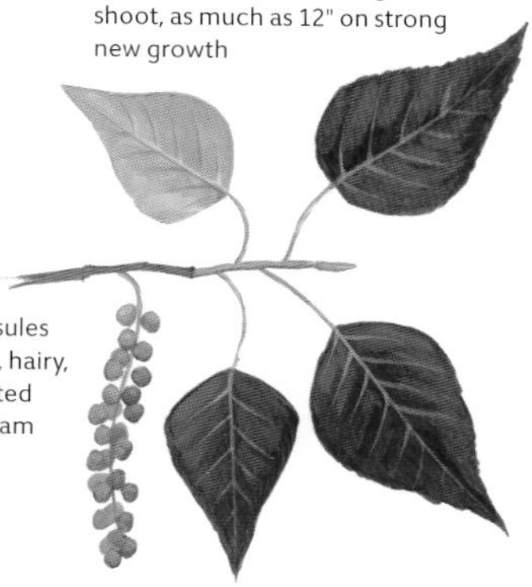
leaves vary from 4–8" long on one shoot, as much as 12" on strong new growth
fruit capsules 3-parted, hairy, less pointed than Balsam

twig yellowish to red-brown
buds sticky, resinous, gummy, fragrant in spring

Hybrids with Balsam Poplar are common where range meets. Black differs primarily in having 3-parted fruit capsules that are more rounded (vs. 2-parted and more pointed) and on average Black has larger leaves with paler underleaf.

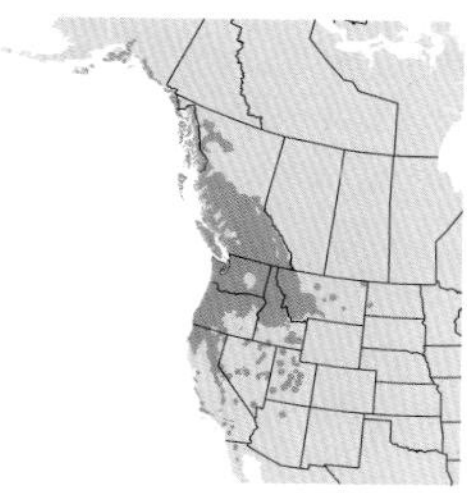

Common and often forms nearly pure stands in clearings, edges, river floodplains. Very rarely cultivated even within native range.

Narrowleaf Cottonwood

Populus angustifolia

WILLOWLEAF POPLAR

Deciduous. Medium to large tree often 60' tall (max. 105'); closely related to Balsam Poplar and Black Cottonwood, but with much narrower leaves.

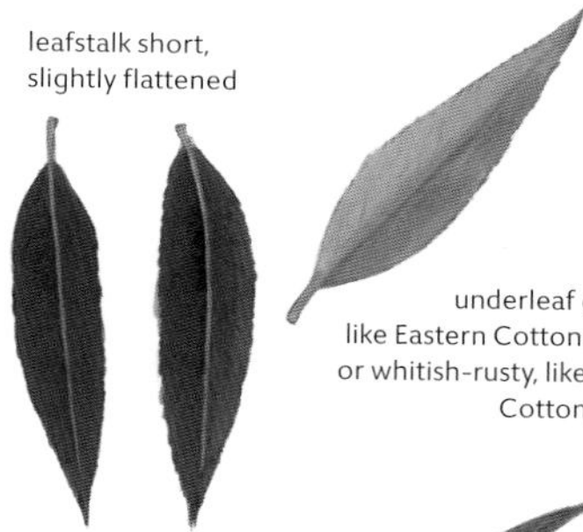
leafstalk short, slightly flattened
leaves 4", narrow, toothed
underleaf green, like Eastern Cottonwood, or whitish-rusty, like Black Cottonwood

leaves narrow, short stalked

twigs slender, pale pinkish

Hybridizes commonly with Eastern Cottonwood where range overlaps. The hybrids have been named 'Lanceleaf' Cottonwood (*Populus* × *acuminata*). These trees have intermediate leaf shape and are commonly cultivated in and near their native range. Hybridizes also with Black Cottonwood where range overlaps.

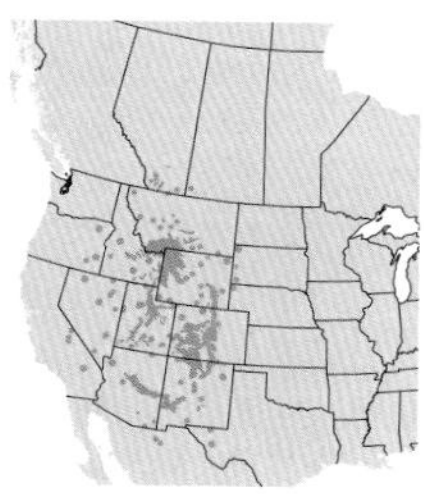

Common along watercourses. Commonly cultivated (zone 3–8).

Willow Family: Willows

The willows (genus *Salix*) include 300–500 species worldwide with about 100 species native to North America. The genus grows more widely in North America than any other type of tree-like plant, ranging from the Arctic to the desert to the subtropics. No matter where you are in North America, chances are there is a native willow growing nearby.

Most willows are shrubs with multiple tall straight stems that growing in dense thickets along streams and in wet areas. A few species are merely dwarf, creeping shrubs that form mats (thick tangles) on arctic or alpine tundra. Many species are occasionally tree-like in favorable conditions, and only a few species are commonly tree-like.

The line between trees and shrubs is particularly blurry in willows. Willows nearly always have multiple trunks, and continue to sprout from the base, even when mature. In order to call almost any willow a tree, the single stem criterion in the definition of a tree must be ignored.

Given the large number of similar shrubby species, this book makes no effort to distinguish the smaller willows. If you wish to work on identifying the willows in your area, look carefully at leaf size and shape, the presence or absence of stipules (small leaf-like structures at the base of the leafstalk), leaf hairiness, and other features. Even insect galls and fungal diseases can be species-specific and helpful for identification. Consult a detailed guide to the plants of your region to identify willows to species, and use this guide for more general identification of willows.

All willows have buds covered by a single scale, looking smooth and sleek compared to other trees. Sycamores also have single bud scales, but are easily distinguished by other features. Twigs can be a variety of colors, including dark brown, red, orange, green or yellow, even within a single species. Some species (and most cultivars) show a narrower range of color variation, but in general twig color is not very reliable for identifying species. Willows have separate male and female flowers and blossom on separate plants.

Willows generally do not grow large enough to be useful for lumber, but they grow quickly, and willow wood is light and flexible. The practice of coppicing (cutting a plant to the ground and later harvesting long slender sprouts) is used to produce large quantities of straight slender willow twigs, used for basket-making and other crafts. One cultivar of White Willow is the source of most cricket bats in Britain. The main ingredient in aspirin (salicylic acid) was first found in willow bark. Willows are used for erosion control, and many animals and birds rely on willow bark and buds for winter food, particularly in their far northern range.

Willow fruit is a two-parted pointed capsule. It splits open to release many tiny seeds with cottony hairs, helping the seeds to float on the wind for wide dispersal.

Willow Oak and Desert-willow are unrelated, but have willow-like long narrow leaves. Russian-olive and several other unrelated species also have willow-like leaves.

Willow twigs are slender, flexible, and whiplike. Their color is extremely variable, although fairly consistent within a single species.

A few species of native willows have very narrow leaves, such as Sandbar Willow and Hinds Willow.

Most willows have narrow leaves. Narrow-leaved species, nearly as large as Black Willow, include Coastal Plain Willow in the Southeast, Peachleaf Willow in mid-continent, and Pacific Willow in the West.

Willows with broad leaves include widespread species, such as Pussy Willow and Bebb Willow, both mainly northern and eastern, and Scouler Willow, mainly western, along with many other species. Willows with broader leaves tend to be smaller and shrubby, only rarely tree-like to 30' tall. The underleaf of many broad-leaved species is fuzzy and pale.

The Pussy Willow and several other species have silky, gray-white hairs on the emerging male flowers. These appear in early spring as short silky catkins, commonly known as "pussy-willows." The catkins soon lengthen and open into flowering catkins with protruding yellow stamens, like other willow species.

Bay-leaved Willow

Salix pentandra

LAUREL WILLOW, BAY WILLOW, EUROPEAN BAY WILLOW

Deciduous. Shrub or small tree often 30' tall (max. 70'); compact oval form. Valued as an ornamental for shiny dark leaves and cold-hardiness. Some hybrids with White or Weeping Willows also cultivated.

leaves 4", dark glossy green
underleaf
glaucous green

Native to Europe and western Asia. Commonly cultivated and locally naturalized in moist soils, wetland margins, roadsides (zones 2–5).

Black Willow

Salix nigra

Deciduous. Medium tree often 30–50' tall (max. 140'). Usually messy-looking, multi-trunked, and leaning with irregular clumps of twigs; the largest native willow and the only willow important for lumber. Taller and with darker foliage than most other willows.

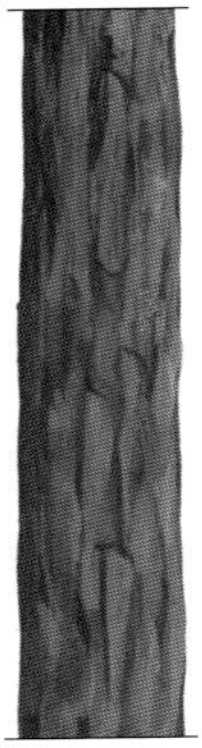

bark of young trunks smooth brown, soon developing thin ridges

mature bark dark brown, roughly-ridged

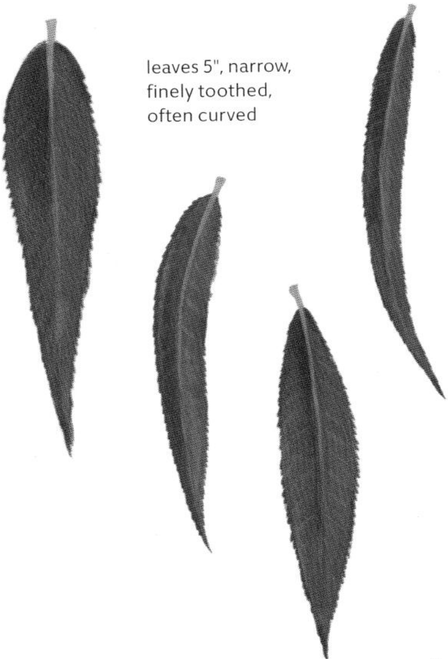

leaves 5", narrow, finely toothed, often curved

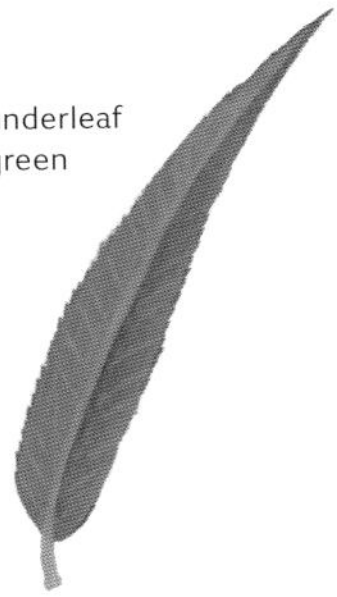

underleaf green

fall color pale yellow-brown

narrow leaves arranged loosely around twig, pointing toward tip

female flowers in greenish catkins

flowers spring (Apr–Jun) later than cultivated tree-sized willows

twigs reddish to grayish

buds relatively short

male flower catkins bright yellow when releasing pollen

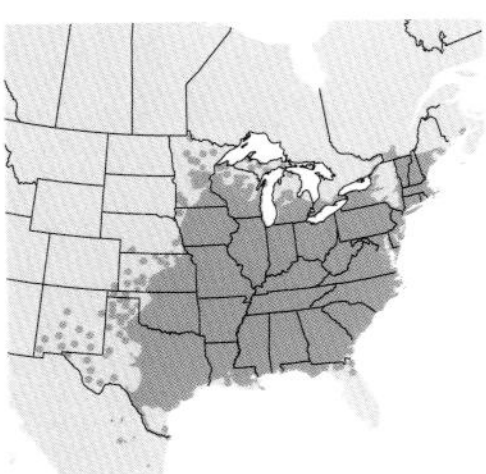

Common in open wet areas, river banks, pond and swamp margins, roadsides. Rarely cultivated.

Crack Willow

Salix fragilis

BRITTLE WILLOW, SNAP WILLOW

Deciduous. Small to medium tree usually under 50' tall (max. 122'), but large trees may be hybrids. Named for the brittle twigs, which snap off at the base rather than bending (but some other weeping willows are equally brittle).

fruit capsules open in summer to release tiny seeds with cottony fluff

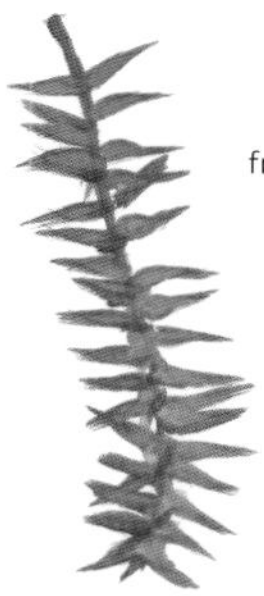
fruit capsules of all willows similar to poplars, but very narrow, pointed

leaves 5", narrow, often curved, coarsely toothed
underleaf pale, sometimes whitish

twigs relatively stout, greenish brown
buds hairy, small and slender

Native to central Europe and southwestern Asia. Commonly cultivated and naturalized (zones 3–6).

a crooked, leaning tree with untidy dense clumps of twigs and sprouts; twigs overall orange-brown

Gooding Willow

Salix gooddingii

SOUTHWESTERN BLACK WILLOW

Deciduous. Small to medium tree usually under 45' tall. Southwestern form of Black Willow, sometimes considered a separate species; differs from typical Black Willow in smaller, duller leaves, paler yellow-gray twigs, and minor differences in fruit capsules.

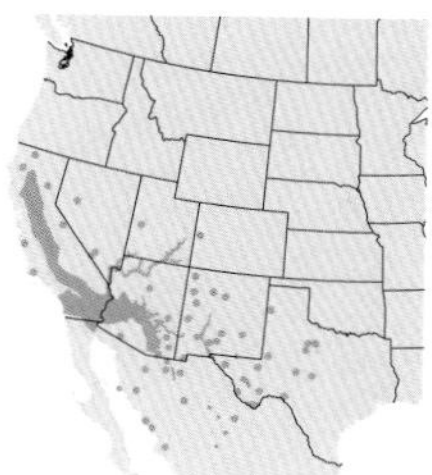

Common along streams, pond margins, marshy areas. Rarely cultivated.

Cultivated Willows

The taxonomy of cultivated willows in North America is very complex. Crack Willow, European White Willow, and Weeping Willow are commonly cultivated, but variation, and hybridization makes identification difficult. Even specialists disagree, and the following should be considered informal labels and used with the understanding that many other variations may be seen.

'GOLDEN' WEEPING WILLOW (var. *'chrysocoma'*), hybrid of Weeping × European White Willow. Large tree to 88' tall; the most commonly cultivated Weeping Willow, very common in North. Twigs bright yellow to reddish, become brighter and quite striking in late winter, leaf out early, stays green late into fall, leaves finely-hairy beneath.

'WISCONSIN' WEEPING WILLOW (*Salix × pendulina*), probably a hybrid of Weeping × Crack Willow; commonly cultivated (zones 4–7). Large tree not strongly weeping, twigs green to yellow-brown, leaves hairless.

'RINGLEAF' WILLOW ['Ram's Horn' Willow, 'Screwleaf' Willow] *'crispa'* or *'annularis'*—a variant of Weeping Willow or hybrid Weeping × White Willow, uncommon in cultivation. Small tree to 40' tall, not weeping; gray-green leaves tightly curled in loops close to twigs.

PEKING WILLOW (*Salix matsudana*) is rarely seen in its typical form (very similar to Weeping Willow), but one common cultivar, known as 'Corkscrew' Willow or 'Dragon's Claw' Willow *'tortuosa'* has curly twigs and leaves. Leafs out early and stays green late. Hybrids of this with 'Golden' Weeping Willow have weeping, twisted, golden to red twigs and are reportedly commonly cultivated.

White Willow

Salix alba

EUROPEAN WHITE WILLOW

Deciduous. Medium to large tree often 60' tall (max. 133'). Low, long branches and flexible twigs form broad rounded crown; some hybrids have strongly weeping form.

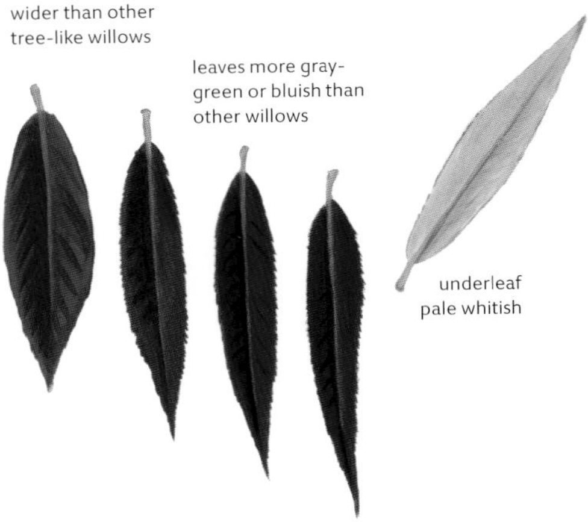
leaves 3", silky-hairy, wider than other tree-like willows
leaves more gray-green or bluish than other willows
underleaf pale whitish

short, stout trunk divides into broad, spreading crown with long, pendulous, yellowish twigs
trunk short and stout

twigs greenish-brown to yellow to reddish

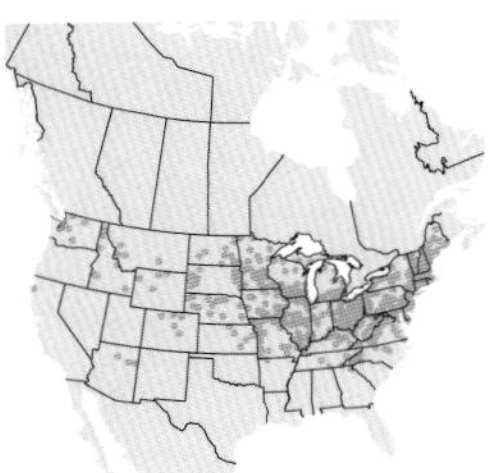

Native to Europe, northwestern Africa, western Asia. Commonly and widely cultivated and naturalized (zones 2–8).

Weeping Willow

Salix babylonica

BABYLON WEEPING WILLOW, CHINESE WEEPING WILLOW

Deciduous. Medium tree often 30–50' tall (max. 134'), but large trees may be hybrids. Low and broad with long flexible twigs hanging gracefully straight down (but other cultivated hybrids can be equally "weeping"). One of the world's most celebrated and distinctive trees.

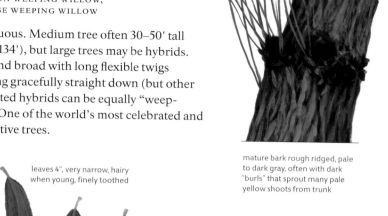

mature bark rough ridged, pale to dark gray, often with dark "burls" that sprout many pale yellow shoots from trunk

leaves 4", very narrow, hairy when young, finely toothed

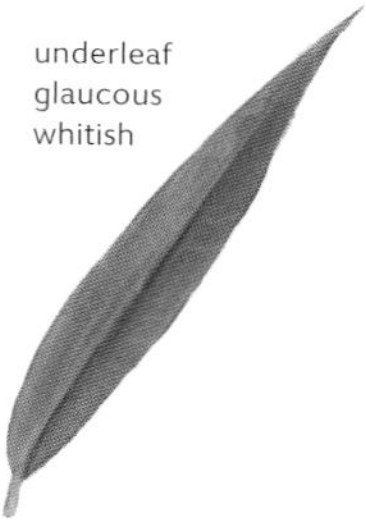

underleaf glaucous whitish

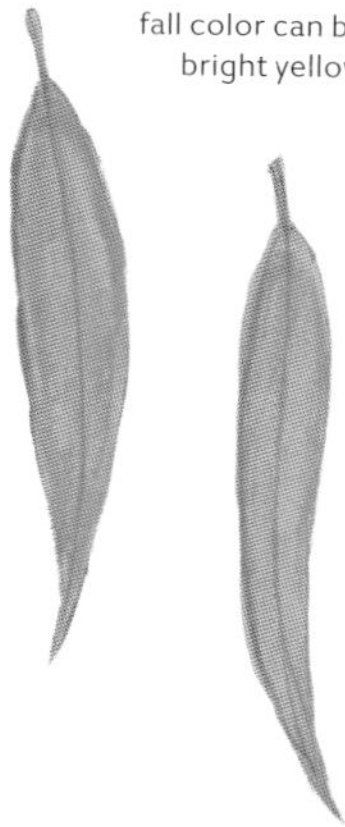

fall color can be bright yellow

long slender twigs, leaves hang down

twigs greenish, olive-gold, or reddish-brown, weeping to ground, long and slender

buds long

Native to western China. Commonly cultivated and naturalized, but less cold-hardy than some "weeping" hybrids (zones 5–8).

usually low and spreading; twigs very long and flexible, hanging straight down to form rounded crown and curtain-like screen of foliage

Oleaster Family

The oleaster family (Elaeagnaceae) includes about seventy species of shrubs and small trees, most of which are in the genus *Elaeagnus*. A few species of native shrubs are in the oleaster family, but only one cultivated species is commonly tree-like.

Most species have leaves and twigs covered with minute silvery scales. Fruit is a small berry, sweet, edible, and high in antioxidants. A few species are cultivated for fruit in China; in North America oleasters are primarily planted as an ornamental or windbreak tree.

bark on young trunk dark gray with pale lenticels

bark on older trunk dark, rough, shreddy

Russian-olive

Eleagnus angustifolia

OLEASTER, SILVER TREE, WILD OLIVE, JERUSALEM WILLOW, TREBIZOND GRAPE

Deciduous. Shrub or small tree usually 10–15' tall (max. 65'); usually branching low with short trunk and broad low crown of small pale leaves.

slender leaves tend to stick out stiffly from twigs

flowers tiny, yellowish, inconspicuous clusters in leaf axils, early summer, sweetly fragrant

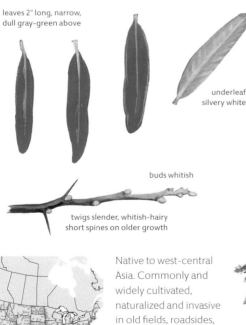

leaves 2" long, narrow, dull gray-green above

underleaf silvery white

fruit small berries, ½", whitish to red

buds whitish

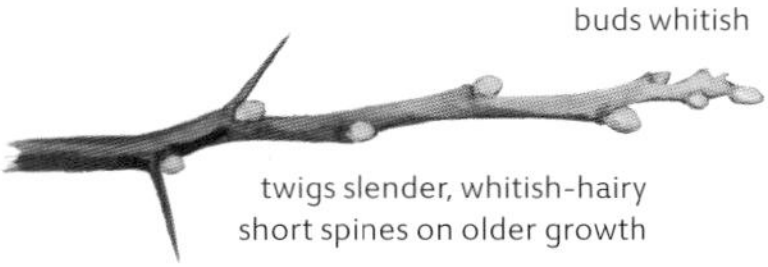

twigs slender, whitish-hairy short spines on older growth

short-trunked with spreading crown of dense thorny twigs, gray-green foliage

Native to west-central Asia. Commonly and widely cultivated, naturalized and invasive in old fields, roadsides, especially along streams in Northern Plains (zones 2–7).

Mulberry Family

The mulberries (family Moraceae) numbers about 1,000 species worldwide, mainly in tropical and subtropical regions. It includes such well-known plants as figs, breadfruit, and the mulberries. In North America, a total of six species in four genera (three native species in two genera) are tree-like and cold-hardy and are covered in this guide. All have milky sap and compound fruit.

The mulberries (genus *Morus*) include three species, two native and one commonly cultivated. Their broad heart-shaped leaves with three main veins from the base are superficially similar to basswoods, but mulberry leaves are often lobed with more symmetrical bases than basswoods, and have milky sap.

Mulberry fruit is a compound cluster of multiple individual berries, sweet and juicy, but not cultivated commercially in North America.

leaves with 3 main veins from base; milky sap
like basswoods, but more symmetrical bases, often lobed
leaves usually unlobed on vigorous twigs, lobed on older and less vigorous growth

White and Red mulberries are similar to each other and both are variable with many cultivars and hybrids complicating identification. White is best distinguished from Red by having leaves more glossy above, and more coarsely toothed with lobe tips more rounded. Fruit color of both ranges from whitish to blackish, although White Mulberry fruit is more often whitish, while Red Mulberry fruit is usually dark purple-black.

Texas Mulberry

Morus microphylla

MEXICAN MULBERRY, MOUNTAIN MULBERRY, LITTLELEAF MULBERRY

Deciduous. Usually a multi-stemmed large shrub, occasionally tree-like to 25' tall. Closely related to Red Mulberry, but with much smaller leaves, smaller flowers and fruit.

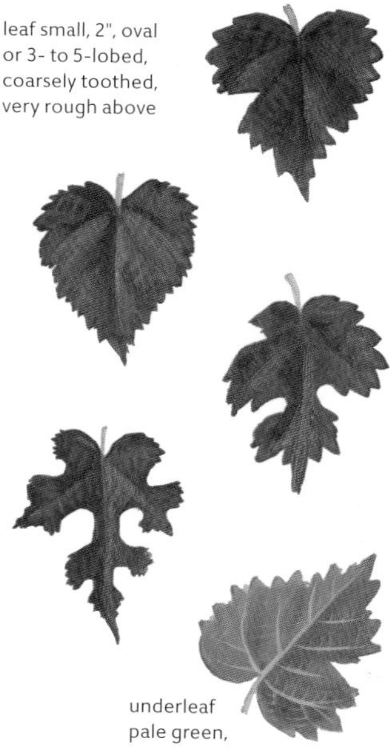
leaf small, 2", oval or 3- to 5-lobed, coarsely toothed, very rough above
underleaf pale green, rough

fruit small, ½", red to black, round, sour
flowers and fruit similar to Red Mulberry but smaller

twigs usually slow-growing, stout, zigzag

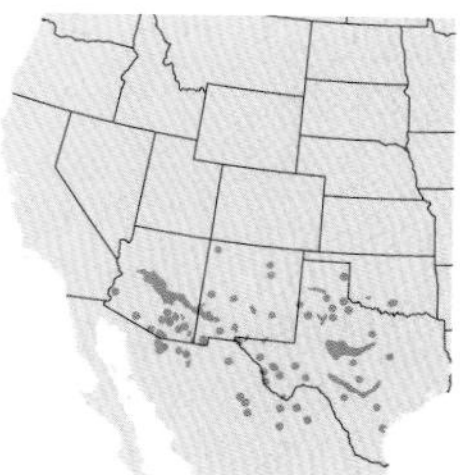

Locally common in dry well-drained soils, usually along streams. Not cultivated.

Red Mulberry

Morus rubra

PURPLE MULBERRY, AMERICAN MULBERRY

Deciduous. Medium tree often 50' tall (max. 63'), largest in Ohio and Mississippi River Valleys; dense, round-topped crown; more open and irregular than White Mulberry.

bark of young trunk pale orange-brown with small lenticels

bark tinged orange-red with broad scaly ridges

usually rough sandpapery above

leaves large, 5½", dark green with coarse teeth

leaves vary from unlobed to 2- or 3-lobed

underleaf more or less hairy

fall color yellowish

flowers in short dangling catkins male narrow, 2¼"

female catkins oblong, 1", pale greenish; early spring with leaves

fruit red-black, 1¼", long-stalked; like elongated blackberry, sweet and juicy

twig brownish

buds dark greenish-brown, divergent

shape like apple tree, lacks dense twigginess of White

Common in fertile moist soils of lowlands. Occasionally cultivated for fruit, but not for ornament and rarely outside of natural range (zones 5–9).

White Mulberry

Morus alba

RUSSIAN MULBERRY, SILKWORM MULBERRY, WEEPING MULBERRY

Deciduous. Medium tree often 40' tall (max. 59'); long-cultivated for fruit and as the host plant of silkworms. Very similar to Red Mulberry, and both species variable.

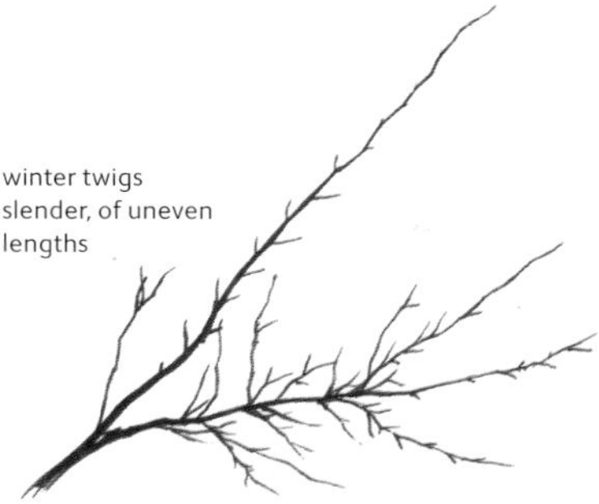
winter twigs
slender, of uneven
lengths

leaves smooth
glossy above
leaves tend
to curl up

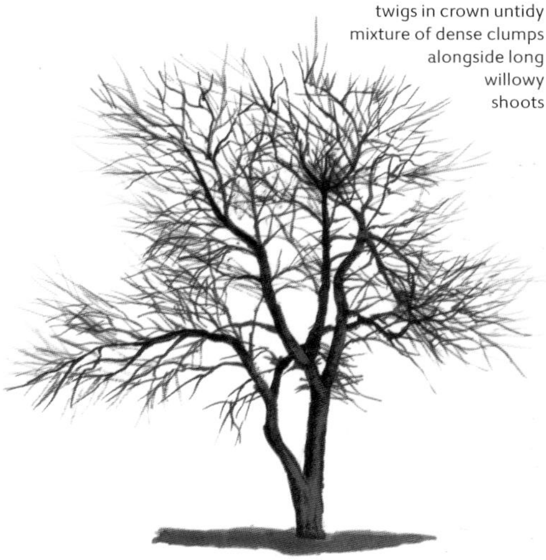
twigs in crown untidy
mixture of dense clumps
alongside long
willowy
shoots

mature fruit ¾",
whitish to red
to occasionally
blackish, ripe in
mid-summer

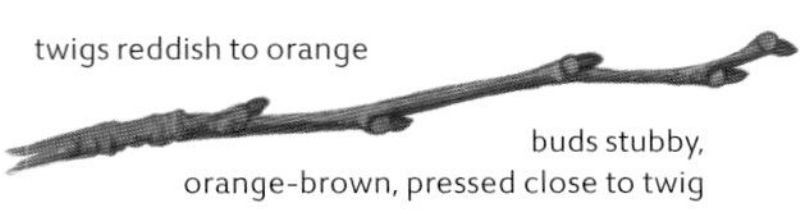
twigs reddish to orange
buds stubby,
orange-brown, pressed close to twig

Native to China. Commonly cultivated and naturalized (zones 5–8) in woods edges and thickets. More common than Red Mulberry in most urban and suburban settings.

Black Mulberry

Morus nigra

Similar to White Mulberry (sometimes considered the same species) and many reports of this species in North America are apparently due to confusion. White Mulberry can have blackish fruit, and Black Mulberry is distinguished mainly by having leaves rarely lobed, which emerge later in spring and stay later in fall than either White or Red mulberries. Native to central Asia and commonly cultivated for fruit in Europe, but only rarely cultivated in North America, mainly on the Pacific Coast (zones 5–9). Another related species, Chinese Mulberry (*Morus bombycis*), is native to east Asia and is commonly cultivated (zones 6–9), mainly as a shrubby cultivar with contorted and twisted branches.

Paper-mulberry

Broussonetia papyrifera

TAPA CLOTH TREE

Deciduous. Large spreading shrub or low-branched tree often 45' tall (max. 75'). Similar to true mulberries with milky sap, but female flowers and fruit a round ball; leaves sometimes opposite (one of the few trees that can have both alternate and opposite leaves). Paper made from bark.

most leaves unlobed, deeply 3- to 5-lobed leaves mainly on vigorous shoots
leaves 6", similar to Red Mulberry;
leaf base often unequal
leaves rough above
underleaf gray-hairy

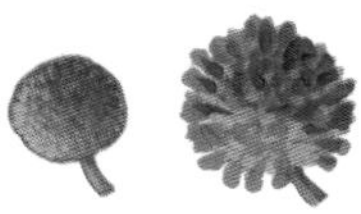

fruit red to orange, round, about 1" fleshy, ripe in late summer or fall

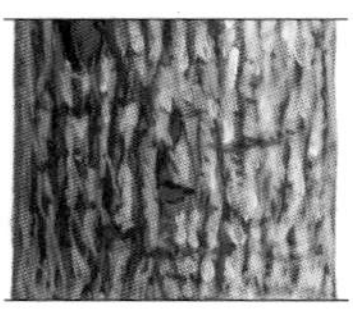

bark thin, yellow brown with smooth ridges and lenticels, trunk becoming burly with age

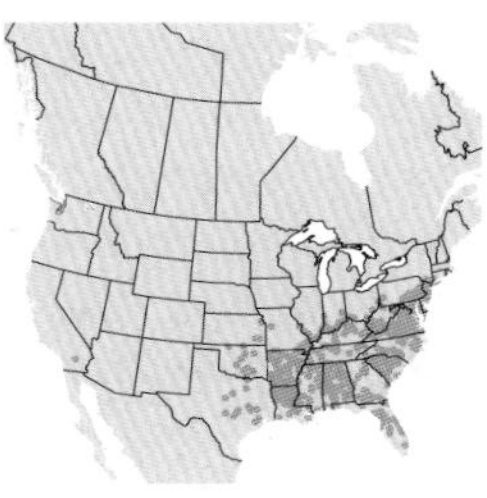

Native to Asia. Commonly cultivated and widely naturalized to fencerows and old fields (zones 6–10) but only a shrub in the north; ornamental plantings are mainly male trees.

Common Fig

Ficus carica

EDIBLE FIG

Deciduous. Shrub or small tree usually low, spreading and rounded under 20' tall, but can be much larger and wide-spreading (max. 80' tall or 150' wide). This species is the source of commercial figs, and the most cold-hardy species of this diverse tropical genus.

leaves 9" long and wide, dark green, palmately 3- to 5-lobed, wavy margins, thick, hairy

fruit pear-shaped 3", purplish, yellow, or green when ripe

twigs very thick

Other species of *Ficus*, large evergreen trees in warm regions, are commonly cultivated. Two species are native in southern Florida, and several exotic species have become naturalized.

Native to eastern Mediterranean, long-cultivated and among the first trees introduced to North America around 1577. Commonly cultivated and locally naturalized (zones 7–10).

Osage-orange

Maclura pomifera

BOIS D'ARC, BODARK, HEDGE-APPLE

Deciduous. Small to medium tree usually under 40' (max. 60'), often forms thickets. Only species in its genus; distinctive with large unusual fruit, pointed glossy leaves, and thorny twigs.

bark splits into broad flat ridges, often peeling in strips with orange highlights

leaves glossy dark green above, untoothed
leaves 5", pointed

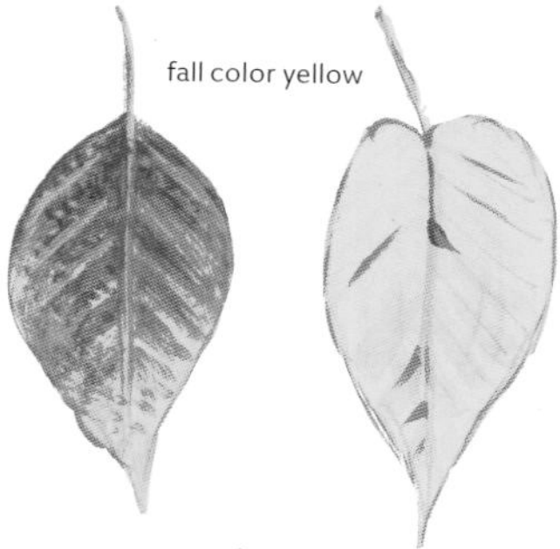
fall color yellow

flowers in leaf axils after leaves appear (late spring)

fruit a hard and heavy green ball 5", ripe in autumn
fruit can weigh over 1 pound

many short stout spur branches
leaves often clustered on stubby lateral branches
leaves with fairly long stalk and slender base, hang loosely from twigs

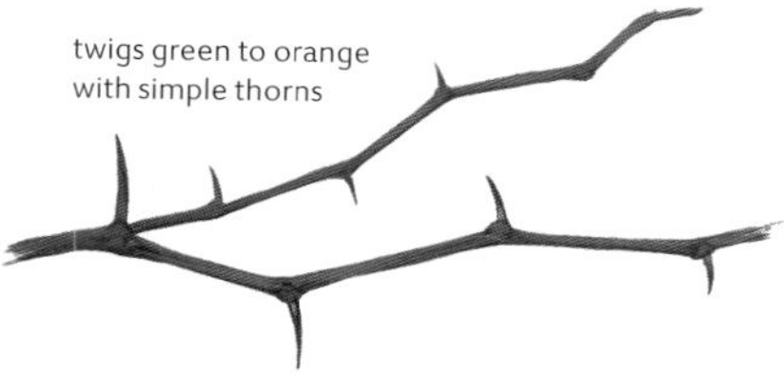
twigs green to orange with simple thorns

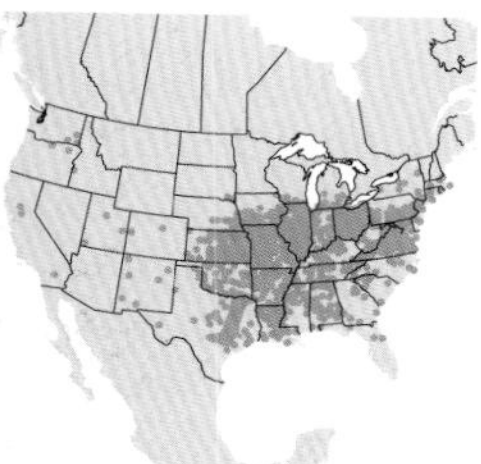

Common, especially in moist sites in fields and edges, but tolerates drier soils. Commonly cultivated and naturalized well-beyond original native range (zones 4–9).

The hard, resilient, and rot-resistant wood of this species found many specialized uses. The colloquial French name, *bois d'arc,* means "wood for bows". Often planted as a "living fence" due to its sharp spines and thicket-forming habit.

Buckthorn Family

The Buckthorn family (Rhamnaceae) includes about 900 species of mostly shrubs and trees worldwide. Eight species (four native) in four genera are tree-like and cold-hardy enough to be included in this guide. All have simple leaves and berry-like fruit. Leaves can be alternate or opposite. Generally too small to be important for lumber, species in this family are valued as ornamentals, as the source of some yellow and green dyes, and buckthorns (genus *Rhamnus*) made the best charcoal for gunpowder production.

The buckthorns and false-buckthorns (genus *Frangula*) were formerly combined in the genus *Rhamnus* with about 150 species worldwide. Two species of Buckthorns (one native) and three species of false-buckthorns (two native) are included here.

Buckthorns differ from false-buckthorns in having thorny twigs, scaled buds (vs. naked), and rough ridged bark (vs. smooth). Buckthorn leaves have three main veins from the leaf base, and veins curving along the edge of the leaf (vs. straight, pinnate veins), and flowers with four tiny petals (vs. five).

Hollyleaf Buckthorn

Rhamnus crocea

Evergreen. Shrub or occasionally a small tree to about 30' tall; most often tree-like on the Channel Islands and adjacent mainland of southern California. Hollyleaf Cherry and some oaks have similar evergreen spiny leaves, but lack thorns and have very different flowers and fruit. Common in canyons and foothill chaparral. Not cultivated.

leaves ¾", small, round, leathery with parallel veins and spiny toothed edges

European Buckthorn

Rhamnus cathartica

COMMON BUCKTHORN, EUROPEAN WAYTHORN

Deciduous. Shrub or small tree usually 12–20' tall (max. 61'); usually short or leaning trunk with low, rounded crown of tangled twigs and small dark leaves.

leaves smaller and more rounded than other buckthorns

leaves 2" long, egg-shaped, dark, bright green, finely toothed, often with 3 main veins from base and veins follow leaf edges

fruit small round blackish, on thorny twigs; persists into winter

twigs thorny

buds scaled

bark of small stems with obvious white lenticels

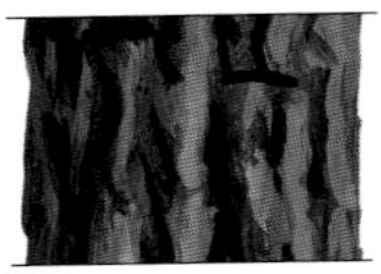

bark of mature trunk dark, rough, ridged and scaly

Native to Europe, West and North Asia, North Africa. Commonly cultivated, naturalized and invasive in fence-rows, field edges, open woods, since the 1800s (zones 3–7).

Carolina False-buckthorn

Frangula caroliniana

INDIAN CHERRY, TREE BUCKTHORN, YELLOW BUCKTHORN, YELLOWWOOD

Deciduous. Shrub or small tree usually 10–15' tall (max. 43'); the only tree-like buckthorn native to Southeast.

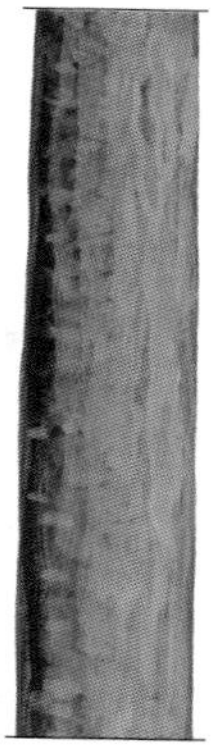

bark ash-gray, smooth to slightly furrowed

leaves 4", oval, pointed with prominent pinnate veins and few teeth

leaves more tapered than Cascara

flowers small yellow-green in small branched clusters in leaf axils in spring

twigs of false-buckthorns opposite, slender, curve out and up

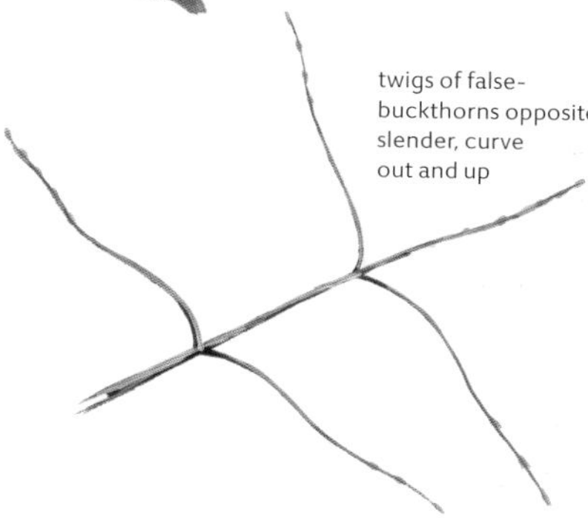

fruit ⅓", small berries, green ripening to red, then blackish; all colors evident together, ripe in Aug–Oct

twigs slender, grayish with pale lenticels

buds naked, yellow-brown

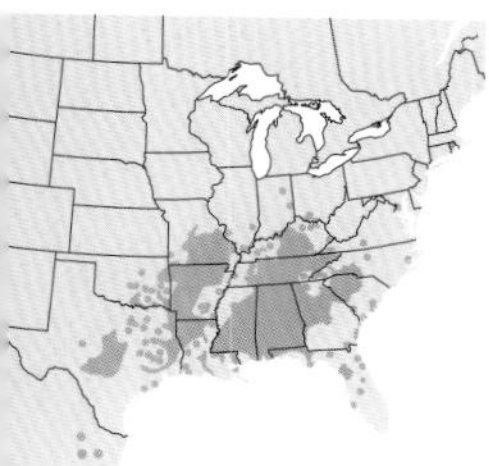

Uncommon in stream valleys and other moist deciduous woodlands. Rarely cultivated (zones 5–9).

Birchleaf False-buckthorn

Frangula betulifolia

Deciduous. Shrub or small tree to about 20' tall. Very similar to Carolina False-buckthorn and sometimes considered the same species. Range overlaps with California False-buckthorn (*Frangula californica*), but that species is very rarely tree-like, and has smaller evergreen leaves.

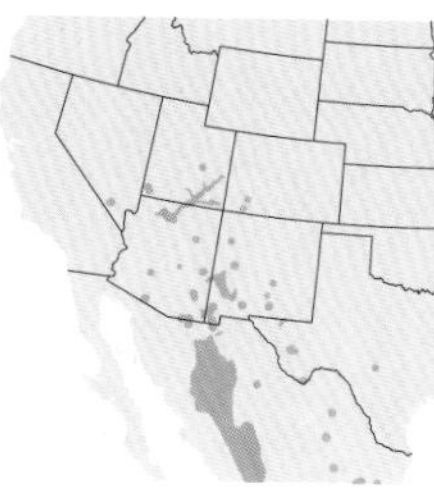

Common in moist canyons. Not cultivated.

Cascara False-buckthorn

Frangula purshiana

OREGON BEARWOOD, BITTERBARK, CHITTAM, COFFEETREE

Deciduous (or young trees evergreen). Shrub or small tree usually 15–30' tall (max. 70'); branches upswept forming neat oval crown. Differs from Carolina False-buckthorn in having flowers on very short stalks. Bark is harvested from wild trees and processed for commercial laxatives.

leaves 5", 10–17 pairs of straight pinnate veins; rounded fine teeth, margins curled under

Five additional species of buckthorns are native to North America and occasionally tree-like (and four others are shrubs). Most are very similar to Carolina and Cascara.

Fairly common in moist valleys and canyon bottoms, very shade-tolerant, growing in understory often with Red Alder. Rarely cultivated.

Glossy False-buckthorn

Frangula alnus

ALDER BUCKTHORN

Deciduous. Shrub or occasionally a small tree 12–20' tall (max. 34'). Similar to Carolina Fasle-buckthorn but leaves smaller, untoothed, and flowers solitary on short stalk (vs. branched stalk).

leaves 2", untoothed, 8–12 pairs of pinnate veins

The genus *Ceanothus* includes about fifty species of shrubs, three of which have been recorded as small trees. They are related to buckthorns and are found mainly in California, where they are an important component of the foothill chaparral community. Leaves are small and oval with three main veins from the base (like Common Jujube); tree-like species have leathery evergreen leaves. Flowers appear in clusters at twig tips, and fruit is a tiny three-parted capsule, blackish when ripe.

Ceanothus leaves leaves small, 1", creased along three main veins, dark green, glossy

Native to western Eurasia, Commonly cultivated, naturalized and invasive in damp woodlands, wetland borders, roadsides; often with alders (zones 3–7).

Common Jujube

Ziziphus jujuba

ZIZIPHUS ZIZYPHUS, CHINESE DATE

Deciduous. Shrub or small tree usually 15–20' tall (max. 50'); suckers to form thickets. Many cultivars developed for edible fruit, grown commercially in China, mainly for ornament in North America.

leaves dark, glossy, 2", with three main veins from base

fruit oval to rounded, 1½", usually reddish-brown, date-like, ripe in fall (Aug–Dec)

flowers tiny, yellow-green, profuse (Mar–Jul) in leaf axils, fragrance like grapes

twigs can be thorny

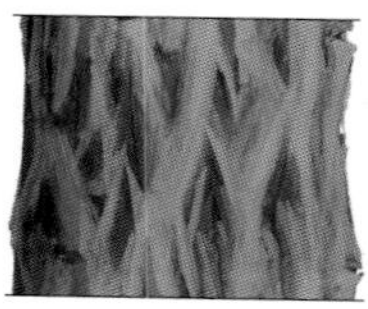

bark rough with deep furrows like Black Locust

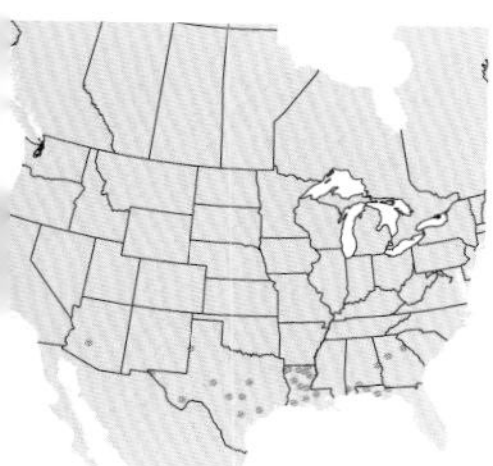

Native to southeastern Europe, Asia. Uncommonly cultivated especially in hot, dry sites; naturalized locally in South (zones 6–9).

Japanese Raisintree

Hovenia dulcis

HONEY TREE

Deciduous. Small to medium tree usually 20–30' tall (max. 88'); oval crown with ascending branches. Named for unusual fruit.

leaves resemble poplar, but twig lacks true terminal bud, end bud axillary

leaf 6½", broad with long pointed tip

underleaf paler green

flowers small, white-green in 3" clusters in leaf axils (Jun–Jul)

fruit small berry on fleshy edible stalk, ripe in Sep–Oct

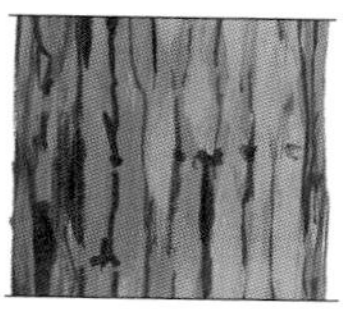

bark gray with narrow, shallow, dark furrows

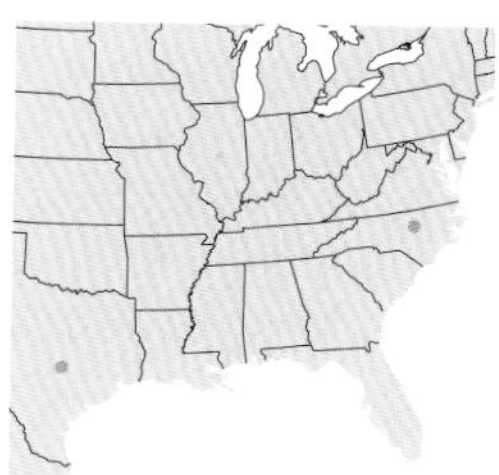

Native to China. Uncommonly cultivated and locally naturalized in southeast (zones 5–7).

Rose Family

The rose family (Rosaceae) includes about 3,000 species of herbs, shrubs and trees worldwide. A total of seventy species are illustrated in this guide (forty-seven native and twenty-three exotic species). Hundreds more tree-like species have been recognized in North America, mostly hawthorns, which are the subject of an ongoing taxonomic debate.

Flowers of all species in the rose family are radially symmetrical with five petals, and in almost all species the petals are showy and white (sometimes pink). Flowers can be single or in axillary or terminal clusters. On many species these clusters are on short lateral spur twigs, opening early in spring either just before or just after the leaves emerge.

Fruit of nearly all Rosaceae illustrated in this guide is round and berry-like with sweet to sour flesh, but the arrangement of seeds inside the fruit varies within the family. Three genera found in the Southwest—*Vauquelinia*, *Lyonothmnus*, and *Cercocarpus*—have small woody fruit capsules rather than the round fleshy fruit of other genera.

Four genera—plums and cherries (*Prunus*), apples (*Malus*), hawthorns (*Crataegus*), and pears (*Pyrus*)—are very similar in general appearance, but differ consistently in some details illustrated here.

Apples and pears have a distinct core with seeds inside 5 thin-walled cavities (left). Plums and cherries have a single stone embedded in the center of the fruit (middle), and hawthorns have multiple stones (up to 5) in each fruit (right).

Flower petals are white on most species in the family (American Plum, top). The only native species that show pinkish flowers are three of the crab apples (Prairie Crab Apple, bottom). Brighter pink flowers are seen on many cultivated apples, and most cultivated plums and cherries. Hawthorns and pears rarely or never show pink flowers.

Most species have the pollen-bearing stamens at the center of the flower with yellow or orange tips, but the pears usually have stamens tipped dark purple (Callery Pear, above).

Flower clusters appear mostly on lateral spur twigs in cherries, pears, and apples (Pin Cherry, above), but more often at the ends of twigs in hawthorns (hawthorn species, below).

Several genera in this family have the ability to reproduce asexually through a form of self-pollination known as apomixis. Hawthorns, serviceberries, and mountain-ashes all have this ability, which leads to the creation of local populations of clones that are distinguishable from other such populations. For over a century, taxonomists have debated how to treat these "micro-species," and even though research has improved the understanding of their relationship to other plants, the complexity still exists and the designation of species limits is somewhat arbitrary.

The rose family includes virtually all of the fruit-producing trees of cooler temperate zone climate, so that the general term "fruit trees" is used to refer to the several genera of the rose family. Many are grown commercially: apples, cherries, plums, peaches, apricots, almonds, pears, and loquat. In addition, shrubby and herbaceous species in the rose family include raspberries, blackberries, strawberries, and quince.

This family is also extremely important as cultivated ornamental plants with cherries, crabapples, pears, mountain-ash, and others (including the namesake rose bush), all cultivated for their showy spring flowers and in some cases for attractive displays of fall and winter fruit.

Black Cherry grows large enough to be used for lumber and its hard reddish wood is highly sought-after for furniture. It is harvested from the wild, not grown commercially. Birds and other wildlife use the fruit of all rose species for food, and birds are the primary dispersers of seeds. Each group is introduced as follows:

Rose Family: Plums and Cherries

Plums and cherries are the largest genus (*Prunus*) in the rose family. Thirty species of trees (seventeen native and thirteen exotic) in the genus are covered in this guide.

All plums and cherries have a distinctive bitter almond odor to broken twigs, and all have showy flowers with white or pink petals, and round berry-like fruit with a single seed. Bark of some species remains smooth into maturity with horizontal lenticels, while related trees, such as apples, pears, and hawthorns quickly develop scaly bark.

Species of plums and cherries are very similar within each group and can be difficult to identify with minor differences between them and many hybrid trees.

The genus *Prunus* is subdivided by botanists into six subgenera. For identification purposes it is practical to use four groups:

PLUMS AND APRICOTS (subgenus *Prunus* with peaches and almonds, subgenus *Amygdalus*) Individual flowers and fruit on short stalks; differ from all other groups in having fruit grooved on one side, stone rough or ridged.

TRUE CHERRIES (subgenus *Cerasus* with Dwarf Cherries, subgenus *Lithocerasus*). Differ from all others in the genus by having individual flowers and fruit on long stalks; this group and all other cherries differs from plums in having round fruit without groove, stone smooth.

BIRD CHERRIES (subgenus *Padus*) Flowers and fruit short-stalked in elongated, branched clusters, appearing in late spring on new leafy shoots (unlike plums and true cherries, which flower in early spring).

LAUREL CHERRIES (subgenus *Laurocerasus*) Flowers and fruit short-stalked in elongated, branched clusters like bird cherries, but leaves leathery, evergreen.

American Plum

Prunus americana

RED PLUM, YELLOW PLUM

Deciduous. Shrub or small tree usually under 25' tall (max. 48') often forming thorny thickets.

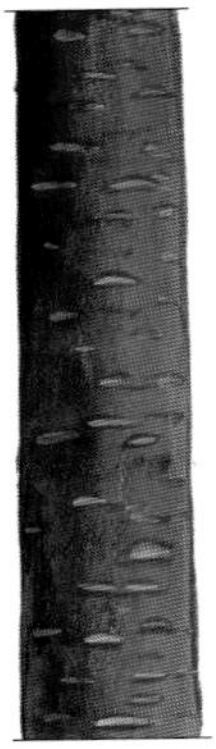

bark thin, smooth, brown with horizontal lenticels

bark on older trunks becoming scaly

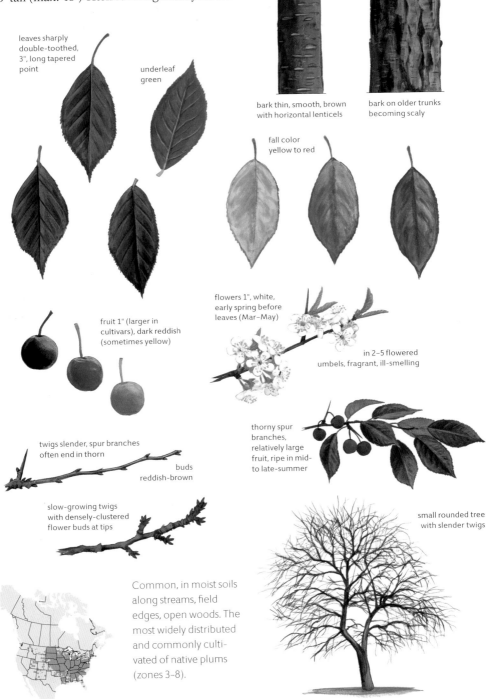

leaves sharply double-toothed, 3", long tapered point

underleaf green

fall color yellow to red

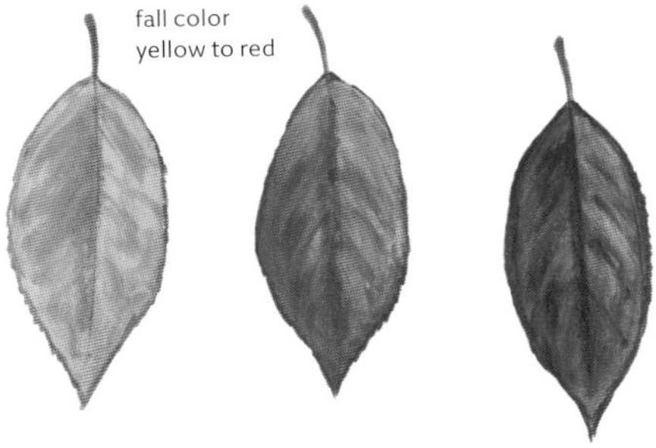

fruit 1" (larger in cultivars), dark reddish (sometimes yellow)

flowers 1", white, early spring before leaves (Mar–May)

in 2–5 flowered umbels, fragrant, ill-smelling

thorny spur branches, relatively large fruit, ripe in mid- to late-summer

twigs slender, spur branches often end in thorn

buds reddish-brown

slow-growing twigs with densely-clustered flower buds at tips

Common, in moist soils along streams, field edges, open woods. The most widely distributed and commonly cultivated of native plums (zones 3–8).

small rounded tree with slender twigs

Mexican Plum

Prunus mexicana

BIGTREE PLUM, INCH PLUM

Deciduous. Shrub or small tree to 20' (max. 36'); solitary, not suckering or thicket-forming. Very similar to American Plum, but with two small glands on leafstalk, dark purple fruit, and underleaf usually hairy.

leaves 3½",
sharply-toothed
underleaf
hairy

fruit 1", usually purplish-red, sometimes yellow; thick sweet flesh

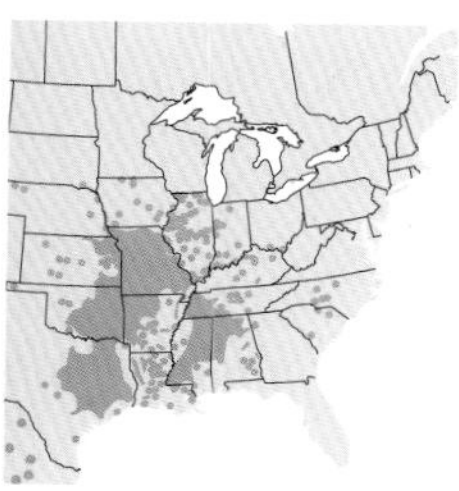

Common but usually scattered in moist to dry habitats. Widely cultivated in central and eastern Texas and Louisiana (zones 6–8).

Canada Plum

Prunus nigra

HORSE PLUM, RED PLUM, WILD PLUM

Deciduous. Shrub or small tree often 25' (max. 51'); short trunk, upright. Very closely related to American Plum, and sometimes considered simply the northern form, best distinguished by two tiny gland-dots on leafstalk (usually lacking on American Plum), and by grayish buds.

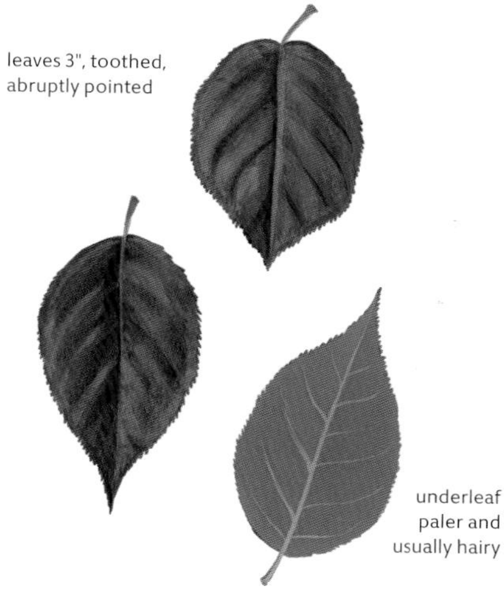
leaves 3", toothed,
abruptly pointed
underleaf
paler and
usually hairy

fruit 1", red to yellowish, sometimes oval

Canada Plum flowers average larger than American Plum, and tend to be more pink (turning pink as they age). Pink flower color is apparently linked to cold winter temperatures, as it is reported that northern flowers are more often pink, and that a cold winter to the south leads to pinker flowers in spring.

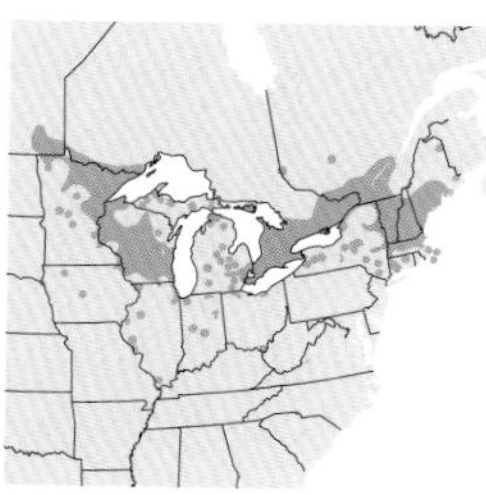

Common in moist soils of valleys and slopes. Rarely cultivated (zones 2–6).

Wildgoose Plum

Prunus munsoniana

MUNSON PLUM, POTOWATAMIE PLUM

Deciduous. Shrub or small tree often 20' tall (max. 36') often forming thickets. Fruit juicy and sweet, used for jelly and sought-after by wildlife.

leaves 3", long and narrow, angled up from midvein

flowers white, ½", appear before or with leaves

fruit small, ⅝", slightly elongated, bright red, sweet; ripe in early summer

narrow curved leaves tend to hang loosely from twig

twigs shiny reddish, sometimes thorny

Uncommon on stream-banks, rich woods, hedgerows. Commonly cultivated with several popular cultivars and hybrids grown for fruit and locally naturalized (zones 6–9).

Hortulan Plum

Prunus hortulana

MINER PLUM, WILD PLUM, WILDGOOSE PLUM

Deciduous. Shrub or small tree usually under 20' (max. 27'); not suckering or thicket-forming. Similar to Wildgoose Plum, but with larger leaves and fruit, leaves flat (not folded) with fewer and larger teeth, flowers appear after leaves and fruit ripens later.

leaves 3½", flat (Wildgoose has leaves folded up along midvein)

flowers white, ½", like Wildgoose, but open later, after leaves

fruit large, round, 1", bright red or occasionally yellow; ripe in late summer

Uncommon in habitats like Wildgoose Plum. Commonly cultivated for fruit, and established widely beyond native range (zones 6–8).

Chickasaw Plum

Prunus angustifolia

SAND PLUM

Deciduous. Shrub or occasionally a small tree usually under 20' (max. 32'); suckers from roots to form large thickets.

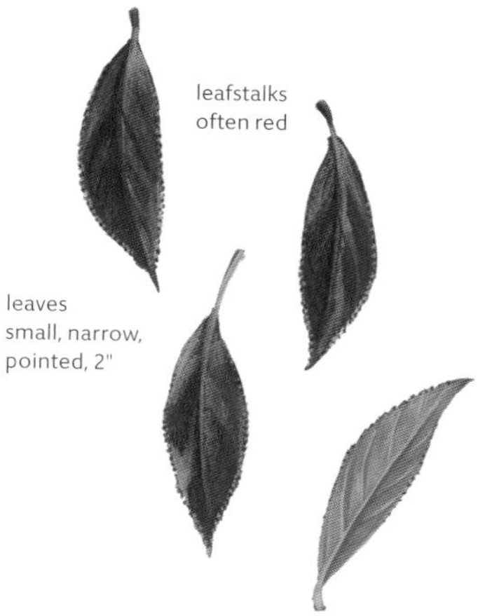
leafstalks often red
leaves small, narrow, pointed, 2"

flowers small, ¼", white, before or with leaves

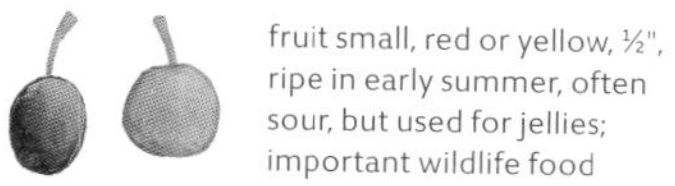
fruit small, red or yellow, ½", ripe in early summer, often sour, but used for jellies; important wildlife food

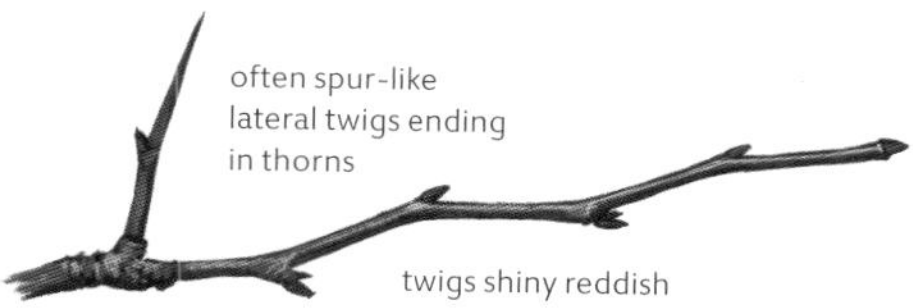
often spur-like lateral twigs ending in thorns
twigs shiny reddish

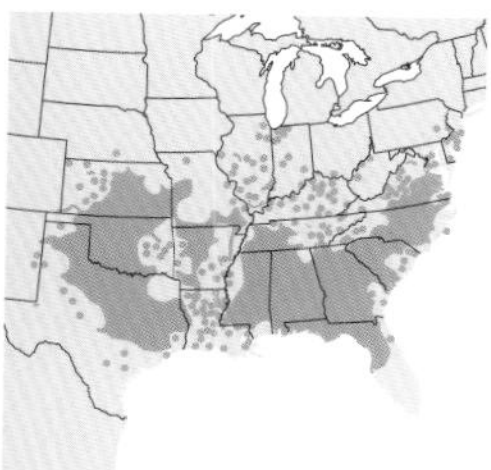

Common in sandy, moist soils in hedgerows, old fields, woods edges, possibly spread by Native Americans from natural range. Uncommon in cultivation (zones 5–9).

Flatwoods Plum

Prunus umbellata

HOG PLUM, BLACK SLOE

Deciduous. Large shrub or small tree often 20' tall (max. 30'). Does not sucker to form thickets and is generally solitary; on average has smallest leaves of all native plums. Distinguished from American Plum by smaller flowers, fruit, and leaves; leaves not double-toothed.

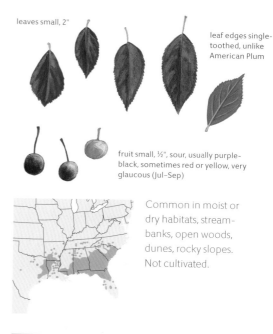

leaves small, 2"
leaf edges single-toothed, unlike American Plum

fruit small, ½", sour, usually purple-black, sometimes red or yellow, very glaucous (Jul–Sep)

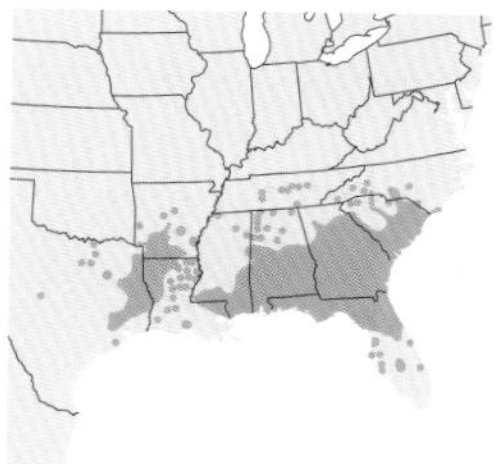

Common in moist or dry habitats, streambanks, open woods, dunes, rocky slopes. Not cultivated.

Allegheny Plum

Prunus alleghaniensis

Plants growing in scattered wetlands in Appalachians and in Michigan have been separated as Allegheny Plum. Average larger leaves than Flatwoods, but apparently distinguishable only by range. This and several other varieties are often considered part of Flatwoods Plum.

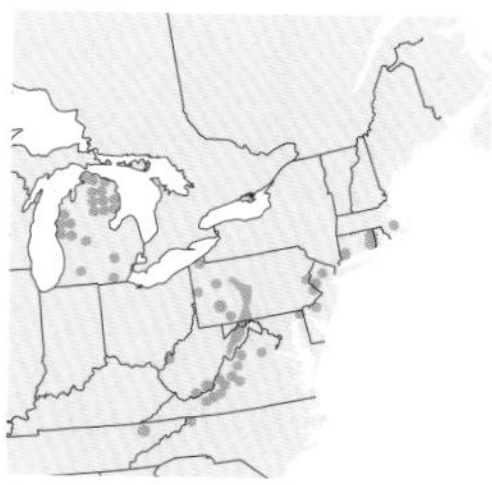

Klamath Plum

Prunus subcordata

SIERRA PLUM, PACIFIC PLUM, WESTERN PLUM

Deciduous. Small tree usually under 20' tall (max. about 30'); often forming thickets with stiff, thorny, horizontal branches. Distinguished from other plums by oval fruit and round leaves.

leaf base often heart-shaped
leaves 2", broad with rounded tip

flowers white, ½"

fruit ¾", dark purple-red, occasionally yellow, oval to round; ripe in late summer

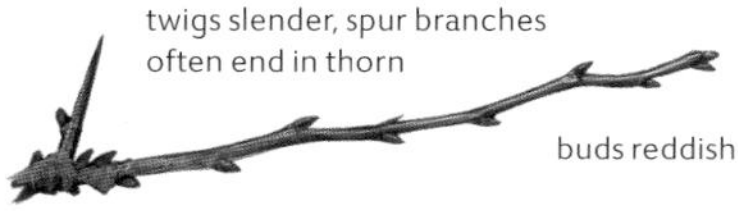
twigs slender, spur branches often end in thorn
buds reddish-brown

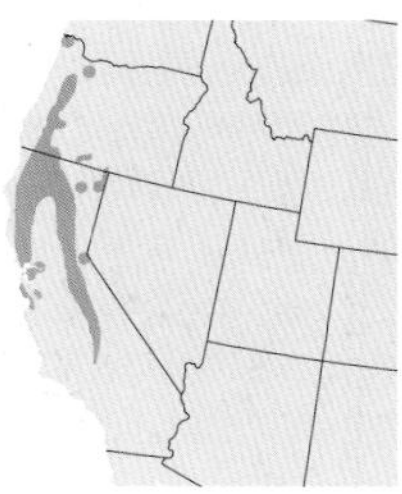

Common in a variety of habitats from streambanks to dry rocky slopes. The only plum native to western states. Not cultivated.

'Garden' Plum

Prunus '× domestica'

EUROPEAN PLUM, COMMON PLUM, PRUNE PLUM, DAMSON PLUM, BULLACE PLUM

Deciduous. Shrub or small tree (max. 45'). Very closely related to Cherry Plum, this widely-cultivated "species" provides commercially-grown plums and prunes.

leaves 2¼", blunt

fruit large, 2¼", blue-black to red or greenish

Many common cultivars include familiar names 'Bullace' and 'Damson' Plums. In general the variations of 'Garden' Plum are selected for fruit, while Cherry Plum cultivars are selected for ornament. Still, varieties of the two overlap, and can be very difficult to distinguish. In addition, several other species of Eurasian plums are cultivated more or less commonly in North America.

Apparently a Eurasian domestic hybrid of complex and ancient origins; unknown in the wild. Very common in cultivation (zones 4–9).

Cherry Plum

Prunus cerasifera

MYROBALAN, FLOWERING PLUM, PURPLELEAF PLUM

Deciduous. Small shrubby tree 15–30' (max. 40'). This species and 'Garden' Plum are among the most commonly cultivated small trees.

bark relatively smooth gray with horizontal lines of branch scars and lenticels

leaves small, 2", (larger in most cultivars)

purple leaves on many cultivated trees, often turning green in summer

flowers small, white, profuse, early spring before or with leaves

purple-leaved cultivars with pale pink flowers among emerging purple leaves

fruit 1", yellow to red or purple; ripe in late summer

Among the many cultivars of Cherry Plum, the most popular are purple-leaved varieties. These can have white or pink flowers. Other cultivars can have weeping habit and other variations.

twigs relatively slender for a plum

small spreading tree with long shoots, some with dark purple leaves

Apparently an ancient domestic hybrid originating in Eurasia. Very commonly cultivated and widely naturalized (zones 4–8).

Desert Apricot

Prunus fremontii

Deciduous. Shrub or rarely a small tree to 15' tall; a small spreading thorny tree.

leaves small, 1", oval to round, finely toothed
underleaf paler green

flowers ¾", white with orange and pink center

fruit ½", oval to round, yellow-green and fuzzy; creased on one side

Uncommon and local in arid sandy washes within its limited range. Uncommonly cultivated near native range.

Common Apricot

Prunus armeniaca

Deciduous. Small spreading tree usually under 20' tall (max. 48'). Generally a stouter and larger tree than Peach with smaller fruit and round leaves; flowers very pale pink in early spring.

leaves 3", broad round to heart-shaped

fruit like a small peach, 1¾"

Native to Manchuria and Korea, commonly cultivated for edible fruit (zones 4–9).

Japanese Apricot (*Prunus mume*) is a small tree native to Japan. It is uncommonly cultivated, but while the Common Apricot is cultivated for its fruit, this species is cultivated for its flowers, and is more likely to be seen as a garden tree. It differs from Common Apricot in having less rounded leaves, but abruptly narrowed at the tip, and flowers appear in late winter.

Peach

Prunus persica

COMMON PEACH, NECTARINE

Deciduous. Small, spreading tree usually under 20' tall (max. 39'). Told from all native plums by woolly buds, very short-stalked flowers and fruit, and long slender leaves.

flowers spectacular, pink
(or white or red in cultivars)
in early spring (Feb–Apr)
before leaves

Among the many common Peach cultivars are trees with flower color ranging from white to red, double flowers, and many variations of fruit (including hairless fruit, such as nectarine). Weeping or purple-leaved cultivars are less commonly planted. Several related species are also cultivated as ornamental trees in yards, gardens, and parks.

leaves slender,
6", often curved

fruit large,
3½", round, very
short stem

slender leaves
curve and droop
from twigs

twigs reddish, buds fuzzy whitish

Native to China. Commonly cultivated for fruit and ornament, occasionally naturalized (zones 5–9); more than 2,000 fruiting cultivars named.

Almond

Prunus dulcis

Deciduous. Small tree usually under 20' tall (max. 38'). Closely-related to Peach and Apricot, but flesh of fruit is thin and sour; grown commercially for edible nut at center of fruit.

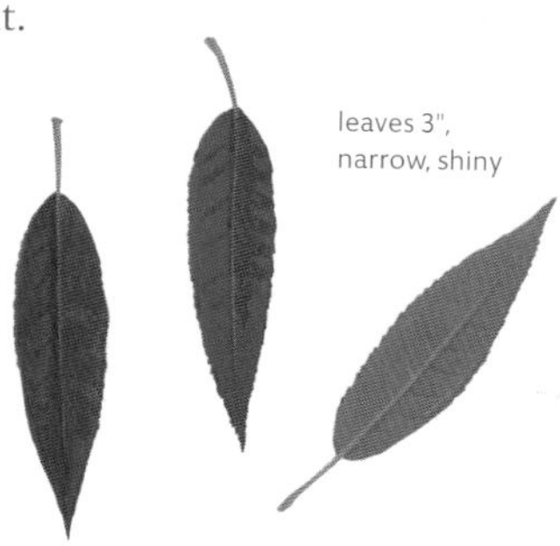
leaves 3",
narrow, shiny

fruit 1½",
greenish, like
a small peach

Native from northern Africa to Syria. Commonly cultivated for nuts and for ornament (zones 6–9). Many ornamental cultivars are actually hybrids with Peach.

Black Cherry

Prunus serotina

WILD BLACK CHERRY, RUM CHERRY, CABINET CHERRY, MOUNTAIN BLACK CHERRY

Deciduous. Medium to large tree often 60' tall (max. 145'), largest of all *Prunus*. Hard reddish wood is prized for furniture-making, while fruit is avidly consumed by birds, who spread the seeds widely.

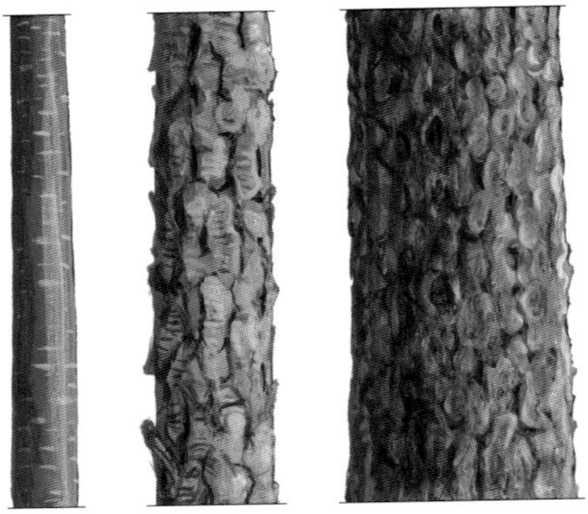
bark of young trees smooth, dark gray
bark dark gray and scaly on older trees

leaves narrow, oval, 4", finely toothed

fall color yellow to orange red, late

fruit ⅓", red to purplish black; ripe in late summer

flowers late spring (Mar–Jun) after leaves
flowers white, small, ⅓", in terminal spikes 5" long

twigs slender, dark, with small dark buds
buds often clustered at twig tips

emerging leaves often reddish

Four varieties are often recognized, but differ only in minor details such as leaf hairiness and leaf shape.

Very common and widespread in open woods, old fields, hedgerows, yards. Commonly cultivated as shade tree and naturalized well beyond native range (zones 3–9).

winter twigs slender, curved, irregular

This species is the primary host for Tent Caterpillar, and web "tents" are often conspicuous in branch angles. Black Cherry (along with Choke and European Bird Cherries) is also frequently infected with black knot disease, a fungus that causes a thickened black woody growth along the twigs. Both of these afflictions can be useful identifying features at a distance.

leaves can be relatively flat and straight or curved and folded along midvein

Chokecherry

Prunus virginiana

BLACK CHOKECHERRY, CALIFORNIA CHOKECHERRY

Deciduous. Large shrub or small tree usually under 20' tall (max. 73') often forming thickets. Very closely-related to Black Cherry, but usually a smaller tree with sharper leaf teeth and blunt sepals on flowers.

can be a well-formed tree with several main upright branches, or a more irregular contorted tree without strong central axis

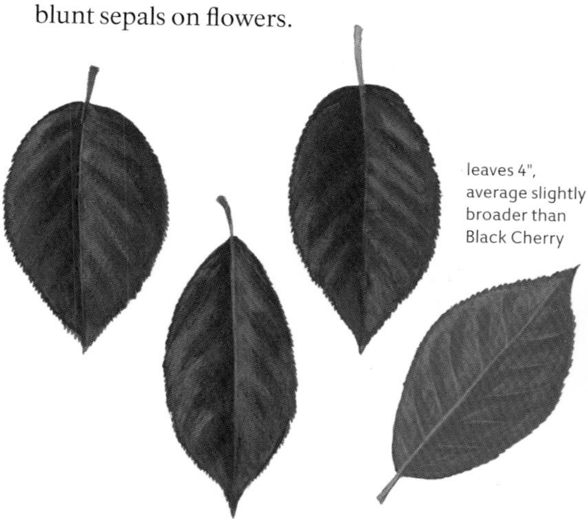

leaves 4", average slightly broader than Black Cherry

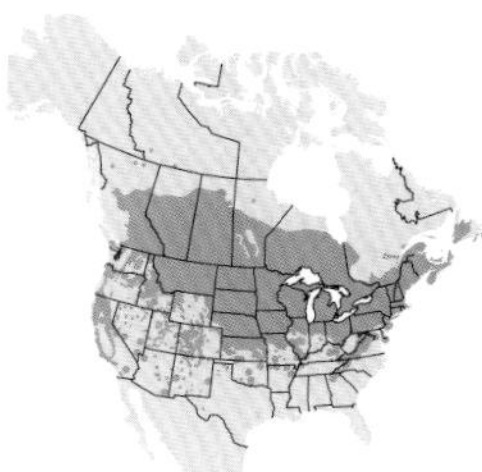

Common in open woods, edges, hedgerows, often near water. Often cultivated within native range, seldom elsewhere; (zones 2–6). Several cultivars include purple-leaved.

European Bird Cherry

Prunus padus

MAYDAY TREE, CLUSTER CHERRY, HAGBERRY

Deciduous. Small, low-branched tree usually under 30' tall (max. 54'). Closely-related to Black and Choke Cherry with similar flower and fruit. One of the first trees to leaf out in spring.

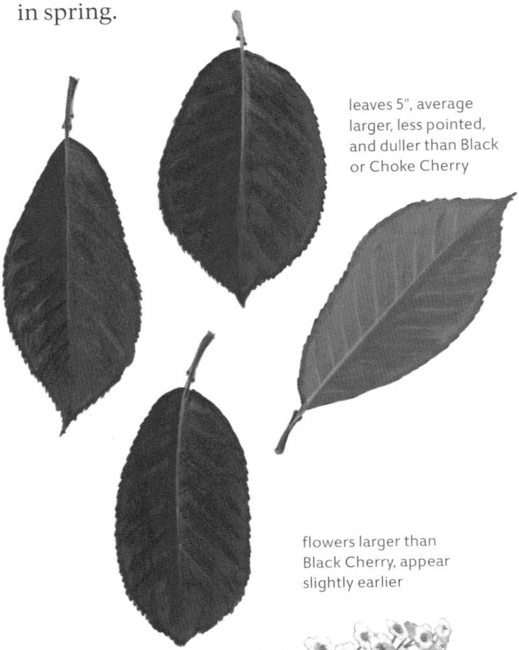

leaves 5", average larger, less pointed, and duller than Black or Choke Cherry

flowers larger than Black Cherry, appear slightly earlier

fruit small, ⅓", red to blackish

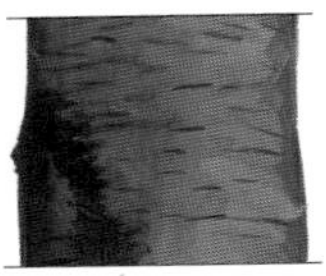

bark gray with dark lenticels

Native to Eurasia. Commonly cultivated and locally naturalized (zones 3–6). Many cultivars, including purple-leaved with purple flowers, are generally rare.

Manchurian Cherry

Prunus maackii

GOLDBARK CHERRY, MONGOLIAN GOLDBARK CHERRY, AMUR CHOKECHERRY

Deciduous. Rounded, dense-branching tree usually under 30' tall (max. 40'). Related to European Bird Cherry, but more cold-hardy and with golden-brown bark, smaller flowers and fruit. Native to Manchuria, Korea, Russia. Uncommon in cultivation (zones 3–6).

leaves 4", oval, similar to European Bird Cherry

Sour Cherry

Prunus cerasus

PIE CHERRY, MORELLO CHERRY

Deciduous. Shrub or small tree usually under 20' tall (max. 41'); similar to Mazzard Cherry but shorter with smaller leaves and fruit. Sometimes placed with dwarf cherries, in a separate group.

leaves glossy dark green, 3", smaller and narrower than Mazzard Cherry with fewer veins

fruit red, smaller than many Mazzard

Domestic origin in Europe, possibly from hybrids involving Mazzard Cherry. Commonly grown for fruit and widely naturalized in North America (zones 3–8).

Mazzard Cherry

Prunus avium

WILD SWEET CHERRY, GEAN

Deciduous. Small to medium tree, usually under 40' tall (max. 100'); upright and often conical with short, crooked trunk. The ancestor of cultivated domestic cherry.

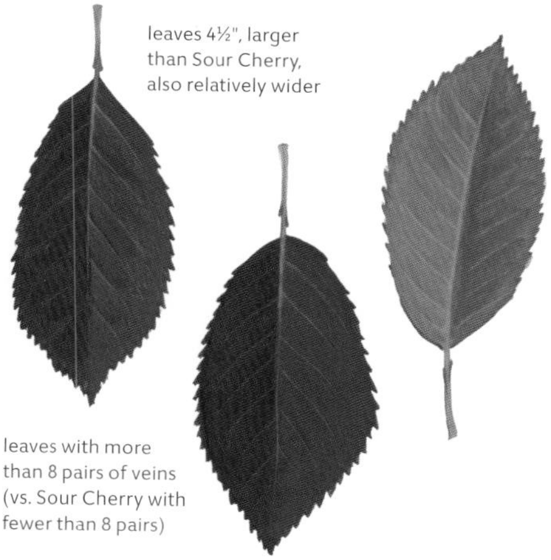

leaves 4½", larger than Sour Cherry, also relatively wider

leaves with more than 8 pairs of veins (vs. Sour Cherry with fewer than 8 pairs)

flowers 1", white, in early spring, just before or with leaves

fruit ripens early summer, red to black, 1" on cultivars selected for fruit, smaller on other trees

twigs reddish gray, buds burgundy

buds clustered on short spur twigs

Native to temperate Eurasia; common in cultivation and widely naturalized in North America (zones 3–8).

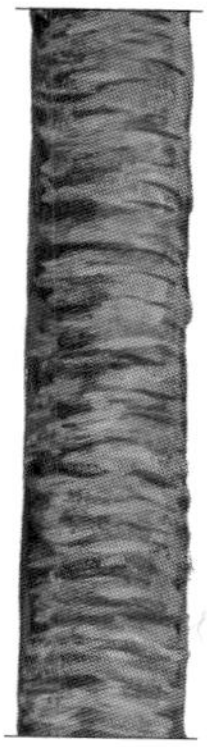

bark of young trunks smooth reddish to gray with obvious lenticels

mature trunks smooth gray-brown, sometimes peeling with obvious horizontal bands

Mahaleb Cherry

Prunus mahaleb

PERFUMED CHERRY, ROCK CHERRY, ST LUCIE CHERRY

Deciduous. Small broad tree usually under 25' tall (max. 44'), short, crooked trunk. Distinguished from other cherries by small, round leaves, often yellowish-green, by very fragrant flowers that open relatively late (Apr–May), and by small black fruit in loose clusters.

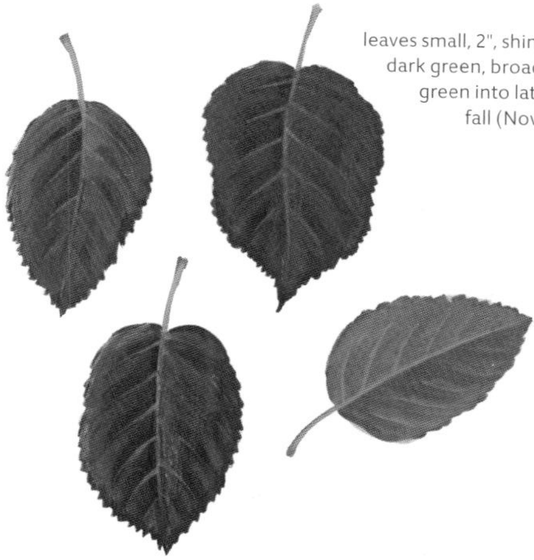

leaves small, 2", shiny dark green, broad, green into late fall (Nov)

Native to Europe, southwest and central Asia. Common in cultivation, and used as rootstock for cultivars of other cherries, widely naturalized (zones 5–8).

Bitter Cherry

Prunus emarginata

QUININE CHERRY, WILD CHERRY, FIRE CHERRY, WESTERN PIN CHERRY

Deciduous. Shrub or small slender tree usually under 30' tall (max. 103'), often forms thickets; closely related to Pin Cherry.

bark on young trunks shiny red, soon turning gray

older trunks brownish or grayish with horizontal orange lenticels

leaves 2", broader, more round-tipped than Pin Cherry with 1–4 dark glands at base

very short stalks

flowers small, ⅜", in dense clusters, appear when leaves half-grown

fruit ½", red to black

small green fruits visible early summer, in small clusters along twigs

twig often bright red with pale lenticels and short spur branches

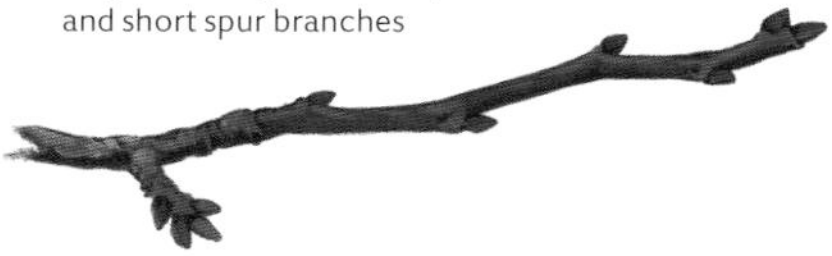

ripe fruit red, turning blackish in mid-summer

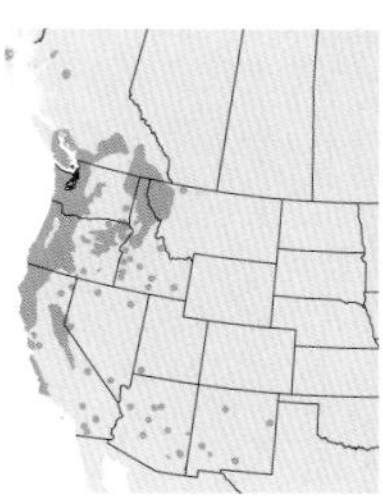

Common in open areas, clearings, disturbed areas; rarely cultivated (zones 6–9).

Pin Cherry

Prunus pensylvanica

FIRE CHERRY, WILD RED CHERRY, NORTHERN PIN CHERRY, PIGEON CHERRY, BIRD CHERRY

Deciduous. Small, upright shrub to small slender tree, usually under 25' tall (max. 85'), often in clumps. Closely-related to Bitter Cherry with distinctive dark red trunk and twigs.

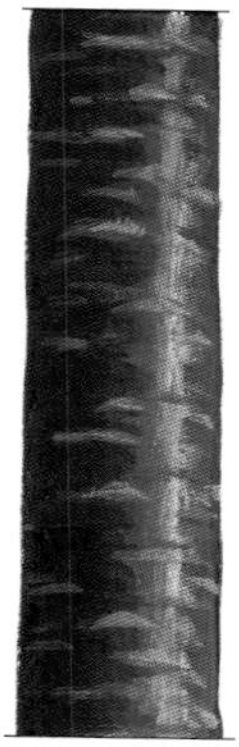

bark on young trees dark red-brown, smooth

older trunks with papery horizontal plates

leaves 3½", slender and long-pointed

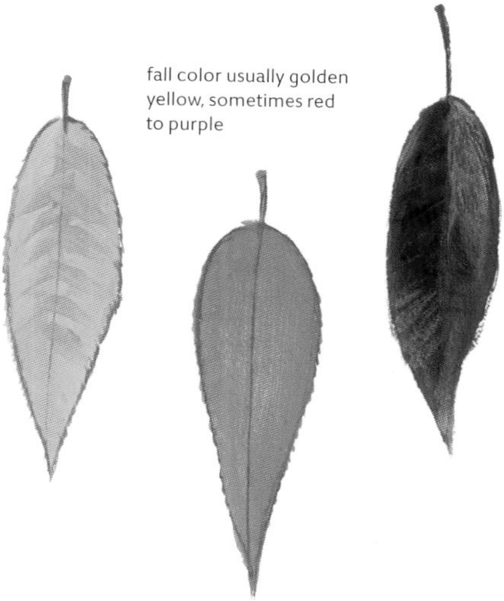

fall color usually golden yellow, sometimes red to purple

fruit bright red, ⅓", ripe Jul–Aug, acid taste

flowers small ½", white to creamy-white in small clusters like apple; Apr–late Jun with or after leaves

twigs glossy bright red, with orange lenticels, many spur branches

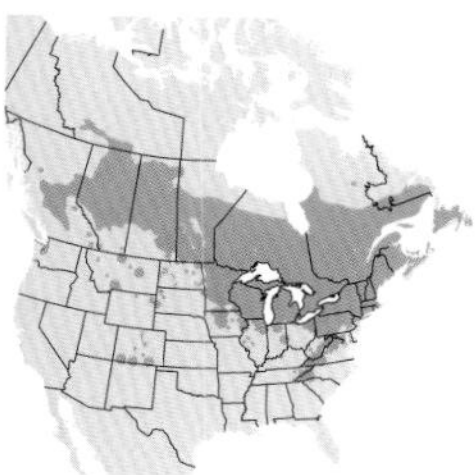

Common along roadsides and in clearings; a short-lived species colonizing recently-disturbed areas, seeds often spread by birds; rarely cultivated (zones 2–5).

This short-lived species rapidly colonizes disturbed ground, such as road sides, burned areas, and clear-cuts. When it ripens in late summer, the fruit is a favorite of birds.

Japanese Flowering Cherries

Prunus species

Deciduous. Small spreading trees often 20–30' tall, rarely over 45' tall. Many varieties have been developed for spectacular spring flowers; some have weeping habit.

bark varies with cultivar from shiny red with horizontal bands to gray and slightly scaly

leaves 4½", usually relatively large and broad, coarsely-toothed

most cultivars flower in early spring before or with leaves

flowers profuse, large, and showy, long-stalked in clusters along twigs, white to deep pink, some creamy-yellow

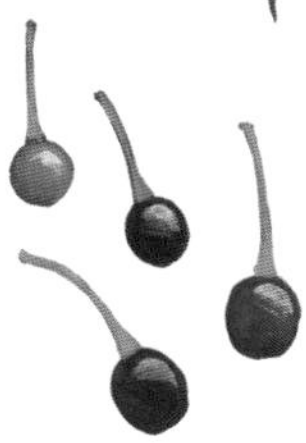

fruit ⅜", red or purple to black, shiny, in general the hybrids and cultivars produce little or no fruit, and flowers are scentless

buds orange-brown to reddish

twigs reddish to gray

some cultivars, both red and white forms, have double flowers with extra petals

Most cultivars of Japanese flowering cherry are derived from hybrids involving species from Japan and adjacent regions, only a few species are cultivated in typical form. As a group, the Japanese cherries are very commonly cultivated (zones 4–8, depending on cultivar). None are known to be naturalized.

Carolina Laurel Cherry

Prunus caroliniana

CAROLINA CHERRY, MOCK-ORANGE, WILD PEACH

Semi-evergreen. Large shrub or small tree often 25' tall (max. 55'); shiny dark foliage. Similar to Common Cherry-laurel, but smaller leaves and flower clusters.

young trunks smooth, with prominent horizontal lenticels

older trunks dark gray, becoming rough in thin squarish plates

leaves glossy, bright green, smooth, 4", sometimes with a few short, sharp teeth

flowers in small tight clusters, short racemes, fragrant, creamy white (Feb–Apr)
fruit often persists into flowering season

fruit small, ½", oblong, blackish, flesh thin, dry, inedible

twig and buds bright reddish

red twig with glossy dark green leaves held stiffly upright

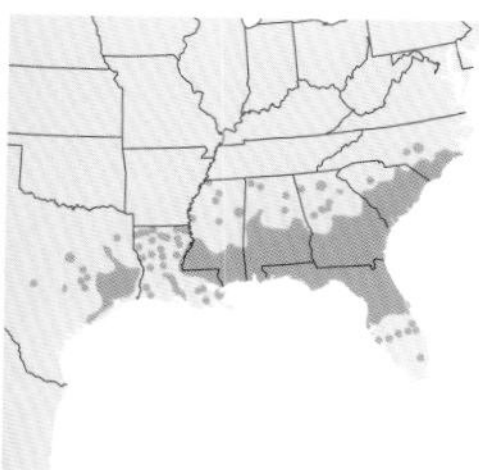

Common, often forming thickets. Common in cultivation, and cold-hardy well beyond its native range; planted widely for hedges in South (zones 7–10).

Hollyleaf Cherry

Prunus ilicifolia

EVERGREEN CHERRY, ISLAY

Evergreen. Shrub or small tree to 25' (max. 56'). Small and compact with dense crown of spiny leaves.

bark dark reddish-brown, fissured and checkered

leaves holly-like, 1½", coarsely-toothed, stiff, leathery, curled

Hollyleaf Cherry with its evergreen, spiny, curled leaves, is the most distinctive North American cherry. Closely related to Catalina Cherry, both are dense shrubs in chaparral on dry rocky slopes and tree-like in sheltered canyons.

fruit ½", red or black, ripe in late fall (Oct–Nov)

some fruit may persist until next season's flowers

flowers ⅓", white, in short spikes 2" long (Mar)

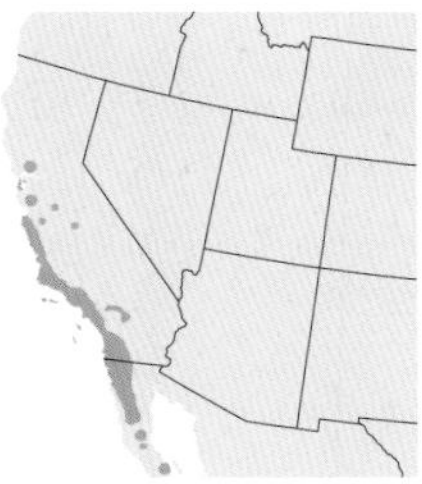

Locally common in coastal foothills. Commonly cultivated in California, rarely elsewhere (zones 8–10).

Catalina Cherry

Prunus lyonii

Evergreen. Low bushy tree with stout trunk usually under 30' (max. 75'). Very closely related to Hollyleaf Cherry with larger, untoothed leaves, and larger fruit.

leaves 4", larger than Holly leaf, only occasionally toothed

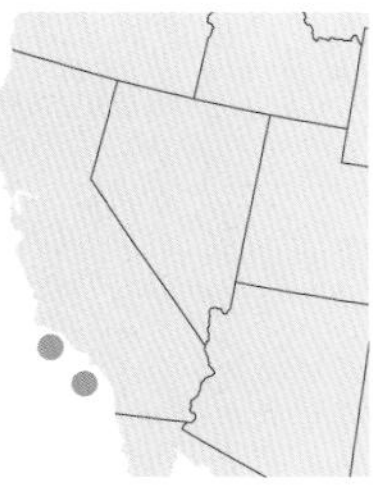

Native only on Channel Islands off southern California; commonly cultivated in California (zones 9–10) many cultivated plants are hybrids with Hollyleaf.

Common Cherry-laurel

Prunus laurocerasus

COMMON CHERRYLAUREL, CHERRY LAUREL, ENGLISH LAUREL

Evergreen. Spreading shrub or occasionally a low tree, usually under 20' tall (max. 44'). Popular hedge plant with many cultivars. Differs from native laurel cherries in elongated flower spike.

leaves 7", larger than Carolina Laurel Cherry

fruit a purplish-black cherry, ripe in fall, sought by birds

flowers white, in spikes 4½" long, (Mar–late May)

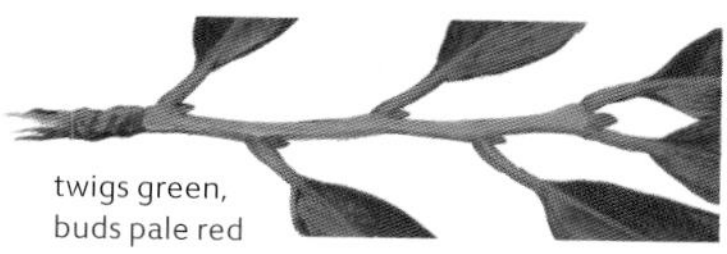

twigs green, buds pale red

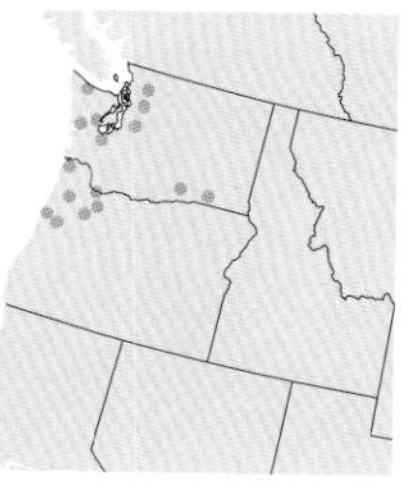

Native to southeastern Europe and adjacent Asia; very common in cultivation and locally naturalized.

Portugal Cherry-laurel

Prunus lusitanica

Evergreen. Usually a large shrub but can be tree-like in cultivation (max. 59'). Similar to Common Cherry-laurel but with shorter leaves, longer flower spikes.

leaves dark and glossy, 4" with purplish-red stalk

leafstalk longer than on Common Cherry-laurel

Both of the European cherry-laurels shown here have escaped from garden plantings and in a few areas are considered invasive. The plants are tolerant of shade, drought, and salt-spray. Once established, their dense evergreen foliage prevents native plants from growing in the soil beneath them. The best way to control the spread of invasive species in natural areas is with early detection and removal.

flowers in long slender clusters 7" long (May–Jun), very fragrant (Hawthorn-scented)

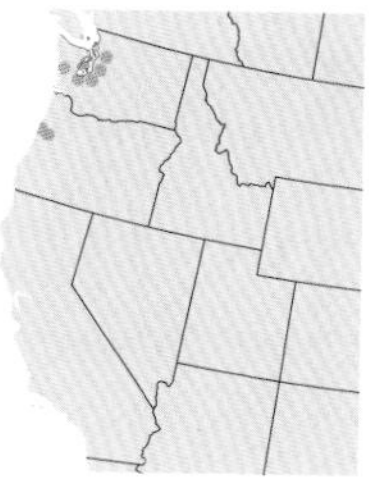

Native to southwestern Europe. Common in cultivation, naturalized in places on Pacific Coast (zones 7–9).

Rose Family: Hawthorns

While hawthorns are relatively easy to distinguish from other genera—they are most similar to crabapples—identifying species of hawthorns is extremely complex and is best left to specialists. Overzealous botanists in the early 1900s named over 1,100 species of hawthorns in North America alone! This was certainly too many, especially given that the differences between most are minute and variable. However, it is undeniable that hawthorns display a very diverse mosaic of variation, especially across the eastern United States.

Variation in hawthorns is attributed to the fact that they are species of clearings and edges, and must have spread quickly with the leveling of eastern forests by European immigrants, leading to rapid adaptation and hybridization. Since hawthorns can reproduce asexually, local mutations or hybrids could then be perpetuated unchanged in subsequent generations.

Most experts now agree that under 100 species of hawthorns is a more practical number, but others still argue that forcing all trees to fit such a limited number of names obscures real variations. This book shows the features that identify hawthorns as a genus with descriptions of a few prominent species, but it does not cover the identification of hawthorn species in any comprehensive way.

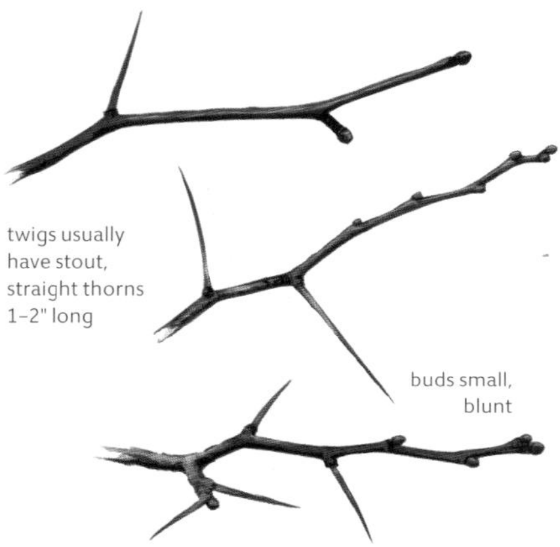
twigs usually have stout, straight thorns 1–2" long
buds small, blunt

Hawthorns

Crataegus species

MAYHAW, THORN-APPLE, HOG-APPLE

Deciduous. Shrub or small tree usually 15–25' tall (max. 52'); short trunk, branching low with dense crown of tangled twigs sometimes showing horizontal layers.

leaves extremely variable, toothed or lobed, 1–3"
some large and rounded with or without prominent lobes
some small, narrow-based, unlobed
fall color yellow-orange to red

Common in varied settings (combined range of all species shown here), often forming dense thickets in openings, field edges. A few species are commonly cultivated (zones 3–7).

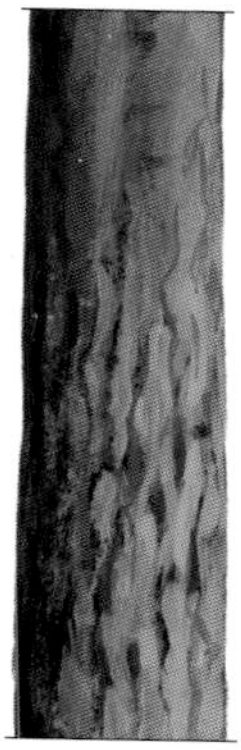

bark of young trunks gray, splitting into long thin scales

some species have bark in rough blocks

older trunks scaly and weakly ridged, often fluted or with obvious knots and burls

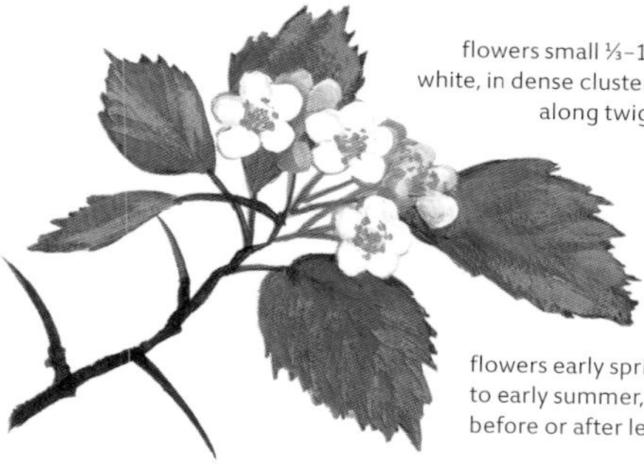

flowers small ⅓–1", white, in dense clusters along twigs

flowers early spring to early summer, before or after leaves

many species have larger toothed and lobed leaves, similar to crabapple

some species, e.g., Littlehip Hawthorn, have small, short-stalked leaves

fruit ⅓–⅔", small, apple-like, round to oval, red to yellow

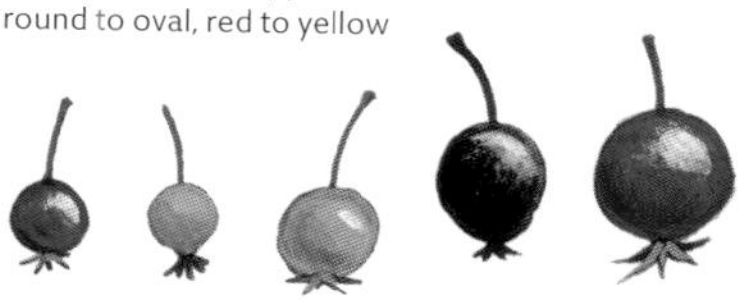

Hawthorns differ from apples in having many long thorns (and no leaves on thorns), later flowers, and fruits have one to several seeds without the apple's 5-parted seed chamber.

fruit hangs from long stems, like crabapple, more clustered

fruit ripe in summer or fall, sometimes persist into winter

usually spreading with broad low crown, tangled twigs

some trees relatively upright with narrow crown

May Hawthorn

Crataegus aestivalis

MAY HAW

Deciduous. Small tree often 30' tall. Flowers relatively few and large, open early, before leaves (Feb–Apr) and fruit ripens earlier than other hawthorns in early summer (Apr–Jul).

leaves 1 ½", usually unlobed
fruit ⅓", red

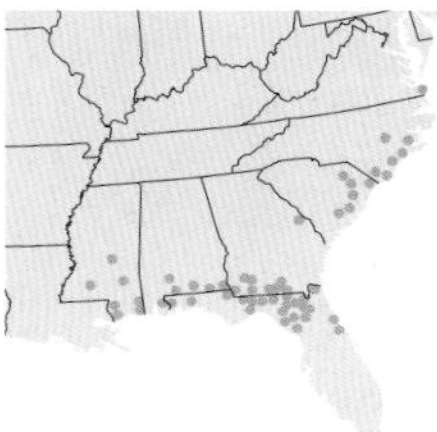

Common in swamps, pond margins, wet woods. Commonly cultivated. Several cultivars are grown for fruit production.

Parsley Hawthorn

Crataegus marshallii

PARSLEY HAW

Deciduous. Shrub or small tree occasionally 30' tall; easily recognized by deeply-cut leaves. Flowers white (Mar–May).

leaves small, 1 ½", parsley-like
fruit small, ¼", oval, red, ripe (Sep–Oct)

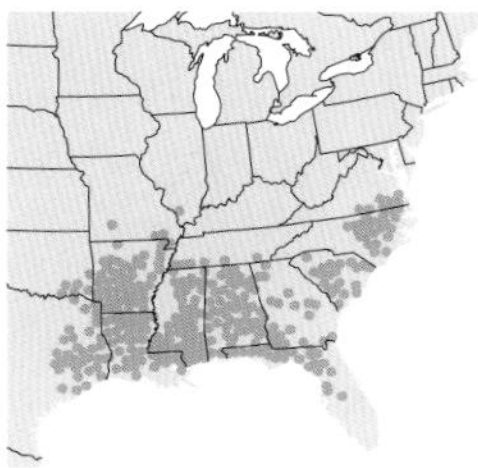

Common in moist floodplain forest. Very rare in cultivation.

Washington Hawthorn

Crataegus phaenopyrum

Deciduous. Small tree often 25' tall. Flowers relatively late (late May–early July, latest of all native hawthorns), and bad-smelling. Small red fruit ripens in winter.

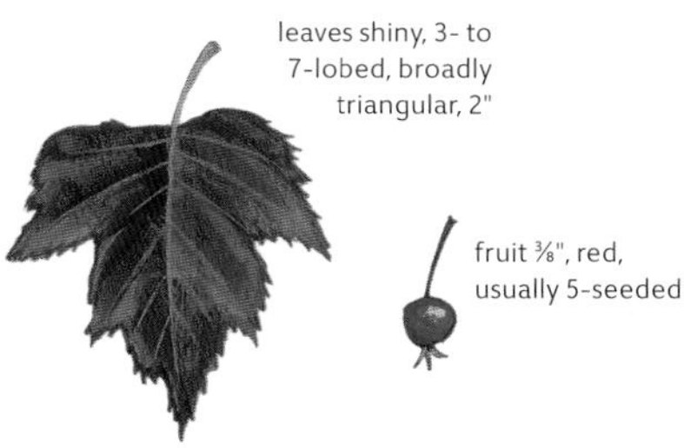
leaves shiny, 3- to 7-lobed, broadly triangular, 2"
fruit ⅜", red, usually 5-seeded

Common in well-drained or sometimes in moist soils. Very common in cultivation. Several cultivars include a thornless variety.

Cockspur Hawthorn

Crataegus crus-galli

Deciduous. Usually a small tree to 30' tall. Flowers ½" (May–Jun); can have very long thorns up to 8" and branched.

leaves dark and glossy
leaves 2 ½", thick, wedge-shaped
fruit ½", rather dull red, usually 2-seeded

Common in well-drained upland soils of open woods, old fields, fencerows. Commonly cultivated with several cultivars.

Black Hawthorn

Crataegus douglasii

Deciduous. Shrub or small tree to 25' tall; flowers ½" (May–Jun after leaves).

leaves weakly lobed or unlobed, usually broad and dark, 2"
fruit ½", large and dark, ripe Aug–Sep

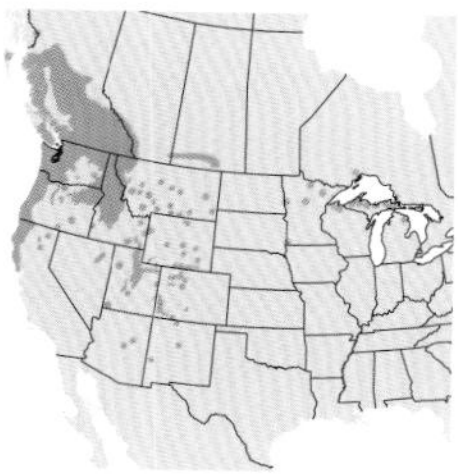

Common in moist soils in pastures, stream banks; the most widespread hawthorn in the west. Very rare in cultivation, mostly in its native range.

Yellow Hawthorn

Crataegus flava

SOUTHERN HAW

Deciduous. Shrub or small tree to about 20' tall. A variable species often split into multiple species. Flowers (Mar–May) and fruit relatively sparse.

leaves 2", usually oval with tapered base
fruit ½", usually red or yellow to dark orange- brown, ripe Aug–Oct, pear shaped or oval

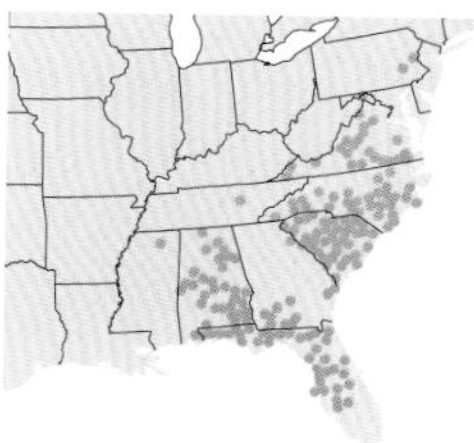

Common in dry well-drained rocky or sandy soils, pine-oak woods. Uncommonly cultivated.

Pear Hawthorn

Crataegus calpodendron

URN-SHAPED HAWTHORN

Deciduous. Shrub or small tree to 20' tall. Flowers late, relatively large, over ½" wide; fall leaf color often bright yellow and red.

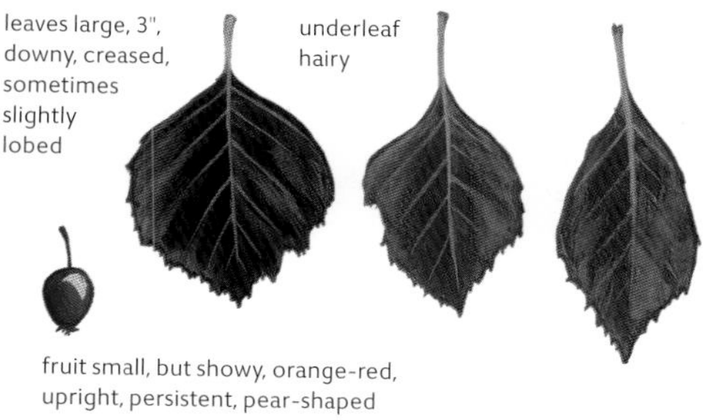
leaves large, 3", downy, creased, sometimes slightly lobed
underleaf hairy
fruit small, but showy, orange-red, upright, persistent, pear-shaped

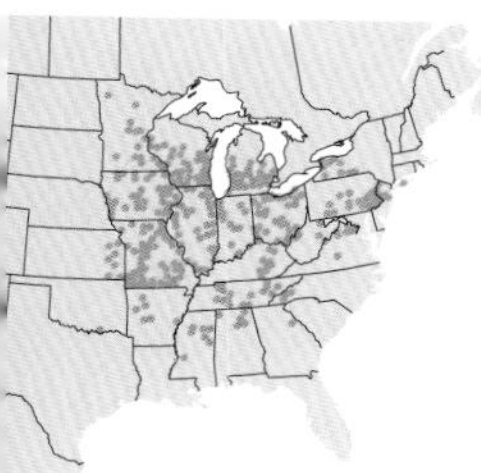

Common in moist, often rocky, soils along streams and in uplands. Not cultivated.

Littlehip Hawthorn

Crataegus spathulata

SPATULATE HAWTHORN

Deciduous. Shrub or small tree to about 25' tall. Flowers small, in dense clusters (Apr–May); small narrow leaves and small red fruit, reminiscent of holly.

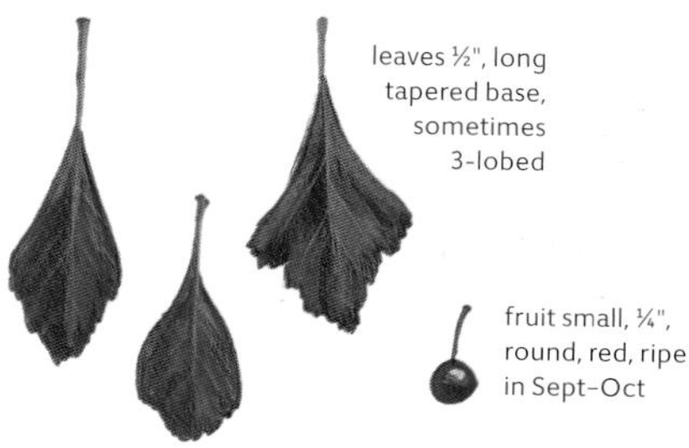
leaves ½", long tapered base, sometimes 3-lobed
fruit small, ¼", round, red, ripe in Sept–Oct

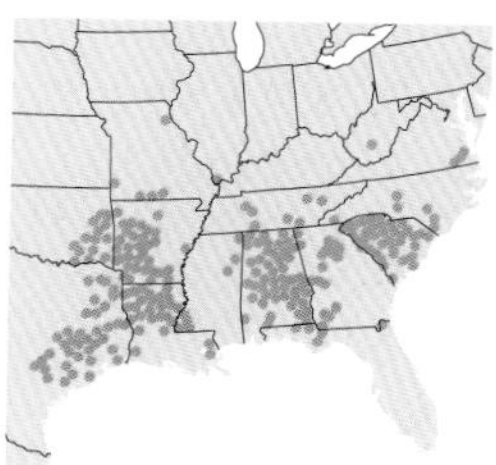

Common in moist or well-drained soils in open woods, edges, fencerows. Not cultivated.

Downy Hawthorn
Crataegus mollis

Deciduous. Small tree often 30' tall; flowers large, ¾" wide, in dense clusters (May–Jun).

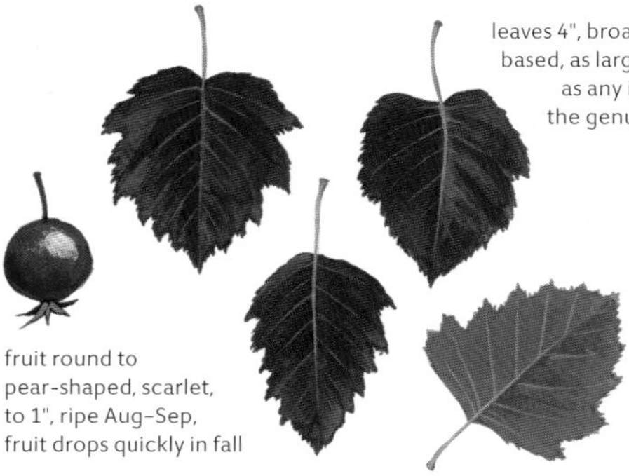
leaves 4", broad based, as large as any in the genus
fruit round to pear-shaped, scarlet, to 1", ripe Aug–Sep, fruit drops quickly in fall

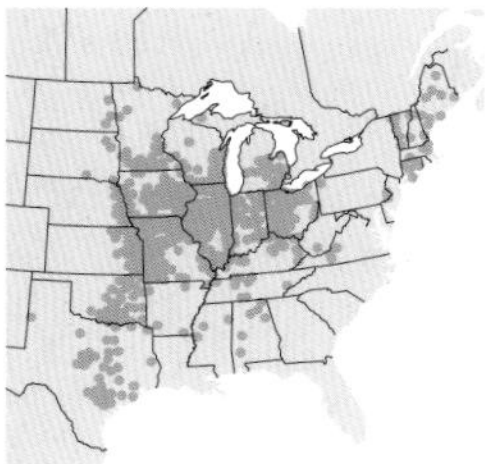

Common in rich soils of bottomlands and streambanks. Widely cultivated with several cultivars frequently planted.

Oneflower Hawthorn
Crataegus uniflora

DWARF HAW

Deciduous. Shrub or rarely a small tree to abou 15' tall; flowers usually solitary (Mar–May).

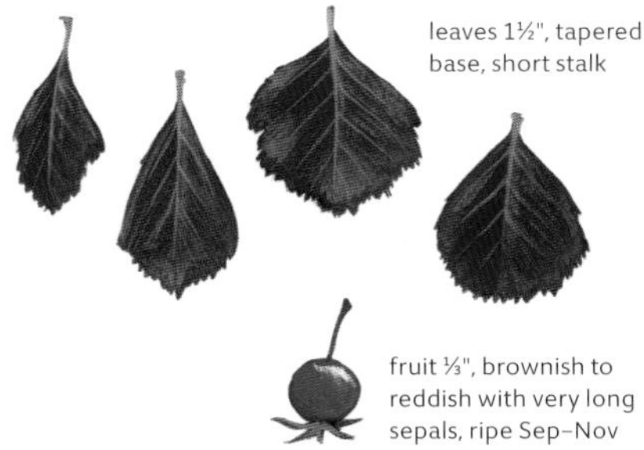
leaves 1½", tapered base, short stalk
fruit ⅓", brownish to reddish with very long sepals, ripe Sep–Nov

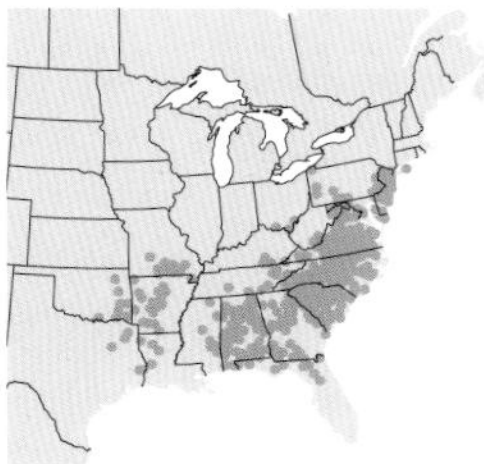

Common, mainly in dry sandy or rocky soils in open woods or edges. Not cultivated.

Beautiful Hawthorn
Crataegus pulcherrima

Deciduous. Shrub or occasionally a small tree to 25' tall; flowers large, about 1" wide, in small compact clusters (Jun).

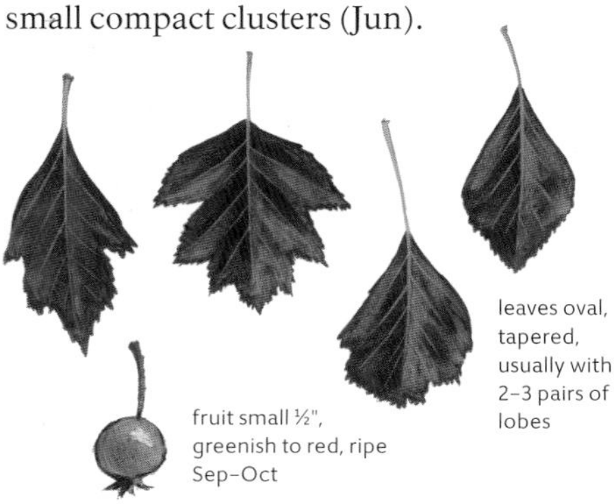
leaves oval, tapered, usually with 2–3 pairs of lobes
fruit small ½", greenish to red, ripe Sep–Oct

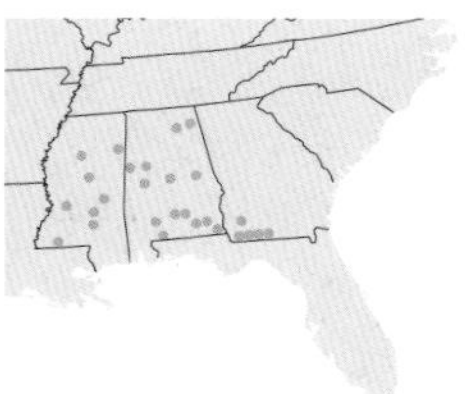

Locally common in damp soils of open woods, swamps and stream banks. Not cultivated.

Dotted Hawthorn
Crataegus punctata

Deciduous. Shrub or often a small tree to 30' tall; flowers ½" wide, in compact clusters.

leaves 3", narrowed near base, broadest above the middle, unlobed; conspicuous straight, closely parallel veins
fruit ¾" wide, dull orange-red to de red, dotted, lightl hairy, ripe Oct

Common and widesprea on rich well-drained soil of hillsides, open woods. Fairly common in cultiva tion. Popular cultivar is small and thornless with bright red fruit.

Fanleaf Hawthorn

Crataegus flabellata

Deciduous. Shrub or small tree to about 30' tall; a variable species often split into many species. Flowers large, ¾" wide (May–Jun).

leaves 2", rounded base, coarsely-toothed and often slightly lobed
fruit ½, red, ripe Sep–Oct

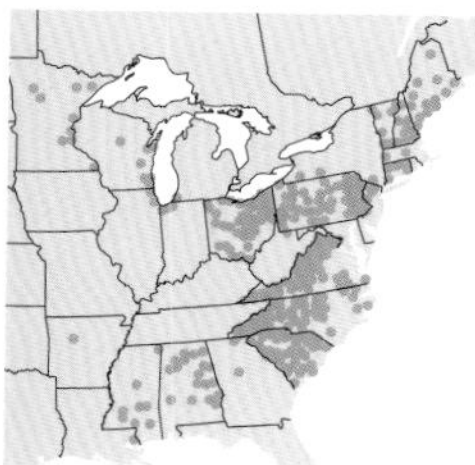

Common, mainly in well-drained rocky soils in open woods, old fields, along streams. Not cultivated.

Oneseed Hawthorn

Crataegus monogyna

COMMON HAWTHORN, ENGLISH HAWTHORN

Deciduous. Shrub or small tree to 20' tall, very similar to English Hawthorn but leaves usually paler below and more deeply lobed; fruit contains only one seed, flowers slightly later than English.

leaves 2", deeply lobed
fruit ½", purple to bright red, usually one-seeded

Native to Europe. The most common hawthorn in cultivation, widely naturalized in North America.

Green Hawthorn

Crataegus viridis

Deciduous. Shrub or small tree to 25' tall; flowers ½" in dense many-flowered clusters.

leaves 2½", usually oval, sometimes slightly lobed
fruit small ⅓", red

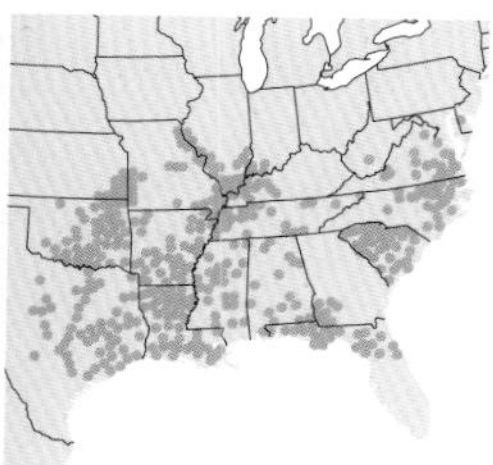

Common in moist open woods of lowlands, pond margins. Common in cultivation

English Hawthorn

Crataegus laevigata

ENGLISH MIDLAND HAWTHORN

Deciduous. Shrub or small tree to 20' tall, flowers ½" similar to native species but can be pink (all native hawthorns have white flowers). Closely related to Oneseed Hawthorn; variable.

leaves darker, less lobed, less hairy than Oneseed
fruit ½", red, 2–3 seeds

Native to Europe. Commonly cultivated, this species and Oneseed account for most cultivated hawthorns.

Rose Family: Apples

The apples (genus *Malus*) include about thirty species of small trees worldwide. Four are native to North America and are included here, along with several other commonly cultivated species. Apple trees have been cultivated for centuries for fruit, and the wood is used for specialty crafts and fuel. Many cultivated varieties are planted for ornament.

Hundreds of small-fruited crab apple cultivars have been developed for their flowers and/or fruit, and can be seen in yards, roadsides, and old homesites across North America. A few are said to be naturalized (along with Common Apple) and can hybridize with each other or with native species producing a range of intermediate plants in the wild.

Some of the apple species in cultivation are Chinese Apple (*Malus prunifolia*); Siberian Crab Apple (*M. baccata*); Japanese Crab Apple (*M. × floribunda*); Toringo Crab Apple (*M. sieboldii*); Hall Crab Apple (*M. halliana*); Tea Crab Apple (*M. hupehensis*); and Sargent Crab Apple (*M. sargentii*). Distinguishing among the many cultivated varieties and hybrids of these and other species is beyond the scope of this guide.

Cultivars vary mainly in details of flower and fruit. In general, exotic species differ from native eastern apples in having smaller and longer-stalked fruit, strongly oval in some varieties with color ranging from brilliant red to greenish yellow. Exotic species and cultivars also tend to flower earlier than natives, and many cultivars have been selected for double flowers with extra or darker pink or red petals, unlike less showy native species. Cultivated apples generally grow well in zones 4–7.

leaves of exotic crab apples are generally simple ovals without lobes; a few cultivars purple-leaved with red flowers.

flowers vary mainly in color, from nearly white to nearly red; many cultivars have been selected for flower display, so flowers are often profuse and large.

some cultivars selected for fruit, with abundant bright red fruit on long red stalks that persists into winter

crab apple fruit varies from ¼" to ¾" in diameter, in shape from narrow oval to round to wide oval, and in color from yellow to dark red

The widespread planting of ornamental fruit trees in the suburbs over the last few decades has created a major source of food for fruit-eating birds. This is almost certainly the reason that American Robins no longer move south from New England in the winter, and can now be seen there in large roving flocks all winter long. The winter distribution of several other fruit-eating birds has also changed dramatically over the years.

Common Apple

Malus pumila

ORCHARD APPLE, DOMESTIC APPLE, MALUS '× DOMESTICA'

Deciduous. Small to medium tree usually under 30' tall (max. 70') but wide-spreading with short, stout trunk. Hard wood is used for crafts and firewood.

Common Apple is presumably a domestic hybrid originating centuries ago in Eurasia, perhaps from European Wild Apple (*Malus sylvestris*) with thousands of cultivars showing a tremendous variety of fruit, leaf, and flower. All well-known edible apples are varieties of Common Apple, while other cultivars have small fruit, like crab apples. They are now planted and naturalized across North America in many cultivated varieties, some of which hybridize with native apples in the wild. All such hybrids tend to resemble the native species, the only barrier to hybridization seems to be flowering time. The European Wild Apple (*M. sylvestris*) with small sour fruit, is rarely cultivated here.

Johnny "Appleseed" Chapman (1774–1845) is known for traveling, mostly on foot, and promoting the establishment of apple orchards from Pennsylvania to Illinois. He distributed seeds that he collected at cider presses. While his efforts were certainly noteworthy, the apple tree was already popular and widely planted long before his lifetime.

leaves 3", finely and regularly-toothed, oval

underleaf and leafstalk whitish-hairy

fruit variable from small and greenish in wild forms to 5" or more; familiar red or green in cultivars

flowers large, about 1¼" across, pink to white; appear in spring with leaves

Apple or crab apple? The conventional rule of thumb is that fruit under 2" indicates a crab apple, fruit larger than 2" an apple. But many trees overlap, and there is simply no botanical distinction between the two.

tree generally low and spreading, with stout twisted trunk and tangled branches

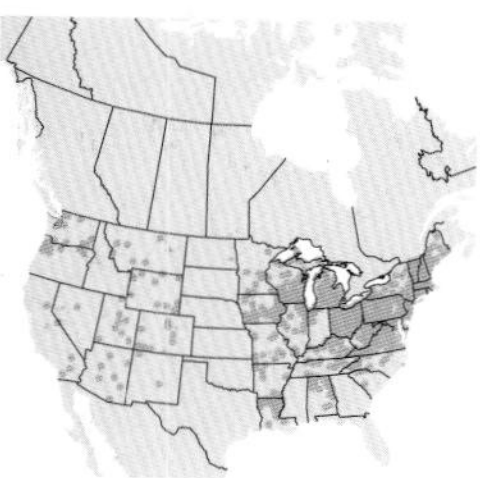

Very commonly cultivated and naturalized in old fields, hedgerows, old homesites (zones 4–7).

Prairie Crab Apple

Malus ioensis

TEXAS CRABAPPLE, WILD CRAB

Deciduous. Shrub or small tree usually under 25' (max. 46'); often thicket-forming. Differs from other native eastern apples in having hairy underleaf (like Common Apple).

bark of young trunk soon developing long gray-brown scales
bark of mature trunk tinged reddish, relatively thin with long narrow scaly strips

leaves 3", average narrower and less-lobed than Sweet Crab Apple
underleaf usually hairy

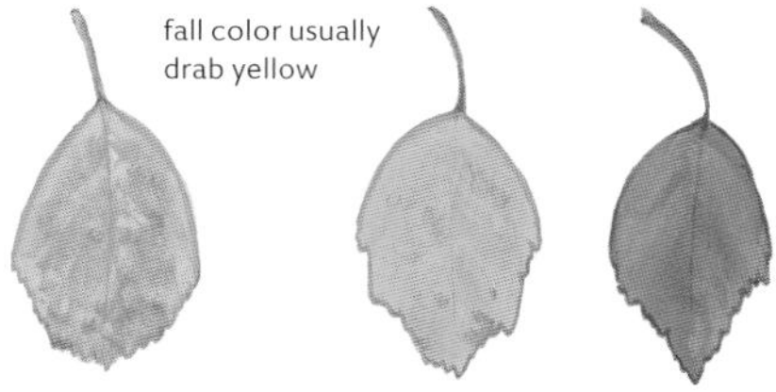
fall color usually drab yellow

fruit 1", pale yellow-green

pink buds open to rosy-white flowers, large, 1" across

Crab apples can have thorns at end of spur twigs, like plums or hawthorns. Thorns appear most often on Sweet Crab Apple and less often on other species.

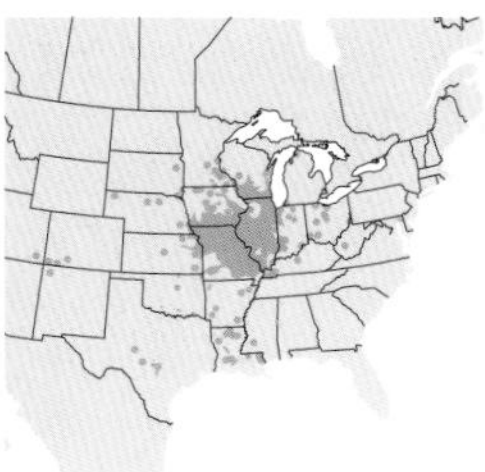

Uncommon in hedgerows, field edges, and open woods, most often in moist settings, Uncommon in cultivation (zones 4–7), including a double-flowered variety.

Southern Crab Apple

Malus angustifolia

Deciduous (semi-evergreen in mild areas). Nearly identical to Sweet Crab Apple and sometimes considered a subspecies. Leaves usually less sharply-toothed, narrower with more wedge-shaped leaf bases; little or no range overlap.

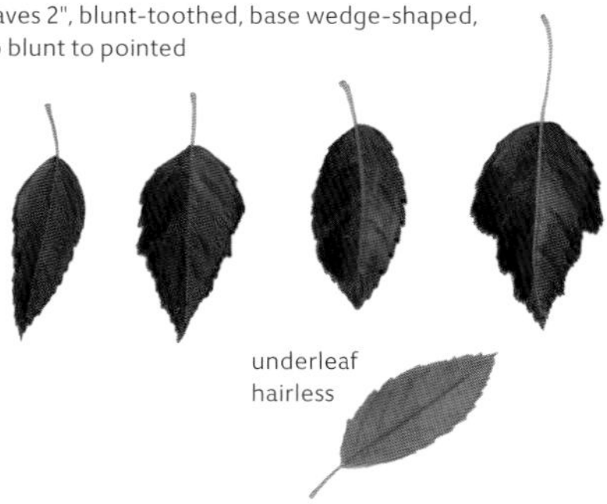
leaves 2", blunt-toothed, base wedge-shaped, tip blunt to pointed
underleaf hairless

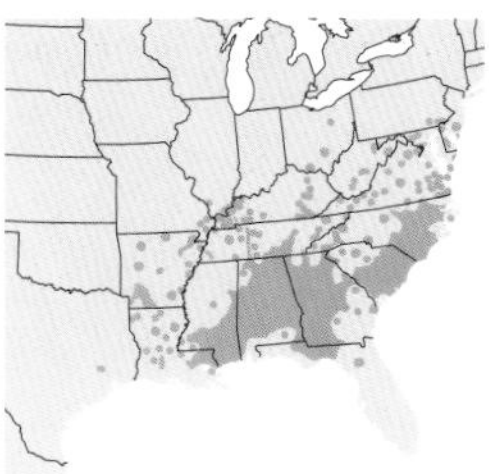

Uncommon in hedgerows, field edges, and open woods, most often in moist settings; occasionally cultivated (zones 4–7).

Sweet Crab Apple

Malus coronaria

GARLAND-TREE, BILTMORE CRAB APPLE, ALLEGHENY CRAB

Deciduous. Shrub or small tree usually under 25' tall (max. 57'); often forms thickets in moist soil. Very similar to Southern Crab Apple with little range overlap. Biltmore Crab Apple (*Malus glabrata*) is now considered part of this species.

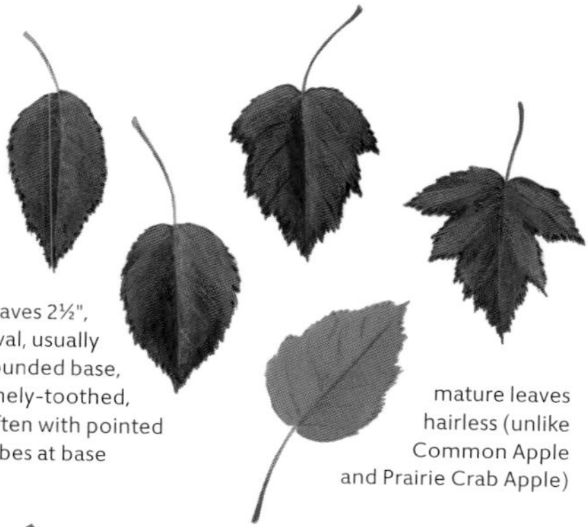
leaves 2½", oval, usually rounded base, finely-toothed, often with pointed lobes at base
mature leaves hairless (unlike Common Apple and Prairie Crab Apple)

fruit pale yellow-green, 1", long-stalked, very sour

pink buds open to pale pink or white flowers 1½" across, appear in spring with leaves (Apr–Jun)

slow-growing twigs stout with spur twigs
twigs grayish, slender

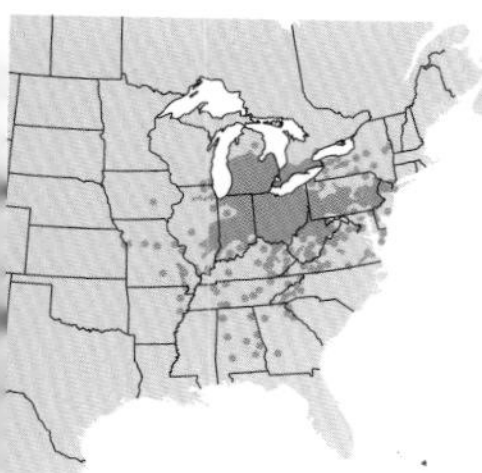

Uncommon in hedgerows, field edges, and open woods, most often in moist settings; commonly cultivated (zones 4–7), some cultivars with pink double flowers.

Oregon Crab Apple

Malus fusca

M. DIVERSIFIOLIA, PACIFIC CRAB APPLE, WESTERN CRAB APPLE

Deciduous. Shrub or small tree usually under 30' (max. 79'), often multi-trunked or thicket-forming. The only native apple with oval fruit; related to Siberian Crab Apple.

leaves 2½", oval or occasionally 3-lobed, base wedge-shaped or rounded

fruit small, ½", oval, yellow-brown to red

flowers small, white, ¾" wide, pale yellow-white centers; in spring with or after leaves

twigs slender, hairy becoming shiny red

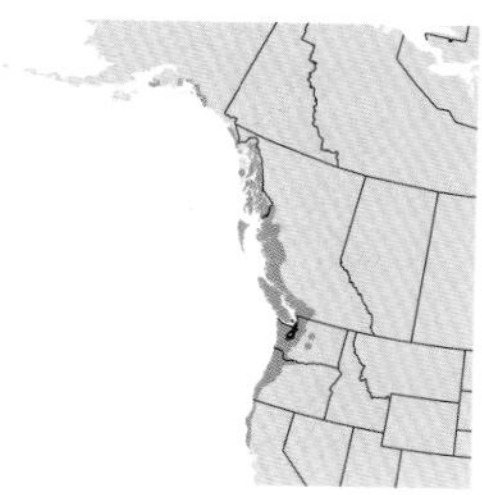

Common, mainly in moist soil along streams and lower slopes. Very rarely cultivated.

Rose Family: Pears

Pears (genus *Pyrus*) include about thirty species of small trees native to Eurasia. Two species are commonly cultivated in North America and are covered here.

Although closely related to apples, pears have granular "grit cells" in their fruit. Common Pear and Callery Pear are closely-related to apples and mountain-ashes. In general, pear trees have small, clustered whitish flowers and inconspicuous greenish fruit, lacking both the spectacular flower displays and decorative fruit of many cultivated trees in related genera.

Pears have less showy flowers than related species like cherries, and are cultivated mainly for their edible fruit or for their dense green summer foliage.

Cultivars of Callery Pear, including 'Bradford' Pear and others, have become very popular street trees in towns and cities for their compact oval shape with dense, dark green foliage, attractive displays of white flower clusters in early spring, and often red to purple fall color. They are very tolerant of pollution and relatively disease-free.

usually more upright habit than apples or plums with very "twiggy" look

Common Pear

Pyrus communis

EUROPEAN PEAR, DOMESTIC PEAR

Deciduous. Small to medium tree typically 30–40' tall (max. 75'); with characteristic pear-shaped fruit. Fall color usually drab yellowish, except some cultivars are orange, red, or purple. Flowers less showy than Callery Pear. Actual origin unknown, presumably a centuries-old domestic hybrid from Europe or western Asia.

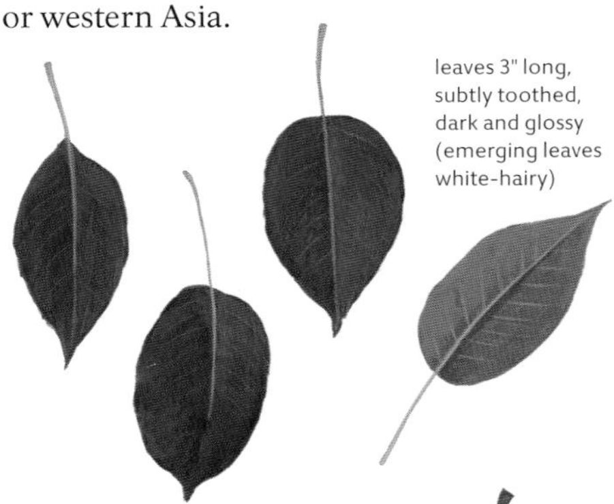
leaves 3" long, subtly toothed, dark and glossy (emerging leaves white-hairy)

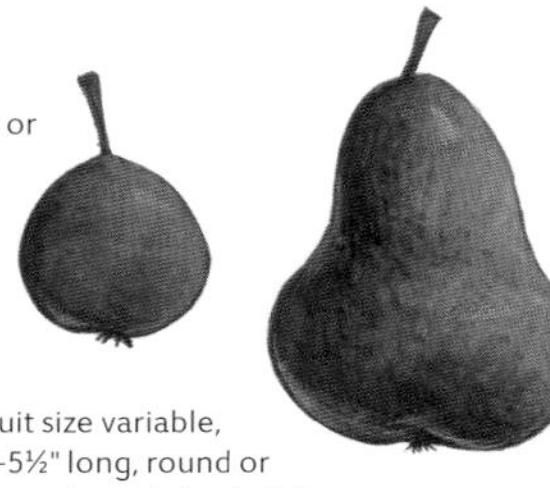
fruit green or yellowish-brown to red or purple
fruit size variable, 2–5½" long, round or pear-shaped; ripe in fall and not persistent

spur branches common, often with small thorns

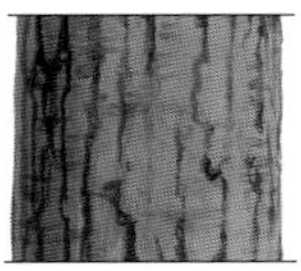
bark smooth, developing narrow cracks with age

Commonly cultivated with hundreds of varied cultivars, grown mainly for fruit and locally naturalized, hedgerows, old fields, and clearings (zones 4–9).

Callery Pear

Pyrus calleryana

FLOWERING PEAR, BRADFORD PEAR

Deciduous. Small to medium tree usually 30' tall (max. 59'); neatly conical to rounded habit, short trunk. Large whitish winter buds with showy white flowers in early spring, and dense dark summer foliage make this a distinctive tree year-round.

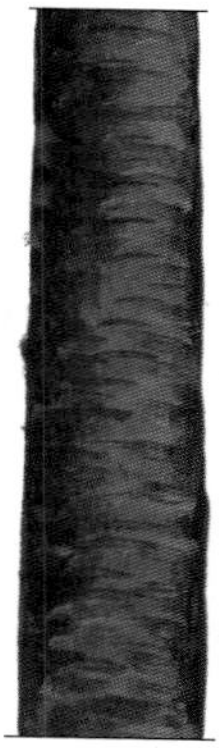

bark on young trees smooth dark gray

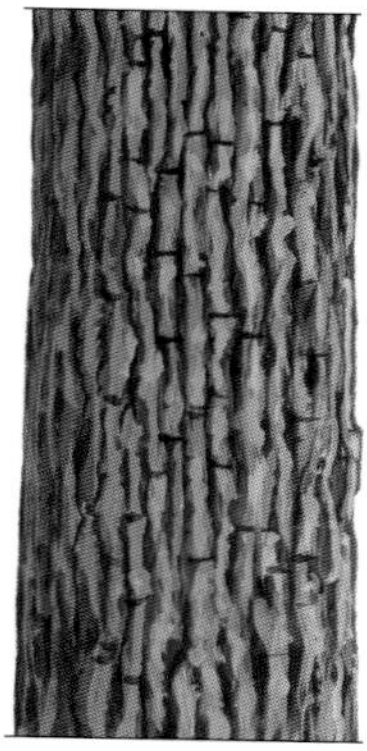

older trunks narrowly and neatly furrowed

leaves small, 2½", rounded, subtly toothed, margins undulating

fall color dark green turning wine red, on some trees brilliant orange-red; relatively late (Oct–Dec)

flowers small, white with dark anthers, in small round clusters

usually dark, glossy and attractive all summer

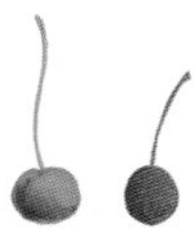

fruit small, ½", round, dull green

fruit on long stiff stalks

small upright tree with dense dark foliage

branches can be somewhat thorny, most cultivars thornless

buds large, whitish-hairy, distinctive

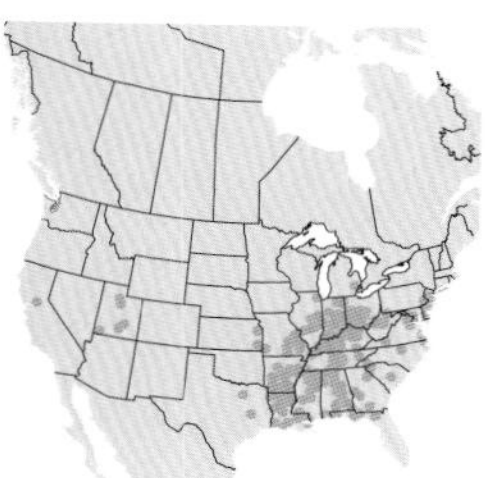

Native to eastern Asia. Very commonly cultivated in yards, streets, and malls, naturalized (zones 5–8).

Rose Family: Serviceberries

Serviceberries are easily recognized by rounded dull green leaves, blueberry-like fruit, slender petals on white flowers early in spring, smooth pale gray bark with darker striations, and long-pointed buds.

Serviceberries can reproduce asexually through apomixis and polyploidy. The resulting microspecies—self-perpetuating local lineages—can also hybridize with each other, and produce a bewildering mosaic of variations. Opinions of the number of serviceberry species in North America have ranged from as many as twenty-five to as few as three. The most authoritative recent review names sixteen species, most of which are known or suspected to hybridize where their range overlaps, and only six or seven of which are sometimes tree-like. Differences between species are slight, mainly involving flowers and emerging leaves, and field identification is extremely difficult for the non-specialist.

usually a small crooked or leaning tree with relatively straight slender twigs

The profuse flowers of serviceberries in very early spring before their leaves, is striking against a still-gray forest.

Eastern Serviceberry

Amelanchier canadensis

THICKET SERVICEBERRY

Usually a shrub growing in alder-like clumps, rarely tree-like to 25'. Closely-related to Downy and Smooth Serviceberry; distinguished by erect flower and fruit clusters (and by minute details of flowers).

leaves 3½" like Smooth Seviceberry

flowers white, in upright clusters

fruit like Smooth but in upright clusters

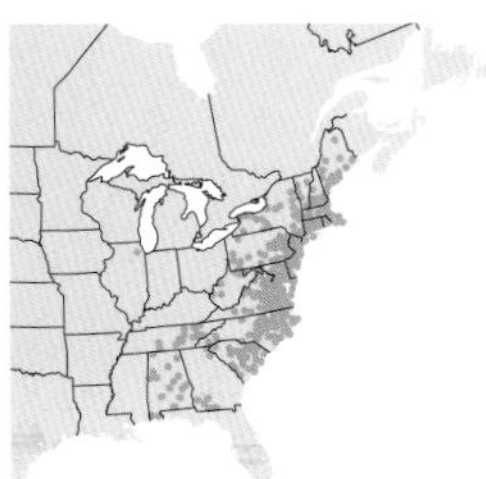

Common in wooded swamps and other wetland habitats. Not cultivated

Smooth Serviceberry

Amelanchier laevis

SHADBLOW SERVICEBERRY, ALLEGHENY SERVICEBERRY

Deciduous. Graceful large shrub or small tree often 30' tall (max. 60'); usually multi-trunked with curving trunks. Very similar to Downy and sometimes considered the same species.

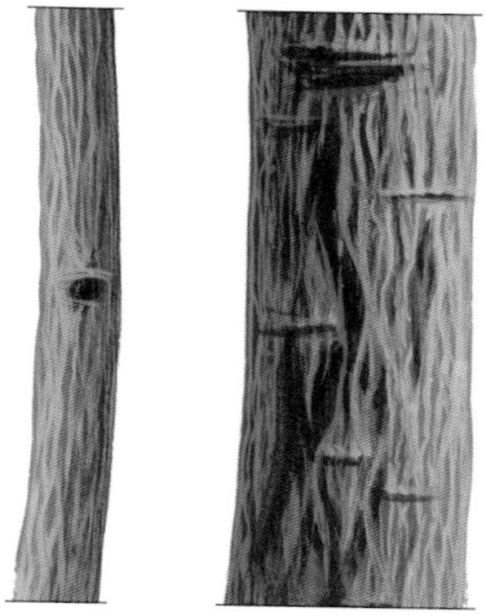
bark on young and old trunks smooth pale gray, with striations

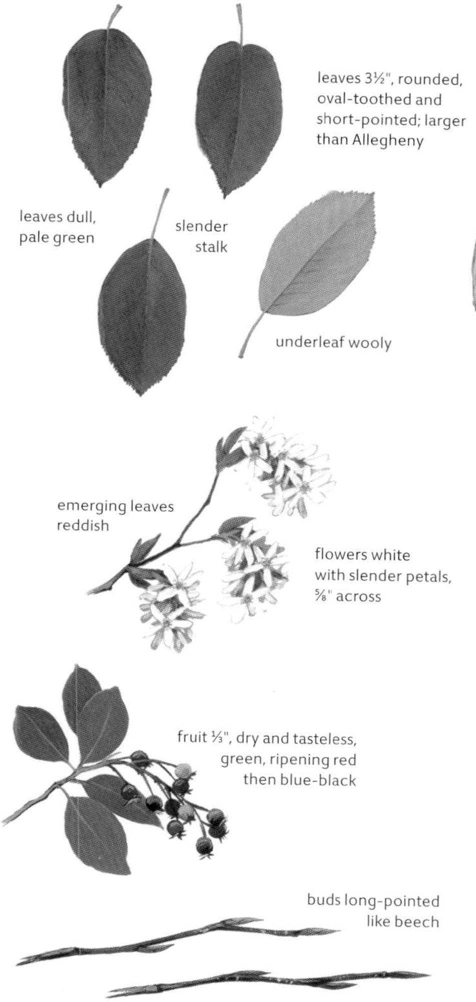
leaves 3½", rounded, oval-toothed and short-pointed; larger than Allegheny
leaves dull, pale green
slender stalk
underleaf wooly
emerging leaves reddish
flowers white with slender petals, ⅝" across
fruit ⅓", dry and tasteless, green, ripening red then blue-black
buds long-pointed like beech

fall color from yellow to red or purple
oval, flat green leaves often nearly 2-ranked

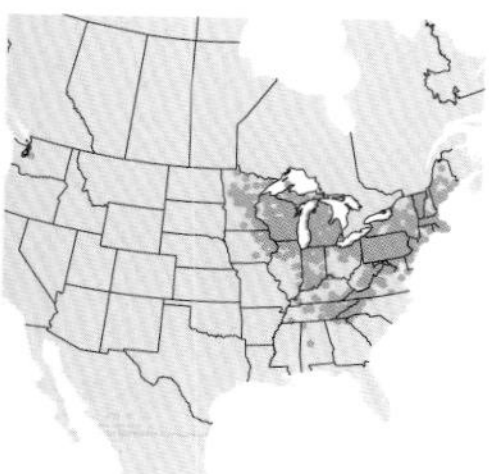

Common in dry to moist deciduous or mixed woods; ridges, streamsides and swamp margins. Commonly cultivated in numerous cultivars (zones 3–8).

Downy Serviceberry

Amelanchier arborea

JUNEBERRY, SARVIS, SHADBUSH, SHADBLOW

Deciduous. Shrub or small tree often 30' tall (max. 48'). Distinguished from Smooth only by green (not reddish) emerging leaves, leaves slightly more round-tipped, flowers average a week earlier, and flowers can be pinkish in southern parts of range. Fruit relatively dry and tasteless.

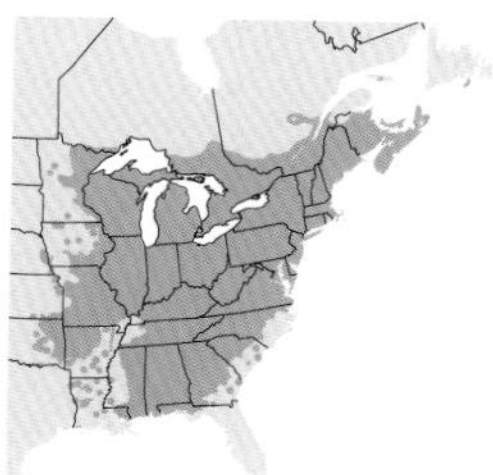

Common in rich moist or dry soils in understory of forest. Uncommonly cultivated (zones 4–9).

Red-twigged Serviceberry

Amelanchier sanguinea

ROUNDLEAF JUNEBERRY, SHORE SHADBUSH, HURON SERVICEBERRY

Deciduous. Shrub or occasionally a small tree to 25'. Similar to Downy, except for rounded leaves with fewer, coarser, teeth. Flowers a few days later than Smooth, up to two weeks later than Downy; flower clusters drooping.

leaves 2", fewer and coarser teeth than Smooth, larger than Western

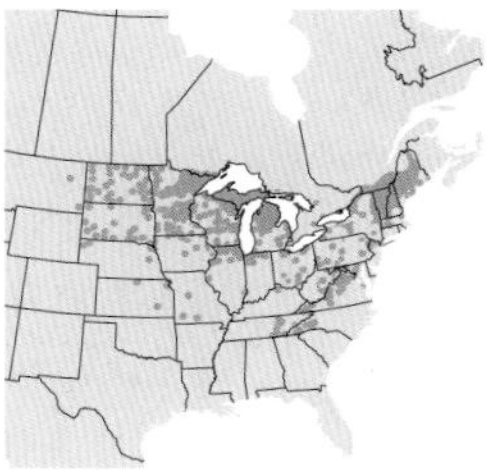

Uncommon on rocky slopes, wetland margins. Not cultivated

Utah Serviceberry

Amelanchier utahensis

Deciduous. Virtually always shrubby under 15' tall. Very similar to Western but with, on average, even smaller leaves, finely hairy leaves and twigs, and short flower petals.

leaf small, round, 1"

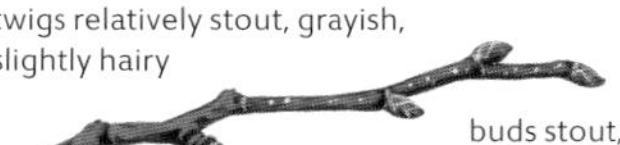
twigs relatively stout, grayish, slightly hairy
buds stout, downy grayish

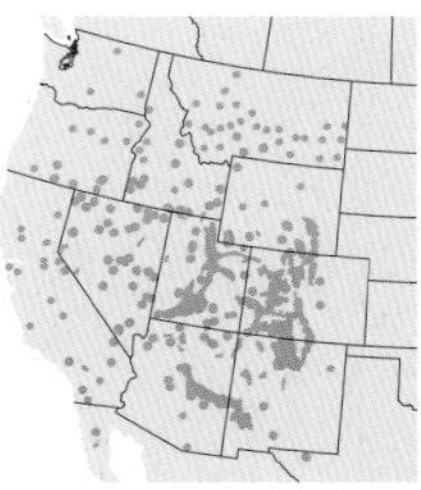

Common and widespread in a variety of habitats from streambanks to rocky slopes. Not cultivated.

Western Serviceberry

Amelanchier alnifolia

PACIFIC SERVICEBERRY, SASKATOON, MANY-FLOWERED SHADBUSH

Deciduous. Shrubby, thicket-forming to 15' tall; occasionally tree-like only in the Pacific Northwest (max. 42'). This species and Utah Serviceberry similar in leaf shape, both have stouter twigs and buds than eastern species.

leaf small, round 2", with coarse teeth

flower clusters erect, leaves fairly well-developed

twigs and buds similar to Utah, but average less stout and less hairy

In general, the variations in serviceberries can be separated into a broad western group—smaller leaves, more coarsely-toothed at tips, veins continuing to leaf edge, and stouter buds—and an eastern group with opposite characteristics.

Common in a variety of habitats from streambanks to rocky or grassy slopes. Uncommon in cultivation but several cultivars grown commercially for fruit (zones 4–5)

Rose Family: Mountain-ashes

The mountain-ashes (genus *Sorbus*) are not related to the true ashes (page 375), although they share superficially similar compound leaves. The genus includes about 150 species of shrubs and small trees worldwide. Seven species are native to North America, all very similar in appearance, but only four are sometimes tree-like. These four, along with two additional cultivated species and a cultivated hybrid, are covered here.

Like hawthorns and serviceberries, the mountain-ashes hybridize freely and are capable of reproducing asexually, leading to very complex patterns of local variation.

Too small to be useful for lumber, these species are valued as ornamental shrubs and trees, and the berries are a favorite winter food of many birds and animals.

Besides American Mountain-ash, three native species are occasionally tree-like:

Showy Mountain-ash (*Sorbus decora*) is found mainly in eastern Canada from Newfoundland to Ontario. It differs from American Mountain-ash in having slightly broader leaflets and slightly larger flowers and fruit.

Two other species in the West can be tree-like to about 20'; range does not overlap with American. Sitka Mountain-ash (*Sorbus sitchensis*) is found along the Pacific Coast from Alaska to California. It is distinguished from other mountain-ashes by its relatively few blunt-tipped leaflets (only 7–11 on each leaf) with no teeth at the base of the leaflet, rusty hair on twigs and buds, and large fruit up to ½".

Greene Mountain-ash (*Sorbus scopulina*) is found mainly in the western mountains from Alaska to New Mexico. It is very similar to American but has slightly larger flowers and fruit.

Alder Whitebeam

Sorbus alnifolia

KOREAN MOUNTAIN ASH, DENSEHEAD MOUNTAIN ASH, ATSUKI PEAR

Deciduous. Small tree usually under 35' tall (max. 70'); pyramidal or oval shape. One of about 30 Eurasian species with simple leaves like alder, but flowers and fruit like mountain-ash. Native to China to Japan. Commonly cultivated (zones 4–7). Some related species with white-hairy underleaf are less commonly cultivated.

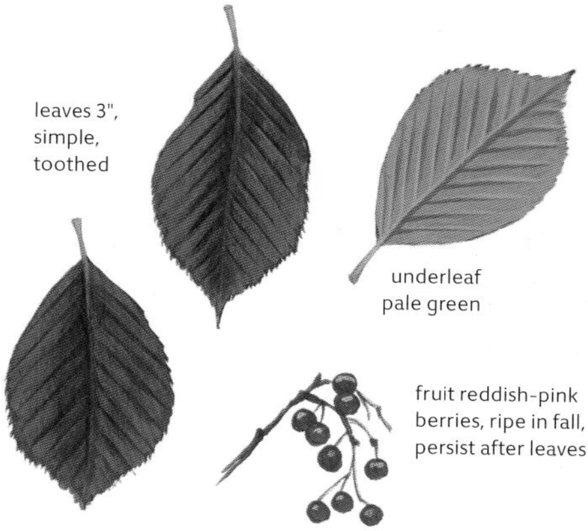
leaves 3", simple, toothed
underleaf pale green
fruit reddish-pink berries, ripe in fall, persist after leaves

'Oakleaf' Mountain-ash

Sorbus '× thuringiaca'

'BASTARD SERVICE TREE'

Deciduous. Small tree usually under 30' tall (max. 56'). Apparently a hybrid of European Mountain-Ash and Whitebeam, but other cultivated hybrids are similar. Of garden origin, commonly cultivated, especially in upright form (zones 4–5).

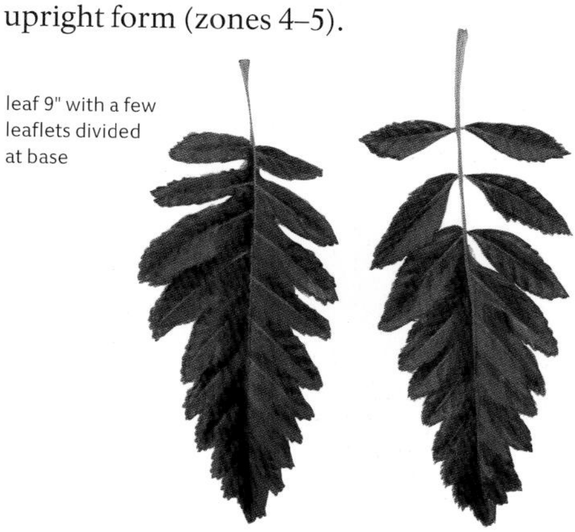
leaf 9" with a few leaflets divided at base

American Mountain-ash

Sorbus americana

MOUNTAIN-ASH, ROUNDWOOD

Deciduous. Round-topped, low tree usually under 30' tall (max. 71'); slender branches forming rather sparse, narrow crown. Largest in northern range, smaller and with narrower leaflets and smaller fruit in Appalachians.

bark on young trunks gray with prominent horizontal lenticels

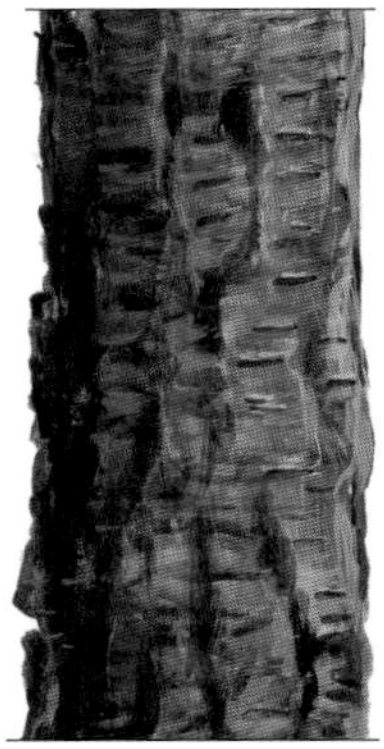

older trunks breaking into scaly ridges

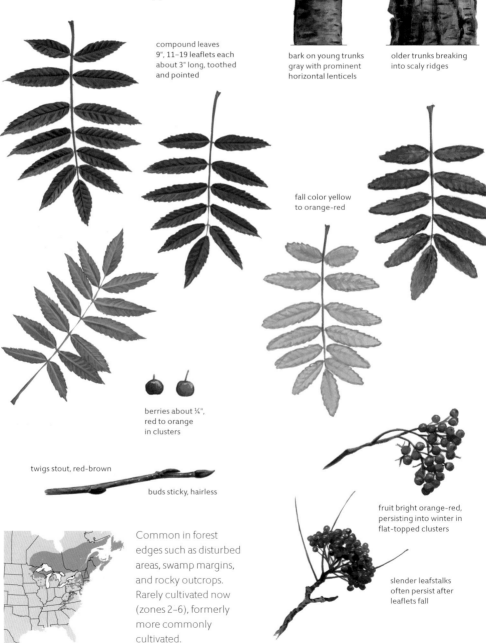

compound leaves 9", 11–19 leaflets each about 3" long, toothed and pointed

fall color yellow to orange-red

berries about ¼", red to orange in clusters

twigs stout, red-brown

buds sticky, hairless

fruit bright orange-red, persisting into winter in flat-topped clusters

slender leafstalks often persist after leaflets fall

Common in forest edges such as disturbed areas, swamp margins, and rocky outcrops. Rarely cultivated now (zones 2–6), formerly more commonly cultivated.

European Mountain-ash

Sorbus aucuparia

ROWAN TREE, COMMON MOUNTAIN ASH, QUICKBEAM

Small tree usually 20–40' tall (max. 85'), usually upright oval shape when young, spreading with age. Distinguished from American Mountain-ash by smaller, blunt-tipped leaflets, pale below, whitish hairy buds.

flowers very small,
white, in broad clusters,
resemble Elderberry

stout, slow-growing twigs show gnarled
scars of previous-years' bud scales
large pointed buds at tips of twigs may be dark
brownish or slightly glaucous gray-brown

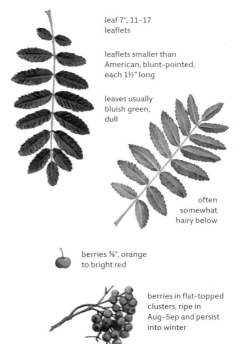

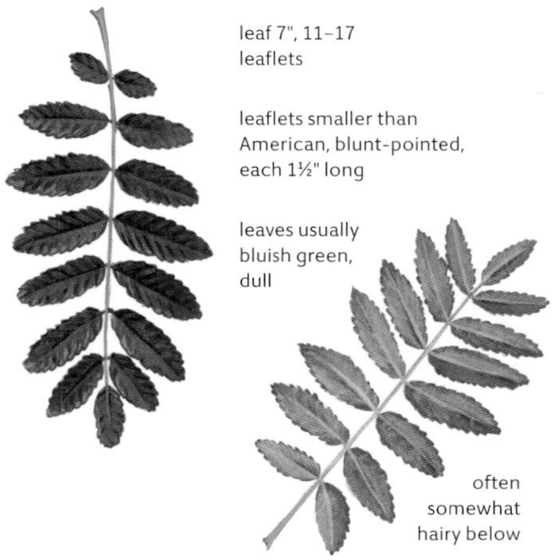
leaf 7", 11–17
leaflets
leaflets smaller than
American, blunt-pointed,
each 1½" long
leaves usually
bluish green,
dull
often
somewhat
hairy below

The flat-topped clusters of orange or red fruit are unique to mountain-ashes, and are a favorite of fruit-eating birds, often attracting large flocks of waxwings and robins in fall and winter.

berries ⅜", orange
to bright red

berries in flat-topped
clusters, ripe in
Aug–Sep and persist
into winter

twigs dull purple-gray
buds hairy, whitish

upright small tree with
gaunt, sparse twigs

Many cultivars include variations in size and color of fruit (red to yellow); as well as cutleaf varieties, upright growth form, and others. However, the most distinctive varieties are uncommon or rare.

Native from Europe and North Africa to Siberia, very commonly and widely cultivated in parks and gardens, and often naturalized (zones 3–6).

Loquat

Eriobotrya japonica

JAPANESE MEDLAR, EVERGREEN MEDLAR

Evergreen. Usually a large, broad-topped shrub, but can be a small tree 15–20' (max. 29') with few stout shoots. Flowers off-white (Aug–Jan), fragrant, in cluster 6" long, covered in dense brown hairs.

leaves large 7" long, dark green, glossy, wrinkled

underleaf brownish-fuzzy

fruit 2", yellow-orange, edible; ripe in spring after flowering

twigs stout, covered with brownish fuzz

Native to China and Japan. Commonly cultivated in gardens (zones 8–10).

Torrey Vauquelinia

Vauquelinia californica

ARIZONA ROSEWOOD

Evergreen. Shrub or occasionally a small tree to 20' tall (max. 47') with stiff, tangled branches. Two other closely related species of *Vauquelinia* are also found in the Southwest, but are rarely tree-like.

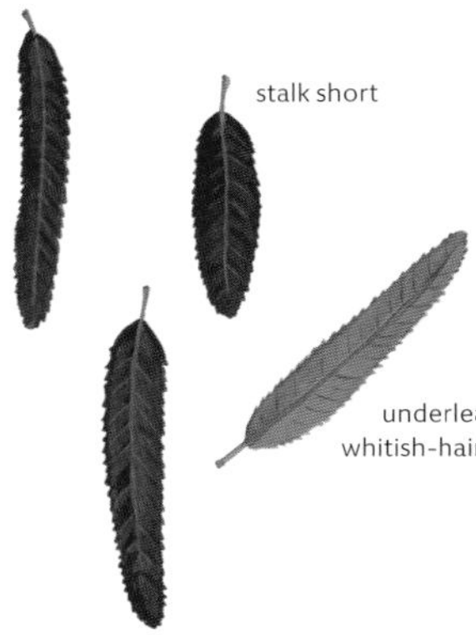

leaves 2½, narrow and blunt-tipped, leathery, alternate, toothed

stalk short

underleaf whitish-hairy

flowers small, white, in broad terminal clusters 2½" across (June)

fruit an oval woody capsule ⅓" splitting into 5 parts (Aug), in clusters persistent through winter

bark scaly or shaggy, dark reddish-brown

Uncommon and local in dry rocky canyons or grassy slopes; tree-like on Santa Catalina Mountains, Arizona. Occasionaly cultivated near native range.

Lyontree

Lyonothamnus floribundus

CATALINA IRONWOOD, SANTA CRUZ IRONWOOD

Evergreen. Small to medium tree usually under 40' tall (max. 46'), often bushy with several trunks. A very distinctive and unique tree native only on California's Channel Islands. Unique leaf shape, persistent fruit clusters and dead twigs create very shaggy appearance.

bark gray, peeling in thin papery strips to reveal reddish inner bark

trees on Santa Catalina Island have leaves 6", narrow, smooth or slightly toothed margins

trees from some islands with leaves 5", compound, 3–7 leaflets with large coarse teeth

flowers white, ⅓", in terminal clusters 6" across

Two subspecies differ dramatically in leaf shape. Simple leaves appear on trees (usually small and shrubby) growing on Santa Catalina Island. Trees growing on Santa Cruz (where they reach largest size), Santa Rosa, and San Clemente Islands have compound leaves. Both forms are cultivated on the adjacent mainland.

leaves turn yellow before falling

fruit ⅓", conical woody capsule, persistent in large clusters

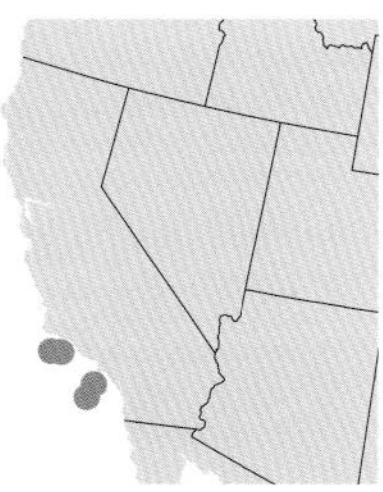

Rare and very local in dry soils in only a few locations on the Channel Islands off southern California. Occasionally cultivated in coastal southern California (zones 9–11).

Alderleaf Cercocarpus

Cercocarpus montanus

TRUE MOUNTAIN MAHOGANY

Deciduous to semi-evergreen. Shrub or occasionally a small tree to 20' tall (max. 21'). Wood hard, heavy, and brittle with dark brown color, thus, alternate name "mahogany." Valued for fuel and for carved small wooden trinkets.

short stalk
leaves small, 1", coarsely-toothed at tip
leaves leathery with straight parallel veins

flowers, small, tubular, greenish-white, clustered in Alderleaf, solitary in Curl-leaf, early spring

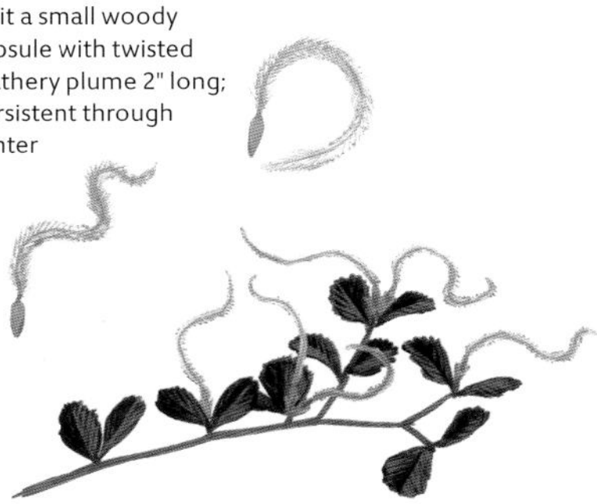
fruit a small woody capsule with twisted feathery plume 2" long; persistent through winter

This genus has been split into as many as 17 species in North America, but all are very similar, and modern authors generally recognize only 2–5 species. The two species shown here are common and represent the extremes of the genus; other species are intermediate.

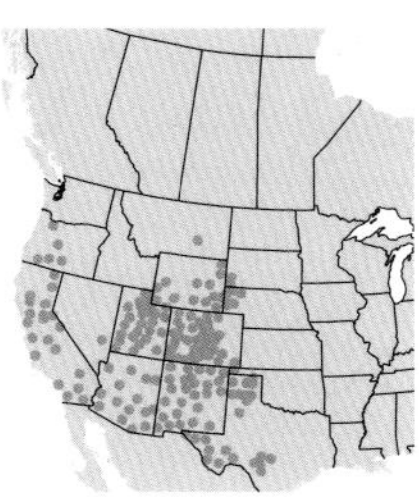

Common on dry rocky slopes. Not cultivated.

bark on young trunks smooth brown with pale lenticels
older trunks dark, rough narrow ridges

small twiggy tree with tiny leaves

Curlleaf Cercocarpus

Cercocarpus ledifolius

CURLLEAF MOUNTAIN-MAHOGANY, DESERT CERCOCARPUS

Evergreen. Shrub or small tree often 25' tall (max. 40'). Largest of the genus and most likely to be a tree. Told from Alderleaf by leaves with flowers usually solitary and later in summer (Jul–Aug).

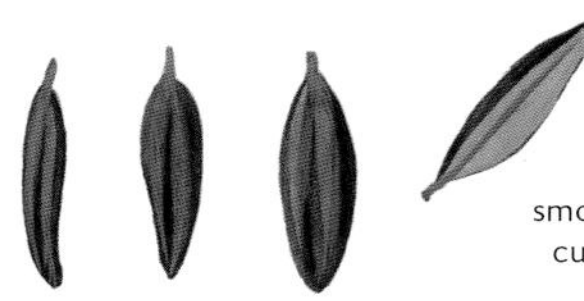
leaves 1", smooth edges curled under

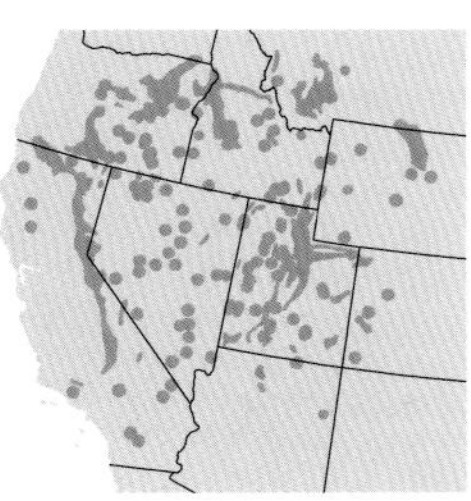

Common on arid mountain slopes. Not cultivated.

Toyon

Heteromeles arbutifolia

CHRISTMASBERRY, CALIFORNIA-HOLLY

Evergreen. Shrub or small tree, usually under 20' tall (max. 30'). Dense and dark green leaves form a striking contrast with clusters of red berries in winter.

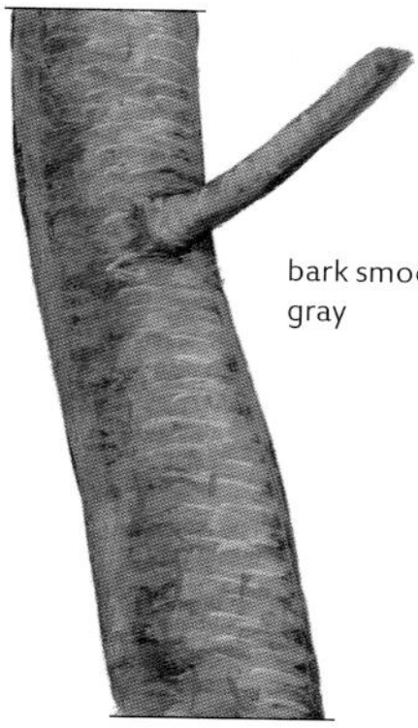
bark smooth, gray

leaves 3", oval, prominently toothed
underleaf paler green

flowers small, white, in terminal clusters 3" long (Jun–Aug)

fruit small, ⅓", pear-shaped, red, rarely yellow (Oct–Dec)

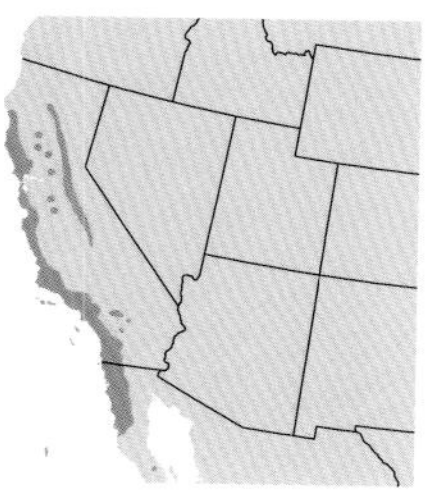

Common on lower slopes and foothills including coastal hills. Commonly cultivated within native range in parks and gardens as an ornamental (zones 8–10).

Chinese Photinia

Photinia serratifolia

Evergreen. Small tree or upright large shrub often 20–25' (max. 48'). Similar to Toyon, except leaves larger, more finely-toothed, flowers spring (Mar–May).

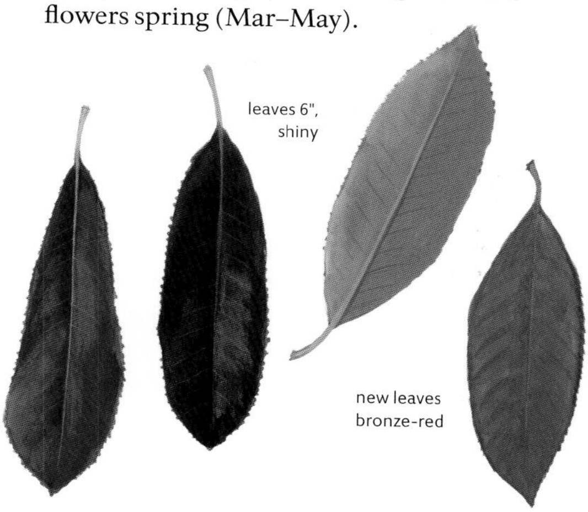
leaves 6", shiny
new leaves bronze-red

The genus *Photinia* is primarily Asian with 40–60 species of shrubs and trees, including many popular ornamental plants. Often cultivated as hedge plants in the South and in the Pacific states. Hybrid cultivars are also very common, the most prevalent is known as 'Fraser' Photinia, a cross of Chinese with another Asian photinia.

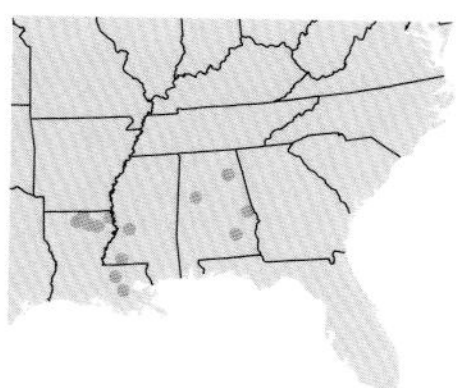

Native to China. Common in cultivation (zones 6–9).

Hemp Family: Hackberries

The hackberries are related to elms and were once placed in the same family (Ulmaceae), but are now considered part of the hemp family (Cannabaceae). This family includes about 100 other species, including well-known genera such as hemp (*Cannabis*) and hops (*Humulus*).

There are about sixty species of hackberries (genus *Celtis*) in temperate and tropical regions worldwide, and six species native to North America. Five of our native species are tree-like and are treated here along with two cultivated species.

All hackberries have tiny, inconspicuous flowers that appear in early spring with new leaves. Leaves are long-pointed, often lopsided with three main veins radiating from the base. Fruit is a small berry, ripe in the fall, persistent into winter, and avidly consumed by birds. Bark is smooth and gray, often developing distinctive warty growths that can form rough ridges in some species.

All hackberry species are very similar, and are distinguished only by minor variations of leaves and fruit.

Hackberries are not important commercially, but do provide valuable wildlife habitat, especially in the arid Southwest, where they form dense thickets that provide food and shelter for many birds and other animals.

hackberry twigs alternate, very slender; often curve back towards trunk

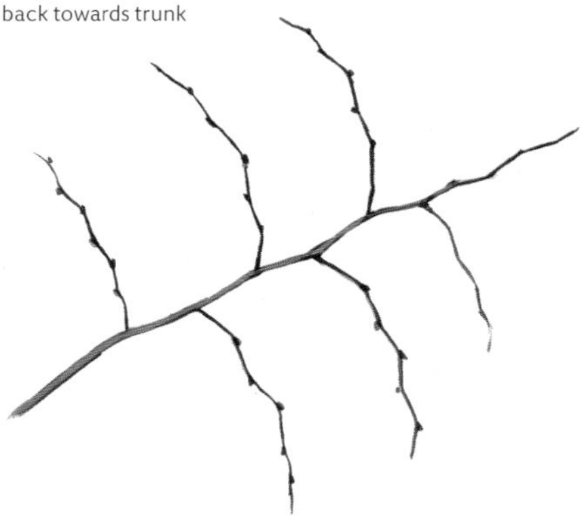

Northern Hackberry

Celtis occidentalis

SUGARBERRY, HACK TREE, NETTLE TREE, FALSE ELM

Deciduous. Medium to large tree often 60' tall (max. 134'). Relatively narrow rounded crown, twigs often clumped in "witch's broom." Size varies greatly depending on habitat.

leaves 3½", long-pointed with broad, uneven base, toothed
leafstalk very short
leaves darker above than Southern Hackberry
underleaf pale green

fruit like Southern but slightly larger, wrinkled when dry (vs. smooth)

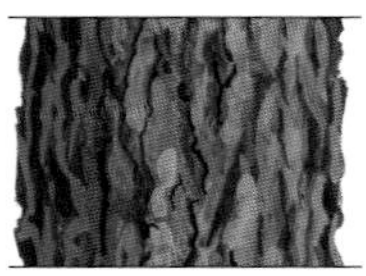
bark often like Southern, but can develop rough warty ridges unlike Southern

Several varieties have been named based on minor differences in size, shape, and hairiness of leaves, but all are variable and poorly defined.

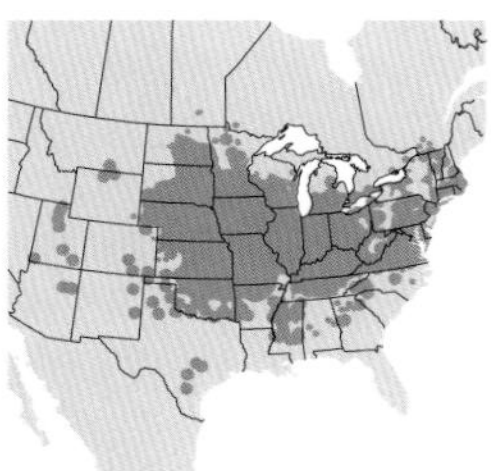

Common in floodplains and along streams, but drought tolerant and also present in dry sandy soils. Commonly planted as a street tree, especially in Midwest (zones 3–9).

Southern Hackberry

Celtis laevigata

SUGARBERRY, LOWLAND HACKBERRY, PALO BLANCO

Deciduous. Small to large tree often 60–80' tall (max. 148'); crowns broad, spreading, branches often drooping. Some small trunks are very warty, while other large trees retain smooth gray bark. Very similar to Northern Hackberry, differing only slightly in leaf, bark, and fruit.

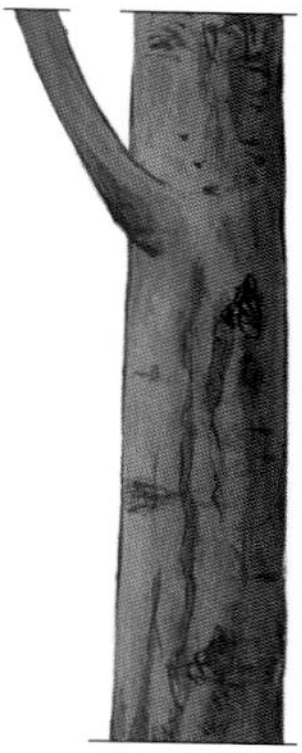

bark of young trunks smooth gray like beech

older trunks gray developing conspicuous warty knobs

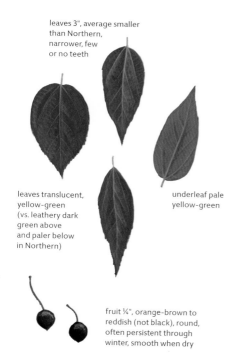

leaves 3", average smaller than Northern, narrower, few or no teeth

leaves translucent, yellow-green (vs. leathery dark green above and paler below in Northern)

underleaf pale yellow-green

flowers inconspicuous, in clusters in leaf axils (Mar–May)

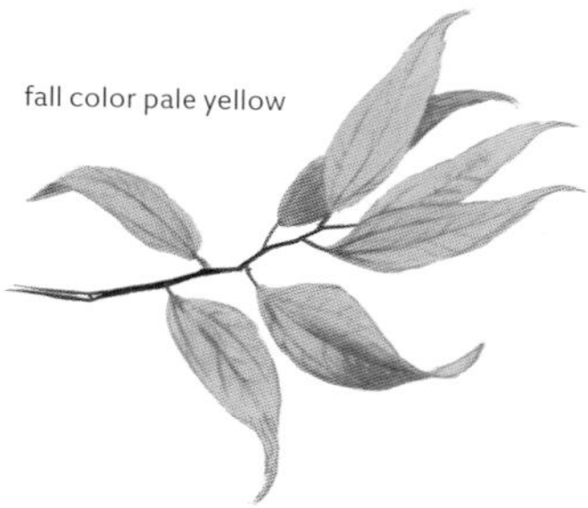

fall color pale yellow

fruit ¼", orange-brown to reddish (not black), round, often persistent through winter, smooth when dry

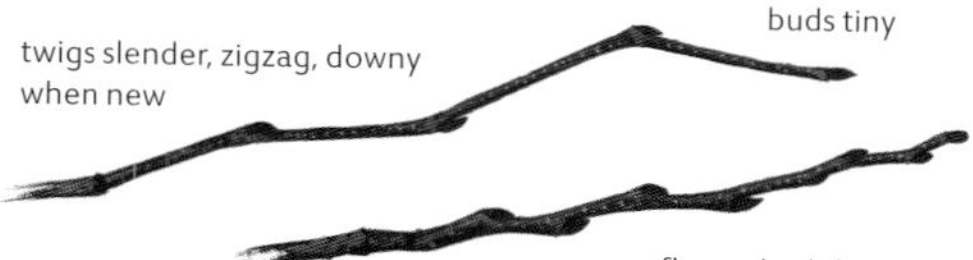

twigs slender, zigzag, downy when new

buds tiny

flower buds larger, rounded, make twigs look "beaded"

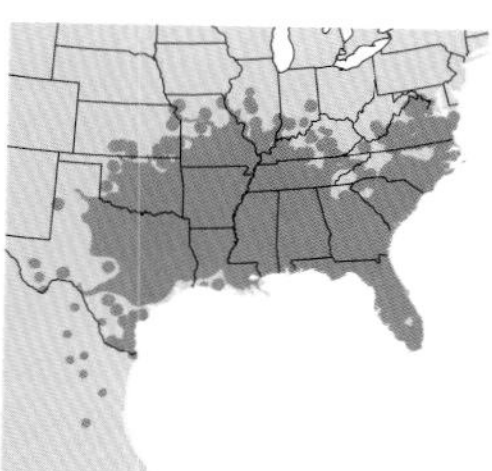

Common in rich bottomlands but also found in rocky or sandy soils. Often cultivated along streets and in parks and yards (zones 5–9).

tree looks unkempt with large contorted branches and dense clumps of fine twigs

Netleaf Hackberry

Celtis reticulata

WESTERN HACKBERRY, SUGARBERRY

Deciduous. Shrub or small tree usually under 30' tall (max. 74'); branches upright and crown more or less rounded. Basically the western form of Southern Hackberry with smaller, hairier leaves.

leaves small, 1½", thick and leathery, few or no teeth, slightly hairy
upperleaf yellow green, rough
underleaf gray green, hairy

fruit ⅓", relatively large, round, smooth when dry

Plants from the western edge of the range of Southern Hackberry are intermediate, tending to show some features of Netleaf Hackberry. They are currently considered a variety of Southern Hackberry (*Celtis laevigata* var. *texana*). Spiny Hackberry (*Celtis pallida*) is a shrub also found in the arid Southwest.

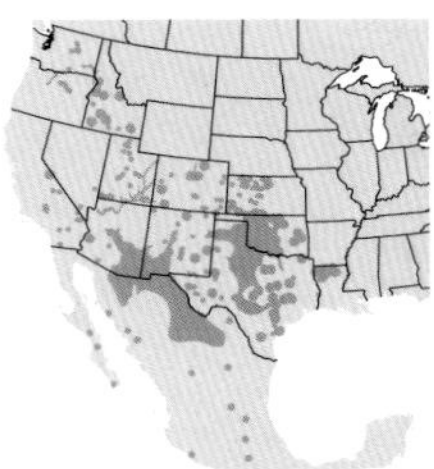

Locally common on dry hills, rocky outcrops, and sandy soils. Occasionally cultivated within its native range.

Dwarf Hackberry

Celtis tenuifolia

UPLAND HACKBERRY, GEORGIA HACKBERRY

Deciduous. Shrub or small tree to 25' tall; tree-like in only a few places. Branches often upright forming narrow, irregular crown. Some plants similar to Northern Hackberry and sometimes considered the same species, but intergrades are relatively few.

base uneven, sparsely-toothed near tip, short-pointed
leaves 2½", relatively small and broad, oval
few leaf veins
upperleaf dark gray-green, rough
underleaf gray-green, hairy

fruit small, ¼", orange to red and glaucous when ripe; dries smooth

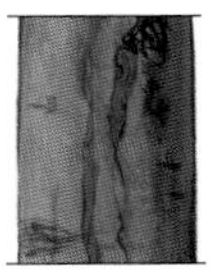

bark on young trunks pale gray

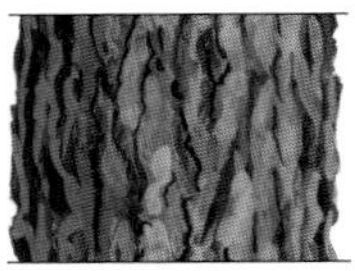

bark on mature trunk develops rough wavy ridges

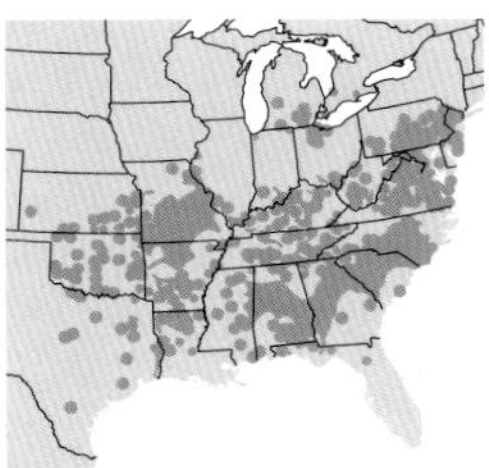

Common in dry soils of slopes and ridges. Not cultivated.

Lindheimer Hackberry

Celtis lindheimeri

Deciduous. Small tree to about 35' tall, branching low with wide spreading crown. Differs from other hackberries in having flowers (early spring) in dense erect clusters of 2–9 from leaf axils.

leaves 3", relatively broad oval, base rounded or heart-shaped, few or no teeth, dark green and rough above
underleaf hairy, pale

fruit ¼", light brown, round

twigs like other hackberries, zigzag with small buds

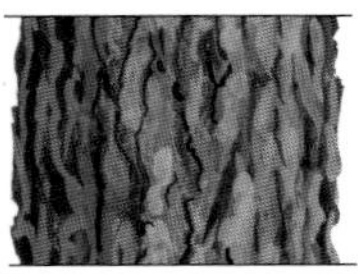
bark pale gray developing rough warty ridges

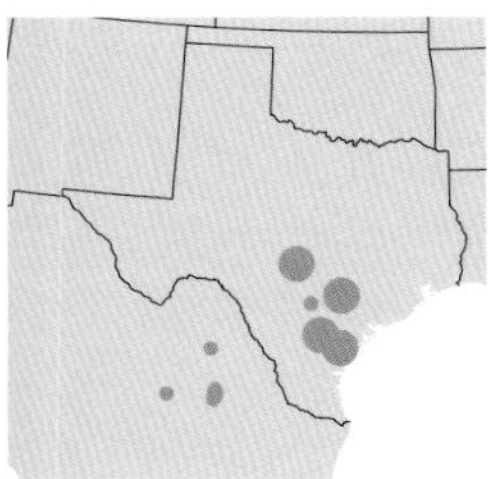

Found only locally in ravines and brushlands of Edward's Plateau, Texas and adjacent Mexico, status in Texas poorly known. Not cultivated.

European Hackberry

Celtis australis

MEDITERRANEAN HACKBERRY, SOUTHERN NETTLE TREE

Deciduous. Medium to large tree often 50' tall (max. 94'); similar to native species but leaves with many coarse teeth, fruit larger. Native to Mediterranean region, drought tolerant, occasionally cultivated (zones 7–9) and escaped mainly in California.

leaves 4", sharply toothed
fruit ½", large, blackish when ripe

Chinese Hackberry

Celtis sinensis

JAPANESE HACKBERRY

Deciduous. Small to medium tree often 45' tall (max. 75'); similar to other hackberries, but leaves relatively broad, blunt-toothed, and leathery. Native to east Asia. Occasionally cultivated in West (zones 4–9).

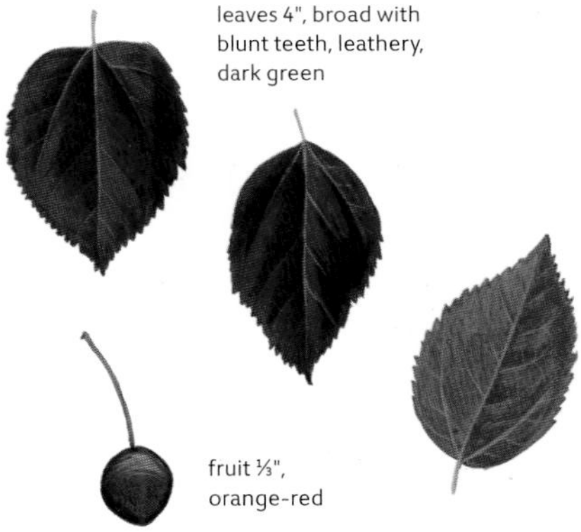
leaves 4", broad with blunt teeth, leathery, dark green
fruit ⅓", orange-red

Elm Family

The elm family (*Ulmaceae*) includes twenty to forty species of deciduous trees worldwide. Six species are native to North America and are covered in this guide along with five commonly cultivated and naturalized species.

All elms have leaves with parallel pinnate veins, short stalks, and often uneven bases. Many species have rough-surfaced leaves. Elm flowers are small and inconspicuous and their fruit is a small flattened seed surrounded by a papery wing.

Cedar, September, and Chinese Elm are distinguished by flowering in the fall. Eight species flower in the spring, four with very short-stalked flowers and fruit—Slippery, Wych, Field, and Siberian Elm. The spring-flowering American, Rock, Winged, and European White Elm have long-stalked flowers and fruit. Some recent research suggests that the fall-flowering Cedar and September Elm are very closely related to the spring-flowering Rock and Winged Elm, forming a group known as the "hard elms."

Elm wood was once important for specific uses, such as chair seats, because it tends not to split, but it is rarely used commercially today. Elms were primarily valued as ornamental trees in parks and along boulevards before the advent of Dutch elm disease. Thought to have originated in the Far East, it was first identified in North America around 1930 and spread rapidly. A new and more deadly strain appeared in the 1960s and continues to spread. Fungi carried by beetles cause the trees to block its own tissue, essentially choking itself to death. Protecting trees from beetles and pruning any dead or infected branches can keep them disease-free. Some regions have not been infected and still support large groves of healthy trees. Asian species such as Siberian and Chinese Elms are resistant to these diseases, and efforts are ongoing to produce a resistant American Elm by hybridization with Asian species.

vigorous shoots have 2-ranked alternate leaves in "ladder" arrangement

leaves variable in size, smaller at base of twig

fall color yellow brown

Many species have "vase" or "bouquet" shape, with tall trunk, spreading crown, drooping twigs; others have a less graceful "oak-like" shape.

American Elm

Ulmus americana

WHITE ELM, GRAY ELM, SOFT ELM

Deciduous. Large tree often 80' tall (max. 160'). Large size and a graceful spreading crown made this a popular shade tree before it was decimated by disease in the mid-1900s. Still common as a small tree, and some large specimens survive in towns and cities.

young trunk
slightly furrowed
with scaly ridges
bark of mature trunks furrowed
in narrow, untidy, interlacing
ridges; each ridge scaly, fallen
scales reveal white patches

stalk short
and stout
many straight
parallel veins
run to leaf
edge
smooth or
rough above
leaf base
very uneven
leaves 5",
oval with short
point
coarsely
double-toothed
underleaf
paler green
to whitish

cross-section of bark in
alternating layers of whitish
and brown, distinctive

flowers drooping
on long stalks, very
early spring before leaves

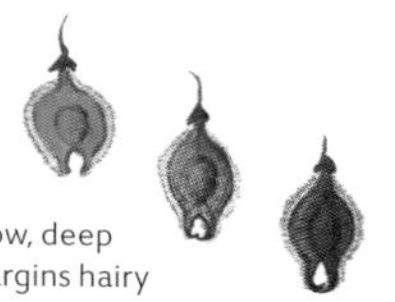
fruit narrow, deep
notch, margins hairy
fruit ½", pale yellow-green,
ripening brown (tinged red
in southern range)

fruit in hanging clusters
ripening as leaves expand

twigs light reddish
to brownish
buds small, pointed,
light brown
flower buds larger, oval

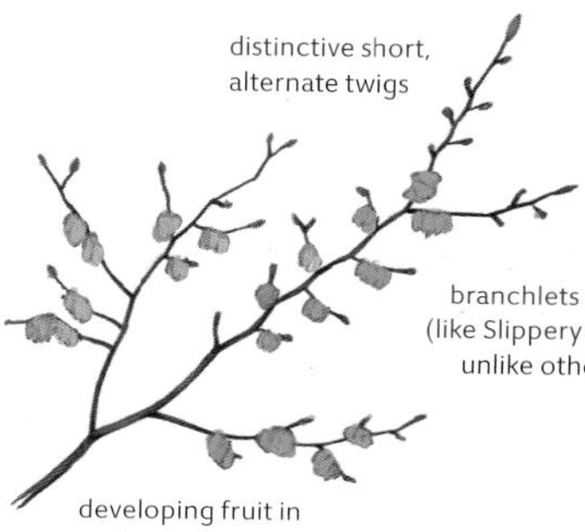
distinctive short,
alternate twigs
branchlets never winged
(like Slippery and Field, but
unlike other native elms)
developing fruit in
early spring before leaves

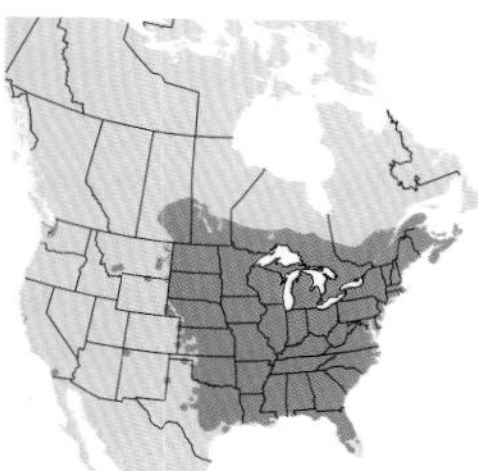

Common in rich soils of river floodplains, swales, streambanks, and other open moist sites. Commonly cultivated (zones 3–9).

Slippery Elm

Ulmus rubra

RED ELM, SOFT ELM, ULMUS FULVA

Deciduous. Medium tall tree often 60' tall (max. 134'). Similar to American Elm, most easily distinguished by short-stalked flowers and fruit. Named for its fragramt and mucilaginous (slippery) inner bark, which is often used medicinally.

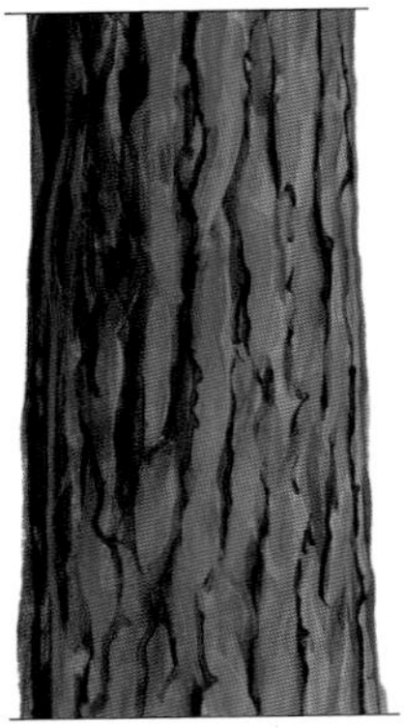
bark of mature trunks dark red-brown in long scaly plates, lacks white patches of American Elm

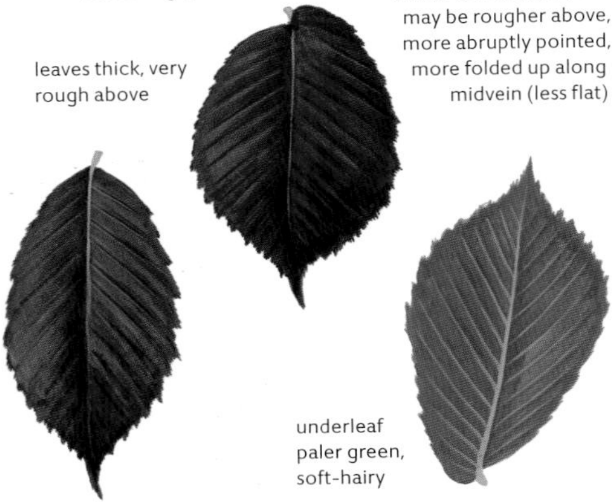
leaves large, 5½"
leaves thick, very rough above
similar to American, but may be rougher above, more abruptly pointed, more folded up along midvein (less flat)
underleaf paler green, soft-hairy

flowers short-stalked, unlike other native elms, except Cedar Elm
flowers very early spring before leaves

fruit pale yellow-green, often darker in center, ripens as leaves unfold

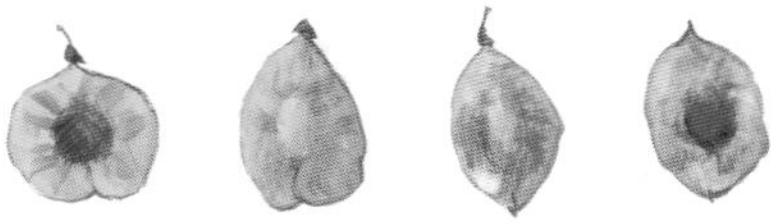
fruit ⅝", rounded, without notch, short-stalked, not hairy on margins (unlike all other native elms)

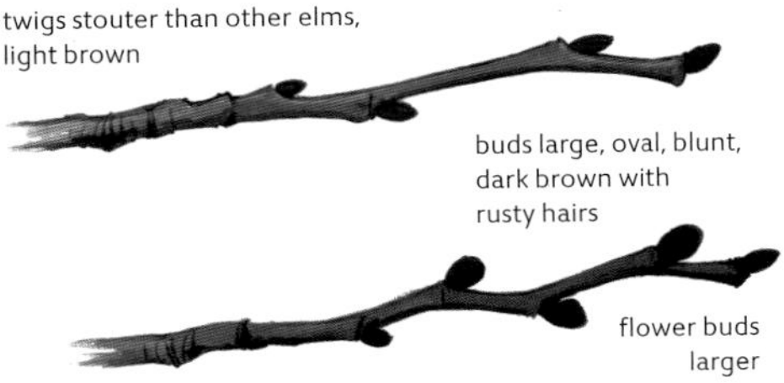
twigs stouter than other elms, light brown
buds large, oval, blunt, dark brown with rusty hairs
flower buds larger

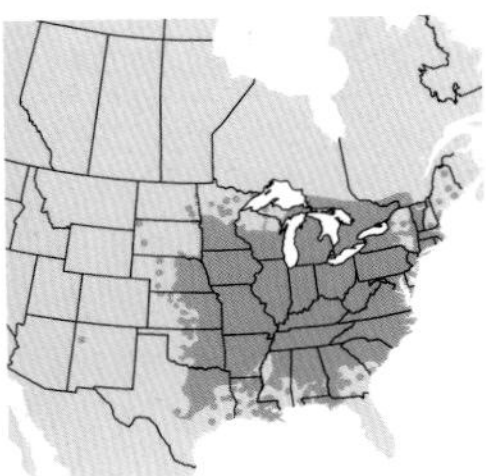

Common, especially in northern and western parts of range; in rich moist soils from stream banks to hillsides. Rarely cultivated.

less graceful and with less arched branches than American Elm

Cultivated Elms

Several species of European elms and their hybrids are cultivated in North America, and several are naturalized. Identification is challenging. The typical leaves and fruit of several are shown here, but many other variations and intermediate trees can be found.

European White Elm

Ulmus laevis

FLUTTERING ELM, HUNGARIAN ELM

Deciduous. Very similar to American Elm with long-stalked flowers and fruit; differing only in more slender and slightly more pointed buds, leaves average broadest near base (vs. broadest near tip), and more asymmetrical. Native to eastern Europe, west Asia. Commonly cultivated at least in some western cities, but identification confused.

leaf 4", oval, base uneven

fruit very similar to American Elm but slightly more circular

'Dutch' Elm

Ulmus '× hollandica'

Name used for some of the cultivars derived from hybrids of Wych and Field Elms. Leaf and fruit are intermediate between the two parent species, but given variation in the hybrids, and the parents, it is exceptionally difficult to identify. Many cultivars are named, and several are commonly cultivated.

leaf 5", oval, base uneven

fruit round, stalkless

Field Elm

Ulmus minor

ENGLISH ELM, NARROWLEAF ELM, HEDGEROW ELM, EUROPEAN FIELD ELM, SMOOTHLEAF ELM

Deciduous. Large tree often 80' tall (max. 165'). The common elm of Britain and Europe, where it spreads by suckering, giving rise to distinctive local clones, many of which have been named and cultivated.

leaf 4", usually smooth above, base usually uneven, but not overlapping leaf stalk

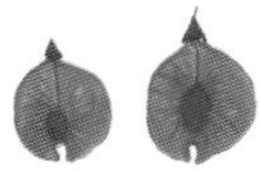

fruit ½", brownish, circular, slightly notched

Native to Europe, north Africa, and southwestern Asia. Some cultivars common in North America (zones 3–7, depending on cultivar).

Wych Elm

Ulmus glabra

SCOTCH ELM, BROAD-LEAVED ELM

Deciduous. Large tree often 80' tall (max. 164'); often multi-trunked, spreading, similar to Slippery Elm, but has entirely hairless fruit, and smooth bark.

leaf large, 5½", usually rough above with uneven base covering leafstalk

fruit ¾", hairless, pale brown, oval, slightly notched

Native to Europe and west Asia. Uncommonly cultivated (zones 4–6).

Winged Elm

Ulmus alata

CORK ELM, WAHOO

Deciduous. Small or medium tree usually 30–40' tall (max. 97'); rounded open crown. Note small asymmetrical leaves. Named for corky wings present on many branchlets, but similar wings can be found on Rock, Cedar, and Field Elm. Flowers in clusters less than 1", not dangling, very early spring.

leaves thick, smooth above
leaves 2", small, narrow
base somewhat uneven
underleaf paler green with some tufts of hair

fruit small, ⅜", narrow, oval with hairy margins, dark, often reddish

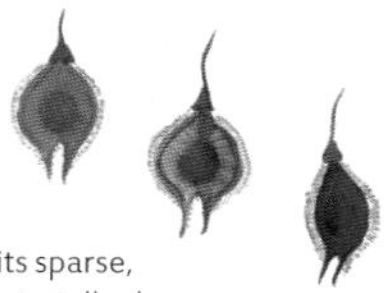

fruits sparse, short-stalked

branchlets often with 2 prominent regular corky wings

twigs reddish brown, hairy or not

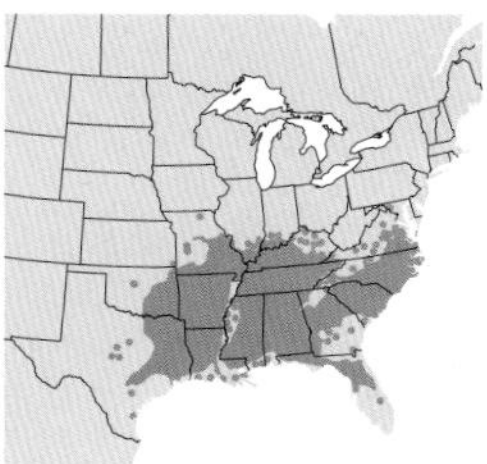

Common in dry to moist sandy soils with other hardwoods, particularly on streamsides and well-drained lowland soils; often cultivated (zones 6–9).

Rock Elm

Ulmus thomasii

CORK ELM, HICKORY ELM, CLIFF ELM

Deciduous. Medium tree often 60' tall (max. 117'); oval crown. Similar to American Elm, but leaves average smaller and more symmetrical, fruit larger, branchlets often with corky wings. Named for hard and heavy wood, but other species (Cedar Elm) have similarly hard wood.

leaves 3½"
base uneven, stalk fairly long
underleaf whitish, downy

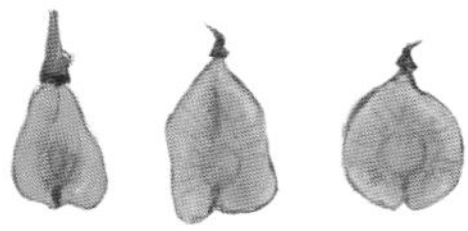

fruit ¾", oval, hairy, pale yellowish-brown

flowers very early spring before leaves

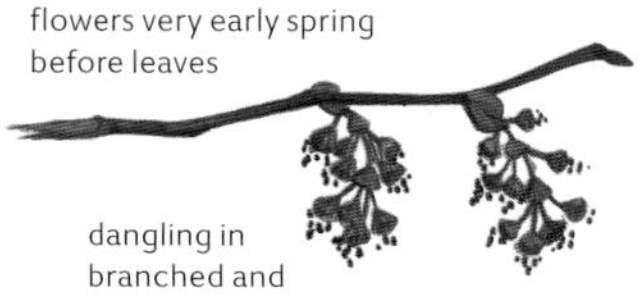

dangling in branched and stalked clusters of 2–4

branchlets have 3–5 corky wings

twigs reddish, hairy

buds brown, oval, pointed

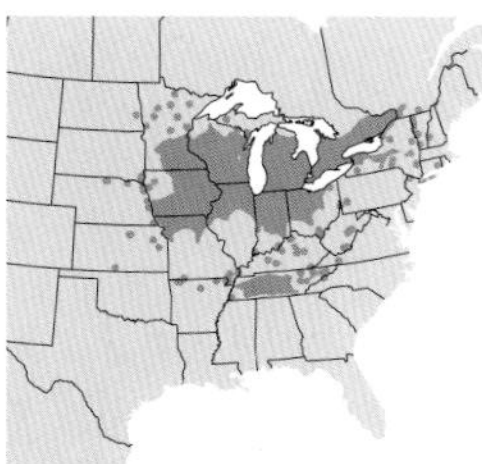

Common on well-drained rocky sites, but also found (and grows largest) in rich moist bottomlands. Rarely cultivated.

Cedar Elm

Ulmus crassifolia

ROCK ELM

Deciduous. Medium to large tree often 60' tall (max. 118'); crown round to narrow with small and narrow leaves (smallest of all elms). Common name refers to close association with juniper (cedar) stands. Flowers in short-stalked clusters in autumn.

leaves small 1½",blunt-tipped
short-stalked with slightly uneven base
leaves thick, rough above
underleaf slightly downy

oval, hairy, light brown, deeply-notched, few in short-stalked clusters in autumn
fruit ⅜"

branchlets often have two corky wings
twigs reddish, downy
buds small, red-brown

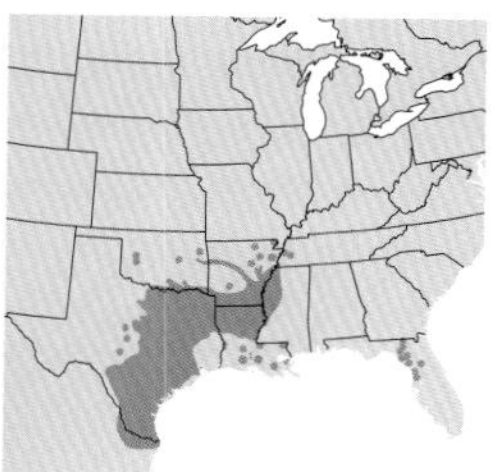

Common in moist bottomlands, streamsides, roadsides; resistant to Dutch elm disease and commonly cultivated as a shade tree, mostly within native range (zones 7–9).

September Elm

Ulmus serotina

RED ELM

Deciduous; usually a small to medium tree under 50' (max. 150'); crown spreading, broad, branches drooping. Similar to Rock Elm but flowers and fruit in autumn (like Cedar and Chinese Elm). Flowers dangling in clusters on long stalks to 2".

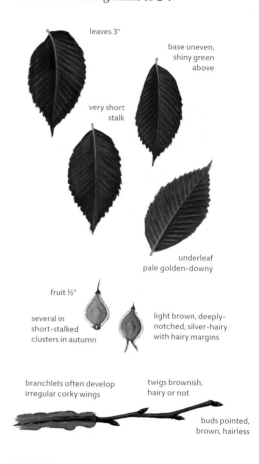

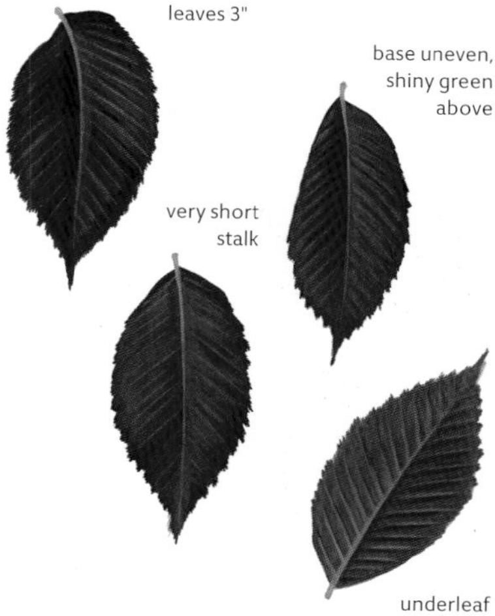
leaves 3"
base uneven, shiny green above
very short stalk
underleaf pale golden-downy

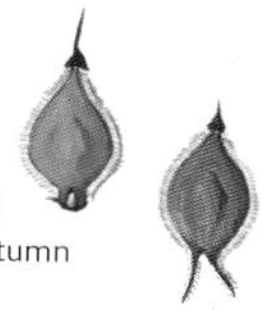
fruit ½"
several in short-stalked clusters in autumn
light brown, deeply-notched, silver-hairy with hairy margins

branchlets often develop irregular corky wings
twigs brownish, hairy or not
buds pointed, brown, hairless

In Oklahoma and Arkansas hybridizes freely with Cedar Elm and many plants there are intermediate.

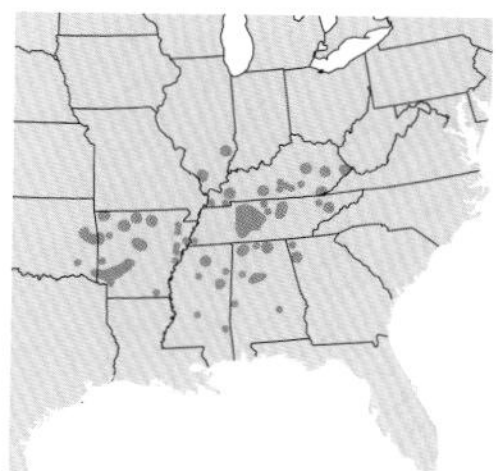

Uncommon and local in moist soils of rich woods especially on limestone outcrops; found mainly in Tennessee. Almost never cultivated.

Siberian Elm

Ulmus pumila

CHINESE ELM

Deciduous, small to medium tree to 50' (max. 146'); crown open, rounded, messy. Note small gray-green leaves, dark rugged bark. Resistant to Dutch elm disease.

bark on mature trunks deeply furrowed with rugged interlacing ridges; similar to Black Locust, but darker

leaves small, 1½", single-toothed, base generally even

underleaf paler green, nearly hairless

flower buds larger, round, blackish

flowers in late winter/early spring before leaves, in tight clusters, blackish and green

Formerly extensively planted as a shelterbelt and shade tree in the Great Plains and arid West, and now one of the most numerous trees there, growing wherever it finds sufficient groundwater.

fruit ½", pale yellowish, circular, hairless with broad wing, deep notch, nearly stalkless; ripens in spring

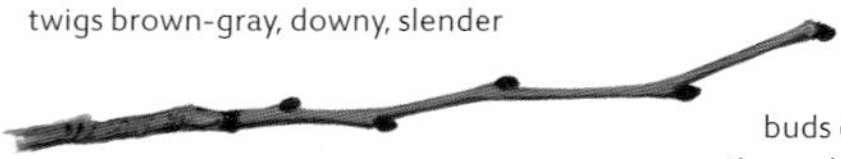

twigs brown-gray, downy, slender

buds dark, tiny, pointed

Native to eastern Asia. Commonly cultivated and widely escaped to roadsides, field edges, old homesites. Thrives in cool dry climates (zones 4–9).

speading crown of irregular branches, many small twigs form dense haze

Chinese Elm

Ulmus parvifolia

LACEBARK ELM

Deciduous (nearly evergreen in warm climates). Medium tree to 50' (max. 95'); crown dense, rounded, branches weeping. Note small leaves and very distinctive bark.

leaves shiny dark green

leaves small, 1½", usually single-toothed with blunt teeth

underleaf pale, hairless

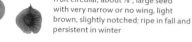

fruit circular, about ⅜", large seed with very narrow or no wing, light brown, slightly notched; ripe in fall and persistent in winter

flowers late summer/ fall, in small clusters, not dangling

twigs brownish, hairy with orange lenticels

buds brown

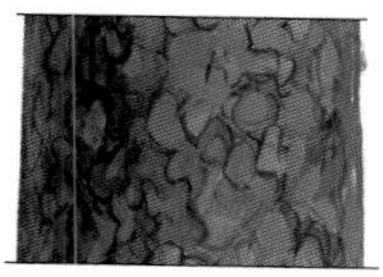

bark of mature trunks smooth gray-green peeling in flakes to reveal orange patches

Native to Asia. Commonly cultivated and widely escaped to field edges and roadsides, (zones 4–9) resistant to Dutch elm disease.

Water-elm

Planera aquatica

PLANERTREE

Deciduous. Small tree often 30–40' tall (max. 106') with slender spreading branches forming a low, broad crown. Seeds are an important food for ducks. The only species in its genus.

leaves small, 2½", dark green with short stalk

underleaf paler green

fruit ⅓", nut-like with leathery, warty husk; ripens in April

small green fruit in leaf axils in early summer (flowers in early spring with leaves)

twigs dark reddish-brown

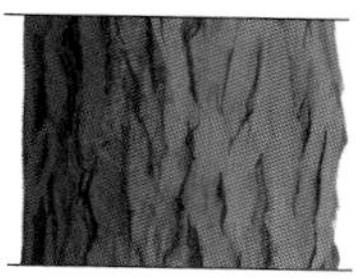

bark thin; peeling in large scales, inner bark reddish

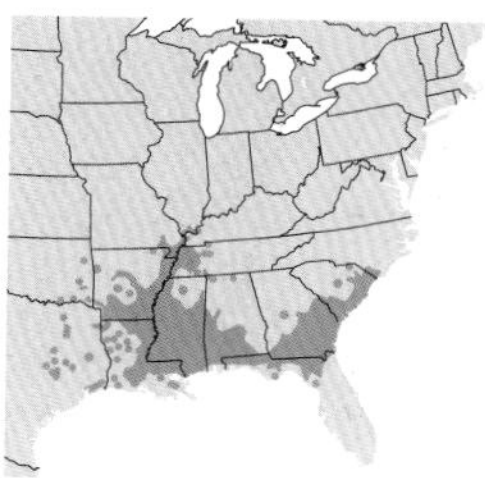

Common and found exclusively in wet sites; river banks and swamps where inundated several months each year. Almost never cultivated.

Japanese Zelkova

Zelkova serrata

KEAKI, COMMON ZELKOVA, ORIENTAL-ELM

Deciduous. Small to medium tree often 50' tall (max. 84') with slender, often drooping twigs forming neat spreading crown, often vase-shaped with small slender leaves neatly arrayed along twigs.

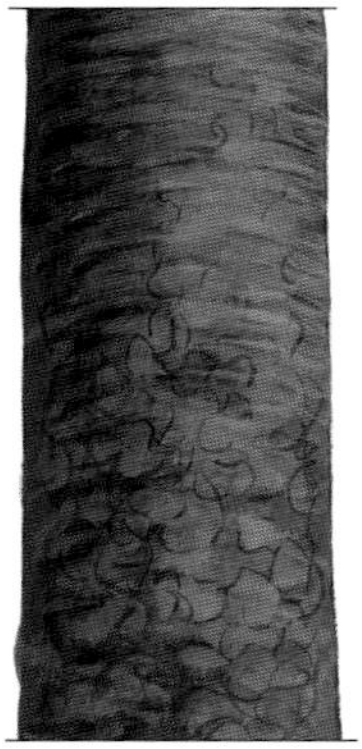

bark pale gray with horizontal lenticels; becoming mottled orange on older trunks

leaves 4", small, narrow

fall color yellow to orange or rusty

flowers tiny and inconspicuous (spring)

fruit very small, berries in leaf axils

rounded crown of very slender twigs

short trunk divides all at once into many straight ascending branches

twigs very slender, gray, curved

buds small

Native to Japan, Korea, Taiwan. Commonly cultivated and locally escaped (zones 5–8). Several cultivars differ in habit and fall color.

Mallow Family: Lindens

The mallow family (Malvaceae), as currently defined, includes over 2,000 species of plants worldwide. Some of the plants in this family are the source of such important products as hibiscus, cotton, okra, and chocolate. Subdivisions of the family are still being studied. In North America, only one genus is native (*Tilia*) and another is cultivated and naturalized (*Firmiana*).

The lindens (genus *Tilia*), also known as limes or basswoods, are deciduous trees found around the northern hemisphere, mainly in Asia. The number of species in the genus is a subject of debate, but most authorities now recognize about thirty species worldwide, one of which is native to North America. All are trees. In this guide, our single native species is covered, along with three commonly cultivated species.

All *Tilia* species found in North America are quite similar and generally can only be distinguished by small average differences in leaf shape and size, leaf hairiness, and details of flowers and fruit. All species hybridize, and cultivated lindens, in particular, can be difficult to identify.

Linden wood is lightweight, but strong and stable, and is popular for various specialized uses, such as model-building and carving, musical instruments, and window blinds. Native Americans used the inner bark of lindens for fibers to make cord (a related Asian species is the source of jute). Flowers are very attractive to honeybees in early summer. Lindens are most important commercially as ornamental shade trees.

Chinese Parasol-tree

Firmiana simplex

FIRMIANA PLATANIFOLIA, JAPANESE VARNISH TREE, PHOENIX TREE, BOTTLE TREE

Deciduous. Small or medium tree usually 20–30' tall (max. 65'). Crown rounded with few stout twigs, flowers yellow-green in large terminal clusters 15" long (Jun–Jul).

leaves large, 1', sycamore-like, with 3–5 lobes, heart-shaped base

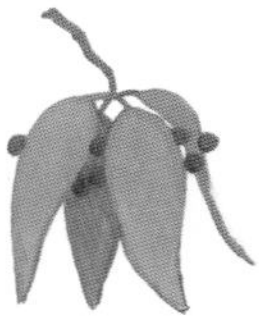
fruit a leathery capsule 3", opening into 5 sections

twigs green
buds large, round

bark smooth, greenish-gray

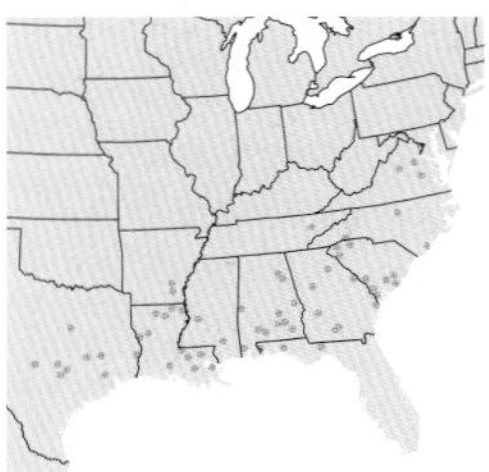

Native to Asia. Widely planted as street tree, locally naturalized and invasive in wet areas and woods (zones 7–9).

American Basswood

Tilia americana

AMERICAN LINDEN, BASSWOOD

Deciduous. Medium to large tree often 50–70' tall (max. 135'). Upright tree with neatly rounded crown; leaf similar to mulberry, but never lobed, and buds have only 1–2 exposed bud scales (5–6 on mulberry).

bark on young trunk smooth
bark of large trunk dark, interlaced

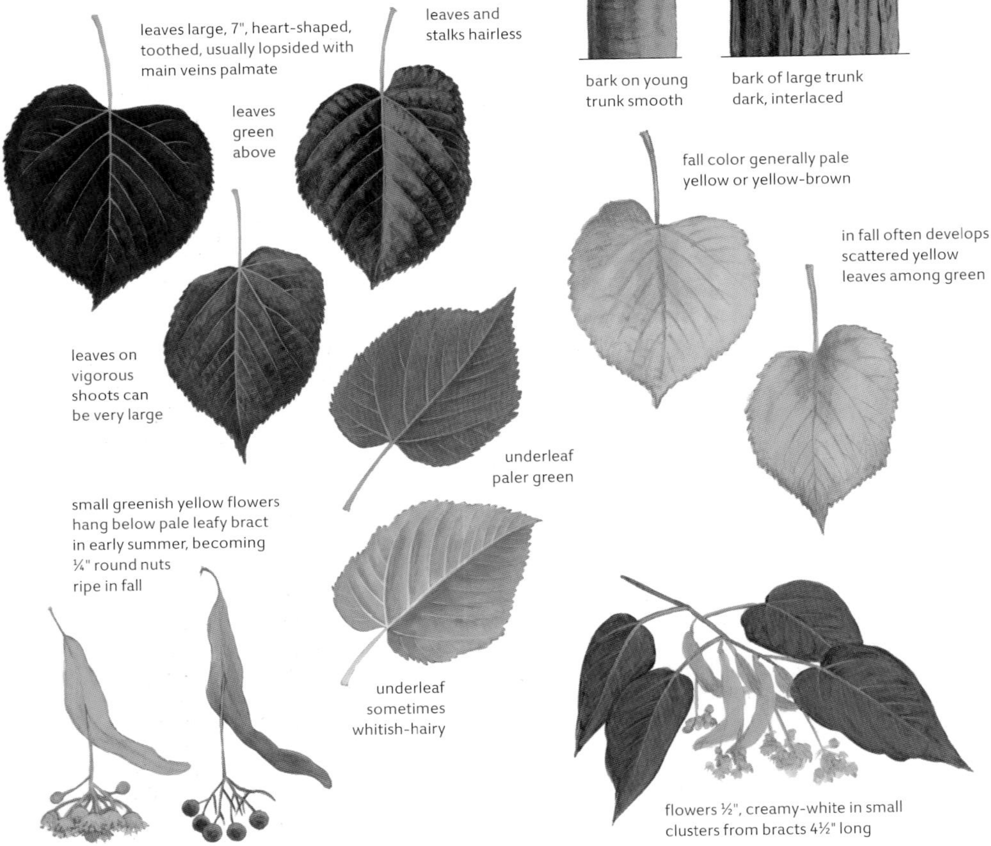
leaves large, 7", heart-shaped, toothed, usually lopsided with main veins palmate
leaves and stalks hairless
leaves green above
fall color generally pale yellow or yellow-brown
in fall often develops scattered yellow leaves among green
leaves on vigorous shoots can be very large
underleaf paler green
small greenish yellow flowers hang below pale leafy bract in early summer, becoming ¼" round nuts ripe in fall
underleaf sometimes whitish-hairy
flowers ½", creamy-white in small clusters from bracts 4½" long

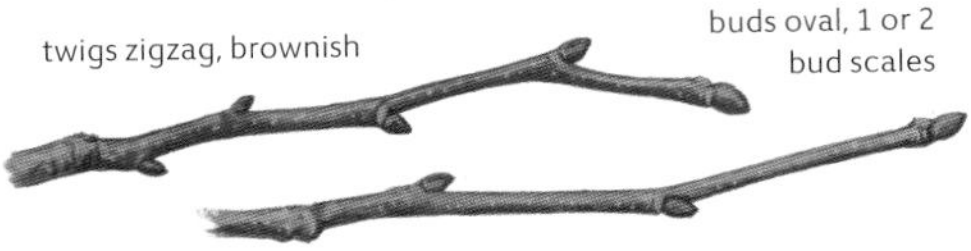
twigs zigzag, brownish
buds oval, 1 or 2 bud scales

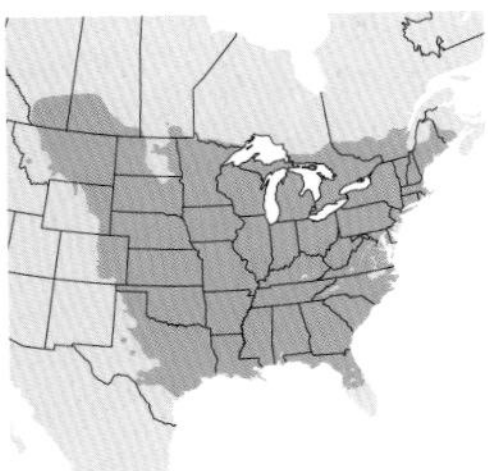

Common in rich soils and in cultivation, but less suited to urban settings than European species (zones 3–8).

Variation in a few features of basswoods has led to recognition of up to a dozen species, but differences are small with many intermediates, and in this guide only a single species is recognized. Two other species sometimes recognized include:

Carolina Basswood (*Tilia caroliniana*) with leafstalk, flower stalk and sometimes underleaf green and slightly hairy; found mainly in southern coastal plain.

White Basswood (*Tilia heterophylla*) with leafstalk, flower stalk and underleaf white hairy; found mainly in Appalachians.

Littleleaf Linden

Tilia cordata

SMALL-LEAVED LINDEN, WINTER LINDEN

Deciduous. Medium tree often 60–70' tall (max. 96').

leaves small, 2½", heart-shaped at base, dark green above
underleaf paler blue-green with orange hair tufts at base

Native to Europe. Commonly cultivated and locally naturalized (zones 3–7); many cultivars differ in habit and branching pattern.

Large-leaf Linden

Tilia platyphyllos

BIGLEAF LINDEN, SUMMER LINDEN

Deciduous. Medium to large tree often 40–60' tall (max 96'); similar to other cultivated lindens, but with larger leaves (although not as big as American Basswood).

leaves large, 6", heart-shaped, toothed

Native to Europe and southwestern Asia. Commonly cultivated and locally escaped (zones 4–6).

Silver Linden

Tilia petiolaris

EUROPEAN WHITE LINDEN, PENDENT SILVER LINDEN

Deciduous. Medium tree 50–70' (max. 125'). Crown very dense, usually rounded with strikingly bicolored leaves dark above and pale below.

leaves fairly small 3½", round, dark green above
underleaf densely white-fuzzy

smooth oval crown, dark reddish arched branches, and slender drooping twigs distinctive

Native to Europe, southwestern Asia. Common in cultivation and naturalized locally (zones 4–7).

Cashew Family

The cashew family (Anacardiaceae) includes about 650 species of plants worldwide, found mostly in the tropics. Several are native to North America, but few are tree-like. Eleven species (six native and five cultivated) are included in this guide.

Most species in the family have pinnately compound, alternate leaves, flowers in terminal clusters, and small flattened nut-like or berry-like fruits.

The family includes such well-known and commercially important tropical trees as Cashewnut and Mango, while sumacs, peppertrees, and smoketrees are popular as ornamental plantings.

Many species in the family exude a blackish resin from broken twigs and develop blackish spots on the leaves. The leaves may turn a distinctive gray color when dry.

Many species in the cashew family—Poison-sumac, Poison-ivy, Poison-oak, and relatives in the genus *Toxicodendron*—have toxic oils in their leaves and stems. They can all cause extreme itching and skin irritation. The largest genus in the cashew family native to North America is the sumacs (*Rhus*), covered on pages 316–317.

Pistachios (genus *Pistacia*) include about ten species of small to medium trees worldwide. One species is native and three others commonly cultivated in North America. All have pinnately compound leaves and nut-like fruits in clusters at the tips of the twigs. Edible commercial pistachio nuts come from the Common Pistachio. Chinese Pistachio is cultivated as an ornamental tree.

Peppertrees (genus *Schinus*) are native to the tropics with about fifteen species worldwide. Only one species is illustrated here. It is barely cold-hardy, but several others are found in the warmest parts of North America.

Smoketrees (genus *Cotinus*) include just two species, both shrubs or small trees, commonly planted as ornamentals.

Texas Pistachio

Pistacia texana

AMERICAN PISTACHIO, WILD PISTACHIO

Evergreen or tardily deciduous. Small tree mostly under 30' tall (max. 39') and usually multitrunked.

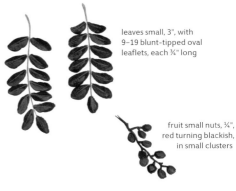

leaves small, 3", with 9–19 blunt-tipped oval leaflets, each ¾" long

fruit small nuts, ¼", red turning blackish, in small clusters

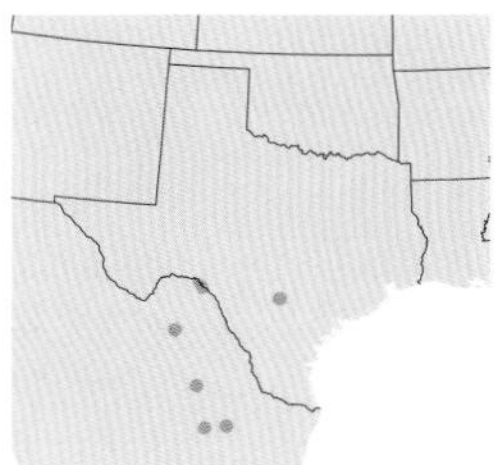

Rare and local in the wild in Texas, mainly along limestone cliffs near confluence of Pecos River and Rio Grande. Uncommonly cultivated (zones 8–10).

Common Pistachio

Pistacia vera

GREEN ALMOND

Deciduous. Small bushy tree with dense crown under 30' tall. Source of all commercial pistachio nuts. Native to west and central Asia. Grown commercially for edible nuts but not cultivated for ornament and not naturalized (zones 8–11).

nuts oval, ¾", pale tan to reddish, in clusters

leaves 8", usually 3 leaflets, rarely 1–7

Chinese Pistachio

Pistacia chinensis

CHINESE PISTACHE, GITTERWORT

Deciduous. Small to medium tree (max. 76'); dense rounded crown, often lopsided, especially when young.

bark finely
checked and
furrowed

leaves 10" with 8–16
pointed leaflets, strong
odor when crushed

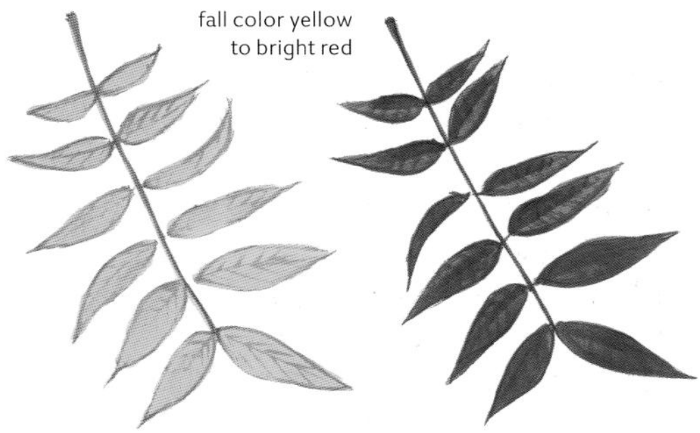
fall color yellow
to bright red

flowers tiny, red to green
in small clusters, like
ashes (Mar–May)

fruit ¼" nuts in loose
hanging clusters, green
turning yellow to red to blue

twig fairly stout,
buds rounded

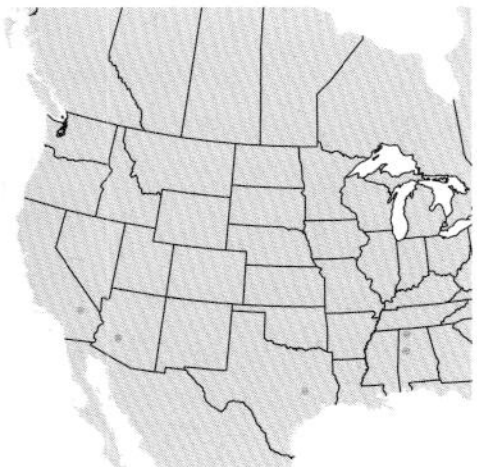

Native to eastern Asia. Commonly cultivated and naturalized in eastern Texas and parts of California (zones 6–9).

Mount Atlas Pistachio

Pistacia atlantica

MOUNT ATLAS MASTICHE

Evergreen or tardily deciduous. Medium tree usually under 40', wide-spreading,

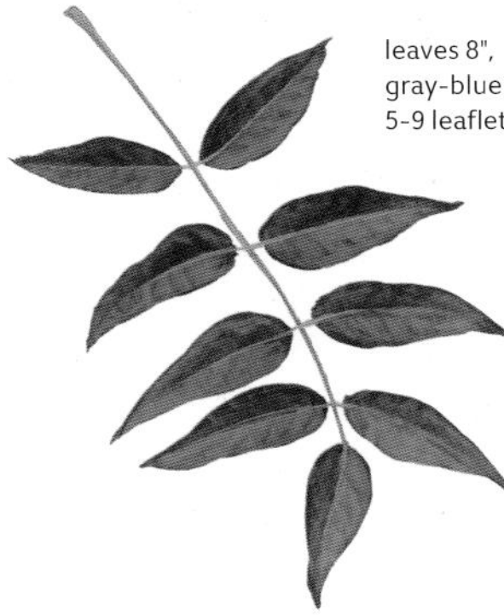
leaves 8",
gray-blue with
5-9 leaflets

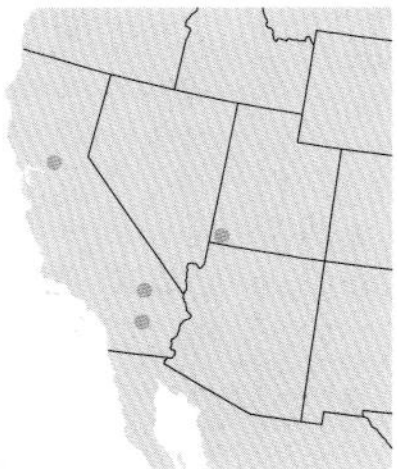

Native from Mediterranean to west Asia. Not cultivated, except as rootstock for commercial pistachio trees. Naturalized locally (zones 7–10).

Peruvian Peppertree

Schinus molle

CALIFORNIA PEPPERTREE, PERUVIAN MASTIC TREE

Evergreen. Shrub or small tree usually 20–35' tall (max. 70'). Short trunk and spreading crown with lacy leaves; twigs hang down in distinctive weeping habit.

bark rough with long shaggy strips

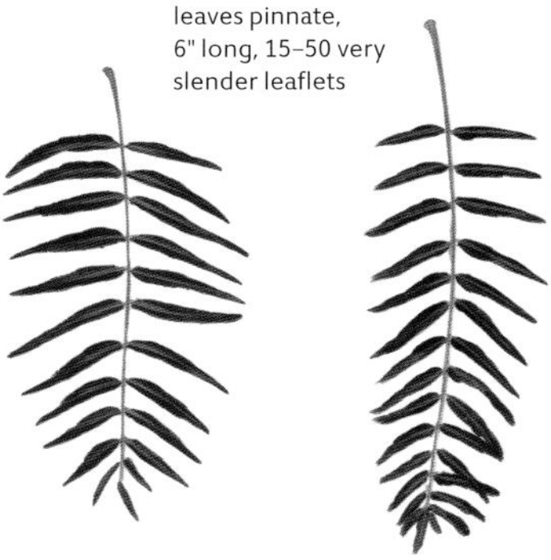
leaves pinnate, 6" long, 15–50 very slender leaflets

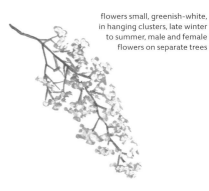

flowers small, greenish-white, in hanging clusters, late winter to summer, male and female flowers on separate trees

fruit small red to pink berries in large loose clusters persistent all year

The fruit of this species is often gathered and sold as "pink peppercorns," which have a somewhat spicy flavor. These peppertrees are not related to Black Pepper (*Piper nigrum*), the source of the common commercial spice; it is a vine distantly related to magnolias.

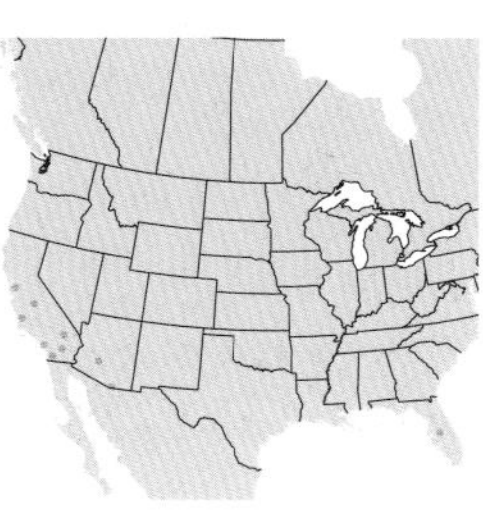

Native to central South America. Commonly cultivated and locally naturalized from California to Florida (zones 8–11).

Other Peppertrees

Three other South American species of the genus *Schinus* are cultivated and naturalized in subtropical regions. All are shrubs or small trees with clusters of red to black berries.

Longleaf Peppertree (*S. longifolius*), cultivated and naturalized in southern Texas.

Brazil Peppertree (*S. terebinthifolius*), commonly cultivated, naturalized and invasive in many habitats in southern and central Florida; planted widely in southwestern states; differs from Peruvian in having fewer and much broader leaflets (5–11 per leaf).

Hardee Peppertree (*S. polygamus*), cultivated and naturalized in southern California. Differs from all other species in the genus in having simple leaves 1½" long (not pinnately compound).

American Smoketree

Cotinus obovatus

CHITTAMWOOD, YELLOWWOOD

Deciduous. Shrub or small tree to 25–40' tall (max. 54') branching low into rounded, open crown. Silky-haired and finely branched flower clusters produce the very distinctive "smoky" appearance, but involve very few actual flowers.

bark light gray, scaly

leaves 5", rounded oval, often bluish-green

fall color brilliant gold to red or purple

after flowering, long silky hairs on flower stalks; hazy or "smoky" effect persists through summer, often from yellowish to pinkish

flowers yellowish, small and sparse on 7" cone-shaped clusters at branch tips, late spring

twig fairly stout, orange or greenish-brown

buds small and dark

Rare and local in dry limestone soils in open woods or edges. Uncommon in cultivation, where much less frequent than European Smoketree (zones 4–8).

European Smoketree

Cotinus coggygria

Shrub usually under 15' tall. Similar to American Smoketree, but only tree-like with constant pruning. Differs in having flower plumes more showy, leaf more rounded, fall color weak. Native from central Europe to China. Commonly cultivated and occasionally escaped from cultivation to woods edges and disturbed areas (zones 4–8). Many cultivars include plants with purple leaves and purplish flowering spikes, unlike any American Smoketree.

Cashew Family: Sumacs

Sumacs (genus *Rhus*) include about 150 species of herbs, shrubs, and trees worldwide. In North America, fourteen species are native, and eleven are at least occasionally tree-like.

None of our native sumacs are commonly tree-like; all are typically small to large shrubs, and several of the most common species form large thickets, often along road cuts or field edges.

Three of the most common and most often tree-like species (Smooth, Shining, and Staghorn Sumac) have deciduous compound leaves. Four species of the Southwest have simple evergreen leaves. Several other exotic species are occasionally cultivated, but are not covered in this guide. This page shows the common features of species in the genus *Rhus*. All have deciduous compound leaves.

Sumacs do not grow large enough to be important commercially for wood, and are valued mainly for providing food and cover to wildlife. The related Poison-sumac is sometimes included in the genus *Rhus*.

bark thin, grayish, smooth with warty horizontal lenticels

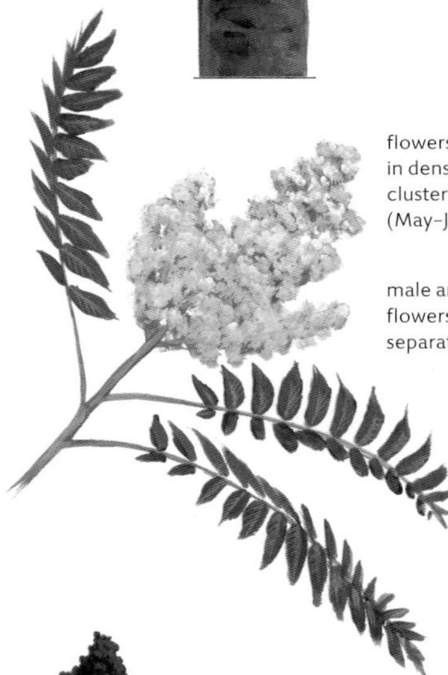

flowers tiny, greenish, in dense pointed clusters at branch tips (May–Jul)

male and female flowers on separate plants

fruit small reddish berries in pointed clusters 6" long at branch tips, persist through winter

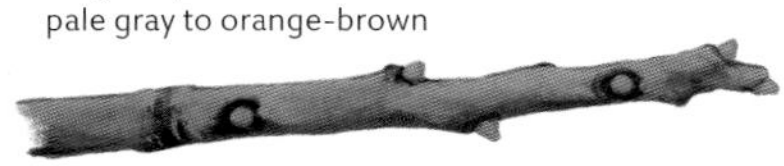

twigs very stout, pale gray to orange-brown

leaves pinnately compound 15", 11–31 narrow, pointed leaflets each 3 ½" long

Shining Sumac with leafstalk winged

fall color brilliant orange to red

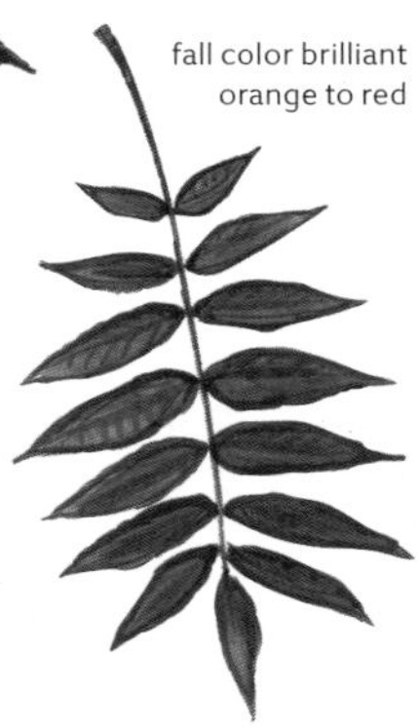

small tree with few branches, female plants have branches tipped with reddish fruit clusters

Smooth Sumac

Rhus glabra

SCARLET SUMAC, SLEEK SUMAC, VINEGAR TREE

Deciduous. Shrub or occasionally a small tree 10–15' tall (max. 45'). Generally suckers to form domed thickets, tree-like plants have leaning, curved trunk and sparse branches.

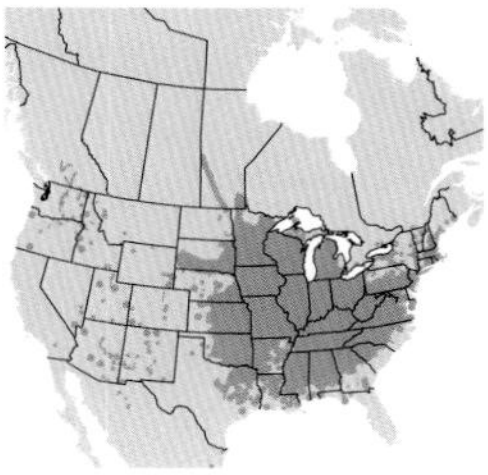

Common and widespread in field edges, hedgerows, road cuts, and other disturbed sites. Commonly cultivated (zones 3–9).

Shining Sumac

Rhus copallina

FLAMELEAF SUMAC, DWARF SUMAC

Very similar to Smooth Sumac, but leafstalk winged between leaflets, twigs and fruit finely hairy, flowers later (Jun–Sep).

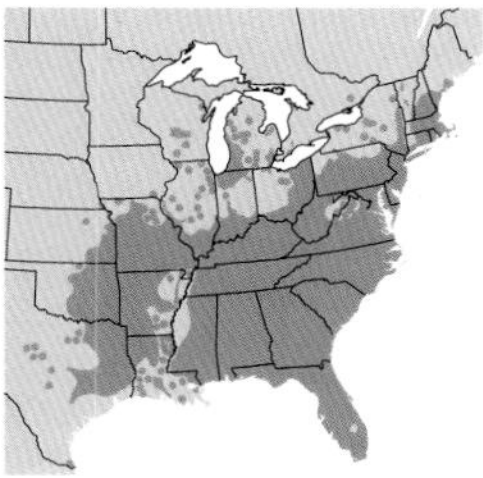

Common in well-drained open areas, roadsides, old fields. Commonly cultivated (zones 4–9).

Staghorn Sumac

Rhus typhina

FUZZY SUMAC, VELVET SUMAC

Similar to Smooth Sumac, but averages slightly larger (max. 61' tall) and has densely fuzzy twigs and fruit clusters.

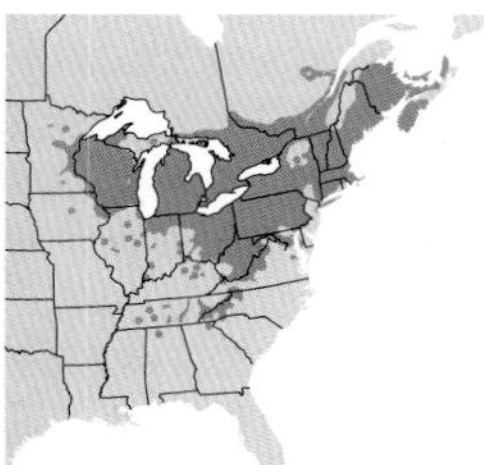

Common and widespread in wet or dry open areas. Commonly cultivated (zones 4–8), including cutleaf cultivars.

Poison-sumac

Toxicodendron vernix

POISON-DOGWOOD, POISON-ELDER, THUNDERWOOD

Deciduous. Slender straggling shrub or occasionally a small tree 12–20' tall (max. 30'). In the same genus with Poison Ivy and Poison Oak; contact with this plant can cause serious skin irritation.

leafstalks often reddish
leaves 10", pinnately compound, 7–15 oval leaflets, well-spaced, each 2 ½" long, shiny green above
fruit a grayish white, berrylike, rounded drupe, ¼" diameter; ripe in fall
fruit on long stalks persists into winter
twigs stout, pale gray, with small buds

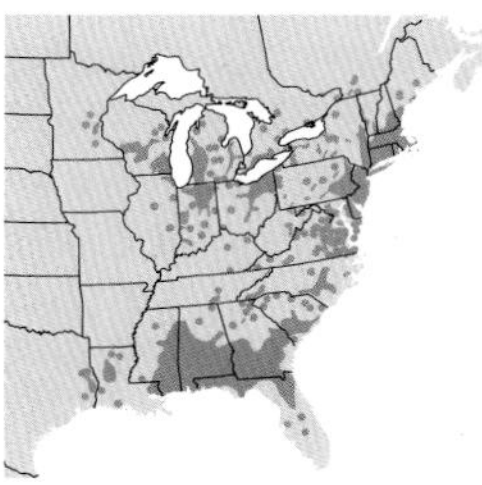

Locally common in wooded swamps, pond and stream margins; exclusively in wetlands. Not cultivated.

Mahogany Family

The mahogany family (Meliaceae) includes about 500 species of mostly tropical trees and shrubs worldwide. Most have pinnately compound leaves and large clusters of flowers at the twig tips. Many species produce valuable lumber. Two species are commonly cultivated in North America.

bark on young trunks brown-gray

older trunks have broad pale gray ridges with orange furrows

Chinaberry

Melia azedarach

BEAD TREE, PRIDE OF INDIA, UMBRELLA TREE, PERSIAN LILAC

Deciduous. Small tree usually under 40' tall (max. 82'); single-trunked with oval crown of stout twigs and large compound leaves. All parts of this plant are poisonous if eaten.

fall color late and drab yellow

flowers delicate purple star-shaped, five petals, in large loose sprays forming hazy mass at twig tips, (Apr–Jun) after leaves

leaves large, 16", bipinnately compound, many dark glossy bluish leaflets, each 2" long, sharply-toothed

underleaf paler green

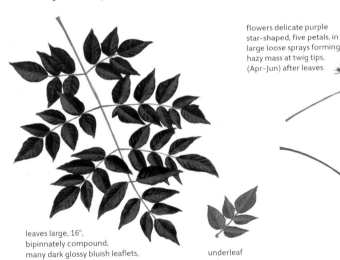

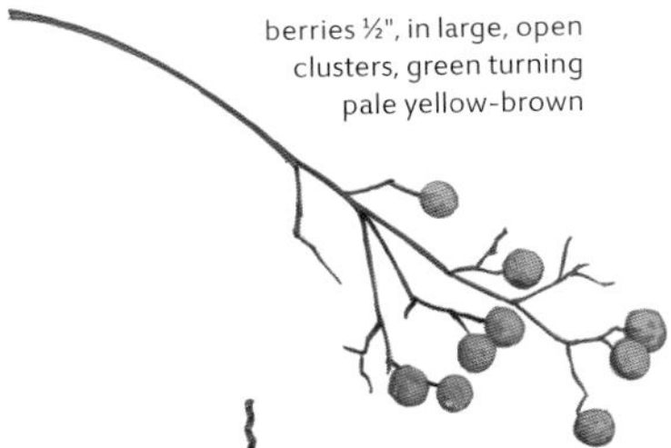
berries ½", in large, open clusters, green turning pale yellow-brown

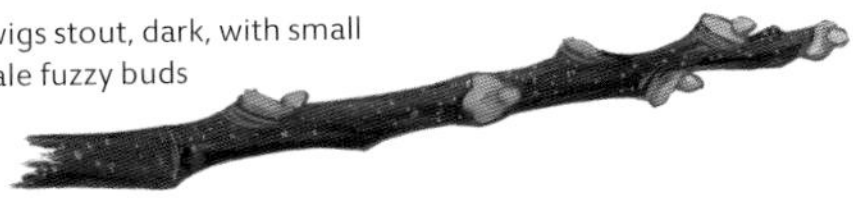
twigs stout, dark, with small pale fuzzy buds

fruit and hanging stal
persistent all winter below stout twig tips

Native from India to China. Commonly cultivated in yards and parks across the South and now commonly naturalized and invasive in many areas (zones 7–10).

Chinese Toon

Toona sinensis

CHINESE CEDAR, CHINESE CEDRELA

Deciduous. Medium tree usually 30–40' tall (max 67'); spreading, gaunt tree single-trunked but with many suckers. Native to China and adjacent regions. Uncommon in cultivation (zone 5-7). The most cold hardy species in the family.

leaves large, 16", pinnately compound with 10 to 22 leaflets, like Black Walnut

leaves smell of onion

flowers white to lavender, in hanging sprays, summer

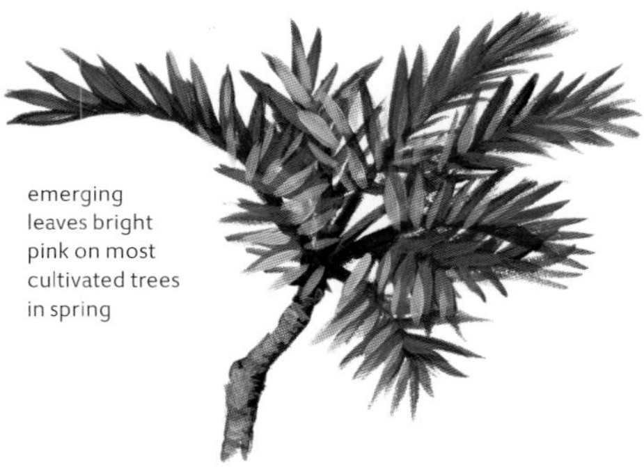
emerging leaves bright pink on most cultivated trees in spring

Rue Family

The rue family (Rutaceae) includes about 1,600 species of herbs, shrubs, and trees worldwide. Closely related to the soapberry, mahogany, and quassia families, the rues include the citrus trees and some popular ornamental trees. Seven species in seven genera (two native) are included here.

The genus *Citrus* may include ten or more closely related species, all originating in southeastern Asia, but these trees have been extensively cultivated for centuries with so many hybrids and cultivars that it is now difficult to classify the existing plants into discrete species.

Oranges were introduced to Europe in the 11th century. Columbus brought citrus seeds to the Caribbean on his second voyage in 1493, and Spanish explorer Juan Ponce de Leon introduced them to Florida in 1513, where some are now naturalized. The grapefruit is a hybrid that originated in Barbados, apparently after Pomelo trees (*Citrus maxima*) brought from Asia in the 1600s cross-pollinated 'Sweet' Orange trees that had been cultivated there since the early 1500s.

The closely related Trifoliate-orange and the kumquats (genus *Fortunella*) are sometimes included in the genus *Citrus*.

Familiar and commonly cultivated citrus include various oranges, tangerine, mandarin orange, lemon, citron, limes (including Key Lime), pomelo, and grapefruit.

Sour Orange is the most cold-hardy citrus. Many cultivars have been developed and are grown commercially in various countries around the world, but less often in North America. The sour fruit of this species is used for marmalade and as flavoring or fragrance in various liqueurs and perfumes. It is also extensively cultivated as rootstock for other, less-hardy varieties of citrus. Compared to 'Sweet' Orange (Citrus ' × sinensis') it tends to have a longer leafstalk, narrower crown, and rougher fruit surface.

Sour Orange

Citrus aurantium

BITTER ORANGE, BIGARADE ORANGE, SEVILLE ORANGE

Evergreen, Shrub or small tree usually under 20' tall (max. about 30'); a low rounded tree with dense dark green foliage. Profuse and strongly perfumed white flowers characteristic of the genus.

leafstalk winged
leaves 4", oval, sharply-pointed
underleaf fairly dark green

white fragrant flowers 1" wide, 5 narrow petals; single or in small clusters in leaf axils
fruit 3", reddish-orange when ripe; rougher skin than commercial oranges

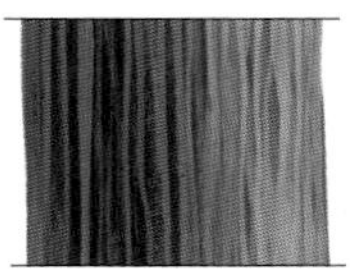
bark thin, striated pale gray and green

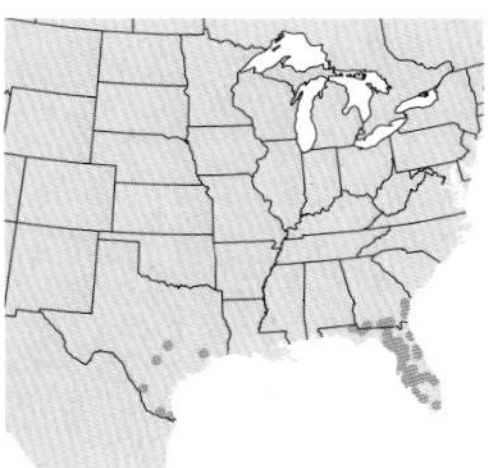

Native to Southeast Asia. Commonly cultivated (zones 9–11) and locally naturalized in a variety of soil types including rich moist soils of lowlands.

Trifoliate-orange

Poncirus trifoliata

MOCK ORANGE, JAPANESE BITTER ORANGE, HARDY ORANGE

Deciduous. Shrub or small tree usually under 12' tall and low-branching (max. 26'); glossy dark green, dense foliage. Flowers white, 1½" across with 5 narrow petals, very fragrant, early spring. Closely-related to *Citrus*, but with compound leaves, vicious thorns, and bitter fruit.

leaves 1½", compound with three leaflets
leafstalk winged

fruit like a small orange, 1½" across, green turning yellow-orange; mature in fall

green twigs armed with very sharp stout thorns

Many cultivars include large- to small-flowered varieties, also used as rootstock for *Citrus* cultivars.

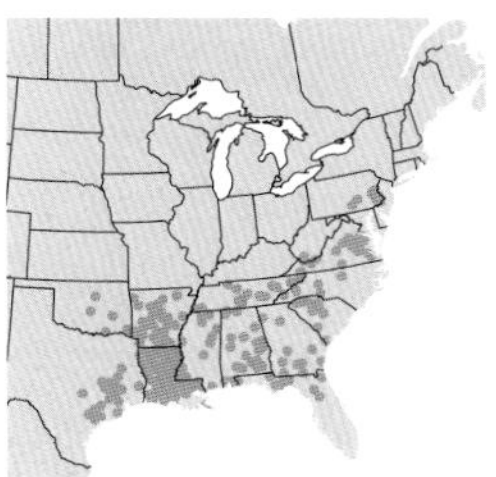

Native to China and Korea. Commonly cultivated as a hedge in the South (zones 5–9) and widely naturalized and sometimes invasive from Texas and Oklahoma to Pennsylvania.

Beebee Tree

Tetradium daniellii

KOREAN EVODIA

Deciduous. Small to medium tree usually 25–30' (max. 75') with broad rounded crown. Flowers very attractive to bees, appearing in late summer when few other flowers are available.

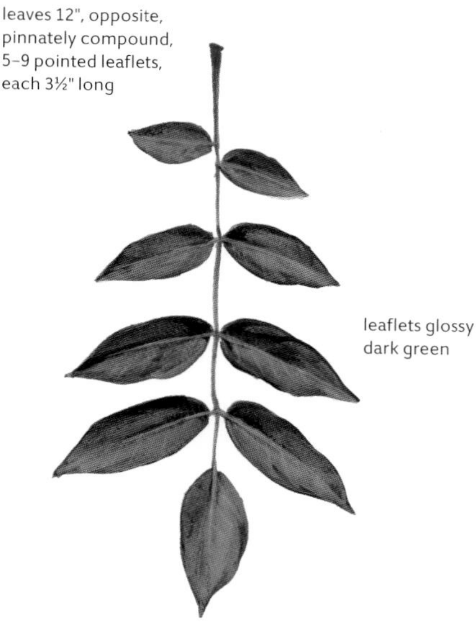
leaves 12", opposite, pinnately compound, 5–9 pointed leaflets, each 3½" long
leaflets glossy dark green

flowers small, whitish, in flat-topped clusters 5" wide (Jul–Aug)

Native to Korea and northern China. Uncommon in cultivation (zones 4–8). Locally naturalized.

Common Hoptree

Ptelea trifoliata

WAFER ASH, HOP TREE, STINKING ASH, SKUNK BUSH, SHRUBBY TREFOIL

Deciduous. Shrub or small tree usually under 20' tall (max. 36'); sparsely-branched, slender, often multi-stemmed and leaning. Distinctive fruit has been used as a substitute for hops. Small greenish flowers in spring have fragrance like orange blossoms.

leaves 5", usually 3 oval leaflets each 3" long, terminal leaflet largest
fruit ¾", round papery samara; persists to late fall

California Hoptree (*Ptelea crenulata*), a similar species native in California, is usually a shrub and rarely tree-like. It differs from Common Hoptree in having smaller leaflets (each 2") with fine wavy teeth on the edges.

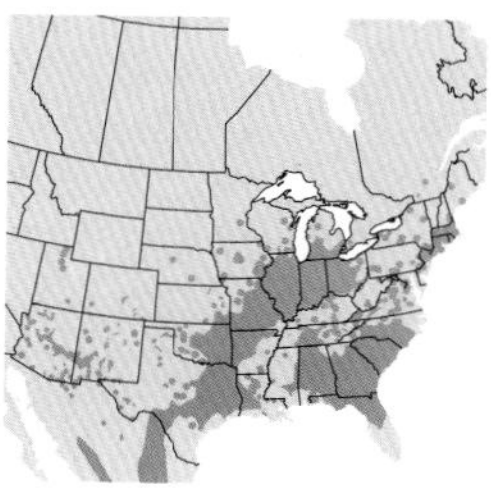

Uncommon in well-drained rich soils, especially in forest edges and rocky slopes; also roadsides, and disturbed areas. Uncommonly cultivated (zones 3–9).

Southern Prickly-ash

Zanthoxylum clava-herculis

HERCULES' CLUB, TOOTHACHE TREE, SEA-ASH, PEPPERBARK

Evergreen or tardily deciduous. Shrub or small tree usually 15–25' tall (max. 65'). Fruits in clusters, small brown husk splits to reveal reddish to black seed, ripe in early summer. Leaves very fragrant; bark has anesthetic properties and was often chewed to numb the pain of toothache.

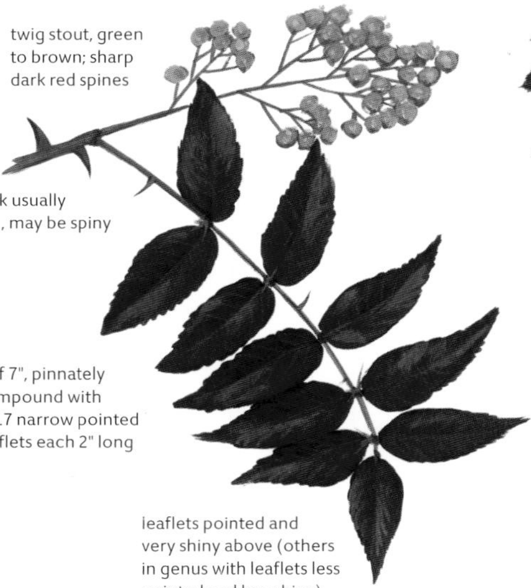
flowers tiny, yellow-green, in broad clusters at twig tips
twig stout, green to brown; sharp dark red spines
leafstalk usually reddish, may be spiny
leaf 7", pinnately compound with 7–17 narrow pointed leaflets each 2" long
leaflets pointed and very shiny above (others in genus with leaflets less pointed and less shiny)

bark gray with spiny knobs

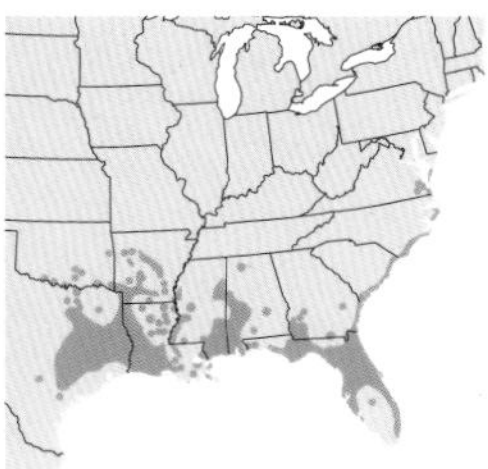

Common in moist soil in forest understory, fencerows, or along waterways, also in coastal sand dunes. Rarely cultivated (zones 7–9).

Castor-Aralia

Kalopanax septemlobus

PRICKLY CASTOR-OIL TREE

Deciduous. Medium to large tree often 40–60' tall (max. 57'); mature trees broad and tropical-looking. Member of the Aralia family (page 393).

leaves 14", very large, palmate, long stalk

flowers small, pale greenish white, in large flat-topped clusters 18" across
fruit small berries, black when ripe

twig stout, greenish with many slender sharp spines

Native to Japan, parts of Russia, Korea, China. Uncommonly cultivated and locally escaped (zones 4–7).

Amur Corktree

Phellodendron amurense

CHINESE CORKTREE, SAKHALIN PHELLODENDRON

Deciduous. Medium to large tree usually 30–45' tall (max. 75'); broad-spreading with massive limbs, often flat-topped. Similar to Kentucky Yellowwood, but note ridged bark, opposite leaves, small flowers, and berry-like fruit. Crushed foliage and fruit have aromatic odor, like turpentine.

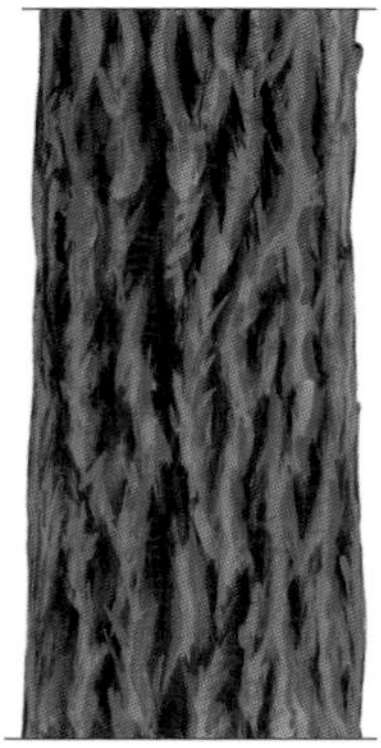

bark deeply furrowed with broad pale ridges, soft and corky

leaves 12", pinnate, 3–11 leaflets each 3½" long; shiny, pointed, twisted with obvious pale veins

fall color briefly yellow

underleaf much paler

flowers green or maroon in upright clusters at twig tips (early summer), male and female flowers on separate trees

fruit small, berry-like, in clusters, green turning dull black

fruit persists into winter, eaten by birds

twigs brown, stout, straight

buds opposite, nearly surrounded by pale leaf scar

Native to Asia. Uncommonly cultivated and locally naturalized and invasive, seeds spread by birds to roadsides and woods in Northeast (zones 3–8).

About 10 closely-related species, or subspecies, of Corktree, are native to Asia and several are reportedly cultivated less frequently in North America. Japanese Corktree (*Phellodendron japonicum*) is reported naturalized in the Northeast. Differences between any of these forms are slight and identification is difficult.

Soapberry Family

The soapberry family (Sapindaceae) includes nearly 2,000 species of herbs, vines, shrubs, and trees worldwide. This guide includes thirty-three species (twenty-one native species) in the soapberry family that are tree-like and cold-hardy in North America.

Recent research has led to the inclusion of both the buckeyes (genus *Aesculus*) and maples (genus *Acer*) in the soapberry family. These two genera are each very distinctive and well-defined; each was formerly placed in its own family. However, detailed studies combined with chemical and DNA evidence confirm a close relationship between them and they are now considered members of the soapberry family.

The three species shown on these two pages represent three other genera in the soapberry family: *Sapindus*, *Koelreuteria*, and *Ungnadia*. With alternate, pinnately compound leaves, they are more typical of the family than the buckeyes or maples (which have opposite leaves with palmate structure). Soapberries (genus *Sapindus*) include about twelve species of shrubs and small trees worldwide (two native). The fruit of soapberries contain a detergent-like compound that produces a soapy lather in water, and the fruit has long been used as form of soap.

One other species of soapberry is found in North America, the Wingleaf Soapberry (*Sapindus saponaria*). It is similar to Western Soapberry, but with broader leaflets and winged leafstalk. It is uncommon and local in Florida.

Western Soapberry bark scaly and reddish brown

Western Soapberry

Sapindus drummondii

CHINABERRY, WILD CHINATREE

Deciduous. Large shrub to medium tree often 20–30' tall (max. 72'), broad, rounded crown and short trunk. Male and female flowers on separate trees; tiny, yellowish-white in 8" clusters (May–Jun), male flowers showier. Fruit produces a soapy lather when crushed.

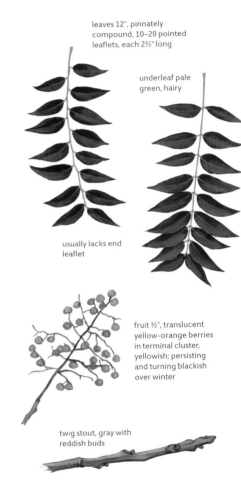

leaves 12", pinnately compound, 10–20 pointed leaflets, each 2½" long

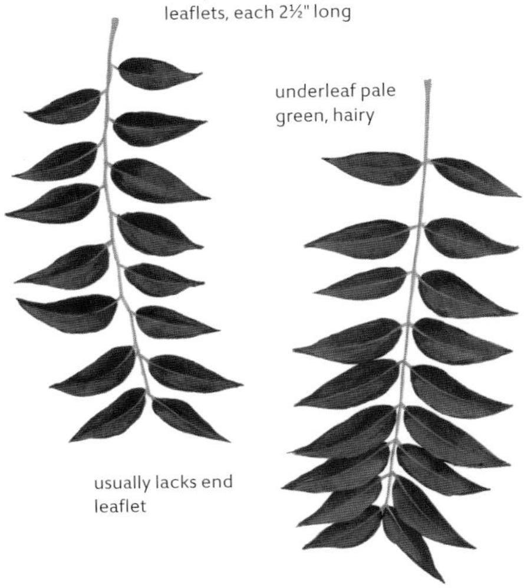
underleaf pale green, hairy
usually lacks end leaflet

fruit ½", translucent yellow-orange berries in terminal cluster, yellowish; persisting and turning blackish over winter

twig stout, gray with reddish buds

Common and widespread along streams, hedgerows, and woods edges. Uncommonly cultivated, mainly in Texas (zones 5–9).

Golden Rain-tree

Koelreuteria paniculata

SHOWER TREE, PRIDE OF INDIA, VARNISH TREE, GATE TREE

Deciduous. Small to medium tree usually 30–40' tall (max. 65'); broad, rounded crown, few branches, short crooked or leaning trunk. Compare Common Laburnum. Two other *Koelreuteria* are less commonly cultivated.

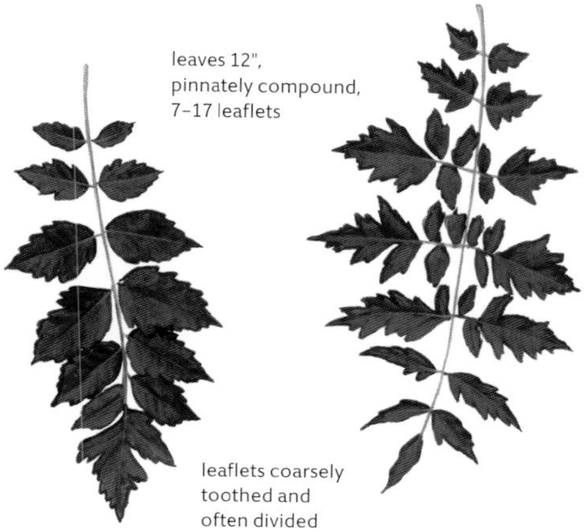
leaves 12", pinnately compound, 7–17 leaflets
leaflets coarsely toothed and often divided

flowers yellow in large loose sprays to 2' long, summer to fall (May–Oct)

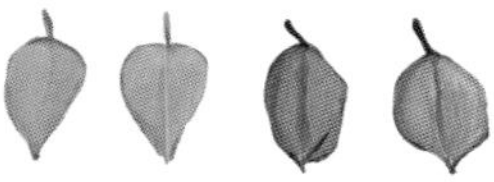
fruit 1½", papery capsule, green then pinkish-brown; hang in loose clusters into winter

twig stout, gray-green

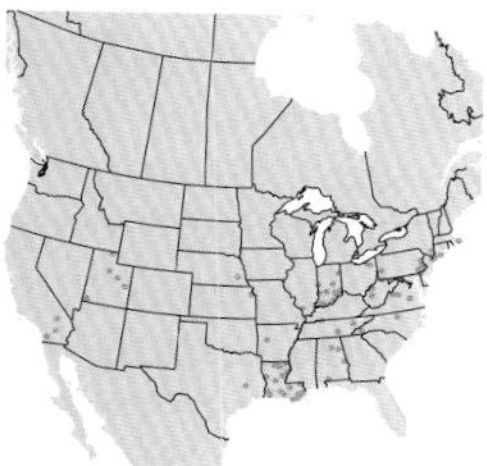

Native to China and Korea. Commonly cultivated as an ornamental yard tree, locally naturalized (zones 5–8).

Mexican-buckeye

Ungnadia speciosa

MONILLA

Deciduous. Shrub or small tree usually 12–15' tall (max. 22') usually multi-stemmed, often leafless. The only species in its genus; fruit similar to buckeyes; pink flowers in early spring reminiscent of redbuds.

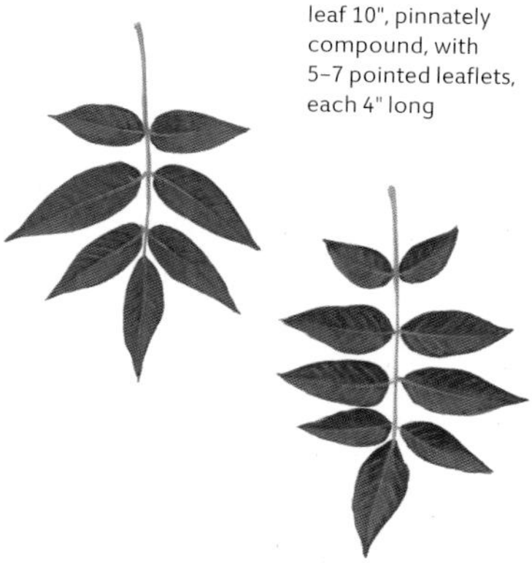
leaf 10", pinnately compound, with 5–7 pointed leaflets, each 4" long

flowers bright pink/lavender, about 1" across, in showy clusters along twigs; early spring before or with leaves

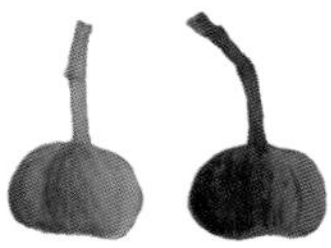
fruit 1½", hanging woody capsule, contains 3 hard round seeds; ripe in early fall and persistent year-round

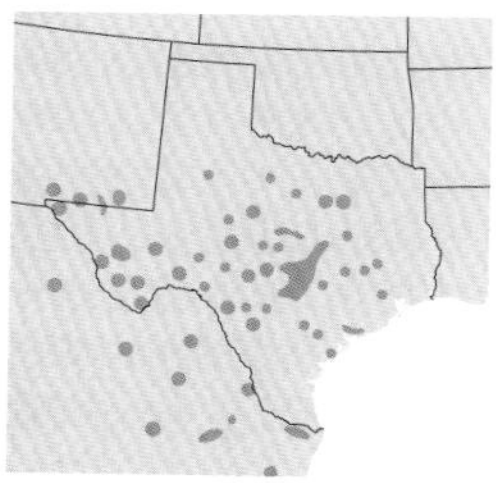

Uncommon and local in canyons and along creeks, often in limestone soils. Uncommonly cultivated mainly within native range (zone 7–9).

Soapberry Family: Buckeyes

The buckeyes and horsechestnuts (genus *Aesculus*) include about sixteen species of trees and shrubs worldwide. In North America, six species are native and are included here, although four are often merely shrubs. One additional Eurasian species is commonly cultivated and naturalized.

Traditionally placed in their own family (Hippocastanaceae), the buckeyes are now considered part of the soapberry family (Sapindaceae) along with maples, despite their distinctive features.

All buckeyes have opposite, palmately compound leaves unique among North American trees. Flowers are showy and tubular, produced in large upright clusters in spring or summer usually with long projecting stamens. Fruit is a large shiny brown seed enclosed in a leathery or spiny husk. Most species hybridize regularly in the wild, wherever their range overlaps, and many garden hybrids and cultivars have been produced. Becasue of hybridization, identification of buckeyes can often be challenging.

The buckeyes native to North America flower in summer, while the species native to Eurasia, known as horsechestnuts, flower in spring. The large, shiny brown seeds of buckeyes appear similar to chestnuts, but are toxic to humans. Toxins can be removed from the seeds through multiple rinses in boiling water, and some Native Americans used this method to make the seeds edible. Animals, such as deer and squirrels, are unaffected by the toxin. The name buckeye refers to the resemblance of the shiny brown seed to the eye of a deer.

The alternate name "conker tree" refers to the British game of conkers, which is played using the seeds.

The wood of buckeyes is relatively soft and little-used; the primary commercial importance of the genus is ornamental.

Common Horsechestnut

Aesculus hippocastanum

CANDLE TREE, CONKER TREE

Deciduous. Medium to large tree often 60' (max. 108'). Attractive tree with large dark leaves in summer, spectacular flowers in spring, and stout upswept twigs in winter. Differs from all native buckeyes in seven leaflets, large sticky buds, and very spiny fruit husks.

leaves large, 14", usually 7 leaflets (vs. 5 in most native buckeyes)
underleaf paler green
leaflets broad and blunt-tipped (vs. tapered and pointed), widest near tip

twigs stout, gray-brown
terminal bud very large, sticky and shiny
buds dark brown, pointed, opposite

Native from Asia to southeastern Europe. Commonly cultivated for shade and ornament; widely escaped from cultivation (zones 4–7).

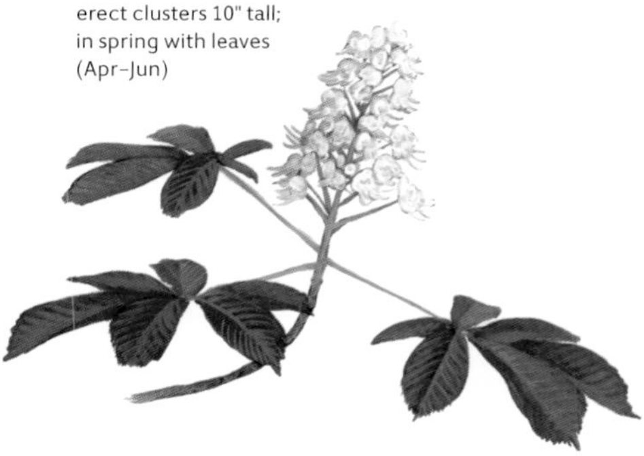

flowers creamy-white in erect clusters 10" tall; in spring with leaves (Apr–Jun)

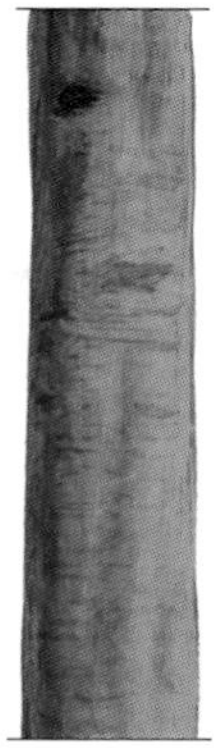

bark smooth on young trunks

older trunks gray-brown, scaly with long thin plates

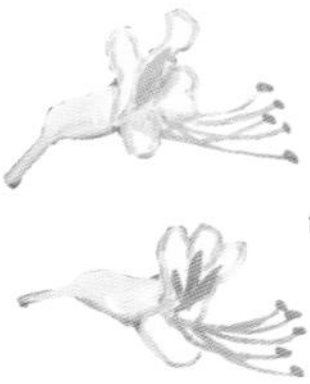

spots inside flowers turn from yellow to reddish after pollination

fall color drab, yellow-brown, late

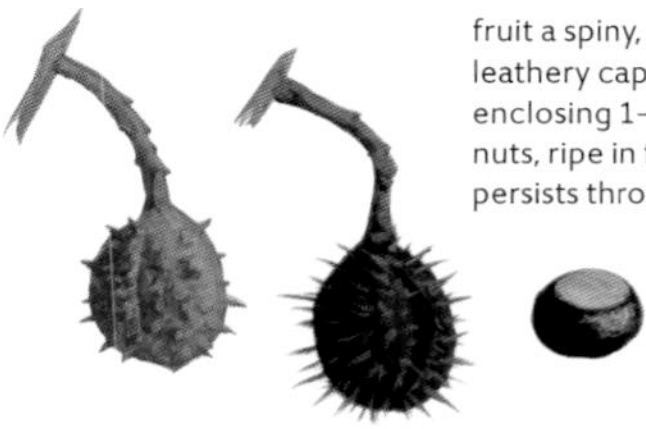

fruit a spiny, 3-parted leathery capsule 2" wide, enclosing 1–3 shiny brown nuts, ripe in fall; often persists through winter

stout contorted branches arched and curved up at tips

'Red Horsechestnut'

Aesculus '× *carnea*'

REDFLOWER HORSECHESTNUT

Deciduous. Small rounded tree usually under 35' tall (max. 69'). Hybrid of Horsechestnut with Red Buckeye commonly cultivated in several different cultivars. The most common large red-flowering tree in temperate zones. Hybrids of Red Buckeye × Yellow Buckeye are also cultivated in many cultivars as *Aesculus* '× *hybrida*.'

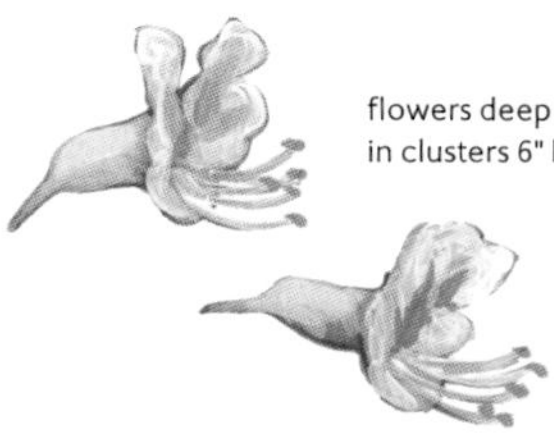

flowers deep pink to red, in clusters 6" long

Yellow Buckeye

Aesculus flava

SWEET BUCKEYE, BIG BUCKEYE

Deciduous. Medium to large tree often 70' tall (max. 136'). Our largest native buckeye; planted frequently as an ornamental tree.

bark on mature trunks relatively smooth, brown and gray with large plates and scales

leaves 9" with 5–7 short-stalked, pointed leaflets

stamens do not project from flower (vs. conspicuous in Ohio and Horsechestnut)

flowers cream to pale yellow in clusters 6" long (Apr–Jun)

fruit large, 2½", with thick smooth husk, 2 seeds

terminal buds large, about ⅔" smaller than Horsechestnut but larger than other buckeyes

trunk divides into relatively straight ascending branches

Common in rich mixed deciduous woods from riverbottoms to mountain slopes; Uncommonly cultivated (zones 4–8).

Ohio Buckeye

Aesculus glabra

FETID BUCKEYE, STINKING BUCKEYE, AMERICAN HORSECHESTNUT

Deciduous. Shrub or small tree often 35' tall (max. 148'); all other buckeyes except Yellow and Horsechestnut are small understory trees or shrubs.

bark thick and furrowed, uneven ridges without clear pattern

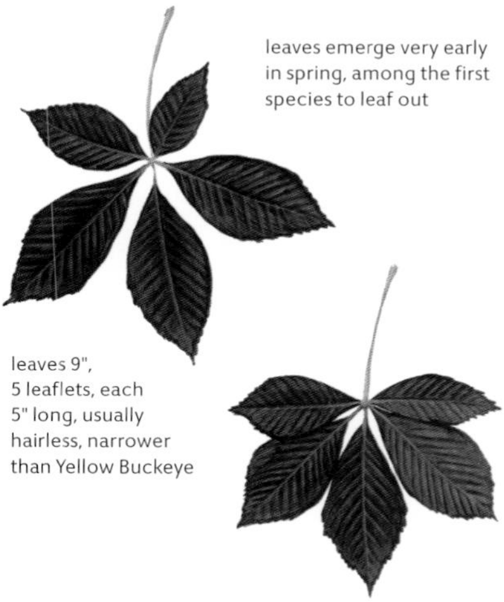
leaves emerge very early in spring, among the first species to leaf out
leaves 9", 5 leaflets, each 5" long, usually hairless, narrower than Yellow Buckeye

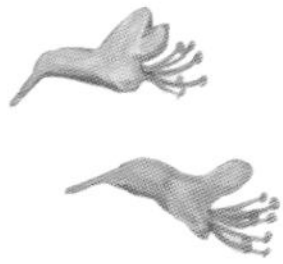
flowers with stamens longer than petals

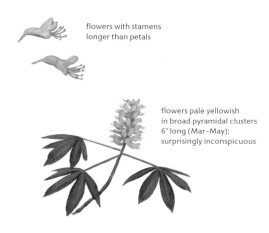

flowers pale yellowish in broad pyramidal clusters 6" long (Mar–May); surprisingly inconspicuous

fruit 2" with short spines; the only native buckeye with spiny husk

twigs stout, yellowish-gray
end buds pale orange-brown
bud scales strongly keeled

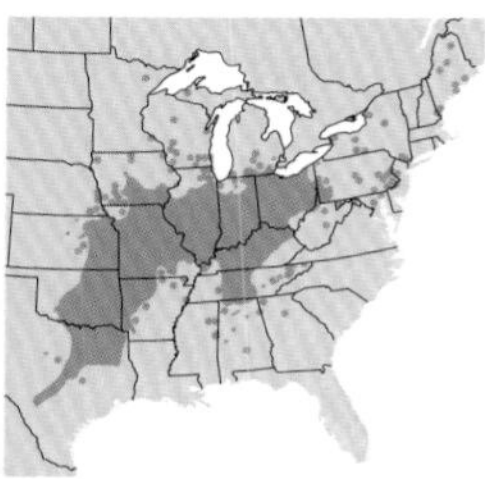

Common in woodland in rich soils, usually as scattered trees but sometimes in shrubby thickets. Commonly cultivated (zones 4–7).

'Texas' Ohio Buckeye

Aesculus glabra var. *arguta*

Similar to typical Ohio Buckeye, but smaller, usually a shrub or small tree 15–20' tall (max. 30') with more and narrower leaflets. Common in rich woods west of the Mississippi River. Uncommonly cultivated (zones 4–8).

leaves 8", 7–9 very narrow leaflets

Red Buckeye

Aesculus pavia

AESCULUS DISCOLOR, SCARLET BUCKEYE, WOOLLY BUCKEYE, FIRE-CRACKER-PLANT

Deciduous. Usually a slender clump-forming shrub, occasionally a small tree to 25' (max. 35'). Larger cultivated trees with reddish flowers are the hybrid 'Red Horsechestnut.'

five leaflets, each 5" long; often with orange midvein; short-stalked

flowers bright red (sometimes yellow), in oblong clusters 7" long (Feb–May)

fruit capsule 1½", smooth, on slender stalk, 1–3 seeds

twigs stout, greenish brown
buds broad, pointed, red-brown

Some Red Buckeyes growing on the Edwards Plateau of Texas have yellow flowers and are considered a subspecies or a separate species.

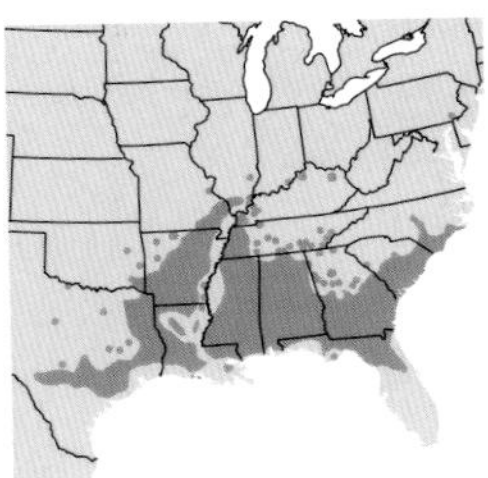

Common in a variety of habitats from bottomlands and stream banks to pinelands or bluffs. Commonly cultivated in gardens (zones 6–9), but less so than 'Red Horsechestnut.'

Painted Buckeye

Aesculus sylvatica

DWARF BUCKEYE, GEORGIA BUCKEYE

Deciduous. Thicket-forming shrub or occasionally a small tree to 30' tall (max. 60'). Similar to Red Buckeye, distinguished by details of flowers and fruit.

five leaflets, each 5" long; often with orange midvein; short-stalked

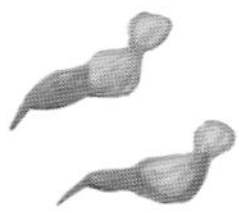
flowers yellow, occasionally partly red or pink; in oblong to pyramidal clusters 6" long (Apr–Jun)
stamens do not project from flower

fruit capsule 1½", smooth, 1 seed

twig stout, orange-brown, buds red-brown

Distinguished from Yellow Buckeye only by smaller size, smaller fruit, smaller buds, and slightly longer leaflet stalks. Known to hybridize with Red Buckeye and with Yellow Buckeye, which complicates identification.

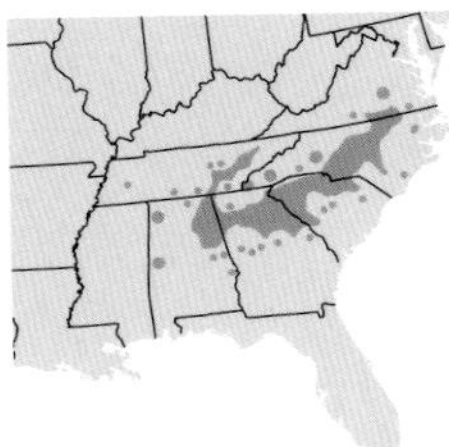

Common, especially as understory plants among pines or deciduous trees on well-drained slopes, less often in bottomlands. Rarely cultivated (zones 6–9).

Bottlebrush Buckeye

Aesculus parviflora

Deciduous. Usually a multi-stemmed shrub, occasionally a small tree to 16' tall (max. about 20'). Often forming dense thickets.

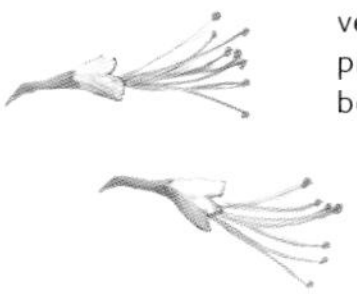
flowers small, white, in tall narrow clusters
very long stamens project well beyond petals

fruit small, about 1"; spineless

terminal buds relatively small, under ½"

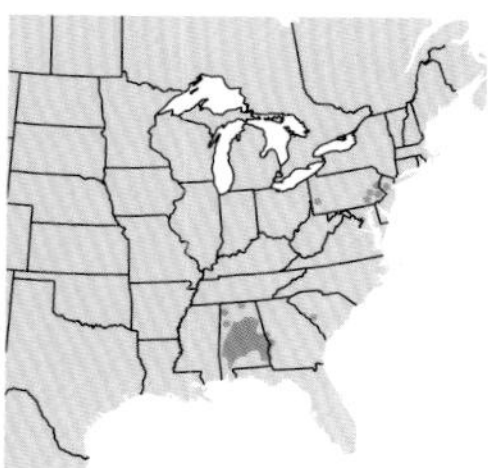

Locally abundant, in rich woods of bottomlands and hillsides. Uncommonly cultivated (zones 4–8).

California Buckeye

Aesculus californica

Deciduous. Large shrub or small tree usually under 25' (max. 48'); spreading with rounded open crown. Differs from other buckeyes in having longer leaflet stalks, resin-coated winter buds, and more oval fruit.

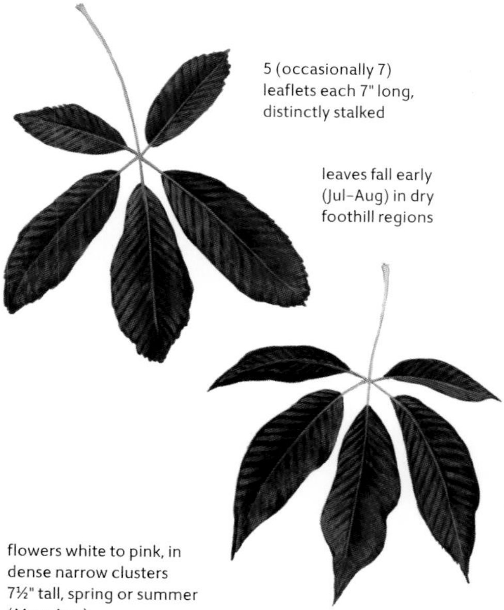
5 (occasionally 7) leaflets each 7" long, distinctly stalked
leaves fall early (Jul–Aug) in dry foothill regions

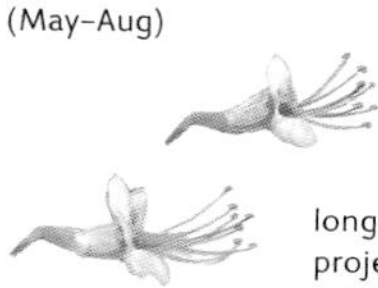
flowers white to pink, in dense narrow clusters 7½" tall, spring or summer (May–Aug)
long stamens project beyond petals

fruit 2", pear-shaped, smooth, 1 seed

buds large, resin-coated

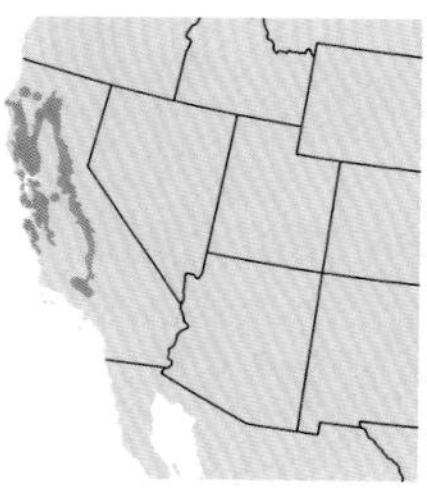

Common in coastal foothills along streams and roadsides; commonly cultivated near natural range (zones 7–8).

Soapberry Family: Maples

The maples (genus *Acer*) include about 125 species worldwide with the greatest diversity in Asia. Most are deciduous trees. Thirteen species are native to North America and all are included in this guide along with ten commonly cultivated species.

The maples have long been placed in their own family (Aceraceae), but more recent research places them in the soapberry family with the buckeyes. To the casual observer there are no other obvious links between these genera, and maples can still be thought of as a very distinctive and well-defined genus of trees.

Maple leaves have long stalks, sometimes the full length of the leaf blade and depending on the species, may be dark or light green or red.

All maples have palmately compound leaves, usually with three or five lobes and long stalks. Maple flowers are small and clustered, but can be quite showy as most species flower before the leaves in spring while the twigs are still bare. Fruit is the familiar "maple key" of paired seeds with papery wings. The wings cause the fruit to spin rapidly in the air, falling

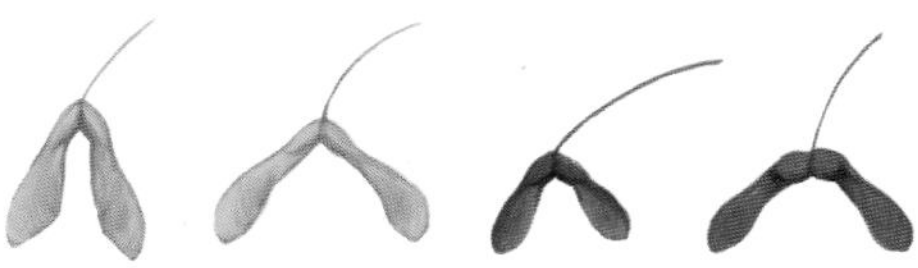

Maple fruit varies in size, color, and in the angle between each winged seed case.

more slowly with the potential to be dispersed on the wind.

Maples can be subdivided into many smaller groups of related species based on their flowers.

Red and Silver maples are closely related and along with Box-elder have tiny long-stalked flowers without petals that appear before the leaves in dense clusters along the sides of the twigs. All other maples have flowers in clusters or spikes at the ends of twigs.

Sugar Maple and its close relatives (Black, Florida, Chalk, and Canyon) have flowers all on long stalks rather than a branched cluster appearing just before the leaves.

All other native maples–Bigleaf, Rocky Mountain, Striped, Mountain, and Vine–have flowers with petals in branched clusters or spikes at the tips of the twigs. In these species the flowers appear with or after the leaves.

Maples are known for their brilliant fall colors. The leaves of most species turn clear bright red or yellow in the fall, and it is the maples, more than any other group of trees, that are responsible for the celebrated fall foliage of New England.

Maple wood (particularly Sugar Maple in North America and Sycamore Maple in Europe) is very hard and is used where extreme

Depending on the species, fall color in maples ranges from pale, clear yellow and orange to scarlet and burgundy.

durability is needed, such as flooring, butcher-blocks, and some specialty products, such as bowling pins. The wood of maples also has excellent sound-conducting properties, and is used for drums and many stringed instruments. Unusual patterns in the grain of maple wood arise occasionally, and are known by descriptive trade names such as 'Tiger,' 'Flame,' and 'Birdseye.' When found, these are particularly valuable and desirable. One of the most unusual commercial uses of the maples is for the production of maple syrup (see page 339).

Most maples are trees of mature forests in moist temperate zones, either as large canopy trees or smaller understory trees. Sugar and Red Maple are very important components of mature rich hardwood forest in the eastern United States. Generally the wetter sites or richer soils support maples, while drier or sandy soils, dry hillsides support pines, oaks, and hickories.

Red Maple (top) and Silver Maple (bottom) are among the earliest-flowering native trees, well before their leaves, and fruit matures in spring as the leaves develop (and their fruit stalks do not persist on twigs). This is presumably an adaptation to spring floods in their preferred wetland and riverside habitats. Fruit that matures and falls in late spring or early summer is more likely to fall into receding flood waters and to a welcoming bed of freshly-deposited moist silt.

Maple branches in sunlight (top) develop leaves arrayed around the twig, often drooping. Shaded branches (bottom), in contrast, hold leaves in a horizontal plane with leaves of different sizes and very different stalk lengths arranged for maximum light-gathering.

The dramatic seasonal change in maple leaf color, and in other plants, is triggered by colder temperatures and shorter daylight hours in the fall. Chlorophyll, along with other pigments, make leaves appear green in the spring and summer and allows them to produce sugars for the tree to grow. When chlorophyll amounts decrease, latent pigments in the leaves make them appear yellow, orange, red, and other colors.

Red Maple

Acer rubrum

SCARLET MAPLE, SWAMP MAPLE, SOFT MAPLE

Deciduous. Medium to large tree often 70' tall (max. 179'). Named for the strong red tones to virtually all parts of the tree, especially twigs, flowers, and fall leaves. One of the widest latitudinal ranges of any North American tree.

bark on young trunks smooth gray
on old trunks bark rough in long narrow plates forming ridges, similar at all ages to Silver Maple, but on average less shaggy

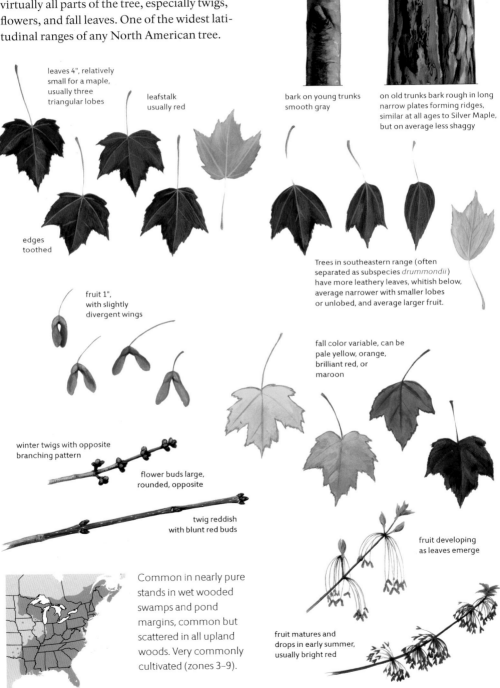

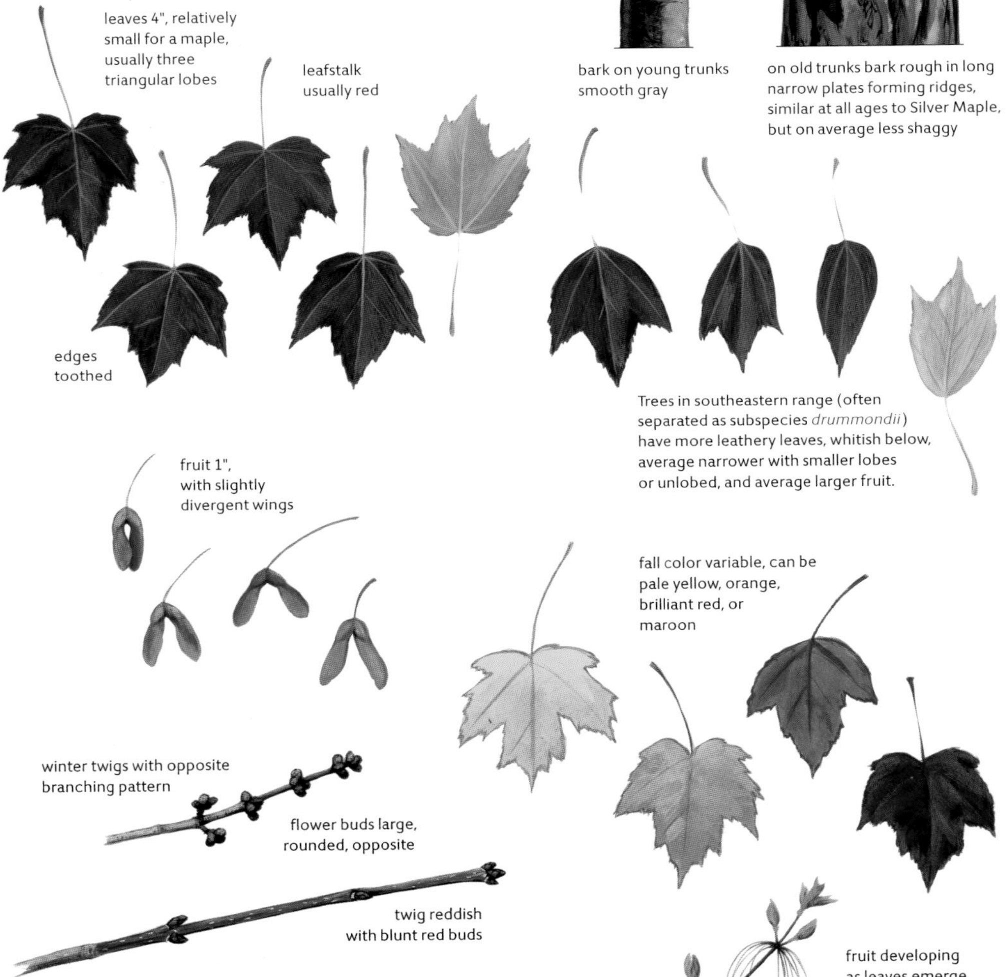
leaves 4", relatively small for a maple, usually three triangular lobes
leafstalk usually red
edges toothed
Trees in southeastern range (often separated as subspecies *drummondii*) have more leathery leaves, whitish below, average narrower with smaller lobes or unlobed, and average larger fruit.
fruit 1", with slightly divergent wings
fall color variable, can be pale yellow, orange, brilliant red, or maroon
winter twigs with opposite branching pattern
flower buds large, rounded, opposite
twig reddish with blunt red buds

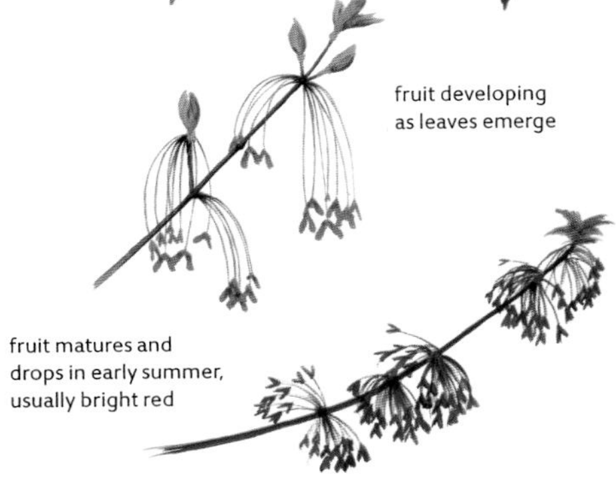
fruit developing as leaves emerge
fruit matures and drops in early summer, usually bright red

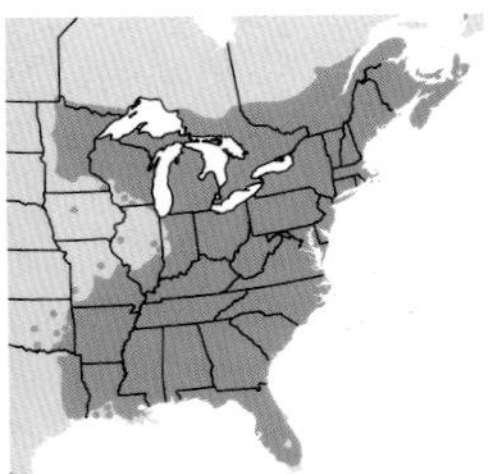

Common in nearly pure stands in wet wooded swamps and pond margins, common but scattered in all upland woods. Very commonly cultivated (zones 3–9).

flower color varies from drab gold to brilliant red

flowers red to yellow, short-stemmed
clusters in very early spring
before leaves

female flowers
usually red, male flowers
usually yellowish

large flower buds
visible all winter
along twigs

new growth
reddish at twig tips
in spring/early summer

summer tree with long leafy branches
extending out all around crown, like Silver
Maple, but unlike more clumped leaves
of Sugar and Norway Maple

slender red twigs
all relatively
straight

natives lose leaves relatively early; cultivated
trees often retain leaves later in fall; most
cultivars with bright red fall color

Silver Maple

Acer saccharinum

SOFT MAPLE, RIVER MAPLE, SWAMP MAPLE, WHITE MAPLE

Deciduous. Large tree often 70' (max. 138') with wide crown of brittle, arching and drooping branches. Closely related to Red Maple, but with delicately divided leaves, little or no red color.

bark pale silvery gray on young trees

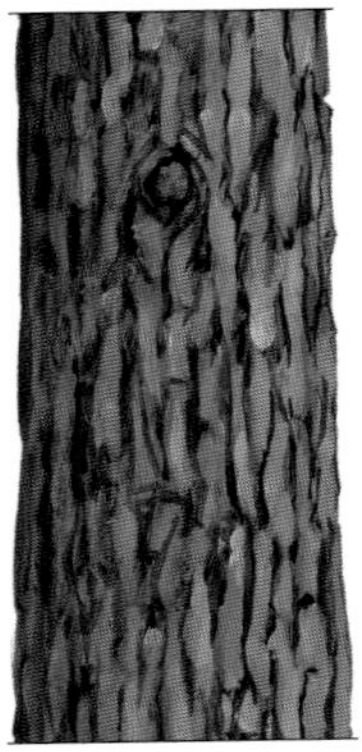

bark on older trees shaggy with narrow strips loose at ends, very similar to some Red Maples

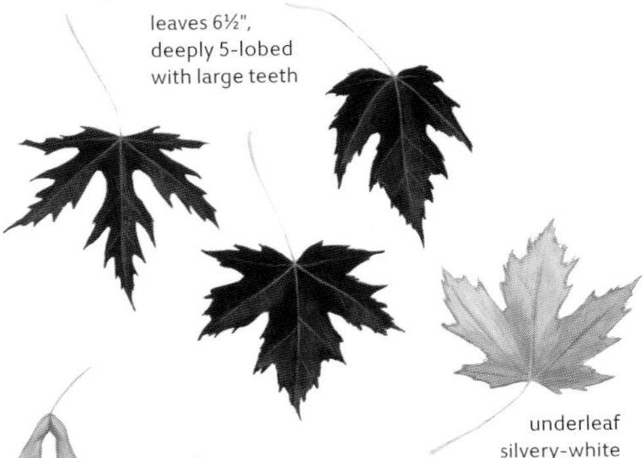

leaves 6½", deeply 5-lobed with large teeth

underleaf silvery-white

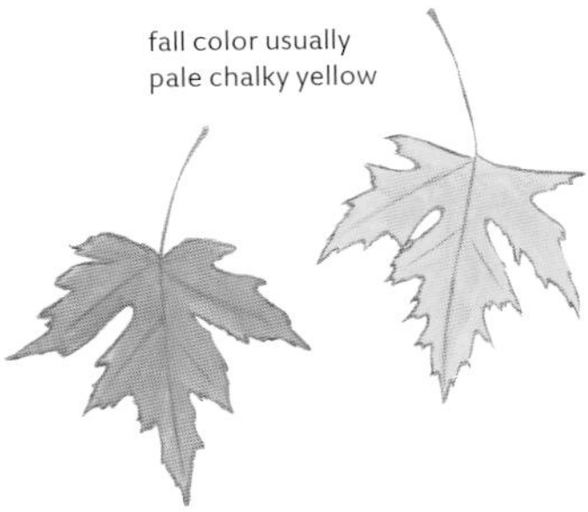

fall color usually pale chalky yellow

fruit large, 1¾", bright pale green, wide spread wings, ripe in spring (May–Jun), largest wings of any native maple

leafy branch like Red Maple, but feathery deeply-cut leaves with contrasting whitish underside

flowers greenish yellow; short-stemmed clusters; very early in spring before leaves

twigs pale brown

buds brownish, blunt

hybrid Silver × Red Maple with intermediate leaf shapes

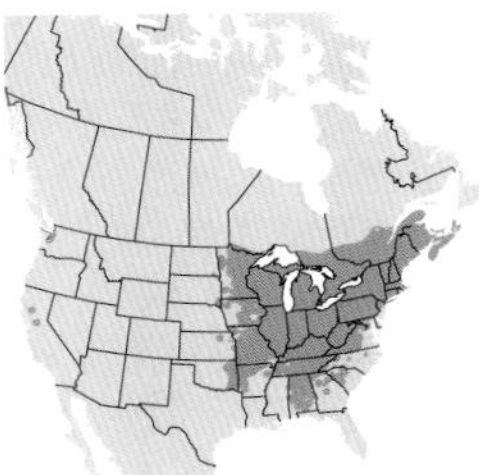

Typical of moist soils, especially riverbanks (Red Maple thrives in swamps), grows rapidly. Commonly cultivated and will grow in a variety of settings in yards and along streets (zones 3–9).

Cultivars of Silver Maple may have more deeply cut leaves, or yellow-bronze emerging leaves, or a more upright habit. Silver Maple × Red Maple hybrids occur naturally, and are also cultivated and frequently planted (known as 'Freeman' Maple).

Norway Maple

Acer platanoides

EUROPEAN MAPLE

Deciduous. Medium to large tree often 60' tall (max. 137'). Typically a dense and well-formed oval of dark green leaves—a classic shade tree.

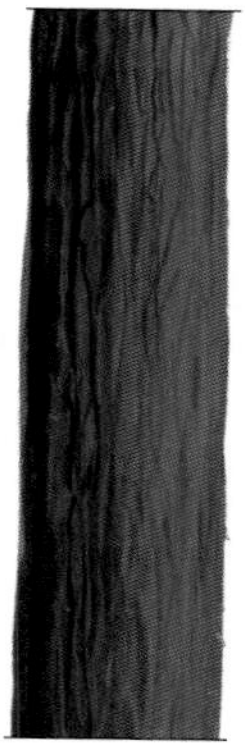

bark of young trunk faintly striped, unlike native maples

bark of mature trunk neatly furrowed like ash

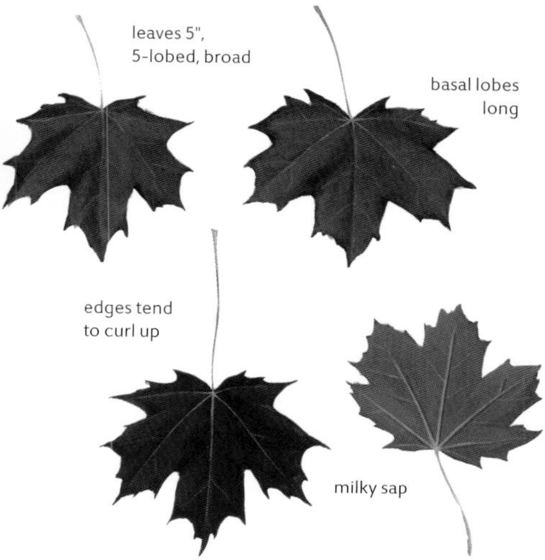

leaves 5", 5-lobed, broad

basal lobes long

edges tend to curl up

milky sap

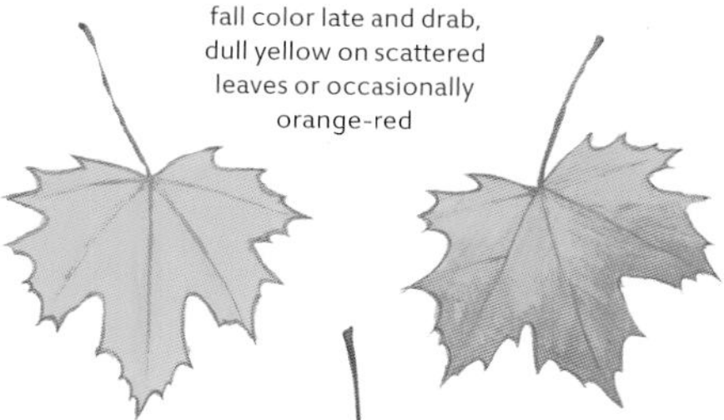

fall color late and drab, dull yellow on scattered leaves or occasionally orange-red

purple-leaved cultivars common

fruit 1¾", spreading, recurved, pale green; ripe in summer

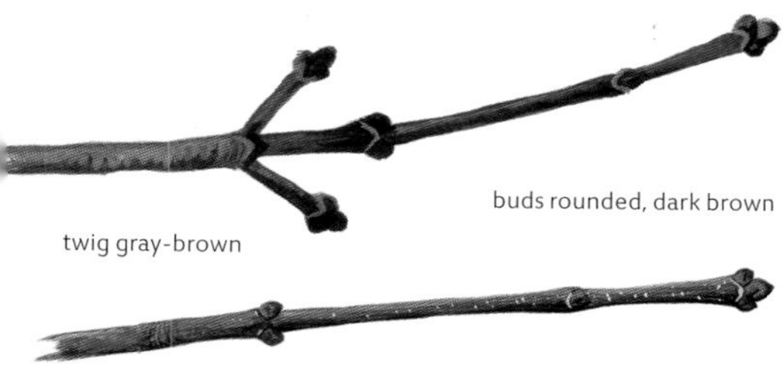

buds rounded, dark brown

twig gray-brown

flowers bright yellow-green, in erect rounded clusters, early spring just before leaves

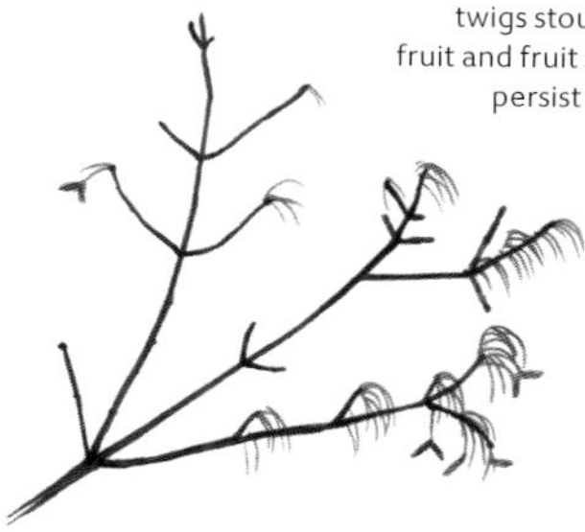

twigs stout, opposite; fruit and fruit stalks often persist into winter

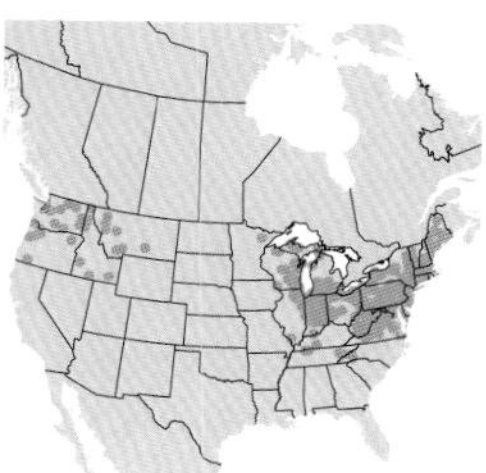

Native from Europe to western Asia. One of the most commonly and widely cultivated and naturalized trees in North America, invasive over much of Northeast (zones 4–7).

Sugar Maple

Acer saccharum

HARD MAPLE, ROCK MAPLE

Deciduous. Medium or large tree often 80' tall (max. 138'). One of the largest and most important commercial hardwood trees in the East—highly prized for wood and its sap is the primary source of maple syrup.

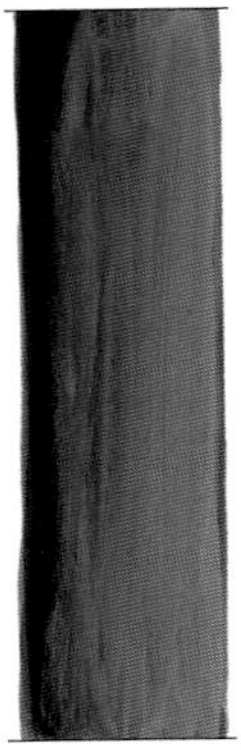

bark smooth gray-brown on young trunk

bark becoming furrowed and plated on older trees

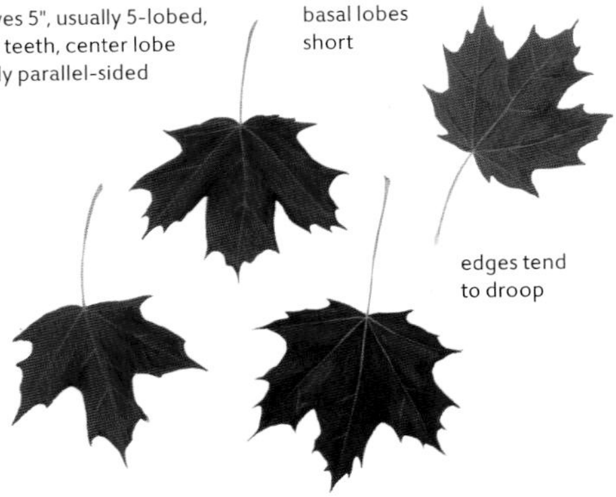

leaves 5", usually 5-lobed, few teeth, center lobe fairly parallel-sided

basal lobes short

edges tend to droop

fall color bright clear yellow to red

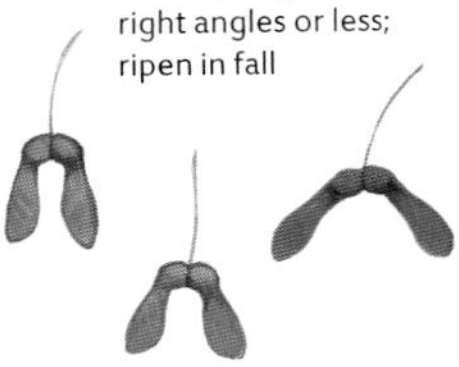

fruit 1", wings at right angles or less; ripen in fall

papery wings turn brown while seeds are still green

buds brownish, pointed

twigs pale brown

flowers pale yellow, dangling on long stalks, early spring with leaves

Many Sugar Maple cultivars include variations in growing form and leaf color, but no purple-leaved variants are known. One cultivar has deeply-dissected leaves.

winter twigs slender, opposite; fruit stalks (but not fruit) often persist into winter

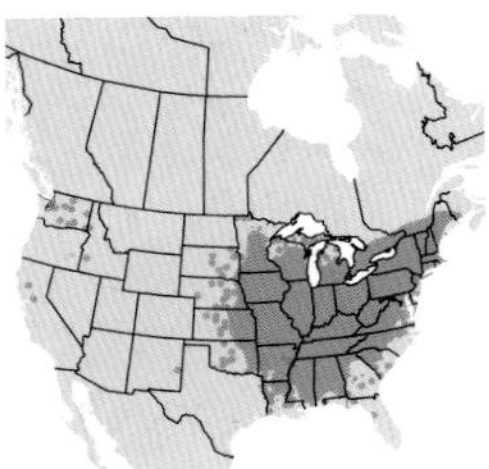

Common in rich, mesic soils on slopes and uplands, and one of the dominant forest trees in its range. Very commonly cultivated in parks and yards (zones 4–8).

In spring, Sugar Maple (right) has paler and more yellowish flowers producing a more hazy effect. Norway Maple (left) has bright green flowers in small round clusters.

Four maple species—Florida, Chalk, Black, and Canyon—are closely-related and very similar to Sugar Maple. All have smooth leaf edges or with few blunt teeth, and all have nearly identical buds, flowers, and fruit. They all hybridize or intergrade with each other, or with Sugar Maple, where their range overlaps. All are sometimes considered merely subspecies of Sugar Maple. They tend to have smaller and less lobed leaves than Sugar Maple with short, acute lobes and also can show smaller fruit wings, and some may average paler bark.

The unusually sweet sap of Sugar Maple was known to Native Americans centuries ago, who collected and concentrated it to make a sweet drink, and taught the technique to the early European settlers. Sugar and Black Maple are still the source of virtually all commercial maple syrup. Sap is collected from the trees in late winter, especially during the brief period when nighttime temperatures are below freezing and daytime temperatures above, just as the trees emerge from winter dormancy. Once buds begin to open, sugar in the sap is metabolized and the resulting byproducts give the syrup an unpleasant flavor, ending the "sugaring" season. Collected sap is boiled to concentrate the sugar (it takes at least 40 gallons of sap to yield one gallon of syrup). Syrup can also be produced from several other maple species, such as Red Maple, Silver Maple, and Boxelder. However, their sap contains less sugar (60 to 80 gallons of sap yield one gallon of syrup) and is palatable for a shorter period as their buds open earlier in spring.

tree usually evenly-proportioned, egg-shaped with dense slender twigs

fall color among the most striking of all trees, luminous green in center of tree, yellow and brilliant red at branch tips

Florida Maple

Acer floridanum

SOUTHERN SUGAR MAPLE, HAMMOCK MAPLE

Deciduous, but dead leaves may persist long into winter on young trees. Usually a small understory tree to 60' tall (max. 126'). Smaller than Sugar Maple with smaller 3-lobed leaves and paler bark.

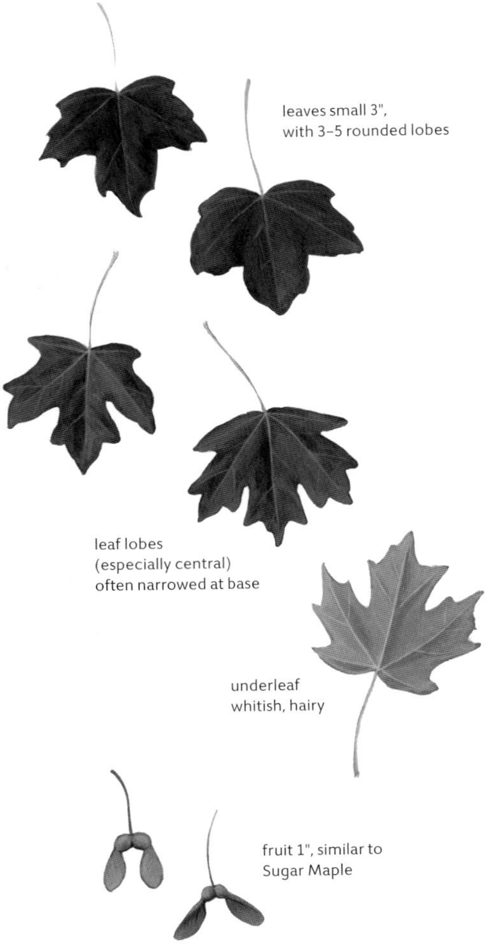
leaves small 3",
with 3–5 rounded lobes
leaf lobes
(especially central)
often narrowed at base
underleaf
whitish, hairy
fruit 1", similar to
Sugar Maple

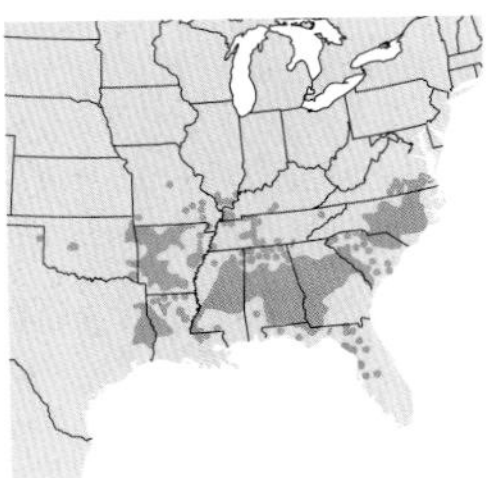

Uncommon in rich soils of valleys and slopes. Occasionally cultivated and often escaped from cultivation in and near native range (zones 7–9).

Chalk Maple

Acer leucoderme

WHITEBARK MAPLE

Deciduous, but some dead leaves may persist through winter. Small to medium tree usually under 25' tall; often multiple crooked trunks and low rounded crown. Small leaves and pale bark like Florida Maple, but underleaf greenish and leaf lobes not narrowed at base.

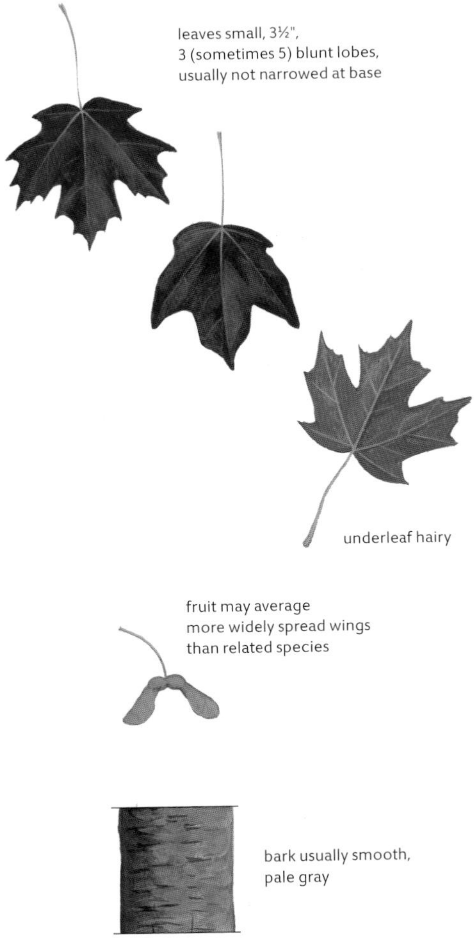
leaves small, 3½",
3 (sometimes 5) blunt lobes,
usually not narrowed at base
underleaf hairy
fruit may average
more widely spread wings
than related species
bark usually smooth,
pale gray

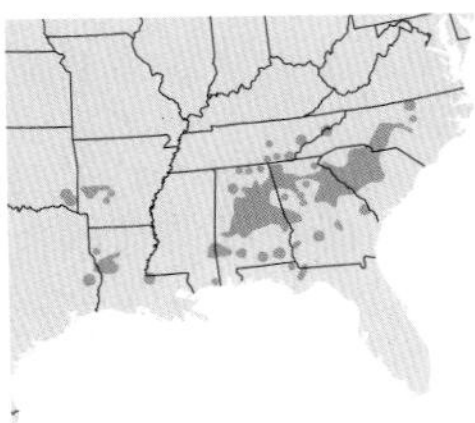

Common understory tree on well-drained streambanks and relatively dry uplands. Rarely cultivated (zones 5–9).

Black Maple

Acer nigrum

BLACK SUGAR MAPLE, IOWA SUGAR MAPLE, HARD MAPLE, ROCK MAPLE

Deciduous. Medium to large tree often 60' tall (max. 118'). Very similar to Sugar Maple, and sometimes considered the same species; many trees are intermediate. Leaves usually 3-lobed, edges curve down, somewhat hairy below (buds, flowers, and fruit identical to Sugar).

leaves 4",
usually 3-lobed
leaf edges
curl down
underleaf
slightly hairy
fruit 1", identical
to Sugar Maple

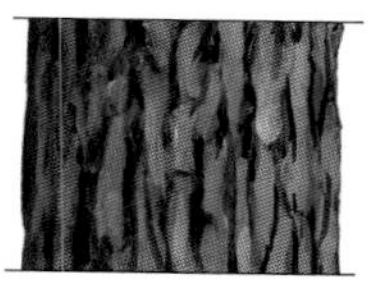
bark may be darker
or rougher, more
deeply-furrowed, than
typical Sugar Maple

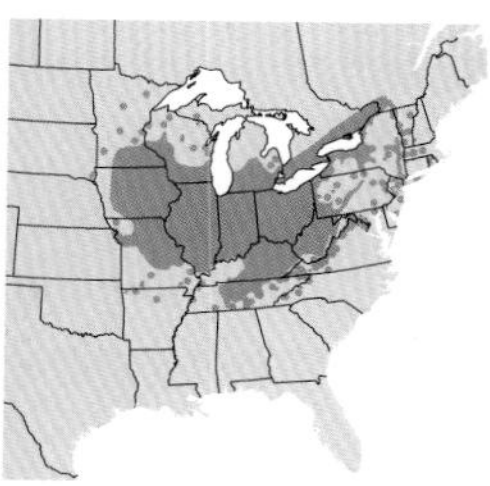

Common in moist river-bottom to drier upland sites, where range overlaps with Sugar Maple, Black is found in hotter, drier sites. Commonly cultivated in several cultivars (zones 4–8).

Canyon Maple

Acer grandidentatum

BIGTOOTH MAPLE, SUGAR MAPLE, UVALDE BIGTOOTH MAPLE

Deciduous. Small tree to 40' tall (max. 68'). Related to Sugar Maple and sometimes considered a subspecies; the only wild western maple with small blunt-toothed leaves and pointed 4-scaled buds.

leaves small, 3½",
3-lobed (sometimes 5),
a few blunt teeth
fruit 1",
U-shaped (Jun-Sep)

Uncommon and local in moist soils along canyon streams; occasionally cultivated (zones 3–8).

Bigleaf Maple

Acer macrophyllum

BROADLEAF MAPLE, OREGON MAPLE

Deciduous. Medium to large tree often 50' tall (max. 158'). Open-grown trees have dense rounded crown on short trunk. Wood important for furniture-making and syrup has been made from sap.

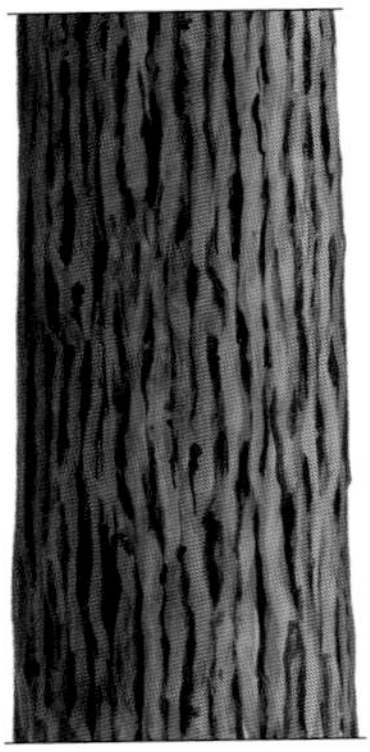
bark smooth, greenish-brown on young trees, becoming blackish, deeply ridged on mature trunks

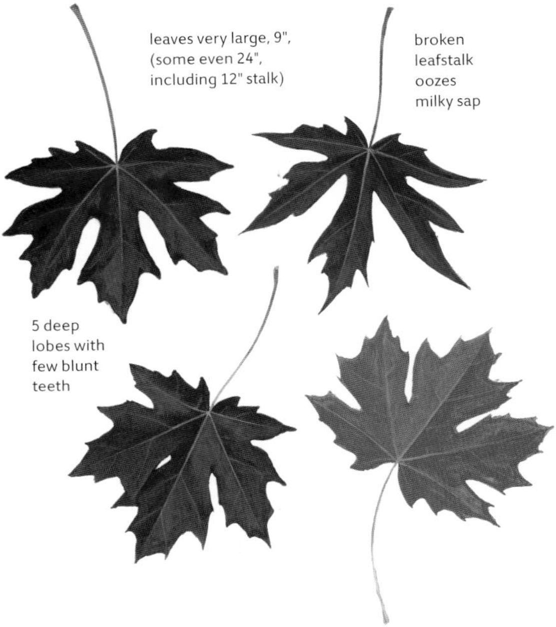
leaves very large, 9", (some even 24", including 12" stalk)
broken leafstalk oozes milky sap
5 deep lobes with few blunt teeth

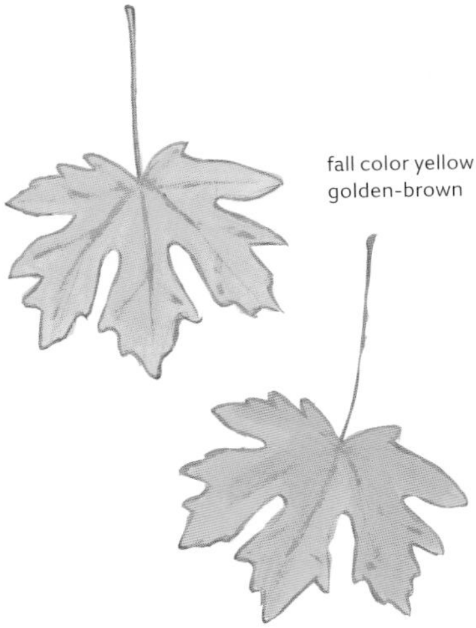
fall color yellow to golden-brown

fruit 1¾", slightly divergent wings, mature in fall

flowers yellowish, in drooping spikes with leaves

twig stout, green to brown
buds blunt

fruit in elongated hanging cluster

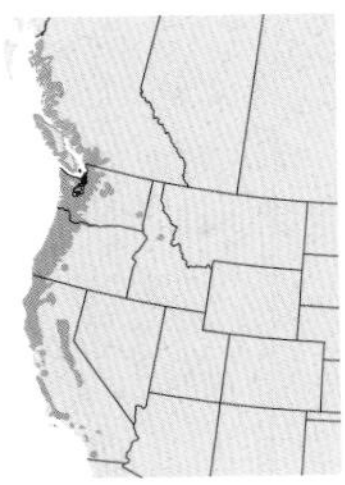

Common locally in moist shaded canyons of coast ranges; uncommonly cultivated mostly within native range (zones 6–9).

Rocky Mountain Maple

Acer glabrum

WESTERN MOUNTAIN MAPLE, DWARF MAPLE, SIERRA MAPLE, DOUGLAS MAPLE

Deciduous. Shrub or small slender tree occasionally 20–30' tall (max. 80'); often multi-trunked. Told from Canyon Maple by sharply-toothed leaves and blunt buds.

bark smooth,
becoming
narrowly-furrowed

leaves 5", 3–5
lobes, many small
sharp teeth
leafstalks
red-green
leaves sometimes
divided into
3 leaflets
especially
on vigorous
shoots

fall color
red and yellow

fruit hangs in small
clusters from
branched stalks, wings
may be reddish

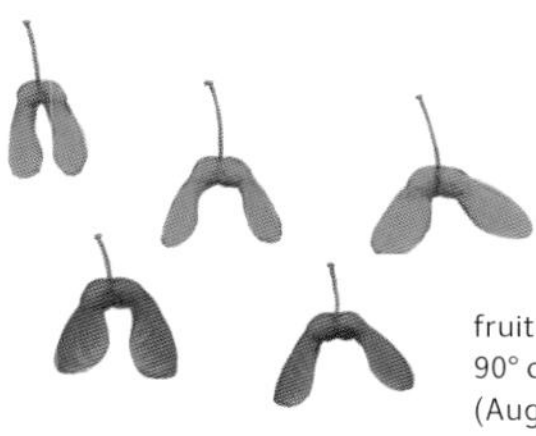
fruit wings spread
90° or less
(Aug–Sep)
fruit green or red,
turning brown
when dried

flowers pale green,
in clusters 2" long
(May–Jul)

twig reddish to brown
buds blunt

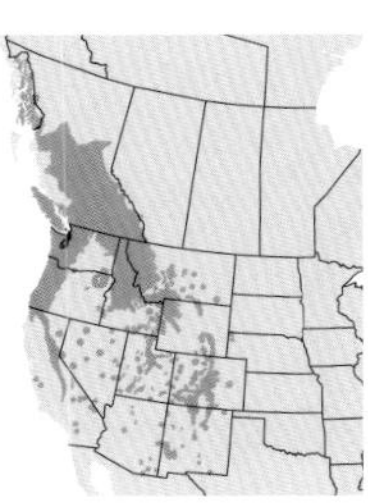

Common on moist sites within the oak and coniferous forests of the western mountains. Uncommonly culti-vated (zones 3–7).

Trees in the Pacific Northwest from Alaska to Oregon tend to have less deeply-lobed leaves and broader seed wings that average closer together. They are distinguished as 'Douglas' Maple (*Acer glabrum* var. *douglasii*). Other regional varieties that differ slightly in leaf shape and size include var. *greenei* in southern California, var. *torreyi*, in northern California, Nevada, and Oregon, and var. *neomexicanum* in Arizona and New Mexico.

Striped Maple

Acer pensylvanicum

MOOSEWOOD, GOOSEFOOT MAPLE, WHISTLEWOOD

Deciduous. Small understory tree usually under 30' (max. 77'). Large three-lobed leaves and striped bark distinctive.

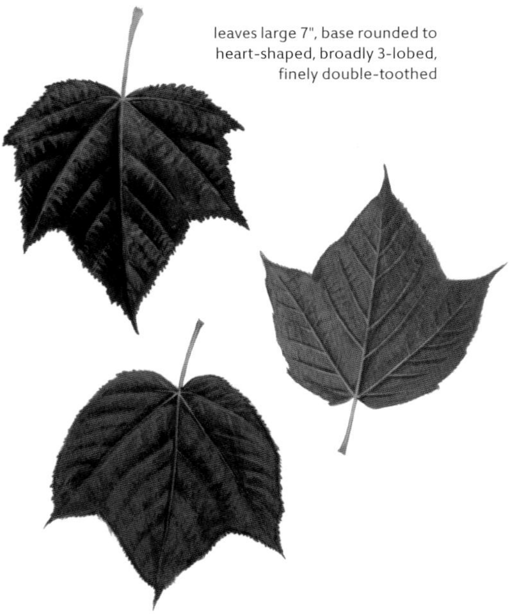

leaves large 7", base rounded to heart-shaped, broadly 3-lobed, finely double-toothed

bark on young trees smooth green and orange with gray stripes

bark on mature trees can be grayish, warty

fall color usually pale clear yellow

flowers bright yellow in slender, drooping clusters 5" long, appear in spring when leaves nearly grown

fruit with wide-spreading wings, 1"; ripe in late summer or fall

Several Asian species similar to Striped Maple are common in cultivation. Known as 'Snakebark' maples, distinguishing bertween the 14 or so cultivated species (and many cultivars) is difficult.

twigs smooth, reddish-brown

buds stalked, large and pointed

Common understory tree in cool moist sites in rich forest, such as well-drained north-facing slopes. Occasionally cultivated but short-lived (zones 3–7).

short trunk and slender, straight ascending branches; as an understory tree often with a sparse crown

Mountain Maple

Acer spicatum

EASTERN MOUNTAIN MAPLE, MOOSE MAPLE

Deciduous. Shrub or small tree often 25' tall (max. 58'); leaning twisted trunk. Often found near Striped Maple, but note much smaller leaves, flowers and fruit in upright clusters, and bark not striped.

leaves 6" with 3 (sometimes 5) lobes, coarsely toothed

fall color red to yellow

fruit ½", somewhat divergent wings, green to rosy-red; ripe in late summer

twigs finely hairy

buds stalked, small, pointed

flowers yellow, in erect spikes, male above and female below, appear early summer after leaves

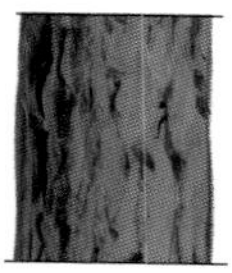

bark thin, reddish-brown to pale gray, scaly to slightly furrowed with dark pits

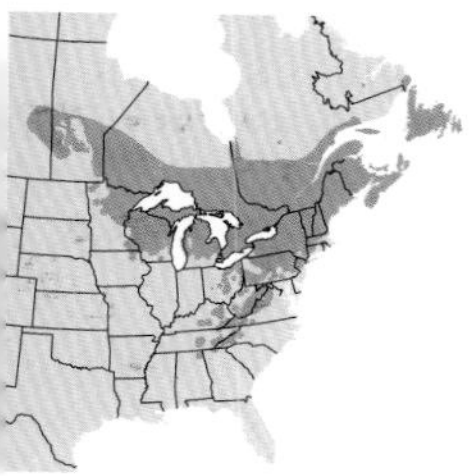

Common understory tree in rich soils of cool moist sites, especially on rocky slopes. Rarely cultivated (zones 2–7).

Vine Maple

Acer circinatum

Deciduous. Large multi-trunked shrub or occasionally tree-like, rarely to 30–40' tall; weak and often reclining trunk can even be vine-like. Often forms dense thickets on logged land; a favorite food of deer.

leaves 4", 7–9 pointed lobes, toothed margins

fruit ¾", widely divergent purple-red wings, ripen in fall

twig reddish

buds rounded

flowers purple-red, in clusters in spring when leaves half-grown

bark smooth, greenish to reddish-brown

Common understory tree within its limited range in wet shady coniferous forest. Rarely cultivated outside native range (zones 6–9), several cultivars available.

Boxelder

Acer negundo

MANITOBA MAPLE, ASHLEAF MAPLE, THREELEAF MAPLE

Deciduous. Medium tree often 60' tall (max. 110'); usually low and spreading with multiple leaning trunks. The only maple that regularly has more than three leaflets. Told from ash by leaflets with few or no teeth, paired fruit, and greenish or bluish twigs.

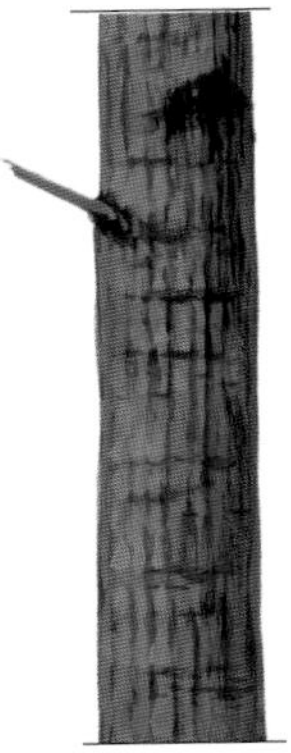

bark slightly ridged on young trees

bark heavily furrowed on old trunk

leaves compound with 3–5 leaflets (sometimes 7, usually 3 in California), each leaflet 3½", hairless with a few large jagged teeth

leaflets small, relatively narrow and pointed

leaves relatively pale yellow-green, dull

fall color yellow

fruit 1¾", V-shaped with narrow seeds

twigs green, bluish, or purplish, often with glaucous bloom

buds oval, whitish

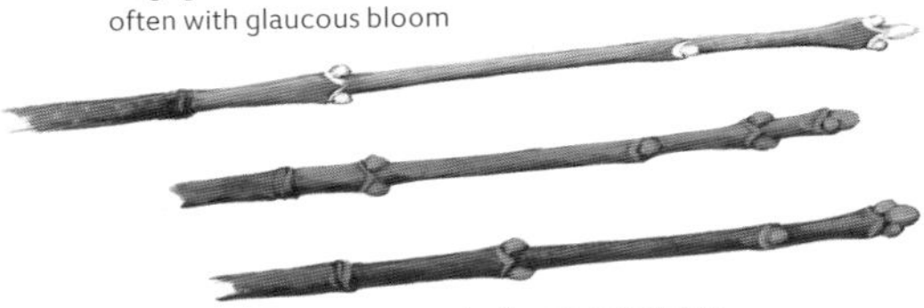

leaf scars meeting in raised point (unlike ash)

dried pale brown fruit often persists all winter on twigs

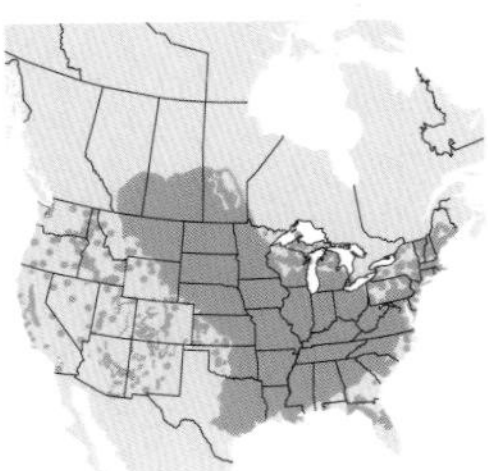

Common (local in Southwest), mainly in moist soils along streams, pond margins. Commonly cultivated and naturalized outside native range (zones 3–9).

Boxelder is one of the few maples that is completely dioecious (separate male and female flowers on separate trees). The male and female flowers appear similar, but only female trees develop fruit. Flower color ranges from violet to reddish to green, unrelated to sex.

several cultivars have variegated green and white leaves; similar variegated colors shown by some Norway Maple cultivars

flowers on long stalks in drooping clusters; can be pale greenish-yellow or reddish, early spring before leaves (Mar–Apr)

Boxelder is one of the only trees that occurs naturally across the entire breadth of North America. Maligned by landscapers as "weedy" or "scraggly" for its susceptibility to insects, tendency to drop twigs and branches, and leaves that curl up and turn brown during dry spells. Despite all this, it grows quickly and vigorously, and has been extensively planted as a shade and windbreak tree. The seeds are a favorite food of Evening Grosbeaks, and the sap has been used to make maple syrup.

usually short-trunked or multi-trunked, spreading with untidy clumps of twigs

pointed leaflets hanging in clumps, bright-green or blue green on new growth; older growth often with dead twigs and year-old fruit stalks, look shaggy

Sycamore Maple

Acer pseudoplatanus

PLANETREE MAPLE, GREAT MAPLE, GREY HAREWOOD, SCOTTISH PLANE

Deciduous. Medium to large tree often 60' tall (max. 110'). Similar to Norway Maple (and in similar sites), but with coarser, toothed leaves, smooth scaly bark, hanging clusters of flowers and fruit.

bark on mature trunks scaly, flaky, gray to tan

leaves 5", 3–5 lobes, coarsely toothed
leafstalk often red
underleaf rough with obvious veins

fall color late and usually drab golden-yellow
several common cultivars have underleaf purple (but with dark green upperleaf)

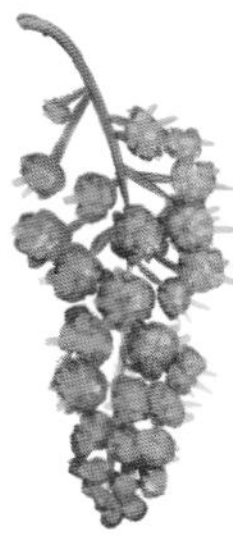
flowers pale yellow in hanging clusters 4½" long, early summer after leaves

fruit wings 1¾", spread 90° or less

fruit hangs in clusters in the late summer

twigs brownish
buds large and blunt

Native from Europe to western Asia. Commonly cultivated and naturalized (zones 4–7); thrives in coastal northeast especially Long Island and Cape Cod.

This is the original sycamore, named in Britain centuries ago. That name was later applied to American trees of the genus *Platanus* (presumably because of their similar leaves), even as those species went by the name "planetree" in Britain.

Hedge Maple

Acer campestre

EUROPEAN FIELD MAPLE, ENGLISH CORK MAPLE, SMALL-LEAVED MAPLE

Deciduous. Small tree to 30' (max. 83'). Related to Norway Maple, and basically a smaller-sized and smaller-leaved version with milky sap, clustered green flowers, and wide-spreading fruit wings.

leaves small 2½",
3–5 lobes with
rounded teeth

fruit 1¼", wings
about 180°

branchlets often have corky ridges

Native to Europe; commonly planted in North America and naturalized locally (zones 5–8).

Trident Maple

Acer buergeranum

Deciduous. Small tree usually under 30' tall (max. 60'). Native to China and Korea; uncommonly cultivated (zones 5–9).

leaves smooth-edged,
3-lobed, glossy
dark green

fruit green to
reddish

Shantung Maple

Acer truncatum

PURPLEBLOW MAPLE

Deciduous. Small to medium tree often 30–40' tall (max. 56'). Related to Norway Maple, but smaller with more rounded crown; star-shaped leaves distinctive. Native to China. Uncommonly but increasingly cultivated especially in warmer regions (zones 4–8).

leaves 4", 5–7
tapered lobes,
no teeth

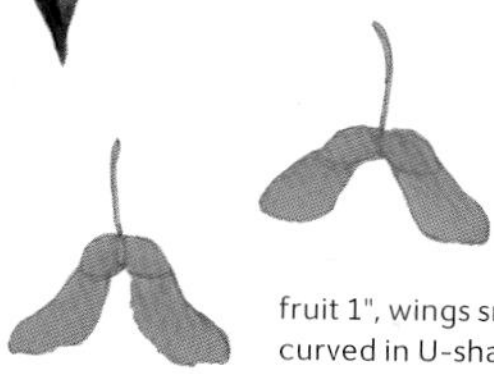
fruit 1", wings small,
curved in U-shape
or in some cultivars
curved out

Amur Maple

Acer ginnala

SIBERIAN MAPLE

Deciduous. Generally a suckering bushy tree under 20' tall (max. 33'); often multi-trunked, resembling a lilac shrub in general form.

leaves 2½", narrow, 3-lobed, toothed

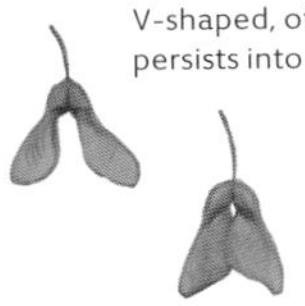

fruit wings 1", V-shaped, often persists into winter

flowers yellow, clustered

Native to eastern Asia. Commonly cultivated, locally naturalized (zones 3–8). Several cultivars available, some only shrubs.

Tatarian Maple

Acer tataricum

Deciduous. Shrub or small tree usually under 20' tall (max. 36'). Closely-related to Amur Maple; flowers pale greenish.

leaves 3", broader than Amur, usually unlobed, dull

fruit persists into winter

Native to western Asia. Less frequently cultivated than Amur Maple, but more often naturalized in several northeastern and midwestern states (zones 3–8).

Paperbark Maple

Acer griseum

Deciduous. Shrub or small tree often 30' tall (max. about 50'), compound leaves with three leaflets and peeling orange bark distinctive. Native to western China. Commonly cultivated in recent years, but not escaped (zones 5–7).

leaves 5", 3 coarsely-toothed leaflets each 2½" long

fruit with broad rounded wings at 90°or less

bark orange-brown or cinnamon with thin layers peeling and curling

Japanese Maple

Acer palmatum

SMOOTH JAPANESE MAPLE

Deciduous. Small shrubby tree usually under 20' tall (max. 50'). Usually a very picturesque small tree with contorted trunk and branches, leaves in horizontal layers. Flowers purple in erect clusters; fall color red, late.

Japanese Maple is one of the most varied tree species in cultivation. It is widely cultivated in many varieties—at least 130 tree-size cultivars are available in North America. Most are rare, and only a few are mass-produced by nurseries. At least 40 cultivars are in the 'Atropurpureum' group of reddish or purple-leaved trees.

leaves 3", deeply-lobed,
5–9 pointed and toothed lobes
fruit small,
wings ¾", wide
spreading wings

cultivars often with purple leaves;
vary from relatively broad lobes and
shallow sinuses to narrow and incised
lobes divided to base

twigs slender, reddish with tiny buds

Native to Japan. Very commonly cultivated and locally naturalized (zones 5–8), many cultivars with red or purple leaves.

Fullmoon Maple

Acer japonicum

DOWNY JAPANESE MAPLE

Deciduous. Usually a tree-like shrub under 30' (rarely to 50'). Distinguished from the more common Japanese Maple by larger leaves with more lobes and hairy stalks.

leaves typically
almost circular with
many short lobes
short leafstalk
usually red

fruit with
wide-spreading wings

Native to Japan. Commonly cultivated but rarely escaped (zones 5–7), mainly as one cultivar with more deeply lobed leaves.

Quassia Family

Ailanthus and Corkwood are both in the quassia family (Simaroubaceae), which includes nearly 100 mostly tropical species worldwide. Ailanthus is one of about eight species in its genus, all native to Asia and Australia. Corkwood is the only species in its genus and has long been given its own family, but recent research places it with the quassias.

bark on young trunk with small pits

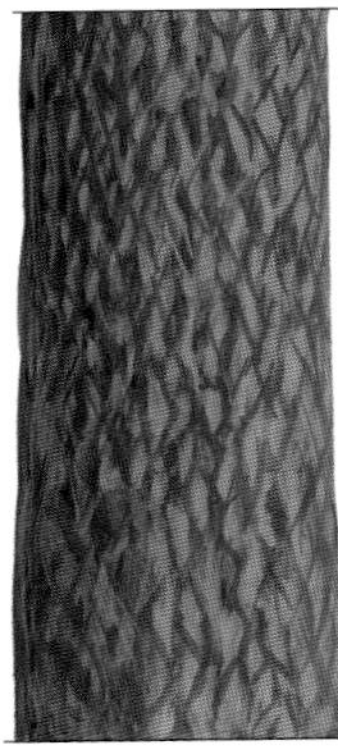

bark on mature trunk relatively smooth gray with short interlacing ridges

Ailanthus

Ailanthus altissima

TREE-OF-HEAVEN, CHINESE SUMACH, COPAL-TREE, STINK TREE, VARNISH TREE

Deciduous. Medium to large tree usually 40–60' tall (max. 89'); open crown with sparse, heavy twigs and very large pinnate leaves. Small trees can be a single unbranched stem.

fruit papery samaras, slightly twisted, hanging in dense clusters

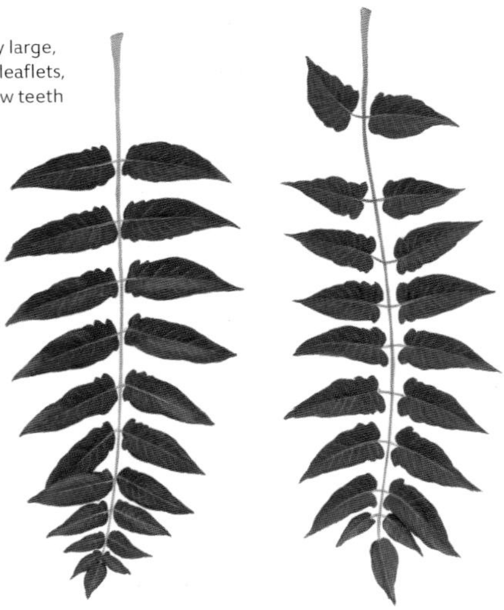

leaves very large, 24", many leaflets, each 4", few teeth at base

fall color dull yellow, late

underleaf paler green

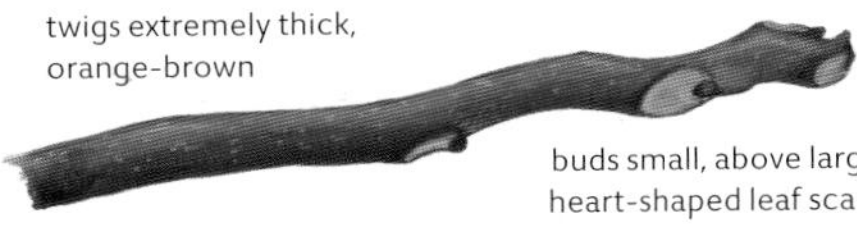

twigs extremely thick, orange-brown

buds small, above large, heart-shaped leaf scars

flowers tiny, yellow-green, in large conical clusters at twig tips; early summer (Jun–Jul), usually male and female on separate trees

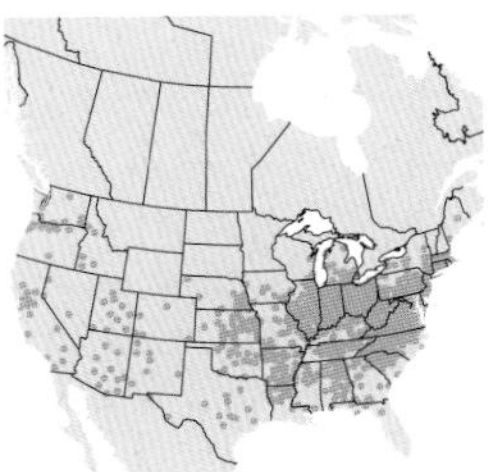

Native to China and Taiwan. Very commonly cultivated, naturalized and invasive in roadsides, waste places, especially in cities (zones 4–8).

female trees retain large bunches of straw-colored samaras through winter; many retain rounded cluster of fine seed stems at tips of twigs, but no seeds

new leaves in spring emerge reddish in large tufts at branch tips

Ailanthus was introduced to North America in 1784 and became very popular and widely planted in the early 1800s. This species is the title subject of the book *A Tree Grows in Brooklyn* by Betty Smith. It is tolerant of pollution and other urban conditions, reseeding, sprouting and suckering to conquer new territory. Trees have been known to sprout from roots 150' away from the original trunk, and grow over 12' in a year. This vigorous growth has made it one of the most invasive plants in temperate North America. This tree's height (over 100' in the wild) has given it the colloquial name "tree-of-heaven" and the scientific name *altissima*, but its aggressive spread has caused environmentalists to label it "tree-of-hell."

Corkwood

Leitneria floridana

Deciduous. Usually a sparsely-branched tree-like shrub under 12', rarely a small tree (max. 20'); most often in dense suckering thickets. Named for its very light wood, lighter than cork and used locally for fishing "bobbers."

leaves 4½", leathery, relatively narrow, tapered to tip and base, hairy below, smooth and glossy above; stay green late into fall

male and female flowers on separate plants, appear before or with leaves in early spring (Feb-Mar)

flowers in upright scaly catkins, male at twig tips, female below twig tips

fruit ¾", leathery, flattened oval drupes, green, becoming reddish brown; ripe in spring before leaves fully-grown

twigs stout, reddish-brown with pale lenticels, hairy when young

buds hairy, grayish, pointed, clustered at twig tips

bark smooth reddish brown with numerous pale lenticels

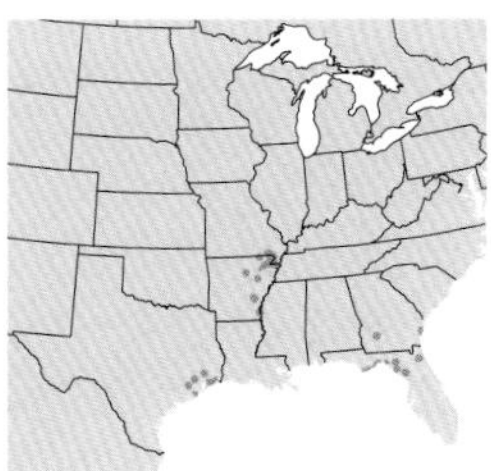

Rare and local in scattered locations in swamps, streambeds, and other wet locations. Rare in cultivation, but can be grown in dry soils and well north of native range; (zones 5-9).

Dogwood Family

The dogwood family (Cornaceae) includes about 120 species of shrubs, trees, and a few herbs worldwide with its highest diversity found in Asia. In North America, most species are shrubs or only rarely tree-like.

The dogwoods in the genus *Cornus* include about forty species worldwide with sixteen native to North America. Most native species are shrubs, rarely or never trees, but four native species, and one commonly cultivated exotic species are regularly tree-like and are covered here.

As a group, dogwoods can be recognized by their curved leaf veins, which follow the leaf edge back towards the mid-vein, opposite leaves (in most species), and berry-like fruit in clusters. Dogwoods can be separated into three groups based on flower structure.

FLOWERING DOGWOODS (subgenus *Benthamidia*) have inconspicuous stalkless flowers surrounded by large showy bracts. This group includes Flowering, Pacific, and Kousa Dogwood.

SHRUB DOGWOODS (subgenus *Swida*) have small, usually white, flowers in branched clusters without conspicuous bracts. This group includes Alternate-leaf, Rough-leaf, and other native shrubby dogwoods.

CORNELS (subgenus *Cornus*) have short-stalked flowers (yellow to greenish-white) with small bracts. This group includes Cornelian-cherry and one shrubby native species, Black-fruit Dogwood (*Cornus sessilis*).

The wood of dogwood trees is not important commercially, as the trees are small. A few species are very popular ornamentals and are grown commercially. The shrubby species are important understory and wetland thicket plants, and the berries, ripe in summer, are devoured by birds.

Dove Tree

Davidia involucrata

HANDKERCHIEF TREE, LAUNDRY TREE, GHOST TREE

Deciduous. Small to medium tree (max. 55'); upright with short trunk and oval crown of large leaves. The large creamy-white flower bracts are showy in spring. Native to western China. Uncommonly cultivated, (zones 6–7).

leaves large, 7", obvious teeth, heart-shaped base

flowers in clusters with two large white bracts 6" long, hanging loosely like cloth (May)

fruit a large round berry 1" on 2" stalk, green to red-brown

The Dove Tree is actually more closely related to tupelos, which are included with dogwoods in the family Cornaceae in this guide, but are often separated as the tupelo family (Nyssaceae) with about ten species worldwide.

Alternate-leaf Dogwood

Cornus alternifolia

PAGODA DOGWOOD, BLUE DOGWOOD, GREEN OSIER, PAGODA-CORNEL

Deciduous. Shrub or small tree usually 15–20' tall (max. 48'). Often multi-stemmed, with broad flattened crown usually wider than tall, branches clearly arranged in horizontal layers.

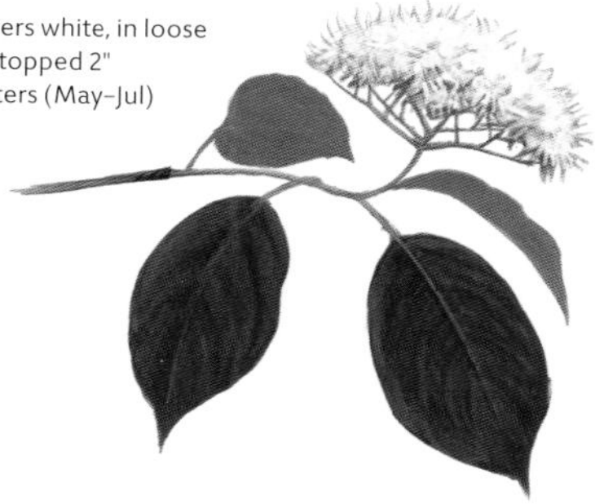

flowers white, in loose flat-topped 2" clusters (May–Jul)

leaves 6", like other dogwoods, but alternate

fruit ⅓", blue-black berry (Jul–Aug), in flat-topped cluster on reddish stalks

twigs zigzag due to alternate buds, unlike all other dogwoods

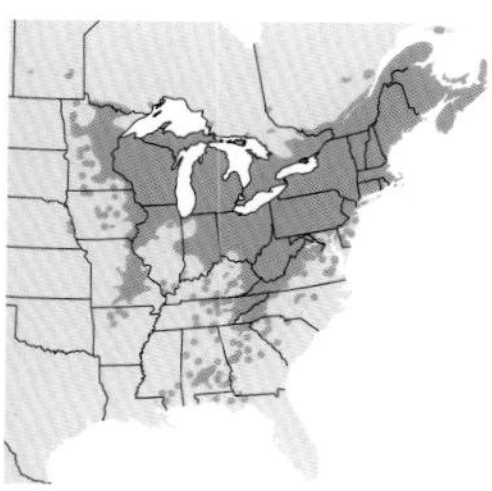

Uncommon in understory of broadleaf or coniferous woods, moist to dry soils. Commonly cultivated (zones 3–7).

Rough-leaf Dogwood

Cornus drummondii

Deciduous. Shrub or small tree usually under 20' tall (max. 22'); a slender understory tree or multi-stemmed shrub. Differs from other dogwoods in having rough upper surface of leaves and fruit white when mature.

leaves 3", slightly hairy and rough-textured

underleaf pale grayish

fruit ¼", small berries, white when mature in late summer

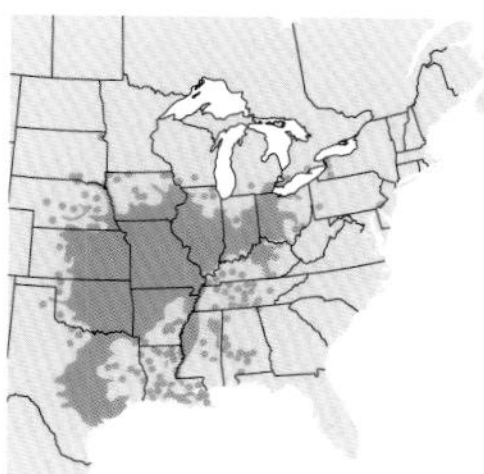

Common in rich woodlands; uncommonly cultivated (zones 4–8).

Ten additional species of smaller dogwoods are native to North America and usually shrubby (seven are occasionally small trees). Two more species in the genus are herbaceous. All can be recognized as dogwoods by leaf veins curving to follow edge, opposite leaves and twigs, and flowers and fruit clusters similar to Rough-leaf and Alternate-leaf Dogwood.

Flowering Dogwood

Cornus florida

CORNEL, BOXWOOD

Deciduous. Small tree usually 15–30' tall (max. 55'); short trunk and oval or spreading crown with relatively sparse leaves arranged in layers.

developing flower cluster with small green bracts beginning to expand
new leaves in spring stand straight up at twig tips

The "flower" of Flowering, Pacific, and Kousa-Dogwoods is really of a cluster of small greenish flowers surrounded by showy white bracts. These bracts emerge slowly over a period of several weeks, first small and greenish, then full-size and whitish, often becoming slightly pinkish as they age. Other dogwoods, such as Alternate-leaf, lack the showy bracts, and instead have a cluster of small flowers each with white petals.

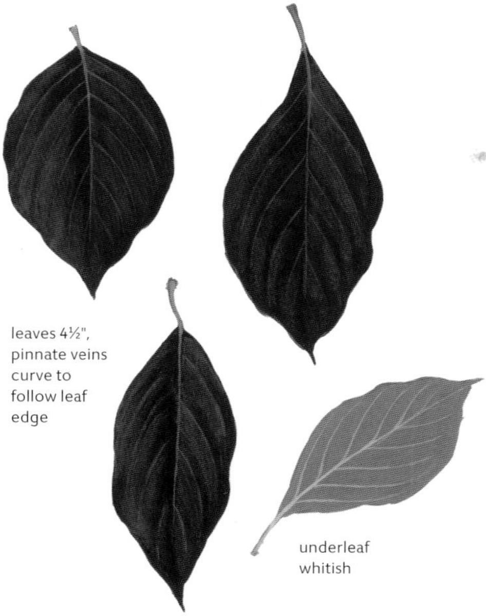
leaves 4½", pinnate veins curve to follow leaf edge
underleaf whitish

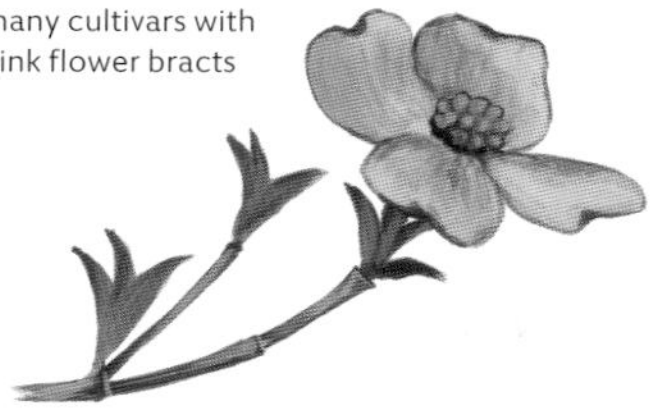
a few wild trees and many cultivars with pink flower bracts

flower cluster with 4 whitish bracts with notched tips (Feb–Jun)

leaves opposite

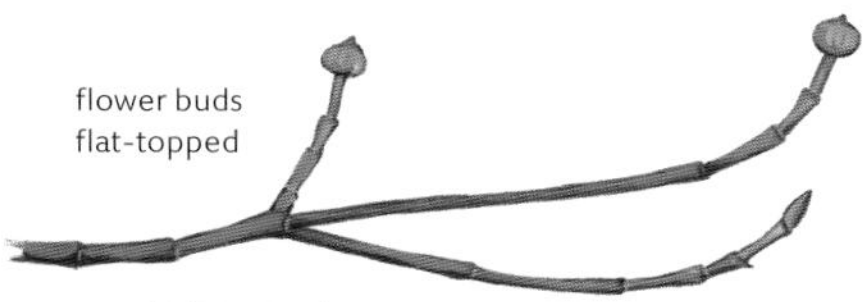
flower buds flat-topped
twigs green to purple, curving up at tips

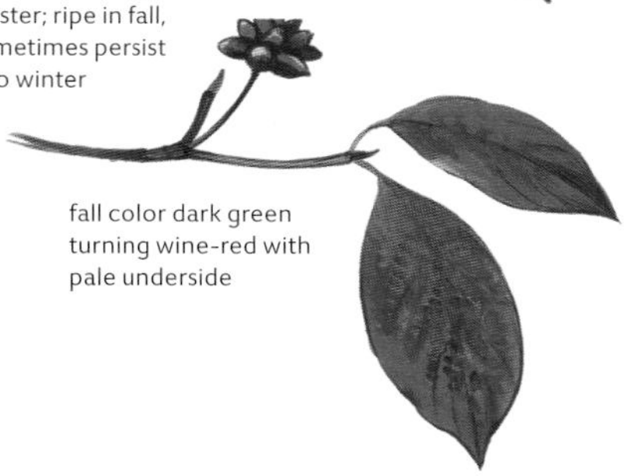
fruit ½" red berry, stalkless in compact cluster; ripe in fall, sometimes persist into winter
fall color dark green turning wine-red with pale underside

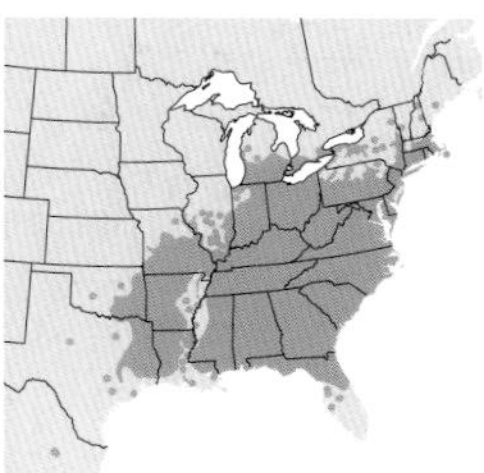

Common in understory of open rich woods. Commonly cultivated with many cultivars (zones 5–8).

Pacific Dogwood

Cornus nuttallii

WESTERN FLOWERING DOGWOOD,
MOUNTAIN DOGWOOD

Deciduous. Small to medium tree to 60' tall (max. 100'); on average a larger tree with narrower pyramidal crown than Flowering Dogwood.

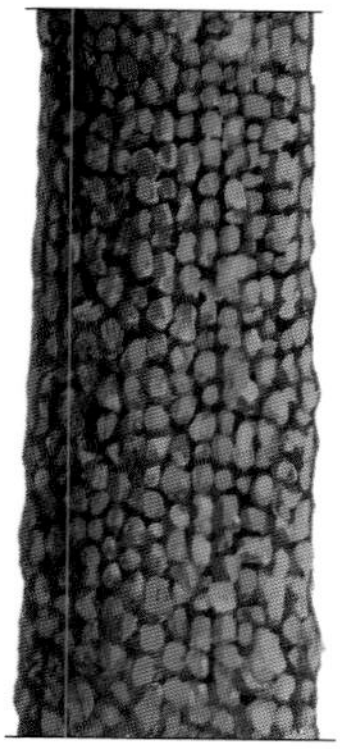
bark breaks up into small
square blocks even
on fairly young trunks

leaves 5½", like
Flowering Dogwood,
but average larger,
more oval

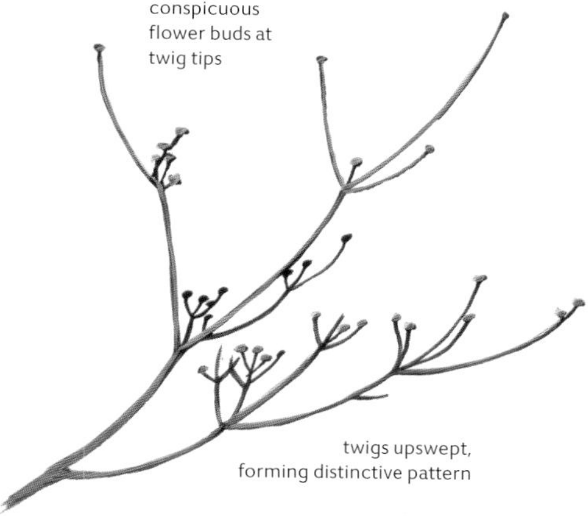
conspicuous
flower buds at
twig tips
twigs upswept,
forming distinctive pattern

flower cluster larger
than Flowering
Dogwood, tinged
purple
usually 6 white
bracts with
blunt tips

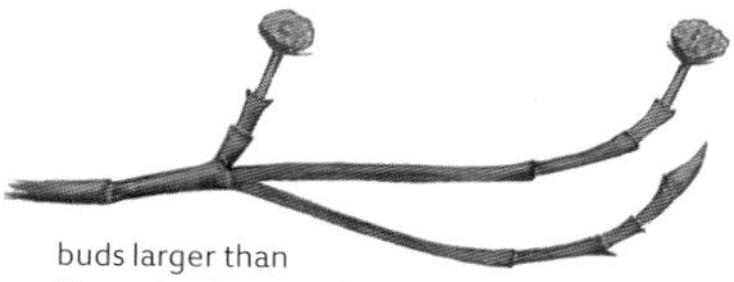
buds larger than
Flowering Dogwood

small rounded tree
with somewhat "layered"
branches

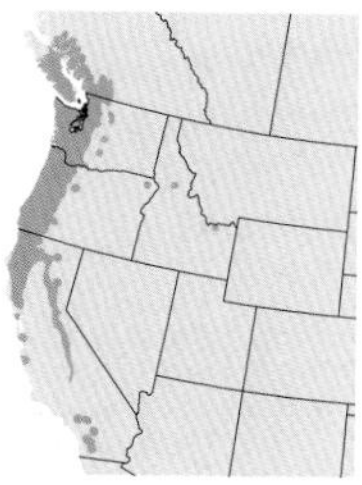

Common understory tree in open forest at low elevations, especially on well-drained slopes. Uncommonly cultivated mainly in native range (zones 7–9).

Kousa Dogwood

Cornus kousa

JAPANESE DOGWOOD, KOREAN DOGWOOD

Deciduous. Small to medium tree usually 20–30' tall (max. 41'); with short trunk and oval to spreading crown; branches often conspicuously layered with dark green foliage.

bark thin, orange, gray, and brown with peeling scales

leaves 4", pointed
underleaf pale green

flower bracts white, pointed, appear after leaves

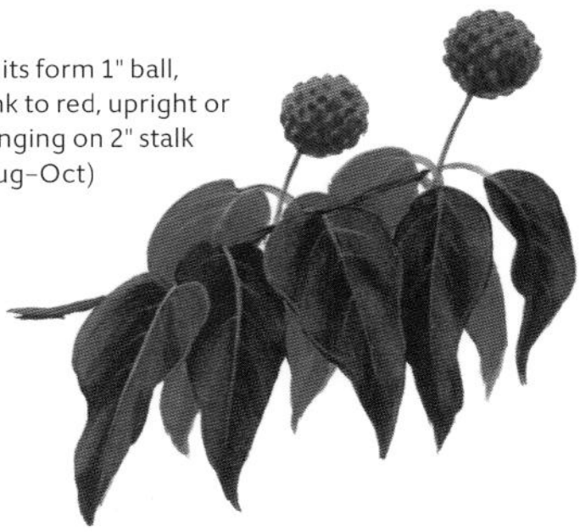
fruits form 1" ball, pink to red, upright or hanging on 2" stalk (Aug–Oct)

Many commercially available dogwood cultivars are hybrids of Kousa × Flowering Dogwood. These hybrids can have unusually wide or narrow flower bracts, while other features are intermediate between the parent species. Several other species of Eurasian dogwoods are fairly commonly cultivated in North America, but are usually shrubby.

twigs light brown, greenish or purplish
flower buds large, pointed

small rounded tree with profuse white flowers in early summer lined up along dark green layers of foliage

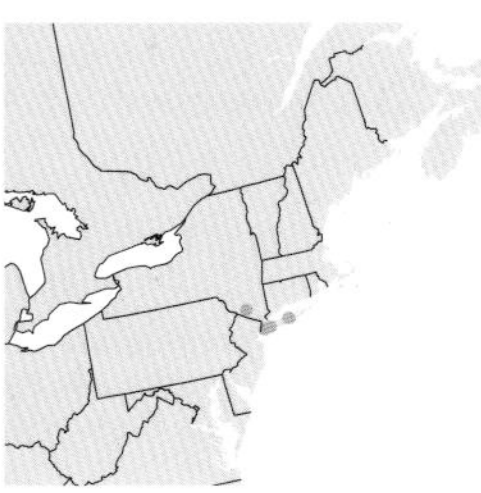

Native to China, Korea, and Japan. Many cultivars, including hybrids with both Flowering and Pacific Dogwoods (zones 5–8).

Tupelo Family

The tupelos (genus *Nyssa*) include about ten species of trees worldwide, four of which are native to North America and are covered here. The tupelos are related to dogwoods, but are often placed in a separate family (Nyssaceae) along with Dove Tree and two other Asian genera.

All of the tupelos are associated with wet soils, especially swamp margins and seasonally-flooded bottomlands. These trees can grow even in standing water (although more slowly). The four native species are all very similar, and differ mainly in details of fruit (including the shape of the seed) and buds.

Tupelo wood is relatively soft, but is harvested commercially and used for shipping containers, plywood backing, paneling, and paper pulp. It is also one of the woods preferred for artistic carvings, such as waterfowl decoys. In some areas, especially the Florida Panhandle, tupelo trees occur in sufficient density that honeybees can produce the celebrated "tupelo honey," which has a mild flavor and relatively high fructose content.

Tupelo trees are often planted as ornamentals for their spectacular red fall color.

base of tupelo trunks often buttressed (like many trees that are periodically flooded)

Water Tupelo

Nyssa aquatica

COTTON-GUM, SOURGUM, TUPELO, WATER-GUM

Deciduous. Medium to large tree usually 60–80' tall (max. 124'). Compared to Black Tupelo has leaves larger and more often toothed; buds close against twigs, larger fruits borne singly.

underleaf whitish
leafstalk long, often red
leaves large, 6", pointed, occasionally toothed or lobed

fruit large, 1", dark purple-black, single on short to long stalk

twigs pale greenish or orange-brown; buds darker brown

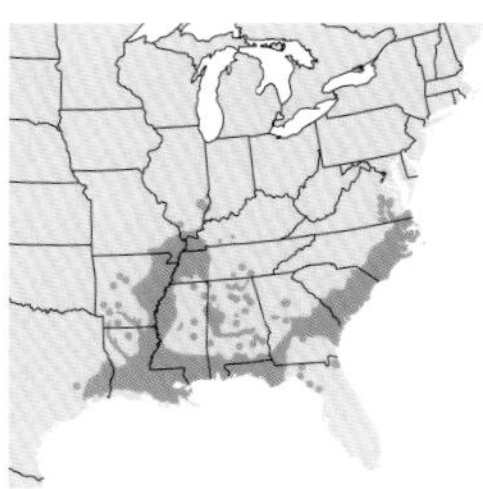

Locally common in swamps, usually in standing water seasonally. Rarely cultivated (zones 6–9).

Black Tupelo

Nyssa sylvatica

BLACKGUM, SOURGUM, PEPPERIDGE, BEE GUM, UPLAND YELLOW GUM

Deciduous. Medium to large tree usually 40–60' tall (max. 141') with single straight trunk. Can be confused with Common Persimmon, but note many spur twigs, different fruit and flowers, and green underleaf.

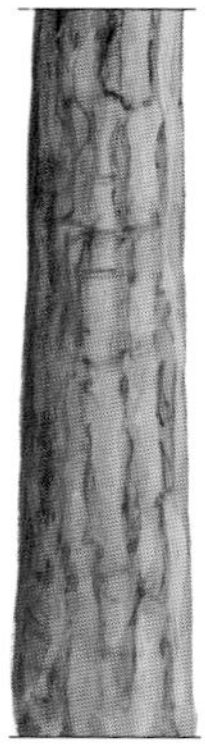
young trunk soon develops rectangular gray ridges

older bark deeply furrowed and checked, chunky

leaves 4", oval, glossy dark green, sometimes with a few teeth
short leafstalk
underleaf pale green

fall color brilliant yellow to red

fruit ½" berry, dark blue-black, oval, 1–5 on long stalk, usually 3 or more; ripe Nov–Jan

twig greenish, becoming red-brown to gray

Common in open woods, usually in well-drained soils at edges of swamps. Commonly cultivated (zones 4–9) mainly in moist soils, several cultivars available.

often flat-topped with jagged angles and many short spur twigs

emerging leaves bright green, standing up in clusters at twig tips
male flowers in dense clusters

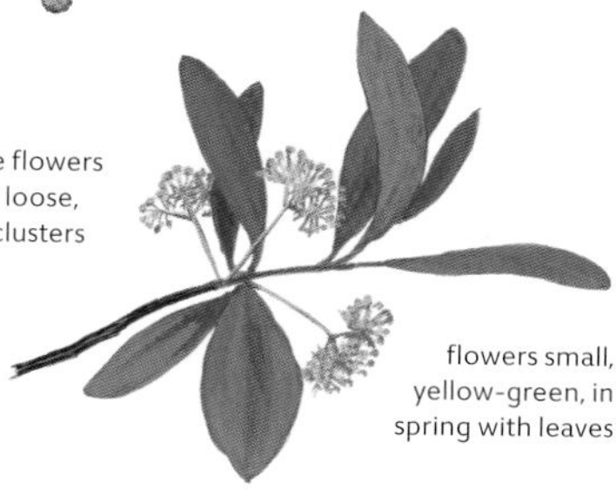
female flowers tiny, in loose, open clusters
flowers small, yellow-green, in spring with leaves

Swamp Tupelo

Nyssa biflora

Deciduous. Medium to large tree 30–60' tall. Very similar to Black Tupelo and sometimes considered the same species, but differs slightly in leaves and fruit, is found in wetter habitats, and has seeds more strongly ribbed.

leaves 3½", blunt-tipped, widest near tip (vs. widest at middle on Black Tupelo), and rarely toothed

fruit single or double on short or long stalk

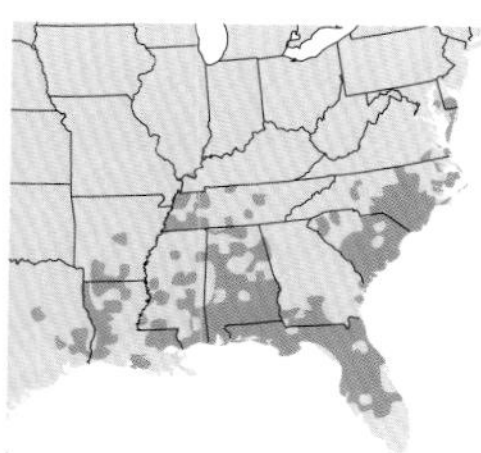

Common, often in pure stands in poorly-drained swamps, bogs, pond edges, on coastal plain from Maryland to Texas. Not cultivated.

Ogeechee Tupelo

Nyssa ogeche

OGEECHEE LIME, SOUR TUPELO, WHITE TUPELO

Deciduous. Shrub to medium tree usually 30–40' tall (max. 93') usually with several crooked and leaning trunks. Similar to Water Tupelo, identified by details of leaf and fruit, also by winged seed (inside fruit), underleaf and twigs velvety-hairy.

leaves 4½", often narrow, usually blunt-tipped

fruit 1", on very short stalk, reddish, single
fruit sometimes persists into winter

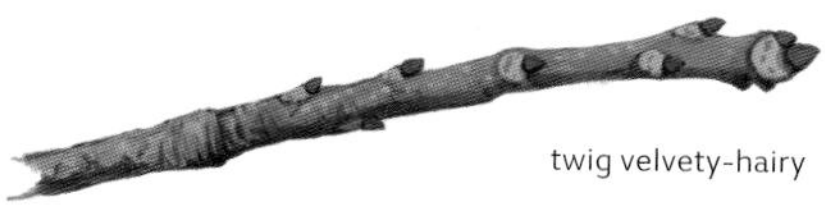
twig velvety-hairy

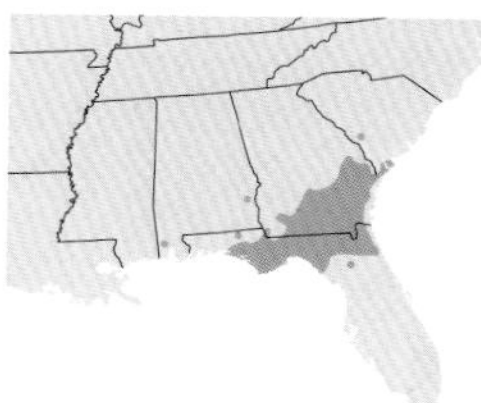

Locally common in swamps, floodplains, and other wet habitats. Not cultivated (zones 6–9).

Cyrilla Family

The cyrilla family (Cyrillaceae) includes just three species in two genera, all native to North America. They are closely related to the heath family (Ericaceae), which includes Sourwood, Madrone, and sparkleberry, as well as to the family Clethraceae (all shrubs), such as Sweet Pepperbush (*Clethra alnifolia*).

Buckwheat-tree

Cliftonia monophylla

BLACK TITI, IRONWOOD

Evergreen. Shrub or occasionally a small tree to 18' tall (max. about 30'). Related to Swamp Cyrilla, and often found with it, but differs slightly in leaves, flowers, and fruit.

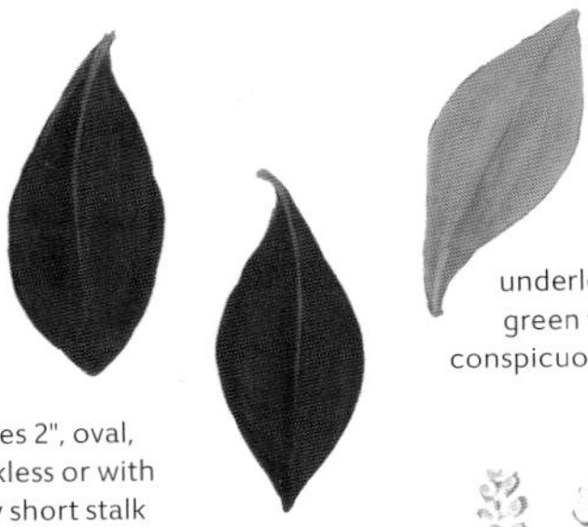
underleaf pale green without conspicuous veins
leaves 2", oval, stalkless or with very short stalk

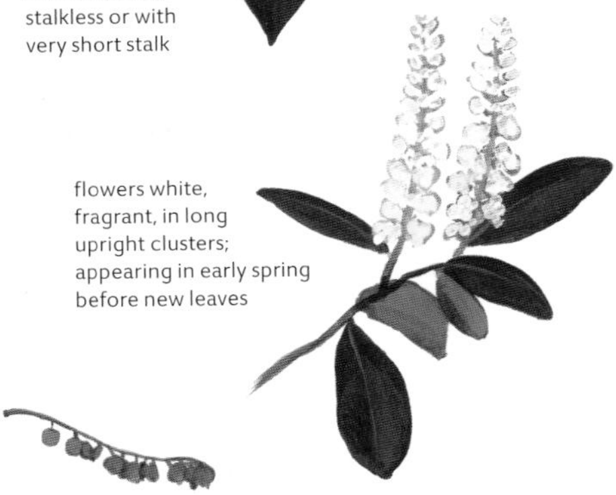
flowers white, fragrant, in long upright clusters; appearing in early spring before new leaves
fruit small, 3-angled, leathery, golden-amber in color, on long spike, some persist year round

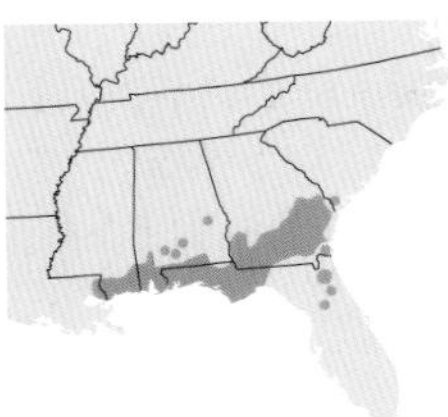

Common in wet soils in open bay swamps and edges of pine flatwoods. Uncommonly cultivated (zones 7–9).

Swamp Cyrilla

Cyrilla racemiflora

TITI

Deciduous to semi-evergreen. Shrub or small tree usually 10–15' tall (max. 58'), usually spreading, twisted, thicket-forming.

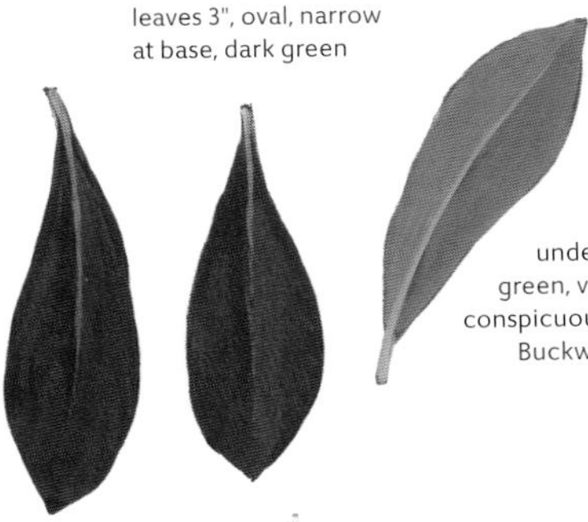
leaves 3", oval, narrow at base, dark green
underleaf pale green, veins more conspicuous than on Buckwheat-tree

flowers white, in 5" spikes diverging from base of current year's growth (May-Jul)
fruit small 2-parted oval capsules on long spike, mature in fall and persist year-round

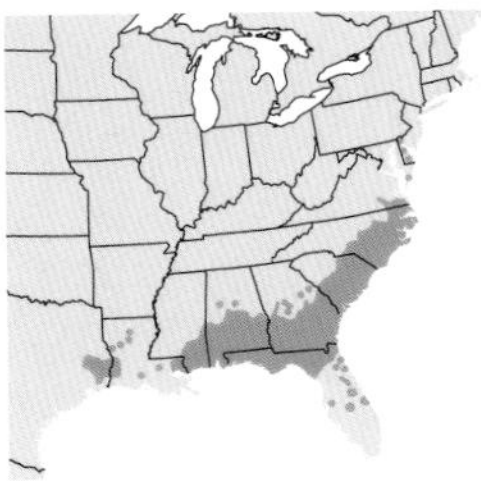

Common in swamps, streambanks, and other wetlands. Commonly cultivated, growing in dry sites as well as wet (zones 6–11).

Littleleaf Cyrilla

Cyrilla parvifolia

LITTLELEAF TITI

Sometimes considered a subspecies of Swamp Cyrilla, but intermediates are scarce. Has smaller leaves 1½" long, flower spikes fewer and shorter, 2½" long, fruit more round. Rare in wet depressions in southern Georgia and northern Florida. Rarely cultivated.

Sapodilla Family

The sapodilla family (Sapotaceae) includes about 800 species of trees and shrubs in about sixty genera worldwide, mainly in the tropics. Five genera are native to North America, but only one, the bullies (genus *Sideroxylon*) are cold-hardy enough to be included here. Bullies are shrubs or small understory trees; six species are native and two are cold-hardy and sometimes tree-like.

Buckthorn Bully

Sideroxylon lycioides

BUCKTHORN BUMELIA, SMOOTH BUMELIA

Deciduous. Shrub or small tree (max. 31'). Similar to Gum Bully, but leaves larger, pointed, hairless; fruit larger, twigs more spiny.

leaves 4½", pointed
underleaf not hairy

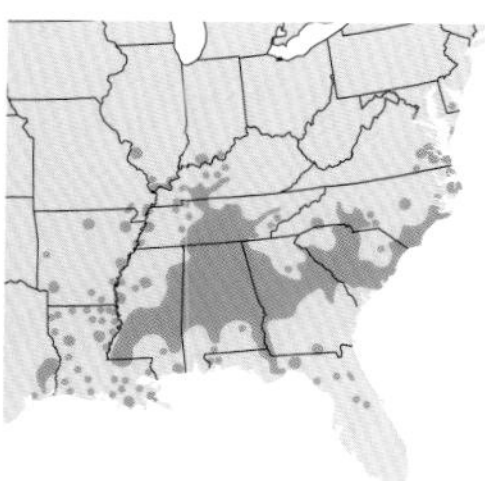

Rare and scattered in understory of woods along pond and swamp margins, less often in uplands. Not cultivated.

Gum Bully

Sideroxylon lanuginosum

GUM BUMELIA, WOOLLY BUCKTHORN

Deciduous to nearly evergreen. Shrub or small tree usually 15–25' tall (max. 55'); narrow crown of stiff spiny branches. Flowers small, white, clustered in leaf axils.

leaves 3½", narrow-based, curved, broad-tipped
leaves alternate, grow in bunches and often appear whorled
fruit ½", oval, blackish
underleaf whitish or brownish, woolly

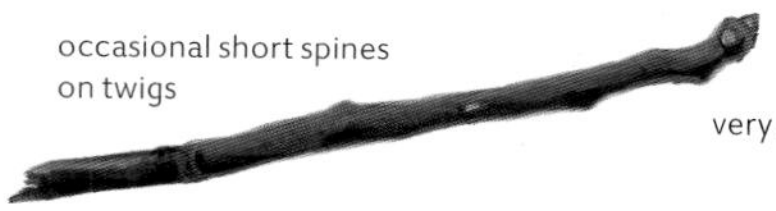
occasional short spines on twigs
buds very small

bark dark, scaly, fissured

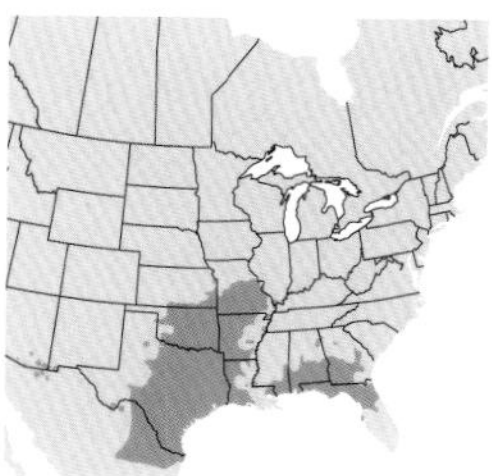

Common in well-drained sandy or rocky soils, often along margins of ponds or swamps. Not cultivated.

Ebony Family

The ebony family (Ebenaceae) includes about 500 species of shrubs and trees worldwide. Nearly all are persimmons (genus *Diospyros*), found mainly in the tropics. Two species are native to North America and are covered here along with a cultivated Asian species. The other genus in the family (*Euclea*), found in tropical Africa and Asia, is the source of ebony wood.

male and female flowers on separate trees; male flowers tubular, in clusters

female flowers white to greenish yellow, solitary

Chinese Persimmon

Diospyros kaki

JAPANESE PERSIMMON, TOMATO TREE, CHINESE FIG

Deciduous. Small tree usually under 25' tall (max. 27'), usually low and spreading with drooping twigs; larger leaves, buds, and fruit than native persimmons. The source of commercial persimmons. Native to northern India, China, and Korea. Commonly cultivated for fruit and, increasingly, for ornament (zone 7–9).

leaves large, 7", pointed tip

orange fruit variable, about 2½" across, round to oval

Texas Persimmon

Diospyros texana

BLACK PERSIMMON, MEXICAN PERSIMMON

Deciduous to evergreen (in warmer climates). Shrub or small tree usually under 20' tall (max. 26'), usually multi-trunked. Heavy wood sinks in water.

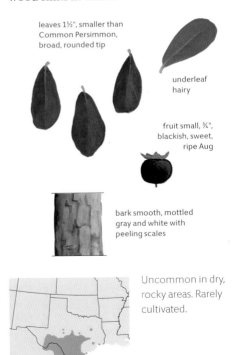

leaves 1½", smaller than Common Persimmon, broad, rounded tip

underleaf hairy

fruit small, ¾", blackish, sweet, ripe Aug

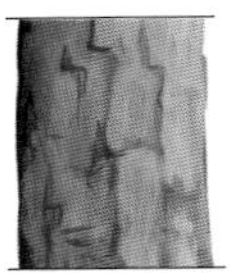

bark smooth, mottled gray and white with peeling scales

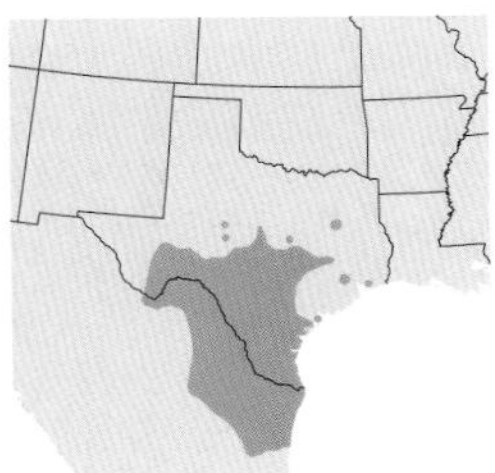

Uncommon in dry, rocky areas. Rarely cultivated.

Common Persimmon

Diospyros virginiana

EASTERN PERSIMMON, POSSUMWOOD

Deciduous. Small to medium tree usually 25–45' tall (max. 132'), usually upright oval with open crown of contorted branches.

bark on mature trunk dark and broken into small, rectangular blocks

leaves 4½", oval, rounded base and pointed tip

leaf edges wavy

underleaf pale whitish (unlike similar Black Tupelo)

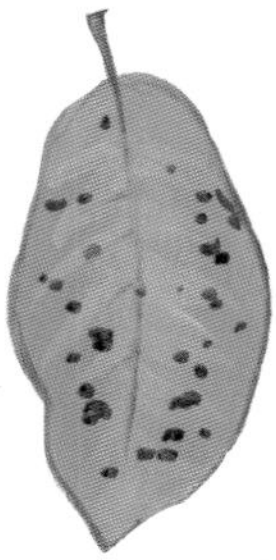

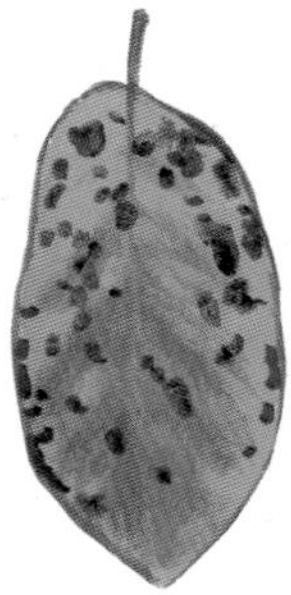

fall color orange to red, leaves spotted black

twigs relatively straight, stout, fruit persists into winter

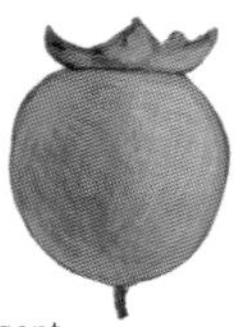

fruit 1½", orange to red-purple when ripe, round, edible

fruit is astringent when green, sweet when ripe in late fall after frost

twig light brown, zigzag

buds broad, dark red-brown

Common in open woodlands and abandoned fields, varied habitats. Uncommonly cultivated (zone 4–9).

relatively narrow tree with crooked trunk and contorted branches

Heath Family

The heaths (family Ericaceae) includes nearly 4,000 species of herbs, shrubs, and a few trees worldwide, including such well-known plants as blueberries, heathers, mountain-laurels, and rhododendrons. Several hundred species are native to North America. Six native species in four genera are commonly tree-like and are included in this guide.

Many species have showy flowers in long spikes and smooth reddish bark. Heaths grow in acidic soils, forming a symbiotic relationship with a root fungus that allows them to extract nutrients from the soil.

None of the heaths grow large enough to be important for lumber, but many species are valued for fruit or showy flowers. The madrones grow larger than other species in the family, but their trunks are usually crooked and not suitable for lumber. The wood burns hot and is valued for fuel in the Pacific Northwest, where native Americans also used the bark and leaves for various medicinal preparations.

Relatives of Tree Sparkleberry in the genus *Vaccinium* include many species with sweet edible berries, such as blueberries, huckleberries, cranberries, lingonberries and others. Fruit of madrones is edible but not very sweet and is consumed mostly by birds. The fruit of Sourwood and Georgia Plume is in dry capsules rather than fleshy berries.

Important ornamental shrubs include the Mountain-laurels (genus *Kalmia*) with several native shrubby species, and rhododendrons and azaleas (genus *Rhododendron*), which includes about twenty-five native species of shrubs. Three species of rhododendrons are reported to be only occasionally tree-like.

Tree Sparkleberry

Vaccinium arboreum

FARKLEBERRY

Deciduous in northern range to nearly evergreen in southern range. Shrub or occasionally a small tree usually under 20' tall (max. 29'); slender or spreading with crooked and leaning trunk topped by dome of small leaves.

leaves 2", oval with small point, somewhat stiff, untoothed

flowers small, white, profuse, bell-shaped, on long stalks from leaf axils

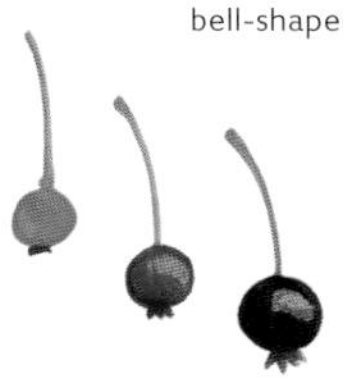

fruit typical of other blueberries, ¼", 5-pointed sepals persistent, green turning red to glaucous black at maturity; ripe in late summer

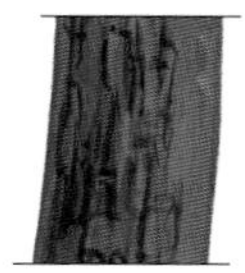

Tree Sparkleberry bark thin, orange-brown, flaking off in long scales

twig slender, orange-brown

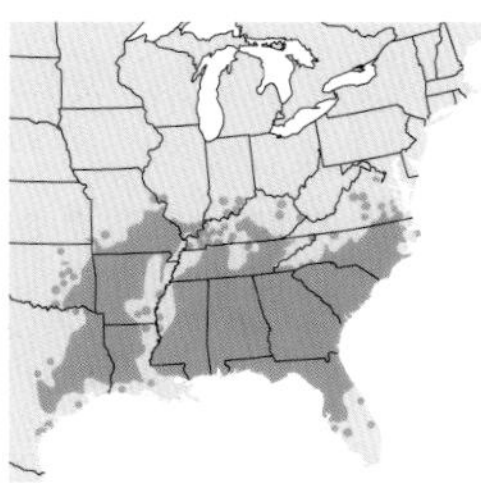

Common in understory of dry woodlands, hammocks, and clearings. Commonly cultivated, but far less common than blueberry cultivars selected for fruit (zones 7–9).

Sourwood

Oxydendrum arboreum

SORREL TREE, SORRELWOOD, LILY-OF-THE-VALLEY TREE, TITI

Deciduous. Small to medium tree usually 25–40' tall (max. 118'), slender with leaning trunk and narrow crown.

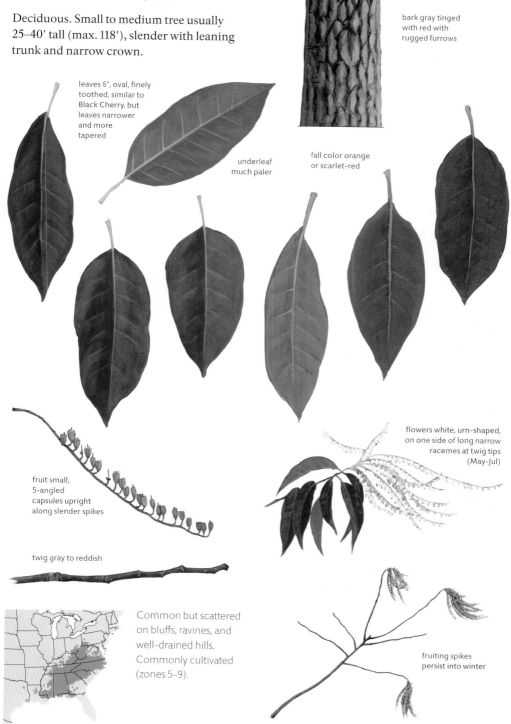

bark gray tinged with red with rugged furrows

leaves 6", oval, finely toothed, similar to Black Cherry, but leaves narrower and more tapered
underleaf much paler
fall color orange or scarlet-red

fruit small, 5-angled capsules upright along slender spikes

flowers white, urn-shaped, on one side of long narrow racemes at twig tips (May-Jul)

twig gray to reddish

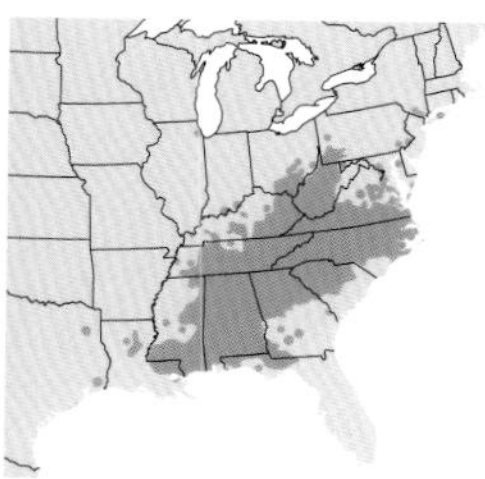

Common but scattered on bluffs, ravines, and well-drained hills. Commonly cultivated (zones 5–9).

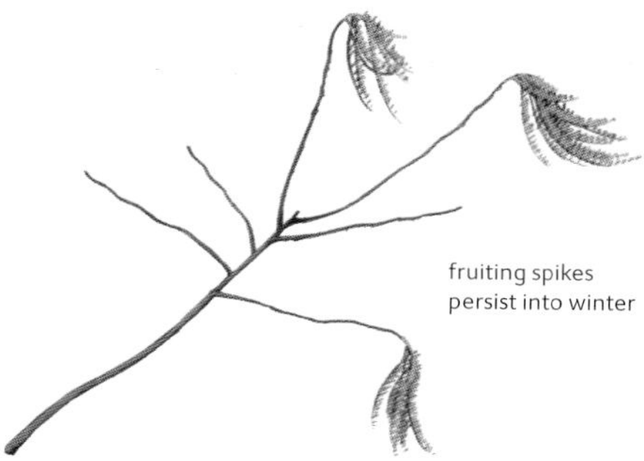
fruiting spikes persist into winter

Pacific Madrone

Arbutus menziesii

PACIFIC MADRONA, COAST MADRONA

Evergreen. Shrub to medium or large tree usually 20–60' tall (max. 131'); form variable, can have tall straight trunk in redwood forests, smaller and often shrubby in other habitats.

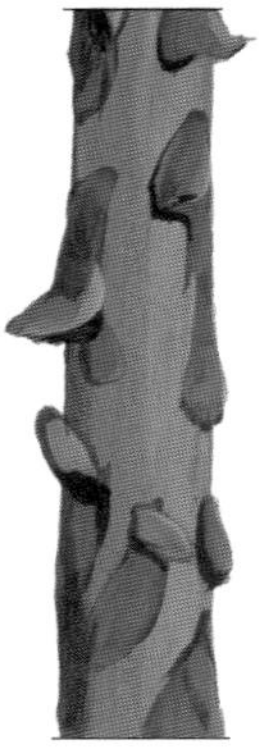

bark red-brown, peeling in thin strips to expose greenish inner bark

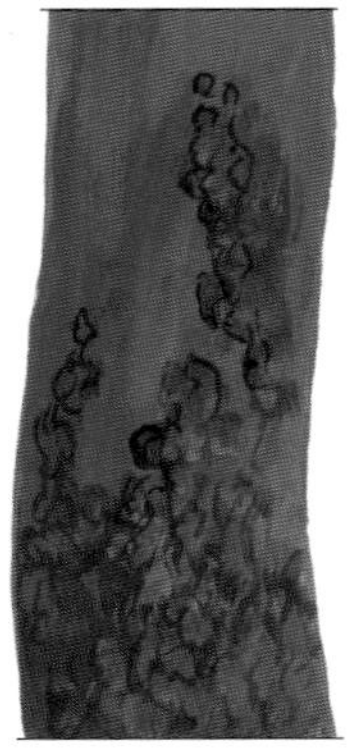

bark on large trunks smooth reddish-brown with rough gray scales

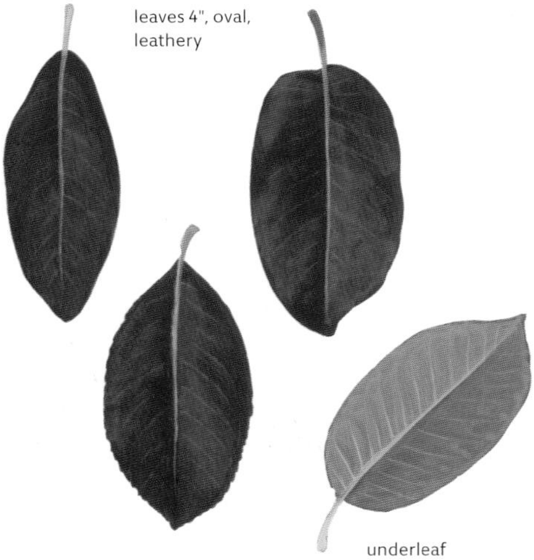

leaves 4", oval, leathery

underleaf paler green

flowers ⅓", small, white, urn-shaped in panicles 6" long (Mar–May)

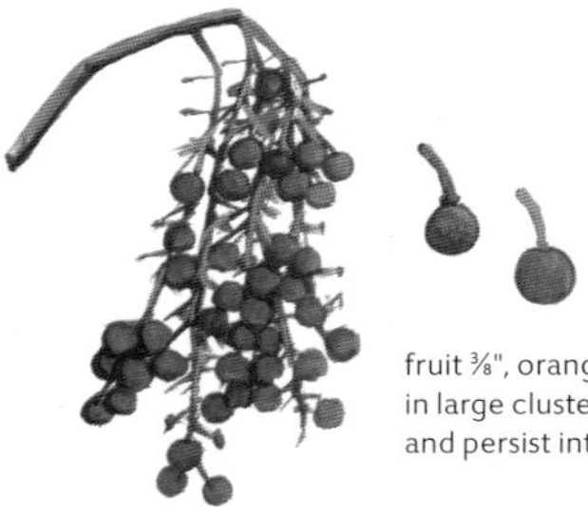

fruit ⅜", orange-red, in large clusters; ripe in fall and persist into winter

twigs reddish

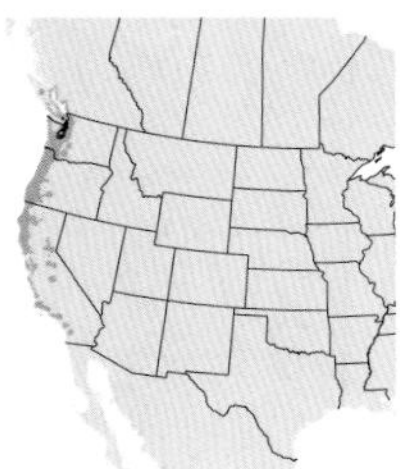

Common in coastal mixed forest. Uncommonly cultivated within native range (zone 6–8).

Strawberry Tree

Arbutus unedo

LILY-OF-THE-VALLEY TREE

Evergreen. Shrub or occasionally a small tree closely related to native madrones. Differs from native species in larger fruit, about 1", bark more shreddy, less attractive, and usually flowers in fall (Oct–Nov) rather than spring. Native to the Mediterranean region. Commonly cultivated and locally escaped (zone 7–9) in various hybrids and cultivars.

About 40 species of manzanitas (genus *Arctostaphylos*) are found in southwestern foothill chaparral, mainly in California. They have smooth reddish bark similar to the madrones, but are shrubs, rarely short-trunked spreading trees.

Arizona Madrone

Arbutus arizonica

ARIZONA MADRONA

Evergreen. Small to medium tree usually under 30' tall (max. 53'); very similar to Pacific Madrone, but with smaller and narrower leaves.

leaves 2½", slender
underleaf
pale green

bark red like Pacific
Madrone, but often
more scaly gray

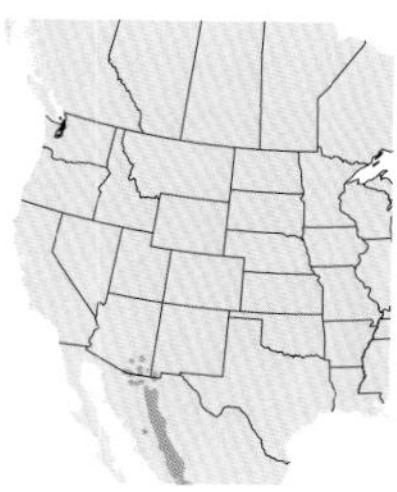

Locally common in mixed oak/conifer forest on canyon slopes. Not cultivated.

Texas Madrone

Arbutus xalapensis

TEXAS MADRONA, LADY LEGS, MANZANITA

Evergreen. Shrub or occasionally a small tree to 20' tall (max. 36'); usually broad with multiple short crooked trunks. Similar to other native madrones, but shorter with hairy underleaf, flowers, fruit clusters, and smaller leaves.

leaves 2",
small

Uncommon and local in dry soils of limestone bluffs and canyon slopes. Rarely cultivated in Southwest and California (zone 8).

Georgia Plume

Elliottia racemosa

SOUTHERN PLUME, ELLIOTTIA

Deciduous. Shrub or small tree often 20' tall (max. 47') with showy spike of white flowers in spring. Apparently dependent on fire; extremely rare and declining in the wild, and now known from only a few locations in Georgia in moist sandy soils. Rarely cultivated.

flowers white, 1", in narrow
upright spike 6" long (Jul),
developing round woody
fruit capsules ½",
leaves 4", oval

Snowbell Family

The snowbell family (Styracaceae) includes about 160 species of trees in eleven genera worldwide. Two genera are native to North America. Snowbells (genus *Styrax*) include about 130 species of shrubs and trees worldwide, mainly in Asia with four species native to North America, but only one commonly tree-like. The silverbells (genus *Halesia*) include four species worldwide, three native in North America.

Few species in this family attain tree size, so these plants are not important for lumber, but many are popular as cultivated ornamental plants. In Asia, the bark of snowbell trees is processed to extract "benzoin resin," an aromatic resin used in incense and perfumery.

Three similar species of snowbells are native to North America, all shrubby. Two additional species from eastern Asia are commonly cultivated and more often tree-like than any native species.

Fragrant Snowbell

Styrax obassia

BIGLEAF SNOWBELL TREE

Deciduous. Shrub or small slender tree to 30' (max. 50') with very large leaves, like Catalpa, 8" long, broad, fuzzy. Native from northern China to Japan. Uncommon in cultivation, but becoming more common in the Northwest (zones 5–8).

Japanese Snowbell

Styrax japonicus

JAPANESE SNOWDROP TREE, JAPANESE STORAX

Deciduous. Shrub or small tree with short, twisted trunk, spreading and low-branched to 30' tall (max. 49'). Leaves small, 3", dark glossy green, flowers and fruit longer-stalked than native species. Native to Japan, Korea, and China. Commonly cultivated; naturalized in New York and Pennsylvania (zones 5–8). Many cultivars include pink flowers.

Bigleaf Snowbell

Styrax grandifolius

SNOWBELL, STORAX

Deciduous. Shrub or rarely a small tree to 18' (max. 22'); leaves and twigs similar to Silverbells, distinguished by fruit and flowers.

leaves 5", finely toothed or not, broad at tip
underleaf white-hairy

flowers May–Jun after leaves
flowers 1", white, 5-lobed, bell-shaped, in drooping clusters 6" long

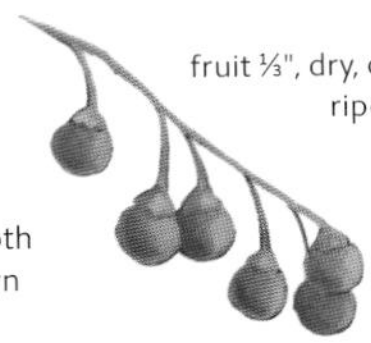
fruit ⅓", dry, oval, hairy; ripe Sep–Oct

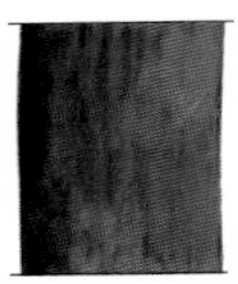
bark smooth gray-brown

twigs zigzag, hairy or scaly, buds lack scales

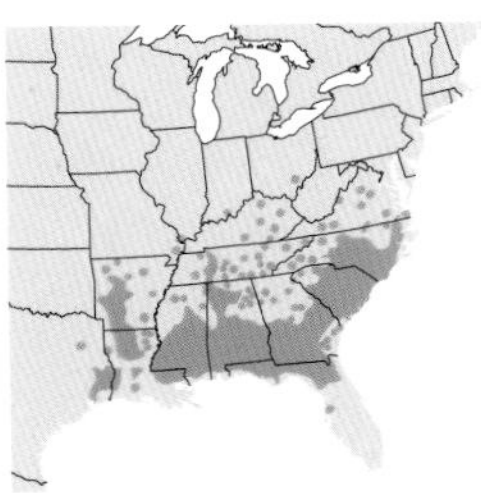

Uncommon in understory of woods, usually in well-drained, rich soils, less often in wet sites. Rarely cultivated.

Mountain Silverbell

Halesia tetraptera

SILVERBELL TREE, SNOWDROP TREE, OPOSSUM WOOD, CALICO WOOD, BELL TREE

Deciduous. Shrub or small tree usually under 40' tall (max. 104').

bark of young trunk smooth, striped pale gray and green

bark of older trunk furrowed with flat, smooth ridges

leaves 6", pointed

fall color yellow

flowers ¾", white, dangling from leaf axils in clusters of 2–6 (Mar–Jun), in spring with leaves

fruit 1½", 4-winged, pale green to brown; ripe in fall

twig slender, brownish

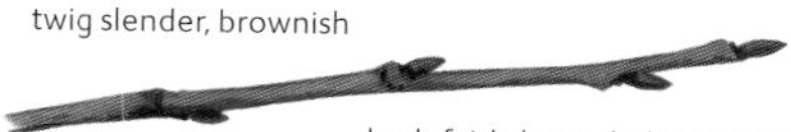

buds fairly long, dark red-brown

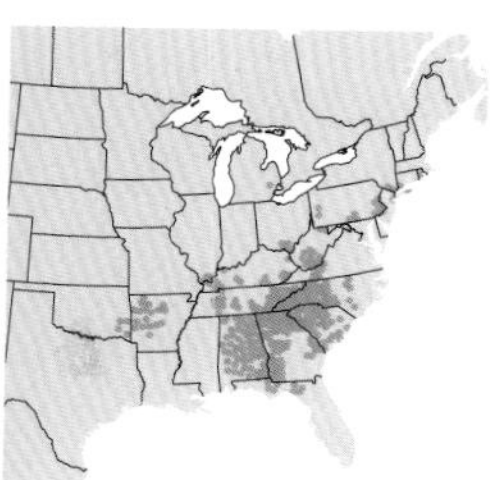

Locally common understory plant in rich soils along streams and on wooded slopes. Commonly cultivated (zone 4–8) and several cultivars.

Two other species of silverbells are native to the southeastern region and rarely cultivated. Both are multi-stemmed shrubs that are rarely tree-like, and both are very similar to Mountain Silverbell. Carolina Silverbell (*Halesia carolina*), which is often considered the same species as Mountain, is a smaller plant with smaller leaves, flowers and fruit. Two-wing Silverbell (*Halesia diptera*) is a shrub to 12' tall, also sometimes considered the same species but differs in having the fruit with only two wings instead of four.

Tea Family

Franklinia and Loblolly-bay are in the tea family (Theaceae), which has about 200 species worldwide. The tea family also includes the familiar camellia, a shrub, commonly cultivated in warmer areas (zones 7–9). The closely related genus *Stewartia* is represented in North America by two native species, which are rarely small trees: Virginia Stewartia (*S. malacodendron*) and Mountain Stewartia (*S. ovata*). Several Asian species and hybrids are cultivated.

Franklinia

Franklinia alatamaha

FRANKLIN TREE

Deciduous. Shrub or small tree usually 10–20' tall (max. 38'); upright spreading branches and open crown reminiscent of Sweetbay Magnolia. Flowers 3½" across, white with orange center (Jul–Sep), similar to Loblolly Bay.

leaves 7", narrow base, shiny dark green above
underleaf paler green, hairy
fruit ¾", a 5-parted woody capsule

twig green to brown, silky
terminal bud silky-hairy, elongated into narrow point

Native to Georgia, but not seen in the wild since 1790; survives only in cultivation mainly as clones of the original tree. Uncommonly cultivated (zones 5–8).

Loblolly-bay

Gordonia lasianthus

HOLLY BAY, BLACK LAUREL, SUMMER CAMELLIA

Evergreen. Small to large tree, often 60' tall (max. 100'). Columnar growth with crown typically pointed, spine-like.

leaves 5", narrow, elliptical, shiny dark green
underleaf paler green

flowers showy, 2½", white, long-stemmed (May–Oct)

fruit a small pointed capsule

terminal bud blunt

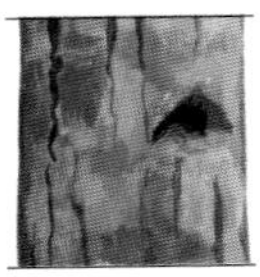
bark reddish to gray, developing narrow cracks

Common in wet soils in swamps, pond margins, low woods. Uncommon in cultivation (zones 8–9).

Four Families

The following four species are in four different families:

HARDY RUBBER TREE is the only species in the family Eucommiaceae.

COMMON SWEETLEAF is in the sweetleaf family (Symplocaceae) with about 320 species worldwide and only one native to North America. It is related to the snowbell family.

ANACUA is in the borage family (Boraginaceae) with about 2,000 species worldwide; includes many familiar garden plants such as forget-me-nots, Comfrey, and heliotropes, but few trees.

BUTTONBUSH is in the madder family (Rubiaceae) with about 13,000 species worldwide, including gardenias and coffeas.

Hardy Rubber Tree

Eucommia ulmoides

GUTTA PERCHA TREE

Deciduous. Small to medium tree usually 40-60' tall (max. 49'); dense oval crown, low branches.

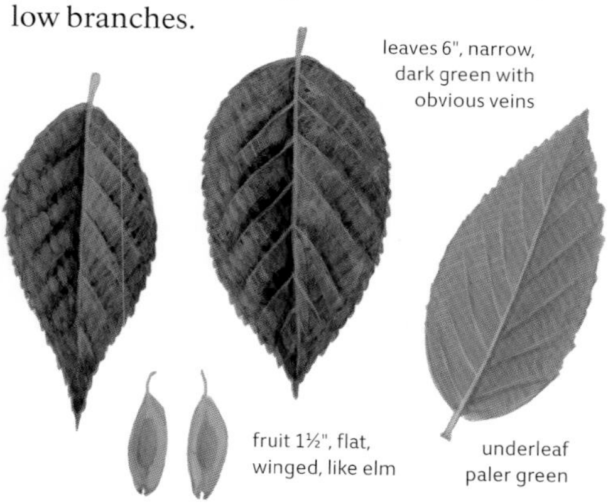
leaves 6", narrow, dark green with obvious veins
fruit 1½", flat, winged, like elm
underleaf paler green

Native to China. Commonly cultivated (zone 4–7).

Common Sweetleaf

Symplocos tinctoria

Deciduous or semi-evergreen. Shrub or small tree often 25' tall (max. 70'); ascending branches and spreading crown. Named for the sweet flavor of leaves.

leaves 5 ½", narrow, somewhat leathery; yellow midvein
underleaf pale hairy

flowers in dense round clusters ½" across, in early spring with new leaves; old leaves may or may not persist through winter

fruit ½", oval capsule, green then brown, in small clusters

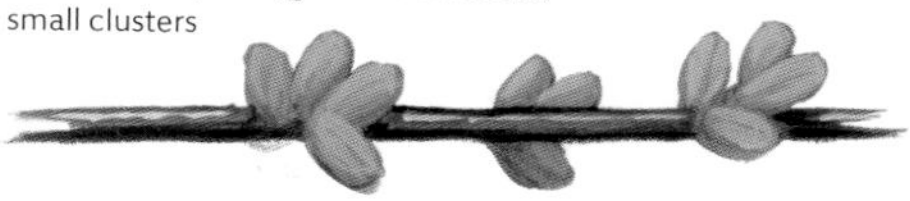

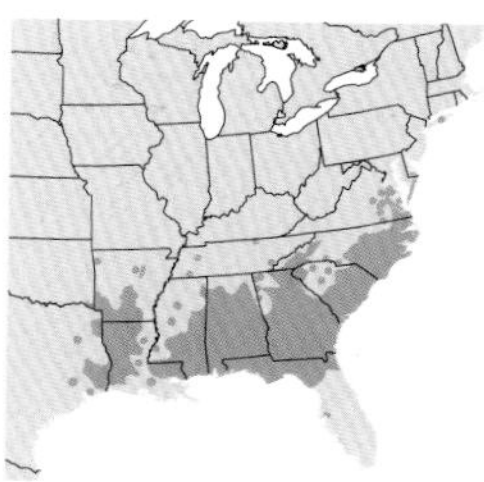

Uncommon and scattered in understory of woods, mostly in moist sandy soils, streambanks, bottomlands. Rarely cultivated (zones 7–9).

Anacua

Ehretia anacua

SANDPAPER-TREE, SUGARBERRY, KNACKAWAY

Tardily deciduous. Shrub or small tree usually 15–25' tall (max. 42') often with several trunks.

leaves 3", oval, dark green with sandpapery texture above

flowers small, white, star-shaped, in small clusters at twig tips, early spring

fruit ¼", round, yellow to orange, ripe in summer

bark gray to reddish, scaly and furrowed

Common in evergreen broadleaf riparian woodlands of southern Texas; uncommonly cultivated and only near native range (zones 8–10).

Buttonbush

Cephalanthus occidentalis

Deciduous. Shrub or occasionally a small tree 10–15' tall (max. 20'), often disheveled, scrubby with dead twigs.

leaves opposite or whorled, oval, 5", rounded base, glossy dark green

fruit in round cluster, persistent through winter

flowers 1", white in dense balls on long stalk (Jun–Aug)

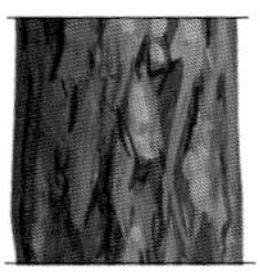

bark rough, furrowed

Common in wet swamps, sunny pond and stream margins, shrub swamps, usually in shallow water, exclusively in wetlands. Occasionally cultivated (zones 5–11).

Olive Family

The olive family (Oleaceae) includes about 600 species of shrubs and trees worldwide. Several familiar and important genera are in this family, including forsythia, privet, olive, jasmine, lilac, and ash. All have opposite leaves.

Nineteen native tree-like species in three genera are included in this section along with six additional exotic species (in two more genera), which are commonly cultivated, cold-hardy and tree-like. The forestieras (genus *Forestiera*) with four native species, are shrubs and only rarely tree-like.

The primary genus in the olive family in North America is ashes (genus *Fraxinus*). This genus includes about fifty-five species of trees worldwide with seventeen native and four commonly cultivated species covered in this guide. All ashes are quite similar in leaf and fruit characteristics with opposite leaves, and all but one have pinnately compound leaves. Fruit of all ashes is a slender seed with a long papery wing, similar to a maple key, but single (not paired). Most ashes have very inconspicuous flowers with male and female flowers on separate trees, appearing in very early spring before the leaves. The notable exceptions to this are two southwestern species with showy white flowers.

male flowers green and purple in small dense clusters

female flowers in delicate sprays, green

The Emerald Ash Borer is a glossy green beetle about ¾ inch long. It was introduced from Asia to the United States, where it was first detected in Michigan in 2002. The larvae make tunnels through ash wood just beneath the bark, disrupting the flow of sap and killing the tree within two to three years. The beetles have already killed millions of ash trees in Michigan, and have now spread to adjacent states and provinces and eastward to Maryland, Pennsylvania, and Quebec, and threaten to spread through the entire continent. Large-scale efforts to limit the spread and impact of the beetles are underway.

Ash wood is very strong and resilient and is used for tool handles, baseball bats, and similar applications. It is also used for some musical instruments, for veneers on furniture, and makes very good firewood. In some ash species the wood separates easily along growth rings into long thin strips or slats which have been traditionally used for basket-making.

Other genera in the family include:

LILACS (genus *Syringa*) with about twenty-five species of mostly shrubs worldwide. Lilacs are one of the most commonly cultivated flowering shrubs in North America with showy cone-shaped clusters of white, pink, or lavender flowers in early spring, but only one Asian species is tree-like and commonly cultivated here.

FRINGETREES (genus *Chionanthus*) with about eighty species of shrubs and small trees mostly in the tropics worldwide. Two species are native to North America, but only one is tree-like.

OLIVES (genus *Olea*) with about twenty species of shrubs and trees native to warmer parts of Eurasia and Africa. One species is the source of all commercial olives and olive oil, and is commonly cultivated in North America.

OSMANTHUS (genus *Osmanthus*) includes about thirty species of shrubs and small trees native to Asia, and one native to North America.

White Ash

Fraxinus americana

AMERICAN ASH, BILTMORE ASH

Deciduous. Medium to large tree usually 50–80' tall (max. 152') with long straight trunk and deeply furrowed bark. Often a larger and taller tree than Green Ash.

bark on young trunks
smooth grayish
mature bark gray,
diamond furrows

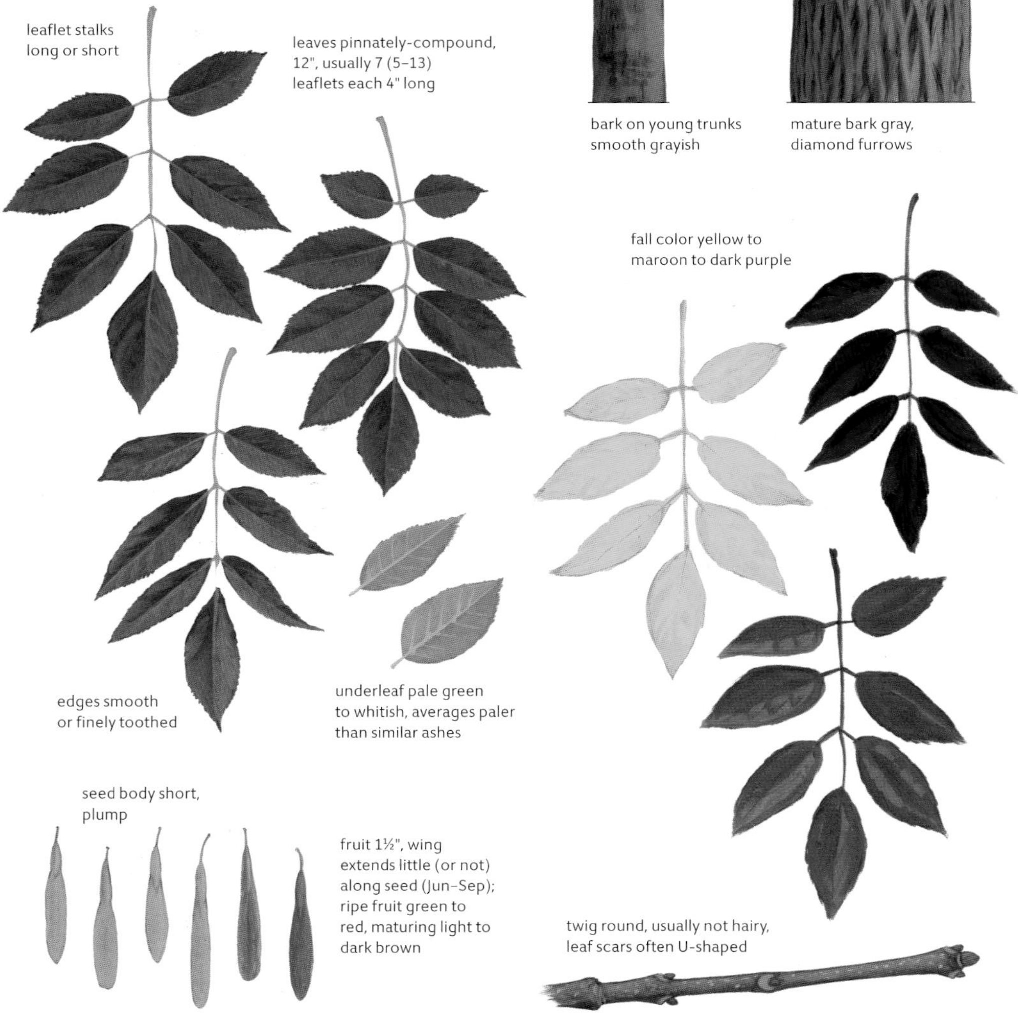
leaflet stalks
long or short
leaves pinnately-compound,
12", usually 7 (5–13)
leaflets each 4" long
fall color yellow to
maroon to dark purple
edges smooth
or finely toothed
underleaf pale green
to whitish, averages paler
than similar ashes
seed body short,
plump
fruit 1½", wing
extends little (or not)
along seed (Jun–Sep);
ripe fruit green to
red, maturing light to
dark brown
twig round, usually not hairy,
leaf scars often U-shaped

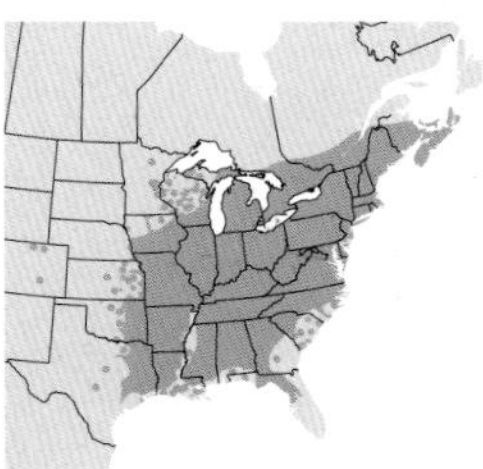

Common in rich deep soils in well-drained uplands. Commonly cultivated; many cultivars (zones 4–9).

In the past, many minor variations of both White Ash and Green Ash have been named as varieties. The distinguishing features are small and variable (mostly involving hairiness of leaves and twigs, or details of leaf or fruit structure). Many trees are intermediate, and most modern authorities do not recognize any of the formerly named varieties.

Green Ash

Fraxinus pennsylvanica

RED ASH, DARLINGTON ASH, WHITE ASH, SWAMP ASH, WATER ASH

Deciduous. Medium to large tree usually 40–60' tall (max. 145'); a variable species, very similar to White Ash and occurring together over a wide area. Habitat is a useful clue for identification and fall color almost always yellow. The only native ash in the Great Plains.

bark of young trunks pinkish with dark joints of branches

mature bark gray, diamond furrows

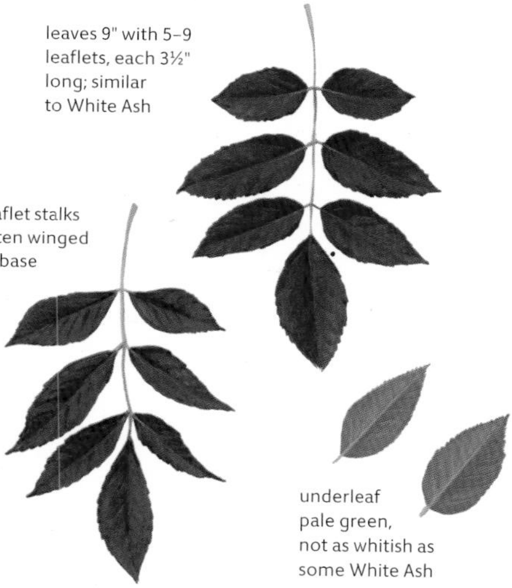

leaves 9" with 5–9 leaflets, each 3½" long; similar to White Ash

leaflet stalks often winged to base

underleaf pale green, not as whitish as some White Ash

flowers after leaves begin to unfold, slightly later than White Ash

male flowers in dense purple and green clusters at twig tips

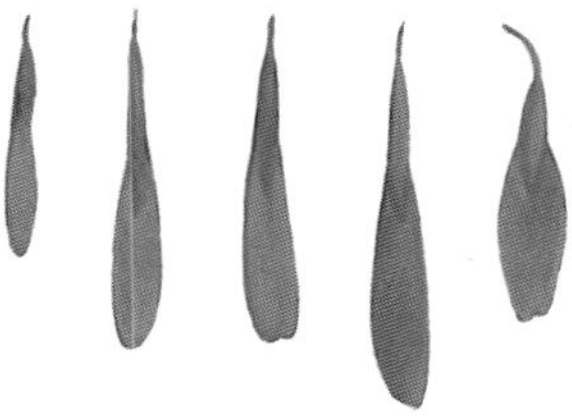

fruit similar to White Ash, but seed longer with wing extending nearly to base

in winter, note stout, straight, opposite twigs and clusters of persistent drooping fruit stems

new twigs can be woolly (smooth on White Ash)

leaf scars not U-shaped

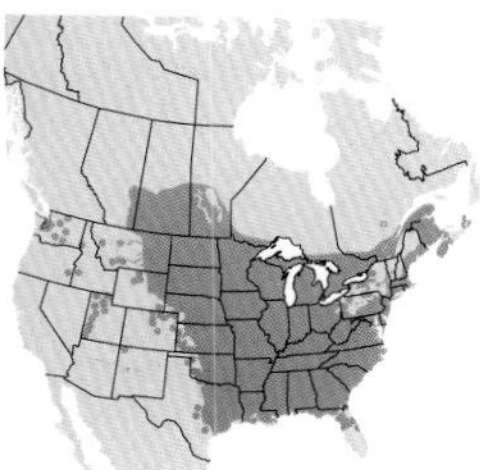

Common in moist to wet woods, wooded swamps, pond and stream margins, bottomlands and river terraces. Very commonly and widely cultivated (zones 3–9).

Carolina Ash

Fraxinus caroliniana

POP ASH, WATER ASH

Deciduous. Small to medium tree usually under 35' (max. 80'); variable, but usually multi-trunked with leaning trunks, buttressed where flooded. Distinguished from other ashes by wet habitat, multiple trunks, wings along entire seed, greenish underleaf.

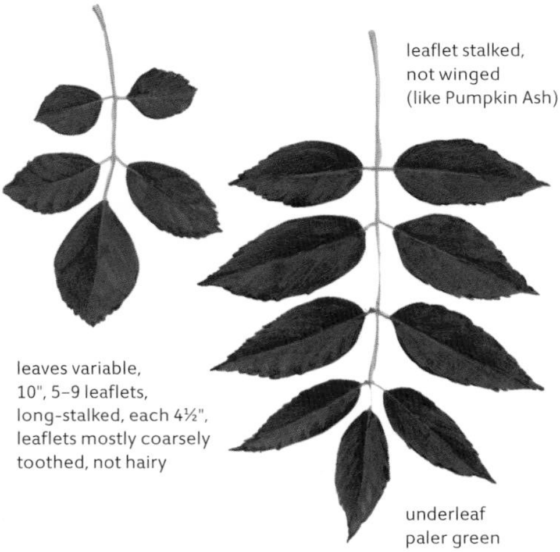
leaflet stalked, not winged (like Pumpkin Ash)
leaves variable, 10", 5–9 leaflets, long-stalked, each 4½", leaflets mostly coarsely toothed, not hairy
underleaf paler green

fruit with seed surrounded by wing

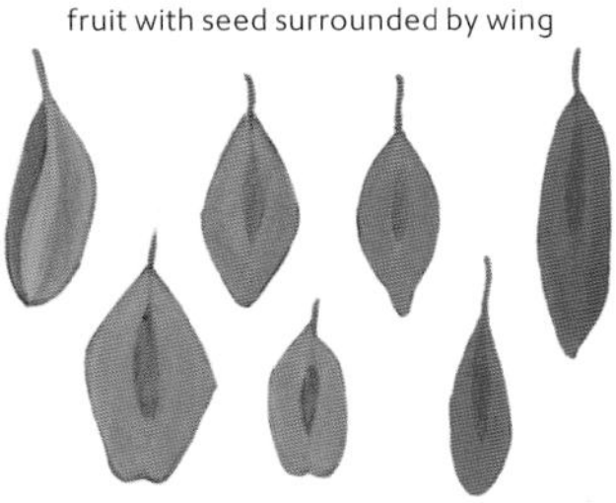

fruit extremely variable; to 2", sometimes 3-winged, seed flattened, more than half as long as entire fruit

Trees in northern Florida tend to have whitish underleaf, narrower fruit wing with notched tip, and single trunk. These are sometimes separated as Florida Ash (*Fraxinus pauciflora*) but most current authorities do not recognize this species.

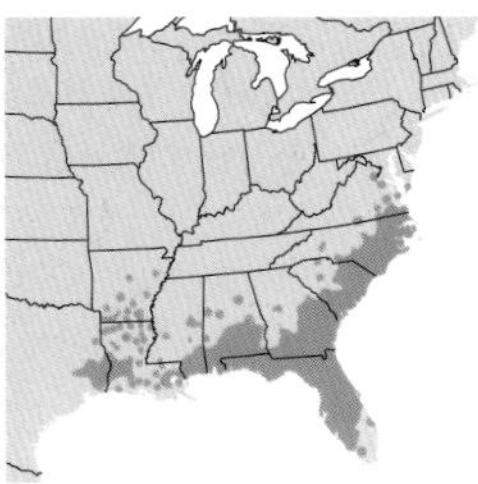

Common in wet habitats, swamps and pond margins, often inundated for long periods. Not cultivated.

Pumpkin Ash

Fraxinus profunda

FRAXINUS TOMENTOSA

Deciduous. Medium to large tree usually 60–90' tall (max. 133') with open, narrow crown. Often found with Carolina Ash, but underleaf pale green and seed plump; fall color bronze-red to purple.

leaves 12", usually 7 (5–9) leaflets oval, pointed, not toothed, each 6" long; hairy below
leaflets stalked
fruit large, narrow, 2¾", seed plump, ¼–⅓ of total length; winged to base of seed

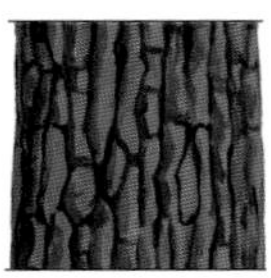

bark ridged and furrowed in interlaced diamond pattern

Uncommon, restricted to deep muddy swamps and seasonally inundated river floodplains; exclusively in wetlands. Not cultivated (zones 5–9).

Oregon Ash

Fraxinus latifolia

Deciduous. Medium to large tree usually 50–70' tall (max. 111'); long clear trunk on good soils, crooked on poor sites. The only native ash in Northwest; closely related to Green Ash but no range overlap.

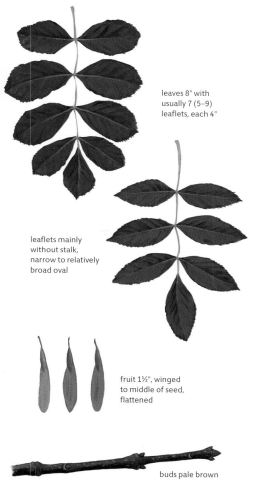

leaves 8" with usually 7 (5–9) leaflets, each 4"

leaflets mainly without stalk, narrow to relatively broad oval

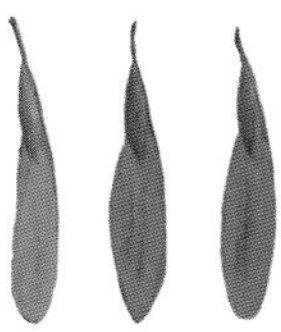

fruit 1½", winged to middle of seed, flattened

buds pale brown

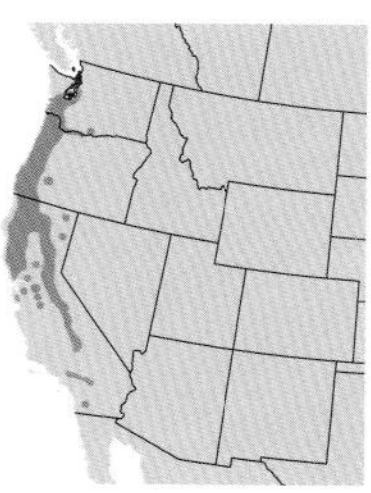

Common in rich moist soils in river valleys, along streams, margins of swamps and woods edges. Very rarely cultivated.

Velvet Ash

Fraxinus velutina

ARIZONA ASH, DESERT ASH, FRESNO

Deciduous. Small tree usually 20–35' tall (max. 85'). Variable and could be considered part of a continent-wide species including Green and Oregon Ash. Told from Berlandier Ash by range, by hairy underleaf, and seed partly winged.

leaves 4½" with 5 (1–9) leaflets, each 2" long; often toothed above middle, velvety-hairy below

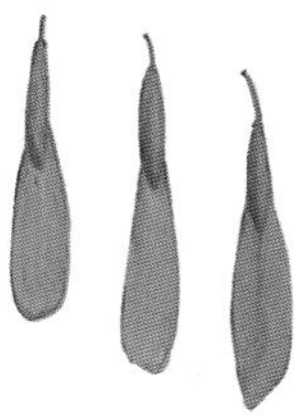

fruit 1", winged only ¼ along seed, seed plump

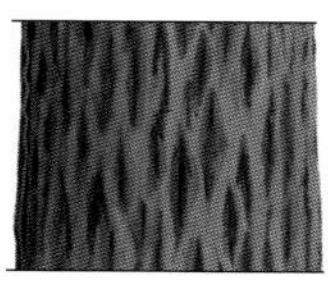

bark gray, ridged, like Green Ash

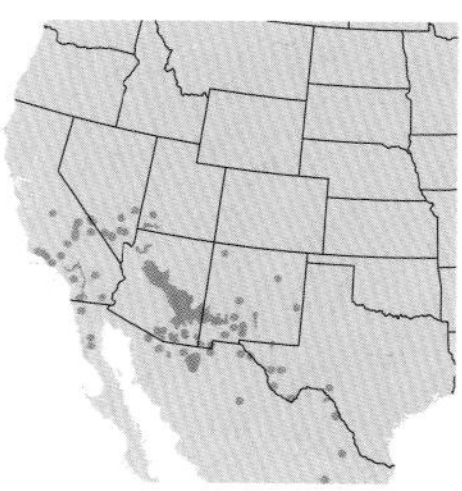

Locally common along watercourses and washes. Commonly cultivated as an important shade tree tolerant of dry climate and alkaline soils in the Southwest (zones 7–9).

Singleleaf Ash

Fraxinus anomala

Deciduous. Shrub or small tree usually under 20' tall (max. 31'). Unique among ashes in usually simple leaves, not compound. This species and Lowell Ash have slightly square twigs with 4 ridges, or lines.

leaves usually simple, 2½", or occasionally compound with 2–3 leaflets, blunt teeth or none
underleaf pale green, hairless

fruit to ¾", winged to base
seed flattened

twigs pale gray, square in cross section
buds orange-brown

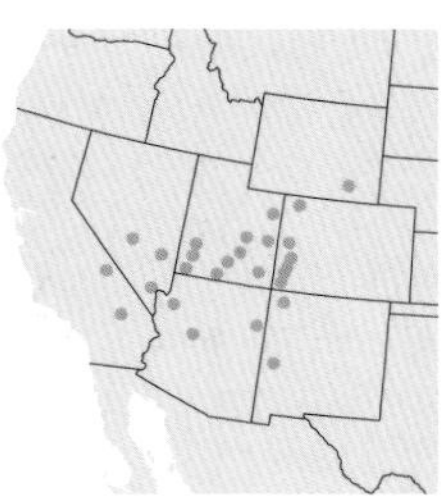

Locally common along watercourses and dry washes in dry rocky soil. Not cultivated.

Lowell Ash

Fraxinus lowellii

Deciduous. Shrub or small tree very similar to Singleleaf Ash and sometimes considered the same species. It differs in having larger leaves with more leaflets, and larger fruit. Distinguished from Velvet Ash by broader leaflets with shorter stalks, flattened seed with wider wings extending to base.

leaves 4½" with 3–7 leaflets

fruit 1", winged to base, seed flattened

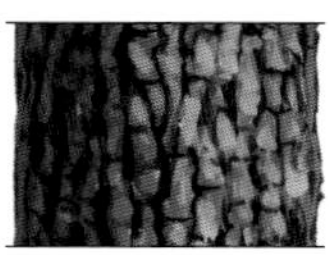
bark forming scaly ridges

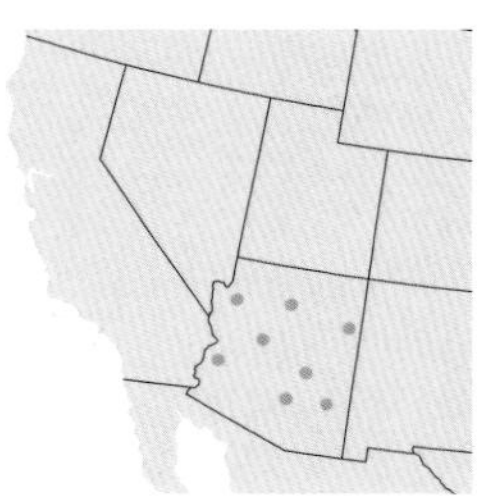

Found only in northern and central Arizona along watercourses. Not cultivated.

Gregg Ash

Fraxinus greggii

Deciduous to semi-evergreen. Shrub or small tree usually under 15' tall (max. about 20').

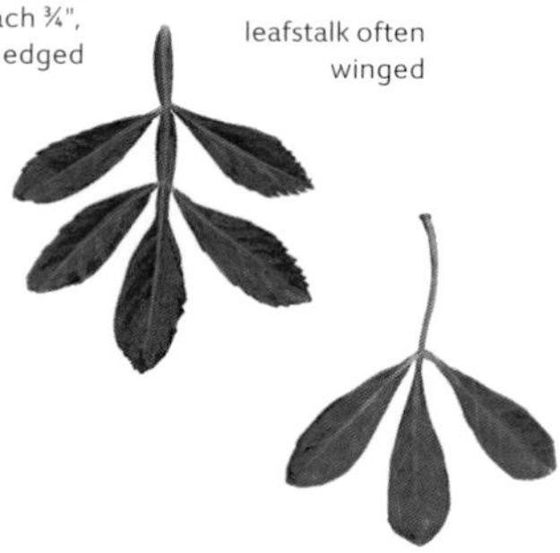
leaves small, 1¾", usually 3 (3–7) leaflets each ¾", leathery, smooth edged
leafstalk often winged

fruit to ¾", winged to middle of seed

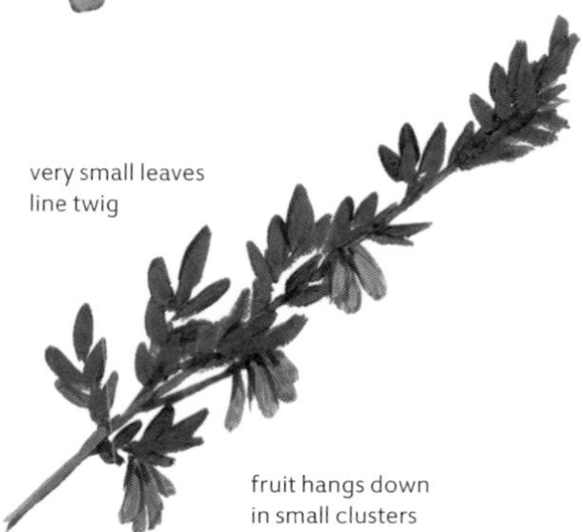
very small leaves line twig
fruit hangs down in small clusters below twigs

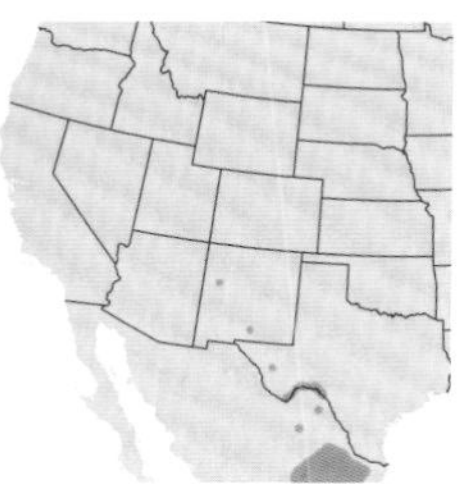

Locally common along streams, limestone canyons, and rocky slopes. Occasionally cultivated.

Goodding Ash

Fraxinus gooddingii

Evergreen to deciduous. Shrub or small tree to 20' tall (max. 25'). Very similar to Gregg Ash with very small leaves and winged leafstalks, but leaves longer, slightly hairy, more toothed, more often evergreen, and broader blunter fruit wing.

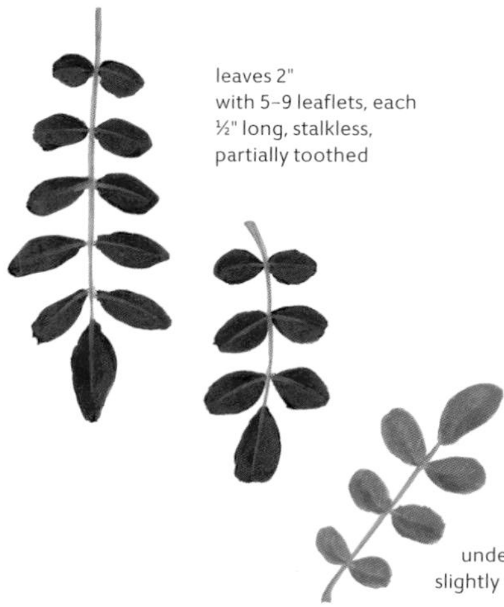
leaves 2" with 5–9 leaflets, each ½" long, stalkless, partially toothed
underleaf slightly hairy

fruit ¾", wing broad and blunt, longer than seed and extending almost to seed base

twigs relatively slender, wooly
buds divergent, gray

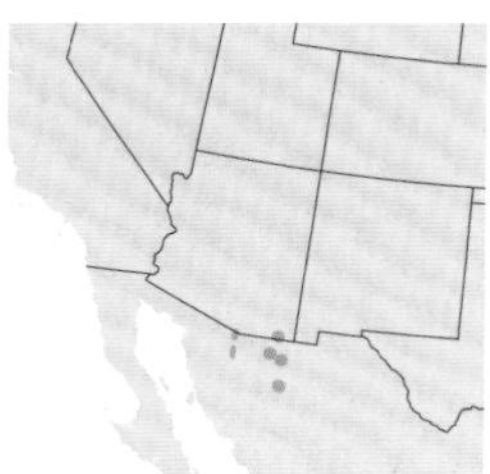

Local and uncommon in its very limited North American range on dry rocky slopes and canyons, not closely tied to water. Rarely cultivated.

European Ash

Fraxinus excelsior

COMMON ASH, ENGLISH ASH

Deciduous. Medium to large tree usually 60–80' tall (max. 93'). Told from Green Ash by leaf margins toothed, buds black, fruit relatively short and broad.

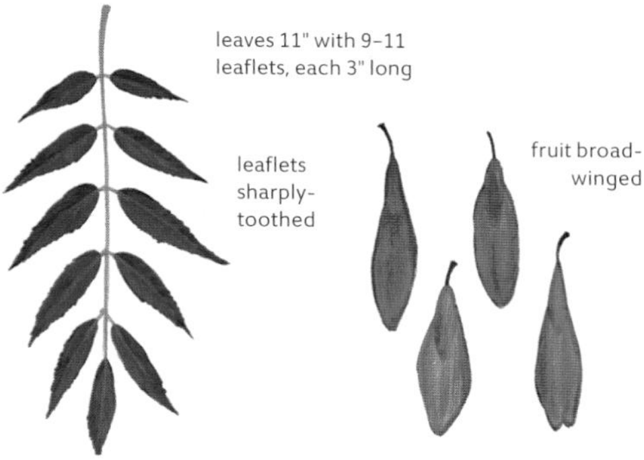
leaves 11" with 9–11 leaflets, each 3" long
leaflets sharply-toothed
fruit broad-winged

Native to Europe. Uncommonly cultivated and locally naturalized; mostly Canada and Pacific Coast and mostly as cultivar with blue-green leaves (zones 5–7).

Evergreen Ash

Fraxinus uhdei

SHAMEL ASH, MEXICAN ASH

Deciduous or semi-evergreen. Medium tree often 30–50' tall. Related to White Ash and other native species.

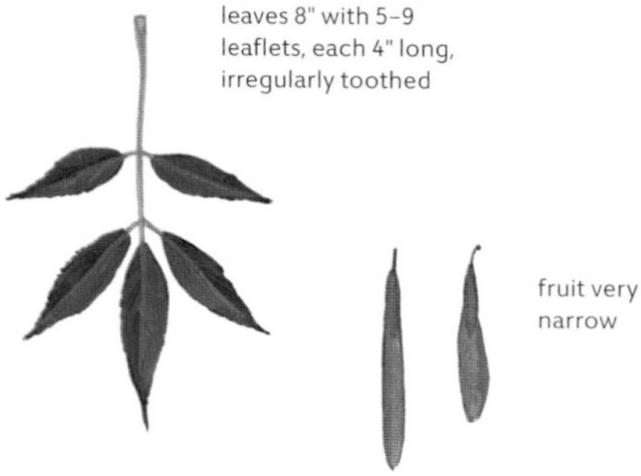
leaves 8" with 5–9 leaflets, each 4" long, irregularly toothed
fruit very narrow

Native to Mexico, Central America; uncommon in cultivation and naturalized in southern California (zones 8–10).

Narrowleaf Ash

Fraxinus angustifolia

MORAINE ASH, CAUCASIAN ASH, PERSIAN ASH, RAYWOOD ASH

Deciduous. Tree usually 40–60' tall (max. 93'). Closely related to European Ash, but with smaller leaves, brownish buds. Native to southern Europe, northern Africa. Commonly cultivated (zones 5–6).

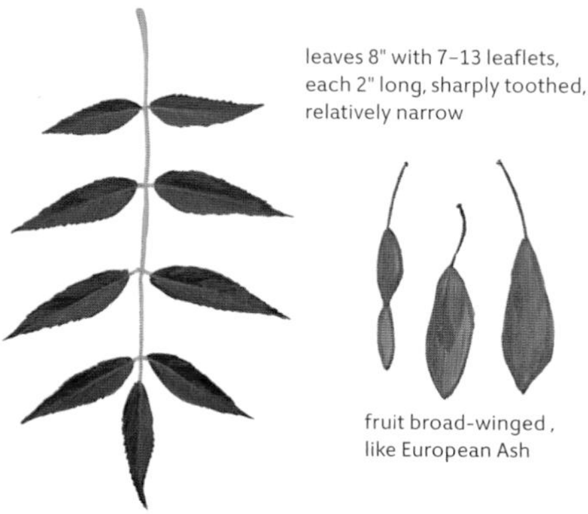
leaves 8" with 7–13 leaflets, each 2" long, sharply toothed, relatively narrow
fruit broad-winged, like European Ash

Manna Ash

Fraxinus ornus

FLOWERING ASH

Deciduous. Small to medium tree usually 30–50' tall (max. 69') with showy white flowers like Fragrant Ash. Native to southeastern Europe and western Asia. Occasionally cultivated and locally common, e.g. in Victoria, British Columbia (zones 5–6).

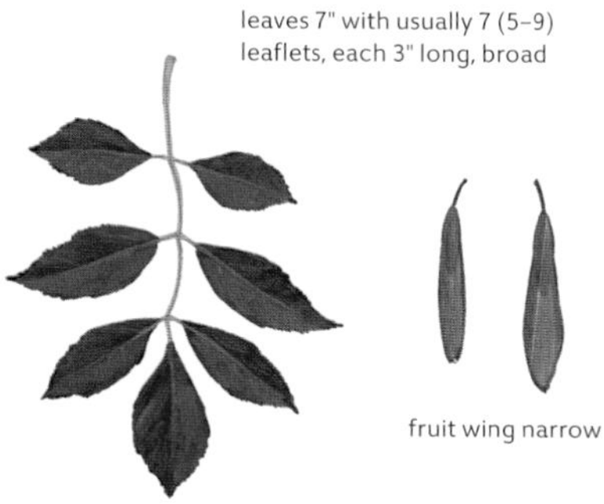
leaves 7" with usually 7 (5–9) leaflets, each 3" long, broad
fruit wing narrow

Two-petal Ash

Fraxinus dipetala

FOOTHILL ASH, CALIFORNIA FLOWERING ASH

Deciduous. Shrub or occasionally a small tree to 20' tall (max. 32'). With Fragrant Ash, the only native ashes with white flowers; this species has twigs square on cross-section, blunt-tipped leaflets, only two petals, and non-fragrant flowers.

leaves 4½" with 3–7 leaflets, each 1½" long, stalked, sharply-toothed, hairless
underleaf pale green

seed flattened
fruit to 1¼", winged to base of seed

flowers ½", with two wide, white, petal-like lobes, in drooping, 4½" long clusters, not fragrant

Locally common on dry slopes of foothills and canyons. Occasionally cultivated (zones 7–10).

Fragrant Ash

Fraxinus cuspidata

FLOWERING ASH

Deciduous. Shrub or small tree to 20' tall (max. 40'). Unique among all ashes, this species has fragrant flowers with a corolla tube divided into four showy white lobes (similar to Fringetree). Flowers appear as terminal clusters on new leafy twigs, whereas all other ashes have flowers arising directly from previous season's twigs, not at tips of new growth.

leaves 5" with 3–7 leaflets, each 2" long, leaflets long-stalked, narrow, pointed

fruit oval, 1", winged nearly to base

flowers ½", white, 4 narrow petal-like lobes in loose cluster 4" long; appears with leaves (Apr), fragrant

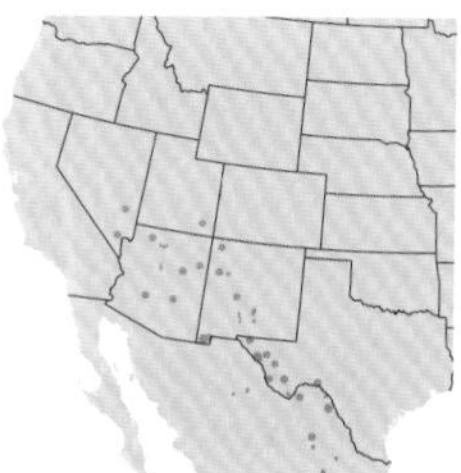

Uncommon on rocky slopes and dry ridges in mountains. Occasionally cultivated (zone 5–9).

Japanese Tree-lilac

Syringa reticulata

GIANT TREE LILAC

Deciduous. Small tree usually 15–30' tall (max. 40'). Spreading and upright branches form oval crown; with age develops more arching branches and graceful appearance.

bark smooth, gray-pink
with horizontal lenticels
like cherry

leaves 5", rounded
or broadly wedge-
shaped at base

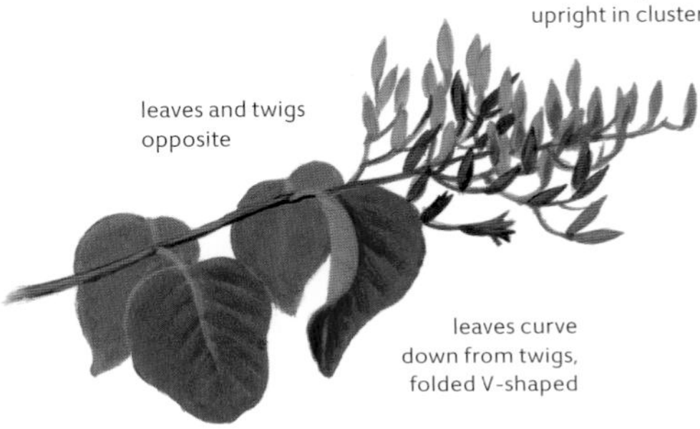
fruit ¾", capsule,
upright in clusters
leaves and twigs
opposite
leaves curve
down from twigs,
folded V-shaped

leaves open
early in spring

flowers creamy-white in
dense terminal clusters
9" long (May–Jul)

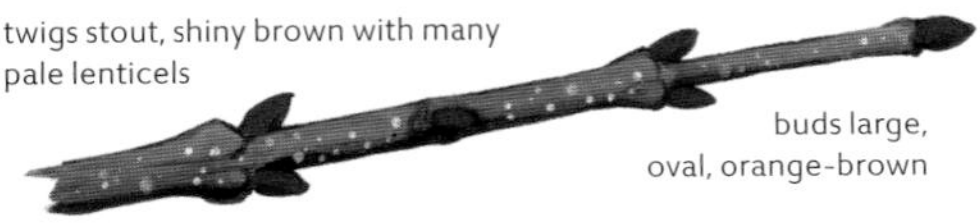
twigs stout, shiny brown with many
pale lenticels
buds large,
oval, orange-brown

Native to Japan. Commonly cultivated in yards and streets, locally escaped from cultivation (zone 3–7).

Several other species of lilacs are commonly cultivated with an incredible diversity of hybrids and cultivars. All are shrubby, rarely or never tree-like. The related Chinese Tree Lilac (*Syringa pekinensis*) is uncommonly cultivated (zones 4–7) and differs from Japanese Tree Lilac in having small leaves about 3", more narrowed at the base, flowers clusters smaller and drooping.

American Fringetree

Chionanthus virginicus

GRANDSIE-GRAY-BEARD, OLD MAN'S BEARD, SNOWFLOWER TREE

Deciduous. Shrub or occasionally a small tree usually 15–25' tall (max. 41'). Low, short-trunked and spreading, general habit and leaf size reminiscent of 'Saucer' Magnolia.

bark gray-brown,
smooth becoming
slightly furrowed

leaves opposite, 6",
smooth or wavy edge

underleaf
paler and slightly hairy

fruit ¾", oval, dark purple,
sometimes glaucous; ripe
Aug–Sep, eaten by birds

twigs stout, green, tan, or dark purple
buds small,
green-brown

Plants in southern parts of its range may have longer and narrower leaves, sometimes distinguished as var. *henryi*, but not clearly separable. Plants vary from low open form to dense and compact to upright and definitely tree-like. A rare pink-flowered form has also been reported.

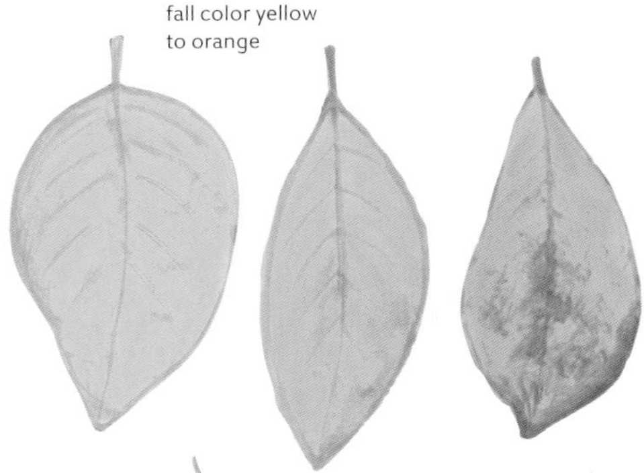
fall color yellow
to orange

flower 1½",
fragrant, white,
4–6 narrow
petals

leaves open late
in spring
flowers in large lacy clusters
8" long on previous year's
twigs (Mar–Jul), open
with leaves

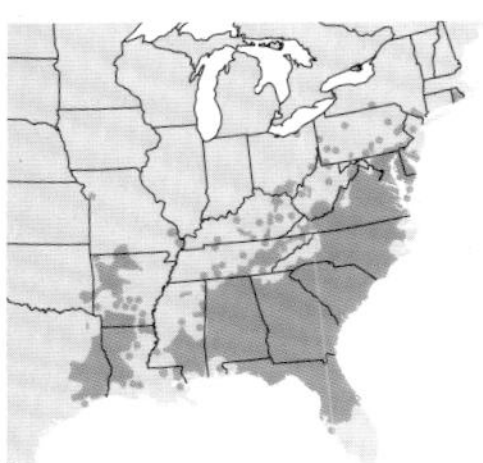

Uncommon in the wild, usually an understory plant in dry or rocky soils. Commonly cultivated as ornamental (zone 4–9).

A related species, Chinese Fringetree (*Chionanthus retusus*), is occasionally cultivated, shrubby and sometimes tree-like (zone 6–8). It differs from American Fringetree in smaller leaves (3" long) and flowers in terminal clusters (not axillary).

Common Olive

Olea europaea

Evergreen. Shrub or small tree (max. 51'). Low and spreading with gnarled trunk; flowers small, inconspicuous, yellow-white, in small hanging clusters, in summer. Commercial olives come from various cultivars of this species; other varieties are selected for ornament and produce no fruit.

leaves 2", narrow, leathery, dark gray-green above
leaves opposite
underleaf pale gray-white

fruit to 1½", familiar hard oval, green sometimes turning black

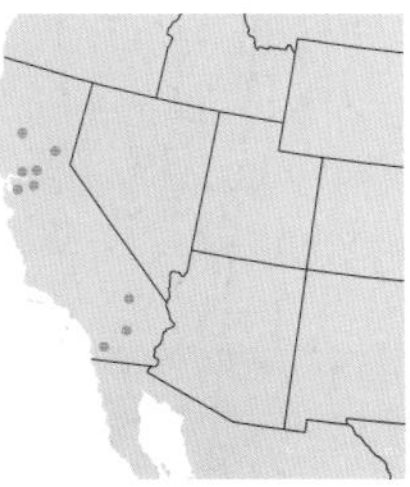

Long cultivated, presumably native to southwestern Asia. Commonly cultivated and locally naturalized in dry regions (zones 7–10).

Devilwood

Osmanthus americanus

WILD OLIVE

Evergreen (leaves persist 2 plus years). Shrub or small tree usually 15–25' tall (max. 46') with open, narrow crown. Leaves somewhat holly-like but opposite; flowers small, whitish, in axillary clusters in spring

leaves 3", opposite, oval; smooth, curled margins, dark olive-green
underleaf paler green

fruit ¾", oval, dark blue; ripe in fall and some persistent through winter

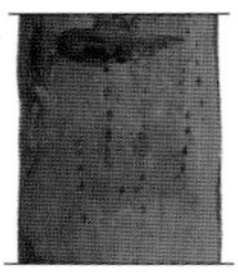
bark pale gray-brown, thin, smooth to slightly scaly

The Common Osmanthus (*Osmanthus heterophyllus*) native to Japan, is commonly cultivated but usually a large shrub. It differs from the native Devilwood in having most leaves with large spiny teeth, and flowering in fall.

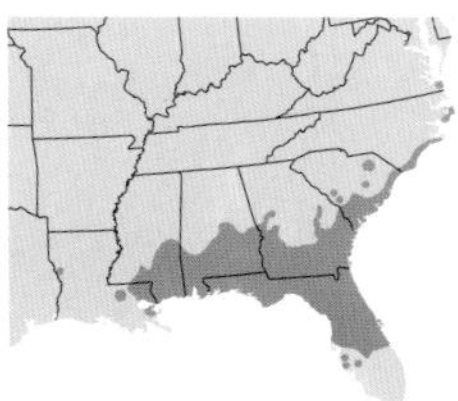

Common in moist soils along streams, swamp margins, wet woods. Occasionally cultivated (zones 5–9), less frequent in gardens than Asian species.

Trumpet Creeper Family

The trumpet creepers (family Bignoniaceae) includes about 700 species of mostly trees and shrubs worldwide. Many species in the family are found in the tropics and subtropics, including popular ornamental trees such as Jacaranda, Calabash, and Sausage-tree. These and others are commonly cultivated in southern Florida, but none grow in the region covered by this guide. Three native tree-like species in two genera are covered here.

The Desert-willow is the only species in its genus, and is found in desert washes in the Southwest. The catalpas (genus *Catalpa*) include eleven species worldwide, mainly in the West Indies and Asia with two species native to North America.

Plants in this family are relatively little-used by humans. Catalpa wood is said to make good durable fenceposts, but the primary use of catalpa is ornamental. A few tropical species provide high-quality lumber in limited amounts, and for a few other specialized uses.

The original range of our native catalpas was very limited. Northern Catalpa grew only along the major river valleys from southern Indiana to northwestern Missouri, and Southern Catalpa from southern Mississippi to southwestern Georgia. As can be seen from the range maps in the native catalpa accounts on the pages that follow, both species have now escaped from cultivation and spread far beyond their native range. Many other species in this guide have undergone a similar human-assisted range expansion, but catalpas provide a particularly dramatic example.

Desert-willow

Chilopsis linearis

Deciduous. Shrub or small tree usually 15–25' tall (max. 68'); twisted trunk and open, airy crown of slender leaves.

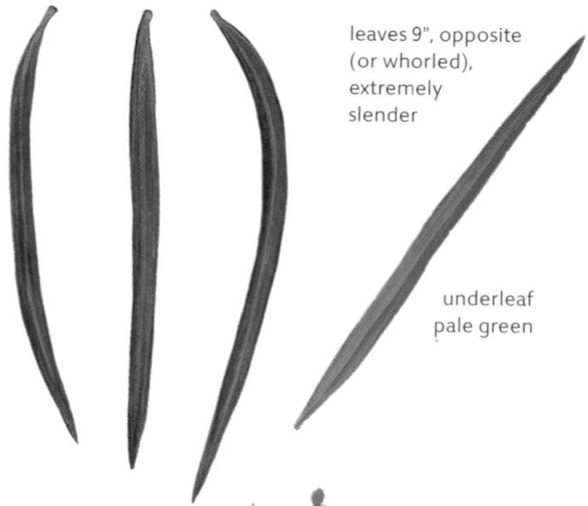
leaves 9", opposite (or whorled), extremely slender
underleaf pale green

flowers 1¼", white to pink with rose and purple markings inside; in loose terminal clusters in summer (Jun–Aug)

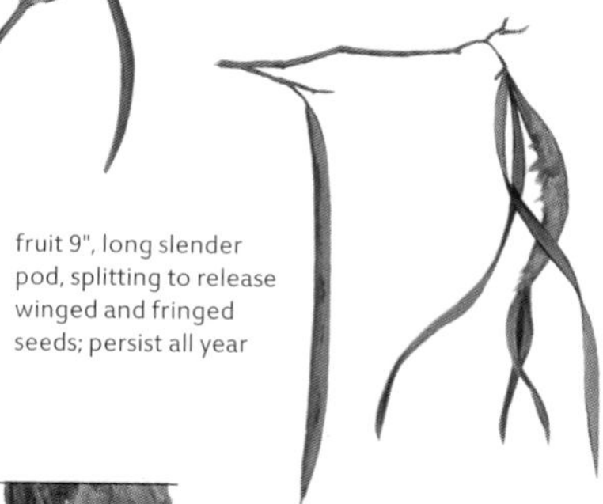
fruit 9", long slender pod, splitting to release winged and fringed seeds; persist all year

bark gray, shaggy

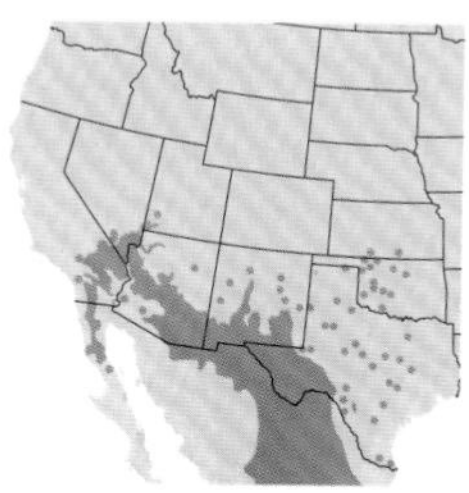

Common in sandy and rocky soils, desert washes. Commonly cultivated (zones 7–9), but only in arid climate and dry soils.

Northern Catalpa

Catalpa speciosa

WESTERN CATALPA, HARDY CATALPA

Deciduous. Small to medium tree usually 30–60' tall (max. 107'); upright with twisted trunk thick at base, but tapering quickly. Leaves emerge late in spring and grow slowly, remaining bright yellow-green after most or all other trees have hardened dark green leaves.

bark furrowed

leaves 8", very large with long stalk, opposite (or whorled)

underleaf pale green

flowers white with yellow and purple markings, bell-shaped

flowers very large, but few per cluster (Apr–Jun)

fruit 14", long, slender, cylindrical pod, green turning dark brown

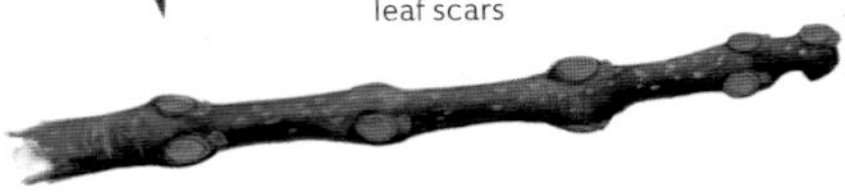

twig stout, gray with large round leaf scars

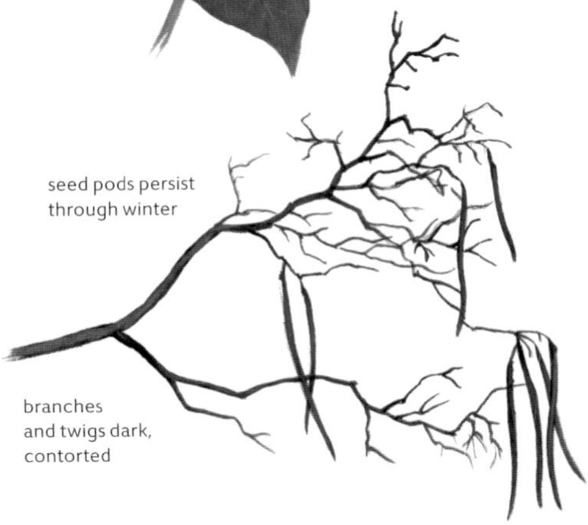

seed pods persist through winter

branches and twigs dark, contorted

Uncommon in the wild along streams, lakeshores, swamp margins. Commonly cultivated and widely naturalized beyond native range to roadsides and waste places (zones 4–8).

Southern Catalpa

Catalpa bignonioides

CATAWBA TREE, CATERPILLAR TREE, INDIAN BEAN, CIGAR TREE

Deciduous. Medium tree usually 40–50' tall (max. 91'); broad spreading crown. Differs from Northern Catalpa in shorter points on leaves, flowers smaller with more purple spots, open about 2 weeks later, pods thinner, and bark scaly.

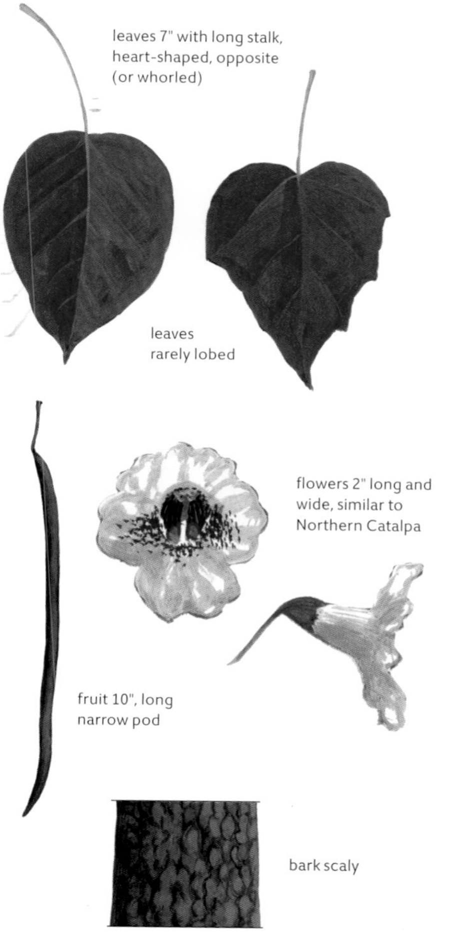
leaves 7" with long stalk, heart-shaped, opposite (or whorled)
leaves rarely lobed
flowers 2" long and wide, similar to Northern Catalpa
fruit 10", long narrow pod
bark scaly

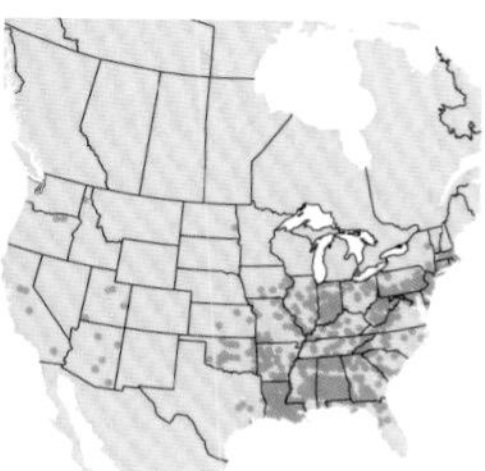

Uncommon in the wild in wet soils of flood-plains and riverbanks. Commonly cultivated and widely naturalized beyond native range to roadsides and waste places (zones 5–9).

Chinese Catalpa

Catalpa ovata

JAPANESE CATALPA

Deciduous. Small to medium tree usually 30–45' tall (max. 73'). Distinguished (with difficulty) from native catalpas by having hairless underleaf, pods more slender, leaves often lobed, flowers creamy-white and less showy.

leaves 7", often with 3–5 obvious lobes, hairless, opposite (or whorled)
flowers creamy-white (Jun–Aug), smaller and less showy than native species

Hybrid Southern × Chinese Catalpa is commonly cultivated. New leaves are reddish or purple in cultivars with leaf and flower features intermediate. Flower display lasts longer than either parent.

Native to China, uncommonly cultivated but locally naturalized to roadsides and waste places (zones 5–8).

Paulownia Family

The paulownia family (Paulowniaceae) includes a single genus of about twelve species of trees native to Asia. One species is introduced and invasive in North America.

bark gray with broad green-gray ridges and shallow orangey furrows, similar to Ginkgo

---

Royal Paulownia

Paulownia tomentosa

EMPRESS TREE, PRINCESS-TREE, FOXGLOVE TREE, BLUE CATALPA

Deciduous. Medium to large tree usually 40–60' tall (max. 105') with sparse stout twigs and unkempt appearance. Main branches and trunk rather contorted with many stout vertical smaller branches and twigs.

flowers large, 2", in large upright clusters, pale purple or blue, in spring before leaves (Apr–May)
fruit 1½", small oval pod

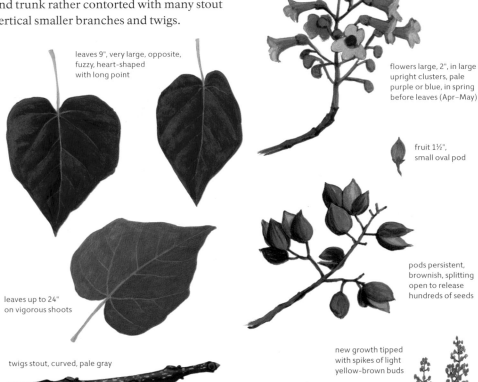

leaves 9", very large, opposite, fuzzy, heart-shaped with long point
leaves up to 24" on vigorous shoots

pods persistent, brownish, splitting open to release hundreds of seeds

twigs stout, curved, pale gray

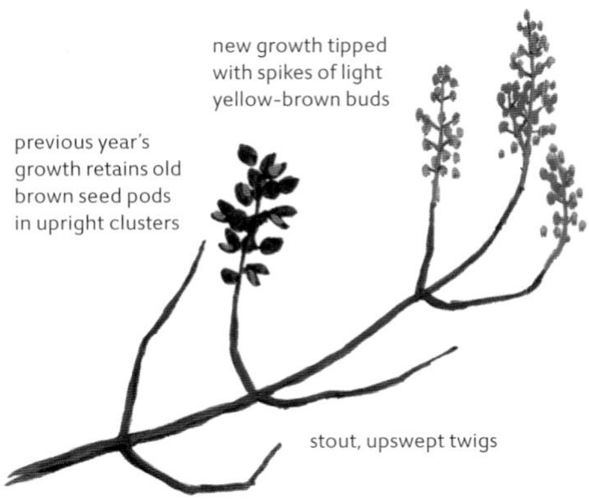
new growth tipped with spikes of light yellow-brown buds
previous year's growth retains old brown seed pods in upright clusters
stout, upswept twigs

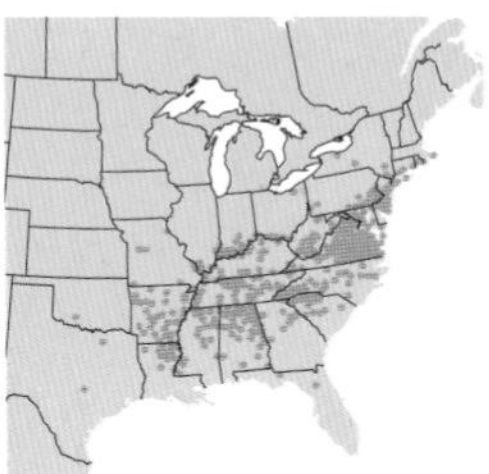

Native to China and Korea. Commonly cultivated and widely naturalized, especially along roadsides and field edges in Appalachian/Mid-Atlantic region (zones 6–9).

Aralia Family

The aralia family (Araliaceae) includes about 250 species of shrubs and trees worldwide. One tree-like species is native to North America and one is commonly cultivated.

Devil's Walkingstick

Aralia spinosa

HERCULES CLUB, PRICKLY ASH, PRICKLY ELDER

Deciduous. Shrub or small tree usually 15–25' tall (max. 60'). Sparsely-branched, sometimes unbranched single stem; often forms dense thickets. Huge leaves and broad clusters of tiny whitish flowers and blackish fruit distinctive.

bark gray, thin with narrow furrows, scattered strong prickles

fruit ¼", small black berries on red stems, in broad cluster 15" across, ripen in fall, quickly devoured by birds

leaves 48", huge, bipinnately or tripinnately compound, each leaflet 3" long

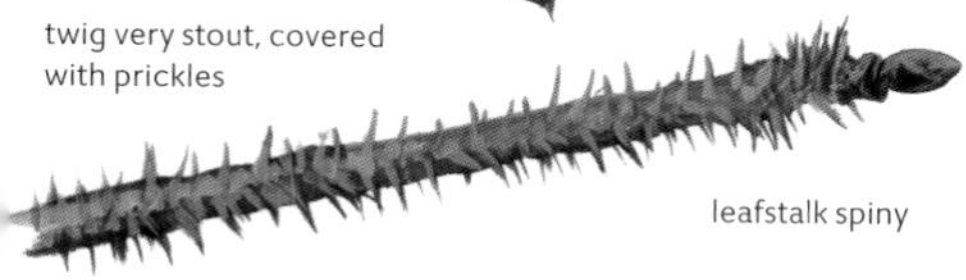

twig very stout, covered with prickles

leafstalk spiny

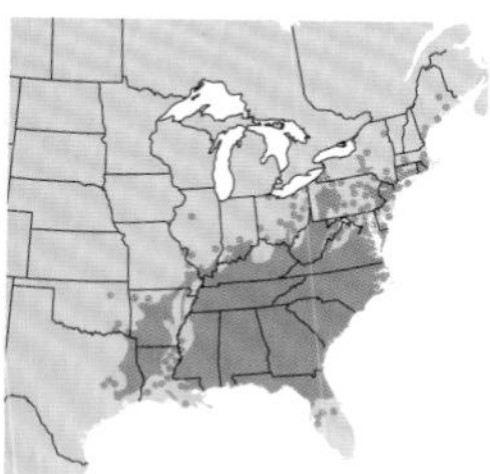

Common in a variety of habitats, especially understory in moist soils in open woods. Uncommonly cultivated, outnumbered by and confused with Asian species (zones 4–9).

Castor-Aralia (page 322) is also in the aralia family, and shares spiny twigs and large terminal flower clusters with Devil's Walkingstick. The prickly-ashes (page 322, family Rutaceae) are superficially similar to Devil's Walkingstick, but have much smaller flower and fruit clusters, and bipinnately compound leaves. Several of the listed alternate names are used for both Devil's Walkingstick and for prickly-ash.

Japanese Angelica Tree

Aralia elata

Deciduous. Shrub or occasionally a small tree to 25' (max. 45'). Differs from Devil's Walkingstick in being less spiny with leaves smaller (26" long) and leaflets shorter-stalked, thicker, and rougher; shorter flower cluster. Native to Japan and Korea; very commonly cultivated and locally naturalized (zones 3–8).

Holly Family

The hollies (family Aquifoliaceae) include about 600 species worlwide. All hollies are in the genus *Ilex*, the only genus in the family. Fourteen holly species are native to North America, but most are shrubs and only a few are commonly tree-like.

The familiar spiny evergreen leaves are shown by the native American Holly and the commonly cultivated English and Chinese Hollies. Three other native species (including Dahoon) are evergreen, but have small leaves without teeth. Ten native species are deciduous. These tend to be shrubs (rarely tree-like), and to have larger, thinner, more pointed leaves than the evergreen species.

Flowers are tiny, greenish to whitish, and appear in the axils of new leaves in spring. Hollies have male and female flowers on separate trees, so only female trees produce the showy red berries, and male trees must be planted near females for pollination.

Fruit is a small round berry, usually red, clustered along the twigs of female plants and ripe in winter. Berries are mildly toxic to humans, but are an important food for birds.

The wood of hollies is pale, dense, and can be polished very smooth, so it is ideal for loom parts, chess pieces, and other specialized purposes. The leaves of many species have a high caffeine content, and are used to brew various teas. The evergreen leaves and red berries are a traditional Christmas decoration. The primary commercial value of hollies is as ornamental trees and shrubs in yards and parks, and hundreds of cultivars are available.

There are no native hollies in Hollywood California, and the name may come from the superficially similar dense green foliage and red berries of the Toyon, but it is also reported that the name comes from the cultivated hollies then growing in Los Angeles. Other species with holly-like leaves include several oaks and laurel cherries.

English Holly

Ilex aquifolium

EUROPEAN HOLLY, HOLM, HULVER

Evergreen. Shrub or small tree (max. 35'). Very similar to American Holly. Hundreds of cultivars, mostly shrubby with variations in leaf size, shape, and color.

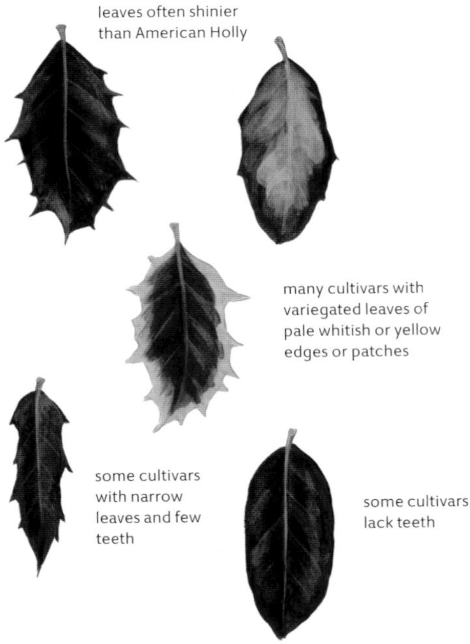
leaves often shinier than American Holly
many cultivars with variegated leaves of pale whitish or yellow edges or patches
some cultivars with narrow leaves and few teeth
some cultivars lack teeth

Hundreds of cultivars of English Holly include many hybrids. Cultivated hybrids of English × Madeira Holly (*Ilex aquifolium* × *perado*) known as 'Highclere' hollies—*Ilex* × *altaclerensis* are diverse and common in cultivation. Cultivated hybrids of English × Chinese Holly (*Ilex aquifolium* × *cornuta*) are also diverse and very commonly cultivated. In addition, several other species of Eurasian hollies are commonly cultivated; Chinese Holly is locally naturalized in Southeast, but all are only occasionally tree-like.

Native to Europe, North Africa, and West Asia. More commonly cultivated than American Holly, naturalized in Pacific Northwest (zones 6–9).

American Holly

Ilex opaca

HOLLY, WHITE HOLLY

Evergreen. Shrub or small tree usually 20–40' (max. 100'). Generally upright with short trunk and branches to ground; fairly dense narrow crown of small dark green leaves.

bark smooth gray

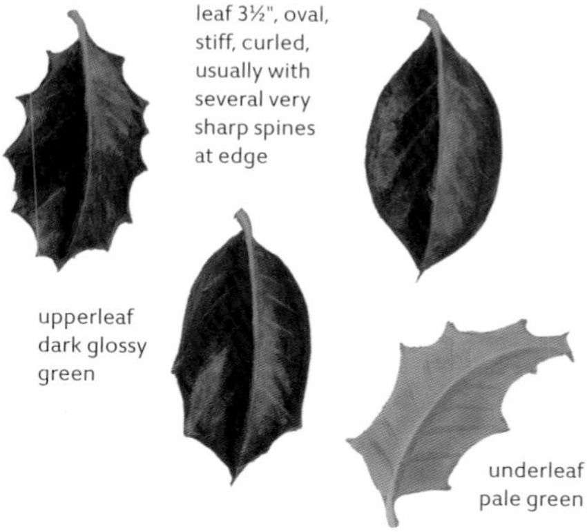
leaf 3½", oval, stiff, curled, usually with several very sharp spines at edge
upperleaf dark glossy green
underleaf pale green

A subspecies of American Holly, known as 'Scrub' Holly, or 'Hummock' Holly (var. *arenicola)*, is a shrub or small tree found in drier and more open sandy habitats. Its leaves are stiffer, smaller, and more yellowish-green than typical American Holly.

flowers tiny, greenish, on new growth (May–Jun)

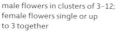

male flowers in clusters of 3–12; female flowers single or up to 3 together
old leaves turn yellow and fall with flowers in spring

fruit ⅓", berries in small clusters, usually red but sometimes yellow

conical upright tree with dense dark green foliage and pale gray trunk

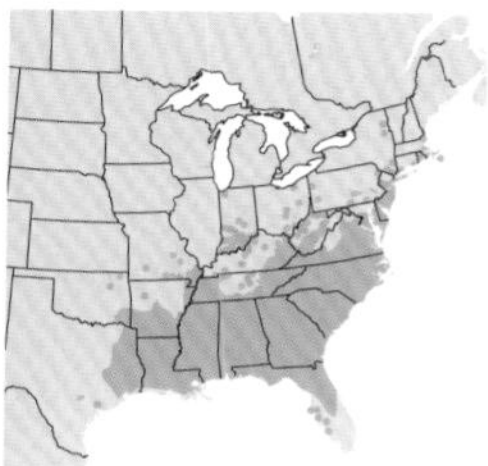

Common in understory of open woods, mainly in sandy soils of coastal plain. Commonly cultivated, but less so than English Holly; dozens of cultivars (zones 5–9).

Dahoon Holly

Ilex cassine

ALABAMA DAHOON, CHRISTMAS-BERRY, HENDERSON-WOOD

Evergreen. Shrub or occasionally a slender small tree to 25–30' tall (max. 72'), usually slender and scrawny, but foliage may be dense.

leaves 2", narrow, blunt-tipped, without spines
fruit small red berries clustered along twigs

Uncommon understory plant in moist soils of swales, pond margins, swamps. Uncommonly cultivated within native range (zones 7–9).

'Topel' Holly

Ilex '× attenuata'

Evergreen. Small tree up to 25' tall (max. 50') with narrow crown. Hybrid of American with Dahoon; occurs naturally in the wild and commonly cultivated. Some cultivars known as 'Foster's' Holly; many trees sold as American Holly are actually hybrids.

leaves 2½" with narrow base, spiny or not

Mountain Winterberry

Ilex montana

MOUNTAIN HOLLY

Deciduous. Shrub or occasionally a small tree to 25' tall (max. about 38'), usually shrubby with multiple slender stems. Named for the bright red fruit that persists into winter, favored by birds. Closely related to several other species of deciduous hollies and can be difficult to distinguish.

leaves 4", larger, longer-stalked, and less leathery than evergreen species

fruit ⅓", bright red, clustered along twigs; persistent into winter
fall color yellow

Common in moist woodlands, slopes, streambanks. This and similar species commonly cultivated (zones 3–9).

Muskroot Family

The muskroots (family Adoxaceae) include about 200 species worldwide in four genera, mostly shrubs. Two genera are native to North America: elders (genus *Sambucus*) and viburnums (genus *Viburnum*). These genera were formerly included in the honeysuckle family (Caprifoliaceae), but were recently moved to the muskroots.

The elders, or elderberries, include seven native species of shrubs (one commonly cultivated) with five species sometimes tree-like.

The viburnums include about twenty-one species of shrubs native to North America, of which six are known to attain tree size. Several Eurasian species are also commonly seen here in cultivation (zones 3–9). All have opposite leaves, small whitish flowers in terminal clusters, and small round or oval berries red to black. The most common native species is covered here.

Elder

Sambucus species

ELDERBERRY

Deciduous. Occasionally small tree to 20' tall (max. 48') suckering to form multi-stemmed sprawling thickets. Fruit small purplish black berries in flat-topped clusters, ripe mid- to late-summer; collected for jellies, pies, and drinks, and devoured by birds.

flowers small, creamy-white, arranged in large showy flat-topped clusters 8" across (May–Jul)
leaves 8", opposite, pinnately compound
5–9 (3–13) leaflets, each 4", narrow, opposite, pointed

Rusty Blackhaw

Viburnum rufidulum

RUSTY HAW, SOUTHERN BLACK HAW, RUSTY NANNYBERRY

Deciduous. Shrub or small tree usually under 18' tall (max. 40'). Similar to dogwoods with opposite leaves, clusters of flowers, and fruit, but leaf venation and buds very different.

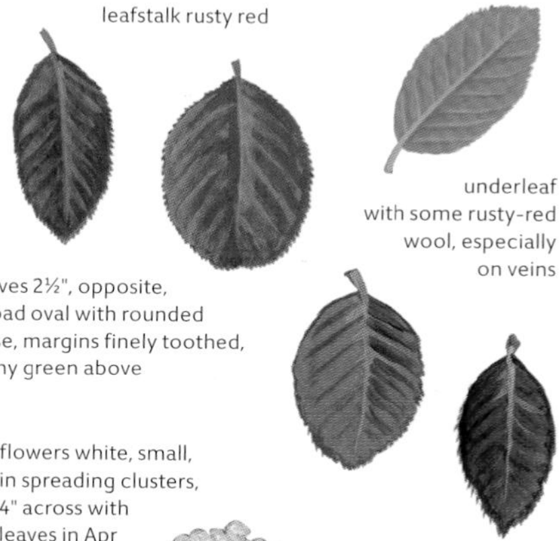
leafstalk rusty red
underleaf with some rusty-red wool, especially on veins
leaves 2½", opposite, broad oval with rounded base, margins finely toothed, shiny green above

flowers white, small, in spreading clusters, 4" across with leaves in Apr

fruit ⅜", oval, purple, glaucous, in spreading clusters

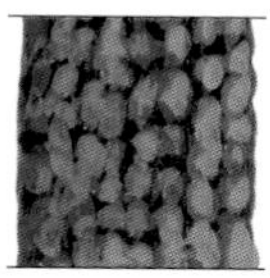
bark checkered in small blocks; resembling Common Persimmon and Flowering Dogwood

young twigs rusty-red

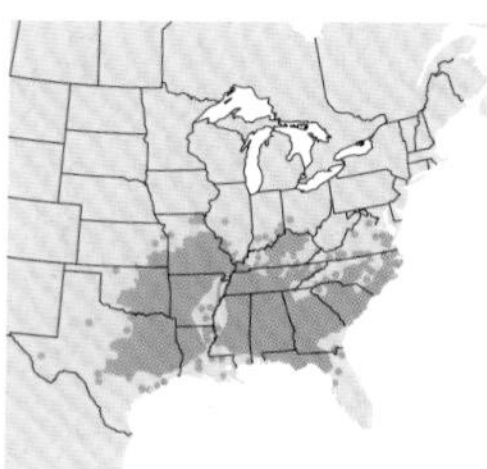

Uncommon in well-drained uplands and uncommonly cultivated (zones 5–9).

Acknowledgments and References

As always, a book like this is an incremental step in an ongoing process. Much is already known about tree identification. This book is based on that knowledge and will hopefully lead to further advances. I owe a huge debt of gratitude to all of the people who have taken the time to publish their observations about trees. Many books were helpful to me in the course of this work, but I should single out *The Guide to Trees of Canada and North America* (with David More's wonderful illustrations), *Trees in Winter*, *The Urban Tree Book*, and *North American Landscape Trees* as four that really inspired me to attempt a tree guide and helped to shape the finished product.

Special thanks to Taber Allison, Robert Bertin, Will Cook, John Kartesz, John Peterson, Rick Radis, and Alan Weakley for answering questions and for taking time to read the finished manuscript and point out all of my mistakes. Thanks to Alexander Krings, Harry LeGrand, Jeffrey Pippen, and Bruce Sorrie for answering my various questions about trees and botany. Their time and effort substantially improved the book.

Thanks to the editing and design team of George Scott and Charles Nix at Scott & Nix for a superhuman effort to put this book together and meet a seemingly impossible deadline. To Ken Schneider, Susan Ralston, Andy Hughes and others at Knopf for allowing me to make the book I wanted and doing their best to keep me on schedule (sort of) while also being flexible.

Thanks to Steve Holzman for tackling the daunting task of creating all of the maps for this guide, and making it look easy, and to John Kartesz and Misako Chu of the Biota of North America Program for making available all of their extensive data on tree distribution.

Thanks to my agent, Russell Galen, for deftly steering another one of my projects through the intricacies of the book business.

And finally, thanks to my family: to my parents for encouraging my interests in nature and drawing, and to Joan, Evan, and Joel for indulging my new fascination with leaves, twigs, bark, and all things tree-like.

The following is a list of the most helpful reference books that I found, and I highly recommend them all.

BLAKESLEE, A.F. AND C.D. JARVIS. 1920. *Trees in Winter*. New York: MacMillan Co.

DIRR, MICHAEL A. 1998. *Manual of Woody Landscape Plants*. Champaign, IL: Stipes Publishing.

———. 1997. *Dirr's Hardy Trees and Shrubs: An Illustrated Encyclopedia*. Portland, OR:Timber Press

DUNCAN, W.H. AND M.B. DUNCAN. 1988. *Trees of the Southeastern United States*. Athens, GA: University of Georgia Press.

JACOBSEN, ARTHUR LEE. 1996. *North American Landscape Trees*. Berkeley, CA: Ten Speed Press.

JOHNSON, OWEN, AND DAVID MORE. 2004. *Collins Tree Guide*. London, UK: Collins.

KURZ, H, AND R.K. GODFREY. 1962. *Trees of Northern Florida*. Gainesville, FL: University of Florida Press.

LITTLE, ELBERT L. JR. 1979. *Checklist of United States Trees (Native and Naturalized)*. Washington, DC: Agriculture Handbook No. 541, Forest Service, USDA.

MCMINN, H.E. AND E. MAINO. 1963. *An Illustrated Manual of Pacific Coast Trees*. Berkeley, CA: University of California Press.

MITCHELL, ALAN. 1987. *The Guide to Trees of Canada and North America*. London, UK: Dragon's World.

MORE, DAVID, AND JOHN WHITE. 2002. *The Illustrated Encyclopedia of Trees*. Portland, OR: Timber Press.

PEATTIE, DONALD C. 1991. *A Natural History of Trees of Eastern and Central North America*. Boston, MA: Houghton Mifflin.

PLOTNICK, ARTHUR. 2000. *The Urban Tree Book: An Uncommon Field Guide for City and Town*. New York: Crown Publishing Group.

PRESTON, R.J. JR. AND V.G. WRIGHT. 1982. *Identification of Southeastern Trees in Winter*. Raleigh, NC: North Carolina Agricultural Extension Service.

SARGENT, CHARLES S. 1922. *Manual of the Trees of North America*. Boston, MA: Houghton Mifflin Co.

SEILER, JOHN R., J.A. PETERSON, AND E.C. JENSEN. 2005. *Woody Plants in North America*. 3 CDs. Dubuque, IA: Kendall Hunt Publishing.

SUDWORTH, GEORGE B. 1908. *Forest Trees of the Pacific Slope*. Washington, DC: USDA Forest Service.

SYMONDS, GEORGE W.D. 1958. *The Tree Identification Book*. New York: Quill.

WEAKLEY, ALAN S. 2008. *Flora of the Carolinas, Virginia, and Georgia, and Surrounding Areas*. Chapel Hill, NC: UNC Herbarium, North Carolina Botanical Garden, University of North Carolina at Chapel Hill.

Scott & Nix, Inc.

George Scott and Charles Nix extend many thanks to Russell Galen of Scovil, Galen, Ghosh Literary Agency, Inc., North Market Street Graphics, and the entire publishing tream at Alfred A. Knopf, including Andy Hughes, Ken Schneider, Kathy Zuckerman, Pat Johnson, Tony Chirico, Sonny Mehta, and Paul Bogaards. We thank Steve Holzman for his expert work on the range maps in the guide and designer Jason Ramirez for his many hours of work laying out the early galley passes. We thank Pamela Nelson for editorial assistance, and the following individuals for their help in the preparation of files, texts, lists and other contributions: David Fusilier, May Anuntarungsun, Elizabeth Drolet, James Montalbano, Sarah Halbert, Alexandra Zsigmond, and Gary Ide.

Species Checklist

This checklist includes all trees featured in full species accounts in this guide and is organized in book order by family.

Yew Family

- ☐ Pacific Yew, *Taxus brevifolia*
- ☐ California Torreya, *Torreya californica*
- ☐ Florida Torreya, *Torreya taxifolia*

Pine Family

- ☐ Eastern White Pine, *Pinus strobus*
- ☐ Western White Pine, *Pinus monticola*
- ☐ Sugar Pine, *Pinus lambertiana*
- ☐ Limber Pine, *Pinus flexilis*
- ☐ Southwestern White Pine, *Pinus strobiformis*
- ☐ Whitebark Pine, *Pinus albicaulis*
- ☐ Colorado Bristlecone Pine, *Pinus aristata*
- ☐ Intermountain Bristlecone Pine, *Pinus longaeva*
- ☐ Foxtail Pine, *Pinus balfouriana*
- ☐ Two-needle Pinyon, *Pinus edulis*
- ☐ Mexican Pinyon, *Pinus cembroides*
- ☐ Singleleaf Pinyon, *Pinus monophylla*
- ☐ Papershell Pinyon, *Pinus remota*
- ☐ Border Pinyon, *Pinus discolor*
- ☐ Parry Pinyon, *Pinus quadrifolia*
- ☐ Bhutan Pine, *Pinus wallichiana*
- ☐ Macedonian Pine, *Pinus peuce*
- ☐ Korean White Pine, *Pinus koraiensis*
- ☐ Japanese White Pine, *Pinus parviflora*
- ☐ Swiss Stone Pine, *Pinus cembra*
- ☐ Lacebark Pine, *Pinus bungeana*
- ☐ Italian Stone Pine, *Pinus pinea*
- ☐ Aleppo Pine, *Pinus halepensis*
- ☐ Bosnian Pine, *Pinus leucodermis*
- ☐ Japanese Red Pine, *Pinus densiflora*
- ☐ Mugo Pine, *Pinus mugo*
- ☐ Patula Pine, *Pinus patula*
- ☐ Maritime Pine, *Pinus pinaster*
- ☐ Chir Pine, *Pinus roxburghii*
- ☐ Lodgepole Pine, *Pinus contorta* var. *latifolia*
- ☐ 'Shore' Lodgepole Pine, *Pinus contorta* var. *contorta*
- ☐ Jack Pine, *Pinus banksiana*
- ☐ Virginia Pine, *Pinus virginiana*
- ☐ Sand Pine, *Pinus clausa*
- ☐ Scotch Pine, *Pinus sylvestris*
- ☐ Spruce Pine, *Pinus glabra*
- ☐ Table Mountain Pine, *Pinus pungens*
- ☐ Pitch Pine, *Pinus rigida*

- ☐ Pond Pine, *Pinus serotina*
- ☐ Loblolly Pine, *Pinus taeda*
- ☐ Longleaf Pine, *Pinus palustris*
- ☐ Slash Pine, *Pinus elliottii*
- ☐ Shortleaf Pine, *Pinus echinata*
- ☐ Red Pine, *Pinus resinosa*
- ☐ Austrian Pine, *Pinus nigra*
- ☐ Japanese Black Pine, *Pinus thunbergii*
- ☐ Ponderosa Pine, *Pinus ponderosa*
- ☐ Arizona Pine, *Pinus arizonica*
- ☐ Washoe Pine, *Pinus washoensis*
- ☐ Jeffrey Pine, *Pinus jeffreyi*
- ☐ Chihuahua Pine, *Pinus leiophylla*
- ☐ Apache Pine, *Pinus engelmannii*
- ☐ Coulter Pine, *Pinus coulteri*
- ☐ Gray Pine, *Pinus sabiniana*
- ☐ Torrey Pine, *Pinus torreyana*
- ☐ Monterey Pine, *Pinus radiata*
- ☐ Bishop Pine, *Pinus muricata*
- ☐ Knobcone Pine, *Pinus attenuata*
- ☐ Deodar Cedar, *Cedrus deodara*
- ☐ Atlas Cedar, *Cedrus atlantica*
- ☐ Lebanon Cedar, *Cedrus libani*
- ☐ Western Larch, *Larix occidentalis*
- ☐ American Larch, *Larix laricina*
- ☐ Subalpine Larch, *Larix lyallii*
- ☐ European Larch, *Larix decidua*
- ☐ Japanese Larch, *Larix kaempferi*
- ☐ Eastern Hemlock, *Tsuga canadensis*
- ☐ Carolina Hemlock, *Tsuga caroliniana*
- ☐ Western Hemlock, *Tsuga heterophylla*
- ☐ Mountain Hemlock, *Tsuga mertensia*
- ☐ Blue Spruce, *Picea pungens*
- ☐ White Spruce, *Picea glauca*
- ☐ Engelmann Spruce, *Picea engelmannii*
- ☐ Sitka Spruce, *Picea sitchensis*
- ☐ Brewer Spruce, *Picea brewerana*
- ☐ Red Spruce, *Picea rubens*
- ☐ Black Spruce, *Picea mariana*
- ☐ Norway Spruce, *Picea abies*
- ☐ Serbian Spruce, *Picea omorika*
- ☐ Oriental Spruce, *Picea orientalis*
- ☐ Bigcone Douglas-fir, *Pseudotsuga macrocarpa*
- ☐ Common Douglas-fir, *Pseudotsuga menziesii*
- ☐ 'Rocky Mountain' Common Douglas-fir, *Pseudotsuga menziesii* var. *glauca*
- ☐ Balsam Fir, *Abies balsamea*
- ☐ Fraser Fir, *Abies fraseri*
- ☐ Subalpine Fir, *Abies lasiocarpa*
- ☐ Rocky Mountain, Alpine Fir, *Abies bifolia*

- ☐ Noble Fir, *Abies procera*
- ☐ California Red Fir, *Abies magnifica*
- ☐ Colorado White Fir, *Abies concolor*
- ☐ Sierra White Fir, *Abies lowiana*
- ☐ Grand Fir, *Abies grandis*
- ☐ Pacific Silver Fir, *Abies amabilis*
- ☐ Bristlecone Fir, *Abies bracteata*
- ☐ European Silver Fir, *Abies alba*
- ☐ Nikko Fir, *Abies homolepis*
- ☐ Caucasian Fir, *Abies nordmanniana*

Cypress Family

- ☐ Monterey Cypress, *Cupressus macrocarpa*
- ☐ Arizona Cypress, *Cupressus arizonica*
- ☐ Baker Cypress, *Cupressus bakeri*
- ☐ Gowen Cypress, *Cupressus goveniana*
- ☐ Tecate Cypress, *Cupressus forbesii*
- ☐ MacNab Cypress, *Cupressus macnabiana*
- ☐ Sargent Cypress, *Cupressus sargentii*
- ☐ Italian Cypress, *Cupressus sempervirens*
- ☐ Eastern Redcedar, *Juniperus virginiana*
- ☐ Rocky Mountain Juniper, *Juniperus scopulorum*
- ☐ Utah Juniper, *Juniperus osteosperma*
- ☐ Western Juniper, *Juniperus occidentalis*
- ☐ California Juniper, *Juniperus californica*
- ☐ Ashe Juniper, *Juniperus ashei*
- ☐ Drooping Juniper, *Juniperus flaccida*
- ☐ Oneseed Juniper, *Juniperus monosperma*
- ☐ Alligator Juniper, *Juniperus deppeana*
- ☐ Redberry Juniper, *Juniperus coahuilensis*
- ☐ Pinchot Juniper, *Juniperus pinchotii*
- ☐ White Cypress-pine, *Callitris columellaris*
- ☐ Japanese-cedar, *Cryptomeria japonica*
- ☐ Chinese-fir, *Cunninghamia lanceolata*
- ☐ Northern White-cedar, *Thuja occidentalis*
- ☐ Western Redcedar, *Thuja plicata*
- ☐ Incense-cedar, *Calocedrus decurrens*
- ☐ Port Orford-cedar, *Chamaecyparis lawsoniana*
- ☐ Atlantic White-cedar, *Chamaecyparis thyoides*
- ☐ Alaska-cedar, *Callitropsis nootkatensis*
- ☐ Baldcypress, *Taxodium distichum*
- ☐ 'Pondcypress', *Taxodium distichum* var. *imbricarium*
- ☐ 'Montezuma' Baldcypress, *Taxodium distichum* var. *mucronatum*
- ☐ Dawn Redwood, *Metasequoia glyptostroboides*
- ☐ Redwood, *Sequoia sempervirens*
- ☐ Giant Sequoia, *Sequoiadendron giganteum*

Monkey-puzzle Family

- ☐ Monkey-puzzle Tree, *Araucaria araucana*

Umbrella-pine Family

☐ Japanese Umbrella-pine, *Sciadopitys verticillata*

Podocarp Family

☐ Bigleaf Podocarp, *Podocarpus macrophyllus*

Ginkgo Family

☐ Ginkgo, *Ginkgo biloba*

Palm Family

☐ Rio Grande Palmetto, *Sabal mexicana*

☐ Cabbage Palmetto, *Sabal palmetto*

☐ California Fan Palm, *Washingtonia filiferia*

☐ Mexican Fan Palm, *Washingtonia robusta*

☐ Saw-Palmetto, *Serenoa repens*

☐ Canary Island Date Palm, *Phoenix canariensis*

☐ Jelly Palm, *Butia capitata*

☐ Mazari Palm, *Nannorrhops ritchiana*

☐ Chinese Windmill Palm, *Trachycarpus fortunei*

☐ Chilean Wine Palm, *Jubaea chilensis*

☐ European Fan Palm, *Chamaerops humilis*

Agave Family

☐ Joshua Tree, *Yucca brevifolia*

Cactus Family

☐ Saguaro, *Cereus giganteus*

Laurel Family

☐ Camphor-Tree, *Cinnamomum camphora*

☐ California Laurel, *Umbellularia californica*

☐ Bay Laurel, *Laurus nobilis*

☐ Sassafras, *Sassafras albidum*

☐ Red Bay, *Persea borbonia*

☐ Silk Bay, *Persea humilis*

☐ Swamp Bay, *Persea palustris*

Custard-apple Family

☐ Common Pawpaw, *Asimina triloba*

Magnolia Family

☐ Cucumbertree, *Magnolia acuminata*

☐ Fraser Magnolia, *Magnolia fraseri*

☐ Pyramid Magnolia, *Magnolia pyramidata*

☐ Bigleaf Magnolia, *Magnolia macrophylla*

☐ Ashe Magnolia, *Magnolia ashei*

☐ Umbrella Magnolia, *Magnolia tripetala*

☐ Southern Magnolia, *Magnolia grandiflora*

☐ Sweetbay, *Magnolia virginiana*

☐ 'Saucer' Magnolia, *Magnolia '× soulangiana'*

☐ Star Magnolia, *Magnolia stellata*

☐ Tuliptree, *Liriodendron tulipifera*

Katsura Family

☐ Katsura Tree, *Cercidiphyllum japonicum*

Sycamore Family

☐ 'London Planetree', *Platanus '× acerifolia'*

☐ American Sycamore, *Platanus occidentalis*

☐ California Sycamore, *Platanus racemosa*

☐ Arizona Sycamore, *Platanus wrightii*

Witch-hazel Family

☐ Persian Ironwood, *Parrottia persica*

☐ American Witch-hazel, *Hamamelis virginiana*

Sweetgum Family

☐ Sweetgum, *Liquidambar styraciflua*

Tamarisk Family

☐ Tamarisk, *Tamarix species*

Myrtle Family

☐ Longbeak Eucalyptus, *Eucalyptus camaldulensis*

☐ Cider Gum, *Eucalyptus gunnii*

☐ Bluegum Eucalyptus, *Eucalyptus globulus*

Loosestrife Family

☐ Crape-myrtle, *Lagerstroemia indica*

Legume Family

☐ Honey Mesquite, *Prosopis glandulosa*

☐ Screwbean Mesquite, *Prosopis pubescens*

☐ Velvet Mesquite, *Prosopis velutina*

☐ Littleleaf Leucaena, *Leucaena retusa*

☐ Tenaza, *Havardia pallens*

☐ Ebony Blackbead, *Ebenopsis ebano*

☐ Huisache, *Acacia farnesiana*

☐ Gregg Catclaw, *Acacia greggii*

☐ Wright Catclaw, *Acacia wrightii*

☐ Silver Wattle, *Acacia dealbata*

☐ Australian Blackwood, *Acacia melanoxylon*

☐ Blue Paloverde, *Parkinsonia florida*

☐ Yellow Paloverde, *Parkinsonia microphylla*

☐ Jerusalem Thorn, *Parkinsoniana aculeata*

☐ Kentucky Coffeetree, *Gymnocladus dioicus*

☐ Honeylocust, *Gleditsia triacanthos*

- ☐ Waterlocust, *Gleditsia aquatica*
- ☐ Desert Ironwood, *Olneya tesota*
- ☐ Smokethorn, *Psorothamnus spinosus*
- ☐ Mescalbean, *Sophora secundiflora*
- ☐ Eve's Necklace, *Styphnolobium affine*
- ☐ Pagoda Tree, *Styphnolobium japonicum*
- ☐ Black Locust, *Robinia pseudoacacia*
- ☐ New Mexico Locust, *Robinia neomexicana*
- ☐ Clammy Locust, *Robinia viscosa*
- ☐ Bristly Locust, *Robinia hispida*
- ☐ Kentucky Yellowwood, *Cladrastis kentukea*
- ☐ Common Laburnum, *Laburnum anagyroides*
- ☐ Amur Maackia, *Maackia amurensis*
- ☐ Eastern Redbud, *Cercis canadensis*
- ☐ 'Texas' Eastern Redbud, *Cercis canadensis* var. *texensis*
- ☐ California Redbud, *Cercis occidentalis*
- ☐ Silktree, *Albizia julibrissin*

Bayberry Family

- ☐ Odorless Bayberry, *Morella inodora*
- ☐ Southern Bayberry, *Morella cerifera*
- ☐ Pacific Bayberry, *Morella californica*

Walnut Family

- ☐ Black Walnut, *Juglans nigra*
- ☐ Arizona Walnut, *Juglans major*
- ☐ Little Walnut, *Juglans microcarpa*
- ☐ Northern California Walnut, *Juglans hindsii*
- ☐ Southern California Walnut, *Juglans californica*
- ☐ Butternut, *Juglans cinerea*
- ☐ Japanese Walnut, *Juglans ailantifolia*
- ☐ English Walnut, *Juglans regia*
- ☐ Shagbark Hickory, *Carya ovata*
- ☐ Shellbark Hickory, *Carya laciniosa*
- ☐ Mockernut Hickory, *Carya tomentosa*
- ☐ Pignut Hickory, *Carya glabra*
- ☐ Scrub Hickory, *Carya floridana*
- ☐ Black Hickory, *Carya texana*
- ☐ Sand Hickory, *Carya pallida*
- ☐ Pecan, *Carya illinoinensis*
- ☐ Water Hickory, *Carya aquatica*
- ☐ Bitternut Hickory, *Carya cordiformis*
- ☐ Nutmeg Hickory, *Carya myristiciformis*
- ☐ Chinese Wingnut, *Pterocarya stenoptera*

Birch Family

- ☐ Paper Birch, *Betula papyrifera*
- ☐ Heartleaf Birch, *Betula cordifolia*
- ☐ Kenai Birch, *Betula kenaica*
- ☐ Resin Birch, *Betula neoalaskana*
- ☐ Gray Birch, *Betula populifolia*
- ☐ European Weeping Birch, *Betula pendula*
- ☐ Manchurian Birch, *Betula platyphylla*
- ☐ Downy Birch, *Betula pubescens*
- ☐ Water Birch, *Betula occidentalis*
- ☐ Yellow Birch, *Betula alleghaniensis*
- ☐ Murray's Birch, *Betula murrayana*
- ☐ Virginia Birch, *Betula uber*
- ☐ Sweet Birch, *Betula lenta*
- ☐ River Birch, *Betula nigra*
- ☐ Smooth Alder, *Alnus serrulata*
- ☐ Red Alder, *Alnus rubra*
- ☐ White Alder, *Alnus rhombifolia*
- ☐ Arizona Alder, *Alnus oblongifolia*
- ☐ Speckled Alder, *Alnus incana*
- ☐ 'Thinleaf' Speckled Alder, *Alnus incana tenuifolia*
- ☐ Green Alder, *Alnus viridis*
- ☐ Seaside Alder, *Alnus maritima*
- ☐ European Alder, *Alnus glutinosa*
- ☐ Italian Alder, *Alnus cordata*
- ☐ Chisos Hophornbeam, *Ostrya chisosensis*
- ☐ Knowlton Hophornbeam, *Ostrya knowltonii*
- ☐ Eastern Hophornbeam, *Ostrya virginiana*
- ☐ Japanese Hornbeam, *Carpinus japonica*
- ☐ European Hornbeam, *Carpinus betulus*
- ☐ American Hornbeam, *Carpinus caroliniana*
- ☐ Beaked Hazel, *Corylus cornuta*
- ☐ Turkish Hazel, *Corylus colurna*
- ☐ Giant Hazel, *Corylus maxima*

Beech Family

- ☐ European Beech, *Fagus sylvatica*
- ☐ American Beech, *Fagus grandifolia*
- ☐ American Chestnut, *Castanea dentata*
- ☐ Allegheny Chinkapin, *Castanea pumila*
- ☐ Ozark Chinkapin, *Castanea ozarkensis*
- ☐ Chinese Chestnut, *Castanea mollissima*
- ☐ Japanese Chestnut, *Castanea crenata*
- ☐ European Chestnut, *Castanea sativa*
- ☐ Golden Chinkapin, *Chrysolepis chrysophylla*
- ☐ Tanoak, *Lithocarpus densiflorus*
- ☐ Northern Red Oak, *Quercus rubra*
- ☐ Eastern Black Oak, *Quercus velutina*
- ☐ Pin Oak, *Quercus palustris*
- ☐ Scarlet Oak, *Quercus coccinea*

- ☐ Jack Oak, *Quercus ellipsoidalis*
- ☐ Shumard Oak, *Quercus shumardii*
- ☐ Maple-leaf Oak, *Quercus acerifolia*
- ☐ Southern Red Oak, *Quercus falcata*
- ☐ Cherrybark Oak, *Quercus pagoda*
- ☐ Buckley's Oak, *Quercus buckleyi*
- ☐ Texas Red Oak, *Quercus texana*
- ☐ American Turkey Oak, *Quercus laevis*
- ☐ Bear Oak, *Quercus ilicifolia*
- ☐ Georgia Oak, *Quercus georgiana*
- ☐ Blackjack Oak, *Quercus marilandica*
- ☐ Darlington Oak, *Quercus hemisphaerica*
- ☐ Swamp Laurel Oak, *Quercus laurifolia*
- ☐ Willow Oak, *Quercus phellos*
- ☐ Water Oak, *Quercus nigra*
- ☐ Shingle Oak, *Quercus imbricaria*
- ☐ Arkansas Oak, *Quercus arkansana*
- ☐ Bluejack Oak, *Quercus incana*
- ☐ Myrtle Oak, *Quercus myrtifolia*
- ☐ California Black Oak, *Quercus kelloggii*
- ☐ Silverleaf Oak, *Quercus hypoleucoides*
- ☐ Graves Oak, *Quercus gravesii*
- ☐ Emory Oak, *Quercus emoryi*
- ☐ Slender Oak, *Quercus graciliformis*
- ☐ Sonoran Oak, *Quercus viminea*
- ☐ Robust Oak, *Quercus robusta*
- ☐ Lateleaf Oak, *Quercus tardifolia*
- ☐ Coast Live Oak, *Quercus agrifolia*
- ☐ Interior Live Oak, *Quercus wislizeni*
- ☐ Shreve Oak, *Quercus parvula*
- ☐ Canyon Live Oak, *Quercus chrysolepis*
- ☐ Channel Island Oak, *Quercus tomentella*
- ☐ Palmer Oak, *Quercus palmeri*
- ☐ Eastern White Oak, *Quercus alba*
- ☐ Basket Oak, *Quercus michauxii*
- ☐ Overcup Oak, *Quercus lyrata*
- ☐ Swamp White Oak, *Quercus bicolor*
- ☐ Burr Oak, *Quercus macrocarpa*
- ☐ Chestnut Oak, *Quercus montana*
- ☐ Common Chinkapin Oak, *Quercus muehlenbergii*
- ☐ Oglethorpe Oak, *Quercus oglethorpensis*
- ☐ Chapman Oak, *Quercus chapmanii*
- ☐ Common Post Oak, *Quercus stellata*
- ☐ Sand Post Oak, *Quercus margarettae*
- ☐ Swamp Post Oak, *Quercus similis*
- ☐ Scrub Oaks, *Quercus* species
- ☐ Bluff Oak, *Quercus austrina*
- ☐ Vasey Oak, *Quercus vaseyana*
- ☐ Pungent Oak, *Quercus pungens*
- ☐ Durand Oak, *Quercus sinuata*

- [ ] Lacey Oak, *Quercus laceyi*
- [ ] Gambel Oak, *Quercus gambelii*
- [ ] 'Wavyleaf' Oak, *Quercus 'undulata'*
- [ ] Sonoran Blue Oak, *Quercus oblongifolia*
- [ ] Engelmann Oak, *Quercus engelmannii*
- [ ] Arizona Oak, *Quercus arizonica*
- [ ] Gray Oak, *Quercus grisea*
- [ ] Netleaf Oak, *Quercus rugosa*
- [ ] Mexican White Oak, *Quercus polymorpha*
- [ ] Mexican Oak, *Quercus carmenensis*
- [ ] Chihuahua Oak, *Quercus chihuahuensis*
- [ ] Valley Oak, *Quercus lobata*
- [ ] Oregon White Oak, *Quercus garryana*
- [ ] California Blue Oak, *Quercus douglasii*
- [ ] Southern Live Oak, *Quercus virginiana*
- [ ] Sand Live Oak, *Quercus geminata*
- [ ] Texas Live Oak, *Quercus fusiformis*
- [ ] English Oak, *Quercus robur*
- [ ] Holm Oak, *Quercus ilex*
- [ ] European Turkey Oak, *Quercus cerris*
- [ ] Sawtooth Oak, *Quercus acutissima*
- [ ] Cork Oak, *Quercus suber*
- [ ] Chinese Evergreen Oak, *Quercus myrsinifolia*
- [ ] Japanese Blue Oak, *Quercus glauca*

Spurge Family

- [ ] Tung-oil Tree, *Vernicia fordii*
- [ ] Chinese Tallowtree, *Triadica sebifera*

Willow Family

- [ ] White Poplar, *Populus alba*
- [ ] Quaking Aspen, *Populus tremuloides*
- [ ] Bigtooth Aspen, *Populus grandidentata*
- [ ] European Aspen, *Populus tremula*
- [ ] Eastern Cottonwood, *Populus deltoides*
- [ ] Fremont Cottonwood, *Populus fremontii*
- [ ] Black Poplar, *Populus nigra*
- [ ] 'Carolina' Poplar, *Populus '× canadensis'*
- [ ] 'Balm-of-Gilead' Poplar, *Populus '× gileadensis'*
- [ ] Swamp Cottonwood, *Populus heterophylla*
- [ ] Balsam Poplar, *Populus balsamifera*
- [ ] Black Cottonwood, *Populus trichocarpa*
- [ ] Narrowleaf Cottonwood, *Populus angustifolia*
- [ ] Bay-leaved Willow, *Salix pentandra*
- [ ] Black Willow, *Salix nigra*
- [ ] Crack Willow, *Salix fragilis*
- [ ] Goodding Willow, *Salix gooddingii*
- [ ] White Willow, *Salix alba*
- [ ] Weeping Willow, *Salix babylonica*

Oleaster Family

- ☐ Russian-olive, *Eleagnus angustifolia*

Mulberry Family

- ☐ Texas Mulberry, *Morus microphylla*
- ☐ Red Mulberry, *Morus rubra*
- ☐ White Mulberry, *Morus alba*
- ☐ Black Mulberry, *Morus nigra*
- ☐ Paper-mulberry, *Broussonetia papyrifera*
- ☐ Common Fig, *Ficus carica*
- ☐ Osage-orange, *Maclura pomifera*

BuckthornFamily

- ☐ Hollyleaf Buckthorn, *Rhamnus crocea*
- ☐ European Buckthorn, *Rhamnus cathartica*
- ☐ Carolina False-buckthorn, *Frangula caroliniana*
- ☐ Birchleaf False-buckthorn, *Frangula betulifolia*
- ☐ Cascara False-buckthorn, *Frangula purshiana*
- ☐ Glossy False-buckthorn, *Frangula alnus*
- ☐ Common Jujube, *Ziziphus jujuba*
- ☐ Japanese Raisintree, *Hovenia dulcis*

Rose Family

- ☐ American Plum, *Prunus americana*
- ☐ Mexican Plum, *Prunus mexicana*
- ☐ Canada Plum, *Prunus nigra*
- ☐ Wildgoose Plum, *Prunus munsoniana*
- ☐ Hortulan Plum, *Prunus hortulana*
- ☐ Chickasaw Plum, *Prunus angustifolia*
- ☐ Flatwoods Plum, *Prunus umbellata*
- ☐ Allegheny Plum, *Prunus alleghaniensis*
- ☐ Klamath Plum, *Prunus subcordata*
- ☐ 'Garden' Plum, *Prunus '× domestica'*
- ☐ Cherry Plum, *Prunus cerasifera*
- ☐ Desert Apricot, *Prunus fremontii*
- ☐ Common Apricot, *Prunus armeniaca*
- ☐ Peach, *Prunus persica*
- ☐ Almond, *Prunus dulcis*
- ☐ Black Cherry, *Prunus serotina*
- ☐ Chokecherry, *Prunus virginiana*
- ☐ European Bird Cherry, *Prunus padus*
- ☐ Manchurian Cherry, *Prunus maackii*
- ☐ Sour Cherry, *Prunus cerasus*
- ☐ Mazzard Cherry, *Prunus avium*
- ☐ Mahaleb Cherry, *Prunus mahaleb*
- ☐ Bitter Cherry, *Prunus emarginata*
- ☐ Pin Cherry, *Prunus pensylvanica*

- ☐ Japanese Flowering Cherry, *Prunus* species
- ☐ Carolina Laurel Cherry, *Prunus caroliniana*
- ☐ Hollyleaf Cherry, *Prunus ilicifolia*
- ☐ Catalina Cherry, *Prunus lyonii*
- ☐ Common Cherry-laurel, *Prunus laurocerasus*
- ☐ Portugal Cherry-laurel, *Prunus lusitanica*
- ☐ Hawthorns, *Crataegus* species
- ☐ May Hawthorn, *Crataegus aestivalis*
- ☐ Washington Hawthorn, *Crataegus phaenopyrum*
- ☐ Parsley Hawthorn, *Crataegus marshallii*
- ☐ Cockspur Hawthorn, *Crataegus crus-galli*
- ☐ Black Hawthorn, *Crataegus douglasii*
- ☐ Pear Hawthorn, *Crataegus calpodendron*
- ☐ Yellow Hawthorn, *Crataegus flava*
- ☐ Littlehip Hawthorn, *Crataegus spathulata*
- ☐ Downy Hawthorn, *Crataegus mollis*
- ☐ Beautiful Hawthorn, *Crataegus pulcherrima*
- ☐ Oneflower Hawthorn, *Crataegus uniflora*
- ☐ Dotted Hawthorn, *Crataegus punctata*
- ☐ Fanleaf Hawthorn, *Crataegus flabellata*
- ☐ Green Hawthorn, *Crataegus viridis*
- ☐ Oneseed Hawthorn, *Crataegus monogyna*
- ☐ English Hawthorn, *Crataegus laevigata*
- ☐ Common Apple, *Malus pumila*
- ☐ Prairie Crab Apple, *Malus ioensis*
- ☐ Southern Crab Apple, *Malus angustifolia*
- ☐ Sweet Crab Apple, *Malus coronaria*
- ☐ Oregon Crab Apple, *Malus fusca*
- ☐ Common Pear, *Pyrus communis*
- ☐ Callery Pear, *Pyrus calleryana*
- ☐ Eastern Serviceberry, *Amelanchier canadensis*
- ☐ Smooth Serviceberry, *Amelanchier laevis*
- ☐ Downy Serviceberry, *Amelanchier arborea*
- ☐ Red-twigged Serviceberry, *Amelanchier sanguinea*
- ☐ Utah Serviceberry, *Amelanchier utahensis*
- ☐ Western Serviceberry, *Amelanchier alnifolia*
- ☐ Alder Whitebeam, *Sorbus alnifolia*
- ☐ 'Oakleaf' Mountain-ash, *Sorbus '× thuringiaca'*
- ☐ American Mountain-ash, *Sorbus americana*
- ☐ European Mountain-ash, *Sorbus aucuparia*
- ☐ Loquat, *Eriobotrya japonica*
- ☐ Torrey Vauquelinia, *Vauquelinia californica*
- ☐ Lyontree, *Lyonothamnus floribundus*
- ☐ Alderleaf Cercocarpus, *Cercocarpus montanus*
- ☐ Curlleaf Cercocarpus, *Cercocarpus ledifolius*
- ☐ Toyon, *Heteromeles arbutifolia*
- ☐ Chinese Photinia, *Photinia serratifolia*

Hemp Family

- ☐ Northern Hackberry, *Celtis occidentalis*
- ☐ Southern Hackberry, *Celtis laevigata*
- ☐ Netleaf Hackberry, *Celtis reticulata*
- ☐ Dwarf Hackberry, *Celtis tenuifolia*
- ☐ Lindheimer Hackberry, *Celtis lindheimeri*
- ☐ European Hackberry, *Celtis australis*
- ☐ Chinese Hackberry, *Celtis sinensis*

Elm Family

- ☐ American Elm, *Ulmus americana*
- ☐ Slippery Elm, *Ulmus rubra*
- ☐ European White Elm, *Ulmus laevis*
- ☐ 'Dutch' Elm, *Ulmus '× hollandica'*
- ☐ Field Elm, *Ulmus minor*
- ☐ Wych Elm, *Ulmus glabra*
- ☐ Winged Elm, *Ulmus alata*
- ☐ Rock Elm, *Ulmus thomasii*
- ☐ Cedar Elm, *Ulmus crassifolia*
- ☐ September Elm, *Ulmus serotina*
- ☐ Siberian Elm, *Ulmus pumila*
- ☐ Chinese Elm, *Ulmus parvifolia*
- ☐ Water-elm, *Planera aquatica*
- ☐ Japanese Zelkova, *Zelkova serrata*

Mallow Family

- ☐ Chinese Parasol-tree, *Firmiana simplex*
- ☐ American Basswood, *Tilia americana*
- ☐ Littleleaf Linden, *Tilia cordata*
- ☐ Large-leaf Linden, *Tilia platyphyllos*
- ☐ Silver Linden, *Tilia petiolaris*

Cashew Family

- ☐ Texas Pistachio, *Pistacia texana*
- ☐ Common Pistachio, *Pistacia vera*
- ☐ Chinese Pistachio, *Pistacia chinensis*
- ☐ Mount Atlas Pistachio, *Pistacia atlantica*
- ☐ Peruvian Peppertree, *Schinus molle*
- ☐ American Smoketree, *Cotinus obovatus*
- ☐ European Smoketree, *Cotinus coggygria*
- ☐ Smooth Sumac, *Rhus glabra*
- ☐ Shining Sumac, *Rhus copallina*
- ☐ Staghorn Sumac, *Rhus typhina*
- ☐ Poison-sumac, *Toxicodendron vernix*

Mahogany Family

- ☐ Chinaberry, *Melia azedarach*
- ☐ Chinese Toon, *Toona sinensis*

Rue Family

- ☐ Sour Orange, *Citrus aurantium*
- ☐ Trifoliate-orange, *Poncirus trifoliata*
- ☐ Beebee Tree, *Tetradium daniellii*
- ☐ Common Hoptree, *Ptelea trifoliata*
- ☐ Southern Prickly-ash, *Zanthoxylum clava-herculis*
- ☐ Amur Corktree, *Phellodendron amurense*

Soapberry Family

- ☐ Western Soapberry, *Sapindus drummondii*
- ☐ Golden Rain-tree, *Koelreuteria paniculata*
- ☐ Mexican-buckeye, *Ungnadia speciosa*
- ☐ Common Horsechestnut, *Aesculus hippocastanum*
- ☐ 'Red Horsechestnut', *Aesculus '× carnea'*
- ☐ Yellow Buckeye, *Aesculus flava*
- ☐ Ohio Buckeye, *Aesculus glabra*
- ☐ 'Texas' Ohio Buckeye, *Aesculus glabra* var. *arguta*
- ☐ Red Buckeye, *Aesculus pavia*
- ☐ Painted Buckeye, *Aesculus sylvatica*
- ☐ Bottlebrush Buckeye, *Aesculus parviflora*
- ☐ California Buckeye, *Aesculus californica*
- ☐ Red Maple, *Acer rubrum*
- ☐ Silver Maple, *Acer saccharinum*
- ☐ Norway Maple, *Acer platanoides*
- ☐ Sugar Maple, *Acer saccharum*
- ☐ Florida Maple, *Acer floridanum*
- ☐ Chalk Maple, *Acer leucoderme*
- ☐ Black Maple, *Acer nigrum*
- ☐ Canyon Maple, *Acer grandidentatum*
- ☐ Bigleaf Maple, *Acer macrophyllum*
- ☐ Rocky Mountain Maple, *Acer glabrum*
- ☐ Striped Maple, *Acer pensylvanicum*
- ☐ Mountain Maple, *Acer spicatum*
- ☐ Vine Maple, *Acer circinatum*
- ☐ Boxelder, *Acer negundo*
- ☐ Sycamore Maple, *Acer pseudoplatanus*
- ☐ Hedge Maple, *Acer campestre*
- ☐ Trident Maple, *Acer buergeranum*
- ☐ Shantung Maple, *Acer truncatum*
- ☐ Amur Maple, *Acer ginnala*
- ☐ Tatarian Maple, *Acer tataricum*
- ☐ Paperbark Maple, *Acer griseum*
- ☐ Japanese Maple, *Acer palmatum*
- ☐ Fullmoon Maple, *Acer japonicum*

Quassia Family

- ☐ Ailanthus, *Ailanthus altissima*
- ☐ Corkwood, *Leitneria floridana*

Dogwood Family

- ☐ Alternate-leaf Dogwood, *Cornus alternifolia*
- ☐ Rough-leaf Dogwood, *Cornus drummondii*
- ☐ Flowering Dogwood, *Cornus florida*
- ☐ Pacific Dogwood, *Cornus nuttallii*
- ☐ Kousa Dogwood, *Cornus kousa*

Tupelo Family

- ☐ Dove Tree, *Davidia involucrata*
- ☐ Water Tupelo, *Nyssa aquatica*
- ☐ Black Tupelo, *Nyssa sylvatica*
- ☐ Swamp Tupelo, *Nyssa biflora*
- ☐ Ogeechee Tupelo, *Nyssa ogeche*

Cyrilla Family

- ☐ Buckwheat-tree, *Cliftonia monophylla*
- ☐ Swamp Cyrilla, *Cyrilla racemiflora*
- ☐ Littleleaf Cyrilla, *Cyrilla parvifolia*

Sapodilla Family

- ☐ Buckthorn Bully, *Sideroxylon lycioides*
- ☐ Gum Bully, *Sideroxylon lanuginosum*

Ebony Family

- ☐ Chinese Persimmon, *Diospyros kaki*
- ☐ Texas Persimmon, *Diospyros texana*
- ☐ Common Persimmon, *Diospyros virginiana*

Heath Family

- ☐ Tree Sparkleberry, *Vaccinium arboreum*
- ☐ Sourwood, *Oxydendrum arboreum*
- ☐ Pacific Madrone, *Arbutus menziesii*
- ☐ Strawberry Tree, *Arbutus unedo*
- ☐ Arizona Madrone, *Arbutus arizonica*
- ☐ Texas Madrone, *Arbutus xalapensis*
- ☐ Georgia Plume, *Elliottia racemosa*

Snowbell Family

- ☐ Fragrant Snowbell, *Styrax obassia*
- ☐ Japanese Snowbell, *Styrax japonicus*
- ☐ Bigleaf Snowbell, *Styrax grandifolius*
- ☐ Mountain Silverbell, *Halesia tetraptera*

Tea Family

- ☐ Franklinia, *Franklinia alatamaha*
- ☐ Loblolly-bay, *Gordonia lasianthus*

Hardy Rubber Tree Family

- ☐ Hardy Rubber Tree, *Eucommia ulmoides*

Sweetleaf Family

- ☐ Common Sweetleaf, *Symplocos tinctoria*

Borage Family

- ☐ Anacua, *Ehretia anacua*

Madder Family

- ☐ Buttonbush, *Cephalanthus occidentalis*

Olive Family

- ☐ White Ash, *Fraxinus americana*
- ☐ Green Ash, *Fraxinus pennsylvanica*
- ☐ Carolina Ash, *Fraxinus caroliniana*
- ☐ Pumpkin Ash, *Fraxinus profunda*
- ☐ Blue Ash, *Fraxinus quadrangulata*
- ☐ Black Ash, *Fraxinus nigra*
- ☐ Chihuahua Ash, *Fraxinus papillosa*
- ☐ Texas Ash, *Fraxinus texensis*
- ☐ Berlandier Ash, *Fraxinus berlandierana*
- ☐ Oregon Ash, *Fraxinus latifolia*
- ☐ Velvet Ash, *Fraxinus velutina*
- ☐ Singleleaf Ash, *Fraxinus anomala*
- ☐ Lowell Ash, *Fraxinus lowellii*
- ☐ Gregg Ash, *Fraxinus greggii*
- ☐ Goodding Ash, *Fraxinus gooddingii*
- ☐ European Ash, *Fraxinus excelsior*
- ☐ Narrowleaf Ash, *Fraxinus angustifolia*
- ☐ Evergreen Ash, *Fraxinus uhdei*
- ☐ Manna Ash, *Fraxinus ornus*
- ☐ Two-petal Ash, *Fraxinus dipetala*
- ☐ Fragrant Ash, *Fraxinus cuspidata*
- ☐ Japanese Tree-lilac, *Syringa reticulata*
- ☐ American Fringetree, *Chionanthus virginicus*
- ☐ Common Olive, *Olea europaea*
- ☐ Devilwood, *Osmanthus americanus*

Trumpet Creeper Family

- ☐ Desert-willow, *Chilopsis linearis*
- ☐ Northern Catalpa, *Catalpa speciosa*
- ☐ Southern Catalpa, *Catalpa bignonioides*
- ☐ Chinese Catalpa, *Catalpa ovata*

Paulownia Family

- ☐ Royal Paulownia, *Paulownia tomentosa*

Aralia Family

☐ Castor-Aralia, *Kalopanax septemlobus*

☐ Devil's Walkingstick, *Aralia spinosa*

☐ Japanese Angelica Tree, *Aralia elata*

Holly Family

☐ English Holly, *Ilex aquifolium*

☐ American Holly, *Ilex opaca*

☐ Dahoon Holly, *Ilex cassine*

☐ 'Topel' Holly, *Ilex '× attenuata'*

☐ Mountain Winterberry, *Ilex montana*

Muskroot Family

☐ Elder, *Sambucus* species

☐ Rusty Blackhaw, *Viburnum rufidulum*

Species Index

Entries in bold indicate a main species account.

C

D

E

N

O

P

Quick Index

See the Species Index for a complete listing of all trees in *The Sibley Guide* by standard English and scientific name.

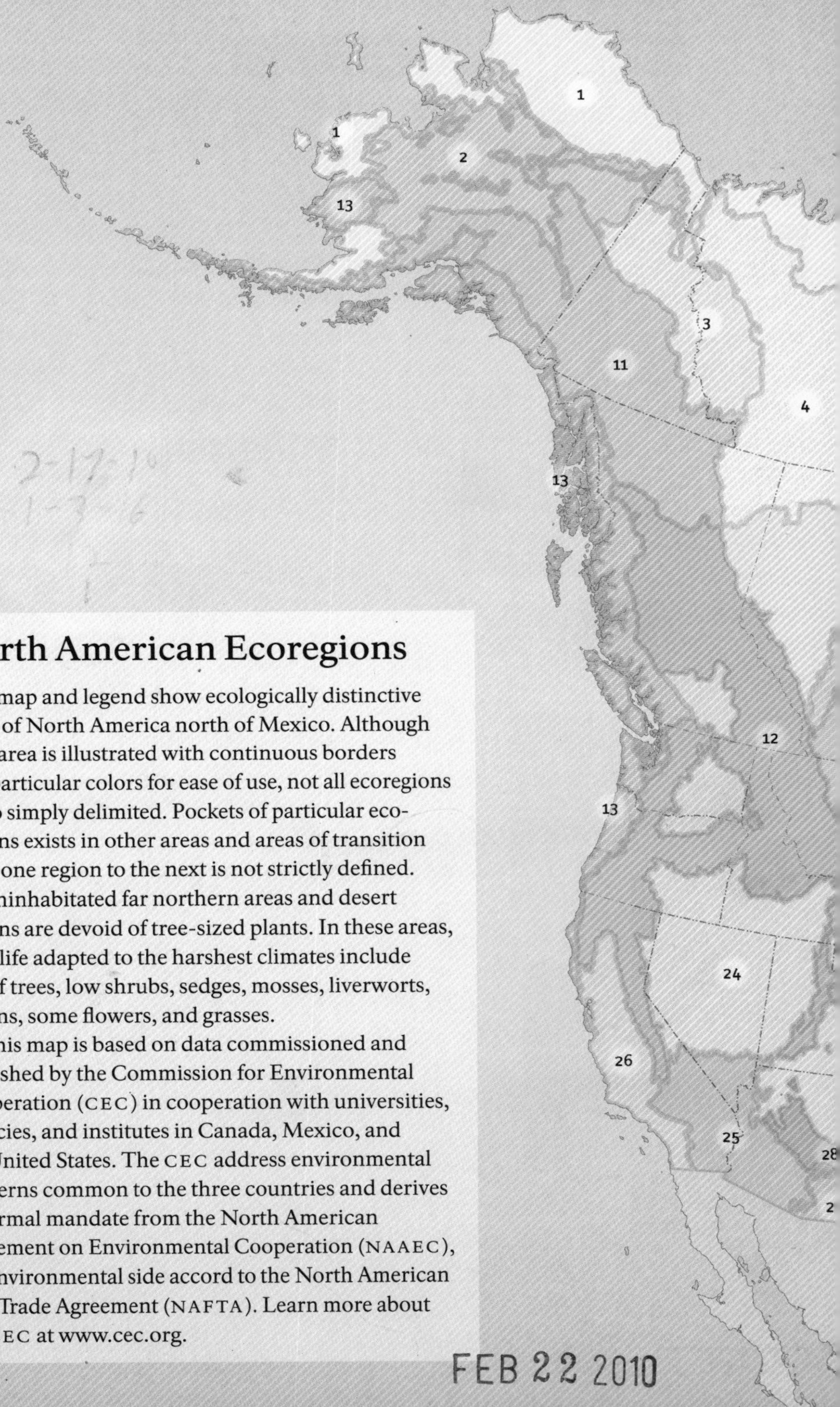
1
1
2
13
3
11
4
13
12
13
24
26
25
28
2

North American Ecoregions

This map and legend show ecologically distinctive areas of North America north of Mexico. Although each area is illustrated with continuous borders and particular colors for ease of use, not all ecoregions are so simply delimited. Pockets of particular ecoregions exists in other areas and areas of transition from one region to the next is not strictly defined.

Uninhabitated far northern areas and desert regions are devoid of tree-sized plants. In these areas, plantlife adapted to the harshest climates include dwarf trees, low shrubs, sedges, mosses, liverworts, lichens, some flowers, and grasses.

This map is based on data commissioned and published by the Commission for Environmental Cooperation (CEC) in cooperation with universities, agencies, and institutes in Canada, Mexico, and the United States. The CEC address environmental concerns common to the three countries and derives its formal mandate from the North American Agreement on Environmental Cooperation (NAAEC), the environmental side accord to the North American Free Trade Agreement (NAFTA). Learn more about the CEC at www.cec.org.